Courts.Net
http://www.courts.net
Provides links to numerous court sites; has state court decisions and provides sources for legal information

Crime Statistics Site
http://www.crime.org/links.html
Provides information about university and college crime in the United States, together with other general statistical information about U.S. crime

Crime Stoppers International, Inc.
http://www.c-s-i.org/stats.htm
Reports information about various crime stopper programs in the United States; examines various types of crime prevention programs and their viability for different communities

Court TV Library
http://www.courttv.com
Provides information about high-profile criminal cases, Supreme Court cases, and death penalty cases

Database on U.S. Supreme Court Opinions
http://www.usscplus.com/
Research site providing valuable information about active criminal cases in federal courts

Drug Enforcement Administration (DEA)
http://www.usdoj.gov/dea/
Supplies information about illegal drugs in the United States and their distribution; acts as an interdiction agency and works with other federal agencies to combat drug trafficking

Federal Bureau of Investigation
http://www.fbi.gov
Enforcement arm of the U.S. Department of Justice; enforces all federal criminal laws

FBI Academy
http://www.fbi.gov/academy/academy.htm
Training center for all new FBI agent recruits

FBI Laboratory
http://www.fbi.gov/lab/report/labhome.com
Investigative center that analyzes data from various federal and state crime scenes; one of the most up-to-date crime laboratories and forensic centers in the world

FBI Law Enforcement Bulletin
http://www.leb@fbiacademy.edu
Publication producing research and interesting articles about all aspects of law enforcement at all levels, including local, state, and federal

Federal Bureau of Prisons (FBOP)
http://www.bop.gov
Organization that oversees the federal prison system

Federal Judicial Center
http://www.fjc.gov
Disseminates information about judicial administration and issues reports from the Administrative Office of the U.S. Courts and U.S. Sentencing Commission

Federal Justice Statistics Resource Center (FJSRC)
http://fjsrc.urban.org/
Maintains Bureau of Justice statistical information about suspects and defendants being processed in the federal criminal justice system

FEDSTATS
http://www.fedstats.gov
Provides search utilities to persons interested in locating information from any federal agency concerning crime statistics and other agency data

Financial Crimes Enforcement Network (FCEN)
http://www.ustreas.gov/fincen/
Investigates and reports fraud and other business-related crimes

Fraud Information Center
http://www.echotech.com/
Clearinghouse for information about business fraud and illegal business practices

Freedom of Information Act (FOI
http://www.citizen.org
Act permitting citizens broad access to public records for inspection

Immigration and Naturalization Service
http://www.ins.usdoj.gov/
Agency that enforces immigration laws and operates the Border Patrol and other services to prevent illegal aliens from entering the United States

The International Association of Chiefs of Police
http://www.theiacp.org/
International body of police chiefs that shares information about police organization and operations

Justice Research and Statistics Association (JRSA)
http://www.jrsainfo.org
Provides information about the collection and analysis of data concerning crime at the state level

Law and Society Association
http://www.webmaster@lawandsociety.org
Group of scholars from diverse fields and countries interested in the place of law in social, political, economic, and cultural life; holds annual meetings to discuss social and legal issues

National American Indian Court Judges Association
http://www.naicja.org
A national voluntary association of tribal court judges primarily devoted to the support of American Indian and Alaska Native justice systems through education, information sharing, and advocacy, with a mission to strengthen tribal justice systems

National Archive of Criminal Justice Data (NACJD)
http://www.icpsr.umich.edu/NACJD/home.html
Contains more than 500 data collections relating to criminal justice that may be downloaded for research purposes

address court manage
issues in federal, state, and local courts; publishes the *Court Manager;* assists court managers to determine their own conduct as well as design programs for their courts

National Association for Justice Information Systems (NAJIS)
http://www.statesattorney.org/nhome.htm
Disseminates ideas among professionals and organizations at the local, state, and federal levels concerning the operations and management of criminal justice information systems

National Association of Counsel for Children
http://www.naccchildlaw.org
Organization dedicated to quality representation to protect children in the legal system; assists attorneys and other professionals in their work with children in the legal system

National Association of Pretrial Services Agencies
http://www.napsa.org
National professional organization for the pretrial release and pretrial diversion fields; serves as a national forum for ideas and issues in the area of pretrial services; promotes research and establishes a mechanism for exchanges of information; consists of pretrial practitioners, judges, and lawyers

National Association of State Information Resource Executives (NASIRE)
http://www.nasire.org
National organization designed to shape federal, municipal, and international governmental policies through collaborative partnerships, information sharing, and knowledge transfer between jurisdictional and functional boundaries

ADMINISTRATION OF CRIMINAL JUSTICE

STRUCTURE, FUNCTION, AND PROCESS

DEAN JOHN CHAMPION

TEXAS A & M INTERNATIONAL UNIVERSITY

Prentice Hall

Upper Saddler River, New Jersey 07458

Library of Congress Cataloging-in-Publication Data

Champion, Dean John
    Administration of criminal justice: structure, function, and process/Dean J. Champion.
        p. cm.
    Includes bibliographical references and index.
    ISBN 0-13-084234-6
    1. Criminal justice, Administration of. I. Title.

HV7419 .C478 2003
364—dc21

2002017688

Publisher: Jeff Johnston
Executive Editor: Kim Davies
Assistant Editor: Sarah Holle
Managing Editor: Mary Carnis
Production Editor: Linda B. Pawelchak
Production Liaison: Barbara Marttine Cappuccio
Director of Manufacturing and Production: Bruce Johnson
Manufacturing Buyer: Cathleen Petersen
Art Director: Cheryl Asherman
Cover Design Coordinator: Miguel Ortiz
Cover Design: Anthony Inciong
Cover Illustration: Rosanne Percivalle, SIS/Images.com
Marketing Manager: Jessica Pfaff
Interior Design: Molnica Kompter
Composition: Clarinda Company
Printing and Binding: The Courier Companies

Pearson Education LTD., *London*
Pearson Education Australia PTY. Limited, *Sydney*
Pearson Education Singapore, Pte. Ltd.
Pearson Education North Asia Ltd., *Hong Kong*
Pearson Education Canada, Ltd., *Toronto*
Pearson Educación de Mexico, S.A. de C.V.
Pearson Education—Japan, *Tokyo*
Pearson Education Malaysia, Pte. Ltd.
Pearson Education, *Upper Saddle River, NJ*

1 0 9 8 7 6 5
ISBN 0-13-084234-6

For my wife, Gerri

CONTENTS

CHAPTER 8

Motivation, Satisfaction, and Morale of Employees   154

CHAPTER 9

Police and Sheriffs' Departments   175

CHAPTER 10

Court Organization and Administration   204

CHAPTER 11
Jail and Prison Organization and Administration   236

CHAPTER 12
Community Corrections Organizations   265

CHAPTER 13
Juvenile Justice Organizations and Their Administration   288

CHAPTER 14
Evaluating Organizational Effectiveness   320

Read

PREFACE

Administration of Criminal Justice: Structure, Function, and Process examines all aspects of the criminal justice syystem from an organizational perspective. It is important to portray all criminal justice agencies and organizations within a general open-systems context, in which community, state, and national inputs can be indicated and their impact on individual agencies assessed. A fundamental assumption of this book is that criminal justice organizations can be understood best by placing them within the existing constraints of the larger environment of external organizations and public interests. Thus, individual behaviors and group conduct can be seen as greatly influenced by forces external to organizations as well as by internal organizational phenomena.

An overview of the book's contents follows. Chapter 1 describes what is meant by the administration of justice or justice administration. The units of analysis (individuals, groups, and organizations) commonly used to investigate justice administration topics are presented. Chapter 2 describes organizational theory and open-system and closed-system organizational models. These include the rational bureaucratic model and the goals and systems models. Chapter 3 describes several nonrational models, including human relations and organizations as natural systems. The relationship between theories and models of organizations is explained and illustrated by contemporary examples. Several popular organizational typologies are presented to provide students with a grasp of how different kinds of criminal justice organizations can be arranged. These arrangements include different sets of defining criteria showing how typologies meaningfully relate to what occurs in different organizational contexts.

Chapter 4 identifies and describes several important organizational variables used for research purposes. Organizational variables are divided according to structure, control, change, and behavior. Organizational structural variables include organizational size, complexity or differentiation, and formalization. Organizational control variables include the size of the administrative component, bureaucratization, centralization, and levels of authority and span of control. Organizational change includes labor turnover, organizational conflict, flexibility, growth, and succession. Organizational behavioral variables include organizational climate, goals, and effectiveness.

Chapter 5 describes several important interpersonal variables, including work group cohesiveness and supervisor-subordinate relations. Individual variables are also presented and include descriptions of employee attitudes about their work, job characteristics, and methods of evaluating work roles and worker effectiveness. The interrelatedness of these variables is explained. Assessing organizational effectiveness involves paying attention to these different variables in a variety of institutional and organizational contexts. Students can obtain a clearer picture of how different actors in the criminal justice system are affected by different organizational dimensions and even by factors external to their own organizations.

Chapter 6 examines leadership in organizations. Traditional power typologies are presented, including examples from the works of Max Weber, French and

Raven, and Amitai Etzioni. Legitimate authority types, the bases of social power, and the compliance-involvement typology are discussed to highlight different motivational methods used by supervisors and administrators to induce employees to act in given ways. A careful examination of employee involvement is offered to show that different means of inducing compliance also induce different types of involvement. Depending on the nature of employee involvement, worker performance and attitudes will be affected either positively or negatively.

Chapter 7 examines several different types of communication systems in organizations, including a discussion of formal and informal communication networks. Communication patterns are closely linked with hierarchies of authority, and several parallels between these concepts are drawn. Both the functions and dysfunctions of formal and informal communication networks are described and discussed.

Chapter 8 examines the factors that impact the motivation, satisfaction, and morale of organizational personnel. How are work satisfaction and motivation related to organizational effectiveness and work output? Several important dimensions of worker satisfaction are explored, including various styles of leadership and supervision, work group cohesion, workload and pressure, the prestige and status of the job, type of reward structure, and participation in decision making. The complexity of explaining worker motivation is described.

Chapter 9 is a description of police and sheriffs' departments. The chapter begins with an overview of the history of law enforcement. The goals and functions of police and sheriffs' departments are presented, together with their liaison with federal agencies. The divisions of labor of these different types of organizations are described, and a full description of the recruitment and selection processes is given for each. The chapter examines several important law enforcement issues, including controlling law enforcement officer performance through better training and selection methods. Professionalization and police-community relations are examined as issues confronting different police agencies. Different forms of officer misconduct are described, as well as the methods used by police departments and public entities to deter or minimize misconduct. Included is a discussion of civilian complaint review boards and their various functions.

Chapter 10 describes the organization and operation of federal, state, and local court systems. The important role of judges is addressed, including how judicial nominees are selected. The roles and responsibilities of prosecutors at all jurisdictional levels are described, along with the methods for selecting prosecutors as well as a consideration of their ethical responsibilities and codes of professional conduct. Prosecutors' case processing and prioritizing functions are examined, and the work of other court employees also is considered. The relationship between prosecutors and the court is described, including the diverse functions associated with these important criminal justice roles. Prosecutorial and judicial misconduct are also examined, including various methods used to detect and sanction such misconduct.

Chapter 11 describes and differentiates jails and prisons and provides a brief history of each. These descriptions also include an examination and profile of both jail and prison inmates. The administration of jail and prison systems is considered, and methods of selecting and recruiting jail personnel and prison correctional staff and administrators are discussed. Selected jail and prison issues are described, including overcrowding, inmate rights, privatization, and the legal liabilities of jail officers and correctional officers.

Chapter 12 describes community corrections, including an examination of probation and parole services and their organization and administration. Other community services are described, including work/study release and furlough programs, home confinement programs, electronic monitoring supervisory methods, and halfway houses. The legal liabilities of different actors who work in or administer community corrections programs are examined, and the use of volunteers and paraprofessionals in community-based programs is considered. The changing nature of community corrections also is described.

Chapter 13 presents an overview of juvenile justice organizations, beginning with a history of juvenile courts. Different types of juvenile offenders are delineated, including delinquents, status offenders, and children in need of supervision. Juvenile court procedures are presented, including a discussion of types of dispositions available. Various types of corrections for juvenile offenders are described, including industrial schools. The blended sentencing statutes that are increasingly important and popular for dealing with more violent juvenile offenders are explained. Several important issues relative to juveniles are examined, including overcrowding, deinstitutionalization of status offenders, escalating violence and the accompanying sanctions imposed by juvenile courts, due process and the get-tough movement, and the legal rights of juveniles. Various community agencies that cater to different youthful offenders also are described.

Chapter 14 concludes the text with an examination of how organizational effectiveness is measured. How do we know that our organizations and policies are effective? Are the goals established by different organizations realized or achieved? Various methods of evaluating organizational performance are presented. Such descriptions are provided successively for law enforcement, prosecution and the courts, and corrections. Evaluation research and public policy are interconnected, and the nature of this relationship is described. The ideal-real dilemma frustrates the efforts of more than a few actors in the criminal justice system, as policy decision making often is at odds with public interests or the vested interests of political subgroups. Organizational effectiveness is examined in retrospect.

Throughout this book, boxes highlight key terms and concepts. These boxes are mostly adaptations of stories that have been featured in international and national news services bulletins, such as those of the Associated Press. They feature current events and vignettes that illustrate different criminal justice agencies in action or underscore particular issues or incidents. Another type of box presents various actors in law enforcement, the courts, and corrections who provide biographical sketches that examine why they became involved in their particular careers and provide advice to students seeking careers in particular fields of criminal justice.

Another feature of the text is the inclusion of case studies that accompany each chapter. These case studies have been drawn from actual events that have occurred in different jurisdictions throughout the United States. Fictitious names and places are used, however, in order to protect innocent parties and to preserve the integrity of others who have acted responsibly in those jurisdictions. The purpose of these case studies is to elicit discussion and argument about why the situation occurred and what strategies might be used to resolve the problems described. The case method is particularly useful for learning how to apply various concepts covered in each chapter. Therefore, an attempt should be made to apply chapter concepts and examples as a part of one's analysis of the case facts. It should be noted that there are no perfect solutions to any particular case. Every scenario may be approached from different perspectives, and more than one solution may be feasible. Class discussion or written responses to questions following these cases should generate a variety of solutions. It is important to provide a rationale for any solution proposed. That is simply saying, "If I were so-and-so, I would do this or that," is insufficient. Students are encouraged to back up their recommendations with their own rationales for the solutions they propose.

Finally, this book is the result of the collective efforts of many people, ranging from the production and editorial staff at Prentice Hall to various reviewers and contributors of box materials. I want to thank all of these people for their individual contributions to the final product. The reviewers for this text were Kevin Bryant, University of West Florida; Bryan D. Byers, Ball State University; Larry Mays, New Mexico State University; Michael Meyer, University of North Dakota—Grand Forks; and Gennaro Vito, University of Louisville. This project has received the strong support of Kim Davies. I want to thank Kim for having faith in my work. I also want to thank Linda Pawelchak, who has headed up the production process and facilitated the completion of this project. I always marvel at her steadfastness, persistence, patience, and attention to details that authors often overlook. In the final analysis, I bear full responsibility for any errors of fact, although I have done my best to ensure the accuracy of all information presented. Thanks everyone, again, for your efforts on my behalf.

Dean John Champion
Laredo, Texas

ABOUT THE AUTHOR

Dean John Champion is Professor of Criminal Justice at Texas A & M International University, Laredo, Texas. Dr. Champion has taught at the University of Tennessee–Knoxville, California State University–Long Beach, and Minot State University in North Dakota. He earned his Ph.D. from Purdue University and B.S. and M.A. degrees from Brigham Young University. He also completed several years of law school at the Nashville School of Law.

Dr. Champion has written and/or edited 30 texts and maintains memberships in 11 professional organizations. He is a lifetime member of the American Society of Criminology, the Academy of Criminal Justice Sciences, and the American Sociological Association. He is former editor of the ACJS/Anderson series on *Issues in Crime and Justice* (1993–1996) and the *Journal of Crime and Justice* (1995–1998). He is a contributing author for the *Encarta Encyclopedia 2000* for Microsoft. He was the Visiting Scholar for the National Center for Juvenile Justice in 1992 and is president of the Midwestern Criminal Justice Association.

Among his published books for Prentice Hall are *Basic Statistics for Social Research* (1970, 1981); *Research Methods for Criminal Justice and Criminology* (1993, 2000); *The Juvenile Justice System: Delinquency, Processing, and the Law* (1992, 1998, 2001); *Corrections in the United States: A Contemporary Perspective* (1990, 1998, 2001); *Probation, Parole, and Community Corrections* (1990, 1996, 1999, 2002); and *Policing in the Community* (with George Rush) (1996).

Dr. Champions's primary research interests relate to attorney use in juvenile justice proceedings and plea bargaining.

CHAPTER
1

CRIMINAL JUSTICE ORGANIZATIONS
AND THE ADMINISTRATION OF JUSTICE

KEY TERMS

Administration of justice
Change agent
Client system
Criminal justice
Criminal justice organization
Criminal justice system
Criminology
Formal organization

Individual unit of analysis, level of
    analysis
Interpersonal unit of analysis, level of
    analysis
Justice administration
Latent social identities
Levels of analysis, units of analysis
Models

Organizational unit of analysis, level of
    analysis
Syntality
Typologies
Units of analysis
Variables

CHAPTER OBJECTIVES

The following objectives are intended:

1. To understand the meaning of the administration of justice
2. To define what is meant by criminal justice organizations

3. To provide a rationale for why criminal justice organizations should be studied
4. To describe the different units or levels of analysis for those who study justice administration

INTRODUCTION

This chapter is about the administration of criminal justice, how it is defined, and what it encompasses. The criminal justice system is a vast and complex network of persons, agencies, and institutions. This system may be conceptualized as various segments involved in processing offenders. When someone commits a crime, the criminal justice system responds. One

segment of this system, law enforcement, seeks to detect and apprehend criminal suspects, as well as to prevent the occurrence of crime. Once criminal suspects have been apprehended, they are screened for prosecution by state's attorneys or prosecutors.

Many offenders are charged with one or more crimes, and they are entitled to a trial. Judges preside at such trials, and either judges themselves or juries decide the guilt or innocence of criminal defendants. If defendants are found guilty of the crime(s) with which they are charged, they are sentenced. Another segment of the criminal justice system, corrections, will supervise sentenced offenders in various ways. Some offenders are placed on probation. Others are institutionalized in jails or prisons. Most offenders sentenced to jail or prison will eventually serve their time or be paroled. Many convicted offenders will be sentenced to probation. Both probationers and parolees will be supervised by a segment of corrections known as community corrections. About 65 percent of all convicted offenders presently are under some form of correctional supervision within their communities. Probation or parole officers supervise them.

All of these segments compose a criminal processing system that requires a fairly high degree of coordination between its individual components. This chapter explores the general nature of criminal justice organizations and why it is important to study them. Our interest is in explaining the administration of these organizations as well as in describing the levels of analysis that account for what occurs in them. Organizations of any kind do not exist in a vacuum. There is both an external environment, such as the United States itself, individual states, and local governments, and an internal environment, including individuals who perform a variety of tasks related to offender processing. These environments are described and their interrelatedness is delineated. The chapter concludes by explaining the general approach taken throughout the text. This is the strategies approach, which involves acquiring a basic understanding of different types of organizational operations to improve our ability to think about organizational events and develop explanations for their occurrence.

One or more case studies appear at the end of each chapter as examples of incident process analysis, which features a variety of scenarios derived from the real world of criminal justice organizational operations. Questions are posed at the end of each case. Alternative solutions to these cases require the application of information learned from the chapter. There are no correct answers to these questions in any absolute sense. Rather, the intent is to cause the reader to think about why certain events occurred and how various problems can be resolved. Different consequences result for those involved, depending on the suggested solutions. Each chapter, therefore, assists in devising case explanations and anticipating possible outcomes depending on the solutions proposed.

1. DIFFERENT WAYS OF HANDLING SPEEDERS? YOU DECIDE.

- You are speeding, going 80 mph on a two-lane road in West Virginia where the speed limit is 55 mph. Suddenly, you see the flashing lights of a patrol car in your rearview mirror. You pull over and a deputy sheriff approaches your car and asks for your driver's license and car registration. The deputy says, "You were going a little fast there, weren't you?" You agree and give some lame excuse such as "I wasn't paying attention to the speedometer." The deputy smiles and says, "Look, given that it's a nice day and all, just be careful from here on out. Don't let me catch you speeding through here again. Have a good day." You drive off and that is the end of the incident.

- You are going 80 mph in a 55 mph zone on Interstate 10 approaching Los Angeles when a California Highway Patrol officer pulls you over. The officer checks your driver's license and registration, and after a few minutes, she issues you a citation for speeding. She says that either you should appear at a downtown Los Angeles courtroom on a certain date, or if that is inconvenient, you can call a number on the back of the citation and a clerk will advise you of the fine amount that you can send in by mail. She wishes you a happy day and admonishes you to drive safely. You make the call the next day and are told that the fine for the speeding offense, which is listed as a seven-digit number, is $175. You are advised that you must remit this amount within 30 days or a warrant will be issued for your arrest. You mail in a check for $175 and that is the end of the incident.

2. DIFFERENT WAYS OF HANDLING BAD CHECK WRITERS? YOU DECIDE.

- You are from Carlsbad, California, and have been arrested for writing a bad check in Billings, Montana. You cashed a worthless check for $150 at a grocery store. While you are waiting at the cash register, a police officer approaches you and places you under arrest for fraudulently writing a bad check. The store manager called your California bank and determined that your supposed checking account did not exist. Later, with a public defender present, the Billings prosecutor says that if you pay a $2,500 fine in cash and plead guilty to a misdemeanor, they will let you go. You wire a close friend in Carlsbad, California, and the fine amount is wired to the Billings court. You sign some papers and leave the city with a criminal conviction.

- You live in Knoxville, Tennessee. You have been out of work for two months and have no money. Your checking account at the bank has been closed because there is no money in it. Yet you go to a store to buy groceries and write a worthless check for $150. You are arrested shortly thereafter and taken to jail, where you are booked and scheduled for a preliminary hearing. At the preliminary hearing, your public defender pleads with the court to show you leniency, citing your unemployment and desperation as reasons for writing the bad check. The judge decides to place you on diversion for six months and temporarily suspends prosecution of your case subject to paying restitution to the grocery store for the bad check and $250 in court fees. A friend of yours pays the court costs and reimburses the store for the worthless check. Six months later, the charges against you are dismissed. You do not have a criminal record.

3. DIFFERENT WAYS OF HANDLING PROBATION AND PAROLE VIOLATIONS? YOU DECIDE.

- You are a probationer who has been convicted of possession of illegal drugs. Instead of a three-year sentence, the judge orders you to probation. One of your program conditions is that you attend Narcotics Anonymous meetings twice a week. One evening your probation officer pays you a surprise visit, and he informs you that he has learned that you have missed several Narcotics Anonymous meetings in direct violation of your probation program conditions. He advises you that if he hears of further absences from those meetings, he will consider turning you in to the judge for program violations. He says you may have to go to prison if you don't "watch your step." He leaves your premises and nothing more is heard of the incident. You are compliant and attend the rest of your Narcotics Anonymous meetings.

- You are a probationer, having been convicted of sexual battery. You were sentenced to three years in prison, but that sentence was suspended by the judge and you were placed on probation. As part of your probation program, you must work at a job and observe a 7:00 P.M. curfew. You have been late by as much as 20 minutes on at least three occasions over the last six months. One evening a probation officer is sitting on your front doorstep as you return from work at 7:10 P.M. You stopped for some cigarettes and are 10 minutes late, in violation of your curfew. You explain to the probation officer why you were late, but he is very upset with you.

"This is the fourth time you've come home late," he says. "I'm not going to tolerate that. You have plenty of time to get home before your curfew, and you chose to be late. That means you're going to suffer the consequences." He advises that he is going to report this program violation to the judge and you will be ordered to appear at a later date. Subsequently, you appear in court before the judge and your probation program is revoked. You are ordered to prison to commence your three-year sentence.

4. DIFFERENT WAYS OF TREATING PRISON INMATES? YOU DECIDE.

- You are serving a six-year prison term in the state penitentiary for the statutory rape of a 16-year-old girl. One day you fall and fracture your arm while moving around in your cell. You call for one of the corrections officers and one appears in front of your cell door. You hold up your bleeding, broken arm with part of the bone protruding through the skin and ask to be taken to the infirmary where it can be treated. The officer says, "I'll be back in a while." About six hours later, another corrections officer shows up at your cell and says, "I heard you had an accident." You show him your broken arm, which by now is becoming infected. The officer hands you your food tray and two aspirin. He says, "Take these and I'll have someone stop by in the morning." The next morning when the new shift officer comes to your cell, he says, "What's wrong with your arm?" By now, your arm is red up to your shoulder. The officer eventually has two other officers join him, and they escort you to the infirmary. The physician examines your arm and asks the officers, "When did this happen?" The other officers reply, "We don't know. We just saw it." The physician directs that the man needs immediate emergency surgery at a local hospital. The inmate is eventually transported to a nearby hospital, where it is determined that the infection is so severe that the arm will have to be amputated. It is informally known among the correctional officers that they do not like rapists. Because of the statutory rape charge, they thought you were a child molester. They were punishing you by ignoring your injuries.

- You are serving a six-year term in the state penitentiary for embezzlement. One day you fall and break your arm. You yell out for assistance and a corrections officer comes to your aid. He has other officers transport you to the prison infirmary immediately, where a physician is able to set your compound fracture and apply medicines to prevent possible infection. Within eight weeks, your arm is healing nicely.

Have you ever wondered about unfairness throughout the criminal justice system and why it occurs? These scenarios are but a few of the millions of annual instances of the American criminal justice system in action. Although these examples involve speeders, bad check writers, parolees and probationers, and prisoners, they all relate to how justice in the United States is administered under different circumstances and how various types of offenders are treated. Considerable variation exists among local, state, and federal jurisdictions about how different situations are or should be handled. The swiftness of justice frequently depends on who you are, where you are, and what you have done. From these examples, it is clear that some unfairness exists relating to how persons are treated by police, the courts, probation and parole officers, corrections officers, and others. People in different parts of the country who are in similar circumstances seem to be treated differently. It is sometimes difficult for us to understand why this apparent unfairness exists. We might think that something ought to be done about it, but those in positions to make policy changes and oversee their enforcement do not seem to care. Life goes on and unfairness continues.

What these scenarios show is that persons in similar positions or circumstances but in different parts of the country are subject to a wide range of treatment or processing by others who are affiliated with one or more components of the criminal justice system. Why aren't all speeders treated the same? Why does a bad check in Montana result in a criminal conviction, but a bad check in Tennessee results in diversion, restitution, and no criminal prosecution or record? Why are some probationers who violate one of their program conditions, such as curfew, sent to prison, whereas others who miss required Narcotics Anonymous meetings suffer no consequences? Why are some inmates in prisons treated in a negligent manner and others receive proper care from their supervising correctional officers?

Although this book is not about unfairness in the criminal justice system, these examples do illustrate that police officers have much latitude or discretion in treating law violators. Jurisdictions also show differential discretion about how bad check incidents are handled, as do probation officers in how they relate to their clients when program infractions are detected, and correctional officers in how they exercise discretion relating to treatment of inmates' injuries.

Each of these scenarios involves different organizations or agencies, different policies and procedures, and different personnel with varying responsibilities and duties. In order for us to understand why these different events occur, regardless of their degree of formality, discretion, or fairness, we must first understand their respective organizational contexts. These incidents occurred in different police systems, court systems, probation systems, and correctional systems. In virtually every incident described earlier, individual decision making or discretion was at work to influence the final outcome. The individual actors in each of these scenarios may or may not have been performing their jobs as required by their respective organizations or agencies. Different police officers exercised their discretion by either ignoring or ticketing speeding motorists. Different prosecutors exercised their discretion by either prosecuting or diverting two bad check writers. Different probation officers chose to report or ignore client program violations. And different correctional officers were indifferent to or sought treatment for inmates with injuries.

We must consider different organizations and agencies as well as the different personnel who have various duties and responsibilities in these organizations and agencies. Understanding why all of these persons choose to exercise their discretionary powers in different ways requires us to understand the organizations themselves, the policies followed by each organization, and the social and psychological characteristics of the organizational membership. This is the subject matter of greatest interest to those involved in justice administration.

THE ADMINISTRATION OF JUSTICE

Criminal Justice, Criminology, and the Administration of Justice

The **criminal justice system** is a more or less integrated process consisting of a vast network of agencies, organizations, and individuals who attempt to control crime through detection and apprehension of alleged criminals. The system processes these individuals through a sequence of legal events that eventually leads to a determination of their guilt or innocence. Subsequently, for those found guilty of crimes, the system supervises and enforces their punishment and/or rehabilitation.

Criminal justice is an interdisciplinary science, including but not necessarily limited to law, sociology, psychology, political science, public administration, history, and economics. By 2002, over 3,000 criminal justice programs had been established at different colleges and universities in the United States, serving the needs of over one million students.

Closely related to criminal justice is criminology, which is the study of crime and criminal behavior. **Criminology** describes various forms of crime, attempts to explain its etiology, and examines criminality and societal reaction to it. More than a few criminologists consider criminal justice to be nothing more than applied criminology, connoting action or practical application. Therefore, those who actually do something about crime and criminals are criminal justicians, whereas those who are primarily concerned about theorizing about crime and its causes are criminologists. Despite the fact that criminal justice and criminology are not synonymous, substantial overlap does exist between the two disciplines.

The key components of the criminal justice system are law enforcement, prosecution and the courts, and corrections. Each of these components is multifaceted, meaning that each consists of numerous organizations, associations, and persons who perform duties specific to these components.

The administration of justice focuses directly on the functional workings of each of these criminal justice system components and their different organizations and elements. For our purposes, the **administration of justice,** or **justice administration,** is the description and elaboration of the structural, functional, and managerial processes involved in the coordination of activities related to determining the incidence of criminal conduct, the detection and apprehension of alleged criminals, an assessment of the credibility of evidence against the accused, a formal judgment about that conduct, and how that conduct is punished.

Essentially, those studying justice administration want to know what is happening in organizations and why. Most of us have a pretty good idea about the general purposes of each criminal justice system component. For instance, we know that the police are interested in investigating crime and catching criminals. We know that prosecutors and the courts are interested in prosecuting alleged law violators and determining their guilt or innocence in court. We know that a lot of people who are convicted of crimes will serve some time in a jail or prison. We know that jails and prisons are populated with inmates. We also know that many of those convicted of crimes do not go to jail or prison. Rather, they are placed on probation and

live in their communities under some form of supervision by probation or parole officers.

Beyond these superficial observations about what each component of the criminal justice system does, we have only a limited understanding of how each of these organizations operates. For instance, we seldom concern ourselves with how people are recruited and trained by police departments. We do not know how shift-work responsibilities in these organizations are allocated or why certain patrol methods are chosen and used. We do not know how policy decisions are made or implemented. We have little or no grasp of the important responsibilities of police executives or those in charge of police departments and other law enforcement agencies.

We lack knowledge about how prosecutors and judges attain their positions, although some of us believe that these persons are often elected to serve for various terms. We do not know how prosecutors decide which cases to prosecute or why certain prosecutors are chosen to represent the state in criminal matters. We do not know about the policy formulation or decision making in prosecutors' offices or how these policies are carried out. We are not well informed about the similarities or differences among state or federal judges, we do not know about their backgrounds or qualifications, and we are not aware of their different courtroom styles. We do not understand why offenders are sentenced in particular ways, or why judges differ in the type of instructions they give to juries before deliberation in each criminal case.

Similarly, we do not know how corrections officers are selected and trained or how jails and prisons are organized and why they operate in different ways. We cannot explain why certain prisons have more frequent rioting among inmates compared with other prisons. We are not aware of the pressures and tedium of correctional work. We do not know about the administrative responsibilities of running jails or prisons. We just assume that there are persons out there who make things run certain ways. Further, we do not know how probation or parole agencies are configured. We are not informed about how probation and parole officers are recruited and trained, nor do we know how they are assigned their clients. We do not know about office policies or the relationships probation and parole officers have with police officers to further law enforcement. Justice administration is intended to bring us up close and personal with this subject matter and more.

Diverse Agency Goals and the Means of Goal Attainment

Justice administration is concerned with several things. If we consider the individual components of the criminal justice system—the police, the courts, and corrections—each of these components has a mission and established objectives. In fact, almost all police departments, court systems, and correctional institutions have evolved goals and mission statements over the years that are used to focus the activities of the personnel who work in these organizations or institutions and provide them with a purpose for performing their tasks. Detecting and apprehending criminals are two of several goals of police organizations. Prosecuting and judging those accused of crimes are two of several goals of court systems. Managing and supervising convicted offenders are two of several goals of corrections organizations. Thus, each of these components is concerned to a degree with offender processing.

But each of these components has other organizational goals. Besides crime detection and control, police departments seek to prevent crime. They invest a considerable amount of time in crime prevention programs. They send police officers to elementary and secondary schools to educate and inform students about drugs, drug trafficking, and the adverse effects of drugs. Police departments sponsor various community programs for youths and others. They offer their assistance to the public in many ways. Many departments have public relations officers to act as liaisons between the department and the community. During the past several decades, many large-city police departments have had to become multicultural and expand their services to accommodate larger numbers of persons of different races and ethnicities. Thus, police departments and individual officers have been encouraged to become more involved in the social and political affairs of cities and communities in various ways.

Prosecutors and the courts have had to deal with a larger volume of criminal cases. Furthermore, the profile of crimes to be prosecuted has been changing gradually. New crimes have emerged as important, such as hate crimes and cyberterrorism. Since most state courts are permitting greater media access through closed-circuit television, court systems have gradually undergone a metamorphosis. Judges, prosecutors, and defense counsel are increasingly conscious of their public image and how their behavior will be interpreted by the media. Some critics have contended that prosecutors and judges are more interested today in processing larger numbers of criminal cases more efficiently than they are with ensuring that justice is obtained for those accused of crimes. Greater social awareness of what goes on in the courtroom has attracted greater attention to what goes on outside the courtroom, including the personal lives of judges and jury members.

Plea bargaining, which accounts for about 90 percent of all criminal convictions in the United States annually, is under attack from various quarters. Prosecutors want more convictions and criminals want greater leniency when punished. The compromise is often a plea bargain agreement that many citizens believe underpenalizes guilty defendants and subverts the justice system in different ways. Various groups insist that criminal defendants should receive their day in court and that plea bargaining ought to be banned in every jurisdiction. Such bans have occurred in several jurisdictions without a great deal of interruption in court affairs. No bans have been successful in eliminating plea bargaining completely from American courts, however.

Institutional corrections does much more than contain criminals for various sentence lengths. The public expects corrections to correct offenders who are accommodated in jails and prisons. Institutional corrections administrators must work with limited budgets that restrict the programs that can be approved and applied in prison settings, however. Furthermore, jail and prison programs are only as effective as inmates want them to be. In most instances, inmates cannot be compelled to involve themselves in self-help programs, despite administrative incentives to do so. Jail and prison overcrowding are pervasive in all jurisdictions. Overcrowding contributes significantly to inmate discontent and violence. Further, the effectiveness of prison programming is undermined, since adequate rehabilitative services cannot be provided for all inmates who may desire them. Only about 20 percent of all U.S. inmates have opportunities to work in prison jobs, for example.

Despite ambitious and large-scale jail and prison construction programs in all jurisdictions, no system can keep up with the growing number of offenders who deserve to be incarcerated. We would now have to construct at least five times the amount of existing prison and jail space to house everyone who deserves to be locked up for various periods. But the money is simply not there for such ideal expansion. Furthermore, if such expansion in prison and jail construction were suddenly to occur, together with an increase in qualified staff to operate such facilities, where would we house *tomorrow's* offenders? It is a fact of life that jail and prison overcrowding will always exist. In recent years, however, private enterprise has increasingly encroached into the corrections field, and several prisons and jails are operated privately now under the watchful eye of the states and federal government.

Apart from institutional corrections is community corrections, to which the bulk of offenders are assigned by judges and parole boards. Community corrections is a rapidly growing enterprise that is operated largely by local, state, and federal governments. As with institutional corrections, private enterprise has become increasingly visible in providing supervisory and monitoring services for correctional clients. Community corrections oversees probationers, parolees, and divertees. A wide variety of programs fall within the community corrections rubric, including home confinement programs; electronic monitoring programs; halfway house operations; furlough programs; educational release programs; work release programs; drug, alcohol, and gambling rehabilitation and counseling programs; day reporting centers; victim compensation and restitution programs; day fine programs; community service programs; and boot camp programs. Because all of these programs function within community settings, many citizens are apprehensive about how they are or should be operated. Real concerns have been raised about public safety. Thus, those involved in community corrections must relate in meaningful ways with the public on a day-to-day basis and keep them informed about new rehabilitative and reintegrative strategies, their purposes, and their implementation.

Another dimension of justice administration focuses on how these agencies, systems, and institutions are organized so that their goals can effectively be attained. Many ideas have been offered about how police departments, criminal courts, and correctional institutions and agencies should be organized and operated. Some of these ideas about organizational operations are better than others for achieving particular objectives. Not all of these ideas are evenly applicable to all organizations in every jurisdiction. Therefore, it is not unusual to find considerable diversity among police department organizations and operations throughout the United States. No two police chiefs or sheriffs have identical views about how their departments should be operated and which policies should be established to govern employee activities. It is also common to find great variation among different state and federal

court systems in how prosecutors determine which cases should be prosecuted and which protocols should be followed by the courts when determining guilt or innocence. No two judges are exactly alike at the state or federal level. Even among the federal judiciary, where the greatest court similarities are found, federal judges are as complex and different from one another as are any two people. Considerable variation also exists among correctional organizations. No two prisons or jails are exactly alike. All are operated in accordance with the individual policies and standards of jail and prison administrators, despite the existence of uniform jail and prison standards, regulatory agencies, and U.S. Supreme Court proclamations that attempt to level the playing field for all concerned.

WHAT IS A CRIMINAL JUSTICE ORGANIZATION?

Any **criminal justice organization** is a predetermined arrangement of persons whose interrelated tasks and specialties enable the total aggregate to achieve goals. It is further characterized by provisions for the replacement of members who resign, transfer, die, or retire; a system of rewards and benefits that accrue to each member in return for services; a hierarchy of authority that allocates power and delegates duties to be performed by the membership; and a communication system that transmits information and assists in the coordination of the activities of the membership.

This book examines criminal justice organizations primarily from the sociological perspective. Although several different themes may be used as subapproaches within sociology, it is generally accepted that social scientists focus on the structural and functional components of social systems (patterns of association among people) within different organizational contexts. Social interaction is a primary target. Therefore, the types of social interaction that occur in criminal justice organizations are described and analyzed. Social scientists frequently ask questions that pertain to organizational structure, such as "What kinds of structural patterns are generated from particular kinds of social interaction?" and "How does organizational change modify existing social arrangements?"

In contrast, psychologists might examine worker aspirations and attitudes and the complex personality systems that are a part of all organizations. Which factors motivate persons to work harder and produce more, or which factors help persons adjust to their jobs, or what are the psychological dimensions of job security, interpersonal relations, and worker anxiety? How employees and other organizational workers orient themselves to their work and clientele has a great deal to do with their personal work effectiveness. In turn, their personal work effectiveness influences overall organizational effectiveness in different ways. Thus, we focus on employee motivations and various factors that affect attitudes and orientations toward work performed.

Social interaction in any criminal justice organization involves individuals with differing personality systems. Several implications for organizational structure stem in part from such factors. Nevertheless, the primary emphasis of this book is on the structure and dynamics of social interaction within criminal justice organizations.

WHY SHOULD WE STUDY CRIMINAL JUSTICE ORGANIZATIONS?

Why should we study criminal justice organizations? Organizational researchers have diverse interests regarding their investigations of organizational phenomena. Some investigators specialize by limiting their analyses to bureaucratic structures and the implications of such structures for the organizational membership at various authority levels. Highly organized and regimented probation or parole offices (POs), for instance, might supervise probationers and parolees more closely. Rule-oriented POs may detect greater numbers of technical program infractions, such as violating curfew or failing drug or alcohol checks. Greater friction between POs and their clients may generate resentment among probationers and parolees. In turn, these feelings of resentment may jeopardize attempts by POs to assist their offender-clients in different ways. Clients may refrain from becoming involved in self-help programs, optional counseling, or other possible treatment. If probation or parole departments require and enforce formal relations between employees and evaluate their staff according to offender recidivism rates, interpersonal frictions among POs themselves will occur and become counterproductive in their efforts to help their clients. Requiring staff to adhere closely to the formal authority hierarchy when submitting monthly reports may cause some POs to distrust other POs or compete with them in adverse ways. Studying how these departments are structured and operate, therefore, can reveal much about why these organizations are or are not effective relating to clients served.

Others researchers study the factors that bring about changes in the sizes and shapes of organizations. How do changes in the crime rate of a particular city change the nature and size of police services, for instance? When new administrators are brought into organizations in order to streamline and improve them, how are the changes these administrators make received by existing officers and staff? For instance, during the 1990s, the New Orleans (Louisiana) Police Department (NOPD) was identified as a department marred by corruption and scandal. Several police officers were arrested for murdering innocent civilians and for trafficking in illegal drugs. Some officers committed perjury when testifying in criminal cases. Subsequently, citizens serving as jurors were more inclined to believe the testimony of defendants accused of crimes rather than the police officers who were testifying against them. There was considerable fear of the police. More than a few citizens were advised by citizen action groups that if they were followed by NOPD cruisers and the officers wanted them to pull over, then they should drive to the nearest police station before stopping. This action stemmed from the fear that certain police officers might assault them sexually or in other ways out on lonely highways. These fears were not without foundation.

Complaints by citizens to the NOPD were referred to the Internal Affairs Division, which tended to ignore or not act on these complaints. Individual officers named in citizen complaints would soon learn about these complaints as well as the names of complaining citizens. Retaliation by these officers against complaining citizens was swift and sometimes fatal. Complainants were threatened, intimidated, or as a last resort, killed. The problem of police corruption and misconduct in the NOPD was so widespread that at one point, the federal government came close to intervening and using federal officers to enforce New Orleans laws. But a new police chief was hired to change things.

The new police chief relocated the Internal Affairs Division to a separate geographical location apart from central headquarters. Confidentiality standards were implemented to protect the identities of citizens making complaints against individual police officers. Citizen complaint review boards were established to provide external monitoring, since the public did not trust that police investigators could monitor their own officers impartially. Further, the new police chief imposed more stringent background checks on new police recruits, and it was soon determined that among the ranks of the NOPD officers were several persons with serious criminal histories. These officers were fired. Other officers suspected of corruption or misconduct were transferred to different shifts and paired with officers who were believed to be untainted by corruption. Personnel changes at all levels were extensive. Not everyone within the NOPD agreed with the new policies of the police chief, but the results-driven chief wanted to bring about positive changes and eliminate the prospect of outside federal intervention in NOPD operations. Over the next few years, overt corruption and misconduct subsided, and the number of citizen complaints against individual officers declined. The NOPD adopted the strategy of community policing in an attempt to rebuild public trust among New Orleans residents.

Organizational researchers not only have different interests concerning the topics to be investigated, but frequently they select different approaches for examining organizational settings. These differences arise in part because of the variety of reasons why investigators conduct their research. The list of specialty areas within justice administration is fairly extensive. No single reason for studying this subject will satisfy all concerned at any given time. Therefore, we will identify several popular reasons at the outset that include the interests of most investigators. The reasons given here are intended to be representative rather than providing an exhaustive compilation. Some of the more common reasons for studying justice administration are the following:

1. Organizations should be studied systematically since we are related to them, directly or indirectly, during most of our lives. Most people either work for, or otherwise belong to, organizations. A greater understanding of the structure and functioning of organizations would be advantageous for many employees. A knowledge of how a person's job fits into the overall organizational work pattern may enable that person to assign greater significance to the work performed. Many parallels exist between criminal justice organizations and other types of organizations, such as department stores, hospitals, fire departments, stock brokerage firms, textile mills, military bases, grocery stores, and manufacturing companies. For instance, automobile manufacturer Henry Ford frequently invited his workers from the assembly lines to visit his office in order to acquaint them with various aspects of automobile manufacturing. He would show them where their particular job fit into the entire process of automobile assembly. This personalized expression of Ford's concern with workers gave their jobs greater meaning, and these workers were increasingly satisfied with the importance of their work tasks and responsibilities. In criminal justice organizations, many administrators have used Ford's methods or similar strategies for enabling their employees to understand the importance of their jobs and instilling within them greater commitment and loyalty. In turn, many employees have improved their individual performance levels and have carried out their tasks more effectively.

2. Organizational leadership can benefit from organizational research that will enable them to plan more effectively whenever changes in organizational structure are anticipated or occur. Organizations are dynamic entities and continually change in response to environmental conditions in an effort to achieve organizational objectives more effectively. Understanding the dynamics of change within organizations can lead to better planning and coordination when implementing new policies or changing organizational leadership and administration. Dealing more effectively with the potential problems associated with changing organizations can significantly reduce the cost of change by improving the efficiency of employees' role performance and the nature of interaction among many work roles. Also, anticipating potential problems can help to improve manager-employee interactions and can lead to a more accepting work climate as employees are given greater consideration in the crucial planning stages. Ultimately, both the administration and employees realize benefits such as increased productivity and greater satisfaction with the conditions under which they perform their jobs.

3. Some persons prefer to investigate the theoretical relations among various aspects of organizational environments. Some researchers believe that it is important to study relationships among organizational factors solely for the purpose of knowing about them. In effect, this is the accumulation of organizational knowledge for the sake of knowledge. Many practitioners find it difficult to understand and relate to the work of theorists. Practitioners want to know how knowledge gained from theorizing can be applied in practical ways. They want answers to the following types of questions: How can changing the method for assigning client caseloads to probation officers maximize their effectiveness? How can improving the job satisfaction of correctional officers reduce labor turnover costs? How can plea bargaining reduce court delays in case processing? How can modifications in police patrol styles result in crime reduction in particular

neighborhoods? Can community policing improve citizen-officer relations and decrease citizen fear of crime? What strategies can be used to detect when police officers are experiencing stress and perhaps are inclined to commit suicide? How can we reduce labor turnover in probation and parole agencies? How can we encourage correctional officers to be more sensitive to the needs of inmates they supervise? How can probationer and parolee recidivism be reduced?

All of these questions are practical ones. Theorists are not concerned with such questions except perhaps in an abstract sense. But we can learn much from the work of theorists. For instance, theorists originally conjectured that if employees are more involved in decision making that affects their work roles, then they might have a greater interest in their work, they might work harder, and they might work more effectively. Subsequently, this theory of worker involvement was practiced in actual work settings and had positive results. Today, it is fairly common for many organizations to involve their employees when making decisions affecting their work, since employers understand that such worker involvement will enhance both employee and organizational effectiveness. A majority of researchers investigating organizational problems adopt a balanced position regarding their immediate and apparent research objectives. They ask *both* kinds of questions: "What are the theoretical relationships among the various aspects of organizations?" and "How can this information be of use to others in dealing with their organizational problems?"

4. Organizations may be studied in ways so that the findings from one investigation can be generalized to several other settings. For instance, counselors and therapists working with drug-dependent parolees and probationers in the community may obtain insights into problems associated with their own subject areas by examining research in correctional institutions about drug-dependent inmates and their characteristics. They may find answers to questions such as "Which counseling methods or treatment therapies seem to work most effectively in causing drug-dependent clients to overcome their dependencies and adopt law-abiding behaviors?" Architectural innovations and experiments have been instrumental in bringing about changes in correctional settings. In many institutions such as jails and prisons, architectural changes and innovations have been implemented so that there are fewer areas that cannot be observed directly by corrections officers. More effec-

tive monitoring methods through direct supervision and/or remote video cameras have reduced inmate assaults and illicit drug transactions appreciably. Correctional officers are now in more strategic positions to observe inmate interactions and respond more quickly to different types of incidents requiring officer intervention and control.

5. Explanatory schemes for individual behaviors can be enhanced by a study of the structure and dynamics of organizations. The impact of organizational structure on the attitudes of individuals is of interest to social researchers. Although criminologists and criminal justicians are perhaps most concerned with these interactions, other persons from related disciplines (e.g., political science, public administration, sociology) frequently use these variables to explain organizational phenomena. Some of the questions these persons might ask are "To what extent does personality influence the structure of organizations?" or "To what degree does the organization bring about changes in the personalities of the staff who comprise it?"

UNITS OF ANALYSIS

The study of justice administration may be approached from several different **levels of analysis** or **units of analysis.** The term *unit* is sometimes used instead of *level* when making these distinctions. Three units of analysis are (1) the individual; (2) the small interpersonal work group; and (3) the formal organization.

The Individual and Interpersonal Units of Analysis

THE INDIVIDUAL UNIT OF ANALYSIS. The **individual unit of analysis** or **individual level of analysis** focuses on the behaviors and attitudes of specific persons. The following kinds of questions might be asked by persons interested in studying organizations at the individual unit of analysis (the examples are fictitious): What makes Judge Joe Smith act in a particular way? How can we motivate state's attorney Joe Smith to work harder? Why does probation officer Joe Smith have a lot of recidivism among his probationer-clients? Why does police officer Joe Smith have so many citizen complaints filed against him? Why is attorney Joe Smith so difficult to get along with when trying to work out a plea bargain agreement? Why does social worker Joe Smith have such a hard time working with juvenile delinquents?

When organizations are examined at the individual unit of analysis, specific persons performing different work roles are described. What are the organizational factors that affect personnel, including their morale, job satisfaction, and work performance? The working personality of police has been investigated extensively for several decades (Goldsmith and Goldsmith, 1974). Individual employees also are described, and their personality systems become the focus of attention for some researchers. For instance, police officers often have been characterized as having a working personality, which suggests that police officers have similar and distinctive cognitive tendencies and behavioral responses, as well as a particular lifestyle (Skolnick, 1994). This working personality is formed through a combination of two main variables: danger and authority. Police officers are trained to be suspicious of others, and the element of danger inherent in police work distinguishes police officers from those who are not exposed to such dangers. Furthermore, police officers are vested with arrest powers and authority. The power and authority they wield distinguish police officers from other citizens, because the police are expected to enforce laws that regulate the flow of public activity and morality (Baker and Meyer, 1980:102–103).

Several studies of police officer candidates have described a fairly strong pattern of self-discipline or control, tough poise, and low anxiety as police officer personality characteristics (Lorr and Stack, 1994). However, other studies indicate that one's personality characteristics may change over time, as officers acquire greater work experience. Some investigations reveal that officers with more than 12 years' experience on the force tend to be cynical, aloof, tough-minded, independent, aggressive, hostile, and more authoritarian when compared with those officers with less work experience (Evans, Coman, and Stanley, 1992). Thus, the amount of time on the job might lead to less flexibility among officers when they are exposed to various stressful experiences.

Some evidence suggests that as police officers mature in their work roles, they are exposed to a greater variety of stress-producing experiences. Involvement in assorted traumatic incidents may lead to emotional problems and special circumstances that may impair an officer's ability to perform effectively on the job. Various stages and corresponding behaviors that officers can experience during their careers are widely documented, from the probation-ary period to the honeymoon period to disillusionment and finally to burnout (Kirschman, 1997). The realities of police work include long hours, shift work, unpredictability, public scrutiny, organizational stress, and personal injuries. Domestic abuse, alcoholism, and suicide are some of the outcomes of untreated stress and burnout, although organizational administrators may be able to mitigate some of this stress and burnout with effective planning, education, and therapeutic counseling. Many officers shun professional help in the form of psychological counseling, however, since this is sometimes interpreted by fellow officers as a sign of weakness. Often, officers most in need of psychological counseling and other forms of social assistance may reject this help because they fear ostracism and scorn from other officers.

Police professionalism is also a variable investigated at the individual unit of analysis. Professionalism is an elusive concept, however, and there have been few attempts to define it precisely or give it a consistent interpretation (Skolnick, 1994). Professionalism signifies the attainment of at least five general objectives: (1) a clearly defined body of knowledge; (2) a code of ethics; (3) ongoing education; (4) uniform standards of excellence for selection, education, and performance; and (5) an unequivocal service orientation (Shigley, 1987). If these standards are applied strictly to law enforcement, it is questionable if professionalism among police officers has ever been fully realized. Increasingly, law enforcement officers are expected to pursue a higher level of education and to take in-service training. In many jurisdictions, educational courses relevant for police officers are recommended but not required. Greater amounts of training and education tend to be equated with greater professionalism, although the type and amount of training or nature of education are often vaguely defined or unspecified.

Improving the professionalism of the rank-and-file police officer means several things. Most large police departments use psychological screening devices to select their police recruits. Many of these departments also use professional psychologists as members of their oral screening boards to assist in candidate interviews and selections (Pollock and Becker, 1995). Minimum educational requirements have been established as prerequisites for employment in many municipal police departments. Also, there are stringent physical standards to be achieved, and the prospective candidate must stand the test of a thorough investigation and background check. In most states, the

BOX 1.1 PERSONALITY HIGHLIGHT

LLOYD W. HALVORSON
Criminal Investigator and Accreditation Manager, Bismarck Police Department, North Dakota

Statistics: Associate of Arts (liberal arts), UND-Lake Region; B.S. (criminal justice), Minot State University; M.S. (criminal justice), Minot State University

Awards and Accomplishments: Safe Driving Award, Bismarck Police Department, 1998; Police Officer of the Year, Bismarck Police Department, 1995; Life Saving Awards, North Dakota Police Officer's Association, 1993–1994; Reserve Law Enforcement Officer of the Year, 1991; Distinguished Student Achievement Award, Minot State University, 1991

Previous Training and Employment: Reserve Law Enforcement Officer, Ward County Sheriff's Department, Minot, North Dakota; Coordinator, Bismarck Area Gang Task Force; Field Training Officer; Certified Law Enforcement Instructor; Specialized Training in Gang Identification, Methamphetamine Investigations, Intoxilizer Operation, and DUI Apprehension

Interests: I became interested in law enforcement while in junior high school. About that time, the city of Devils Lake, North Dakota, where I spent the first 20 years of my life, hired a new chief of police, Chris Mathieson, who moved next door to us. I remember seeing him in his new uniform and observed how he commanded respect simply by his presence. I knew at that moment that I wanted to be a police officer. When I was in the eighth and ninth grades, Chief Mathieson started an Explorer chapter at the police department and I immediately joined up. I still have the patches from my first Explorer "uniform." Chief Mathieson moved away before I graduated from high school, but I never gave up my desire to become a police officer.

Background and Early Experiences: I was fortunate to be raised in a very stable and nurturing home, with two wonderful parents and four brothers and sisters. It took me until the end of my probationary period as a rookie police officer to realize that not everyone is as fortunate as I was. I was extremely naive, in that I had no idea of the circumstances in which some people choose to live or the circumstances and environment that some persons (mainly children and the elderly) are forced to endure. This was probably the most interesting realization I have made as a police officer. Seeing this firsthand sparked not only my advanced academic study, but it also gave me a heightened awareness and cultural sensitivity. (Remember that I grew up thinking that everyone grew up like I did.)

The dynamics of child abuse, neglect, poverty, homeless drunkenness, domestic violence, and gangs are so complex and rooted in so many social problems that they pose a threat to society as a whole. Most often the criminal justice system (and in large part many police departments) are faced with the task of dealing firsthand with these problems. It is frustrating to see police departments work without adequate personnel or resources, so that all they can do is react to the problems. Rarely is the police officer afforded the opportunity to bring people to the table and solve the problems so we can stop reacting to them. Most police officers today are educated professionals who are capable and willing to help solve problems. Instead, the "mediate-negotiate-and-calm-the-situation-so-we-can-react-to-it-again-tomorrow" mentality prevails. Although this is changing with the new momentum toward the community policing and problem-solving philosophy, there is still a long way to go.

I have found that being a police officer is a rewarding and satisfying career. Although frustrating at times, the job as a whole is filled with excitement, humor, camaraderie, and friendship that cannot be explained easily. In addition, the uniform provides a sense of security and confidence in your own ability, and at the same time, it provides a sense of respect, trust, and understanding from the public that no other category of public employee is afforded.

Advice to Students: This is my advice to a newly graduated college student: Do not give up. Becoming a police officer in a major city is not an easy task. Competition is tough, and you will probably spend a year or two testing everywhere and anywhere, just hoping someone will give you a chance. Perseverance usually will help you prevail. I remember beginning my job search, testing in several North Dakota cities (and beyond) and a few state and federal agencies. It seemed like I was getting letters every week telling me that I did not qualify for an interview, or I did not pass this or that portion of a test, or when I did pass, that I was too far down the list to become eligible for employment with the police agency. Although not every applicant will have a successful ending to their job search, most will sharpen their skills, get better at the interviewing process, and finally obtain that sought-after job offer.

prospective recruit must be certified by a regulatory board before being hired. All of these criteria are associated with the improvement in quality of the rank-and-file police officer.

THE INTERPERSONAL UNIT OF ANALYSIS.   The **interpersonal unit of analysis** or **interpersonal level of analysis** is concerned with group interactions and processes. The individuals who make up groups are certainly important, but of greater interest are group characteristics. The following types of questions are often asked by those interested in the study of organizations at the interpersonal unit of analysis (these sample questions are fictitious): Why does the group of probation officers in Birmingham, Alabama, have such excellent rapport with their probationer-clients, such that their clients have very low rates of recidivism? And why does the group of probation officers in Montgomery, Alabama, have such a poor working relationship with their probationer-clients, who have high recidivism rates? Why do the district attorneys in the Los Angeles County office have such low conviction rates, whereas the district attorneys in the San Francisco office have such high conviction rates? Why does it take an average of six days to hold trials in Dade County (Florida) criminal courts, but it takes an average of only three days to hold trials in Volusia County (Florida) criminal courts? Why is there high labor turnover among corrections officers in the correctional facility in Carson City, Michigan, but there is low labor turnover among corrections officers in the E.C. Brooks Regional Facility in Muskegon Heights, Michigan?

Focusing attention on groups of persons as a special interest includes an examination of the following variables: group cohesion, or the extent to which groups on the job band together to promote mutual interests; informal relations in the work group, or the extent to which small work groups in the business-industrial setting are able to complement the formal arrangement of things in the organization; the output or productivity of the work group, or the number of products produced, the amount of paperwork completed, or the number of services performed; and the composition of the work group (e.g., gender, age, and educational homogeneity and socioeconomic status differentials).

For instance, there is a pervasive esprit de corps that binds police officers with one another (Bittner, 1970:63). Police officers often remark that one of the most cherished aspects of their occupation is the spirit of "one for all, and all for one." To the extent that the fraternal spirit binds police officers together, it also serves to segregate them from others in society (Bittner, 1970:63–64). A code of silence exists among police officers in many police departments, and this code can create a situation in which certain police officers will not incriminate other police officers if they observe those officers violating departmental rules or the law. The code of silence is somewhat pervasive among police officers in departments throughout the United States. Police officers close ranks whenever one of their own is criticized or comes under fire from investigative agencies or the public. The informal rules that govern interpersonal police secrecy are violated if one officer discloses the misconduct of fellow officers to others. Such is the strength of interpersonal bonds among officers. This phenomenon is also an important reason why police corruption and misconduct are difficult to identify and eliminate by administrators and others.

Most close friends of police officers are other police officers, although this is not particularly atypical of other professions or occupational categories (Skolnick, 1994). This pattern of social interaction continues over time and gives outsiders the impression that police have their own subculture. This view is similar to George Homans's theory of interactions, activities, and sentiments (Homans, 1950). Although somewhat oversimplified, this theory is that persons who engage in similar activities and interact with one another frequently will develop similar sentiments or attitudes about things. When applied to police officers and the associations they develop with one another, this theory suggests the existence of a rather unique police subculture or police family (Drummond, 1976). This police subculture has many of the same characteristics as societal culture, with special rules to govern one's conduct; a system of rewards and punishments for conformity or rule violations; ways of obtaining recognition, esteem, and promotion; and methods for supporting or excluding those who choose to conform or deviate from established group norms.

The group counterpart of personality for the individual is syntality (Cattell, 1951). **Syntality** is literally the personality of the group. Researchers have found that work groups have characteristics that are different from the simple sum of personality characteristics of the individuals who make up the groups. Police officers evolve subcultures with distinct characteristics, and groups of police officers exhibit a particular syntality or group personality. The same phenomenon is observed among court officers, such as judges, defense counsel, and prosecutors. These persons tend to associate with others like them. Over time, these groups acquire a personality of their own.

Several factors may account for this subculture and its perpetuation over time. For one thing, police officers are selectively recruited and screened through interviews and psychological tests and measures. Most officers are conservative and conventional. Unconventional types of persons probably would be excluded from the selection process in hiring prospective police recruits. It may be that certain types of persons are attracted to police work (e.g., persons who want to exert authority over others, who want to control the actions of people, or who want absolute power) (Bonifacio, 1991).

Sometimes specific individual characteristics are overshadowed by group power and interpersonal factors. Prison superintendents or wardens and police managers often refer to groups of their employees as behaving this way or that, rather than describing the behaviors of individual officers. To a great extent, the group is treated as an independent entity. The group

thinks. The group acts. Social scientists sometimes use the term *reification* to describe this practice. Reification means to treat groups as real rather than as simple aggregates or collectivities of individuals or interacting personality systems. In subsequent chapters, it will be interesting to observe the significance attached to small work groups in police organizations, courts, jails and prisons, and community corrections, and to investigate the degree to which these collectivities play important parts in the growth and development of their respective organizations.

Organizations and Organizational Environments

The unit of analysis of greatest importance to justice administration is the organization. The **organizational unit of analysis** or **organizational level of analysis** concerns the organization in its entirety. Persons interested in studying organizations as organizations are not especially concerned with the individuals or groups within these organizations. Rather, their attention is focused on the organizations themselves. It is as if the organizations are living, breathing entities. The following types of questions might be asked (the examples are fictitious): Why is the annual rate of prison escapes considerably higher in California than in Nebraska? Why does it cost more to operate the Oregon Department of Corrections compared with the Utah Department of Corrections, when both departments are of similar sizes? Why do New York criminal courts have slower case processing time compared with New Jersey criminal courts? Why does the Texas Department of Criminal Justice have more lawsuits filed against it annually compared with the Arkansas Department of Corrections? Why does the New York City Police Department have more widespread corruption compared with the Dallas Police Department? Why is there greater recidivism among Georgia juvenile parolees annually compared with the annual recidivism of Mississippi juvenile parolees?

All organizations, regardless of their complexity or magnitude, are made up of individuals performing roles that are functionally interrelated with other roles. Furthermore, all organizations have one or more work groups of varying sizes. Although our discussion of what occurs in organizations could be limited entirely to describing the behaviors of individuals and small groups, our analysis would be incomplete if we ignored the characteristics of organizations themselves in our description of what is going on and why.

BOX 1.2 HOT PURSUIT: JUST FOLLOWING THE DEPARTMENTAL RULES?

Hot Pursuit in Centreville. In Centreville, Illinois, police officers are authorized to engage motorists in high-speed pursuits whenever motorists attempt to elude them. On Saturday, June 29, 1996, a speeder was clocked by a traffic officer, Sgt. Robert Stadler, traveling 55 mph in a 35 mph zone. The driver stopped, but as Sgt. Stadler got out of his cruiser and approached, the driver suddenly drove off again. Sgt. Stadler pursued the speeding vehicle. About two miles down the road, two other vehicles were coming the other way, returning from a church service. In one car was Clementine Peals, 66, and three of her friends. In the other car, her daughter, Lavon Peals, was following. Clementine Peals had no chance to evade the oncoming speeding car. The speeder slammed into Clementine Peals's car as he attempted a tight turn. The result-ing collision killed the speeding driver and a companion as well as Clementine Peals and her three friends. The Centreville police chief, Curtis McCall, said that the pursuing officer acted in accordance with departmental rules. Thus, his actions were authorized. Lavon Peals had another opinion, however. "The police were negligent. My mother was killed over a damn traffic stop!" said Lavon Peals when interviewed.

What can police administrators do to ensure that high-speed pursuits are controlled or highly regulated? Can policies be developed concerning high-speed chases that will be followed by individual officers? How can administrators regulate the behavior of their officers concerning high-speed chases? What do you think?

Source: Adapted from the Associated Press, "Car Chase Leads to Six Deaths," July 2, 1996.

Organizations as systems of persons have unique qualities and characteristics in much the same sense as individuals and work groups possess certain characteristics. In fact, most organizations may be compared with one another according to specific characteristics that are common to all of them. For instance, we may estimate the size of an organization by counting all employees on the organizational payroll, by observing the numbers of police officers who receive salaries from their departments, by determining the number of inmates accommodated by a jail, or by counting the number of inmate beds in a penitentiary. We might also look at organizational budgets or how much is allocated for organizational expenditures to allow the organization to function over time. Other organizational characteristics might include the centralization of authority and decision-making power, the specialization of tasks and the functional complexity of task interrelationships, and the proportionate size of the administrative component. In subsequent chapters, detailed descriptions and definitions of these variables and others will be presented.

One primary objective of students of justice administration is to explain and possibly predict social phenomena by investigating their relationships with these major organizational properties. Therefore, one important task of organizational researchers is to de-scribe these important characteristics and focus on their interrelationships with other formal organizational properties and their impact, directly or indirectly, on social and individual behaviors.

These different units or levels of analysis are not mutually exclusive. They may be treated and analyzed as separate dimensions of organizational life, however. In fact, there is a great deal of interdependence among these three units of analysis. Organizational changes in size, structure, and complexity influence work groups and worker interactions. In turn, individual employees are affected by change in various ways. By the same token, employees bring their personality systems to their jobs. They cannot compartmentalize their personal attitudes and feelings while performing their work. The organizational theorist Alvin Gouldner (1954) has sometimes referred to this phenomenon as **latent social identities.** All persons have latent social identities. These identities follow them wherever they go and affect whatever they do. Thus, if certain employees are performing poorly or having negative interactions with other work staff, the effects of these poor performances or negative interactions may affect the organization itself. A single act by a correctional officer, such as mistreating or discriminating against a particular inmate, may trigger a wholesale prison riot. Individual employees easily can influence organizations in various ways. We may conclude that a

■ **TABLE 1.1** THREE UNITS OF ANALYSIS OF ORGANIZATIONS AND SOME SPECIFIC INTEREST AREAS AS SUBCATEGORIZATIONS

INDIVIDUAL	INTERPERSONAL	ORGANIZATION
1. Personal motivation	1. Incentives of work groups	1. Organizational commitment
2. Personal productivity	2. Output of work groups	2. Organizational effectiveness
3. Personal goals	3. Goals of work groups	3. Organizational goals
4. Personal adaptability	4. Informal group sanctioning system, flexibility of work group	4. Organizational adaptability

Source: Compiled by author.

two-way relationship exists among these different units or levels of analysis.

Throughout this book, the organizational unit of analysis will be emphasized whenever possible and selected aspects of interaction between this unit and the individual and small group units or levels of analysis will be described. The influence of organizational variables on individuals and work groups will be explained as each criminal justice system component is presented. Table 1.1 summarizes the three units of analysis and depicts some of the major differences between them.

THE OBJECTIVES OF THIS BOOK

The objectives of this book are to

1. *Define criminal justice organizations and why they should be studied.* Defining organizations necessarily involves an examination of various units or levels of analysis, such as organizations as total entities and organizational environments, groups, and individuals. It is presumed that all units of analysis are interrelated. Thus, some attention will be given to the development and evolution of organizational theories as they seek to explain and predict relations between organizational, interpersonal, and individual variables.

2. *Describe the different characteristics shared by criminal justice organizations.* This involves an examination of several types of organizations, including prisons, parole and probation departments, jails, courts, social service institutions, community agencies, state highway patrols, county sheriff's offices, and police departments. Our investigations will include every setting in which the social interactions and procedural arrangements are consistent with the definition of a formal organization. A **formal organization** is a predetermined arrangement of departments and work roles governed

by rules and related so as to achieve one or more goals; members are selected based on their expertise and qualifications for performing work roles.

3. *Identify the unique structural and process-related features of criminal justice organizations that explain these institutions and our understanding of them.* Criminal justice organizations are dynamic entities. As Hall (1972) indicates, however, every social phenomenon may be viewed as static at any given point in time. A static analysis allows us to study which organizational characteristics are interrelated. This approach also provides possible explanations for why and how these organizations have evolved into their present forms.

4. *Describe different* **models** *and* **typologies** *of organizations.* Models enable us to conceptualize organizations in different ways. Utilizing the systems perspective, organizations may be viewed as either closed-system or open-system entities. Some organizations are highly regimented and rooted in predictability and rationality, whereas other organizations are conceived best as human relations oriented with certain nonrational features. Typologies of organizations seek to group them into different categories so that those sharing certain characteristics or qualities can be viewed as somewhat unique from other types of organizations with different sets of characteristics. Models and typologies of organizations operate in tandem to yield interesting explanatory schemes for how organizations go about achieving their goals.

5. *Describe key* **variables** *used in the study of organizations.* Traditional variable categorizations are presented. An array of important variables is introduced according to different organizational dimensions, including structure, control, behavior, and change. Interpersonal and individual variables are presented as well, including group cohesiveness, value similarity, and selected job characteristics, such as decision-making power and job satisfaction.

6. *Examine authority hierarchies and communication networks in organizations.* All organizations have authority hierarchies and a division of labor, complete with formal and informal communication patterns. Various factors interact with superior-subordinate relationships to influence organizational goal attainment. Thus, various styles of leadership and supervisory behavior will be examined. Several types of communication networks are presented as a means of highlighting the importance of this variable for maximizing organizational effectiveness.

7. *Describe the administration of law enforcement systems, the courts, and corrections.* Each of the key components of the criminal justice system is analyzed systematically in separate chapters in order to highlight their unique organizational features. All criminal justice organizations share a common set of characteristics at a general level. Each criminal justice system component has different responsibilities and duties as a part of offender processing, however. Thus, there are separate sets of issues unique to each component that will be highlighted in individual chapters. Law enforcement agencies at all levels are examined, and contemporary issues involving these types of organizations are discussed. The courts are described with a presentation of issues relevant to court processes and functions. Finally, corrections organizations are featured, including descriptions of jails, prisons, and community corrections. In each case, unique problems and issues are presented and discussed. A presentation of the juvenile justice system is included to round out all dimensions of criminal justice.

8. *Describe organizational effectiveness and policymaking in different organizations.* Each criminal justice system component has established policies and protocols for offender processing and general systemic functioning. The legal and political ramifications of policymaking are presented, together with a discussion of the far-reaching impact of policymaking on organizations themselves and the general public served. It is also important to examine the methods that are used to evaluate organizations to determine if they are effective and whether or not their goals are attained over time. Assessing organizational effectiveness is somewhat subjective, although social research and scientific inquiry are used to gauge whether or not each criminal justice system component's aims and mission are realized in given time intervals.

9. *Highlight contemporary issues and trends in criminal justice organizations.* Key issues overlapping all criminal justice system components include holding individual actors more accountable for their actions relating to offender processing. Mechanisms are being established continually to heighten the accountability of all organizations throughout the criminal justice system. Additionally, the legal liabilities of individuals working in different agencies are increasingly scrutinized by a critical public. Standards of professional responsibility and conduct are evolving from various organizations affiliated with law enforcement, the courts, and corrections. New codes of ethics are emerging and innovative policies are being developed to improve community relations and public understanding of the criminal justice process.

THE STRATEGIES APPROACH

One orientation for acquiring organizational information presented in this book is the strategies approach. The strategies approach is not the only approach we could use to present information about organizational events. But it does have its practical uses and applications. This approach views as important the development and cultivation of theoretical and methodological skills as strategies designed for organizational problem solving.

The strategies approach is not altogether different from the approaches used to solve problems in relationships between doctors and their patients, or lawyers and their clients, or correctional officers and their inmates, or police officers and citizens. In each of these interactions, the objective is to devise solutions to problems for the purpose of curing (doctor-patient), assisting (lawyer-client), managing (correctional officers–inmates), or serving (police officers–citizens). In each situation, there is a client system experiencing difficulty: an illness, a lawsuit, behavior management or modification, or public relations and order maintenance. The change agent in each case applies his or her skills to help the client system in various ways. For instance, when you read the different cases at the ends of chapters in this book, you are asked to apply what you have learned from the particular chapter.

Essentially, you are placing yourself in the role of a **change agent** whenever your advice is sought. Change agents are persons who have some amount of expertise concerning individual, interpersonal, or organizational problems. They may be consultants who are asked to solve organizational problems. They provide possible solutions to problems, and organizational members rely on their advice to remedy existing problems. In a sense, each reader is a potential advice-giver or change agent in relation to some **client system** (an individual, a group, or an organization). One acquires a set of useful strategies for the purpose of developing a greater awareness and understanding of the nature and operations of organizations. You may be asked to analyze an organizational problem based on the facts presented and then devise one or more alternative solutions for these problems. Your solutions may or may not be the correct ones, but the important thing is that you are learning about different ways of analyzing these cases and why certain incidents have occurred. Although you may never hire yourself out as an organizational expert and consultant, at the very least you will have acquired greater knowledge and skill in thinking about organizational problems and possible solutions for them.

Problem solving is somewhat difficult at the individual level. Accordingly, at the organizational level, investigators encounter different kinds of problems, but they may have at least the same seriousness and magnitude as individual problems. Some investigators argue that organizational problem solving is less complex compared with individual problem solving. But one thing is clear, regardless of the position one takes: Workable solutions to organizational problems are difficult to formulate and implement. You will experience this problem firsthand as you delve into the different cases presented for written or oral discussion at the end of each chapter.

The use of a strategies approach in our assessment of organizational problems and identification of interpersonal interrelations among phenomena will assist us in examining organizations from a variety of perspectives. One objective of this approach is to develop an impression of the relative strengths and weaknesses of alternative competing explanations for problems. At first it may seem that one must memorize several strategies that may function as a "bag of tricks," and that these tricks can be applied categorically as we shift from one organization to the next in a helping capacity. Although it is useful to have a fund of knowledge about several aspects of organizational activity, the role of the change agent and advice-giver is far more involved than simply dispensing theoretical cures for organizational problems. Change agents not only must assess the organization and its dilemmas, but they also must consider seriously their own capabilities and potential contribution toward solving existing problems. It is not uncommon for change agents (sometimes professional consultants to organizations) to find that the information they have acquired previously in the classroom is of little or no value for specific types of organizational problems. In that event, it is necessary for change agents to be flexible and creative and devise unique solutions for the problems they observe.

Change agents are like artists, therefore, who study the unique qualities of each organization. Through a close collaborative association with the client system, they become increasingly sensitive to whether or not the organization as a client system has the skills and capabilities to deal successfully with its own problems. Their job is to assist client systems to determine if change is necessary, and if so, what the direction and nature of change should be, as well as to provide a reasonable forecast of the possible theoretical and substantive implications of change (Gluckstern and Packard, 1977).

Change agents most capable of benefiting client systems are usually those with (1) the most strategies, (2) the skills to apply the strategies in useful ways, and (3) the insight to counsel with client systems concerning the potential implications of organizational changes they propose. They must be good teachers, good critics, and good listeners. Above all, they must be flexible in their thinking and must not allow themselves to be drawn toward one solution too quickly before considering the merits of alternative solutions.

SUMMARY

The administration of justice or justice administration is an interdisciplinary science that focuses on the functional workings of criminal justice system components and their different organizations and elements. It is the description and elaboration of the structural, functional, and managerial processes involved in coordinating activities related to determining the incidence of criminal conduct, the detection and apprehension of criminals, an assessment of the credibility of evidence against the accused, a formal judgment of that conduct, and how that conduct is punished. Those who study justice administration want to know what is going on in criminal justice organizations and why.

The criminal justice system consists of law enforcement, prosecution and the courts, and corrections.

BOX 1.3 PERSONALITY HIGHLIGHT

SCOTT R. WESTON
Crime Prevention
Sergeant, Minot Police
Department

Statistics: B.S., Minot State
University

Interests: When I was a freshman in high school, I became interested in law enforcement as a career. In my home county, I knew several of the deputies and local law enforcement officers. That curiosity and a sense of serving and protecting the people of this state led me to take criminal justice classes when I enrolled in college.

Once in the college classroom, I was hooked on becoming a member of a law enforcement agency. In Devils Lake, ND, my instructor, Astrid Anderson, was able to put us in contact with many of the law enforcement officers in the Lake Region area. I had positive contacts with these people, and this encouraged me to further my criminal justice education.

I had many positive contacts with instructors and students enrolled in the Criminal Justice Program at Minot State College. For my field experience, I went back to my home county and was able to work with the people who had influenced me in my high school years. Giving back to the communities that had raised me was a very gratifying experience.

After graduation from Minot State, I did not find full-time employment, so I took a summer position with the U.S. Customs Service. This experience helped me to become a more mature law enforcement officer. I took that experience with me when I tested for the Minot Police Department, and I know it helped my chances of being hired by the department. At this time, my fiancée was attending college in Minot, which provided me with additional incentive to remain in this area.

Originally I did not plan to stay at the Minot Police Department for 14 years, thinking I would move on to a federal or state job. I have stayed because of the high caliber of my coworkers. When I leave, this will be my last law enforcement job. I will take my education degree and enter the world of a classroom teacher, my second ambition in life. My first ambition was to be a cop!

Most Interesting Event on the Job: I was on duty as a security officer at Minot State University when George Burns entertained at a Hostfest crowd at the Dome. I was able to "guard" Mr. Burns in the Beaver Booster room before he went on stage. He was watching the baseball playoffs while enjoying a martini and a cigar. I observed a young boy approach him and ask for an autograph, saying it was for his mother. Mr. Burns complied. I looked at my fellow officer and whispered, "If it worked for him, maybe it will work for me." I approached Mr. Burns and asked for his autograph, telling him, "It is for my mother." He looked me up and down and then signed my Minot Police Department notebook. I still have that notebook and the autograph of this fine entertainer.

Other Experiences: One of the good things that has happened to me during my years of service was receiving the North Dakota Peace Officer's Life Saving Award with fellow officers Fred Debowey and Dan Strandberg. Officer Debowey came across a car that had struck a concrete barrier and a tree near Oak Park in Minot. The car was in flames, with a man trapped inside. His legs were stuck between the collapsed dash and the front seat. Officer Strandberg and I arrived at the scene, and along with Officer Debowey, the three of us tried to pry open the passenger door in order to remove the man. The front area of the car was getting very hot. We were afraid the car might blow up, resulting in injury or possible death for all of us. In a final desperate act, all three of us pulled down on the partially opened car door. The effort caused the door frame to bend and shattered the window. We then reached into the burning car, freed the victim's feet, and carried him across the street to safety. The Minot Fire Department arrived and put out the fire. Arriving on the scene, another officer saw that the door had been bent literally in half, and he asked how the fire department had accomplished that. We told him that it was caused by three adrenaline-filled officers. He could not believe it. We came from this experience with a sense of accomplishment and self-satisfaction in that we had probably laid our lives on the line for a total stranger.

On the bad side, unfortunately, there also have been too many instances when I wish I had chosen another line of work. The foremost incident that pops into my mind is the Lipp double murder and suicide. Officer Steve Niebuhr responded to a suspicious incident call at a Minot address. I went to this location as a backup officer. At this residence, Officer Niebuhr discovered a two- to three-month-old baby with its head crushed. On my arrival, we did a protective sweep of the house.

With weapons drawn, using our SWAT training, we systematically searched every room for possible suspects or additional victims. After securing the room of the murdered infant, we went into the basement, where we discovered a dog, beaten to death. We then found the newly adopted baby's mother in her bed. She had been savagely beaten in the head and body with a claw hammer, which was later found. The last room we came to was an upstairs bathroom. Since this room was locked from the inside, we knew the suspect must be there, possibly waiting for us. I jimmied the lock to the door. Officer Niebuhr entered the room and discovered that the husband, the murderer, had slit his wrists and died as the result of these wounds. After the house was secure, I found that I could barely walk. I experienced dry heaves for the first time while on duty. Days later I was still experiencing nightmares about the incident. Although several years have passed, I can still remember parts of the incident as if it happened yesterday.

Advice to Students: Anyone who enters the law enforcement field needs to be aware of the ups and downs of the job. If you know in advance that you will go through emotional highs and lows, professional triumphs and losses, liking your job and hating it, you will be able to prepare yourself to be a good cop. I would suggest that, along with your criminal justice degree, you take another concentration of study. Having this additional background provides you with an alternative choice in the event law enforcement is not what you want to do for the rest of your life.

I would suggest joining an Explorer's Post or a Reserve Officer program. In this way, you will get a taste of this line of work and of the people you will work with on a day-to-day basis. I also would suggest that you sit down and discuss with your family, spouse, or future spouse what this job may ask of you. Shift work, stress, missed birthdays, missed holidays, and the seductions of the job may not be what your family expects from this role as keeper of the peace.

And finally, you will need a commitment to the job. After all the whining and complaining and poor pay, you still need the will and the heart to go out and do the job. You need to care, and you need to have that desire to serve and protect the people in your community and country.

Criminal justice and criminology focus, respectively, on how criminals are processed and why criminals engage in criminal behavior. Each of the three criminal justice system components consists of a network of organizations and agencies designed to achieve goals. The methods of goal attainment for each organization and agency vary, depending on the jurisdiction examined.

Organizations generally are predetermined arrangements of persons whose interrelated tasks and specialties enable the total aggregate to achieve goals. Organizations are also characterized as having provisions for the replacement of members who resign, transfer, die, or retire. They have a system of rewards and benefits that accrue to each member in return for services, a hierarchy of authority that allocates power and delegates duties to be performed by the membership, and a communication system that transmits information and assists in the coordination of the activities of the membership.

Any organization may be viewed from several levels or units of analysis. These units of analysis are the individual, interpersonal, and organizational. The individual unit of analysis consists of persons as personality systems. Attitudes and personal behaviors are fundamental objects of inquiry at the individual level of analysis. Variables of interest to those studying individual employees include job satisfaction, work performance, and morale. The interpersonal unit of analysis consists of groups of persons who interact as a unit within organizational environments. Social interaction among groups of employees are targets of interpersonal inquiry. Variables of interest include work group cohesiveness or cohesion, informal relations among work group members, work group output or productivity, and work group homogeneity. The organizational unit of analysis consists of the organization in its entirety. Although people and groups make up organizations, these units or levels of analysis are secondary considerations. Organizations themselves are the primary objects of inquiry. Organizational size, complexity, structure, effectiveness, and change interest those who study organizations at the organizational level of analysis. All three units or levels of analysis are meaningfully interrelated. Each unit may be studied separately, but it is more realistic to consider that individuals, groups, and organizations have mutual impact or effect.

It is important to study the structural and process-related features of criminal justice organizations because all of us are affected to a degree by one or more of them almost daily. Further, organizational administration can benefit from research about these organizations in order to understand why particular events occur and how changes may be controlled. Organizational research for theoretical purposes may have significant applications, and it may be possible to generalize these applications to a variety of organizations at different times. Additionally, explanations for individual, group, and organizational behaviors can be generated to suggest answers to our questions about what is going on and why. Our general understanding of organizational phenomena also can be improved.

QUESTIONS FOR REVIEW

1. What is the administration of justice? How does it differ from criminology and criminal justice?

2. What are criminal justice organizations? What are some general features these organizations share?

3. Why should we study criminal justice organizations?

4. What are units or levels of analysis? What are three major units of analysis used in organizational research? In what ways are they linked to one another?

5. What is meant by syntality? In what respect do organizations have personalities? Explain.

6. What is the difference between criminology and criminal justice?

7. How do criminal justice and criminology complement the work of justice administration?

8. Why does so much variation exist among jurisdictions with regard to how police departments and correctional institutions are structured and operated?

9. Why is public relations such an important feature of most criminal justice organizations?

10. What is meant by latent social identities? What are some implications for latent social identities for influence on group behaviors as well as on the organization itself?

SUGGESTED READINGS

Cole, David (1999). *No Equal Justice: Race and Class in the American Criminal Justice System.* New York: Free Press.

Polinsky, A. Mitchell, and Steven Shavell (1999). *The Economic Theory of Public Enforcement of the Law.* Cambridge, MA: National Bureau of Economic Research.

Stojkovic, Stan, David Kalinich, and John Klofas (eds.) (1998). *Criminal Justice Organizations: Administration and Management.* Belmont, CA: West/Wadsworth.

• CASE STUDIES •

1. THE HIGH POINT BOOT CAMP

Frank Sweeny is the director of High Point Boot Camp, a state-operated juvenile facility designed to foster discipline, self-control, and law-abiding behavior among 50 juvenile delinquents, ages 14 to 17, who have been sent to the boot camp as an alternative to a secure juvenile facility or prison for juveniles. The High Point Boot Camp has been operating for 15 months and has processed 163 youths. Sweeny, 46, was selected by the Department of Corrections in the state to oversee boot camp operations. Sweeny is a former corrections officer, having served as a sheriff's deputy for six years, a jail officer for four years, and a correctional officer for one of the state prisons for 12 years. While at the state prison, Sweeny was promoted to lieutenant and placed in charge of 14 correctional officers. He prides himself in his ability to work with people, and he has defused several tense inmate situations with his calm demeanor. Under his watch, no officer assaults or serious prisoner fights occurred. Sweeny has a master's degree in criminal justice that he acquired while working as a prison correctional officer. Sweeny's previous work, therefore, has been exclusively limited to adult offenders.

Among Sweeny's responsibilities in his new job as director of High Point Boot Camp was the hiring of 12 staff members. Sweeny believes that education is an important prerequisite to performing corrections work, and he thinks that the principles he has learned and practiced in his jail and prison experiences will work also at High Point. Therefore, he has chosen only applicants with some college, preferably college graduates, to work under him at the new boot camp. Six of the 12 new recruits have had military experience and have received honorable discharges from the service. He has chosen them to act as boot camp instructors to instill discipline within the juveniles under his supervision. Therefore, these instructors conduct daily drills, which involve considerable exercise, marching, and other physical activities. None of these instructors has any experience in dealing with juvenile delinquents. The other employees are in charge of educational programming and instruction, meal preparation, and personal and psychological counseling or related services. One employee is a nurse who handles minor physical injuries. A local hospital nearby is available if someone becomes seriously ill or requires medical attention.

Sweeny has conducted several orientation sessions for his staff members. These have consisted of three eight-hour sessions in which he has outlined the state guidelines for boot camp operation and the protocol he would like his staff to follow. He distributed literature to all staff members concerning the boot camp philosophy and expectations. State guidelines were also included. He advised that as long as everyone went "by the book," they would have no trouble from him. He said that he wanted things to run smoothly, but that he didn't want these juveniles coddled in any way. They weren't sent to the camp to be pampered. He said that he was determined to make a difference in their lives for the good, no matter what it took. He ended his speeches to his staff by saying, "I want the best boot camp in this state. I don't want anyone dropping out or flunking out. Do whatever you have to do, within reason, to get the job done. These kids need to learn discipline because it's obvious they've never had any. Show 'em who's boss. And don't come running to me every time you have little problems. Work them out on your own. You're all educated enough to know what to do. See that you do it."

Juveniles sent to the boot camp have been directed there by three different juvenile courts in nearby cities. Typically, juveniles will spend at least three months at the boot camp. If they successfully complete the program, they graduate and receive a boot camp diploma. The training is rigorous, and the education received by these juveniles is first rate. Both male and female juveniles are accommodated at High Point, and separate dormitories are provided for their use. Their activities are monitored continuously by several of the instructors. They are not permitted to leave the boot camp for any reason. If they attempt to escape from it, they will be placed in a secure juvenile institution for at least a year. Most of these juveniles have committed property crimes, such as burglary, vehicular theft, and larceny, although there are some violent offenders who have been sent there as well.

As a part of their training, the juveniles are supposed to take occasional long hikes in areas surrounding the boot camp. These hikes are usually distances of 5 or 10 miles, and juveniles are permitted several rest pauses and lunch. One hot July afternoon, an instructor, Joe Brooks, was leading a 10-mile hike with 15 juveniles, three of whom were girls. Each juvenile was carrying a backpack filled with 40 pounds of rocks. The rocks-in-the-backpack idea was Joe's, since he was a former drill instructor for the U.S. Marines. He figured that if it was good enough for the Marines, it would be good enough for these juveniles. Brooks didn't clear the plan with anyone. He just did it on his own, and he believed that it would make the juveniles appreciate the value of hard work. Each juvenile was given a small canteen for water. The hike was over rough terrain and Brooks only permitted one rest pause. About two hours into the hike, one girl, a 16-year-old, was lagging behind the other juveniles. Brooks approached her and berated her for holding up everyone. He said that if she did not catch up with the others, then he would put another 10 pounds of rocks in her backpack. The girl was somewhat overweight and perspiring profusely. He told her to take a drink of water and get the lead out.

The girl continued to lag behind, and so, true to his promise, Brooks made her stop. He picked up a few nearby rocks and dumped them into her backpack. "Now handle that," he said. The girl was crying and wheezing, but Brooks ignored it. He believed that juveniles should not be coddled. The girl got up and hefted the heavier backpack on her shoulders. She hiked another few hundred yards, and then suddenly she collapsed. Everyone stopped and stared at the fallen girl. Brooks walked up to her and kicked her in the posterior. "Get up and get moving," he barked. But the girl was still. She was very pale. Brooks leaned over for a closer look. The girl was not breathing. Brooks suddenly began to panic. He pulled the girl over to the shade of a large tree and began performing CPR, but the girl did not respond to his efforts.

Next, Brooks called the boot camp headquarters on his cellular telephone and reported the incident. He said that they needed some immediate transportation to take the girl to the hospital. About 30 minutes later, a helicopter arrived from the hospital. Paramedics examined the girl and determined that she was hardly breathing. They airlifted her to the hospital but she died en route. Subsequent investigation revealed that the girl's medical records, which had been received by the boot camp secretary, disclosed that she had a history of asthma and high blood pressure. Somehow these conditions were overlooked by the new staff. They had just assumed that all of the juveniles who had been sent to them were healthy, and that the judge never would have ordered anyone with known physical ailments to boot camp.

Questions for Discussion

1. Who do you think is to blame for the girl's death? Should Sweeny have had physicians give all youths physical examinations before entering the High Point Boot Camp? What responsibility did Sweeny have to determine the health status of the different juveniles under his supervision?

2. What level of analysis do you believe is most useful for analyzing this particular situation? Why do you think the level of analysis you have chosen is most appropriate?

3. What do you think about Sweeny's concern for hiring educated staff? Are highly educated staff necessarily better than less-educated staff when it comes to operating a facility like a boot camp? Discuss.

4. Joe Brooks's idea to put 40 pounds of rocks in the juveniles' backpacks for their hike was his own. What justification can you provide for Joe's actions? What are some of the criticisms you might lodge against Joe, considering that these were juveniles and not Marine recruits? What disciplinary measures should be taken against Joe for his treatment of the juveniles under his supervision?

5. What administrative procedures could Sweeny implement to make sure that such incidents do not happen in the future? Should they close the boot camp because of this incident? How would you establish policies to govern how juveniles are treated while at the boot camp?

2. THE GRIFFIN POLICE DEPARTMENT

The Griffin Police Department (GPD), located in Okashawa County, is a medium-sized organization in a midwestern state, about 10 miles south of Interstate 70. It serves the city of Griffin, population 65,000. There are 165 police officers and 40 auxiliary personnel. The department has three detectives and a juvenile unit. Most crime in Griffin is property crime, with some delinquency and status offending. The chief of police is Dan Ainsworth, who has been on the job for the past 32 years. Ainsworth worked his way up through the ranks, starting out as a rookie cop with the GPD and moving up in rank over the years. Ainsworth has a high school diploma and no college experience. He is now 61, but he plans on working until age 70. He does not intend to do anything differently, since what

he has done in the past seems to have worked well. He gets along well with the Griffin mayor and city council. His approval rating is high. His police department is running smoothly, and everyone is doing what they are supposed to do. Turnover among officers is quite low, since most officers are satisfied with their jobs.

One day an agent with the Bureau of Criminal Investigation (BCI) pays a visit to Ainsworth. William Frawley has been with the BCI for 12 years and works in the gang task force. Frawley informs Ainsworth that there is a significant and growing methamphetamine problem in and around Griffin, especially on some of the sparsely populated farms in the surrounding countryside. Frawley wants Ainsworth to assign some of his juvenile officers to work with Frawley's agents as well as with some of the Okashawa County Sheriff's Department juvenile officers in an effort to combat this growing drug problem. The last thing Ainsworth needs right now is the visibility of a major gang-related drug problem right in his own backyard. Thus far, his own juvenile unit has said nothing to him about drugs and juveniles as major Griffin problems. He says as much to Frawley.

Frawley produces some documents to show that an increasing number of communities, especially those along major interstate highways such as I-70, have been targeted by juvenile gangs for locating methamphetamine labs for production and distribution. Furthermore, the BCI has an undercover officer pretending to be a gang member. The undercover officer says that Griffin is a major distribution point for much of the methamphetamine and other drugs, such as cocaine and heroin, that are making their way to Chicago, Oklahoma City, Detroit, and Omaha. Ainsworth advises Frawley that it seems that the county boys and the BCI have the situation well in hand. Further, Ainsworth cannot spare any of his limited juvenile officers to work on any task force. He says that he does not see how this is his problem anyway, and he believes that the BCI can handle it without his assistance. He says to Frawley, "Listen, Bill, I'll tell you what. The first inkling my officers have of drugs in Griffin, we'll get together, have a conference, and decide whether we ought to get involved. Right now, I'd just as soon not bother the mayor or city council and scare them with the idea that drugs are all over Griffin. Let's just leave things as they are." Frawley leaves, thinking that he is not going to get any cooperation from Ainsworth.

Questions for Discussion

1. Why do you believe Ainsworth is reluctant to become involved in an antigang task force to combat the spread of methamphetamine and other drugs in Griffin?

2. What are some alternative ways that Frawley could have approached Ainsworth or other officials in Griffin in order to alert them to the dangers of drug manufacture and distribution that were encroaching into their community?

3. What level of analysis is most appropriate for analyzing this particular case? Why?

4. Could the representative from the Bureau of Criminal Investigation and the sheriff of Okashawa County approach the Griffin mayor and city council with their request for police assistance and bypass the police chief entirely? What do you think would be the consequences of such contact?

5. Since the activities of gang members in and around Griffin appear to be affecting drug trafficking in cities in other states, should the BCI network with the Federal Bureau of Investigation or Drug Enforcement Administration to enlist their manpower and assistance in combating this local problem? Why or why not?

CHAPTER
2

ORGANIZATIONS AS CLOSED AND RATIONAL SYSTEMS

KEY TERMS

Bureaucracy
Bureaucratic model
Classical model
Closed-system model
Decision model
Division of labor
Empirical generalizations
Frame of reference

Goals model
Grapevines
Hierarchy of authority
Machine model
Nepotism
Nonrational model
Open-system model
Organizational effectiveness

Organizational goals
Organizational model
Rational model
Scientific management
Theory
Traditional model

CHAPTER OBJECTIVES

The following objectives are intended:

1. To define organizational theory and show how it differs from organizational models

2. To differentiate between open-system and closed-system models and their chief features

3. To present several popular closed-system rational organizational models and describe their primary characteristics and uses

4. To provide a general background for the development of the bureaucratic model, including a discussion of machine theories and the emergence of scientific management

5. To describe the bureaucratic model and examine its characteristics

6. To illustrate why the bureaucratic model is the most popular organizational model and how group and individual behaviors are influenced or affected

7. To contrast the bureaucratic model with the goals and decision models

INTRODUCTION

This chapter is about theories and models of organization. These terms, although sometimes used synonymously, are quite different. **Theories** are integrating mechanisms that seek to tie together different variables in predictable ways, whereas *models* (introduced in Chapter 1) are ways of characterizing organizations in order to view them scientifically. Thus, the same theory of an organization might be used with several different organizational models, depending on the preferences of the researcher and the kinds of organizations studied.

The first part of this chapter examines several popular organizational models that have been used for many decades. Models are classified as either closed or open, depending on whether we use external events or refer to the outside environment of organizations when explaining what is going on and why. Closed-system models are self-contained in that they rely almost exclusively on the internal dynamics and components of organizations to explain organizational, group, and individual behaviors. Open-system models are those in which variables or events that occur outside of the organization (the external environment of an organization) are believed to influence what is going on within the organization and to explain why. Open-system models are more realistic in the sense that no organization exists in a vacuum totally unaffected by the outside world. But closed-system models are used almost all of the time when explaining organizational events. This is because closed-system models are much easier to deal with theoretically, since we do not have to take into account environmental variables in our explanations of organizational events. In order to understand what is going on in a prison and to explain why, for example, we would focus exclusively on what is happening within the prison. We would look at the prison warden, prison policies, correctional officers, inmate culture, officer-inmate interactions, and other organizational components of the prison itself. We would not be concerned with the external environment of the prison, such as the community where the prison is located, the state legislature, the governor, the director of the department of corrections, external food suppliers, and local politicians and judges.

Models also are divided according to whether they are rational or nonrational, meaning that the organizational events that occur are either the result of deliberate, planned initiatives of others or occur naturally or spontaneously. The key rational models of organization are bureaucracy and scientific management. Other rational models include the goals model and the decision model.

ORGANIZATIONAL THEORY

Understanding the seemingly complex networks of interrelations among the various dimensions of organizations is simplified to a degree through the use of theoretical frameworks or logical explanatory schemes. Such frameworks enable us to structure relationships between things in a consistent and systematic fashion. Therefore, organizational phenomena can be examined within the context of a logical scheme that includes a pattern or map of relationships between organizational events or characteristics. In a general sense, a *theory* is defined as an integrated body of assumptions and propositions that are related in such a way as to explain and predict relations between two or more variables (adapted from Merton, 1957:96–99). The elements contained in theories are assumptions and propositions.

Assumptions

Assumptions are analogous to **empirical generalizations** or observable regularities in human behavior (Merton, 1957:95–96). Assumptions imply regularly recurring relationships between things. For instance, some assumptions pertaining to organizations might be (1) a hierarchy of authority relations exists in all organizations, (2) a division of labor exists in all organizations, and (3) a functional interdependence exists between roles in organizations. Such statements need little or no confirmation in the real world. They are statements about the observed nature of things that have been confirmed repeatedly so that little or no exception to them is encountered. We have much confidence in assumptions and take their validity for granted. Let us consider some corroborative evidence of the truthfulness of the three statements made previously.

1. A **hierarchy of authority** exists in all organizations. All police organizations have hierarchies of authority. At one extreme, we have the New York Police Department, with over 27,000 officers. The NYPD is divided into precincts and other divisions, all with elaborate authority hierarchies. At the other extreme are one- and two-person police departments. Such police departments are not exceptional. In one midwestern community, for instance, a two-person department is comprised of the chief, who is a lieutenant, and the subordinate, an officer at the rank of sergeant. It may seem peculiar, but there is a fixed and formal authority hierarchy even in this small department.

All jails and prisons, regardless of their size, have authority hierarchies. The Los Angeles County Jail is one of the largest in the United States, with an elaborate authority hierarchy. In 1998, over 4,100 inmates were housed there, with approximately 1,000 jail officers and staff. There are numerous one- or two-officer lockups in rural counties in every state, however. Someone is in charge, and schedules of rotating shifts govern who does what and when. Regardless of the magnitude or the scale of the organization, a hierarchy of authority is present and dictates lines of power among superiors and subordinates (American Correctional Association, 2000:54).

2. A **division of labor** exists in all organizations. The Federal Bureau of Prisons is one of the most elaborate correctional organizations, with a centralized chain of command as well as a division of labor. This division of labor oversees all aspects of federal corrections, including the different federal correctional institutions and medical centers. An inspection of the American Correctional Association's *2000–2001 Directory* discloses a host of different positions at each federal facility, regardless of its size (American Correctional Association, 2000). Some personnel supervise inmates, and others prepare meals and launder dirty clothes, blankets, and sheets. On-call physicians are available to treat inmate ailments. There are different levels of command and areas of responsibility. Again, even one- and two-person lockups and police departments have such divisions of labor.

Remote counties in Virginia and Tennessee have justices of the peace and other officials who preside at informal proceedings to fine speeders or petty offenders. The courtrooms may be trailers near farmhouses. Justice is swift and certain. A clear division of labor is observed, regardless of how simple it appears to us. *Court TV* overwhelms us with courtroom dramas daily, and we are impressed with the formality of the proceedings presented. A clear division of labor is apparent in most city courtrooms where serious criminal defendants are being tried. At one end of the courtroom spectrum are full-scale courts, complete with juries, prosecutors and defense counsel, and a host of court officers. A trial may transpire over several days or weeks. At the other end of the spectrum are courts such as those portrayed on television. *Judge Judy* is a popular television courtroom show in which civil cases of limited jurisdiction are dispatched without juries or other fanfare at the rate of 15 minutes each or less. Even in these smaller-scale courts, a persistent formality can be observed between the judge and the respective litigants. The simplest division of labor preserves the formal mechanism of judicial decision making and the presentation and evaluation of evidence.

3. There is functional interdependence between roles in organizations. When police officers make arrests, they take arrestees to city or county jails for booking. At these jail facilities, jail officers fingerprint and photograph those booked. Other personnel determine whether those booked should be placed in cells or released on their own recognizance. In situations in which serious charges have been filed, defendants may appear before magistrates or judges and bail is determined. Some jail officers have responsibility for transporting inmates to courts for periodic appearances, such as preliminary examinations or arraignments. Judges rely on others to make sure prisoners are in court on time. Other jail officers oversee inmates accommodated in cells and cell blocks. Considerable interdependence can be found among work roles in police organizations, jail settings, and courtrooms.

Therefore, assumptions about organizations are at the level of factual detail and need little if any corroboration. We make many assumptions about criminal justice settings and what goes on in these settings. Assumptions are the bedrock foundation of theories about organizations. In a theory, assumptions provide a foundation for the development of an explanatory framework that will lead to the deduction of more tentative statements that can be tested in actual organizational situations. These statements are called *hypotheses*. Hypotheses are statements that can be subjected to empirical test to ascertain the validity of the theory from which they were deduced.

Propositions

Propositions differ from assumptions in degree; they have not yet achieved the generality and consistency of assumptions. Yet propositions do provide somewhat tentative reflections of the real world. If we were to place propositions on a continuum with assumptions, it might look something like the following:

Certainty←——(Assumption)—
—(Proposition)——→Uncertainty

This continuum suggests that we can differentiate between assumptions and propositions according to their respective degrees of certainty or uncertainty. Compared with propositions, assumptions have a greater degree of certainty attached to them. Not all researchers are in agreement about which statements should be labeled as assumptions and which ones should be labeled as propositions at any given time, however.

Some examples of propositions follow: (1) Increases in police officer professionalism reduce the number of citizen complaints against police officers;

(2) The effectiveness of correctional officers increases as they are given more important responsibilities; and (3) Judges make more objective sentencing decisions relative to one's race, ethnicity, and gender to the extent that they become aware of how these factors influence their sentencing decision making.

We are uncertain about the first statement, and this uncertainty also might exist for the other two statements. For instance, police officers may acquire greater professionalism through different activities, such as taking college coursework and specialized law enforcement courses. But although these officers may acquire the tangible criteria of professionalism, they may not practice good human relations skills with the public. Thus, public complaints against officers may continue at previous complaint levels, despite greater police professionalism.

Also, we might think that if we give correctional officers greater responsibilities, they may become more effective in their work. But greater responsibilities for some officers may heighten their anxiety over work. They may be unable to cope with the difficult demands of greater responsibilities. One reaction might be to do most or all of their work poorly, since they are overwhelmed by additional responsibilities.

And what makes us believe that judges suddenly will sentence offenders impartially if they are made aware of their racial, ethnic, or gender biases? Some judges who make disparate sentencing decisions and are clearly influenced by racial, ethnic, or gender factors believe that there is not a single prejudiced bone in their bodies. Thus, merely making judges aware of their sentencing disparities attributable to race, ethnicity, or gender will not necessarily make them better judges who will make more impartial decisions.

Each of these statements lacks the degree of certainty that characterizes assumptions. We may believe that in many instances, these propositions are valid. We may believe that more professional police officers will relate better with the public and generate fewer citizen complaints. We might believe that giving correctional officers more responsibilities might also heighten their work effectiveness. We might even think that most judges who become sensitive to race, ethnicity, and gender in their own sentencing decisions might change their behaviors and conduct themselves more impartially. But there are too many exceptions to these statements. Thus, we label them propositions instead of assumptions.

Theorists construct theories consisting of both assumptions and propositions. By carefully integrating empirical generalizations with less certain statements, the theorist is able to advance a theory to a level at which phenomena can be explained or understood. The theorist makes the most significant contribution to organizational theory at this juncture by extending the more certain knowledge about things into areas that lack satisfactory explanations or have been studied only infrequently. Some more general examples of propositions are (1) group cohesion varies directly with goal clarity, (2) the frequency of communication varies directly with type of authority, and (3) productivity varies directly with type of supervision. Again, researchers exercise judgment in determining which statements will be labeled as propositions and which ones will be labeled as assumptions or hypotheses.

In the context of uncertainty and certainty, hypotheses are closest to the uncertainty end of the continuum. Propositions may be former hypotheses that have been supported by empirical testing in past studies. Assumptions are placed more toward the certainty end of the continuum, and therefore they are often the foundations of our theories. We need building blocks as supports for more tentative statements about events. Our scientific knowledge tends to move gradually toward certainty through continuous reexamination of particular phenomena in real-world social situations.

Some Problems with Our Definitions of Organizational Phenomena

One of the problems with trying to label particular statements as propositions or hypotheses or assumptions is that there is ongoing research in organizations that produces new information and refines and modifies our explanations of organizational events. Therefore, what is a proposition today might develop into an assumption tomorrow. This is simply the result of an accumulation of knowledge in given subject areas. The more we know about certain organizational phenomena, the more certainty we acquire about how different variables are related with one another. Furthermore, new ideas have the effect of altering our current definitions of things as well as changing our opinions about them and the strategies we use to investigate them. The more we learn about a given phenomenon, the better we are able to evaluate statements related to it as being either propositions or assumptions.

Reviewing the research literature on a variety of criminal justice topics sensitizes us to the fact that not all topic areas are researched equally. Some topics have received considerable attention in recent years, such as boot camps, police use of deadly force, prosecutorial discretion and misconduct, and electronic monitoring/home confinement, but other topics have been investigated less frequently or not studied at all. For example, little is known about campus theft or the effect of probation officer use of firearms on the job. As a result, we know much more about boot camps than we do about campus thefts. Our theorizing about boot camps and boot camp organization logically will be more sophisticated, since we know more about the subject because of the extensive research work of investigators. Thus, our knowledge about different topics in organizational analysis evolves or develops unevenly.

Another difficulty is that various researchers using the same statement or statements in their theoretical formulations may choose to use the statements differently. For example, some investigators may believe that the information currently available about a particular phenomenon is insufficient to make a strong assumption about it, whereas other researchers might readily include the same statement in their theoretical schemes as an assumption without question. Different uses of identical statements create different kinds of theoretical and methodological problems for investigators who study the same dimension of an organizational phenomenon. Such inconsistency promotes conflict, confusion, and disagreement among these researchers. Some amount of disagreement will always occur among researchers concerning how much is known about specific topics and how the results from different investigations over time should be interpreted and evaluated.

Although justice administration currently reflects some amount of consistency concerning how organizational phenomena should be defined, much disagreement and inconsistency still exist with respect to research findings and their systematic interpretation. It will become increasingly evident that justice administration offers investigators an endless reservoir of phenomena to study and explain. Also, we will see that a wide variety of approaches (theoretical, methodological, or both) to organizational research problems are accepted and applied within this flexible domain of social activity.

Levels of Theory

In the same sense that there are different levels or units of analysis for investigating justice administration, there are also different levels of theory. In fact, investigators construct theoretical schemes to fit the particular unit of analysis they choose for describing organizations. As a result, researchers who study individuals tend to devise theoretical schemes to account for relationships between individual motives and subsequent work actions or between work attitudes and subsequent job effectiveness and work performance. Researchers who study small groups of employees tend to focus on the nature of interpersonal relations, and they devise theoretical schemes to account for these associations.

Researchers who study organizations in their entirety tend to develop theories to account for general organizational activities. Their explanatory schemes often include such variables as organizational size, complexity, and levels of supervision, as well as the functional autonomy of organizational roles and the division of labor. As the level of analysis moves from the individual to the work group to the organization at large, psychological explanations of individual behaviors on the job are gradually replaced with sociological explanations of organizational phenomena.

Some theoretical schemes attempt to integrate all units of analysis with one another. These theoretical formulations are more difficult to construct, but they have the advantage of accounting for a greater share of organizational behavior more effectively than any single unit of inquiry considered separately. The organizational unit of analysis will be emphasized throughout this book, although we will not ignore the important contribution and influence of other units or levels of analysis.

A theory about an organization is different from a model of it. Our conceptions of theories and models of organizations are sometimes blurred because these two terms are frequently used synonymously. For instance, one researcher has said, "There are many different theories or models of organizations . . . [and] they tend to fall into two broad generic types" (Litterer, 1965:147). Another investigator says, "There will be little need to separate a theory from a model" (Krupp, 1961:54).

Highlighting meaningful differences between theories and models, Rubenstein and Haberstroh (1966:18) have said that

> Theories are structured such that the conclusions derived from them can be placed into . . . empirical hypotheses and confirmed or refuted by experiments. Models, on the other hand, are systems standing in the place of another, usually more complicated, system or object. Models have structures such that their premises are interpreted. A

theory can be refuted by a single contradictory empirical finding; a model is not exposed to refutation, but it is used as long as any benefit can be derived from it. A model can continue to be useful even though it yields many conclusions which are clearly wrong, provided only that they yield some conclusions that are correct or useful. A theory is expected to yield only true conclusions.

In this book, a sharp distinction is made between organizational theories and models. Theories are interrelated sets of assumptions and propositions arranged so that a logical explanatory and predictive scheme is established from which testable hypotheses can be derived. A model refers to a set of organizational characteristics that permit portrayal of an organization or organizations from a particular viewpoint or dimension. For instance, correctional institutions and agencies manage inmates, probationers, and parolees in different ways. These organizations are almost always faced with inmate overcrowding or high probation or parole officer caseloads. The effectiveness of correctional institutions and probation/parole agencies often is measured by the recidivism rates of these inmates or clients. One way of looking at these types of organizations is in terms of what these organizations must do to minimize inmate/client recidivism rates. Our attention would be focused on the extent to which different departments within these organizations perform functions to assist overall organizational performance with respect to reducing recidivism rates. Sometimes, researchers have labeled this view of organizations as either the goals model or the survival model (Hudzik, 1987).

If we agree that organizations are predetermined arrangements of persons whose interrelated tasks and specialties enable the overall organization to achieve its goals, then this definition is consistent with the goals model. Models direct our attention toward certain dimensions of these organizations so that our theorizing about them can be enhanced.

Some departments in correctional institutions operate vocational/technical training and educational programming for inmates. Other departments offer counseling and therapy. These departments are designed to offer various types of rehabilitative assistance such that an inmate's success chances are improved on parole. We evaluate the effectiveness of these organizations by paying attention to the quality of their products, released inmates. Do released inmates have high success rates? Do they manifest low

recidivism? Viewing these organizations in terms of what they must do to survive, or what they must do to achieve goals, means that we can gain a better appreciation for different kinds of problems faced by these organizations and departmental units within them.

Organizational models function as schemes in which theories can be classified and constructed. Therefore, if we choose to view an organization from a particular perspective, such as applying model *X*, a goals or survival model, what can we theorize about interrelationships among various organizational variables? If we use an alternative organizational model, such as model *Y*, then our attention might be focused on other factors. For instance, we might view correctional institutions in the context of an equilibrium model, our model *Y*. In the context of the equilibrium model, our attention is focused on what the organization must do to maintain the status quo or some type of equilibrium.

For example, some people have characterized prisons as warehousing violence. Our prisons are warehouses, according to these observers. Violent offenders are warehoused for a period of time, shielded from the public. The public is protected, although warehoused inmates are merely maintained, fed, watered, and clothed, like cattle. There is little or no concern for inmate rehabilitation. No one is concerned about the recidivism rates of these inmates, since their incapacitation is the realized goal. Do these organizations maintain prisoners adequately? The federal penitentiary at Florence, Colorado, is considered a maxi-maxi, admin max, or supermax prison, where inmates are under lockdown for 23 hours a day. There are no rehabilitative programs or services offered to these inmates. They merely exist from day to day until they are released. Some of these inmates are serving life-without-the-possibility-of-parole sentences. As long as these inmates are accommodated with minimal provisions for their physical comfort and safety, the correctional organization is considered effective simply by maintaining its equilibrium over time. Thus, our model *Y*, the equilibrium model, causes us to view correctional organizations in a way (inmates are incapacitated) different from our model *X*, the goals or survival model, in which our concern is with product (inmate) quality (low recidivism rates, high success rates, rehabilitation).

Models and theories complement one another. Although models and theories are not identical in either form or function, they are very much related to one another in other respects. Certainly we would not call a

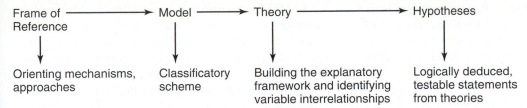

FIGURE 2.1 The Relation Among Frames of Reference, Models, Theories, and Hypotheses.

Source: Compiled by author.

frame of reference a theory. The frame of reference, or the particular way someone chooses to look at a research problem, does not necessarily convey the explicit explanatory scheme involved in linking the explanation of the event with the event itself. The relation between frames of reference, models, and theories is illustrated in Figure 2.1.

In sum, justice administration has many organizational models that emphasize different dimensions of organizations. By contrast, we have relatively little information that can be labeled as organizational theory. Organizational theory in the formal sense is conspicuously absent in justice administration research today. More often than not, classification schemes or models are passed off as theories, when in fact, they have little or no explanatory or predictive value.

MODELS OF ORGANIZATION AND THEIR CLASSIFICATION

A long time ago, an Indian tsar summoned several blind men together and asked them to describe an elephant that they were allowed to touch. Each blind man touched a different part of the elephant (i.e., legs, trunk, tail, head, tusks, and sides), and, as a result, each gave a different account of what an elephant was like (Tolstoi, 1928:439–440). One blind man who felt the elephant's tail said, "An elephant is like a rope." The blind man who touched the elephant's legs said, "An elephant is like a tree."

In some respects, this story may be adapted to fit organizational researchers who select different approaches for investigating organizational behavior. Depending on the model chosen for analysis, a different view of organizational phenomena will be obtained. A model functions, in part, to provide the researcher with a way of looking at organizations.

Each **organizational model** stresses a particular dimension or characteristic of organizations. To a degree, models complement one another in that some of them focus on aspects of organizations that other models tend to ignore. Organizational models are used because of the unique explanatory advantages they give to social investigators as they attempt to account for the observed conditions of organizational structures, whether they are prison systems, police departments, or courts.

Given the rather large number of organizational models, a question arises concerning which model is best to use under most organizational conditions. Although this question is easily asked, it is not easily answered. Currently there are several barriers that prevent unanimity regarding which of several organizational models is most productive and universally acceptable. Some of the more significant barriers follow.

1. All organizational models are replete with exceptions. Thus far, organizational models are either too narrow in application (i.e., they fit a limited number of organizations but do not apply to the rest of them) or too broad (i.e., they are so generally descriptive that they are of little value to researchers in explaining the differences between two or more organizations that appear on the surface to be identical with one another). Researchers who use organizational size as a classification characteristic find that a sufficient number of organizational properties exist to contaminate relationships between the size factor and other dimensions. For instance, two police departments, police department A and police department B, may be the same size, with 200 full-time officers each. However, police department A may have 10 supervisory levels, whereas police department B has only five supervisory levels. With 10 supervisory levels in police department A, more supervisors are available to supervise officers. Generally, officers in police department A may feel closely supervised, since their supervisors have a great deal of time to supervise them. These officers may have some resentment and may believe they have less autonomy to function as officers. They may think that supervisors are constantly reviewing their work and checking up on them. In police department *B*, however, the fewer supervisory personnel do not have time to closely supervise their officers. As a result, the officers believe they have quite a bit of autonomy to do what they want and to practice their crime-fighting skills such as drug interdiction or prevention. Thus, two similar organizations can be identical in size but have very dissimilar job satisfaction levels among their respective police officer groups (Benson, Rasmussen, and Sollars, 1995; Dantzker, 1993).

2. All models emphasize different dimensions of organizations. Many of these dimensions are equally important. Therefore, the deliberate inclusion of particular characteristics and the systematic exclusion of others render most, if not all, models inadequate for analyzing organizations. Two different criminal courts in Virginia may be viewed quite differently by different researchers. One researcher may view criminal courts as a system of structures and functions. Another researcher will look at the court as an input-output system. The view that courts are systems of structures and functions stresses court organization and the interplay among judges, prosecutors, defense counsels, and court officers (Sloan and Miller, 1990). The view that courts are input-output systems focuses our attention on numbers of case filings and case processing time (Nelson, 1992). Little attention is focused on the interplay between court actors, the structure of courts, and the functions of various court officers (Knepper and Barton, 1996). Two independent explanations for case processing might be described, with each differing according to the researcher's view of court organizations.

3. Many models are derivatives and modifications of others. The terminology used to describe the resulting subclassifications of certain organizational models is inconsistent and confusing. Should a researcher talk about classical organizational models, or machine models, or traditional models, when all of these refer to the same thing? Or should the investigator refer to goals models, rational models, effectiveness models, professional models, or human relations models when discussing bureaucratic models? The overlapping nature of models poses a significant problem for those who want to make decisions about which models to use for organizational analysis.

4. Many organizational models are designed for examining static organizational arrangements. Given the fact that all organizations are constantly changing in different ways, some models are unrealistic and eventually become inapplicable as organizations change in size, complexity, and function.

5. All models vary according to the primary unit of analysis selected for investigation. Motivational models, which emphasize personal willingness to become involved in organizational activity and to pursue the organization's goals, focus on the individual as the unit of analysis (Florida Office of Program Policy Analysis and Government Accountability, 1996b). The human relations model focuses primarily on the unit of the work group. The equilibrium model selects the entire organization as the basic analytical unit.

6. Models constructed many years ago continue to generate criticism and dialogue in contemporary justice administration literature. More recently developed schemes also are subjected to the same type of scrutiny and criticism. The uneven utilization of models in research has no doubt contributed to the extensive investigation of the validity of a few types, whereas other models have not as yet been exposed to specific research applications. Many researchers have legitimately proclaimed that, at least for now, we do not have sufficient information about these models to make competent judgments about their usefulness as analytical tools. We are still in the process of inventing new models and conducting ad hoc investigations of these as well as older models.

Since the development of organizational theory is heavily dependent on a satisfactory organizational model, the present theoretical void in organizational analysis is not entirely surprising. Given the existing conceptualization and theoretical inadequacies of formal organizational research, an attempt will be made here to place several organizational models in proper analytical perspective in relation to one another. Accompanying each of these models in the following presentation will be brief discussions of their relative usefulness. Justice administration is an art, in that decisions about interrelationships among variables in the social world are not always clear-cut. Rather, the process of determining causal relationships between things is complex and tedious, and it frequently demands that the researcher use some degree of imagination to locate the best approach for studying the problem as well as the best solution for it. The assessment of various models or strategies for analyzing organizational arrangements is equally arduous. The researcher compares and contrasts, ultimately selecting a model that offers the most strategic explanatory advantage.

The state of organizational analysis is such that classificatory schemes are needed in every facet of social life for thought and action (Hall, 1972:78). Despite the need for typologies, no adequate scheme for organizations is currently available. One obvious implication of this statement is that we currently have a collection of inadequate models for organizational analysis. In fairness to existing schemes, it would be more accurate to say that all schemes exhibit weaknesses as well as strengths, especially in relation to particular organizational theorists, given the shortcomings of our technology and theoretical sophistication. Although organizational theorists attempt to develop all-encompassing models in their endeavors, they are usually among the first to catalog the weaknesses, inconsistencies, and inadequacies of their own schemes.

In contrast to the "without exception" criterion used to assess the adequacy of models, we will assume that each scheme selected for discussion here possesses both weaknesses and strengths complementary to other schemes. A reprise of an earlier observation about models is that they can continue to be useful even though they yield many conclusions that are clearly wrong, provided only that they yield some conclusions that are correct or useful (Rubenstein and Haberstroh, 1966:18).

The classification of models is almost as difficult as developing the models themselves. This is particularly true when we consider the pressure on theorists to make original contributions to their field. In spite of this pressure, there are continuities among various models developed to date. Although some models are distinct from the rest and are not amenable to easy grouping, others may be categorized conveniently under several general headings. For instance, all organizations, regardless of their degree of complexity, formality, or size, may be viewed as social systems of interaction. One of the basic assumptions of this book is that meaningful explanations of organizational behavior cannot be provided without due consideration given to the processes of social interaction within organizations.

All organizational models reflect particular ways of looking at organizations and the groups within them. At least 18 basic premises and orientations in theories of organization have been identified that serve to illustrate the differentiation between various organizational schemes. For instance, groups can be viewed as (1) cultural products, (2) agents of exchange with their environment, (3) independent agencies, (4) systems of structures and dynamic functions, (5) processing and input-output systems, (6) structures of subgroups, (7) biological-social entities, (8) collections of individual members, or (9) summations of member characteristics (Stogdill, 1974:4). It has been suggested that which concepts and problems are regarded as important in the study of organizations is determined in part by the philosophical and professional schools espoused by individual researchers, and in part by individual conceptualizations investigators want to advance (Stogdill, 1971:3–4).

SOME FUNCTIONS OF MODELS

Organizational models are different from theories of organizations, but they do perform several important functions. The most significant function of models is that they permit investigators to structure organizational components into meaningful patterns that are useful in developing theoretical schemes. Each successive model that is developed becomes the basis for explanations of organizational events.

Another function of organizational models is that they sensitize us to particular aspects of organizations that we might ignore if we applied some alternative model. If we consider several competing and alternative models when viewing the same organization, we get different impressions of the organization by viewing it from these different perspectives. This is comparable to examining a topographical map from different positions. What may not be clear according to one view may become clearer when viewed from another angle. Models, therefore, are the means by which we structure our thinking about organizations and systematize our investigations of them scientifically.

Models have several limitations. Each model focuses our attention on specific dimensions of organizations, but we tend to ignore other equally important dimensions of organizations. Thus, our organizational models act like blinders on horses: We see events quite clearly when they are directly in front of us, but we do not recognize other equally important events or dimensions as significant or important. Any one particular model for analyzing organizations and their structures and operations will have an upside and a downside. Therefore, there are both positive and negative implications for using models. Sometimes researchers will consider an organizational structure from several different perspectives in order to determine which orientation yields the best vantage point for assessing problems within the organization. Later we see that many organizational models exist and that they overlap one another to some degree. The weaknesses of some of these models may be offset by the strengths of other models. Some limitations and some strengths will always accompany each model selected for organizational analysis.

CLOSED-SYSTEM AND OPEN-SYSTEM MODELS

Models can be either **closed-system models** or **open-system models** (Katz and Kahn, 1966:18). Closed-system models rely almost wholly on internal organizational processes to account for organizational behavior. For example, many penitentiaries are self-contained, largely self-sufficient entities, complete with food services, medical facilities, recreation, vocational/educational training, and personal or group counseling (North Carolina Bar Association, 1971). What goes on in penitentiaries might be explained by exploring only those processes and aspects that occur within the penitentiaries themselves. We would not pay attention to the state legislature or state policy governing the state penitentiary. We would not search for newspaper articles that describe how the penitentiary is being managed or report on the nature of prisoner rioting or discontent. We would not focus on how inmates in other penitentiaries are treated. We would concentrate only on internal prison operations and procedures to account for any observed events (Surette, 1979). This method is reflective of the closed-system perspective.

In contrast, open-system models stress the interrelationships of organizations with their greater external environment and seek to explain organizational behavior by using factors and events that occur both within and outside of the organization. In the state penitentiary example, if prisoners riot and we want to know why, we would not limit our investigation to strictly internal phenomena, such as the presence or absence of inmate grievance councils or infringements of inmate rights or maltreatment of particular inmates or correctional officer misconduct. Rather, we would consider all factors, including how inmates at other prisons are treated. It makes sense that prison inmates read newspapers, watch television and news broadcasts, and are acutely aware of the treatment inmates receive in other prisons (Kelly and Ekland-Olson, 1991). If there are major discrepancies in how inmates at two or more different prisons are treated, then some amount of rioting can be explained. Organizations do not exist in a vacuum. Rather, they exist in an environmental context with other organizations (Shichor, 1993). Thus, if we are trying to explain courtroom actions, police department policies and police officer actions, or prison inmate rioting, it is realistic to consider both internal and external factors occurring in the lives of inmates that may affect or influence their conduct (Londard and More, 1993).

We do have a choice of which types of models to use, closed-system or open-system models, but closed-system models are easier to work with theoretically (Munro, 1974). This is because we do not have to weave external factors and other organizations from the environment into our explanations of events within a single organization. Open-system models are more realistic, however, in that they recognize the presence and significant influence of external factors that impinge on organizations at all times. Two researchers have described the difference between closed-system and open-system models as follows:

> The simplest and perhaps most widely used and most valuable application of the systems concept is that of closed-system analysis. Notice that a closed system is a hypothetical construct. Closed systems do not exist in reality. There never was, and probably never will be, a completely closed system, because components are always influenced by forces not being considered—that is, by forces outside the system itself. But closed-system analysis as a way of *thinking about* the interaction of components is extremely useful. (Rice and Bishoprick, 1971:164–165)

Using the closed-system and open-system classification distinction, we can generate two orientation groupings, shown in Table 2.1 (p. 36).

A simple frequency count of these different views under the closed-system and open-system distinction provides tentative support for the contention that closed-system analysis is most widely used in research (Rice and Bishoprick, 1971:164). Certainly the research advantages of studying an organization without considering external factors as causes of organizational behaviors contribute strongly to the use of closed-system analysis. Another advantage is the increased simplicity of explanatory schemes of organizational phenomena that do not have to utilize and account for the effects of external factors.

Several popular organizational models have been selected and grouped under the closed-system and

BOX 2.1 HOW MUCH COMMUNICATION IS THERE AMONG PROSECUTION, THE COURTS, AND CORRECTIONS?

Rehabilitation or Fixed Amounts of Incarceration as Punishments? Mixed messages are being sent from out there in corrections-land. On the one hand, prosecutors convict and put away the criminals, usually for fairly long incarcerative periods. On the other hand, prison officials establish rehabilitative programs to turn criminals around and make law-abiding citizens of them. Rehabilitation is based in part on an incentive system. Prisoners are encouraged to enroll in self-help programs to the extent that the programs offer them something in return. In some cases, prison authorities can reward prisoner participation in rehabilitation programs by paroling them earlier than might otherwise be the case if they do not participate in such programs. In Mandan, North Dakota, for instance, a program has been established to assist nonviolent first-time felons and persons who have committed drug-related property crimes. Prisoners are chosen for the legislature-approved program according to objective criteria and their prospects for self-improvement. They receive treatment through the state hospital and counseling services. They generally spend between 60 and 90 days in the program, according to Tracy Stein, a release program manager for the state corrections department. Officials have provided figures to show that 154 prisoners participated in the program during 1999. Of the 113 who were eventually released from prison after completing the program requirements, only 20 have been arrested for committing another crime. This is a recidivism rate of just 17 percent. A program coordinator, Rick Hoekstra, says that "Our goal is to send prisoners out with the tools and skills they need to make the change to law-abiding behavior." Warren Emmer, state parole and probation director, says that "We want the toughest, most risky people to have room in the prison system. We can't build ourselves out of overcrowding. There's a lot of material out there today that suggests what works is treatment." Prison overcrowding has not always been a problem in North Dakota. Until 1994, when North Dakota implemented President Bill Clinton's Crime Bill provisions pertaining to "truth in sentencing," North Dakota inmates were serving an average of 40 percent of their maximum prison sentences before being paroled. After adopting the sentencing guidelines in the Crime Bill,

North Dakota inmates now must serve a minimum of 85 percent of their maximum sentences before becoming eligible for parole. During the 1999 legislative session, the North Dakota legislature set aside $2 million for alternatives to prisons, including a community program in Jamestown.

Not everyone is enthusiastic about prisoner rehabilitation. Ask any prosecutor and they will tell you what they think about it. Burleigh County Assistant State's Attorney Rick Volk said that he prosecuted one defendant who was sentenced to two years in prison for eight felonies, including burglary and theft. The man was placed in the rehabilitation program and was out in 120 days. "It seemed incredible that someone with that amount of felony convictions would be out that quickly," Volk said. Other prosecutors echo Volk's concerns. Barnes County State's Attorney Robin Huseby says that the rehabilitation program often nullifies plea agreements reached by prosecutors and defendants. Huseby also says that the rehabilitation program defeats mandatory sentencing laws by allowing offenders to serve less time if the parole board approves. Prosecutors say that although the rehabilitation objectives of correctional officials are well-intentioned, corrections is diminishing the punishment and deterrence aspects of longer sentences. Cass County State's Attorney Birch Burdick says, "It doesn't seem to me that the criminal justice system is intended to rehabilitate and to save prison beds. There is no punishment aspect. We're just going to have to sentence people locally to get any punishment."

Warren Emmer said that "We never intended to undermine anything prosecutors do in their offices. This rehabilitation program is not a bad one. It's being looked at all around the country as a potential model for other correctional systems." Prosecutors were encouraged by Emmer to work with corrections to form a group to work with other state officials for the purpose of improving the program. One reason prosecutors object to the rehabilitation program is that they are not always told which prisoners are being considered for the program, nor what happens to them once they complete it. They also believe that many criminals who deserve to spend time behind bars are getting off too easily.

What is the answer to this debate? Should rehabilitation, which seems to be working with existing program enrollees, be permitted? Or should prisoners be required to serve long sentences, despite the rehabilitative goals of prison systems? Which priorities should prisons have when warehousing their offenders? How much coordination should exist between the courts, who impose punishments, and corrections, who administers them? Should we view corrections from a closed-system perspective or an open-system perspective? What do you think?

Source: Adapted from Blake Nicholson, "Prosecutors Upset with Prisoner Rehab Program," Associated Press, January 22, 2000.

open-system classification shown in Table 2.2. Several of these models might be grouped under both classifications, given the inherent overlap in them. The grouping in Table 2.2, however, reflects the emphasis of the scheme on primarily internal or primarily external factors as explanatory tools. Table 2.2 has been subdivided further into rational and nonrational systems in the closed-system category. This subdivision evidences the different assumptions about organizational participants held by theorists who must contend repeatedly with the potential outcomes of member interaction in organizations. These distinctions are described next in simplified form.

The **rational model** assumption is that planned (expected or anticipated) outcomes will follow planned organizational structures and processes (Gido, 1998).

TABLE 2.1 ORGANIZATIONAL ORIENTATIONS

CLOSED-SYSTEM ORIENTATIONS	OPEN-SYSTEM ORIENTATIONS
1. Organization as an independent agency 2. Organization as a system of structures and functions 3. Organization as a structure in action over time 4. Organization as a processing system 5. Organization as a system of dynamic functions 6. Organization as a structure of subgroups	1. Organization as a cultural product 2. Organization as an agent of exchange with its environment 3. Organization as an input-output system

Source: Compiled by author.

TABLE 2.2 CLASSIFICATION OF ORGANIZATIONAL MODELS WITHIN A SYSTEMS CONTEXT

ORGANIZATIONS AS SYSTEMS		
CLOSED SYSTEMS		**OPEN SYSTEMS**
Rational	Nonrational	

1. Machine models
  a. Scientific management
  b. Bureaucracy
2. Goals Model
3. Decision model
	1. Human relations model
	2. Professional model
	3. Equilibrium model
		1. Natural systems model

Source: Compiled by author.

This means that if we arrange an organization according to a set of rules, then we can expect certain logical outcomes, such as a smooth-running organization, greater employee effectiveness, and increased productivity. In contrast, the **nonrational model** assumption is that planned organizational structures and processes sometimes have unplanned or unanticipated consequences or outcomes. For example, a public employment agency introduced statistical records to chart the productivity of employee interviews with those in search of jobs. Each interviewer was responsible for finding jobs for unemployed interviewees. The interviewers were divided into two sections, A and B. Members of both sections were assessed in terms of the number of successful job placements over a given time period. The original source is not clear on this point, but apparently interviewers in section B were not evaluated by their supervisors as rigorously as were those in section A in terms of how many job placements they made during a certain period of time. This, combined with greater job security felt by the members of section B, was the apparent reason that the members of section B were less competitive among themselves than were the members of section A. If any interviewer in both sections had a job applicant (job applicants came to all interviewers of both sections according to random assignment), but did not have a suitable job at the moment, it was understood that the interviewer would make known to the other members of the section the availability of the job applicant. On the other hand, the idea of rating employees according to their individual performance actually backfired in section A. Some interviewers there would hoard job descriptions or job applicants from their fellow interviewers. The result was an overall decline in the effectiveness of the employment agency rather than an expected increase in job placements. One of the important reasons given for this decline was that at least one supervisor was using the statistical records as a means of evaluating and promoting agency personnel under his direct control, thus pitting his subordinates against one another rather than encouraging them to work together as a team for the good of the entire agency (Blau, 1955).

Even within those organizations considered to be profoundly goal-oriented and centered on crime fighting, such as police departments, extensive evidence of competition exists. Thus, for a variety of reasons, both vertical and horizontal competition can be found within given police departments. State and federal government finance-assisting strategies including grants are used to induce the adoption of organizational elements to make police departments more effective (Crank and Langworthy, 1997). However, powerful institutional actors such as mayors and city councils influence police department operations and cause different agendas and goals to be adopted and pursued. The fragmented nature of policing in any given police department is evident in inconsistent policies, cross-purpose actions of different subunits within the department, and a lack of coordination among constituencies across different levels of government (Crank and Langworthy, 1997).

Examples of all models discussed in the following section can be found in organizations throughout the criminal justice system today. Some agencies continue to operate on early-1900s managerial assumptions and models that organizational researchers have repeatedly found in empirical investigations to have deleterious effects on the morale and the levels of work performance of subordinates.

CLOSED-SYSTEM RATIONAL MODELS

The Machine Model and Bureaucracy

The forerunner of many organizational schemes today is the **machine model.** Popularly known as the **classical model** or **traditional model,** the machine model is best portrayed in the works of Fayol (1949), Gulick and Urwick (1937), Taylor (1911), and Weber (1947). The machine model views organizations as machines and maintains that just as we build a mechanical device with given specifications for accomplishing tasks, so also do we construct an organization according to a blueprint to achieve a given purpose (Katz and Kahn, 1966:71–72).

The primary objective of the machine model is to maximize organizational effectiveness. Therefore, our attention is directed to those aspects of organizations that can be rearranged and structured to fulfill this objective (Mendelsohn and O'Keefe, 1981). The machine model requires the application of certain management principles, such as a division of labor, authority, discipline, unity of command and direction, subordination of individual interest to general interest, remuneration of personnel, centralization, a chain of command, order, equity, stability of tenure of personnel, initiative, and esprit de corps (Fayol, 1949:20–40). One outcome of the application of these principles is the maximization of efficiency. Two variations of the machine model are scientific management and bureaucracy.

SCIENTIFIC MANAGEMENT.   Perhaps the greatest impact on the entire field of management was exerted by Frederick W. Taylor (1911). Taylor became known as the father of **scientific management.** His ideas were similar to those of Fayol. Taylor believed that organizational effectiveness could be maximized by dividing all production-related tasks into a series of simple movements and operations. Each worker could be trained to perform a few simple operations, and the combined efforts of all workers laboring for the common good would maximize efficiency and productivity. Taylor believed also that the average worker is incapable of being self-motivated. Workers are interested in doing only whatever is minimally required by management. Therefore, in addition to redesigning and simplifying tasks, increased productivity could be achieved by establishing incentives to work harder during the work period.

Taylor advocated using the bonus system to reward workers who exceeded minimal work expectations. For example, workers would receive additional compensation as a bonus for producing 10 units of product per day when their normal production expectation was only eight units. Taylor's most specific contribution was his idea of measuring a suitable day's work, which led to time-and-motion studies and many complex methods of wage payments. In this regard, Taylor said that employees could be directed like robots to perform work at command in a predetermined manner. Adhering to a mandatory schedule of rest pauses and work periods, workers would be at their peak efficiency at all times during the workday. Employees are neither machines nor robots, however. They do not always act in predictable ways like machine parts, and it is not always easy to explain these unanticipated behaviors.

Applying the machine model to a midwestern police department, police administrators were interested in devising an alternative method of evaluating their patrol officers (Lundman, 1979). The administrators observed that there was great diversity among police officers concerning the number of traffic citations issued on a monthly basis. Personnel file notations were made regularly in the files of those officers who issued fewer traffic citations compared with some of the other officers. This information was used later when evaluating certain officers for promotion or advancement. Subsequently, it was decided by the police administration to establish traffic citation quotas for all officers. It was believed that the quota system would prompt all patrol officers to work harder to stop more motorists and issue more citations. In turn, greater enforcement aggressiveness would be rewarded by favorable notations in the officers' personnel files, and advancement potential would be enhanced for officers that met their quotas.

In the actual case, a study was made of this quota system over a 15-month period. Police administrators were surprised to find that most police officers tended to resist the quota system. This was subtle resistance, however, since most officers sought to postpone their traffic patrol assignments until the latter half of each month. This way, they could avoid writing traffic citations altogether during the first half of each month. During the second half of each month, however, patrol officers were aggressive in their issuance of traffic citations and strived to meet their quotas. Investigators designated the first half of each month as "low-quota saliency," and the second half of each month was designated as "high-quota saliency." Evidence revealed that during periods of low-quota saliency, the rate of traffic stops was low, with only 42 percent of all traffic stops ending with traffic citations. In periods of high-quota saliency, 52 percent of traffic stops were concluded with a traffic citation. Interviews with officers later disclosed that officers resented having their discretionary powers and autonomy challenged by administrators. Thus, while the quota system was in effect, it did not have the intended consequences, except during periods of high-quota saliency. Officer autonomy and exercise of discretion were more critical determinants of issuances of traffic citations than the quota system itself, which was regarded as intrusive and burdensome.

BUREAUCRACY.   The most popular and long-lasting machine model is the **bureaucratic model** or **bureaucracy** (Weber, 1947). This model was developed by Max Weber (1864–1920) in the late 1800s. The bureaucratic model prescribes a list of essential components that must be present within organizations in order for them to achieve maximum effectiveness. Weber delineated the following characteristics of an ideally effective organization:

1. Impersonal social relations
2. Appointment and promotion on the basis of merit
3. Spheres of competence
4. System of abstract rules
5. Task specialization

Impersonal Social Relations.   Weber believed that organizational employees should not relate with one another on a personal basis. His emphasis on impersonal social relations was a severe criticism of nepotism prevalent in many organizations in his time. Weber assigned great significance to the importance of laws that govern positions of superiors and decisions made by them. Weber said that an organization should operate according to previously specified laws that would eliminate the potential for favoring one employee over another on the basis of who they know as opposed to how well they can perform the work. This principle would either minimize or eliminate differential favoritism based on familial connections or personal friendships. Maintaining personal distance between oneself and others meant less emotion would be involved when rule enforcement became necessary. The matter of retiring older personnel would be handled impersonally and impartially, and employees could be reprimanded more easily by supervisors. Correctional officers in prisons must maintain social distance between themselves and inmates, for example. Once a correctional officer befriends an inmate, then some degree of control is lost over that inmate. Impersonality is conceived to be a strong defense against the potential loss of power in the event a supervisor should become too friendly with subordinates.

Appointment and Promotion on the Basis of Merit. **Nepotism** is the practice of employing or favoring relatives or close friends. Nepotism was a key target of much of Weber's analysis, and he specified that employees should be hired on the basis of their abilities and promoted according to their performance compared with the performance of others competing for advanced organizational positions. Thus, the possibility of hiring the supervisor's relative just because he is the supervisor's relative is either reduced or eliminated. All persons competing for available jobs are thrown into objective competition for those jobs. Persons rating higher than others on objective performance criteria are ultimately selected, since they are the best qualified for the position, or so it is assumed under the bureaucratic model.

Contemporary hiring practices in police departments, corrections agencies, and other criminal justice organizations have emphasized hiring greater numbers of ethnic and racial minorities and females (Eisenberg, Kent, and Wall, 1973, 1974; Poulos, 1992). Larger organizations have been more responsive over the years in minority recruitment compared with smaller agencies. Although nepotism is less apparent in recent years in hiring law enforcement and corrections personnel, smaller, less formal agencies continue to exhibit some resistance to minority employment (Poulos and Doerner, 1996; Steinman, 1984).

Spheres of Competence. Each employee should have jurisdiction over specific work activity, and the employee should be responsible to a supervisor for role performance. The authority of the position should not change merely because a worker is replaced by another who has resigned, been rehired, or been fired. The position exists independently from the individual personalities filling that position. For instance, there are several expectations of supervisors that do not change as different employees perform the same supervisory job. The person's personal qualities and characteristics should have absolutely no bearing on how the supervisor's job is performed. A person's authority extends to the boundaries of the present position rather than infringing on the work of others.

Accrediting agencies are used increasingly to recruit more qualified personnel for criminal justice agency work. New selection procedures, including heightened educational requirements and a variety of testing techniques for both appointment and promotion, also are being used more frequently. A study of 70 accredited municipal police departments showed greater use of assessment centers for making personnel selection decisions (Baker, 1995). More formal oral interviews, written examinations, and more thorough background checks are being employed for employee screening purposes. Ideally, the most competent personnel will be appointed compared with less formal and inconsistent hiring practices of previous years.

System of Abstract Rules. Weber also believed that rules of law enable persons to make more objective decisions rather than allowing their personal judgments to interfere. Thus, a system of abstract laws exists to enable persons to succeed one another more easily. This characteristic accompanies closely Weber's notion of impersonality. The impersonal implementation of abstract rules or laws in organizational decision making approximates Weber's ideal view of the official behaviors of managers (Steinman, 1984).

National organizations and local boards have been instrumental in vesting many law enforcement agencies with both standards and rules by which to govern employee conduct. In the early 1980s, standards were promulgated for law enforcement agencies by organizations such as the International Association of Chiefs of Police, the National Organization of Black Law

Enforcement Executives, the National Sheriffs' Association, and the Police Executive Research Forum (Commission on Accreditation for Law Enforcement Agencies, 1983). Each standard comprises a standard statement, a commentary, and a level of compliance showing whether it is mandatory, other than mandatory, or not applicable to each of six agency-size categories. A majority of standards are mandatory, and those agencies applying for accreditation are expected to comply with these standards. A team of assessors is sent to different departments by the commission to conduct an on-site assessment and render a report to the accrediting commission. Standards are organized into sections covering the law enforcement role; responsibilities and relationships; organization, management, and administration; the personnel process; law enforcement operations; operations support; and traffic operations.

Task Specialization.   Each person should acquire a high level of competence in a specified task. By dividing the totality of organizational roles into various basic components, each person would be able to maximize job effectiveness. Each person would exercise absolute control over his or her own job-related activities, and a worker would be barred from interfering with others and the way they carry out their specialized activities. Each employee would have a sphere of competence and fixed jurisdiction over his or her own work aspects. In police work, for example, older officers who have longer service records compared with younger officers exhibit greater focus in their assigned work roles and are less inclined to be as active in a broad range of police work (Crank, 1993). Thus, greater task specialization occurs over time with more seasoned officers, at least among those investigated in selected studies. Formal selection criteria have been articulated by many law enforcement agencies throughout the United States, and evidence suggests that persons are assigned tasks most suited to their particular abilities and skills as evidenced by tests and other assessment devices (McLaughlin, 1984).

In addition to these organizational requirements, Weber described several ideal characteristics of officials: (1) The officeholder should view the position as a vocation, (2) the official should enjoy social esteem, (3) the official should be appointed on merit rather than be elected, (4) the position of an officeholder is held for life or until retirement, (5) a fixed salary and fixed security benefits should accompany the office held, and (6) the official should perceive the occupation as a career. In most criminal justice agencies, an emphasis on professionalism suggests that many of these personnel orientations are incorporated into the socialization process during recruitment and training of new personnel (Anderson, 2000; Benson, Rasmussen, and Sollars, 1995; International City/County Management Association, 1991).

Several predictable outcomes were foreseen by Weber, provided that the organization adhered to these requirements. The following list summarizes many of the predictable consequences of the bureaucratic model ideal:

1. The best persons will perform jobs most closely associated with their personal competence.

2. Each person will have jurisdiction over a designated sphere of work activity, thus eliminating duplication of function.

3. Each person logically should be more loyal to the organization as the result of internalizing the career orientation (e.g., the employee might develop strong vested interests in the organization and increased commitment to it through greater loyalty).

4. Each person will be able to predict the economic rewards from one year to the next. Being able to plan ahead reduces employee anxiety and enhances worker security. The organization continues to protect the employee, even following retirement.

5. Each person will obey the system of abstract rules or laws. Management will be able to anticipate that all persons will conform to stated expectations.

6. Management can expect uniform work of high quality from employees who are selected by test and appointed to positions because of their work proficiency and individual skills.

7. The easy replacement of organizational members can be anticipated through selection by test and the system of abstract rules.

8. Overall organizational effectiveness will occur as a result of a combination of the factors stated previously, and the organization will exhibit maximal efficiency.

Some general criticisms of the bureaucratic model are indicated in the following paragraphs. Because the bureaucratic model is the most advanced, popular, and formalized statement of the machine model in application, many of the criticisms leveled against the

BOX 2.2 PERSONALITY HIGHLIGHT

MARILYN BERGEE
University of
Wisconsin–Platteville

Statistics: M.S. (criminal
justice), Illinois State
University

Interests: I teach police function and correctional philosophy at the University of Wisconsin–Platteville. Before working in academia, I held several positions in the corrections field. I became interested in criminal justice in high school due to my involvement with a youth advisory board in Madison, Wisconsin. Each high school in Madison had one or two representatives who met monthly with city officials to look at issues such as underage drinking, truancy, and juvenile gangs.

Background: In 1987, I was accepted to Wheaton College (Illinois) and joined a program called the Institute for Prison Ministries. With this group, I tutored inmates working on their GED at Cook County Jail in Chicago. I also had the privilege of doing a research project on recidivism for the sociology department. This project included interviewing and observing a pilot program for ex-offenders sponsored by the Chuck Colson Scholar Fund at Wheaton College. Then as a senior, I taught D.A.R.E. to fourth- and fifth-grade students for the Glendale Heights (Illinois) Police Department.

After graduation, I received a gubernatorial appointment as a Vito Marzullo Intern with Governor Jim Edgar and the Department of Rehabilitation Services for one year. This opened doors to a career as a correctional officer with the Illinois Department of Corrections. I worked with adult inmates at a co-ed facility. This was a very unique correctional experience, as males and females interacted on a daily basis in a place that has been traditionally a unisex environment.

Some of the common issues facing inmates as they adapt to the prison subculture took on new forms. For example, the pseudofamilies observed in many female prisons had less influence, probably because the opportunity existed to develop actual relationships with men. The male inmates also were less concerned with maintaining strict allegiance to gang activities (e.g., scheduled fights, meetings), because they had girlfriends and did not want to jeopardize their relationships with transfers to anther prison.

In 1997, I worked with juveniles at a detention center as a private investigator while I attended Illinois State University, pursuing a master's degree in criminal justice. After graduation, I accepted my current position instructing undergraduates in policing and corrections. One of my main reasons for obtaining a graduate degree had been to pursue a career as a warden or director of a boot camp; however, the politics of the organizations that I was working with did not promote women or minorities. Equal opportunity applied only to entry-level positions.

Advice to Students: My advice is to carefully select the organizations you apply to. As a student, push yourself to volunteer and intern at as many places as possible. This will not only help you know what kind of work you enjoy, but it will give you the inside scoop on how an agency treats its staff. In addition, having live human beings, who know you and have seen your work, will make all the difference when a job opportunity becomes available.

I find great satisfaction in working in the criminal justice field. I currently serve on a selection committee for a program for ex-offenders called Koinonia House. *Koinonia* means "to bring together." This program bridges the gap between prison and needs, while at the same time restoring the community's needs for trust and safety. My point in sharing this is that the possibilities and variety of places to serve in the criminal justice field are limited *only* by your imagination.

bureaucratic model also apply to the machine model generally.

1. People do not behave like parts in a machine. The expectation that employees will act like robots in an impersonal organizational environment is unrealistic. The cognitive and emotional organizational environment is such that personal feelings and attitudes will always interfere with attempts to realize totally rational behavior. The expected behavior of supervisors in a hierarchy of authority provides an example. According to the machine and bureaucratic models, supervisory behavior is linked closely with several impersonal rules that govern the definition of the supervisor's role. Supposedly, anyone can carry out the supervisor's role effectively, to the extent that the rules governing the role are complied with to the letter. Unfortunately, personality characteristics contaminate the correspondence between what persons are supposed to do in their respective positions and what they actually do.

In probation work, for example, several different styles of supervising offenders have been described to typify the mode of probation officer (PO) supervision. Under conditions in which probationers have high crime or recidivism rates, probation departments may implement policies for their POs that are intended to intensify the monitoring that probationer/clients receive. Presumably, closer monitoring by POs will decrease probationer crime and recidivism. More than a few POs have adopted an enforcer supervisory style, however, devoting considerable attention to probationers and their programs. These POs will subject their probationer/clients to the closest scrutiny and put their behaviors under microscopes. Enforcer POs tend to function like police officers in that they strain to detect any program violation, such as curfew and drug/alcohol checks. One result is that more probationers are caught engaging in minor program infractions, which are not crimes. Nevertheless, one or more program violations may have the same effect as a crime, in that those probationers who are caught may have their probation programs revoked by judges. It may never have been the intention of the probation department to encourage such overly strict enforcement of technical program requirements. But the personalities of some POs inspired them to detect minor program infractions.

In police training programs, field training officers (FTOs) are expected to impart their knowledge and experience to new recruits. However, many field training officers have advised that what is learned "by the book" may be different from actual practice. Thus, FTOs will advise their trainees to use their personal discretion in diverse situations with the public. If a police department has a policy in place concerning high-speed chases, for instance, officers may be admonished not to engage speeders in dangerous high-speed chases if the offense is a mere traffic violation and would result in a small fine. Nevertheless, more than a few officers will engage speeders in high-speed chases despite department policy to the contrary, simply because the officer's authority is being challenged when a motorist does not stop. Emotional involvement by officers involved in high-speed chases often overrides good judgment and common sense, sometimes with lethal consequences that could have been avoided (Los Angeles Independent Commission, 1991).

2. In most organizations, rules cannot be written to govern every situation. Frequently, events occur that are not clearly within any given department's jurisdiction. Also, events may emerge that are clearly within a department's jurisdiction, although no clearcut policy statement exists to indicate how the situation should be handled. If departments act in response to an event that is not obviously within their domain, they may be criticized by higher-ups later for overstepping their authority. As a protective measure against such criticisms, supervisors and other officials may restrict their activities to several well-defined and predictable events, and they may take great pains to avoid any unusual problems that are not clearly within their departmental definition. Almost everyone who has called a large corporation with a specific complaint has encountered the runaround from receptionists. Customers are shuffled from one department to another as each receptionist seeks to avoid responsibility for handling the complaint.

Police officers must operate under diverse circumstances when stopping motorists or making searches incident to arrests. The Fourth Amendment and the exclusionary rule have been addressed and interpreted extensively by the U.S. Supreme Court in recent years. The Supreme Court's rulings and interpretations in this area of law have become exceedingly complex, such that even some law professors find it difficult to understand what officers may or may not do relating to searches and seizures (Heffernan and Lovely, 1991). It is difficult for police departments to adopt consistent policies about Fourth Amendment rules, regulations, and exceptions in view of the fact that the constitutional landscape is constantly changing. Many police officers carry out searches and seizures of suspect contraband under the "good faith" or "totality of circumstances" exceptions to the exclusionary rule. Interestingly, investigations of officer knowledge as well as the knowledge of defense attorneys and prosecutors suggest that at least 25 percent of the time, these actors are mistaken regarding the legality of intrusions governed by specific search and seizure rules. Thus, effective rule writing for every situation is virtually impossible.

3. Conformity to rules and personal expertise can be detrimental as well as beneficial in promoting organizational effectiveness. In fact, the very skills workers acquire to become experts at what they do can work against them (Merton, 1940). Persons become so specialized that they develop trained incapacity, a condition in which they lack flexibility to deal effectively with situations that do not fit precisely within their own job definitions. In short, employees are unable to perform certain jobs or make decisions that differ slightly from their own rigid job description. It has been said that if people adopt measures in keeping with their past training, and that under new conditions that are not recognized as significantly different, the very soundness of this training may lead to the adoption of the wrong procedures. In effect, people may be unfitted by being fit in an unfit fitness. Their training may become an incapacity (Burke, 1935).

One implication of this overconformity is resistance to change. Since organizations are generally dynamic and responsive to innovation both internally and externally, bureaucratic rigidity through strict obedience to rules or laws is in direct opposition to organizational progress.

An example of absolute conformity to rules is the establishment of mandatory arrest policies by different police departments in spousal abuse incidents. Mandatory arrest policies direct police officers to make an arrest of one spouse or the other whenever they respond to a domestic violence complaint. Prior to the implementation of mandatory arrest policies, police officers were permitted wide latitude in deciding whether or not to make arrests of either spouse. Much of the time, informal adjustments and cooling-off periods were permitted, and the officers left both spouses to work out their differences without further violence. Since mandatory arrest has become the rule rather than the exception in many police departments, however, there have been more than a few unanticipated consequences. These unanticipated consequences include increased violence and harassment by batterers, more stalking of spouse-victims,

and the development of alternative forms of abuse by perpetrators (Buzawa, Hoteling, and Klein, 1998).

4. Departmental activities, in time, may be devoted to perpetuating the department rather than benefiting the organization as a whole (Selznick, 1966). Each department in an organization has subgoals that contribute to the achievement of overall organizational objectives. At some point, however, the subgoals may be elaborated and exist as the prime motivators of the behavior of the employees. The department exists, therefore, to achieve the goals of the department. This condition is not necessarily undesirable unless the effectiveness of goal attainment for the entire organization is threatened. When separate departments begin to view their own activities apart from the activities of other departments, the danger arises that they will lose sight of the overall organizational goals toward which their separate activities are directed.

Attempts by different police departments and other agencies to develop codes of ethics and establish behavioral standards for persons in leadership positions may inadvertently contribute to perpetuating the status quo, which may include abuses of discretion by officers and others. Questionable practices relating to criminal suspects may be continued within the context of noble-cause corruption, in which it is believed that the ends justify the means. If illegal contraband, such as crack cocaine or heroin, is found as the result of an illegal search, some departments may regard the drug discovery as justification for violating the constitutional rights of criminal suspects. Many ethical dilemmas arise in the course of law enforcement and in other sectors of the criminal justice system (Anderson, 2000; Crank and Caldero, 2000; North Carolina Bar Association, 1971).

5. Informal groups in formal organizations can modify existing impersonal social arrangements. The formal hierarchy of authority and communication channels often are discovered to be in competition with informal grapevines. **Grapevines** are informal communication patterns that exist within the formal communication network. Informal leaders emerge who do not have the same degree of official job status as the formal leaders but who nevertheless exert significant influence on employees' attitudes toward their jobs. Every organization creates an informal structure, and the process of modifying organizational goals is effected through such structures (Selznick, 1943). Some of the characteristics of informal group structure include codes of conduct for group members; schemes of ideas, beliefs, and values that underlie and support the codes of conduct; and the informal communication system that is vital to group solidarity and action (Goldsmith and Goldsmith, 1974).

One implication of the presence of informal groups in organizations is that rule enforcement is often subject to informal workers' codes and approval. Supervisors frequently find themselves bargaining with subordinates outside of the formal chain of command. The replacement of individuals in various organizational positions is often facilitated or hindered by acceptance or rejection by informal workers' aggregates.

6. The bureaucratic model of organization, although characterized by high productive efficiency, generates low innovative capacity. In an increasingly competitive economic environment, organizations must manifest some adaptability to change if they are to remain viable. Organizations that are more bureaucratic than others (i.e., those that possess more characteristics of a bureaucracy) appear to be less responsive to internal or external change. Organizations must change in response to innovation, invention, or new product markets if they are going to compete successfully and survive (Welsh and Farrington, 2000). Since it has been shown that many bureaucratic departments in organizations are intent on perpetuating the organizational status quo, the bureaucratic model would pose certain structural obstacles that would seriously restrict the introduction of any innovation.

7. The bureaucratic model fails to take into account the interrelations among the various subsystems in an organization. The machine model usually does not deal adequately with the problem of intraorganizational conflict of interests in defining limits of organizational behavior (March and Simon, 1958:33). The interdependency of departments suggests that the lack of exchange of mutually beneficial information on a give-and-take basis, which is necessary for the satisfactory progression of the organization, is not seriously considered as problematic by the bureaucratic model.

8. The integrity of individuals as autonomous decision makers is completely overlooked by the bureaucratic model. Persons functioning in various organizational roles have little latitude for varying their behaviors from previously established role definitions. Individual manifestations of innovation for circumventing red tape or unnecessary paperwork are often suppressed by higher-ups for fear of disrupting the rational order of things. To an extent, the innovation

means disorder, a condition that is not compatible with the bureaucratic model.

In 1984, for example, the Comprehensive Crime Control Act was passed by the federal government. This act authorized government seizure of assets linked with illegal drug transactions, including homes, automobiles, and cash. Many state and local law enforcement agencies capitalized on the provisions of the act to shift their law enforcement priorities more dramatically toward drug enforcement, a major source of federal asset confiscations. After 1984, local law enforcement agencies increased arrests for drug offenses relative to arrests for property and violent crimes. This shift in the reallocation of state and local law enforcement resources generated immense revenues for police agencies, which have typically been underfunded and understaffed. The new financial incentives under the asset forfeiture provisions of the Comprehensive Crime Control Act caused many changes in police behavior that were unrelated to general departmental law enforcement policies and individual personalities. Today, many smaller communities finance almost their entire police operations with revenue generated from asset forfeitures related to greater enforcement of drug laws (Benson, Rasmussen, and Sollars, 1995). Police behaviors in these jurisdictions are driven almost completely by departmental dependency on drug money. In more than a few instances, innocent citizens have had their assets seized, simply because of police suspicions that they might be involved in drug trafficking, even though no direct evidence had been found to bring criminal charges against these persons (Warchol, Payne, and Johnson, 1999). Although individual police officers may oppose these questionable practices, the departmental bureaucracy overrides their individual discretionary powers and causes them to engage in questionable police practices that are designed merely to generate more departmental revenue (Blumenson and Nilsen, 1998).

9. Selection by test is an inadequate method for replacing employees. There have been wholesale misuses of achievement and interests tests in organizations. Testing is viewed as one of the poorer methods of selecting new recruits or employees, inasmuch as almost everyone today has Internet access to mail-order houses that sell test preparation materials. For a fee, these mail-order houses will furnish reproductions of standardized tests used by various criminal justice organizations, together with the correct answers. Thus, the prospective job applicant comes to the organization primed to give the right answers to test questions.

The test results may suggest that the job applicant fits the job requirements perfectly, when in fact he or she may be a poor fit for the available position. Personality tests, such as the MMPI (Minnesota Multiphasic Personality Inventory) and Cattell's 16 PF (Personality Factor Inventory), also have been widely copied and distributed. Thus, psychological and social adjustment indicated by test results may have nothing to do with the psychological or social adjustment state of particular job applicants. Personality and abilities testing is often a farce.

In addition to the problems of utilizing standard tests for personnel selection, other factors influence how new employees are recruited. For example, affirmative action policies have been implemented in virtually every criminal justice agency, and strong measures have been adopted by different agencies to hire more minorities and women into work roles formerly dominated by males. Although standard selection criteria continue to be used in most agencies, recruitment at the entrance level, personnel responsibilities and functions, lateral entry/transfer, promotion, performance appraisal, appeals and grievances, and organization and management have new and different priorities related more to quota fulfillment than to merit and performance quality (Eisenberg, Kent, and Wall, 1973; Poulos and Doerner, 1996). Pressures to hire larger numbers of minorities also arise from threats of lawsuits or actual suits filed against municipal police departments suspected of discriminatory hiring or promotional practices. Substantial increases in the proportionate representation of racial minorities have been observed to occur over time in jurisdictions such as Atlanta, Georgia, and Toledo, Ohio (Lewis, 1989). Despite affirmative action policies and lawsuits or the threat of them, more than a few municipal police departments and other agencies continue to have low proportionate numbers of women and minorities among the ranks of sworn, full-time personnel (Poulos, 1992).

10. The bureaucratic model is restricted in application to larger organizations. It is widely assumed that an increase in the size and complexity of organizations will increase the likelihood that a bureaucratic structure will eventually emerge. Bureaucracy connotes the proliferation of departments and a fairly complex division of labor. Smaller organizations are less amenable to the use of the bureaucratic model (Crank and Wells, 1991). They tend to have fewer departments, if any, and role interrelations are simple (Steinman, 1984). Increases in the number of departments and the general complexity of the organization create new kinds of coordination problems. The establishment of an authority hierarchy with an explicit division of labor and chain of command is one solution to the problem of coordination of tasks.

The Goals Model

An alternative organizational scheme that is functionally similar to the machine model is the **goals model.** The basic elements of the goals model are that (1) the organization exists to achieve stated goals, (2) the organization develops a rational procedure for goal attainment, and (3) the organization is assessed in terms of the effectiveness of goal attainment. Since all organizations function to achieve different goals, it makes sense to focus our attention on existing **organizational goals** and the means used to achieve them. The problems of organizations become problems of goal attainment.

The goals model is a deceptively simple strategy for approaching organizational problems. One of the more perplexing questions asked is, "What are the goals of the organization?" The identification of true organizational goals is no easy task. An organizational goal is defined by one investigator as a desired state of affairs that organizations attempt to realize (Etzioni, 1961:4). Another researcher says that an organization is merely an abstraction when the assertion is made that the organization has goals and desires (Thompson, 1967:127). Definitions that reify organizations in this sense have little tangible value, particularly if we view the goals of an organization in terms of the accumulated goals of its individual members. A preferred definition is that organizational goals are the future domain desired by those of the dominant organizational coalition (Thompson, 1967).

A third definition is similar to the second. An organizational goal is a shared goal for the organization on the part of its leaders (Vroom, 1960:229). Goals are further differentiated according to each employee's own goal for an organization (the region into which each person wants an organization to move) and the perception of organizational goals (personal estimates of the regions into which it is thought that the leaders of the organization would like it to move).

Vroom's (1960) analysis and criticism of the ambiguity associated with organizational goal definitions highlights the general ambiguity of the goals model. Consider the problems confronting someone who consults with an organization in an attempt to solve its problems. To whom does a change agent turn to determine the organizational goals? If the change agent consults with various supervisors or managers at different levels of the authority hierarchy, several different, possibly contradictory, organizational objectives may be gleaned from the information provided. If the change agent reads published accounts of organizational goals, a discrepancy between what is supposed to be achieved ideally and what actually is achieved may be revealed. The ideal-real discrepancy poses a significant obstacle to deriving adequate organizational goal definitions.

A study of the Virginia State Penitentiary underscores the problem of who defines the goals of the organization. In a study by Seaman (1978), a maximum-security prison was investigated in an effort to determine its goals. The investigation was more complicated than originally envisioned by the researcher, since organizational goals within the prison varied according to the opinions of different subgroups and staff. Questions arose about the nature of the organization of the institution itself, the relationships among different organizational subunits, staff relationships, and staff roles. Goals were subsequently identified according to whether they were official mandates, executive views, or staff perceptions. Although secure confinement was seen as the overall operating organizational goal, this fact did not explain fully the priority or importance given to such factors as the basis for decision making in the daily operations of the institution, the organizational structure of the prison, relationships among different organizational subunits, and staff roles (Seaman, 1978).

The consensus of several researchers suggests that organizational goals are difficult to define and **organizational effectiveness** in goal attainment is equally difficult to evaluate (Cordner, 1989; Rush, 1997; Thomas, 1980). A primary implication for the goals model in organizational analysis is that it is too complex to use on a large scale. The fact that goals may be viewed from multiple positions has led to a proliferation of attempts at classifying goals (Borodzicz, 1996; Wallace, Roberson, and Steckler, 1995). Goals have been categorized as output goals, adaptation goals, management goals, motivational goals, and positional goals (Gross, 1969:286–291). Some writers have distinguished between system goals and product-characteristic goals (Hage and Aiken, 1969:373–374). Others differentiate between operational and nonoperational (March and Simon, 1958). Goals are also distinguished in terms of a time dimension, such as short-range and long-range (Vroom, 1960). Some of the major criticisms of the goals model are outlined next.

1. Goals are difficult to define; therefore, the goals model is difficult to apply. Organizational goals are perceived from several different vantage points (Thomas, 1980). Some organizations exist for years without ever realizing stated goals. Attempts to classify organizational goals have not been very successful from the standpoint of general application to all types of organizations.

2. The goals model makes the unrealistic assumption of a static organization. Describing organizations as though they are static entities simplifies our descriptions of them, but our descriptions fail to take into account the dynamic features of organizations (Duffee, 1975). All organizations are dynamic entities, ever changing in size and complexity as well as in other dimensions (Saari, 1982). Most of the time organizations do not attain their goals in any final sense (Etzioni, 1964:16). The desired state of any organization may be a condition to be maintained daily. The goal, defined as a condition of organizational equilibrium, is a perpetual one. In one sense, goals of this type are reachieved daily or are continually preserved. Existing organizational goals may be supplemented with new ones, modified to fit new markets and service directions, or both (Llynn, 1980). The goals model is not prepared to deal adequately with transformations of organizational goals.

3. The goals model tends to stereotype study findings. The goals model leads to a comparison between ideal and real organizational goals (Allinson, 1983; Frank and Atkins, 1981). The comparison is misleading in a sense because it almost always implies that the organization is not very effective in its goal attainment.

The Decision Model

Three assumptions have been made about employees in organizations that tend to typify managerial views of workers over the years. Employees are (1) passive instruments capable of performing work and accepting directions, but not of initiating action or exerting influence in any significant way; (2) sentiment-laden individuals with attitudes, values, and goals, and they have to be motivated or induced to participate in the system of organizational behavior; or (3) decision makers and problem solvers, with perception and thought processes that are central to the explanation of behavior in organizations. It is likely that manifestations of these three views can be found in many organizations today. The third view, that of identifying organizational members as decision makers and problem solvers, is of most interest to us in defining the essential elements of the **decision model.**

The decision model consists of three important components. Organizations are viewed as rational systems consisting of various parts. Each part, such as a department, makes decisions that affect relations with other parts and the organization as a whole. Organizational problems are accounted for, in part, by the quality of decisions pertaining to the utilization of organizational assets and human resources. The decision model has as its guiding theme the rational selection of the best action from several available alternatives, with some calculated probability of predictable results. In short, this model encourages the selection of the best way to solve problems with the least amount of financial loss to the organization.

Organizations are decision-making structures, and the various dimensions of an organization (e.g., hierarchy of authority, division of labor, specialization of tasks) are designed to enhance the rationality of decision making. Specialization, for instance, acts to confine an employee within a small sphere of activity. The employee is able to have a better grasp of the alternative decisions to select from in order to fulfill the particular decision-making role in the organization. The hierarchy of authority exists to dictate the sphere of activity within which the employee will operate (Simon, 1957).

The decision model is not altogether different from the goals model. Both schemes incorporate the notion of achieving goals. An important difference in these schemes, however, is that the decision model emphasizes the quality of decisions made to achieve goals, whereas the goals model is concerned about any organizational dimension (including the decision-making process implicit in the hierarchy of authority and the division of labor) that is functionally related to goal attainment. Another difference is that the decision model considers as most important the decisions about the means devised for solving problems rather than the actual problem solving, which is of primary importance to the goals model. Several criticisms of the decision model follow.

1. The decision model assumes a static organization. The decision model neglects to consider external factors. The propensity for organizations to change in many crucial dimensions introduces significant factors that influence outcomes and over which workers in the organization have little or no control. For instance,

various state and local public agencies exist to make decisions about out-of-state placement of children in need of supervision. These agencies have jurisdiction concerning child welfare, education, juvenile justice, mental health, and mental retardation. Individual agency policy decision making may be duplicated or contradicted by the actions of other agencies with overlapping jurisdiction (Hall et al., 1982). Also, studies of court systems reveal that we can understand their organization and operations better if we view them as dynamic rather than static entities (Saari, 1982).

2. Interpersonal processes are not treated adequately in the decision model. Administration as a decision-making structure deals largely with the effects of a formal blueprint for decision-making behavior and does not include a systematic analysis of those interpersonal processes that are not a part of formal structure. For example, New Jersey state prosecutors were interested in establishing a comprehensive crime-fighting strategy for combating organized crime. Twenty-one prosecutor's offices throughout New Jersey became involved with various county, state, and federal agencies to coordinate their investigative efforts and conduct joint investigations and greater interagency cooperation. Strictly from a decision model view, these efforts were well-intentioned and appeared to be consistent with moving in a unified direction and purpose at all levels. However, the very nature of the numerous specialized units devoted to organized crime, white-collar crime, and corruption required greater coordination than was originally contemplated by policymakers at the top of the state decision-making apparatus. Little or no provision for interpersonal relations among different units has undermined the overall effectiveness of the state's collective crime-fighting efforts, despite the larger number of indictments and prosecutions conducted (New Jersey Attorney General's Office, 1978).

3. All variables typifying the organization (i.e., hierarchy of authority, span of control of supervisors, communication network) are viewed exclusively in terms of their impact on rational decision making. No consideration is given to the effect that each of these variables has on the others (Blau and Scott, 1962:38). Process-based changes have occurred that relate to the more rapid processing of drug cases in various courts. In New York, for example, felony prosecution priorities shifted substantially during the 1980s from property and violent crimes to drug offenses. This priority shift caused a significant increase in the New York prison and jail population. Prison overcrowding was exacerbated, and judicial sentencing decision making was affected. Thus, although more drug prosecutions and convictions occurred, more serious problems were created in other organizations throughout the New York criminal justice system (Nelson, 1992; New York State Division of Criminal Justice Services, 1992).

4. Few controls exist to ensure objectivity on the part of the decision maker (Jacoby, Mellon, and Smith, 1982). The possibility arises for the individual decision maker to arrive at decisions that are beneficial to a particular department but not to the entire organization (National Center for State Courts, 1990; Sloan and Miller, 1990). The frequency with which individuals act in their own behalf to the detriment of the organization in contrast to the frequency of altruistic, organization-oriented decisions is well-known. Organizational decision making becomes largely an individualized activity in the absence of well-defined guidelines for member behavior. For instance, in Essex County (Newark), New Jersey, during the period 1990 to 1994, a significant backlog of cases and case-processing delays developed. The implementation of certain initiatives to remedy case backlogs and delays included the adoption of expanded early case screening, strict case processing time standards, the establishment of special remand courts, and a sharp reduction of the period during which defendants were permitted to accept plea offers from prosecutors. Case backlogs were reduced by 71 percent (Mahoney and Bakke, 1995). Although these initiatives were beneficial for prosecutors and the courts, corrections agencies were taxed to find more space for greater numbers of convicted felons. Thus, the consequences of actions taken by one or more agencies or institutions in one part of the criminal justice process may have unintended implications for other agencies in other parts of the system.

SUMMARY

Theories of organization are interrelated sets of assumptions and propositions arranged in such a way that a logical explanatory and predictive scheme is established from which testable hypotheses can be derived. Different levels of theory exist. These levels follow closely the levels or units of analysis associated with individuals, groups, and organizations. Assumptions are components of theory that are statements with a high degree of certainty. Their derivation is the product of considerable organizational research. Less

certain statements are propositions. Organizational investigators use these different statements in their theorizing about organizational events, such as statements that declare that all organizations have hierarchies of authority or all organizations show evidence of a division of labor.

Theories are difficult to develop and apply. One reason is that it is difficult to explain all of the events that occur inside and outside of organizations and how these events are interrelated. As an alternative to general theory building, many researchers have chosen to devise scaled-down versions of theories to guide their investigations. They may study interpersonal relations among employees or worker attitudes toward their jobs. They may devise theories of worker motivation to help explain worker productivity and effectiveness.

Assisting organizational researchers in their theory building are organizational models. Models are particular sets of organizational characteristics that permit the portrayal of an organization from a particular viewpoint or dimension. Many different kinds of organizational models exist. Models become orienting mechanisms and cause us to view organizations in particular ways. Models guide theorists who speculate about organizational events and why they occur. Probably the most important function of organizational models is that they enable us to structure organizational environments in certain ways so that they disclose patterns of interaction and general organizational structures and processes.

Some general criticisms of models are that they are replete with exceptions. Furthermore, they emphasize different dimensions of organizations and cause us to ignore equally important alternative dimensions. Many models are derivatives of other models, and thus there is considerable model overlap. Models also envision organizations as static entities, when in fact organizations are dynamic entities. Models also vary according to the unit of analysis chosen by individual researchers.

Models may be divided according to whether they are closed-system or open-system models. Closed-system models view organizations by focusing exclusively on events that occur within the organizations themselves. Open-system models pay attention to both internal and external organizational environments. Open-system models are more difficult to apply, since we must pay attention to numerous external factors occurring outside of organizations. Closed-system models are more simple to work with, since we only need to focus on internal organizational factors. Closed-system models may be further subdivided according to whether they are rational or nonrational. Rational models assume that organizations are structured to deal with predictable, recurring events. Nonrational models assume that organizations are structured to deal with unpredictable and unanticipated events.

The primary closed-system rational models discussed in this chapter include scientific management, bureaucracy, the goals model, and the decision model. Scientific management evolved during the early 1900s and is considered to be a derivative of the machine model or classical model. The bureaucratic model emerged during this same time period, but it has prevailed as perhaps the most popular organizational model today. The key reason for the popularity of the bureaucratic model is that its formulator, Max Weber, paid considerable attention to the details of the model and explored its implications for the organization as well as individual employees. The bureaucratic model describes organizations as having a hierarchy of authority, impersonal social relationships, appointment on the basis of merit, spheres of competence, system of abstract rules to govern decisions and task assignments, and task specialization.

Anticipated outcomes of the bureaucratic model include the following ideas: The best persons will be selected to perform work, each person will have a sphere of competence, each person can predict future organizational rewards, management can expect work of only the highest quality from organizational personnel, replacement of personnel is facilitated through selection by test, and greater organizational loyalty will be elicited from employees. People don't behave like machine parts, however. Rules cannot be written to cover every aspect of organizational activity. Strict conformity to rules may be detrimental to organizational effectiveness. Informal groups exist to interfere with the orderly transmission of information through formal communication networks. Selection by test is circumvented in various ways. And the bureaucratic model is more applicable to larger organizations than to smaller ones.

Other alternative closed-system rational models are the goals model, which assumes that the organization exists to achieve goals and be effective, and the decision model, which views organizations as interrelated departments making independent decisions that combine to influence organizational effectiveness. Similar to the bureaucratic model, the goals and deci-

sion models assume that organizations are static entities. Further, the ways that interpersonal processes affect organizational survival, growth, and effectiveness are not taken into account properly. Further, different employees at different organizational levels have diverse goals and expectations that may be in conflict. Also, the decision model fails to provide for decision-making objectivity among individual organizational actors.

QUESTIONS FOR REVIEW

1. What is organizational theory? What are two important functions of theories?

2. What are two important components of organizational theories? Differentiate between each and give an example.

3. How do different definitions of the same organizational phenomena used by different organizational researchers create problems for theory development?

4. What are three levels of theory? Describe each.

5. What is the general relationship among frames of reference, models, theory, and hypotheses?

6. What are organizational models? What are some key functions of organizational models?

7. What is the difference between closed-system and open-system models? Describe the chief characteristics of each.

8. Why are closed-system models used more frequently than open-system models?

9. What is the difference between scientific management and the machine model?

10. What is meant by bureaucracy? What are its primary characteristics?

SUGGESTED READINGS

Albonetti, Celesta A. (1999). "The Avoidance of Punishment: A Legal-Bureaucratic Model of Suspended Sentences in Federal White-Collar Cases Prior to the Federal Sentencing Guidelines." *Social Forces* **78:**303–329.

Wallace, Harvey, Cliff Roberson, and Craig Steckler (1995). *Fundamentals of Police Administration.* Englewood Cliffs, NJ: Prentice Hall.

Wright, Kevin N., et al. (1997). "Job Control and Occupational Outcomes Among Prison Workers." *Justice Quarterly* **14:**525–546.

1. THE NEW POLICY ON DOMESTIC VIOLENCE CALLS

The Dudley Police Department (DPD), a 135-officer/staff organization, recently held a departmental meeting to issue new guidelines for police officers to follow when responding to calls for domestic disturbances. Chief Harold Knox is a former military man, having served 20 years in the Navy as a commander. He has been with the DPD for 11 years. The DPD is located in a southern state, and the community served has a population of 75,000. During the last five years, the number of calls for service relating to domestic violence has increased.

It has been Chief Knox's custom to allow his officers broad discretion when responding to these calls. His officers have visited fighting spouses and have attempted to resolve situations on-site rather than make an arrest of either spouse. Needless to say, there have been incidents in which one spouse has been arrested for assaulting the other spouse, although the injured spouse seldom has followed through with a criminal complaint. A local women's group, "Women Now," has sent some of its leaders to visit Chief Knox, because two local shelters for battered women have been receiving larger numbers of female victims of apparent spousal abuse. The women have related the same story about what occurred whenever police officers visited their homes in response to domestic violence complaints. The police officers have done little or nothing, other than lecture the spouses and leave. Essentially, the women's group would like Chief Knox to direct his officers to take a more proactive role in monitoring calls for service involving complaints of domestic violence. One of the Women Now leaders is the mayor's niece. She was a victim of spousal abuse herself and now heads one of the shelters for battered women. She also has spoken to her uncle, the mayor, and advised him to "see what he could do" to get some action from investigating officers. In fact, just before the visit from the representatives of Women Now, Mayor Phil Riley called Chief Knox and suggested that he "do something about this domestic violence situation." Knox assured Mayor Riley that he, Knox, would do whatever he could.

At the called meeting of officers, Chief Knox distributed some materials related to spousal abuse, some statistical information, and a profile of batterers that he had obtained from Women Now. He also issued a new policy letter directing that beginning immediately, all police officers who respond to domestic violence calls must arrest one of the spouses and take them to jail. He advised these officers that they should probably arrest the men, since they were most likely to be the batterers in the situation, absent any evidence to the contrary. He labeled the new policy letter the "Mandatory Arrest Policy for the Dudley Police Department." The officers looked around at each other and shrugged. When asked if they had any questions, some of the officers asked the chief if they had to arrest a spouse if the spouses were simply arguing and there was no indication of physical violence. Off the cuff, the chief responded, "Take one in and book 'em regardless. If you've got to go out there, make 'em pay for your time." The officers grumbled, but they left the meeting intent on following the chief's orders.

Over the next month, all officers followed the directive of mandatory arrest in all calls involving domestic violence. Incredibly, 68 spouses were arrested during that 30-day period. Many of these spouses were shocked to be handcuffed, placed in a squad car, and taken to jail. In fact, during that month, many of the other spouses came to the jail to bail out their husbands. Most of them expressed their dissatisfaction over the situation. Many of the women said, "Whose bright idea was that to arrest our husbands? We're not going to press any charges. What's the point, anyway?" The police officers involved would merely say, "It's our new policy. We're just following orders." Many of the women said, "Well, they're stupid orders, if you ask me. It cost me quite a bit of money to get my husband out of jail. Are you guys going to do this every time my husband and I have an argument?"

One of the arrestees was a city councilman. He had been arrested following a fight with his wife. His wife struck him with her fist and bloodied his nose. He tried to keep her from hitting him and held her wrists. She screamed at him, and one of the neighbors who lived nearby called the police. They were there in minutes, and despite his position as a city councilman and his bloody nose, they arrested him and took him to jail. His wife was irate over the incident. One of the first things the city councilman did when he got out of jail was to have a chat with the mayor about the out-of-control police officers under Chief Knox's direction. "What sort of police chief do we have, anyway?

Locking up people for having innocent fights. It's incredible." The mayor sighed and said he would see what could be done. The city councilman said that he was going to bring this matter to the attention of the city council and put some pressure on the police chief to change things.

Questions for Discussion

1. Given Chief Knox's style in allowing his officers considerable discretion when investigating domestic violence complaints previously, did he make the change to a mandatory arrest policy in the right way? Is there any other strategy the chief might have employed to warn fighting spouses in advance that his officers were going to put this new policy into effect?

2. In what ways did Chief Knox's behavior fit the bureaucratic model of organizations? In what ways did his behavior violate the characteristics of the bureaucratic model?

3. Should the new mandatory arrest policy, which seemed to be Chief Knox's initiative, be subject

to the approval of the mayor or city council, or was the chief justified in making the decision to implement a new policy on his own?

4. In what ways is the Dudley Police Department an open system, given the input from the mayor and the leaders of Women Now?

5. How do the goals and decision models apply for the new mandatory arrest policy enacted by Chief Knox?

6. Should Chief Knox have advised the newspapers and the community about his proposed policy change and solicited their reaction to it? Could Chief Knox have learned anything worthwhile from his own officers about their previous handling of domestic violence complaints?

7. What should Chief Knox do now regarding his mandatory arrest policy, and how should he respond to the pending negative reaction from the city council and several citizen complaints? How do you think he ought to handle this delicate situation involving conflicting interests?

2. THE LEGRAND COUNTY JAIL

The Legrand County Jail is located in a northeastern state and serves a population of 100,000. The jail is old, although it can hold up to 400 inmates. Right now, the jail houses about 200 inmates. Most of these are pretrial detainees or persons serving short sentences for misdemeanor convictions. A small cell area separated from the other cells is made available to accommodate 25 female prisoners. Sheriff Jim "Bobo" Snodgrass, 48, has been in charge of the jail for two years. He was elected and was largely unopposed. He has no previous jail experience and has not finished high school. His former job was real estate salesman. He sees his job as mostly a figurehead position, and he hires and fires deputies depending on what he considers to be good or bad performance.

Snodgrass has about 60 deputies on the payroll, and they do cruiser work. He has another 20 jail officers who manage jail operations. There are no female officers working for Legrand County at present, since Snodgrass doesn't think women belong in law en-

forcement. He has made a concerted effort to keep women out of his jail officer pool. Among those hired to act as jail officers is Fred Lincoln, who is Snodgrass's nephew. Lincoln is 28 years old and has had no jail experience. He has a prior record as a juvenile delinquent, with one delinquency adjudication for sexual assault. Snodgrass knows about the record, but he wants to help out his nephew and has assigned him to guard duty.

Other deputies and jail officers know about Lincoln and his relationship to Snodgrass. Therefore, they stay away from him or let him do as he pleases most of the time, since they do not want to cross Sheriff Snodgrass and lose their jobs. On different occasions, some of Snodgrass's deputies have not performed well. As a punishment, Snodgrass has assigned them to a month of guard duty at the jail. Thus, for some of these regular deputies, doing jail guard duty is considered a punishment.

One day, Fred Lincoln approached the chief jailer, Frank Little, and he asked Little if he could guard the female prisoners. Little, who was unaware of Lincoln's record, said, "Sure, why not?" Over the next few months, Lincoln took every opportunity to have conversations with some of the more attractive female inmates. He was virtually alone with them in the wing of the jail where they were held. At one point, he invited one of the female inmates, Mary O'Connell, to join him for lunch in the guard room down the hall. They had lunch together on several occasions over the next few weeks. One day, Lincoln advised O'Connell that he could get her out of jail if she would have sex with him. Initially, O'Connell balked at the idea and asked to be returned to her cell. The next thing O'Connell knew, she was placed in solitary confinement in one of the two empty solitary confinement cells adjacent to the women's cellblock. Lincoln made Mary strip and ordered her into the six-foot by six-foot cell, which was constructed of iron. There was only a water tap in the room and no toilet. Lincoln brought her meals every day and passed them through an iron grate in the cell door. The cell itself was dark except for the occasional light when the iron grate was opened for meals. After a week, Lincoln had Mary leave the cell and take a shower in the guard room down the hall. He asked her again if she would have sex with him. Reluctantly she consented. Lincoln was able to carry on his sexual relationship with O'Connell for about six weeks.

Then another deputy called Lincoln and advised him that Mary O'Connell's sentence had expired and that she was to be released. Lincoln brought Mary into the guard's quarters and advised her that she was about to be released. He claimed to be responsible for that, although Mary knew that she had served her time and had to be released anyway. He told Mary that she shouldn't say anything to anyone about their relationship, because his uncle, Sheriff Snodgrass, had friends in high places and could get her back in jail "right quick." Mary agreed not to say anything to anyone. But when she was free of the jail, she immediately went to an attorney and related what had happened to her. The attorney, Jack Fisher, a criminal lawyer, interviewed her at length. Mary also had several female in-

mates as witnesses, and they could be called to verify that Lincoln had taken her from her cell frequently. Fisher immediately called the Bureau of Criminal Investigation (BCI) for the state. He had a meeting with one of their agents and apprised him of the sexual misconduct of Deputy Lincoln. He also advised that Sheriff Snodgrass was "out of the loop in this matter" because he was Lincoln's uncle and couldn't be trusted to act on this information. The BCI agent said that he would launch an investigation.

A month later, after the BCI agent interviewed several of the female inmates at the Legrand County Jail, he and several other officers appeared at the jail one day with a warrant for the arrest of Lincoln on multiple rape counts. Sheriff Snodgrass was livid and objected strongly to BCI interference in "his jail matters." But the BCI pushed forward and took Lincoln into custody.

Questions for Discussion

1. Given the fact that the Legrand County Jail was a medium-sized facility, what sort of administrative controls should the chief jailer have implemented to guard against sexual assaults of women by deputies under his supervision?

2. How is the problem of Fred Lincoln a function of poor bureaucratic administration?

3. How could an application of the bureaucratic model in the Legrand County Jail perhaps have avoided the incidents of sexual assault between the jail officer and the female inmate?

4. Since Sheriff Snodgrass knew about his nephew's delinquency and the sexual assault charge, should he have been informed by the chief jailer about Lincoln's assignment to the women's wing of the jail?

5. How is the Legrand County Jail a closed system in an organizational sense? How does the intervention of the Bureau of Criminal Investigation change this closed-system perspective?

CHAPTER 3

ORGANIZATIONS AS OPEN AND NONRATIONAL SYSTEMS

KEY TERMS

Compliance-involvement typology

Equilibrium model

Hawthorne effect

Hawthorne studies

Human relations model

Human relations school

Initiating structure

Motivational model

Natural-system model

Organizational typologies

Prime beneficiary typology

Professional model

Showing consideration

Survival model

Theory *X*

Theory *Y*

Theory *Z*

Total quality management (TQM)

CHAPTER OBJECTIVES

The following objectives are intended:

1. To describe several nonrational closed-system organizational models, including Theory *X* and Theory *Y*

2. To describe the human relations model, the historical context of its emergence, and its contemporary importance and application

3. To examine Theory *Z* and Total Quality Management (TQM) as interesting alternative nonrational organizational models

4. To examine the professional and equilibrium models in contrast to the human relations model

5. To describe the natural-system model, its application, and its weaknesses and strengths

6. To describe and explain several key organizational typologies used for categorizing organizations according to several salient and shared characteristics

INTRODUCTION

This chapter describes another class of organizational models. The organizational models introduced here assume that organizations are nonrational entities and that they are not designed for the purpose of dealing with rational, anticipated events. In Chapter 2, rational organizational models, such as the bureaucratic model, presumed that organizations are tightly organized structures, with predetermined arrangements among different organizational members. Each person working for the organization was considered a specialist and had considerable control over his or her work. The work performed by individual members was routine, anticipated, or predictable. Thus, everyone was highly trained and had his or her own sphere of competence that did not overlap the spheres of competence of other employees. A rigid hierarchy of authority was in place and abstract rules governed how the business of the organization was conducted. Persons related with one another on an impersonal basis, and nepotism was discouraged.

The organizational models presented in this chapter are in sharp contrast to the features of the bureaucratic model and other rational models that were described earlier. Nonrational models are based on the assumption that organizations are dynamic entities and must deal with numerous nonrational or unpredictable events on a daily basis. Organizational rules are relaxed to a degree, and the importance of social skills and interpersonal relations among organizational members is emphasized. Considerable attention is paid to one's emotional state, and great value is placed on each employee's feelings and attitudes toward his or her job.

The chapter begins with a description of several popular and early models of organization that emphasize individual dispositions toward work. The first two models presented are known as Theory *X* and Theory *Y*. Theories *X* and *Y* focus on individuals as personality systems. Several assumptions are made about individuals and the work they perform in their organizations. Organizational effectiveness is viewed as dependent on how workers orient themselves toward their jobs. These theories, which in effect are organizational models that focus on the individual unit or level of analysis, provide the framework for a description of the most popular nonrational organizational model, the human relations model.

The human relations model emerged in large part as the result of a series of experiments conducted at the Hawthorne, Illinois, plant of the Western Electric Company during the late 1920s. The Hawthorne plant employed many people who performed various tasks associated with telephone equipment and relay systems. Social scientists focused on the Hawthorne plant for their investigations of worker productivity and how worker output might be influenced by environmental factors such as workroom lighting, temperature, and rest pauses. Subsequently, it was discovered that workers at the Hawthorne plant modified their behaviors and produced more, but only because they considered themselves special in the eyes of organizational administrators. This special consideration was a new phenomenon for management, and over the next

30 years or so, the human relations school of management was born. Today, the human relations model is one alternative way of viewing organizational systems. It has undergone substantial modification since its inception. The Hawthorne experiments will be described as well as the human relations model itself.

In subsequent decades other organizational models were devised. During the 1980s, for instance, Theory *Z* was formulated. Theory *Z* is considered a nonrational organizational model in that it emphasizes employee participation in decision making that affects their work and a managerial concern for their welfare as well as their families. Closely related to Theory *Z* is Total Quality Management or TQM, which is an organizational model focusing on quality leadership, worker participation in decision making, open communication between supervisors and subordinates, and more creative incentives pertaining to work performed. Both Theory *Z* and TQM are discussed in this chapter.

Two additional nonrational organizational models are presented and described. These include the professional model and the equilibrium model. The professional model actually is regarded by some investigators as a synthesis of the best elements of bureaucracy and the human relations approach. This model was established during the 1950s and attributes at least some of its popularity to the increased general education of the workforce. As the workforce in business and industry acquired additional education following World War II and the Korean War, workplaces throughout the United States were populated increasingly with persons with college degrees. Many of these college graduates expected more from the work they performed. Furthermore, they were increasingly regarded by their employers as valuable sources of new information about how organizations should be structured and operated. Their counsel was sought more often by higher-level administrators, and it became evident that many employees believed that they were entitled to greater involvement in organizational decision making as professionals. The professional model is described in some detail in the chapter.

Another nonrational organizational model is the equilibrium model. This model, sometimes called the survival model or motivational model, stresses the importance of individual motivation and employee involvement in organizational decision making. The equilibrium model views organizational members as participants who work together in concert to bring about a type of homeostasis or status quo. Organizations viewed from the framework of the equilibrium model stress the interrelatedness of work tasks and departments in much the same sense that different organs must function properly in order for the human body to survive over time. The essential elements of this model are presented.

Another section of this chapter focuses on the natural-system model. This model conceives of organizations as systems comprised of numerous codependent parts. The natural-system model is different from the equilibrium model because it also considers important the external environment of the organization itself. Some investigators have used an organic analogy to describe this model, although its proponents reject such a comparison. The parallels and differences between organizations and human systems are presented. Both the weaknesses and strengths of the natural-system model are discussed.

The chapter concludes with a description of two popular organizational typologies. Typologies of organizations seek to categorize organizations in terms of their structural and functional similarities. Typologies of organizations are different from organizational theories and models in that they merely seek to categorize rather than provide explanations for organizational phenomena and employee actions. Some theorists believe that our generalizations are more effective if we limit them to organizations of particular types. Thus, we might profit more by making generalizations about the military, police departments, and fire departments rather than clutter our typologies by adding Sears, JC Penney, and hospitals in our groupings or categorizations. Two typologies described here include Amitai Etzioni's compliance-involvement typology and Peter Blau and Richard Scott's prime beneficiary typology.

NONRATIONAL MODELS: THEORIES X, Y, AND Z AND HUMAN RELATIONS

Theory X and Theory Y

During the early 1900s, few workers and employees in business and industry were educated beyond the elementary school level. For many workers, high school was a luxury. A college education was beyond the means of most persons except the affluent. Thus, the workforce generally was dominated by managerial philosophies that emphasized worker control. Most

workers were paid minimum wages and struggled to make ends meet. Worker unionization was poorly organized and in its infancy. Organizational leaders gave little or no consideration to worker sentiments and attitudes. The philosophy of administrators was that workers were paid to do their jobs and nothing more. If workers were not producing as administrators expected, then management focused on various incentives to increase worker output. These incentives were often mere wage increases and did little or nothing to modify the work environment of most employees. In this context the machine model was most effective. The bureaucratic model was also popular for visualizing organizations and how they should be structured.

Douglas McGregor (1960) characterizes this early view of workers in the organization by describing a set of beliefs labeled as **Theory X.** Under the assumptions of Theory X, persons have an inherent dislike of work and will avoid it if they can. Because of this human characteristic of dislike of work, most people must be coerced, controlled, directed, and threatened with punishment to get them to put forth sufficient effort toward the achievement of organizational objectives. The average human being prefers to be directed, wants to avoid responsibility, has relatively little ambition, and craves security above all (McGregor, 1960:33–34).

In contrast, McGregor devised **Theory Y.** Theory Y depicts an emerging conception of workers that focuses on worker attitudes, sentiments, and social environment. According to Theory Y, the expenditure of physical and mental effort in work is as natural as play or rest. External control and the threat of punishment are not the only means to bring about effort toward organizational objectives. Workers will exercise self-direction and self-control in the service of objectives to which they are committed. Commitment to objectives is a function of the rewards associated with their achievement. The average human being learns, under proper conditions, not only to accept but to seek responsibility. The capacity to exercise a relatively high degree of imagination, ingenuity, and creativity in the solutions of organizational problems is widely, not narrowly, distributed in the population. Under the conditions of modern industrial life, the intellectual potentialities of the average human being are only partially utilized (McGregor, 1960:47–48).

Theory Y was unique because it vested workers with attitudes and feelings. Furthermore, it suggested that factors other than orders from superiors and directives from administrators were equally or more important for eliciting greater organizational commitment and productivity from employees. Theory *Y* was influenced greatly by the human relations model.

The Human Relations Model

Traditional organizational models that focus on rational factors are criticized in part because they assume that human beings will perform tasks without emotion. A logical response to this criticism was the establishment of the **human relations school,** which was formally founded in the late 1920s by Elton Mayo (Mayo, 1945). Mayo believed that although organizations exhibit many rational properties, the work attitudes and sentiments of the membership must be considered as primary motivating factors affecting variables such as productivity and morale. The **human relations model** reflects the view that workers are collections of sentiments. These sentiments must be considered as strategic in virtually every phase of organizational planning and change.

The human relations model examines the integration of people into an organization in addition to those factors that motivate them to work together cooperatively and productively. It is action-oriented, relating to people at work in organizations and their economic, psychological, and social satisfactions. It examines variables that contribute toward building a more productive and satisfying worker interrelation (Davis, 1962:18–19). In probation and parole agencies, for example, persistent problems have occurred in certain offices pertaining to administrative and personnel conflicts, role orientations of probation/parole officers with the police, and worker disagreements with supervisors about the objectives of supervision (Takagi and Carter, 1967). Over the years, significant efforts have been made to solicit greater probation/parole officer input regarding the nature of their roles relative to clients and the most workable strategies for providing helpful services (Burns, 1975; Crank, 1996). If individual officers can maximize their personal and professional skills in relation to their clients, worker satisfaction and effectiveness are enhanced accordingly (Takata, 1983).

THE HAWTHORNE STUDIES. Much of the scientific evidence compiled by researchers in the early development of the human relations model focused on a series of investigations conducted at the Hawthorne plant of the Western Electric Company near Chicago,

Illinois, during the years 1927 to 1932. The **Hawthorne studies** are regarded as classics in organizational literature and were described in detail in the work of Roethlisberger and Dickson (1939). It has been said that there can be few scientific disciplines or fields of research in which a single set of studies or a single researcher or writer has exercised so great an influence as was exercised for a quarter of a century by Elton Mayo and the Hawthorne studies (Carey, 1967:403).

The Hawthorne plant was a major assembly point for telephone equipment, including relays and banks of terminals. The studies investigated the impact of the following variables on employee productivity: rest pauses, new work incentive systems, temperature, lighting, length of the workday, humidity, hours of work, pay, and the type of social situation. A series of five separate studies constituted much of the material for the later report by Roethlisberger and Dickson. These five stages were

Stage 1: The Relay Assembly Test Room Study (new incentive system and new supervision)

Stage 2: The Second Relay Assembly Group Study (new incentive system only)

Stage 3: The Mica-Splitting Test Room Study (new supervision only)

Stage 4: The Interviewing Program

Stage 5: The Bank-Wiring Observation Room Study

Stages 1 through 3 contained evidence that presumably led to Elton Mayo's conclusion that social needs and satisfactions are important considerations in explaining employee productivity (Carey, 1967:404).

The technical aspects of the Hawthorne studies are well-known. The major outcome was the discovery of the significance of the **Hawthorne effect** (Etzioni, 1964:33). In a series of illumination experiments, for instance, researchers surmised that if the room lighting were increased with a dimmer switch, then worker productivity would logically increase. Thus, they increased the lighting and observed increased worker productivity. Subsequently, these researchers reasoned that if the lighting were decreased in the room, productivity would decline. When the room lighting was dimmed, however, productivity reached an all-time high. Researchers were flabbergasted by this result and sought to explain it. Workers were interviewed and the answer to high productivity under low lighting conditions became evident. The workers had ignored room lighting changes. They believed that they were special and were receiving special treatment from organization officials. Thus, no matter what the lighting was like in their workroom, they were determined to show management that they could produce at a high rate anyway.

Amitai Etzioni (1964:33) notes that their increased productivity appeared to be one result of increased group cohesiveness among workers, significant modifications and improvements in their levels of psychological satisfaction, and new patterns of social interaction brought about by putting them into the experiment (Relay Assembly Test) room and the special attention they received. The increased participation of workers in decisions affecting their work and a greater identification with managerial goals also contributed substantially to their increased productivity, indirectly lending additional support to the Hawthorne effect.

CHARACTERISTICS OF THE HUMAN RELATIONS MODEL.   Basic characteristics of the human relations model include (1) mutual interest, (2) individual differences, (3) motivation, and (4) human dignity.

Mutual Interest.   This is an assumption of some commonality of interest between employers and employees and among employees. An employee's participation is largely voluntary. No two persons will have identical goals, but they can find mutual interest through an organization. In this way, people are encouraged to fight the problem at hand instead of each other. The existence and influence of unions in criminal justice organizations is prevalent in both law enforcement and corrections. Collective bargaining occurs with some frequency between law enforcement officers and administrators. Although this collective action creates economic benefits for participants, there are positive social consequences as well. Those involved are brought together for a common purpose, and this pursuit of common goals is unifying. Some evidence suggests that one's work performance is positively affected by such collective bargaining (Zhao and Lovrich, 1997).

Individual Differences.   Each person has unique qualities, but they are whole persons, rather than a mass of separate traits. The individual is the unit of feeling, of judgment, of action. They are the ones who determine satisfaction and are motivated. The group is secondary. Only people can take responsibility and make decisions—a group cannot do so. It is powerless until individuals act. If, for example, everyone in a

group waits for the group to act, there will be no action. A person always has responsibility for action. A study of 949 municipal police chiefs found that there is great diversity among these persons with regard to their backgrounds and individual differences. Often, departmental relations are more profoundly influenced by the personalities of police chiefs than by organizational factors, such as size, complexity, and workload (Steinman, 1984). Thus, chiefs play key roles by using their individual attributes, education, and administrative training to influence their subordinates to perform more or less effectively.

Motivation.   Individuals must be encouraged to work together inasmuch as most, if not all, social behaviors are caused by some stimulus or combination of stimuli. Motivation provides a potential cause or initiating factor in this instance. It is the means by which the manager creates and maintains the desire of the subordinates to achieve the planned goals of the organization. In court organizations, for instance, considerable variation exists concerning the efficiency of case processing and success of prosecutions. Attempts to explain variations in case processing among different courts often have focused on processual variables, such as the mechanics of offender processing and accompanying paperwork involved (Cramer, 1981). However, alternative explanations of court effectiveness in case processing have targeted personality systems and informal working relations as instrumental in case outcomes (Burstein, 1980). In fact, some researchers have indicated that the informal work group is the most appropriate concept for explaining both participant behavior in criminal trial courts and trial court output (Clynch and Neubauer, 1981).

Human Dignity.   Most studies of personal needs or wants show that people want to be treated with respect and dignity—to be treated as human beings. The human relations model accepts human dignity as basic (Davis, 1962:14–19). In correctional institutions, such as prisons, for example, organizational structure, operations, and policy changes have been viewed as administratively inspired and directed (Seaman, 1978). However, organizational effectiveness in correctional settings has been positively influenced by use of the human relations model in the treatment of correctional officers and in shaping their attitudes of themselves as well as the value they place on the work performed (Gido, 1998).

From the human relations model perspective, production is the secondary consideration and the individual is the primary one (Brewer, 1995). Organizational structure is designed to accommodate individual attitudes and sentiments. For instance, the nature of supervision over subordinates is employee-centered as opposed to job-centered (Stogdill and Coons, 1957). Another classification of supervisory behavior widely used in research is based on measures of **initiating structure** and **showing consideration** (Maier, 1965:130–131). Each concept is treated as a dimension. The dimension of showing consideration reflects the degree to which the leader establishes two-way communication, mutual respect, and a consideration of the feelings of subordinates. Essentially, it represents a human relations orientation toward leadership. Initiating structure reflects the extent to which the leader facilitates group interaction toward goal attainment. This involves planning, scheduling, criticizing, and initiating ideas (Fleishman and Harris, 1962).

In some probation departments, for instance, probation officer effectiveness is most frequently evaluated by offender recidivism. If offender recidivism is high, then probation officer effectiveness is low. But this is a rather sterile analysis and neglects to include one or more dynamic components associated with the probation officer role (Jester, 1982). Giving probation officers greater latitude in performing their roles and providing them with a sense of greater self-worth rather than manipulating their caseloads enables them to provide their probationer-clients with more focused services and attention (Schmidt, 1989).

The human relations model maintains some of the rationality associated with the bureaucratic model. Selection by test and a hierarchy of authority are basic components, although the emphasis on conformity to abstract rules or laws is relaxed considerably. Decisions made by supervisors or managers depend on personal considerations as well as rationally calculated probable outcomes (Crawford, 1994). Promotions within the organization are dependent for the most part on one's ability to communicate with others effectively. A knowledge of the rules is important, but even more crucial is the human application of them.

CRITICISMS OF THE HUMAN RELATIONS MODEL. Several criticisms of the human relations model are given in the following paragraphs.

1. The human relations model is only selectively applicable. Some organizations simply do not lend themselves to analysis by use of the human relations model. A military organization, for instance, would tend to favor a bureaucratic model in view of the logistical problems of coordinating large numbers of troops. Likewise, prisons are not analyzed easily with the human relations model (Rison, 1996; Seaman, 1978). Social work clinics, on the other hand, perhaps might be more amenable to study by using this model. Although problems of human relations are a part of all organizations, the fact is that better models exist to account for behaviors in a greater portion of organizations.

2. The human relations model places too much emphasis on the importance of social factors. The importance of considering the sentiments of organizational members is self-evident. Certainly the role of the informal group on the job is a significant one. We would be in error, however, if we failed to recognize the significance of attachments that individuals develop to groups or group affiliations external to the immediate organizational setting (Cicourel, 1995).

3. Although the human relations model emphasizes harmonious superior-subordinate relations and close associations within work groups, we must recognize the importance of conflict as a means of promoting eventual organizational progress. Assuming that one intraorganizational objective is cooperation and harmony among the membership, the human relations approach seeks to achieve such a state by reducing or eliminating conflicts between work units through mutual understanding and adjustments in personal interactions (Selke, 1978; Zeidler, 1981).

4. Human relations may bring about a more pleasant social condition within which to work, but this approach does not lessen the tediousness of tasks (Chinoy, 1955). Studies of police cynicism, for example, have shown that although material and social rewards for meritorious conduct and general officer effectiveness are appreciated and desired, they do not by themselves change the routine or stress of police work (Regoli, 1975; Wallace, Roberson, and Steckler, 1995).

5. The human relations model is functional for those kinds of organizations requiring a high degree of social skills and communicative abilities. It has been argued that the human relations model is most appropriate for situations in which tasks are relatively nonuniform and/or involve social skills (Litwak, 1961:182).

Theory Z and Total Quality Management (TQM)

THEORY Z. In the early 1980s, William Ouchi (1981) wrote a book titled *Theory Z* that outlined an approach to management utilizing a new model, **Theory Z,** that emphasized employee job security, participatory decision making, group responsibility and teamwork, increased product and services quality, slower evaluation and promotion policies, broader career paths, and a greater concern for employees' work and familial welfare. Japanese businesses and industries had utilized this model for many decades as a powerful means for motivating employees.

Several of Ouchi's contemporaries, such as Joseph Juran and W. Edwards Demming, developed various principles of statistical quality control and applied these principles to assist Japanese firms in improving worker productivity and effectiveness. It was estimated by Juran that at least 85 percent of worker effectiveness was under the direct control of management. Through a process of continuous improvement, working collaboratively and closely with employees, both product and service quality could be improved substantially.

TOTAL QUALITY MANAGEMENT (TQM). The ideas of Ouchi, Juran, and Demming have been synthesized into a management model known as **total quality management** or **TQM.** TQM is a model stressing high employee participation in the decision-making process. It also stresses teamwork, continuous learning and self-improvement, and the use of the scientific method and statistical quality control to evaluate and improve worker effectiveness. TQM is implemented through (1) developing effective leadership; (2) instilling greater worker commitment to work quality and services; (3) establishing a work atmosphere conducive to self-fulfillment, creativity, and pride in workmanship; (4) using scientific thinking; (5) creating open communication and emphasizing greater honesty and information-sharing; and (6) being citizen-oriented (West, Berman, and Milakovich, 1994).

TQM has been used in the analyses of various criminal justice organizations, such as courts and probation agencies, although some research suggests that

it may not be appropriate for certain types of organizations, such as police agencies, that have adopted the paramilitary model (Fleischman and Aikman, 1993; Janes, 1993). Limitations of the paramilitary model on which many police organizations are based include a general failure to consider important dimensions of organizational behavior and rationality and a failure to recognize the uncertainty inherent in police goals, environment, and technology. Increasing the professionalism of the occupation of policing may make TQM more applicable for explaining the nature of police operations and functions (Fry and Berkes, 1983; Southerland, 1984).

OTHER ORGANIZATIONAL MODELS

Both the bureaucratic and human relations models are efficient for dealing with different, but equally important, types of organizational phenomena. However, the bureaucratic model is most efficient if the organization deals primarily with uniform events and with occupations or professions that stress traditional areas of knowledge rather than social skills. As noted previously, the human relations model works best if an organization deals with events that are not uniform (e.g., community policing, medical treatment, graduate training, designing) and with occupations that emphasize social skills, such as psychiatric social work, sales, and politics (Litwak, 1961:177).

One solution for contemporary organizations that deal with both uniform and nonuniform events simultaneously (e.g., police departments, departments of corrections, probation and parole programs, courtrooms) is the development of a model that permits two conflicting views of organizations to coexist without friction. Thus, such a blended model would generate greater flexibility in internal functioning and services provided by individual organizations. Four mechanisms have been identified that can permit segregation of functioning and services without friction. These are

1. Role separation as a mechanism of segregation. It is necessary to restrict primary group behavior to one set of individuals and formal relations to another.
2. Physical distance as a mechanism of segregation. Depending on the physical facilities of the organization involved, space may not permit great physical distance between departments

geared to handle problems differently. If possible, however, physical separation has the advantage of lessening conflict.

3. Transferral occupations as mechanisms of segregation. Certain individuals in the organization are charged with the responsibility of bridging interest areas (e.g., the differences between pure scientists' work and the production line) without contaminating either.

4. Evaluation procedures as mechanisms of segregation. This requires the creation of a position to determine when social relations should shift from one form to another (Litwak, 1961:182–184).

The Professional Model

Eugene Litwak (1961) has described a **professional model,** which suggests that increased specialization within the organization can be a means of attaining greater flexibility in managing organizational problems. Expanding the training of organizational members to deal with problematic events more flexibly is professionalizing them. Professional persons are typically identified as persons trained in professional schools, possessing complex skills and special knowledge, and equipped with internalized control mechanisms (Scott, 1966:268–269). Professionals are contrasted with bureaucrats who are thought of as relatively specialized in function and as operating in a hierarchical structure under a system of formal rules (Crank, 1993). Scott (1966) warns that as members of organizations become more professional in their abilities and orientations, organizations run the risk of creating new problems as well as resolving old ones. On the one hand, professionals will be able to operate in organizations more effectively by applying greater expertise with respect to task knowledge and social skills. On the other hand, professionals are increasingly likely to resist or reject various bureaucratic rules, resist or reject bureaucratic standards, resist bureaucratic supervision, and reflect only conditional loyalty to the organization (Scott, 1966:269).

BENEFITS OF THE PROFESSIONAL MODEL. For many organizations, the problems of adapting the characteristics of professionals to bureaucratic structure will not emerge because either the organization is able to function adequately without the aid of professionals, or mechanisms of separation of function are instituted that will at least minimize the conflict if not entirely eliminate it. Professionals are likely to establish a more functional set of behavioral expectations. Their expertise entitles them to operate "professionally," without constraining regulations or interference from others (Scott, 1966:270). They resist standards of bureaucratic organizations because, reflecting a cosmopolitan orientation, they adhere to the standards created by the abstract professional aggregate on a national scale (such as the American Bar Association, Academy of Criminal Justice Sciences, Fraternal Order of Police, American Probation and Parole Association, and the American Correctional Association).

CRITICISMS OF THE PROFESSIONAL MODEL. Professionals are increasingly discontent with bureaucratic supervision because in many instances, the supervisors over them are not qualified in their own fields of specialization (Arensberg and McGregor, 1942; Marcson, 1960). The loyalty of professionals toward their employing organizations cannot be predicted absolutely. Professionals increasingly follow the norms and behavioral expectations of their profession at large (provided that their specialty areas have local, state, or national professional organizations), rather than those of the employing organization (Commission on Accreditation for Law Enforcement Agencies, 1983).

The Equilibrium Model

An alternative to the professional model is the **equilibrium model.** The equilibrium model stresses the importance of motivational factors to encourage member participation in organizational activities. Barnard (1938) and Simon (1947) have defined an organization as a system of consciously coordinated activities or forces of two or more persons. The equilibrium model involves an exchange of rewards from the organization for services performed by organizational members. The organization ensures its survival over time by motivating participants to become involved in organizational activities. Thus, sometimes the equilibrium model is also referred to as the **survival model** or the **motivational model.** This is because the model is a statement of the conditions under which an organization can induce its members to continue their participation and assure organizational survival over time. Some writers have described a typical police department as an example of a bureaucracy that has lost sight of its purpose and seeks only to survive. It is concerned with narrow turf interests and measures of production that are worthless to the real crime problem (Lashley, 1995).

BOX 3.1 CAN PROFESSIONALIZING JAIL OFFICERS PREVENT INMATE LAWSUITS?

The Trail County Jail and Leroy Peterson. It happened at the Trail County Jail in North Dakota. Leroy Peterson was arrested in April 1990 for falling behind in his child support payments. A chronic alcoholic, Peterson began to suffer alcohol withdrawal symptoms while jailed. According to jail records, Peterson had been drinking heavily when he was picked up by sheriff's deputies initially. He was placed in a detoxification cell on the Friday night after his arrest. He was transferred the following day to a cell with three other inmates. Peterson was scheduled to be taken to a nearby medical clinic the following Monday, but while he was in the cell, he fell and hit his head. Jail officers approached Peterson at his cell and inquired if they could be of assistance. Peterson could talk and never asked for medical attention. Subsequently, another inmate celled with Peterson, Charles Syvertson, told jail officers that Peterson appeared disoriented, was sick to his stomach, and tried to bathe himself while clothed. Jail officers observed, however, that only Peterson's hands appeared to be shaking and that he refused to eat all of his food. They believed that Syvertson, who was awaiting a 40-year sentence for child molestation, was lying about Peterson and his condition. In February 1995, Peterson filed a lawsuit against jail officials and the Trail County Jail alleging negligence in how he was treated and ignored by jail officers. Peterson's attorneys contended that the county was responsible because of what the jailers didn't do,

that is, take Peterson for medical treatment. A later trial ruled in favor of the county. The posttrial memo from the judge said that "If Peterson's view of the case prevailed, the precedent would be thereby established that immediate medical attention would have to be provided by any and every jail in North Dakota, to any and every prisoner for whom a claim for such services was made." Leroy Peterson died of heart failure shortly after his lawsuit was filed. His widow decided to pursue the case on behalf of her husband's estate, however. The North Dakota Supreme Court ordered a new trial in Peterson's case in October 1999 after hearing former trial evidence and reviewing the first judicial decision. The Supreme Court said, "Certainly passive omissions to act can cause as harmful an injury as affirmative actions. Adopting the county's proposed distinction would encourage employees to fail to act in situations where a duty to do so clearly arises, merely to retain governmental immunity. This result is not only ludicrous, but the consequences could be hazardous or tragic."

In view of the short-term nature of jail confinement, what amount of professional training do you think should be expected of jail officers? What can administrators do to ensure that jail officers are trained to detect and report potential inmate mental and physical problems and deal with them effectively? Is it practical and reasonable to expect that all jail officers should be true professionals? What do you think?

Source: Adapted from the Associated Press, "Supreme Court Orders New Trial in Jail Injury Case," October 22, 1999.

Equilibrium is generally interpreted to mean a state of balance between opposing forces. It implies a perpetuation of the status quo with little, if any, organizational change. Thus, attention is focused on those factors that serve to maintain the organization in some kind of static state. Perhaps organizational leaders and others may believe that the organization is stable and not in need of change. Each part of the organization apparently relates to other parts in a harmonious fashion. Member participation is predictable. Each person does a particular job, each department performs designated functions, and things generally run smoothly (Ulmer, 1995). Similar to the concept of homeostasis in an organism, as long as each bodily part or group member

fulfills its designated tasks, the entire organism or group persists in a constant state. Factors that might upset this homeostasis include increased competitiveness from other organizations or member discontent with work or remuneration. Members who quit, die, retire, or are fired are replaced by others in order to maintain the equilibrium of the organization. Promotions of personnel, transferrals, the phasing out of certain departments, the consolidation of various departments, and changes in the authority pattern or communication network all spell change in the equilibrium of the organization. At the very least, changes of these types can upset organizational equilibrium for a short time. But usually, the organization restores the

BOX 3.2 PERSONALITY HIGHLIGHT

PENNY R. ERICKSON
Jail Commander, Ward County Jail, Minot, North Dakota

Statistics: B.S. (criminal justice), Minot State College and Correctional Officer Basic Training, North Dakota Law Enforcement Academy

I presently hold the position of jail commander of the Ward County Jail in Minot, North Dakota. Prior to this position, I held the positions of shift supervisor and correctional officer. I grew up in Minot, North Dakota, graduated from Minot High School, and attended Minot State College. I graduated with a B.S. degree in criminal justice in 1984.

Background: My career in corrections began just a couple of weeks after graduating from college. It was not necessarily a planned career choice. While attending college, I anticipated working as a juvenile court officer after graduation. About a month before I was to complete my degree, some fellow classmates informed me that hiring would be taking place in the upcoming weeks for correctional officer positions for the Ward County Jail, which was in its final stages of construction at that time. I decided that since I would be graduating in about a month, it would be helpful to have some work experience in the criminal justice field, as well as having my degree. I was hired as a correctional officer in June 1984, and that is when my career in corrections began. I find correctional work to be very interesting and always very challenging.

Work Experiences: Corrections work entails dealing with many different situations and many different types of individuals. I never know exactly what I will encounter when I begin my shift. Some of the most interesting situations have been being involved in thwarting escape attempts by inmates. This includes finding cement cinder blocks that have been loosened by an inmate using a plastic utensil, uncovering written escape plans that at times include diagrams, discovering a knife made from a shower drain cover, finding shattered windows (glass panes that inmates have not been able to break out but have been able to shatter, similar to a car windshield), and finding sheets tied together.

Throughout my career in corrections, I have found that the general public's perception of what corrections work entails often is based on what they have seen on television or in the movies. There are many more aspects of correctional work than what are portrayed in the popular media. Some of the day-to-day duties of a correctional officer are maintaining safety and security of the facility, booking in prisoners (including fingerprinting and mugshots), conducting cell checks, serving inmate meals, conducting inmate recreation, coordinating inmate programs, taking care of inmate visitation, ensuring medical care is provided, dealing with suicidal inmates, and many other duties that are necessary to make sure that inmates are cared for while at the same time maintaining security of the facility.

One of the greatest challenges I have encountered in correctional work is dealing with the negative atmosphere. The challenge is not to let the negativity bring you down in your daily work. It is difficult at times to deal with verbal abuse, and sometimes physical abuse, from an inmate and not let it get you down or interfere with how you deal with the next inmate. Recidivism is very frustrating. It is difficult to have an inmate come through the system over and over again.

Advice to Students: For those interested in a career in corrections, I would suggest that you get some hands-on experience while you are pursuing your education. This kind of experience can be obtained through an internship program in a correctional facility, through a ride-along program, and also by arranging tours of criminal justice agencies. All of the criminal justice agencies work very closely together, and therefore any experience you gain will lend itself to enhancing your career.

status quo fairly rapidly through member replacement, financial rewards, and numerous other adjustments.

Some assumptions of the equilibrium model follow:

- An organization is a system of interrelated social behaviors of several persons who are called participants. A courtroom work group might be one example, in which prosecutors and judges interact with court reporters, defense counsels, and other actors in caseflow management and organization (Ulmer, 1995).

- Each participant and each group of participants receives inducements from the organization in return for individual or group contributions.

- Each participant will continue participating in the organization only so long as the inducements offered are as great or greater, as measured in terms of one's personal values and any options available, than the contributions one is asked to make.

- The contributions provided by various groups in the organization are the source from which the organization manufactures the inducements offered to participants. Thus, organizations are solvent and will continue to exist only as long as the contributions are sufficient to provide inducements in large enough measure to draw forth these contributions. (Simon, Smithburg, and Thompson, 1950:381–382)

The equilibrium model places considerable emphasis on individual attitudes toward organizational participation. The notion of inducement covers a broad range of motivational factors including psychological rewards as well as financial ones. The survival of an organization, however, depends on many additional factors besides individual incentives. For instance, the economic market conditions in any given time period must be considered in an evaluation of the effectiveness of any organization. The factors of size and functional complexity also contribute to organizational equilibrium and to its chances of survival.

The interdependence of members and departments in their cooperative effort to perpetuate the organization also is stressed. The coordination of tasks in the division of labor very well might be handled through skillful planning rather than reliance on highly motivated participants to carry out cooperative functions. The bureaucratic model plays down the role of motivation in relation to the perpetuation of the organization. A system of abstract rules coupled with unconditional compliance with them defines the basic orientation of members within highly bureaucratized institutions. Bureaucracy achieves stability or equilibrium through norms of compliance, whereas the equilibrium model relies on personal incentive factors. Neither the bureaucratic nor the equilibrium model is particularly amenable to changes, however, at least from within the organization. The interdependence of positions allows for the determination of whether or not any particular role is being effectively implemented. Within the context of the equilibrium model, conflict may be interpreted as a discrepancy between individual values and organizational expectations, as manifested by higher-level management.

CRITICISMS OF THE EQUILIBRIUM MODEL. Some of the more important criticisms of the equilibrium model are noted in the following paragraphs:

1. The emphasis on individual motivational factors moves the equilibrium model away from a consideration of organizational factors. Small groups or informal aggregates are not considered as important contributors to organizational stability. Supervisory styles are largely ignored as possible inducements to participate. The psychological dimension is present to such a degree that strong elements of the human relations school are presumed to underlie the equilibrium model. For instance, police officer burnout and stress have been correlated with job demands and the amount of social support among colleagues (Burke, 1987).

2. The equilibrium model gives insufficient consideration to formal labor agreements. An organization is much more than a collection of cooperating individuals. The superior-subordinate relation rests more on objective, contractual guidelines and labor laws than on personal definitions of the value of inducements to participate (Zhao and Lovrich, 1997). Organizational changes are to be expected regularly in a competitive environment. Organizational members are obligated to make adjustments and adaptations to new and improved technologies. Through arbitration between labor and management, agreements are reached concerning wages to be paid and work to be performed. In this sense, whether any given individual perceives the inducements associated with the work performed as adequate or inadequate is quite immaterial. In many organizations today, employee discontentments are taken care of through a simple grievance process. Those grievances that are determined valid by an independent evaluation body or arbiter are brought to management for resolution. Usually, contracts are worked out between the union and management that include guidelines for deciding the fairness of work expectations and labor output. The organization does not become insolvent because of personal discontent. The availability of labor to replace dissatisfied members who quit or are fired is also a significant factor.

3. The equilibrium model largely ignores organizational change from within. According to this model, in order for change to occur, organizations must receive some kind of stimulus from their external environment, such as a competitive challenge from another organization or from advice by outside consultants. Mechanisms for promoting change within the organization itself are conspicuously absent. Organizations are dynamic entities, whereas the equilibrium model connotes a static organizational situation (Llynn, 1980). Organizations want to do much more than simply preserve the status quo, although the maintenance of a formal pattern of interrelations of roles is very important. Modern American police organizations are rationalized, hierarchical arrangements that reflect the influence of classic organizational theory and result in a firmly established, impersonal system that is extremely resistant to change (Angell, 1971).

NONRATIONAL MODELS: THE NATURAL-SYSTEM MODEL

The organic analogy has often been applied in an attempt to describe the **natural-system model** of organizations. In this analogy, organizations are perceived as systems made up of independent parts, each part functioning so that the entire system is perpetuated and survives over time. The system draws its nourishment or energy from sources in its external environment (Cohn, 1977).

The system has built-in mechanisms for maintaining itself and for regulating the relations between its component parts. In the context of the organic analogy, the system develops and grows, becoming increasingly complex (Borodzicz, 1996). Each of the parts adjusts to the contributions of the other parts so that a type of homeostasis is generated. To this extent, at least, the natural-system model is similar to the equilibrium model (Giles, 1983).

Assumptions of the Natural-System Model

The major assumptions of the natural-system model follow:

- The organization is considered as a natural whole.
- The component structures of the system are emergent institutions that can be understood only in relation to the diverse needs of the total system.
- The component parts of an organization are interdependent.
- The organization is an end in itself (Gray and Gray, 1974).
- The realization of goals of the system as a whole is but one of several important needs to which the organization is oriented.
- The organization serves to link parts of the system and to provide avenues for controlling and integrating them.
- Organizational structures are viewed as spontaneously and homeostatically maintained (Selke, 1978).
- The equilibrium of the system depends greatly on the conforming behavior of group members.
- Changes in organizational patterns are considered the results of cumulative, unplanned, adaptive responses to threats to the equilibrium of the system as a whole.
- Responses to problems are crescively developed defense mechanisms being constantly shaped by shared values that are deeply internalized in the members (Gouldner, 1959:405–410).

The natural-system model possesses perhaps the most realistic set of assumptions about organizations compared with other models examined thus far (Wachtel, 1982). All organizations must, in fact, contend with an external environment replete with other competing organizations. In corrections, for instance, prison inmate population growth has escalated to the extent that the privatization of prison operations has become both a significant and viable alternative to strictly state-run or federally operated institutions. Even some of the larger local and regional jails in various counties throughout the United States presently compete by offering accommodations at reduced rates for state and federal prison inmates who are victims of chronic overcrowding. Although the nature of this competition among institutions does not jeopardize the existence of state-run or federally operated prisons, some competition does exist, affecting the quality and variety of inmate services and amenities.

Although the closed-system approach to organizational analysis may offer greater theoretical simplicity, largely because factors external to organizations do not need to be accounted for in the theoretical scheme, it is far removed from the way things are in the real world of organizational activity (Joubert, 1976). Early in their formal training, for instance, police officers learn about conditions under which violence and deadly force may be used to effect arrests. However, street encounters with violent criminals and disparate situations cause more than a few police officers to use excessive force, particularly away from public view. Individual decisions to use violence are triggered by situational circumstances that often are not covered in textbooks or manuals about police training (Ross, 1993). Furthermore, citizen reviews of police officer conduct are becoming standard elements in many larger police departments. Therefore, citizen input is substantial in causing sanctions to be brought against certain officers if allegations or complaints have been made by certain arrestees who believe they have been mistreated or subjected to one or more forms of police misconduct (Walker and Wright, 1995). Citizen input is very much an external factor whose impact on police conduct cannot be taken into account in any closed-systemic view of police organizations.

A major limitation of the natural-system model is its unfortunate association with the organic analogy. Although there are many parallels between a bodily system and an organization, there are also many exceptions, which cause the organic analogy to break down under close scrutiny. An organization does not always die. Neither does an organization operate ineffectively on a permanent basis. Many factors external to organizations generate particular conditions that inject new life into them. New managerial philosophies, new product markets, improved technology, organizational growth, improved training methods for supervisors and lower-level personnel, new and changing organizational structures, and an increasingly educated workforce differentially contribute to organizational effectiveness and survival (Gray, Cochran, and Gray, 1976).

The natural-system model conceives an organization to be the recipient of various inputs from the external environment. A factory is provided with raw materials as inputs from external sources, for example. The organization, in turn, has several outputs, which are fed back into the external environment. The same factory system converts the raw materials into products, which are marketed to the general public through retail outlets.

The various components of an organization are often departments that differentially contribute to the perpetuation of the entire structure. Each department is a vital part of the system. If the advertising department does not perform its function well, organizational sales will likely decline and the institution will not prosper. On the other hand, if a company has excellent advertising, the marketing of faulty products manufactured by careless personnel in the production division of the organization will be detrimental to the system as well.

In juvenile justice, for instance, there has been a dramatic shift over the years away from the rehabilitative ideal toward a law-and-order and justice orientation that emphasizes incapacitation, corrections, punishment, and public safety as key policy priorities. Juvenile justice practitioners have been influenced greatly by environmental pressures of public sentiment and empirical/theoretical evidence about how juvenile offenders should be treated. In many instances, support for particular public policies about juvenile offender management and control are influenced by one's own limited autonomy within the organization. One's own job experience helps to account for support of particular policies about juveniles, although it is clear that the external environment of society is a strong driving force leading to the adoption of particular delinquency prevention and control strategies (Schugam, 1983).

Social theorist Talcott Parsons (1951, 1956a, 1956b) has used the natural-system model in viewing social organizations in general and formal organizations in particular. Parsons adds to the model by describing four kinds of problems that organizations must resolve in order to survive and progress over time. He states that the process in any social system is subject to these four independent functional imperatives or problems, which must be met adequately if equilibrium and/or continued existence of the system is to be maintained (1951:16). These problems are (1) goal attainment, or keeping the system moving steadily toward its goals; (2) adaptation, or the process of mobilizing the technical means to achieve goals; (3) integration, or the process of achieving and maintaining appropriate emotional and social relations among those directly cooperating in the goal-attainment process; and (4) latency, pattern maintenance, and tension management, or making sure that the cooperating units have the time and facilities to constitute or recognize the capacities needed by the system.

Various units within the organization function to ensure that each of these problems is resolved on a continuing basis. Some units have planning and coordinating functions, whereas others have managerial functions (Saari, 1982). Some units oversee the quality control dimension, and others make policy decisions. Using the natural-system model for analyzing organizations, a theorist might pay attention to the functional interrelations between departments as well as the relation of the organization as a whole to its external environment.

Another undesirable outcome when using the organic analogy applied to organizations is the fallacious assumption that an organization has a "natural history" and follows natural laws. In reality, organizations usually have units that make rational decisions about the nature and direction of organizational growth. Rather than following a natural pattern, the destiny of the organization is directed by carefully calculated decisions.

Criticisms of the Natural-System Model

Following are some of the more important criticisms of the natural-system model.

1. Although the natural-system model calls attention to the unplanned and spontaneous nature of organizational structures, it has the disadvantage of de-emphasizing their rational features (Gouldner, 1959:407). Organizations do have many rational aspects that must be considered as important in accounting for organizational behavior (Jester, 1982). The natural-system model includes events that are not touched on at all by any of the rational models, however.

2. The notions of natural laws and natural development are somewhat unrealistically applicable to organizations. The obvious influence of intentional and rational actions by members of various departments in organizations has been observed often in organizational research. Most urban police departments have internal affairs divisions that are intended to heighten officer accountability and impose punishments if officer wrongdoing is proved. We might argue that the rational act of establishing an internal regulatory body to oversee the actions of individual members of police

departments actually may serve to undermine officer morale and esprit de corps. In turn, this may cause officers to distrust one another and create dissension within police officer ranks (Becknell, Mays, and Giever, 1999; Walker and Wright, 1995). These consequences are not intended by internal affairs divisions, although they frequently result anyway.

3. Mechanisms for incorporating planned change into the system are ignored by the natural-system model. No provisions exist for dealing with rational action geared to change the system. The natural-system model views change in the system only as a response to external threats to its survival (Zimmerman, 1988). For example, growing numbers of lawsuits have been filed in federal and state courts by inmates in correctional institutions. The grounds for these lawsuits are diverse, including allegations of civil rights violations and habeas corpus and mandamus actions. In an effort to minimize the frequency of these lawsuits, many prisons have established inmate grievance councils and review bodies to screen prisoner complaints. These inmate review boards are comprised of other inmates who listen to prisoner grievances and complaints. The actions of these boards resolve many prisoner grievances before a lawsuit is commenced against the prison system or prison authorities. But not all prison administrators support such inmate councils. They believe that inmate council members may wield considerable informal power among other inmates, and thus their establishment actually may serve to undermine the prison authority hierarchy and power structure. Thus, some resistance to changes of this sort is expected from at least some institutional leaders, since such changes are regarded as threatening to the organizational status quo.

THEORIES AND MODELS IN RETROSPECT

The different organizational models presented in this chapter describe some of the ways researchers view organizations. Each model stresses different dimensions of an organization, and in this respect, at least, each model competes with others. No single model of organizations has been universally accepted. There are obvious overlaps among models, and some models have serious omissions. Organizational theory is heavily dependent on the construction of a satisfactory model of organizations. Perhaps the best-known model of organizations is the bureaucratic model, which was examined in Chapter 2. Certainly it has received the most comment and discussion in the research literature. Various weaknesses of Max Weber's bureaucratic model have been elaborated, however. Other models, such as the human relations model and professional model discussed in this chapter, appear to address some of these weaknesses. But these models also have inherent weaknesses.

The existence of rational models, including the bureaucratic model, and nonrational organizational models, such as the human relations and natural-system models, either assume that the organization exists as a closed or an open system and is or is not impacted by external factors. We need a model that will take into account both predictable and unpredictable (anticipated and unanticipated) consequences of organizational activity, even though much of it is planned. We have learned much about human beings and how they are grouped and function within organizations. We have observed managers' concepts that employees slowly change, from robots to sentiment-laden creatures to decision makers and problem solvers. And accordingly, we have had to modify our organizational models to fit these changing views of organizational participants.

Models enable us to develop a perspective that is potentially useful in our analysis of organizations. We can consider organizational models as sensitizing constructs that focus our attention on one set of characteristics or another. Models are potentially useful strategies in that they provide us with a way of approaching organizations and making systematic statements about them in the context of certain characteristics or dimensions. Each model, then, is a different strategy for conceiving organizations.

Models focus our theorizing. Every organizational theory makes explicit assumptions about organizations and their operations over time, and every organizational theory reflects a particular organizational model. This is the nature of the important relationship between theories and models. However, some investigators have sought to simplify organizational theory construction even further by elaborating organizational typologies that classify organizations into different categories.

ORGANIZATIONAL TYPOLOGIES

Organizational typologies are ways of describing or labeling differences among organizations. Certain relationships among variables may be true within one type of organization but not necessarily within an-

other. Typologies are useful in that they contribute to explanations of differences between organizations. Although organizational theories are devised and intended to apply to all organizations, the fact that organizations differ in their size, shape, complexity, and a host of other factors often means that our theoretical statements about them will not always be clear-cut. If a theory applies to one organization but not to another, the theorist usually wants to know why. Is the theory only partially adequate or applicable, or is the investigator attempting to apply a theory about oranges to apples? Classifying organizations according to several key criteria enables the investigator to unravel some of the complexities surrounding the systematic analysis of these structures.

For example, suppose we have developed a theory of organizations to describe what goes on in prison settings (Surette, 1979). Prisons are strict places with a relatively permanent clientele. Rule observance in prisons is strictly enforced and punishments are meted out whenever rules are violated. Persons who work in these settings as correctional officers or administrators approach their tasks and relate to their clientele (e.g., the inmate population) in certain ways. Thus, theorizing about how prisons are organized and operate takes into account the nature of the organizational environment.

Would a theory that is applicable to prisons necessarily be applicable to police departments? In police departments, there are numerous divisions and varying numbers of police officers and clerical and administrative personnel. Unlike prison settings, workers may come and go freely, and although rules exist, they are not as strict as prison settings.

What about courts? Are courtrooms like police departments and prisons? Obviously not. Therefore, would an organizational theory about police departments also apply to court settings or prisons? Probably not. Usually we would make a different set of assumptions about the work roles of courtroom actors and the settings of court systems.

Unfortunately, organizational theory is not at the level of sophistication necessary to bridge the theoretical gaps among all organizations. Consequently, many theorists have attempted to devise theories that apply to certain classes or types of organizations (i.e., those that exhibit specific characteristics in common) and not to others. The crucial question raised in the construction of organizational typologies, therefore, is "Which criteria should be used in such classification schemes?" A second question is "How do we know if we have selected the right criteria for our typology?"

Only through systematic research on organizations can this question be answered satisfactorily. Obviously, some typologies are more popular and useful than others. Success is usually defined according to the functional utility of particular typologies when predicting differences between organizations. Researchers tend to be quite pragmatic when it comes to developing an allegiance to one typology or another.

This section examines several popular typologies of organizations. It should be noted that all organizational typologies suffer the same deficiencies and limitations as organizational models. No typology has been devised that is fully comprehensive. All typologies have prominent exceptions. The general usefulness of typologies, however, is that they enable us to sift and sort through the myriad of organizations that exist currently and isolate important similarities among them that have potential theoretical and substantive value. The decision about which typologies should be included here was based in large part on which ones are most frequently cited in the literature. Two typologies will be described, the compliance-involvement typology and the prime beneficiary typology.

The Compliance-Involvement Typology

A classification scheme for organizations has been devised according to the nature of compliance behavior (Etzioni, 1961:3–21). It is called the **compliance-involvement typology.** Compliance is universal, existing in all social units. It is a major element of the relationship between those who have power and those over whom they exercise it. Accordingly, compliance refers to the way an actor behaves in response to a directive from another actor and to the orientation of the subordinated actor toward the power applied (Etzioni, 1961:3).

In all organizations, members are subjected to the orders of members at a higher level in the authority hierarchy. Higher-level members may exercise authority over subordinates through force or coercion, reward or remuneration, or normative means. Also, the recipients of directives, the lower-level participants, vary in the nature of their involvement in the organization according to the nature of the directives aimed at them. For instance, it may be that a person will become alienated within the system because he is forced or coerced into complying with directives from higher-ups. On the other hand, some persons may feel morally obligated to participate and obey the directives from above to the extent that they believe that they are normatively based. Finally, some persons may calculate the benefits they might obtain by complying with remuneratively based directives (Glaser, 1977). A typology of compliance relations has been devised by Amitai Etzioni and is illustrated in Table 3.1.

Table 3.1 shows various possible compliance-involvement patterns that may typify certain types of organizations. Some of these compliance-involvement patterns are considered congruent, in that they are more effective and expected. Types 1, 5, and 9 are congruent. The other types are incongruent. Incongruent compliance-involvement types exist, in part, as the result of external factors that reduce the power of superiors in the organizations (e.g., the membership of lower-level participants in labor unions) and various value commitments.

CONGRUENCIES IN THE COMPLIANCE-INVOLVEMENT TYPOLOGY. A coercive-alienative congru-

---

TABLE 3.1 ETZIONI'S TYPOLOGY OF COMPLIANCE RELATIONS

KINDS OF POWER	TYPE OF INVOLVEMENT		
	ALIENATIVE	**CALCULATIVE**	**MORAL**
Coercive	1	2	3
Remunerative	4	5	6
Normative	7	8	9

Source: Amitai Etzioni, *Complex Organizations* (New York: Holt, 1961), p. 12. Reprinted with permission of Holt, Rinehart and Winston.

ency is best illustrated with a jail or prison setting and the interplay between inmates and correctional officers. Prisoners are coerced into complying, although they resent having to do so. They know that if they do not comply, bad things will happen. They might lose some or all of their good-time credits, and thus, their release from prison may be delayed. Or some inmates may be placed in administrative segregation or solitary confinement. These are some of the powerful incentives for inmates to comply with directives from the institution and correctional officers.

A calculative-remunerative congruency may be illustrated by the interplay between a prosecutor and a defense attorney during plea bargaining (Ulmer and Kramer, 1998). The defense counsel wants the most favorable outcome and sentence for the defendant. A lenient sentence recommendation from the prosecutor is considered a reward if it is accepted, contrasted with the alternative, which might be a trial, conviction, and a more severe sentencing outcome. The defense counsel strikes the best bargain, after weighing the benefits and potential alternative outcomes (Eisenstein and Jacob, 1977).

The normative-moral congruency may be illustrated by the probation officer–probationer relation. Although probationers are required to obey a strict set of behavioral requirements in their probation programs, they are nevertheless relatively free within their communities. Probationers often regard their probation officers as enablers who can give them various forms of assistance, including job referrals and involvement in treatment programs. To the extent that probationers view their probation officers in this fashion and as normative, they might consider good behavior to be morally acceptable.

INCONGRUENCIES IN THE COMPLIANCE-INVOLVEMENT TYPOLOGY. Incongruent types also exist. For instance, the coercive-moral incongruency might be illustrated by someone who is drafted into the army, air force, or some other military branch. The draft is coercive, but involvement in the military for the good of the country is patriotic and morally acceptable. A coercive-calculative incongruency may be the prison inmate who becomes involved in various educational or self-help programs. Essentially a coercive environment, the prison is nevertheless viewed as a place in which rewards can be granted with good conduct or behavior. When parole hearings are convened later, the inmate calculates the possible rewards

that might accrue resulting from involvement in these educational or self-help programs.

The remunerative-alienative incongruent type might be depicted by a soldier of fortune or mercenary who fights for a country for money, not because of any concern for the country's ideals or values. A remunerative-moral incongruency might be illustrated by the director of a funeral home who realizes substantial profits from the funeral business but at the same time realizes the task has moral implications for bereaved families.

The idea of congruent and incongruent types does not necessarily mean that overlaps cannot exist. It is entirely possible for several types of power to be exerted by the same person in relation to others at the same time. It is also possible for persons to have overlapping types of involvement in the activities they are expected to perform.

CRITICISMS OF THE COMPLIANCE-INVOLVEMENT TYPOLOGY. Several criticisms have been made of the compliance-involvement typology. For instance, it has been suggested that schemes that focus on a single dimension of organizational structure or process neglect other, equally important or more important dimensions that should be considered. In the general case, unidimensional schemes tend to be inadequate theoretically and have little explanatory value beyond certain organizational limits. Although multidimensional schemes offer better theoretical promise in this regard, they are considerably more complex to construct. In addition, the question arises as to which variables are most important to include in the typology. On the interpersonal level, however, Etzioni's scheme appears to contribute to an explanation for particular behaviors and attitudes, such as morale, work satisfaction, labor turnover, productivity, and esprit de corps (Thomas, Kreps, and Cage, 1977).

The Prime Beneficiary Typology

The **prime beneficiary typology** is based on the principle of who benefits by the particular organizational activity (Blau and Scott, 1962). Four classes or types of beneficiaries have been defined by Peter Blau and Richard Scott (1962). The different beneficiaries are (1) members or rank-and-file participants, (2) owners and managers, (3) clients, and (4) the general public. For each class of beneficiary, Blau and Scott have indicated a particular type of organization that fits the beneficiary class. If members or rank-and-file participants

■ **TABLE 3.2** THE PRIME BENEFICIARY TYPOLOGY

TYPE OF ORGANIZATION	PRIME BENEFICIARY	EXAMPLES
1. Mutual-benefit	Members, rank-and-file participants	Political parties, labor unions, fraternal orders
2. Business	Owners, managers	Mail-order houses, industrial firms, banks, insurance companies, wholesale/retail stores
3. Service	Clients	Social work agencies, hospitals, schools, legal aid societies, mental health clinics
4. Commonweal	General public	IRS, military organizations, police and fire departments

Source: Adapted from Peter M. Blau and W. Richard Scott, *Formal Organizations: A Comparative Approach* (San Francisco: Chandler, 1962), pp. 42–58.

are the prime beneficiary, then the type of organization is mutual-benefit. If owners or managers are the prime beneficiary, then the type of organization is business. Client prime beneficiaries are associated with service organizations, whereas the general public is associated with commonweal organizations. Table 3.2 shows the prime beneficiary classification scheme devised by Blau and Scott.

Blau and Scott note that their scheme includes potential inconsistencies and understandable overlaps. It should be emphasized, however, that in organizations that appear to benefit several interests, the category of persons that benefits most is designated as the prime beneficiary. Thus, the classification scheme might be useful for investigating the impact of organizational change on the prime beneficiaries. For instance, a legal aid clinic may function for the primary benefit of client/defendants. However, several of the staff may become so engrossed in their own career advancement and legal development that they may fail to provide the necessary services (good legal representation) to clients. The organization slowly drifts from being a service institution to being a business that benefits staff members.

Organizational typologies are classification schemes by which different kinds of organizations may be grouped according to common characteristics. Typologies and models have proliferated for the same reasons. But typologies differ from models in separating organizations; models, by contrast, can be applied to all organizations across all categories.

Organizational typologies are useful for categorizing organizations for the purpose of theorizing about them or devising strategies relating to problem solving. No typology that currently exists is entirely adequate from the standpoint of being universally applicable. All typologies have inherent weaknesses and strengths, and they appear to be differentially appropriate under various organizational conditions. The existence of numerous schemes is indicative of a continuing interest among organizational theorists to develop analytical tools capable of being applied to all organizations.

Competing for recognition are various ways of looking at and classifying organizations. If we consider each of these schemes as an attempt to develop a set of consistent propositions that will contribute to a general theory of organizations, then it is clear that much work remains to be done. The administration of justice is wide open in this respect. Perhaps the primary merit of typologies is that they serve to delimit our theoretical scope and develop singularly useful statements about certain kinds of organizations. And although attempts at constructing typologies have so far been less than perfect, the typologies we have are better than none at all.

SUMMARY

Nonrational organizational models are premised on the idea that organizations must deal with numerous unplanned or unanticipated events on a continuous basis. The ever-changing environmental milieu means that employees must continually adapt and adjust to organizational changes and acquire greater flexibility than might be expected under rational organizational models. In courts, for instance, no two criminal trials are ever identical. Although there is a protocol to follow as well as explicit rules of criminal procedure, there are always unique events that transpire. Defendants may be shot and killed in open court by their victims or the victims' families. Judges may be threatened. Prosecutors and defense counsel may sensationalize various moments during the examination of witnesses or the presentation of evidence.

In police departments, although there is a great degree of predictability regarding what goes on daily, individual patrol officers often are involved in unanticipated and unpredictable events in which their lives or the lives of fellow officers are in jeopardy. A nonrational organizational model is useful in order to understand what is going on in these organizations and why.

Nonrational organizational models have evolved in part because of the pioneering work of Elton Mayo and his associates, who conducted several notable studies of employees in their workplaces. A series of studies was conducted at the Hawthorne plant of the Western Electric Company near Chicago, Illinois. Groups of workers were studied and their attitudes about their work were solicited. A prevalent view of workers at the time was that they were unmotivated and had to be coerced, threatened, and controlled in order to get them to perform their jobs. This was later described as Theory X. The Hawthorne studies changed this view dramatically when it was discovered that paying attention to workers, showing them consideration, and treating them with importance caused them to increase their output and overall work effectiveness. The increased productivity of workers arising from giving them special consideration and attention did not go unnoticed. This phenomenon was termed the Hawthorne effect. Subsequently, an alternative theory, Theory Y, was formulated. Theory Y suggested that workers are self-starters, have minds, and crave responsibility and attention. Within this context, the human relations school of management evolved.

The human relations model has characteristics that emphasize human dignity, mutual interest, individual differences, and motivation. However, some criticisms of this model include that it is only selectively applicable, that it places too much emphasis on the importance of social factors, that the conflict may be productive rather than destructive or counterproductive, that this approach fails to eliminate or minimize the tediousness of tasks performed by individual employees, and that too much emphasis is placed on social skills and communicative abilities.

Derivatives of the human relations model include Theory Z, which stresses participatory decision making, group responsibility and teamwork, broader career paths, and a greater concern for the welfare of employees and their families. Total quality management (TQM) is closely related to Theory Z in that it emphasizes the importance of effective leadership, greater worker commitment to work quality and service, the establishment of a work atmosphere more conducive to self-fulfillment and creativity, and more open communication and information sharing.

The professional model and the equilibrium model also reflect the human relations view. However, the professional model blends selected elements of the bureaucratic model, especially worker expertise, selection by test, and spheres of competence, together with interpersonal and/or social skills. The equilibrium model focuses on motivational factors as crucial. Thus, employees are viewed as interdependent participants in organizations who strive to coordinate their efforts in order to improve organizational effectiveness.

The natural-system model is a nonrational open-system model. This model has an organic analogy, in that organizations are viewed as human beings and individuals and departments have been compared with body parts and organs. All parts must function in some type of homeostatic environment in order for the organization to survive over time. Natural-system organizational model proponents reject the organic analogy and believe that this unfavorable comparison is one reason why this model is not especially popular and widely used. These proponents note that organizations exist in a broader environment in which interactions with other organizations are prevalent. Therefore, the natural-system model conceives of organizations to be the product of inputs and outputs of the organization in interaction with its external environment. Both planned or anticipated and unplanned or unanticipated events are explained in the context of the natural-system model.

Organizational typologies serve to categorize organizations into various divisions. These grouping mechanisms are useful in that they draw together various organizations that share similar characteristics or features. Organizations that share similar characteristics are assumed to react in more uniform ways to both internal and external environmental stimuli. Therefore, organizational theorists derive some value by using typologies in their theorizing about what is going on in organizations and why. Two typologies were described, the compliance-involvement typology and the prime beneficiary typology. The compliance-involvement typology seeks to categorize organizations according to how employees are drawn into compliance by supervisors or administrators. Administrators may use coercion, rewards, or normative pressures to induce compliance. Depending on the method used to elicit one's compliance, predictable types of involvement are evident and easily explained. Three types of involvement are alienative, calculative, and moral. The prime beneficiary typology divides organizations according to the types of persons served by the activities of the organization itself. Categories devised by the prime beneficiary typology are business organizations, commonweal organizations, service organizations, and mutual-benefit organizations.

QUESTIONS FOR REVIEW

1. What are nonrational models of organizations? Describe their primary characteristics and assumptions.

2. What are the primary assumptions about workers made by Theory *X* and Theory *Y*? Which theory seems to account for contemporary workers in organizations? Explain.

3. What were the Hawthorne experiments? Describe them briefly. What is the Hawthorne effect and why was it important in the development of the human relations school?

4. Describe Theory *Z*. How is Theory *Z* useful for explaining administrator-officer relations in a medium-sized police department? Explain.

5. What is meant by total quality management?

6. What is meant by the human relations model? What are some of its primary characteristics? What are several criticisms of the human relations model?

7. Give two examples of superior-subordinate relations from any criminal justice system component (e.g., law enforcement, the courts, or corrections) in which supervisors either show consideration or initiate structure.

8. Are open-system models or closed-system models easier to use in theory building? Why?

9. Compare and contrast the bureaucratic model with the human relations model. Which model best fits court systems? Which model best fits correctional institutions? Which model best fits police organizations? In each case, provide a brief rationale for your answer.

10. Why is the professional model considered to be a blend of the bureaucratic and human relations models?

SUGGESTED READINGS

Carlson, Peter M., and Judith Simon Garrett (eds.) (1999). *Prison and Jail Administration: Practice and Theory.* Gaithersburg, MD: Aspen Publishers.

Karp, David R. (ed.) (1998). *Community Justice: An Emerging Field.* Lanham, MD: Rowman and Littlefield.

Whisenand, Paul M., and Fred R. Ferguson (1996). *The Managing of Police Organizations.* Upper Saddle River, NJ: Prentice Hall.

• CASE STUDIES •

1. THE PROPERTY CLERK AT THE MCNABB POLICE DEPARTMENT

James Riker, 62, has been with the McNabb Police Department (MPD) for 36 years. He started out as a patrol officer, rose quickly through the ranks, and eventually leveled out at captain. At age 60, he was informed by the police chief that because of his age, he was no longer qualified for traditional officer duties in the field. He was offered the choice of retiring or taking over the property room as property clerk for the MPD, since Mary Murphy, the present property clerk, had reached the mandatory retirement age of 70 and was on her way out. Riker reluctantly accepted the new position, which was to start in three weeks. Riker was resentful over what he considered to be a major demotion and an insult to an otherwise successful police career. He craved the action in the field. Frequently in past years, he would visit crime scenes and assist detectives in their investigative work. He would attempt to be involved in any major criminal case that occurred, regardless of who was assigned to handle the case. He would respond to calls for service in his own cruiser despite the fact that the calls were assigned to younger officers near the various crime scenes. Frankly, this irritated investigating detectives and other police officers, since they viewed his intervention and unwanted assistance as interference. Most of them were glad to hear that he was finally going to be out of their hair with his new duties as property clerk at the station house.

When Riker was in the process of taking over his new duties as property clerk, Mary Murphy patiently explained to him how evidence from different crimes should be booked into the property room and where it should be stored. Riker seemed disinterested in Mary Murphy's information about his new job. He kept thinking about what he was going to be missing, and that he was going to be stuck with a desk job for the duration.

When Murphy finally left, Riker began to perform his property clerk duties. Various officers would bring him bagged evidence. He would tag the evidence and store it in designated alcoves in the property room. Illegal drugs seized in raids or confiscated from arrestees went into the property room, which was supposed to be locked at all times when not in use. Riker conscientiously had everyone sign the property book with a description of the evidence they were storing. From time to time, different authorized persons would come to the property room and check out certain evidence. Among those examining crime scene evidence were assistant district attorneys and other personnel.

Riker found that there were long periods where nothing happened in and around the property room. The area was located in the basement of the MPD, and it was very quiet. Riker had a small radio, but listening to music and ball games during the day quickly became boring. One weekend, Riker went to a nearby Radio Shack and bought a police scanner. He brought it with him to the property room the next Monday morning. He was excited with this purchase, since he could follow along and hear police action, a literal play-by-play description of what crimes were happening in the community. This made him long for action on the streets even more.

On one occasion, a bank robbery was reported in progress. The bank being robbed was only a few blocks down the street. Riker couldn't resist. Nothing was happening around the property room anyway, and so Riker closed the property room door without locking it and headed upstairs and outside to his car parked in the police parking lot. He drove to the bank robbery scene and got there just in time to see a shootout between investigating officers and two bank robbers armed with semiautomatic rifles. The two bank robbers were killed in the shootout. After the shooting, Riker moved in closer to see what had happened. One of the senior officers, another captain, O'Rourke, saw Riker and said, "Hey, Riker, I thought you were hanging out in the property room these days. What brings you out here?" Riker quickly responded, "Oh, I'm just taking a lunch break and happened to be in the neighborhood." He quickly returned to the station where he found the door to the property room ajar. He entered the property room and turned on his police scanner again, blissfully listening to more action.

About three days later, an assistant district attorney visited the property room and asked to see a quantity of drugs and a pistol that had been seized in a recent drug bust. Riker went into the property room to retrieve the items, but to his dismay, the evidence was missing. Riker panicked, knowing that in his brief absence from the property room on the day of the bank robbery, someone had entered without his knowledge and made off with at least those drugs and a pistol. He went back to the assistant district attorney and said, "I couldn't find these items. Someone else must have checked them out." An examination of the property log showed that no one had checked out or examined these items since the drug bust. The assistant district attorney was livid, since this evidence was the sole evidence against the arrested suspects. Without the evidence, there would be no case and no conviction. She decided to report the incident to the police chief.

An investigation was launched immediately concerning the missing drugs and gun. As it turned out, other drugs were also missing, as well as three other firearms. When questioned, Riker said that he had no knowledge of these thefts of property, and that he had never left the property room unattended. To his knowledge, no one could have entered the property room and stolen that evidence without his being aware of it. He conjectured that there must be other keys to the property room floating around, and that someone else must have burglarized the property room at night when he wasn't on duty. However, the homicide captain, Mike O'Rourke, told the police chief that he had seen Riker at a bank robbery scene in the middle of the day a week ago, about when the drugs and guns were apparently removed from the property room. Riker was confronted by the police chief and asked to explain why he was absent from his post visiting a crime scene.

Questions for Discussion

1. Was James Riker the best choice for Mary Murphy's replacement as property clerk? Why or why not?

2. Given the abrupt confrontation with Riker concerning his two choices, retirement or property clerk duty, is there any alternative method the chief of police could have used to involve Riker in the decision about his career options?

3. Apply "initiating structure" and "showing consideration" to Riker's case. What strategy may have been more effective? Is there a way Riker could have been induced to view the property clerk duty more favorably? Explain.

4. Apply the human relations model to this scenario. What is the importance of interpersonal processes in this situation?

5. How could the police chief have used Theory Z or total quality management in the reassignment of Riker to his new duties? Can you think of any other job options for Riker that he could have performed other than property clerk duties?

2. EVE JONES, PAROLE OFFICER

Eve Jones, 35, is a parole officer in a western state. She has a master's degree in criminal justice and worked as a police officer in a small police department for nine years before become a parole officer. She did undercover work, and her actions led to several citations for merit. She became disinterested in arresting criminals, however. She had always yearned to be a social worker, but somehow her interests in that area remained unfulfilled. One day she saw an opening with the state parole division and applied for it. Two years ago she became the first female parole officer.

Her first day on the job was a nightmare. She was introduced to eight or nine other parole officers. They acted as though she was an intrusion in their otherwise perfect world. Prior to her first day on the job, Jones had undergone extensive in-service training in a program directed by the state parole department. She quickly became acquainted with the paperwork required, and she determined that this job was going to be a lot different from police work. When she was introduced to the other parole officers, the chief parole officer, Ed Blake, said, "I'd like you to meet Eve Jones.

She's been around the block in law enforcement and has a lot of practical experience that I'm sure can benefit many of you. Besides, she's got a master's degree and that makes her the smartest officer on our payroll. Oh, another thing. The next time you guys go to the can, make sure you knock. You never know who might be in there." And then he chuckled at his own amusing remark and winked at Jones. Jones was somewhat embarrassed over the remarks but let them pass.

Jones was given an initial caseload of the most nonviolent parolees in the department. She was in charge of 35 parolees and was responsible for checking up on them at least twice a month. She had to fill out contact reports with each client, and it was up to her to determine whether any of them had violated their parole conditions. One of her clients was a 22-year-old crack cocaine addict, Alice Marshall, who had been arrested for prostitution and selling crack. She had been sentenced to four years in prison but was paroled after serving only 19 months. She saw Alice Marshall at least twice a month and tried to build some amount of trust between them. On each occasion when she visited Marshall, she would administer a urine test to determine whether Marshall had been using drugs. Most of the time, Marshall would test clean, indicating that she was drug free. On seven or eight occasions, however, Jones determined that Marshall had been using cocaine, at least in small amounts. Each time, she confronted Marshall with this discovery. But instead of reporting Marshall for a parole infraction, she attempted to counsel Marshall instead. Jones didn't want to lose the rapport she had developed with Marshall. She wanted Marshall to trust her and regard her as a friend. Marshall seemed responsive to these sessions and promised each time that she would attempt to remain drug free.

In the meantime, Jones had developed a few friends at the office. She thought that she was getting along well with at least a few of the male officers. Some officers acted as though she was an outsider and a subordinate, however. On numerous occasions, some of the other officers would send her out to get them coffee and sandwiches from a nearby diner. Being good-natured, Jones ran the errand without complaint. She thought that even though it was demeaning, who would it hurt? Maybe it would help her get along better with the other officers. Actually, this activity became somewhat routine.

One day, Jones came into the office and entered the unisex rest room. Shortly thereafter, three parole officers came in and sat at their desks. "Where is our gofer today?" one of them inquired to no one in particular. "I'm hungry. I could use a coffee and a sandwich. Where are these bitches whenever you need them?" "Who knows?" said another officer. "She's probably out with her female thing. Who cares?" The third officer said, "Why they hired a woman to do a man's work is beyond me. I'd hate to have her as backup if I ever had to visit one of my dangerous clients. You just can't count on women when push comes to shove." "Yeah, that's right," the others agreed. Jones was listening to this conversation from behind the rest room door. She waited a minute, cleared her throat loudly so that the other officers could hear her, flushed the toilet, and came out of the rest room into the office area. "Hi, guys. Anything happening?" "Yeah, we're hungry," one man replied. "How about taking a hike over to the diner and getting us some coffee and donuts?" Jones looked at them and said, "Why don't you get your own damned donuts? And when you do, why don't you shove them where the sun don't shine?" Then she stormed out of the room.

After that incident, the atmosphere was tense whenever Jones was in the office. She was doing a good job with her clients, at least in her view. One day, Ed Blake called her into his office and said, "I'm reassigning some of your cases to some of the other officers. Here's a list of your new clients, starting at the first of the month." Jones looked over the list and saw that almost every one of her new clients were the worst parolees from the office. Several rapists, robbers, and murderers were on her new client list. "What about my present load?" she inquired. "We're letting the other officers take up the slack. You'll get more experience with these new ones," Blake said.

Jones was more than a little apprehensive about her new caseload and more dangerous clientele. But even more upsetting was that she was going to have to terminate her working relationship with Alice Marshall, whom she had come to like. Over the next several weeks, she made a point of contacting the new clients on her list. Almost all of them were shocked to see a female parole officer placed in charge of them. Some of them made off-color remarks to her, but she advised them that she expected their full cooperation, just as they had given their former parole officers. Her visits to her new dangerous clients proved uneventful. They came to respect her authority and complied whenever she wanted to search their dwellings or give them drug checks.

About a month into her new assignment, she was called into Blake's office. "Eve," said Blake, "Jerry Granger took over the supervision of one of your clients, an Alice Marshall. Do you know her?" Jones's eyebrows raised a little and she said, "Yes, I know Alice Marshall. I'd been working with her on her drug problem." "Well," said Blake, "apparently you didn't work with her enough. She's in the hospital right now from an overdose of cocaine. Granger went to her apartment and she was spaced out. She told Granger that it was no big deal, that you let her use dope all the time and never did anything about it. Granger was really ticked off and told me that you ought to be canned. I want to know if it's true. Did you know that the Marshall gal used coke and you didn't report it?"

Questions for Discussion

1. When Jones was introduced to the rest of the parole officer staff, was Blake out of line to bring up Jones's former work experience and

education? How do you feel about his remarks under the circumstances?

2. When Jones was visiting Alice Marshall, it was evident that she was attempting to develop some rapport with Marshall for the purpose of helping her. Is the parole officer–client relationship such that officers should seek to improve social relationships with their clients?

3. When Jones did not mention Alice Marshall's drug use in her monthly reports or report Marshall for violating one or more terms of her parole program, to what degree do you believe that this was a professional judgment call on her part?

4. How should Jones have handled the matter of going for coffee and sandwiches for other officers initially? The fact that this activity became routine says much about how the other officers viewed Jones. How much of this problem was Jones's? What could she have done or said

around the other officers to avoid being drawn into that subordinate role?

5. Do you believe that the other parole officers are resentful of Jones and her former accomplishments? Do you think it is because Jones is a woman that she is being isolated from the other officers? As an administrator, how would you overcome resistance from other staff when bringing her into the department?

6. Before bringing Jones into the department, could Blake have used Theory Z or total quality management to address the eventual inclusion of female parole officers into an all-male department? How would the use of these strategies better prepare the other officers for someone like Jones?

7. What do you think of the way Blake is reprimanding Jones for apparently not reporting Alice Marshall's drug use? If you were Jones, how would you respond to Blake's questions?

CHAPTER
4

ORGANIZATIONAL VARIABLES
AND MEASURING
ORGANIZATIONAL EFFECTIVENESS

KEY TERMS

Administrative component
Administrative succession
Bureaucratization
Centralization
Debureaucratization
Decentralization
Formalization
Horizontal complexity

Labor turnover
Levels of authority
Organizational behavior
Organizational climate
Organizational complexity
Organizational conflict
Organizational control

Organizational flexibility
Organizational growth
Organizational size
Organizational structure
Span of control
Technology
Vertical complexity

CHAPTER OBJECTIVES

The following objectives are intended:

1. To present a rationale for studying organizational variables

2. To describe some of the problems associated with variables and how they are conceptualized or defined in organizational research

3. To examine organizational structure and sensitize students to different salient dimensions, including size, complexity, and formalization

4. To describe the primary features of organizational control, including the administrative component, bureaucratization, centralization, and levels of authority

5. To examine organizational change and the influence of variables such as labor turnover, organizational conflict, flexibility, growth, and administrative succession

6. To examine organizational behavior, including variables such as organizational climate, goals, and effectiveness

INTRODUCTION

What goes on in criminal justice organizations and why? What are the relevant variables in studying organizations and how they are related to cause the phenomena under study (Argyris, 1960:6)? How are we to understand patterns among variables whose interdependence is highly complex? These are difficult questions to answer. The variables are so numerous and the interrelationships are so complex that we must be careful lest we miss the very complexity that is so characteristic of organizations.

The systematic study of organizations involves an examination of several key variables. As we have seen, variables are any quantities that can assume more than one value. Some examples of variables in organizational analysis are the span of control, degree of work satisfaction, size of the administrative component, levels of authority, and organizational effectiveness. This chapter examines several important organizational variables. The discussion includes how the variables examined can be empirically measured and how they can be used in theory verification. Several selected variables used most often in organizational research will be highlighted. In most instances, we will present some of the ways each variable has been conceptualized, measured by social scientists, and utilized in actual research.

Researchers new to the study of organizations are frequently unfamiliar with many of the more critical variables that would be useful in their analyses. Although the treatment of variables here is by no means exhaustive, we have attempted to highlight those variables that are used most frequently in the contemporary research literature. This was a primary criterion by which these variables were selected for inclusion.

The variables defined and described in subsequent sections of this chapter are labeled "organizational." This label underscores the fact that each variable is a characteristic of the organization as a unit or level of analysis. Other variables typically associated with other levels of analysis, such as the interpersonal and individual levels, will be discussed in Chapter 5.

The first part of this chapter discusses the importance of organizational variables generally and why researchers take an interest in them. Organizational variables frequently change over time, and these changes often influence the persons and groups within organizations in different ways. Despite the fact that several researchers might study the same organizational variable, how the same variable is conceptualized or defined by various researchers may be quite

different. For example, organizational size sounds simple enough. Doesn't this mean the total number of persons in an organization? Yes and no. Some researchers may measure organizational size by the net worth of an organization. Measures of prison sizes often rely on the number of beds a prison has. Prison size may be whatever an architect has envisioned as the prison capacity when the prison was built. A prison rating official may rate the capacity of a prison differently, however, referring instead to the number of prisoners that may be accommodated in various cells. Yet another gauge of prison size might be the actual operating capacity of the prison, or the total number of prisoners who can be housed without violating their constitutional right against cruel and unusual punishment through excessive overcrowding. In short, it is frequently difficult for social scientists to agree on how a variable as "simple" as organizational size ought to be measured.

Following the discussion of organizational variables, the chapter is divided into four parts. The first part examines variables commonly associated with organizational structure. How are organizations constructed or arranged? These variables include organizational size, organizational complexity or differentiation, and organizational formalization. The second part of this chapter examines variables associated with organizational control. Organizational control refers to the actual operations of organizations, how orders are given, and how the organization actually functions. Organizational control variables include the size of the administrative component, bureaucratization and debureaucratization, centralization and decentralization, levels of authority, and spans of control. The third section describes variables associated with organizational change. These variables include labor turnover, organizational conflict, organizational flexibility and growth, administrative succession, and technology. The final part of this chapter examines variables associated with organizational behavior. These variables include organizational climate, organizational goals, and organizational effectiveness.

ORGANIZATIONAL VARIABLES

All of the variables discussed in this chapter may be viewed as strategies to assist researchers in answering certain questions about organizational behavior. Not all variables examined here are equally useful at any given time for explaining the problems of any particular organization, however. In this sense, the term *organizational problems* refers to any undesirable conditions in organizations as seen by at least some organizational members (e.g., low profits, high labor turnover, low morale, low work satisfaction, high interdepartmental hostility). Assessing organizational problems analytically often involves imaginative combinations of several variables. Researchers are not always able to use the same variable combinations for analyzing different organizations. Therefore, acquiring a knowledge of several key organizational variables that would be potentially helpful in explaining organizational behaviors will not necessarily lead directly to immediate solutions for organizational problems. The reservoir of information compiled will significantly affect an investigator's facility for thinking constructively about organizational problems, however. Classifying variables in organizational research is difficult because of the following factors:

1. Not all organizational researchers agree which variables are organizational and which ones are interpersonal or individual or both.

2. Several measures of the same variable simultaneously used in different studies compete for professional recognition in the field.

3. An excessive number of exceptions to classificatory schemes can be found once they have been constructed and agreed on, and variables are observed to overlap several units of analysis (i.e., the individual, interpersonal, and organizational).

4. Variables take on many different meanings and have any number of different implications depending on the setting in which the research is conducted (e.g., variable X may not exert the same kind of significance or impact on variable Z in a probation office as it does in a police department); therefore, the contextual surroundings act as intervening conditions that must be considered when one is interpreting research results.

5. Organizational investigators adopt contrasting and often conflicting philosophies and frames of reference when researching the same organizational problem, inevitably leading to the use of the same variables in different capacities in similar, yet independent, research investigations.

The following grouping of variables is an attempt to rearrange several key organizational factors into a limited number of applicable categories. This grouping assists us in distinguishing more meaningfully between them and appreciating their differential contributions to the increasing accumulation of organizational literature. Although the array of variables presented here overlap one another to varying degrees and in different ways, four distinct subdivisions will be used: (1) organizational structure, (2) organizational control, (3) organizational change, and (4) organizational behavior.

ORGANIZATIONAL STRUCTURE

Variables in the **organizational structure** category describe the arrangement of formalized positions or departments within an organization. They also describe the amount of differentiation and specialization within organizations. Three important variables pertaining to organizational structure are (1) size, (2) complexity, and (3) formalization.

Size

Organizational size is typically defined as the total number of employees in any organization. However, it can be measured in several other ways (Hall, Haas, and Johnson, 1967). An alternative definition is the total number of full-fledged members in the association. In a study of tuberculosis hospitals and general medicine and surgery hospitals, researchers defined the size of hospital organizations as the annual average daily patient load (Anderson and Warkov, 1961). They also defined size as the total hospital labor force.

In a study of Maryland police departments, organizational size was defined as the total number of full-time officers attached to any given department (Cordner, 1989). Organizational size has been defined similarly in other studies (Regoli, 1975). Sometimes the focus of size is on clientele served by an institution or agency, however. The size of American jails has been conceptualized as the number of inmates a jail is designed to hold. Small jails are defined as holding fewer than 50 inmates, whereas large jails might hold 500 or more inmates and megajails might hold 1,000 or more inmates (Cornelius, 1997). Thus, sizes of organizations may refer to full-time employees or to the numbers of inmates or clients accommodated by an institution or agency.

Since so many different definitions are associated with this single variable, it is not surprising that researchers can arrive at different conclusions when studying essentially the same topics. The issue of size has been a compelling one in organizational analysis (Hall, 1972:109), and one complicating factor is that there are so many different kinds of organizations. The fluidity of membership, the transiency of employees, seasonal employment fluctuations, and the factor of full-time or part-time personnel lend further frustration to researchers intent on conceptualizing this phenomenon (Crank and Wells, 1991).

Complexity or Differentiation

Organizational complexity is as difficult to conceptualize as organizational size. Few attempts have been made to define this variable precisely (Campbell and Akers, 1970:438). Two types of complexity have been identified: horizontal and vertical. **Horizontal complexity** is the lateral differentiation of functions that may be duplicated at all levels of authority in corporate organizations. **Vertical complexity** refers to the extent to which there is differentiated depth or organizational penetration below the most inclusive level (e.g., an organization that includes three or four different levels—national, regional, state, local—is more vertically differentiated and complex than one that has no additional levels below the national).

When hospitals have been investigated, complexity has been defined based on the number of diseases treated. General medicine and surgery hospitals are more complex than tuberculosis hospitals because they treat a greater variety of diseases on a regular basis, including internal diseases and psychiatric illness as well as tuberculosis. Studies of police agencies might focus on the number of different subdivisions or bureaus within any given department. Some departments might be considered less complex if the number of subdivisions or subunits is less than five, whereas departments with more than five subdivisions or subunits might be conceptualized as having more complexity (Langworthy, 1985).

Formalization

Formalization is the extent to which communications and procedures in an organization are written down and filed (Hinings et al., 1967:66). Formalization measures the amount or percentage of rules, procedures, instructions, and communications that are written. In many respects, formalization reflects the bureaucratic model and its emphasis on abstract rules and impersonal relations between work units and positions. For instance, many police agencies are described as formal, because of their military-like structure and organization, regardless of how many full-time personnel might be a part of the organization. Rigid adherence to bureaucratic rules and a high level of formalization are observed in police departments with as few as two officers (Bradley, Walker, and Wilkie, 1986).

ORGANIZATIONAL CONTROL

Associated with **organizational control** are (1) the size of the administrative component, (2) bureaucratization and debureaucratization, (3) centralization and decentralization, and (4) levels of authority (including span of control). These variables are central to the planning and coordinating of tasks within the overall division of labor of an organization. The initiation of directives to subordinate personnel and the formulation and implementation of policy decisions fall within the control realm.

Size of the Administrative Component

The **administrative component** is that part of an organization charged with coordinating, facilitating, and supporting the activities of the rest of the organizational participants (Campbell and Akers, 1970:437). Some researchers use the term *supervisory ratio* to indicate the number of supervisors compared to the total number of members. Supervisors are defined as those individuals whose functional role involves mainly direct interpersonal supervision or key organizational administrative decision making (Indik, 1964:302). This definition excludes rank-and-file workers higher in the organization who perform mainly clerical functions. In police organizations, for example, the administrative component has been conceptualized as the proportion of officers ranked sergeant or higher (Langworthy, 1985). Investigators often are interested in the variation in size of the administrative component in response to other organizational variables, such as size, complexity, formalization, and goals.

Bureaucratization and Debureaucratization

These terms refer to particular conditions of structure and process generated by bureaucracy. **Bureaucratization** is the extension of the bureaucracy's spheres of activities and power either in its own interests or those

BOX 4.1 PERSONALITY HIGHLIGHT

TIMOTHY SCHUETZLE
Director of the Prisons Division and Warden of the North Dakota State Penitentiary

Statistics: B.A. (psychology, distributive science, and education), Gustavus Adolphus College; M.A. (college student personnel administration), Bowling Green State University

Background: I taught science at a small high school for two years before going back to graduate school for my master's degree. After graduation, I started work for Rough Rider Industries, the prison work program at the North Dakota State Penitentiary. My title was janitorial products factory manager, and I was responsible for supervising a crew of inmates in the manufacture of cleaning supplies. From there, I became the administrative officer of the prison, which was an administrative assistant to the warden. My duties were chairing the inmate discipline committee, meeting with inmates, and writing the institution's rules, policies, and inmate handbook. I served in this job for three years, but then I went back to Rough Rider Industries as the director of that program. Three years later I was chosen to be the warden for the North Dakota State Penitentiary, a position I've held for the past nine years. In 1998, we opened a third prison, and I was asked to oversee the operations for all of the penal facilities in the state. We developed a prisons division within the Department of Corrections and Rehabilitation, and I became the director of that division, in addition to serving as warden at the main penitentiary.

To be honest, I never dreamed that I would become a prison warden. In fact, I only accepted the job at the penitentiary because I wanted to live in Bismarck so that I could be close to my girlfriend (who is now my wife of 19 years). My true career goal was to become a dean of students, or perhaps even the president of a college or university. As a young idealist, I knew I wanted a career in which I could make an impact on people's lives and society. My course of graduate study emphasized developing students in all aspects of their lives: intellectually, emotionally, socially, and morally. I believed that I could have the best impact on society by helping college students develop and grow into well-rounded citizens. But after a year of working with convicted criminals, I realized that college kids were a fairly normal group of people. The ones who really needed the help were with me behind the bars.

Additionally, I was seeing almost daily positive changes in the inmates' behavior as a result of working in the industries program. They were learning how to hold a job, experiencing the feeling of pride and accomplishment of seeing the fruits of their labor, and their self-esteem was growing. I became passionate about prisoner rehabilitation. Most people in society believe that all inmates are "bad people" and should be locked up for the rest of their lives, but the reality is that over 90 percent of the inmates will be released back into society. Not all of these people are bad. In fact, the majority are salvageable and can become productive members of society, but they have flaws or deficiencies in their development that first must be identified and then corrected. Keeping prisoners incarcerated is extremely costly to society, and therefore, our goal must be to help correct inmates while they are in prison so that they do not come back a second or third time. If prison administrators can properly identify the inmates' needs and then provide the kinds of rehabilitative programs necessary to address those needs, then we will have a dramatic effect on this cost to society. It is the idea that first turned me on to corrections, and it still keeps me motivated and excited to come to work each day.

Interesting Things That Have Happened to Me at Work: I think every day you can deal with people is always interesting, and I have never had a boring day at work. The most interesting and mentally challenging times for me have been when I have had direct involvement with inmates. Their problems may have a common theme (such as dealing with inmates who are suicidal, assaultive, or need protection), but because I am always working with a different personality, the approach used to resolve the problems is vastly different. As a rule, inmates tend to be very manipulative, and they love to engage staff in con games to try to get their way. You must stay mentally sharp when dealing with them.

I am never surprised at both the good and the bad I have seen on my job. Early in my career, I was threatened with physical harm by two inmates in a secluded part of the prison, but a third inmate stood up for me and got between us so I could radio for help. I have seen one inmate violently assault another with a baseball bat, but I have also seen inmates sit up all night counseling and consoling another inmate who was depressed and suicidal. I have seriously questioned the mental competence of one inmate who cut off part of his body, another who swallowed metal knives and razor blades, and one rebellious diabetic who thought he would get even with the system by refusing to eat or take his insulin. On the other hand, I am amazed at the ingenuity and creativity displayed in some of the escape and contraband smuggling plans we have discovered over the years. I think it is this diversity in human behavior that makes this such an interesting place to work.

Frustrating Experiences: One of the few things I dislike about my job is that people seem to have a morbid curiosity about prisons and prisoners, and therefore, almost everything that happens here is viewed as newsworthy by the media. Especially now that corrections is taking a bigger share of taxpayer's dollars, we are finding ourselves more in the public eye. Your good decisions and your mistakes are both there on the front page for everyone to see. Because we are a part of government, politics also can sometimes get in the way of good correctional decisions. Finally, I do not enjoy having my family, or myself, threatened by some inmate, nor do I enjoy being the principal defendant in all of the prisoners' lawsuits filed annually.

Advice to Students: Unfortunately, I have found that most students who choose to major in criminal justice, and therefore most people who are reading this book, do so because they want to work in law enforcement. Although I believe that all areas of the criminal justice system can make rewarding career choices, I would advise you to keep an open mind about corrections, especially if you have a penchant for helping others, and a dream to try to make a difference in society. A prison can be dangerous and intimidating, but it is never dull, and it is a wonderful environment to observe and study human behavior. I am not saying that prison work is right for everybody, but if you are open-minded and can have compassion for others, then this is a very interesting and rewarding profession.

of some of its elite. In organizations that exhibit bureaucratization, we tend to see greater regimentation of different areas of social life and some extent of displacement of service goals in favor of various power interests or orientations. Abstract rules exist to cover most organizational events, and individuals are expected to follow policies closely. Examples are military organizations that tend to impose their rule on civilian life or political parties that exert pressure on their potential supporters in an effort to monopolize their private and occupational life and make them entirely dependent on the political party (Eisenstadt, 1959:312).

In labor unions, for instance, bureaucratization refers to the development of centralized control by the leadership, which robs union rank and file of most of its influence over policies and decisions (Blau, 1970:150). Bureaucratization means increasing specialization, more rules and paperwork activities, increased complexity of the division of labor, and an expanding number of departments. Any increased emphasis on one or all of these dimensions would be regarded as an increase in bureaucratization. The bureaucratization of parole departments has been described, with numerous adverse consequences for parolees served by these agencies. In agencies in which bureaucratization has occurred, we find a proliferation of paperwork, greater reliance on rules for client processing, and greater formality among colleagues (Kingsnorth, 1969; McCleary, 1978). Similar phenomena have been observed to occur in prison settings (Landau, 1969).

Debureaucratization is the reverse of this process and is defined as the subversion of goals and activities of the bureaucracy in the interests of different groups with which it has close interaction (clients, patrons, interested parties) (Eisenstadt, 1959:312). In debureaucratization, the specific characteristics of bureaucracy in terms of both its autonomy and its specific rules and goals are minimized, even up to the point at which its very functions and activities are taken over by other groups or organizations. Examples of this can be found in cases that involve attempts by an organization (e.g., a parents' association or a religious or political group) to divert the rules and working order of a bureaucratic organization (school, economic agency) for its own use or according to its own values and goals (Eisenstadt, 1959:312).

Centralization and Decentralization

Centralization refers to the amount of power given to organizational subunits, departments, or separate operating units that could be retained by the central organizational hierarchy at the same level as the subunits to which it is distributed (Hall, 1972:228). Centralization also means focused control and an integrated and efficient organization (McMullan, 1984). In Canada, for instance, sexual abuse against children was studied by a government-appointed committee. The committee released a document known as the Badgley Report, which recommended the centralization of control of sexual abuse investigations in application of standards at all relevant levels and sites of the state apparatus (Kinsman and Brock, 1986). The Badgley Report was criticized by local professional and social service workers, since it was interpreted as an infringement on the decision-making powers of local agencies and their individualized supervision and management of sexual abusers. Local agencies perceived this report to be a threat to their individual initiatives and their power to deal with sexual abuse cases. But as far as the government was concerned, centralization was good in that it consolidated policymaking and seemed to make sense for the application of consistent standards. In effect, decision-making power was shifted upward in the authority hierarchy, so that primarily persons in the top administrative posts were in charge of policy formulation and implementation. Less control remained in the hands of individuals within the local agencies.

Decentralization means to distribute the diverse responsibilities of top management either to middle-level managers at the same headquarters or to individual managers of local offices (Blau, 1970:156). Five suburban police departments decentralized their patrol function in Connecticut, North Carolina, California, and Oregon (Kerstetter, 1981). Decentralization involved giving individual patrols greater decision-making responsibilities and diminishing the control of senior-level management. Although some disjointedness arose from this decentralization in most departments, a distinct improvement was seen in police-community relations throughout the jurisdictions studied.

One of the primary means for regulating the level of centralization-decentralization is the method of recordkeeping and paperwork processing used by an agency. Computerized recordkeeping has made substantial differences in the speed with which cases are processed and data are accessed. Theoretically, at least, the availability of computerized records to any given department may signify more power or control potentially manifest by that department. Thus, when computerized recordkeeping has been introduced in different agencies, personnel at different supervisory levels have viewed computerization with some apprehension, fearing perhaps a loss of control and greater centralization. For instance, a large juvenile court established a computerized recordkeeping system (Albrecht, 1976). The effects of this record computerization were studied for a four-year period. The research showed that no changes occurred with respect to the exercise of managerial authority, communication, setting of organizational goals, structure of the organization, budget, cost of services, span of control, or job descriptions. Work flow and the processing of cases were accelerated and made more consistent, however. Organizational theorists surmise that it depends on how computerization of information is handled by any given agency and whether centralization or decentralization will be affected (Albrecht, 1976).

An example of a correctional organization that was highly centralized but underwent a transformation toward greater decentralization is the Ocean County, New Jersey, Department of Corrections (DOC) (Bedea-Mueller and Hutler, 2000). The DOC is comprised of 182 sworn and civilian employees under the authority of a warden. The DOC is divided into the areas of services, operations, and the office of the warden. There are three shifts for the security division, which oversees inmates in a 400-bed county jail. Prior to decentralization, the DOC was characterized as having a formal chain of command and rank structure, and individuals were excluded from the decision-making process. The outdated organizational structure resulted in an inefficient communication process, thereby weakening and fragmenting accountability. An organizational change was suggested, which was fueled by both external and internal forces. The DOC wanted to be accredited, and thus, a change in organizational structure was in order. Budgetary cutbacks also occurred that required the organization to reconsider how manpower was utilized. Further, the criminal justice system complexities were such that DOC managers had to be informed about all legal and operational issues. The change toward decentralization was proposed to improve communications, accountability, interpersonal relations, and productivity within the DOC, and to reduce the unauthorized dissemination of information (gossip, internal leaks, and departmental sabotage). The inclusion of all levels of managerial and supervisory personnel in the decision-making process would probably reduce if not eliminate the aforementioned concerns (Bedea-Mueller and Hutler, 2000:3). A team management concept was incorporated that was geared toward the equalization of power between individuals of equal stature, regardless of rank. The team approach resolved several important organizational issues and improved communication and the dissemination of information. Immediate results of the change toward greater decentralization were (1) increased employee motivation, confidence, and productivity resulting from increased recognition and empowerment; (2) increased cohesiveness among team members; (3) increased orientation toward departmental goals and objectives; (4) increased trust among team members; (5) reduced territorial conflicts between civilian and sworn personnel; and (6) reduced "power-tripping" and personal agendas (Bedea-Mueller and Hutler, 2000:6).

The DOC organizational change occurred during the spring and summer of 1996. Subsequently in 1997, a training session was held with key DOC personnel to assess the implications and impacts of the change to decentralization. Although not everyone was satisfied with the results of the organizational change, the overall results were favorable. It was determined by the DOC that inclusion is paramount to success in today's organizations. Greater trust and job effectiveness follow more open communication. The investigators concluded that through teamwork and greater empowerment, the organization became stronger and greater than the sum of its parts (Bedea-Mueller and Hutler, 2000:18). A direct consequence of decentralization was the improvement of services and attitudes toward inmates as well as attitudinal changes among inmates themselves.

Levels of Authority and Span of Control

Levels of authority refer to the degree of vertical differentiation within an organization. *Levels* connotes layers of different positions, each layer constituting a homogeneous aggregate of employees. The **span of control** is the number of persons or departments under the direct control of a supervisor or individual department. Span of control also may refer to the managerial or supervisory responsibilities and power relative to subordinates in different organizational units (McAulay, 1989).

For instance, a classic study of Sears, Roebuck and Company was conducted by James Worthy (1950:178). The numbers of supervisory levels at various Sears stores was manipulated. In turn, several interesting interpersonal and individual behavioral changes were observed as the numbers of supervisory levels were modified. For instance, in organizations characterized with many levels of supervision and elaborate systems of controls, the individual not only has little opportunity to develop the capacities of self-reliance and initiative, but the system frequently weeds out those who do. A number of highly successful organizations have not only paid little attention to span of control, they actually have gone directly counter to one of the favorite tenets of modern management theory, which holds that the number of subordinate executives or supervisors reporting to a single individual should be limited to enable that individual to exercise the detailed direction and control that is generally considered necessary. On the contrary, these organizations often deliberately give each key executive so many subordinates that it is impossible for them to exercise supervision too closely over the activities of every individual (Worthy, 1950:178).

In the Worthy study of Sears stores, behavior modifications were generated in supervisor behaviors over subordinates when supervisory spans of control were expanded and supervisors were given many persons to supervise. Subordinates reported greater freedom of movement and activity under wider span of control conditions compared with conditions in which their supervisors had few persons to supervise. Thus, wider spans of control made it more difficult for supervisors to supervise any given employee closely. Wide spans of control caused supervisors to supervise generally, thus giving subordinates greater decision-making discretion and latitude.

Some critics say that there may be a limit to the span of control, but it is advantageous to make the spans a great deal wider than any of the numbers usually specified if the work is interrelated (House and Miner, 1969:455). Others believe that the notion of a small span of control is wrong, since it presumes one-on-one relations between supervisors and subordinates, whereas wider spans of control emphasize and promote person-to-group interaction patterns (Likert, 1961).

One of the first persons to propose a science of administration was Henri Fayol. Fayol said that whatever the level of authority, one head should only have direct command over a small number of subordinates, less than six normally. The superior (foreman or the equivalent) should be in direct command of 20 or 30 workers only when the work is simple (Fayol, 1949:98). No conclusive evidence exists to suggest exactly how wide or narrow spans of control should be for any type of organization. Some have suggested that technology may influence the optimum size of span of control in any organization (Woodward, 1965:69–71).

In various sectors of the criminal justice system, such as probation and parole agencies, the span of control for supervisory personnel has been investigated. In California, supervisory caseloads for probation officers were expanded greatly in the late 1970s to early 1980s as a cost-cutting initiative. Large numbers of probation services and programs were eliminated, including delinquency prevention, crisis resolution, specialized supervision and therapy, and diversion programs (Chaiken, 1981). Increasing the span of control of probation officers through increased caseloads had the general effect of decreasing individual officer performance effectiveness in relation to clientele served. Research involving selected police departments has yielded similar findings about the nature of the span of control and officer effectiveness (Souryal, 1977).

ORGANIZATIONAL CHANGE

As organizations grow in size and complexity, new departments are created, membership fluctuates, and technology changes in response to innovation and customer-consumer demand. The variables in this section pertain to various ways of measuring or explaining change and include (1) labor turnover, (2) organizational conflict, (3) organizational flexibility, (4) organizational growth, (5) administrative succession, and (6) technology.

Labor Turnover

The number of persons who leave an organization in the course of one year or some other standardized time interval is referred to as **labor turnover.** Probation and parole agencies typically report their amount of labor turnover annually. There is about a 20 percent turnover rate among persons performing probation and parole work among the states. The turnover rate for federal probation offices is much higher, about 35 percent. However, correctional officer turnover in prisons in the federal system is only 6.6 percent compared with an average state correctional officer turnover rate of 15 percent (Camp and Camp, 1999a).

Labor turnover often is used to determine the potential impact of such factors as the nature of supervision, employees' morale and satisfaction, or administrative behavior. It also can be used as a means of accounting for the heterogeneity of workers, as new employees are introduced into the organizational environment to modify existing formal and informal (interpersonal) interaction patterns.

Labor turnover is one of the easiest organizational variables to measure. It can be assessed by the records of any given organization. Of course, some distinction may be made between those persons who leave voluntarily and those who are fired (Argyle, Gardner, and Cioffi, 1958:31). Those who are laid off, die, retire, or become pregnant may be regarded as a part of the aggregate of involuntary labor turnover.

Organizational Conflict

Organizational conflict refers to tension within the organization. We may observe such tension by paying attention to possible incompatibilities among departments, to incompatibilities among staff members, to complexities of the communication network, and even to the organizational structure itself (Dahrendorf, 1959). The idea of conflict has several meanings. In one sense, conflict may mean feelings of hostility on the part of one person or group toward another or others. It also may mean emotionally hostile and intentional efforts on the part of one person or group to prevent another person or group from attaining the latter's desires or goals.

Organizational conflict has been found related to organizational size, specialization, hierarchy, complexity, staff additions, and heterogeneity (Corwin, 1969:507). Perceived tensions or reports of perceived disagreements and overt disputes also are used to measure conflict. Staff disunity and general disagreement also indicate the presence of organizational conflict.

In some jurisdictions, conflicts arise concerning how criminal offenders should be managed while on probation. Police agencies and officers may have a general distrust of probation officers, who are responsible for supervising and monitoring their probationer-clients. At the same time, probation officers may regard the police role as interfering in the rehabilitative function of probation generally. These differences in orientations and beliefs were the subject of an investigation of 170 constables, sergeants, and inspectors, as well as 109 probation officers, in England (Crawford, 1994). Another type of conflict may arise from within an agency, such as a large police department. Large police departments work toward the attainment of multiple goals. These goals have different priorities for different police chiefs and their subordinates. A study of 52 police chiefs and 92 assistant chiefs involving 55 police departments in the United States revealed that both overt and covert differences of opinion exist about which goals should have priority in fulfilling community and organizational responsibilities, depending on which types of administrators are surveyed (Stamper, 1988). These conflicts may be harmless, although certain adverse consequences for subordinates may occur if they receive mixed messages from two or more persons in authority over them.

Organizational conflict, regardless of its origins, influences such factors as effectiveness, clarity of roles, and work satisfaction. There are at least two potential kinds of organizational conflict, intraorganizational and interorganizational. Intraorganizational conflict is conflict of an interpersonal nature or conflict between departments within the system. Interorganizational conflict is conflict between organizations. Managers and theorists have more frequently been concerned with resolving conflict within organizations rather than conflict between organizations (Assael, 1969:573).

Organizational Flexibility

The degree to which an organization is adaptable to internal changes (e.g., changes in the hierarchy of authority or interpersonal groups) and external changes (e.g., competition with other organizations, changes in the economic market, or marketing innovations) describes **organizational flexibility.** Some organizations, particularly those with built-in research and development divisions, have structural means for implementing changes and modifications in organizational structure and process in response to change. Organizations that are deeply entrenched in departmentalization and routine are difficult candidates for change in the absence of such formal mechanisms for change (Denhardt, 1968).

In corrections, organizational changes are often mandated by the courts through decrees to modify and improve existing prison conditions in compliance with constitutional standards. Court-ordered prison improvements of necessity involve more than a modest amount of organizational change. The Texas prison system, for example, has been under a federal court order to make large-scale reforms relating to the care and treatment of inmates and the various services, both vocational and legal, made available to prisoners. Some changes have involved modifications in technology to deliver high-tech information retrieval in prison library services. Other changes have related to prison governance and the nature of inmate involvement in self-government. As Texas prisons have responded to changes suggested by court decrees, their organizational structures have become more or less centralized, depending on preexisting conditions (Gorton, 1997). Although change has occurred unevenly in different Texas prisons, the overall system has exhibited considerable flexibility in adapting to court-ordered standards and policies.

One difficulty in determining the degree of organizational flexibility is in finding how much coordination among units within the organization is required for substantial changes to occur. One way of assessing the flexibility of an organization is to determine the amount of resistance to change in the form of intraorganizational conflict. A lack of overt conflict will sometimes accompany a resistance to change, particularly in voluntary organizations that do not have effective procedures for working through disagreements. To preserve the semblance of unity, organizational members in such circumstances often avoid dealing with a problem that calls for change for fear that unproductive, hostile disagreement will result, leading to no real resolution of the issue. Organizational flexibility influences the rate of technological change and the implementation of new channels of communication. It is also a by-product of specific organizational structures, administrative patterns, and supervisory practices.

Organizational Growth

Organizational growth is the increase in the number of employees over any specified time period (Haire, 1959). Such a definition is consistent with a biological growth model, that is, the population increase within an organizational context (Draper and Strother, 1963:194). But the biological growth model does not seem valid for describing or predicting organizational growth, nor does it appear to be a source of useful hypotheses for future research.

In the area of youth services, for example, various stages of organizational growth of Omni-House, a youth rehabilitation center in Illinois, have been charted (Llynn, 1980). Three stages of development were identified: the initiation stage, the operational stage, and the organizational maturity stage. Indicators of organizational growth of the Omni-House included more smooth-running social programs for youths, fewer interpersonal conflicts between staff and youthful clients, and a greater success rate among clients served.

Organizational growth may create problems for staff. In prisons and jails, for instance, the inmate populations have escalated during the period from 1980 to 2000. As more prisoners have been added to existing prisons and jails, officials have been forced to place more inmates in cells designed for only one occupant. Cell space for new offenders has become scarce throughout most U.S. jurisdictions, and not a single state prison system can boast that it is presently not overcrowded. In 1999, state prison systems were operating at about 120 percent of their rated and design capacities, holding on the average approximately 20 percent more inmates than they were designed to hold when originally constructed (Maguire and Pastore, 2000). Organizational growth in these institutional settings has been associated with more rioting and inmate-staff assaults, increased lawsuit filings by inmates, and greater labor turnover among correctional staff.

The growth of an organization also may be defined in terms of increases in net assets, the proliferation of departments and job specialties, the increase of contacts with other organizations in symbiotic exchange relations, and the expansion of new product markets. Organizational growth exerts influence on factors such as organizational complexity, the size of the administrative component, and personal alienation. This variable is influenced in turn by the degree of market competition, product innovation, and technological change (Yeager, 1981). In view of the fact that most organizations have the propensity to expand, it is apparent that organizational growth as an exploratory variable is an important consideration in the study of organizational behavior (Barnard, 1938:159).

Administrative Succession

Administrative succession refers to the degree of turnover among administrative heads in an organization. All enduring organizations must cope with succession, and replacement of an individual in a key office is potentially a significant event in the development of an organization (Carlson, 1961:210).

Administrative succession is an important problem in many organizations. In the course of administering an agency or institution, superintendents or managers often devise personalized styles of leadership and ways of orienting themselves toward staff that are not transmitted to their successors. Thus, when administrative change occurs, subordinates are frequently in a state of uncertainty about the expectations and orientations of administrative successors. In the Virginia Department of Corrections, for instance, superintendents of prisons have a profound influence on institutional policies and procedures, and their attitudes affect both subordinate correctional staff and inmates (Rollo and Kalas, 1975). Subordinates, including the inmates themselves, develop an understanding of the expectations and limits of particular administrators. When these superintendents leave and are replaced by others, this change leaves a void that often leads to staff discontent and disagreement about procedural issues. Adjustments must be made when new superintendents are chosen and establish their own way of doing things.

Administrative influence on how domestic violence ought to be addressed by police has been investigated. During the period from 1997 to 1998, 42 police departments in England were studied and surveyed (Plotnikoff and Woolfson, 1998). Domestic violence officers were interviewed concerning administrative expectations about how they were to perform their roles. Wide variation existed among departments concerning performance expectations and monitoring, as well as with regard to the clarity of communication from front-line officers with their superiors. Because the management of domestic violence officers was often blurred, the management of information about domestic violence incidents was lacking, and officers spent more of their time gathering information rather than responding to domestic violence situations.

In selected police departments throughout the United States, the importance of the influence of administration on officer performance has been assessed extensively (Breci and Simons, 1987; Franz and Jones, 1987). Officer demoralization has been reported whenever intraorganizational communication between superiors and subordinates is diffuse or unclear, or if there is a lack of trust in administrative policies and protocol (Franz and Jones, 1987). Although officer behaviors are not entirely dependent on administrative

---

BOX 4.2 NEW PRISON OFFICIALS, NEW RULES ABOUT INMATE HAIR

The Virginia Department of Corrections. The Virginia Department of Corrections implemented a new inmate identification policy when it announced that all prisoners will receive short haircuts and that long hair will not be tolerated. Prison official Larry Traylor said, "We've had a couple of instances where inmates have hidden drugs or weapons in their hair." The new hygiene requirements are aimed at increasing the health and safety of prisoners and at the same time giving them a more uniform look. Under the new rules, hair must be cut above the shirt collar and can be no more than an inch thick. Braids, dreadlocks, ponytails, designs shaved into hair, and other decorative types of hair styles are forbidden.

Any state department of corrections has the right to establish policies and rules that enable the organization to function effectively. Should new prison administrators have the right to order short hair for all prison inmates? How can policies associated with administrative succession best be implemented? What strategies can these organizations use to influence the acceptance of change?

Source: Adapted from the Associated Press, "Prisoners Get New Hairdos," November 17, 1999.

---

orientations and attitudes (Breci, 1986; Breci and Simons, 1987), managerial styles do have a significant impact on how officers perform their jobs as well as their amenability to innovation (Gaines, 1978). In fact, evidence suggests that many police managers deliberately use specific styles of management calculated to modify subordinate behaviors in particular ways (Auten, 1985).

State and federal officials are responsible for selecting superintendents of prisons, agency heads for police departments, and probation/parole services. Outcomes of administrative succession are most frequently studied, including the influence of new administrators on officer performance, organizational effectiveness, labor turnover, and client recidivism (Katsampes, 1981; Swanson, Territo, and Taylor, 1993).

Technology

Some research has examined the effects of technology on organizational structure, interpersonal relations, and individual behavior. In the broadest sense, **technology** refers to the mechanisms or processes by which an organization turns out its product or service (Harvey, 1968:247). Other meanings of technology may include a tool or device, machine, computers, closed-circuit television monitoring, a system of machines, or even certain ideas and strategies.

Because technology can refer to so many things—mechanization, computers, ideas—it is likely that several conceptual problems may be encountered when studying the phenomenon. What is the rate of techno-

logical change, for instance? Does it refer to the amount of invention or innovation within an organization? Does it refer to the number of ideas that are implemented in companies each year to improve communication channels? Each of these changes is a technological change by definition, although each would have decidedly different impacts.

ORGANIZATIONAL BEHAVIOR

The term **organizational behavior** is not intended to personify the organization as an object with emotions and volition: The organization "acts" or "behaves" through the aggregate movements of its living membership. Organizational behavior is more difficult to define than merely accumulating the actions of all persons in an organization and labeling them as organizational behavior, however (Thompson, 1967:127). Organizational behavior is sometimes associated with a power coalition that controls the organization. Expressions about organizational behavior are widespread and are an integral feature of the layperson's vocabulary, such as "The New York Police Department practices brutality against minorities." "This organization doesn't pay me enough for my work." "That store cheats every customer." "This parole agency is very warm and friendly." From these examples, it is apparent that organizations are personified extensively, yet we know that the organization, as an abstraction, does not possess these qualities in the same sense as a living person. An organization takes on characteristics and qualities in the same way that a country develops a national character or a basic personality. Complicating the meaning of organizational behavior further is the fact that much organizational research refers to this phenomenon as covering a wide range of attributes.

Three variables that are not directly connected with structure, control, and change in organizations are (1) organizational climate, (2) organizational goals, and (3) organizational effectiveness. These variables are identified most often as important dimensions of organizational behavior in the collective sense.

Organizational Climate

The establishment of the human relations school in the late 1940s contributed significantly to the development of the concept of **organizational climate.** It has been said that organizational climate is somewhat like the personality of a person. The perceptions that people have of the organization's climate produce its image in their minds. Some organizations are bustling and efficient, whereas others are easygoing. Some are quite human, but others are hard and cold. Organizations change their climate slowly; they are influenced by their leaders and their environment (Davis, 1962:58).

In law enforcement, the entry of full-time, sworn female officers into traditionally male ranks has occurred, but only gradually. Affirmative action has caused significant changes in the proportionate numbers of women in officer ranks. Among the majority of male officers, however, some amount of resistance to change has occurred. Social isolation and rejection of female officers has been reported in some departments. The working environment for them has not been particularly warm or friendly. Interviews with female officers working in predominantly male agencies have revealed that the organizational climates involved have varied in their receptivity to females. Thus, in these situations, female officer perceptions of the work climate have a great deal to do with describing and defining the organizational climate (Poulos, 1992). Interpretations of the organizational climate of police departments have also been made by minorities who have typically been underrepresented in officer ranks (Lewis, 1989; Poulos and Doerner, 1996; Price, 1985).

From the standpoint of examining organizational climate empirically, this variable is difficult to conceptualize. Frequently it is meant to convey the impressions people have of the organizational environment within which they work. It may also be viewed as the degree to which organizational rules are enforced by the administration. It may refer to the extent to which persons are treated like human beings rather than as cogs in a machine.

There are some methodological problems with this term as well. Since climate often is inferred from the subjective impressions workers have of the organizational environment, it is logical to expect that not all individuals will have the same view of that environment. Some will see the climate of a given organization as authoritarian, whereas others will view the same organization as democratic. The location of the defining individual in the organizational hierarchy is an important consideration in understanding the nature of the interpretation. One illustration might be found in an academic department of a large university. If promotions and salary increases are based, for the most part, on the number of publications a professor has, a highly productive professor may see the "publish-or-perish" climate as democratic and rewarding, whereas an unproductive colleague may view the climate as threatening, punitive, and authoritarian, which it is to him.

Organizational Goals

Arguably, the central concept in the study of organizations is the organizational goal (Gross, 1969:277). Little consistent attention has been devoted to giving the concept a clear definition, however. An organizational goal is defined as a state of the organization as a whole toward which the organization is moving, as evidenced by statements people make (intentions) and activities in which they engage.

One problem with defining organizational goals from this perspective, however, is that people at different levels of authority and within different departments of an organization see it in the context of their own role definitions (Thomas, 1980). Differences exist between the goals that members have for an organization and the goals of the organization itself. The goals of particular departments within an organization may not be recognized by the general public as goals of the organization as a whole. The members of each department have in mind a vague conception of the objectives of the organization for which they work, but all too often they see the overall organizational goals from a biased perspective. The department's existence becomes an end in itself.

The difficulties in defining organizational goals methodologically should not obscure the fact that the term *organizational goals,* as used in research, most frequently refers to collective ends or objectives of the organization at large. One analysis of organizational characteristics suggests that we might define organizational goals by paying attention to the definitions provided by the organizational power coalition, a small oligarchy of individuals who establish policy and direct and design the communication networks and mechanisms of conformity to norms within the organization. Sometimes organizations publish brochures or other printed matter outlining the major objectives around which most of their internal activities center.

Thus, organizational goals are shared goals for the organization on the part of the organizational leadership (Vroom, 1960:229). Goals constitute a region of positive valence. A potential discrepancy exists between an individual's definition of organizational goals and certain personal goals he or she might have as a member of a given department. A person's own goal for an organization, therefore, is a region into which that person desires the organization to move. Their perception of the organizational goals represents their estimates of the regions into which they think the leaders of the organization would like it to move (Vroom, 1960:229).

The concept of an organizational goal may be examined more meaningfully and methodologically if we distinguish between system goals and product goals (Perrow, 1967:202). System goals emphasize quantity, substantial profits, and stability, whereas production goals emphasize growth in size, improved product quality, and innovative research and development (Hage and Aiken, 1969:373).

Some organizational goals are easily articulated. In Seattle, Washington, for example, a local task force was created to work with the Federal Arson Task Force to reduce the incidence of arson (National Institute of Law Enforcement and Criminal Justice, 1980). In Rhode Island, California, and Louisiana, a two-year Comprehensive Adjudication of Drug Arrestees (CADA) project was conducted with the primary goal of expediting the processing of drug cases from arrest to final disposition without jeopardizing due process (Henderson et al., 1991). In New York, the New York State Office of Court Administration implemented the Misdemeanor Trial Law (MTL) as a means of eliminating jury trials, reducing case backlog, expediting trials, and reducing the number of inappropriate pleas (Dynia, 1990). In Hennepin County, Min-

nesota, a special night court was established to process less serious cases, but with the specific goal of reducing severe overcrowding at the Adult Detention Center (National Center for State Courts, 1990). Prisons throughout the United States and elsewhere have the goals of providing training, assistance, and aid to prisoners in an effort to make them more employable and less inclined to recidivism (Adams, 1977; Kaiser, 1984).

Organizational Effectiveness

Although it would appear that much more has been written about organizational effectiveness than about organizational climate, the concept is equally difficult to define with precision. Often researchers will use parallel criteria to portray effectiveness. Amitai Etzioni (1959:43) says that organizational effectiveness is the ability of the organization to achieve its goals. Other researchers include derivatives of this definition in their discussions of organizational success or effectiveness.

Different criteria of organizational effectiveness might be used depending on the model of organization used. If rational models are used, then attainment of goals and adaptability will be used to portray organizational effectiveness. The rational model emphasizes achievement of goals, whereas the social system model emphasizes how well the organization can adapt to existing conditions in a competitive environment with other organizations.

Effectiveness is sometimes defined as efficient, productive performance. Performance is closely related to, and usually accompanied by, a high degree of utilization of personnel achieved through job assignments that challenge and utilize the skills available, as well as the cultivation of human resource potential resulting from formal training and reliance on the internal development of current staff (Mahoney and Weitzel, 1969:360). Reliability and cooperation are singled out as two important criteria of effectiveness, although they have only an indirect connection with productivity.

Some examples of organizational effectiveness and its assessment are provided in the criminal justice literature. A police department in a large midwestern city is considered effective if certain numbers of traffic citations are issued and if quotas are fulfilled on a monthly basis (Lundman, 1979). The Texas Board of Pardons and Paroles measures the effectiveness of the

Texas prison system on the basis of the recidivism rates of parolees (Kelly and Ekland-Olson, 1991). The Los Angeles Police Department considers its police system effective on the basis of low numbers of citizen complaints and lawsuits filed against officers in which misconduct or corruption are alleged (Los Angeles Independent Commission, 1991). In Florida, the Florida Community Control Program, which is operated by the Florida Department of Corrections, is considered effective on the basis of the number of program revocations among probationers and parolees (Florida Probation and Parole Services, 1984). And in New York, the courts are judged effective according to the speed with which criminal cases are processed (Nelson, 1992; New York State Division of Criminal Justice Services, 1992).

Chapter 14 examines organizational effectiveness in great detail. Included in that chapter is an examination of evaluation research and how organizations are evaluated in terms of whether or not they achieve their manifest goals. For the present, a summary of some indicators of the effectiveness of organizations is presented next, according to particular criminal justice system components.

LAW ENFORCEMENT.   Law enforcement is an inclusive term that encompasses local, state, and federal agencies. Local police and sheriff's departments, state bureaus of criminal investigation and highway patrols, and numerous federal agencies (e.g., Federal Bureau of Investigation; Drug Enforcement Administration; Bureau of Alcohol, Tobacco, and Firearms; Treasury Department; U.S. Secret Service; U.S. Marshal's Service; Border Patrol; Immigration and Naturalization Service) comprise U.S. law enforcement. Measures of organizational effectiveness for each of these departments or agencies vary according to the stated goals of each organization. Generally, law enforcement effectiveness is assessed according to several criteria, including but not limited to

1. The number of arrests
2. Greater detection of criminal activity
3. The number of crimes solved
4. The amount of drugs confiscated
5. The amount of crime prevented
6. The number of citizen complaints processed and resolved
7. The amount of professionalism among officers

8. The minimization of agency criticism by the public
9. Low numbers of lawsuits against various law enforcement agencies
10. Greater cooperation between the police and citizens in community-oriented policing programs
11. Improvement in public relations between police officers and the public

PROSECUTION AND THE COURTS.   At the local, state, and federal levels, prosecutors, judges, and the courtroom workgroup strive to achieve various goals. Again, organizational effectiveness among prosecutors and judges is measured according to whether certain desired goals are attained. The degree of goal attainment often is determined by but is not limited to the following:

1. Number of cases prosecuted
2. Number of successful convictions
3. Speed of case processing
4. Minimization of judicial decision reversals
5. Minimization of misconduct complaints from citizens or defendants
6. Minimization of trial delays
7. Number of successfully concluded plea bargain agreements

CORRECTIONS.   Local, state, and federal corrections also have explicit goals and mission statements. Perhaps corrections generally is the most overburdened segment of the criminal justice process. Much is expected of corrections at all levels and in all areas. A great deal of pressure is applied by the public for corrections to make changes in offenders' lives. Whether or not correctional organizations of all types are successful in achieving their goals and exhibit organizational effectiveness likely would be gauged according to the following criteria:

1. Low recidivism rates among probationers and parolees
2. Expansion of rehabilitative programs in prisons and jails, including vocational programs, educational opportunities, and interpersonal skills development
3. Low rates of write-ups among inmates of prisons and jails

4. A high degree of program compliance among probationers and parolees, with few technical program violations

5. Low labor turnover among correctional staff in all agencies

6. Low numbers of inmate escapes, riots, or other incidents

7. A high degree of institutional order in prisons and jails

8. Expansion of community services to benefit probationers and parolees

9. More counseling opportunities for correctional clients

10. High employment rates for probationers and parolees

11. Low amounts of drug and alcohol use among probationers and parolees

12. Greater detection of illegal contraband and drugs among inmates in prisons and jails

13. Low numbers of lawsuits against corrections officials

Admittedly, some amount of overlap exists among the various criteria listed here. For instance, the use of recidivism as a gauge of program effectiveness is common. However, there are at least 14 different ways of measuring recidivism (e.g., rearrests, reconvictions for new offenses, probation or parole program violations or infractions, testing positive for drugs or alcohol, being cited for a traffic violation after being released from prison or jail). Recidivism often is used because it is a variable that is easily counted. We can count the number of rearrests; we can count the number of reconvictions. But improved public relations is less easily measured by counting. Often, this and related phenomena are measured by inference or media coverage.

It is clear from this organizational variable presentation that the terminology used to describe organizations has many interpretations and definitions. Not everyone defines all terms in the same way. Not everyone uses any one of these variables in precisely the same manner from study to study. Therefore, inconsistencies in study findings may occur from time to time, even though the same terms are used. The conceptualization of variables, or the conversion of organizational terminology into a functional numerical language for hypothesis testing, is often characterized by bias and subjectivity. Therefore, we must be particularly careful when examining replication research to determine if there is consistency in variable usage and definitions.

SUMMARY

Organizational variables characterize the organization at large. Little if any importance attaches to individuals or small work groups within organizations when examing these variables. The study of organizational variables is interesting but complicated. Not all researchers agree about which variables are organizational and which are interpersonal or individual. Several measures of the same variable exist to cause inconsistencies in our investigations of similar phenomena. Organizational variables have differential importance depending on the organization we are examining. Competing frames of reference or ways of looking at organizations are used, and therefore different and contrary conclusions often are reached by investigators purportedly investigating the same organizational problems.

Organizational variables may be grouped according to different organizational dimensions. One way to examine an organization is to consider its structure. How are organizations structured? Key structural variables that characterize organizations are size, complexity, and formalization. The size of an organization can be measured several different ways. Organizational complexity pertains to the number of different functions performed by organizations, or the degree of elaborate detail associated with the division of labor, or the number of departments or work groups. Organizational formalization is indicated by the extent to which organizations rely on rules and regulations, the amount of impersonality among individual work units, and the officious nature of personnel.

Another dimension is organizational control. Organizational control encompasses the process-based aspects of organizational life and how activities are accomplished. Control variables include the size of the administrative component, the amount of bureaucratization or debureaucratization, centralization and decentralization, levels of authority, and span of control. These variables are among the more important organizational dimensions, since they relate to how the organization actually operates in order to achieve its goals. The nature of the administrative component, coupled with the levels of authority and span of control, say much about the process-based aspects of information processing and work performance. Bureaucratization pertains to the adherence to rules and established patterns for employees to follow. It also focuses on task specialization and spheres of competence as organizational members improve their own performance levels. Centralization of decision making greatly influences the establishment and implementation of organizational policies and procedures for goal attainment.

A third major organizational dimension is organizational change. All organizations undergo one type of change or another over time. The key variables within the scope of this dimension are labor turnover, organizational conflict, organizational flexibility, organizational growth, administrative succession, and technology. Labor turnover is regarded as an indication of whether or not an organization is capable of retaining quality employees for long periods. It is usually expensive for organizations to hire and train new staff. Thus, organizations whose employees have the greatest longevity and whose turnover rate is relatively low are considered successful and effective. Some amount of organizational conflict is anticipated is well. No organizational environment is perfect, and there are bound to be territorial disputes and problems among different departments that see their own roles and objectives in unique ways compared with other departments. Organizations also grow and develop. In order for growth to occur in positive ways that benefit the organization at large, organizations must be flexible and receptive to changes when they occur. Key players in organizational change are administrators. Whenever there is administrative succession, this means that the organizational leadership is changing. Usually, changing leadership signifies changes in managerial philosophies and how the organization should operate. Thus, administrative succession is quite important in considering what is going in organizations and why. Technology is rapidly transforming organizations and streamlining them into more productive entities. The computerization of information has led to more efficient information processing. Virtually every organization has benefitted from improvements in its technological component.

A fourth major organizational dimension is organizational behavior. Key variables within the scope of this dimension include organizational climate, orga-

nizational goals, and organizational effectiveness. The climate of an organization is derived largely from the personal attitudes and dispositions of individuals within the organization. The collective sentiment of organizational members is often described as the organizational climate. The climate of each organization is inextricably connected with other organizational variables, such as bureaucratization, formalization, and complexity. The most important variables associated with organizational behavior are organizational goals and effectiveness. All organizations have goals. The attainment of these goals is often an ongoing process, and the degree of goal attainment is often used as a measure of organizational effectiveness. Organizational goals are as diverse as the organizations examined. Accordingly, organizational effectiveness is also assessed in a variety of ways, again depending on the type of organization we are describing. The ultimate aim of any organization is to be effective and to achieve the goals manifested by its mission statement.

It is important to acquire an understanding of the major organizational variables that characterize criminal justice organizations. In order to appreciate what is happening in organizations and why, we must become familiar with the vocabulary of those who study such organizations. Furthermore, our own perceptions of these organizations are affected by a greater knowledge of key variables that are of interest to organizational researchers. We can learn to appreciate why certain organizations are more or less effective, since we are equipped with a variety of organizational variables that sensitize us to different aspects of organizations that might affect personnel in diverse ways. As we proceed through the chapters to follow, the usefulness of many of the variables discussed here will become apparent. We can utilize these variables to fashion our own explanations for different organizational occurrences. Ultimately, our understanding of justice administration will be maximized as we learn about which variables to investigate and how they respectively impact the persons and groups in those agencies we choose to examine.

QUESTIONS FOR REVIEW

1. What are organizational variables? Why is the classification and utilization of organizational variables somewhat complicated? What are some reasons to explain these complications?

2. What are the four key organizational dimensions? Describe each.

3. What are organizational size, complexity, and formalization? Give examples of each variable and how it might be used in different organizational contexts.

4. What is meant by organizational control? What are several reasons why organizational control is a more important dimension of organizations compared with other dimensions discussed in this chapter?

5. Distinguish between bureaucratization and centralization. How does each influence organizational effectiveness?

6. What is the administrative component of an organization? How do administrative components relate to the hierarchy of authority and the division of labor?

7. What is meant by the span of control within organizations? How does the span of control influence supervisory effectiveness and employee productivity?

8. What is meant by organizational behavior? Does organizational behavior mean that we are regarding the organization as having personal characteristics much like individual personality systems? Why or why not? Explain.

9. What is meant by organizational climate? How is it measured or determined? Why is the climate of an organization considered an important factor that affects work groups and individuals and their organizational commitment and work performance?

10. What are organizational goals? How do organizational goals relate to the effectiveness of organizations?

SUGGESTED READINGS

Idaho Office of Performance Evaluations (1999). *Employee Morale and Turnover at the Department of Correction.* Boise, ID: Idaho Office of Performance Evaluations.

Koehler, Robert (2000). "The Organizational Structure and Function of La Nuestra Familia Within Colorado State Correctional Facilities." *Deviant Behavior* **21:**155–179.

Mitchell, Ojmarrh, Doris Layton MacKenzie, and Gaylene J. Styve (2000). "The Impact of Individual, Organizational, and Environmental Attributes on Voluntary Turnover Among Juvenile Correctional Staff Members." *Justice Quarterly* **17:**333–357.

• CASE STUDIES •

1. THE NEW POLICE CHIEF

Chief Grady Locke of the Metro Police Department (MPD) was retiring. The mayor and city council of Porterville, a community of 75,000 in a midwestern state, announced that applications would be accepted from anyone with policing experience interested in taking over Chief Locke's position in the fall. Thirty applications were received and the field of candidates was narrowed to five. Subsequently, one of the lieutenants in the MPD was chosen to take over the chief's job when Locke retired. Lieutenant Gant was named as Locke's successor. Gant had been a police officer with the MPD for 28 years. He was 53 years old and had a master's degree in public administration from a nearby university. At the time of his application, Gant was chief of detectives, and most others within the department considered him to be the most likely candidate to succeed Locke. He had completed a written test along with the other applicants for the chief's position, and he was judged to have given the best answers. Furthermore, his interview with the mayor's selection committee was the best received. All of this combined with the fact that Gant was intimately familiar with the MPD and its daily operations made him Locke's natural successor.

Chief Locke had been chief of the MPD for 16 years, and he, too, had worked his way up the ranks, starting out as a rookie patrol officer. Locke, too, had a college education and some graduate work in criminal justice. But he never completed the work for his master's degree. Nevertheless, Locke had learned enough from his academic and on-the-job training to know that it was wise to involve his officers in decision making whenever he made changes affecting their work. It was common practice for Locke to hold monthly strategy conferences with everyone from the rank of sergeant on up, and because of Gant's position and seniority, he was a regular participant in these conferences. During these conferences, Locke would make suggestions about how the MPD could improve its public image and fight crime more effectively. He would ask for suggestions from the rest of the officers in attendance. Then he would carefully map out a strategy for change and run it by them during their next regularly scheduled meeting. When he believed that he had sufficient approval from them, he would announce the changes he planned to make through a quarterly newsletter distributed throughout the department by a departmental secretary. Everyone seemed satisfied with how Locke was running things. The MPD was operating smoothly, and interestingly, the MPD had one of the lowest labor turnover rates among police departments throughout the state. It seemed that if you went to work for the MPD, you stayed with them for the duration. Almost no one left the MPD to work elsewhere. This is because the organizational climate was so supportive of officers and their interests.

Locke was also the sort of person who could be approached if any subordinate had a problem, either personal or professional. His door was always open, and he listened to any officer who wanted to discuss his personal or professional problems. Sometimes these problems pertained to off-the-job matters such as family problems. Most of the time, however, these personal visits were to discuss some job-related problem. Sometimes, there might be friction between two or more officers, and they would seek out Locke for his fatherly advice. Locke would give thoughtful suggestions and intervene if he saw the need to do so. Often, however, the problems were resolved through his insightful advice and suggestions.

When Locke finally retired, Gant moved into his office. Within a few weeks following Locke's retirement, Gant began making changes. First, he announced several new policies relating to shift work and shift changes. He called his senior officers together for his own type of conference and informed them of some new policies that he believed would benefit the department. He told them that he was going to run things around the department quite differently from Locke's style. There would be no further monthly conferences, because in Gant's opinion, they were a complete waste of time. He further advised his

officers that major changes in shift assignments were going to be made. He was going to reassign most officers with new partners, and all patrols were going to be changed. His explanation for these reassignments and patrol changes was simple. "Change is good for the system," he said. "People doing the same things over and over again for too long get stale and inefficient. Giving them something different to do will revitalize them." Then he dismissed his officers and said that they would be receiving a list of changes to be made in a week or two.

Within two weeks, Gant distributed departmental reassignments to all officers. In some instances, officers who had been doing graveyard shifts were assigned to day work. Those doing day work were assigned to night patrols. Officers also were assigned new partners. Other changes occurred as well. Gant often was away from his office. He spent a lot of time in his cruiser, riding around the community and checking up on his patrol officers. For instance, he would watch officers take a lunch break at a local diner. On these occasions, he would time them to see how long they took to eat lunch. He checked up on patrols at all hours, including those patrols working the graveyard shift. He discovered that officers were taking extended lunch breaks, and that many of his staff had lengthy conversations with civilians, sometimes for two hours or more. He made notes of his observations.

In the latest departmental bulletin, Gant wrote a policy statement concerning officer laxity and slothfulness, and he specifically referred to extended lunch breaks by his patrol officers. He said that officers were being paid to do police work, not sit around and gab with civilians at diners and restaurants. On several occasions, he called in officers he had observed and reprimanded them for their abuse of lunch hour. He said that these reprimands were going in their permanent personnel file and that if it happened in the future, their jobs would be on the line.

Soon officers began discussing Chief Gant behind his back, wondering how he knew about their long lunch breaks. One officer said that he saw Gant observing other officers having lunch at a diner from his unmarked cruiser one evening. He speculated that was how Gant was learning about these minor violations of departmental policy.

On several occasions when officers wanted to discuss personal problems with the chief, they would

• CASE STUDIES •

walk to his door and ask if he had any time to talk with them. "See the secretary and make an appointment like everyone else," Gant would tell the officers. And then, if an officer did have a conference with Gant, Gant would say, "Listen, don't come to me with your personal business. Solve these problems and leave them at home where they belong. Don't bring your personal problems to work. And if you've got a beef with some other officer, take it up with him. I don't want to hear about it." Soon no officers sought Gant out to discuss their problems, because they found him completely unreceptive.

Over the next year, 11 officers resigned from the MPD. This was unprecedented. Of course, Gant hired 11 new officers to replace them, but he never made any effort to determine why the experienced officers had left. Morale was low around the department. The number of sick calls increased dramatically. Gant was perplexed and wondered why so many of his officers had trouble following orders and doing their jobs.

Questions for Discussion

1. How did the labor turnover among the officers in the MPD relate to administrative succession, when Gant replaced Locke as police chief?

2. Gant seemed to embrace certain bureaucratic principles of his job that he believed should work in the MPD. Why was he unsuccessful in his attempt to bring about nondisruptive changes?

3. What type of leader was Locke? What kind of organizational climate did he create? Did this organizational climate change when Gant took over? Why or why not? Explain.

4. What organizational variables do you view as most important in analyzing this particular case? Why?

5. Was Gant entirely to blame for the fact that 11 officers resigned from the MPD? Compare and contrast the supervisory styles of Gant and Locke.

6. In what ways were both Gant and Locke goal oriented? Both administrators thought that in their own way, they were causing the MPD to be more effective. What are some better ways Gant could have brought about changes within the department that may have been received better by his subordinates? Explain.

2. THE BAYLOR COUNTY PROBATION DEPARTMENT

The Baylor County Probation Department is a small probation department in the Southeast. Although the size of the probation department is not unlike other county probation department sizes throughout the state, President Bill Clinton's 1994 Crime Bill and other legislative actions caused a substantial increase in the number of drug arrests and convictions. The number of new drug offenders was so great that during the past six or seven years, the probation department has had to triple its probation officer staff.

The assistant chief probation officer, R.J. Snell, conferred with the chief probation officer, Robert Sloan, and it was decided that a new position should be created to coordinate more effectively the activities of all probation officers (POs) in the agency. Snell reviewed the records of the existing probation officers to see if anyone was especially qualified to assume the

new coordinator's duties. Since most of the older POs had been with the department for 15 or more years and were familiar with the agency and the various work assignments and responsibilities, Snell's choice of coordinator was difficult to make. Further conferences with Sloan brought Snell to the conclusion that no single PO had all of the necessary skills to perform the new coordinating job adequately.

Sloan instructed Snell to seek a coordinator from outside the probation agency, possibly a person with some experience in human relations and with a task-related administrative background. Sloan further recommended that the person should have some college experience, preferably a bachelor's degree in business, sociology, or psychology, and a strong interest in working with people in a coordinating activity.

Snell contacted other probation agencies around the state, including some of his personal friends who worked in probation departments outside of the state.

Several persons were recommended to him. But of all coordinator candidates, Snell selected Tom Blake, a rising young parole officer from another state. Blake was 29, had an MBA with an undergraduate major in sociology, and had been with the parole department in his state for five years. He was in line for promotion, but because of the seniority system operative in his present position, advancement to a higher parole officer post within his agency was unlikely in the immediate future. Therefore, Snell reasoned, his own probation department could compete successfully for Blake's services. Blake responded positively when approached by Snell a few weeks later. An interview with Sloan proved equally worthwhile. The salary was considerably more than Blake was making as a parole officer in his home state, and the retirement benefits were lucrative. Within 90 days, Blake was on board at work in his new role as coordinator of POs in the Baylor County Probation Department.

Blake was given his own private office and personal secretary, since the governor had recently approved substantially more funding because of the increased volume of probationers. Two POs were assigned to Blake to assist him in his planning and coordinating chores. Blake's official title was Coordinator of Probation Officers and Special Programs, referring to various community programs either developed or about to be developed to serve the needs of probationer-clientele. Blake was introduced to all other POs during the next week or so, and it was understood that all POs, regardless of their seniority with the department, would take orders from Blake concerning their caseload assignments and other PO duties. They were ordered to touch base with Blake before varying their client supervisory routines.

Three senior-level POs, Rogers, Morgan, and Jefferson, assumed that Blake was their new immediate superior and intermediary between themselves and Snell. All of these men were over 40 and none had formal academic training beyond high school. In addition, Rogers, Morgan, and Jefferson were close friends with Snell and had discussed earlier among themselves which of the three would be selected for the new coordinator position. Thus, it was a shock to all three of them when Blake was chosen instead. When this "outsider" was chosen, each of these men was sorely disappointed. From all external appearances, however, no one would have known how each felt about the new situation.

Blake's first official act as coordinator was to call a meeting with all POs in the department. At this meeting, he announced that he wanted to educate them about how he had assisted his former parole department in becoming more efficient in client supervisory practices and techniques. Among other things, he said that he believed in open communication with his subordinates, and he encouraged each of these persons to let him know how they felt at all times about their jobs.

Over the next several months, Blake would announce that he was going to accompany one PO or another on his or her rounds during client visits in the field. On many of these occasions following client contacts, Blake would share his observations with his officers and let them know what he felt was wrong with their interpersonal styles. He made various suggestions about how specific clients might be treated in the future. He even made suggestions that some POs change their supervisory style completely and begin "to act more like probation officers rather than social workers."

Within six months, Blake had compiled information and observations about virtually every PO in the probation office. All the POs, at least in his view, were incompetent. This applied especially to the older POs such as Morgan, Jefferson, and Rogers. One of the records Blake maintained had to do with client recidivism. He noticed that during the past six months, recidivism rates of clients under the supervision of Morgan, Jefferson, and Rogers had risen by 30 percent. In his mind, this was unacceptable. Blake called each of these older POs into his office individually and reprimanded them for not doing a better job monitoring their clients. In his interview with Morgan, he advised Morgan, "You know, we never had recidivism rates that high in my parole department. You must be doing something wrong out there with your clients. You'd better discover what it is and correct it. Otherwise, I'm afraid you're not going to last long around here." Morgan was incensed over this upstart and his interference with how Morgan and others were doing their jobs. Morgan stood up, faced Blake, and said, "You can take your master's degree and your advice and go straight to hell!" Then he stormed out of Blake's office. Blake was flabbergasted at Morgan's outburst. He made up his mind to see Sloan about this problem the next day. In the meantime, Morgan got together with Jefferson and Rogers and sought out Snell, their longtime friend. During the next several hours, they burned Snell's ears with how Blake had been interfering in the performance of their jobs from his first day on the job. Snell listened with interest, and after the lengthy conversation, he said, "We're going to see Sloan first thing in the morning about this. We'll get it straightened out one way or another. Don't worry about a thing. None of you are going to lose your jobs. We just have to put Blake in his place!"

The following day, Blake made an appointment to see Sloan. In his meeting with Sloan, he berated Morgan, Rogers, and Jefferson as being three of the most incompetent POs he had ever seen in all of his years of experience on the job. He said to Sloan, "In my opinion, they're all deadwood and our office would be better without them. My recommendation is that you get rid of all three of them and replace them with younger POs who are more eager to do their jobs the right way." Sloan telephoned Snell, who was in another office, and asked if he could meet with him and Blake. Snell said he'd be right in. Within two minutes, Snell entered Sloan's office. Accompanying him were Rogers, Morgan, and Jefferson. All four men took seats and glared at Blake.

Questions for Discussion

1. If you were Snell, what, if anything, would you say to Sloan about Blake in his presence? How would you account for bringing Morgan, Rogers, and Jefferson along with you when Sloan assumed you were coming alone to meet with him and Blake?

2. If you were Sloan, what should be your opening statement to Snell? Should you have called Snell in Blake's presence? Why or why not? After hearing Blake's complaints, how could you have acted to avert the unpleasant encounter now before you?

3. What organizational variables might be used to explain the higher recidivism rates among the PO clients? Discuss.

4. If you had been the chief probation officer, how would you have handled the process of selecting the new PO coordinator? What would be some of the more important implications of your actions for organizational effectiveness?

5. To what extent do you believe that Jefferson, Morgan, and Rogers should have been consulted in the selection of Blake as the new PO coordinator? Why?

6. Was Blake the right man for the job? Why or why not? What could possibly account for Blake's behavior in relation to the three senior-level POs?

7. How did rapid organizational growth contribute to the present problem? Was the hierarchy of authority observed by any or all participants in this incident? Why or why not?

8. What sort of organizational climate do you believe Blake created by calling a meeting of his "subordinates"? What did Blake do to contribute to decreased organizational effectiveness among the POs and the rising recidivism rate among probationer-clientele? Explain.

CHAPTER 5

INTERPERSONAL AND INDIVIDUAL VARIABLES

INTRODUCTION

Generally, organizations function more or less smoothly, depending on the personnel who make up these institutions. In criminal justice organizations, various agencies and institutions are often in the background, receiving little or no recognition or attention from the media. Our attention is attracted to different criminal justice agencies or organizations whenever something goes wrong or whenever significant events occur, however.

When Rodney King was beaten by four officers in Los Angeles, California, we were exposed to replays of the videotape of that event. The public was critical of the police and said they were out of control. A subsequent Simi Valley, California, trial resulted in acquittals or hung juries for the officers responsible for King's injuries. A federal trial later convicted two of these officers, however. Following the state trial in Simi Valley, black residents of Los Angeles rioted. Several white citizens were critically injured and a number of black individuals were arrested and charged with aggravated assault and attempted murder. These persons were acquitted of all charges. The media played the race card in both incidents. Law enforcement officers in Los Angeles and throughout the rest of the nation were portrayed in a negative light. It did not help that an unarmed citizen was shot to death by several police officers in New York City several years later, and that they escaped punishment through a jury trial. And then the antigang unit of the Rampart Division of the Los Angeles Police Department was accused of stealing drugs and setting up defendants by committing perjury and planting evidence to incriminate them.

Prosecutors and judges have made headlines in various jurisdictions as well. In some instances, prosecutors have withheld crucial exculpatory evidence from the defense or have engaged in malicious prosecutions of innocent defendants. In one case, a district attorney prosecuted a woman falsely for a crime she did not commit because she rejected his sexual advances. Some judges have sexually abused their court officers and others. In one case, the chief justice of the New York Supreme Court stalked and harassed a woman with whom he had had an affair. He sent the woman obscene messages and threatened to kill her daughter. He attempted to extort money from her. FBI agents discovered his identity and made the arrest. He was removed from his high post, convicted, disbarred, and sentenced to prison. Later, he published his memoirs in a tell-all book and had his own New York radio talk show. A circuit judge in Tennessee was convicted of violating the civil rights of several of his clients as well as some of his own female court officers. He would force his female clients and certain female witnesses to have oral sex with him in his chambers, and he would fondle his court reporter during trials. Subsequently, he was charged with various sex crimes and convicted.

In corrections, seven dangerous inmates escaped from a Texas prison in December 2000. They killed a Texas police officer and menaced numerous other people as they moved from state to state in stolen vehicles. In Montana, a child murderer escaped from a van that was transporting him and other dangerous prisoners to a new prison facility more adequately equipped to confine them. In California, several correctional officers staged gladiatorial fights among inmates, leading to at least one inmate death. They were subsequently removed from their posts and prosecuted for staging these events. Various civil lawsuits against these officers were filed.

The point is that all of these organizations have received notoriety, not always negative, through the actions of individual actors within these systems. Either individual officers, prosecutors, judges, or correctional officers did or did not do something they should or should not have done. The result was publicity about the system itself. It is quite evident that individual actors have a great deal to do with public impressions of each criminal justice system component.

This chapter is about groups and individuals who administer or work in different capacities for various criminal justice organizations. We explore variables that are used to describe the interpersonal and individual units or levels of analysis in some detail here. The interpersonal unit of analysis focuses on the social relations among organizational personnel and superior-subordinate relations. Organizations usually consist of various interrelated departments or divisions. These departments or divisions have one or more work groups made up of two or more persons who perform jobs. Interpersonal variables have to do with group characteristics, such as the uniformity or similarity of values shared by group members, or their work group cohesiveness. Also, supervisory-subordinate relationships are important.

The essence of any organization is the individual employee or worker, regardless of his or her responsibilities, level of authority, or work role. Individual actors in organizations often are our only primary contact with the organizations. We read about or learn about certain persons who work for particular organizations. If these persons behave in certain ways, then the organizations for which they work also must be characterized by these behaviors. It does not always work this way, but nevertheless, this is the public view of organizations that the media portrays.

When individuals are examined, they may be described according to different individual dimensions, such as their work attitudes, job characteristics, and the definitions and performance of their work roles. Individual work attitudes described in this chapter include level of aspiration and job satisfaction. Job characteristics that fit particular individuals pertain to their decision-making power, the status of their jobs, and work routine and monotony. Definitions and performance of their roles pertain to individual productivity levels, role specificity, and role conflict.

As has been noted in previous chapters, there is a high degree of interrelatedness among all units of analysis, whether they are organizational, interpersonal, or individual. What happens in organizations at large inevitably filters down and influences work groups as well as individual group members. It is important for us to grasp the important concepts that are used to describe interpersonal and individual characteristics of persons in organizational settings. Throughout the rest of this book, these variables will be used, together with others, to describe various types of organizational settings and explain what is going on and why.

INTERPERSONAL VARIABLES

Variables designated as interpersonal are characteristics of employees' work groups in organizations. These are not necessarily typical of the organization as a unit. Neither do they describe individual behaviors adequately. Many studies focus on work groups or cliques of employees in a business or industrial setting. The classic Hawthorne studies concentrated in part on the cohesiveness of employee aggregates in specific sections of a work plant (Roethlisberger and Dickson, 1939). Among the many questions raised were "How can the output of work groups be increased?" "How can the morale of specific work groups be modified?" "What is the effect of a particular type of supervision on turnover or interpersonal conflict in a work group?"

Three interpersonal variables described here include (1) uniformity or similarity of values, (2) group cohesiveness, and (3) supervisory methods.

Uniformity or Similarity of Values

Similarity of values pertains to the homogeneity of orientations toward the job. How much homogeneity is there among any group of workers or employees? To what extent are the aspirations of workers similar?

Employees who perceive that they share certain interests and ambitions with other members of their work group evidently have a more compatible relation with them. Standards of behavior and productivity for work groups as a whole appear to be more readily enforced to the extent that attitudinal uniformity exists. It has been suggested that groups in general that manifest similar sentiments toward things will interact more harmoniously and participate in greater numbers of activities (Homans, 1950:182).

In criminal justice organizations such as police departments, for example, there have been frequent references to the working personality of police officers (Goldsmith and Goldsmith, 1974; Waddington, 1999). The idea of a police subculture is prevalent in studies of the police, suggesting that there is a particular set of core personality traits and shared values that distinguish police officers apart from others (Buerger, 1998; Herbert, 1998). Investigations of police officers in Scotland, London, and the United States indicate a significant and distinct personality pattern shared by officers in all cultures examined (Harper et al., 1999). And a comparison of sheriff's and highway patrol academy recruits showed more similarities than differences when standardized tests such as the Minnesota Multiphasic Personality Inventory (MMPI) and the California Psychological Inventory (CPI) were used (Hargrave, Hiatt, and Gaffney, 1986).

Herbert (1998) describes a normative order among police officers, which is a set of rules and practices oriented around a central value. Six such orders are crucial to policing: law, bureaucratic control, adventure/machismo, safety, competence, and morality. Some evidence suggests that although differences might be observed among officers in large and small police departments, many value similarities still exist among them and support the idea of a subculture (O'Shea, 1999).

The 1970s movie *Serpico* told the story of one police officer's struggle to combat police corruption in the New York Police Department. Frank Serpico was a loner against a seemingly corrupt law enforcement agency whose tentacles reached the upper echelons of police administration. The movie underscored the code of silence among police officers, signifying that if any officer observed another officer engaging in misconduct or committing any illegal act, then that misconduct or illegal act would not be reported. Interestingly, the Hollywood interpretation of events in the New York Police Department was based on actual fact, and such portrayals of police officers are not limited to New York or even to the United States (Brereton and

Ede, 1996; Chin and Wells, 1998; Klockars et al., 1997; Waddington, 1999).

Frequently, work groups are comprised of members of similar ages, gender, educational level, and/or socioeconomic backgrounds. These similarities often will generate similar outlooks toward things. Workers who come from the same residential areas and who interact with one another both on and off the job socially as well as formally seem more likely to share similar values. Although it is true that groups may be composed of individuals with a variety of individual personality characteristics, some evidence indicates that gradual modifications of individual attitudes and behaviors occur toward a group standard or group norm that typifies none of the individual group members' original dispositions toward things. Group associations, therefore, tend to foster characteristics unique to the group as opposed to describing behaviors of any given individual in the group. It may be that during the process of interactions of work groups, a heterogeneity of attitudes and orientations observed at the outset may be replaced in time by a greater similarity of interests. Formal organizational research conventionally defines attitudinal uniformity as an independent variable.

Group Cohesiveness

A nineteenth-century French sociologist, Émile Durkheim, was one of the first to introduce social scientists to group cohesion, an interpersonal factor responsible for increases and decreases of certain individual behaviors (Durkheim, 1951). The term **group cohesiveness** means the tendency of group members to stick together. It has been variously measured by means of the number of times group members use "we" when referring to their group activities, the number of in-group sociometric choices, and the degree of willingness of group members to leave the group. Some researchers have defined cohesion as the number of times that a work group will process grievances jointly before administrative higher-ups (Sayles, 1958). Group cohesiveness also has been characterized as the attraction of members to the group in terms of the strength of forces on the individual member to remain in the group and to resist leaving the group.

In many respects, group cohesiveness has roots in the subculture of organizational personnel. Cohesiveness generally occurs over time and through close interpersonal interactions and occupational socialization. In a study of 148 police academy recruits, for example, occupational solidarity and cohesiveness appeared positively related to individual characteristics such as race, gender, age, military experience, and level of police experience (Britz, 1997). In fact, police training is often viewed as more education oriented rather than training oriented (Buerger, 1998). To some extent, there are pressures on officers to behave in ways the public expects, particularly in view of media portrayals of them on television and in the movies (Hallet and Powell, 1995). In organizational research, group cohesiveness is often treated as an independent variable, although some attention is also directed toward how group cohesiveness can be improved or increased in various agencies.

Supervisory Style

Supervisory style is predominantly an independent variable in formal organizational research. Although it is true that in most organizations supervisors are obligated to follow certain rules and adhere to specific procedures as a part of the superior-subordinate relation, some latitude generally exists for supervisors to interject personal behaviors into their leadership roles. Supervisory behavior connotes initiating activity for subordinates in the work setting. Leaders must obtain the compliance of lower-level participants in the organization. Since several alterative means may be employed to elicit the compliance of subordinates, many researchers have investigated the diverse reactions of these individuals to differential supervisory behaviors in a variety of organizational settings (Anderson et al., 1966; Lowin et al., 1969; Parker, 1963). The consensus seems to be that differential supervisory behaviors elicit fairly predictable reactions among subordinates. Acting as intervening variables between type of supervisory behavior practiced and reaction of subordinates are such factors as years of education of employees, job seniority, type of work performed, age differences between supervisors and subordinates, and union strength.

Sometimes, researchers have distinguished between showing consideration and initiating structure (Fleishman and Harris, 1962). Consideration includes behavior indicating mutual trust, respect, and a certain warmth and rapport between the supervisor and work group. Structure includes behavior in which the supervisor organizes and defines group activities for subordinates.

Some of the implications for subordinates resulting from a supervisor's exercise of different kinds of power have been described by Etzioni (1961). Power is the supervisor's ability to induce or influence another to carry out directives or any other expected norms. Supervisors may exercise (1) coercive power, in which threat of physical sanctions such as pain, frustration, or death are used to obtain compliance; (2) remunerative power, in which material rewards are used as incentives to obtain compliance from subordinates; and (3) normative power, in which esteem and prestige symbols may be allocated for the benefit of subordinates to enlist their compliance. Following the use of each of these types of power are various kinds of involvement that are predictably expected from subordinates. Subordinates who are coerced into complying with higher-ups may become alienated and have negative orientations or hostile views, whereas those who comply through remuneration will reflect calculative involvement and the expectation of material gain. Finally, those who comply because of normative power are morally involved in their work and have generally positive orientations of high intensity. Loyal follower and leader, parishioner and priest, political party member and candidate are manifestations of moral involvement in contrast to the relationships created by the use of the other types of power.

Although supervisory style is not directly organizational in nature compared with other variables such as organizational size and complexity, the role of this factor in effecting organizational change is equally important and must be accorded adequate treatment in organizational research. In police agencies, for instance, police supervisors have been provided with managerial strategies calculated to enable their subordinates to achieve organizational goals (Brewer, 1995). Enhancing or improving the work effectiveness of individual subordinates is linked closely with improving overall organizational effectiveness (Cordner, 1989; Schmidt, 1989).

Not all supervisory studies are directed at improving the conduct of subordinates. In some instances, supervisory style is studied in relation to particular types of clients, such as probationers, parolees, or juveniles. The get-tough movement has caused increasing numbers of youthful offenders to be placed in adult institutions, such as prisons and jails. More inmates under age 18 are placed legally in adult facilities. However, does this mean that supervisors should treat all inmates the same, regardless of their youthfulness? Bradette Jepsen (1997) has studied supervisory practices of those in charge of institutions in which youthful offenders have been placed. Jepsen says that not all adult correctional staff are able to learn new skills or

modify old ones to be effective with youthful offenders. Thus, staff who work with juveniles need to be educated to use a positive discipline approach to teach juveniles new behaviors and self-control. Jepsen indicates that supervisory training should include such areas as adolescent development, risk factors related to aggressive and violent behavior, behavior of adolescent offenders, the impact of antisocial peer groups, effective communication skills, and crisis intervention techniques (Jepsen, 1997:69). Supervisors may be required to make on-the-spot decisions about whether or not youthful offenders may be sold tobacco products, who can approve a youthful inmate's nonemergency medical care or visiting list, and if youths can file child abuse complaints against prison officials. Therefore, some supervisory behavior is not clear-cut legally, although it might at first appear to be.

Many institutions consider it a luxury to create special areas to house youthful offenders separate from the general adult inmate population. Thus, these separate areas do not exist. Furthermore, programming aimed at youthful offenders, including recreation, education, and cognitive behavioral training, may be sorely needed, but from a budgetary standpoint, this programming may be impractical. Therefore, those supervisors assigned to work with youthful offenders have an additional responsibility to acquire more information about policies and procedures that do not necessarily pertain to general population adult inmates.

INDIVIDUAL VARIABLES

Individual variables depict personal perceptions of the work environment and tasks performed. The employee, worker, or volunteer has numerous attitudes, orientations, and dispositions toward various work roles. It is not uncommon for an employee to define the status of the position in relation to others within the organization. Perhaps the greatest array of variables exists to describe the condition of the organizational member. Three general classifications of individual variables are (1) attitudes of members, (2) job characteristics, and (3) definitions and performance of work roles.

Attitudes of Members: Level of Aspiration

Abraham Maslow (1954) postulated the existence of several needs that are presumed basic to all individuals. These needs include (1) physiological well-being,

(2) security or safety, (3) belongingness, (4) self-esteem, and (5) self-actualization or self-fulfillment. These are popularly known as **Maslow's hierarchy of needs** or simply the **hierarchy of needs.** The idea behind this scheme is that we are motivated to satisfy these needs in our everyday social encounters, and therefore our behavior is in part a manifestation of the attempt to fulfill these needs. Several interesting interpretations can be made of Maslow's notions, but of most interest to us here is the potential impact of these needs on individual behavior in organizational settings. Behavioral variations in work performance are sometimes attributable to Maslow's needs hierarchy. Some workers are highly motivated and produce much. Others are apathetic about their work activity and produce relatively little. Some employees struggle a great deal to advance themselves in their work through promotions. The need for esteem and recognition account in part for their achieving behavior. This variable is sometimes termed the **level of aspiration.**

W.I. Thomas (1923) also espoused a scheme of human wishes or desires not altogether different from Maslow's hierarchy of needs. Thomas said that people have four basic wishes, including new experience, security, recognition, and response or love. The wish for new experience, for instance, may partially account for the frequency with which some persons change jobs or are dissatisfied with their present tasks. The wish for recognition may propel some workers toward their best efforts and output in the work setting, thus enabling them to make good impressions on higher-ups and to obtain their praise (recognition).

Subsequent to **Thomas's four wishes** and Maslow's hierarchy of needs, several organizational researchers have elaborated interesting motivational models. Vroom (1964:6) has outlined the "Vroom model," which defines motivation as a process governing choices made by persons or lower organisms among alternative forms of voluntary activity. Vroom argues that the *valence,* or strength of a worker's desire for a particular outcome, *instrumentality,* or the extent to which one outcome enables a worker to achieve other outcomes, and *expectancy,* or the likelihood that a particular effort will lead to a desired outcome, are important motivational factors that account for individual behavior in organizations (e.g., superior performance leads to promotion within the work setting) (Hunt and Hill, 1969:104).

Interestingly, not all employees of organizations always seek to advance themselves in their respective organizational hierarchies. Some persons achieve positions of leadership in organizations in which they are subjected to intensive stress and conflict, and they may decide to give up their positions in favor of less stressful jobs. For example, a survey of former large-city police chiefs was conducted to determine why they sought jobs as small-town chiefs (Daviss, 1983). Police chiefs interviewed cited several personal reasons for such career shifts, including the need to escape the frantic pace of work, the difficulties of an enormous bureaucracy, and the frustration of city police work. Professional reasons included the desire to be more involved with the community they serve, to bring an element of sophistication to rural law enforcement, and to develop policies that would increase a department's overall sense of professionalism. Although some of the police chiefs interviewed said that they miss the excitement and pace of the big city, most do not. Most agreed that they were giving their families a better quality of life as well as providing their smaller communities with better law enforcement. Thus, there are occasionally very powerful social determinants at work to govern one's level of aspiration in performing the job.

Employees' levels of aspiration are usually treated as independent variables that can be used to account for job satisfaction levels, productivity, and cooperation and conflict among workers. Using this variable in an independent capacity, for instance, Chinoy (1952) has discussed the influence of worker aspirations on interpersonal relations in the automobile industry.

Attitudes of Members: Job Satisfaction

Job satisfaction refers to the degree to which people like their jobs or the actual work performed. Job satisfaction has been linked with numerous variables, including ability, absenteeism, achievement, administration, advancement, aspirations, autonomy, education, experience, fatigue, freedom and independence, health, human relations, job enlargement, marital status, mental health, mobility, motives, occupational level, opportunity to learn, peer group, physical hardships of the work, recognition, responsibility, routine, security, self-esteem, supervision, training, turnover, and working conditions (Dantzker and Kubin, 1998).

Considerable variation in study findings exists because there are so many different definitions of job satisfaction. One measure may emphasize one's satisfaction with the working hours, whereas another measure may emphasize satisfaction with fringe benefits and the retirement package. The importance of this variable in social research is evidenced by the fact that over 12,000 studies had focused on job satisfaction as key variable as of 1996 (Spector, 1996).

Investigations of job satisfaction in criminal justice have been found in virtually every component, including law enforcement, the courts, and corrections. Job satisfaction is almost always regarded as a multidimensional concept, and researchers have found that satisfaction with work varies with several different factors. For example, a study of 199 full-time sworn officers with the Spokane (Washington) Police Department found that police officers' satisfaction with work is associated positively with their perceptions about the importance and significance of their work, the recognition they receive, their autonomy, and the capability to do their work (Zhao, Thurman, and He, 1999:167). Similar findings have been reported in studies of 8,115 employees of the Federal Bureau of Prisons (Wright et al., 1997).

Job satisfaction is used as a dependent variable to measure the effect of other variables such as the type of supervision, quality of job content, and organizational commitment (Lambert, Barton, and Hogan, 1999:96–97). It is also used as an independent variable to account for individual productivity variation and rates of labor turnover.

Early attention to job satisfaction reflected the philosophy that a happy employee is a more productive one. Thus, much attention was devoted to examining this variable under a variety of conditions. However, it has subsequently been determined that more than a few employees may have high job satisfaction but may be somewhat unproductive.

Job Characteristics: Decision-Making Power

Decision-making power is the amount of freedom an employee has to determine how the work should be performed. decision making is the process by which pressures and power are translated into policy. Considerable decision making power is vested in law enforcement officers on beats in some jurisdictions, for instance. Officer autonomy in decision making is regarded as a key factor affecting work motivation and effectiveness. A study of 102 New York City police officers found that although bureaucratic restraints and community expectations did govern officer conduct in the law enforcement process, individual officers were able to exert considerable control over their enforcement patterns through a process of mutually accommodating informal roles. Thus, officers were able to ensure control over their work and preserve their autonomy despite contrary value systems of administrators that tended to stress rational efficiency (Walsh, 1984).

Most widely used as an independent variable in organizational research, decision-making power is closely related to the authority structure of organizations. The question is often asked, "How much decision-making power should employees have?" Some evidence suggests that employees who are more involved in decisions affecting their work will exhibit greater interest in their work (French, Israel, and Aos, 1960; Viteles, 1953).

A study of 194 police officers from a large, urban police department in a midwestern state is one of several research investigations showing that greater participation in decision making improves officer satisfaction with work and individual effectiveness. For instance, those officers who experienced more opportunities to participate in decision making also tended to report higher levels of job satisfaction and organizational commitment (Jermier, 1979). This was true even when levels of danger, career stage, task variability, and role ambiguity were controlled. Officer discontent was related to lack of community support, modest income, promotion-related frustrations, lack of family support, and unpleasant working conditions. Subsequent studies of similar phenomena have reported findings consistent with this investigation (Lambert, Barton, and Hogan, 1999; Zhao, Thurman, and He, 1999).

Job Characteristics: Job Status

Job status is determined by position in the hierarchy of authority. People tend to evaluate one another in an organization according to the amount of power that they can wield over others. Sometimes, knowledge about work and the interrelations of roles becomes a type of status, particularly in the eyes of novice employees. Staff members who have greater seniority than others in some organizations may take great delight in slowly doling out information to new workers, relishing the opportunity to demonstrate that they know more than someone else.

Job status derives directly from the actual work performed. The type of work performed may affect one's attitudes toward other work associates as well as toward clients. For instance, in secure juvenile institutions, confined juveniles are provided not only with supervision from institutional staff, but they are also exposed to a variety of programs designed for their improvement in areas in which they manifest weaknesses. The collective goal of the juvenile detention facility is the treatment of youthful clients. In 1999, Jill Gordon conducted a study of the correctional staff at a juvenile detention facility. The study group consisted of all institutional staff members who occupied treatment or security positions and who had direct contact with youths (Gordon, 1999b:86).

Gordon surveyed a total of 80 staff members, including five state rehabilitation counselors, 10 private chemical dependency counselors, and 62 juvenile correctional officers. Although all staff members were expected to support the therapeutic environment of the correctional center, Gordon found clear differences among the staff. The positions they held clearly influenced whether their outlook toward juvenile inmates was punitive or therapeutic. Juvenile correctional officers tended to reflect a punishment orientation toward juveniles, whereas rehabilitation counselors and chemical dependency counselors were treatment oriented in their approach to their youthful inmates. Staff position seemed to be a good predictor of one's institutional philosophy. Gordon concluded that if certain institutional staff do not support the institutional philosophy, then their actions may be at odds with program strategies. Her research has been consistent with the findings of her own research study of a rehabilitative agency (Gordon, 1999a) and the work of others (Bazemore, Dicker, and Nyhan, 1994).

Job status may be determined by occupational title, income, or surroundings at work. Job status is also heavily dependent on education and former work experience. Almost exclusively an independent variable in most research, job status influences interpersonal relations, job satisfaction, motivation for achievement, and job security. In turn, it is influenced by income, decision-making power, and position in relation to other jobs.

Job Characteristics: Work Routine and Monotony

The amount of **work routine,** monotony, and repetitiveness modifies a worker's satisfaction with his or her job. Too much routine may lead to high labor turnover or lower employee morale. Bureaucratic organizations are notorious for creating positions in-volving repetitive job operations and strict adherence to rules. The routine and monotony associated with any job is defined as an independent variable.

Correctional officers and police officers perform roles with a great deal of routine and monotony. Probation and parole officers also engage in repetitive job operations daily. Probation officers, for example, must write rather lengthy presentence investigation reports, which are more or less a perfunctory part of their work routine. Although these documents are quite important and are considered by judges in the sentencing process, probation officers regard these report tasks as excessive paperwork. These officers can do little to alleviate some of this work routine and monotony, however.

Considerable routine and paperwork also can be found in policing and correctional work. However, police officers are exposed to a wide variety of situations requiring their intervention and apprehension of law violators. Correctional officers also must cope with an increasingly clever inmate population, continually designing ways of beating the system by manufacturing illegal weapons, smuggling contraband, or engaging in some other illegal behavior. Situations that require police officers or correctional officers to deal with interesting or even dangerous circumstances can offset the monotonous or routine aspects of their jobs.

Definitions and Performance of Roles: Productivity

Productivity is defined according to the particular organizational context within which employees are studied. Productivity may be production of so many units of product per day or processing so much paperwork in a given time interval. In research and development laboratories, however, it may never be the case that a particular standard of production is ever achieved. In this respect, the application of effort toward the research objective becomes the measure of group or individual productivity, despite the ambiguity surrounding such a measure.

Productivity is almost always used as a dependent variable in relation to such factors as job satisfaction, supervisory style, and technological change. It is determined by the extent to which an organizational member satisfactorily performs the work role or fulfills the expectations of higher-ups. Individuals who accomplish much in relation to their role expectations are considered high producers. Those who fail to achieve the minimum standards of their role set by administrative definition are regarded as low producers.

This statement simply suggests that productivity is not always a matter of producing things.

Managers and business leaders are perhaps most interested in workers' productivity, since this variable most directly determines the profits and losses of organizations. Different managerial styles, administrative hierarchical models, and fringe-benefit programs for employees have been instituted to influence this variable in an upward direction. The motivational research of the industrial psychologist, for instance, is directed toward discovering those factors that cause the worker to produce more.

Definitions and Performance of Roles: Role Specificity

Role specificity or **role clarity** refers to the perceived degree of familiarity with the requirements of one's work role in an organization. Much agreement can be found among managerial researchers that clear lines of authority and responsibility are desirable, together with clear role definitions (Hickson, 1966:232).

Role specificity has been studied under different names. Sometimes it has been studied as role clarity, and some researchers have referred to role specificity as role expectations. For example, a study of prison superintendents in the Virginia Department of Corrections focused on the role expectations of superintendents as viewed by themselves, their correctional officers, and by inmates. Interestingly, each sample had a different impression of the role of superintendent (Rollo and Kalas, 1975). The vaguely defined role of superintendent was posited by these investigators as one of the primary reasons for institutional conflicts and misunderstandings between correctional officers and inmates, between inmates and administrators, and between superintendents and correctional officers.

In police departments, for example, in which it is logical to assume that official police behaviors are articulated along with formal sanctioning mechanisms for rule violations and misconduct, some aspects of a police officer's role are obscure and difficult to conceptualize. Misconduct, for instance, ranges from trivial incidents and behaviors to gross negligence and dishonesty and corruption. There are not always clear lines to distinguish between trivial and serious forms of misconduct. Equally unclear are the formal sanctioning mechanisms that some departments employ to discipline their officers if misconduct of any kind is detected or reported (Goldsmith, 1988; Kania, 1982).

Role specificity is treated predominantly as an independent variable in relation to such factors as workers' commitment to the job, motivation, and anxiety. One argument is that with high role specificity, there is a reduction in flexibility and hence much frustration. The more clearly the role is defined, the less deviation is expected as a part of the role performance. Highly bureaucratized organizations are known for imposing numerous rules and regulations as role expectations for their members.

Sometimes role specificity is related to certain components of the personality. Some people prefer considerable latitude in their job definitions. Others feel uncomfortable with their work if they do not have a precise knowledge of what their superiors expect of them.

Organizations can be classified according to the amount of role specificity present within them (Hickson, 1966:237). And studies of organizational change examine the impact of modifications of jobs, elimination of jobs, and reassignments on role clarity. Studies of technological change in organizations might consider changes in role clarity as influencing such factors as labor turnover, absenteeism, and low esprit de corps.

Definitions and Performance of Roles: Role Conflict

Role conflict may pertain to any number of things. There may be conflict (1) in the disparity between the demands of two roles that an individual performs; (2) if a person assumes so many roles that he or she cannot possibly fulfill all of the obligations involved; (3) internal to a given role, such as if a person accepts a role and finds that he or she does not have time to meet the demands and does not know how to get out of it, or if a person accepts a role for which he or she has time but then has neither the interest nor the ability to carry out its obligations; and (4) caused by different expectations about how one's role should be carried out (Dyer, 1960).

As role conflict becomes more intensified, workers become increasingly ineffective in role performance (Getzels and Guba, 1954:166). The intensity of perceived role conflict varies according to certain personal and attitudinal characteristics of the organizational member, however.

Numerous instances of role conflict exist in criminal justice agencies. Parole and probation officers vary in how closely they supervise their clients. Technical program violations by parolees or probationers are

BOX 5.1 PERSONALITY HIGHLIGHT

JOSEPH CHARVAT
Correctional Officer II and
Assistant Squad Leader
SORT Team, Alpha Squad,
Department of Corrections
and Rehabilitation, North
Dakota Penitentiary

Statistics: A.A. (criminal
justice), Bismarck State
College, B.S. (criminal
justice), Minot State
University

Background: Like many kids, I always wanted to be a policeman or a fireman. Somewhere along the way I forgot about that and had decided that I wanted to do something in the communication field. I was not sure exactly what I wanted to do or where I wanted to go, and so I enrolled at the local college. During this time, I was approached and accepted an offer to work for a local private security agency. This renewed my long-forgotten interest in law enforcement and I started taking more courses related to that type of work. I still did not know exactly what I wanted to do, but at least I was headed in the right direction.

About a year and a half into my A.A. degree, I decided that I needed to find a job. I went to job services to get some ideas and to fill out the proper forms. I was told that they would contact me if they heard of anything for which I qualified. Living in a town of 70,000 people, the job market was tough but not impossible. The trip to job services did not produce any leads, and so I started looking into other forms of work until they contacted me. I left the job services office and started home. On the way home, I drove past the North Dakota State Penitentiary. I had never thought about going into corrections, but I decided I would see what it was like. It was a good thing they had a wide driveway and that there was no one behind me, because I hit the brakes and turned in. I pulled up to the front gate and was overwhelmed by the fences and concertina (razor) wire. I went to the front desk and asked the officer if they were hiring and if I could get an application. It happened that they were hiring, and two years later, I am

still glad that I made that decision to try something different.

Work Experience: Working in the field of corrections can be a rewarding and fulfilling experience, but it also can be very disappointing. Every day you deal with inmates who have a wide variety of different attitudes, beliefs, and lifestyles, and whose convictions can range from writing bad checks to rape to murder. You are involved in face-to-face contact and situations with them on a daily basis. If you think about the reason why they are there and you let them affect your judgment, you will run into a lot of difficult situations and you run the risk of letting your personal feelings affect the way you perform your duties. You need to be fair and unbiased, as tough as that can be. Remember, they are in prison as a punishment, not to be punished.

Advice to Students: Corrections is not the type of work that is the most glamorous or pays the best, but it is really rewarding when you see a person who walks out of that door after they have completed their sentence, and who never come back. So many times you see the same people come back, time and time again. I would venture to say that corrections could be one of the most dangerous professions. To explain what I mean by this, consider the following scenario: What would the average citizen say if someone proposed that police officers be assigned to a neighborhood that was inhabited by no one except criminals, and those officers would be unarmed, would patrol on foot, and would be heavily outnumbered by the criminals? I wager that the overwhelming public response would be that the officers would have to be crazy to accept such an assignment. Such a scenario is being played out in prisons and jails across the country every day. We are corrections officers, not guards. "Guards" are the people who watch school crossings. Although you will never see us on *911* or *Top Cop*, we are law enforcement professionals. We are the forgotten cop, hidden away from public view, doing a dangerous beat, hoping someday to receive the respect and approval of the public we silently serve.

The corrections industry often is forgotten and overlooked, but a career in this field can be very rewarding in other ways than just money or fame. My advice to students who are interested in corrections, or even those who think they might be, would be to take classes in college that are centered around social work and criminal justice. I say this because when you are working in this type of job, you are the first person dealing with people who have all sorts of problems and you need to be able to help them, or at least point them in the right direction to get help. The biggest asset that you can have going into any criminal justice profession is to be a good person of high moral and ethical character.

supposed to be reported by their officers whenever detected. Some technical program violations are petty or trivial and not worth reporting, however. For instance, if a parolee returns home at 10:05 P.M. instead of 10:00 P.M., this is a violation of a curfew imposed by the parole board. A late bus or any number of legitimate excuses may be given by the parolee. The parole officer is under a duty to report the program infraction, however, regardless of how minor it may appear. But reporting the infraction may create unnecessary hostility between the officer and the client if therapeutic progress has been made in an otherwise successful parole program. What should the parole officer do in this case? Many parole officers would not bother with this trivial infraction. Of course, if this type of infraction (e.g., violating curfew) becomes rather frequent, then formal action would probably be taken.

A different scenario may be more clear-cut. Using our same parole officer and parolee, suppose the parolee tests positive for cocaine use. Drug or alcohol use by any parolee is prohibited, and the parole officer will report it immediately. Thus, officers themselves often devise priorities about which rules and program requirements are more important than other rules.

A patrol officer may stop a car that was traveling 50 mph in a 40 mph zone. Should a traffic citation be issued? Some officers say that it depends on the attitude and demeanor of the motorist. Others say, "Issue the ticket; the speed limit was exceeded. Where's the conflict?"

Now change the scenario to two detectives who are investigating a burglary. They apprehend a fleeing suspect. The suspect has a bag of allegedly stolen items, including some jewelry. The burglary being investigated by the detectives did not report any jewelry missing, and therefore, the detectives assumed that the jewelry was from another unreported burglary. In the course of handling the stolen goods, one of the detectives notices a gold nugget ring, picks it up, and tries it on. He says, "I think I'll keep this, since it fits." The other detective says nothing. Later, the detective in possession of the gold nugget ring offers it to a friend and private citizen for $100, well below the market value of the ring. The private citizen buys the ring, as-

suming that since a detective sold it to him, it must be a legitimate piece of jewelry. At no time in the future is a burglary reported involving the theft of a gold nugget ring. In this case, the detective who took the ring for himself should have turned in all goods recovered as "stolen property." This was not done. The other detective who saw his partner take the ring should have asked him to put it back with the other stolen property. If he did not comply, the misconduct should have been reported. But neither officer said anything. When the detectives were talking about this incident later, one said that this type of conduct, that is, selling off certain items known to be stolen, is more or less common practice. One detective said, "If I didn't take that ring and sell it, someone in the property department would have taken it. It's just how things are done." Incidentally, this was a true incident.

Finally, suppose you are a sex therapist who conducts outpatient therapy sessions for those convicted of various sex crimes. A new member of your group is a probationer who was recently convicted of several sex crimes. One feature of the program is that group members/probationers should disclose their crimes and tell why they committed them. Another feature is that these probationers also should disclose other crimes they have committed but for which they were not detected, apprehended, or prosecuted. The new probationer is encouraged to talk about his crimes, and as the therapist, you ask him to tell about other crimes he may have committed. He admits to three additional crimes that are presently unsolved. One of these crimes involved your cousin, who was seriously injured and traumatized by the incident. You have advised these probationer-clients that these therapy sessions are confidential; yet, you want to serve justice and report this probationer who has gotten away with molesting your cousin. What should you do? This is definitely a role conflict situation and not easily resolved.

It is difficult to study organizational processes without paying attention to the groups and individuals who make up organizations. A view of formal organizations that considered only organizational factors would yield a relatively sterile product. But it also would be unproductive to focus only on interpersonal and individual characteristics. We must acknowledge that all three units of analysis—the organization, group, and individual—are blended if we are able to comprehend organizational structure and processes.

SUMMARY

Interpersonal variables describe social relationships of people in their respective workplaces. Interpersonal variables do not characterize the persons themselves. Rather, the focus is on group characteristics. Groups often share similar values and attitudes about their work. Uniformity or value similarity enables group members to share common experiences with one another. Value similarity can be either good or bad, depending on the values endorsed by the group. If the group places high value on good moral conduct, then the group becomes mutually supportive of one another in the performance of work roles. The group may condone illegal conduct, however. Whether we are examining police officers, prosecutors, judges, or correctional officers and administrators, if there is prevalent corruption or misconduct, then the group itself becomes a proponent and perpetuator of such corruption and misconduct.

Groups also vary in the degree of their cohesiveness. Group cohesion refers to a group's ability to stick together or the extent to which group members are consolidated and act in concert toward particular objectives. Influencing group relations is the supervisory relations between superiors and subordinates. Although bureaucratic organizations are less likely to condone individualized supervisory styles, individual supervisors and administrators cannot avoid manifesting particular characteristics that set them apart from other administrators, even within the same organization. Therefore, different supervisory styles are found in organizations. A relation exists between employee involvement in work activities and the type of supervision received from higher-ups. The nature of the supervisory-subordinate relation can have diverse consequences for subordinates, how they view their jobs, and how effective they are at performing their work tasks.

Individual variables are characterized according to several salient dimensions. These include member attitudes, specific job characteristics, and definitions and performance of work roles. Individual member attitudes include one's level of aspiration and job satisfaction. The level of aspiration an employee acquires says much about his or her motives for work performance. According to various psychologists and other social scientists, individuals have personal needs that are fulfilled to a great degree by what transpires in the working environment. Persons are believed to have needs for recognition, esteem, and self-fulfillment. Therefore, their actions will be directed toward need fulfillment. We can describe persons in organizations and explain their behavior by paying attention to the needs they appear to have and the goals they strive to achieve based on their presumed needs.

Every employee of an organization, from frontline officers to top-level administrators, exhibits a degree of job satisfaction. It is uncertain just how work satisfaction influences job performance or productivity, but we know that job satisfaction might be used to explain one's attitudes about the general nature of the work environment. Traditional thinking about job satisfaction is that it explains directly one's work effectiveness and productivity. Employees who are more satisfied with their jobs are believed to be more productive and effective, although there are many happy yet unproductive employees in all organizations. But job satisfaction has many dimensions. Some researchers claim that it is more important to avoid circumstances that cause employees discontentment than it is to discover circumstances that improve worker satisfaction. This debate remains unresolved.

Job characteristics include decision-making power, job status, and work routine and monotony. It is generally agreed that a majority of workers like to be included in decision making affecting their jobs. The workforce of today is considerably more educated than the workforce 50 years ago. Thus, new employees simply expect more from their jobs than workers may have expected several decades ago. But many of today's jobs lack challenges that prompt employees to be contented with them. To some extent, at least, the amount of challenge associated with one's work contributes in part to labor turnover in many organizations. People are continually seeking more challenging work, more satisfying work, better-paying work, and work that will bring them greater recognition and self-fulfillment. Thus, many employees are motivated to seek promotional opportunities whenever they arise, since they view these opportunities as a means of gaining greater job status and control over whatever they do. But the fact is that most jobs have their repetitive aspects. Over time, employees become bored with their work, although they continue to perform it. This is one reason why administrators attempt to devise new incentive systems as strategies to maintain employees' interest in their work so that individual work effectiveness can be improved.

Definitions and performance of work roles include variables such as productivity, role specificity, and role conflict. Depending on the organization examined, productivity is measured differently. For police officers, productivity may mean how many traffic citations are issued per month. It may mean how many crimes are solved. For prosecutors, productivity may mean how many cases are successfully prosecuted or how many plea bargain agreements are concluded successfully. For judges, productivity may mean expeditious handling of cases and the elimination of case processing delays. For corrections officers, productivity may be measured by an absence of inmate conflicts and low numbers of write-ups for misconduct, or the low frequency of lawsuits filed by inmates against correctional institutions and their officers.

Role specificity pertains to how clearly persons understand their own work roles. In many organizations, although job descriptions or prescriptions are written for each job, more than a few employees have diverse work expectations and lack role clarity or specificity. They may perform work that ought to be performed by others, thus creating a degree of interpersonal friction among departmental units. Role specificity may be too high, such that persons performing certain types of work become incapable of performing simple tasks outside of their immediate spheres of competence. Some observers have termed this phenomenon as trained incapacity.

Role conflict is a bothersome variable, since it almost always exists in the workplace. Role conflict has several different meanings. It may mean a discrepancy between one's personal abilities to do the work and the actual work assigned. Or it may mean internal conflict between what the worker does and what the worker feels ought to be done. The conflict may arise due to overcommitments, that is, a person takes on too much work and does not have time to do all tasks adequately. Or conflict may arise due to a supervisor's expectations about how work tasks should be performed and individual definitions of how they same work should be done. It is virtually impossible to rid organizations of role conflict. Therefore, administrators and supervisors attempt to manage conflict in an effort to minimize its occurrence.

Although we can examine interpersonal or individual variables separately, it makes more sense to consider these variables as interrelated entities. All variables influence other variables in different ways. In turn, most of these variables are influenced by the presence or absence of other variables. We can make important use of these variables in our analyses of organizational events. For instance, what value similarity or role conflict existed among individual officers during the Rodney King incident? To what extent was value similarity a factor? When officers are cited for bravery and other accomplishments, are they motivated by the need for esteem or recognition, or are these unselfish acts? When probationers and parolees fail in their programs and are sent to jail or prison, what variables seem to explain these occurrences? Are organizations and their policies at fault, or are individual officers or groups of officers failing in different ways in the performance of their duties? What about the officer-client relation? Is it effective? Why or why not? What does one's level of aspiration, job status, and work routine and monotony have to do with these events? All of these questions cause us to examine these problems by paying attention to one or more of the variables that characterize organizations, groups, or individuals.

QUESTIONS FOR REVIEW

1. What are interpersonal variables? Identify and describe three important interpersonal variables.

2. How does value similarity or the uniformity of values contribute to job satisfaction? Explain.

3. What is meant by group cohesiveness? Can group cohesiveness be influenced by any particular organizational variable? Why or why not? Explain.

4. Distinguish between job satisfaction and job status. Are these variables related? Explain.

5. How does the nature of supervisory style in the work setting influence worker productivity? Explain.

6. Are employees who are satisfied with their jobs better workers than those workers who are dissatisfied with their jobs? Explain.

7. How is job satisfaction used in criminal justice research to explain other variables and occurrences?

8. What are some similarities and differences between Maslow's hierarchy of needs and

Thomas's four wishes? How are these schemes viewed as motivating forces for workers to behave in given ways?

9. How does participation in decision making affect an employee's job satisfaction level? Do all employees want to be involved in the decision-making process? Why or why not?

10. How is productivity measured in police agencies? How is productivity related to role specificity?

SUGGESTED READINGS

Cordner, Gary W., Larry K. Gaines, and Victor E. Kappeler (1996). *Police Operations: Analysis and Evaluation.* Cincinnati, OH: Anderson Publishing Company.

Fyfe, James J., et al. (1997). *Police Administration* (5/e). New York: McGraw-Hill.

Lovegrove, Austin (1997). *The Framework of Judicial Sentencing: A Study in Legal Decision Making.* Cambridge, UK: Cambridge University Press.

• CASE STUDIES •

1. THE ANGRY MOTORIST

Officer Ron Marks has been with the local police department for five years. Marks is 29, single, and good-looking. He has a reputation among the officers as a ladies' man. Marks has been on patrol during the late evening hours for the past six weeks. One morning, a young woman, Joan Allen, asks to see you, the police chief. Allen wants to complain about how she was treated by one of your officers when stopped for speeding. She says that the officer, Marks, stopped and approached her. He advised her that she had been speeding, doing 45 mph in a 35 mph zone. Allen said that Marks then made certain advances toward her while examining her automobile registration and driver's license. According to the woman, Marks told her that if she would cooperate and have coffee with him at an all-night diner down the road, he might be persuaded to forget about writing her a speeding ticket. She was deeply insulted and adamantly refused to have coffee with him. She said that Marks then issued her a ticket for speeding, which placed her speed at 40 mph over the speed limit. He also cited her for reckless driving. You advise the woman that you will look into these allegations.

When Allen leaves, you summon the watch commander and inquire if he or other officers have heard anything about Marks soliciting female motorists. Two hours later the watch commander advises you that at least three other officers have heard rumors that Marks "comes on" to certain attractive women he stops for traffic violations. Until now, you have unsubstantiated allegations that Marks may be engaging in sexual harassment of female motorists. You want to learn more about these incidents and talk with the officers who

heard these rumors. While you are in the process of contacting these other officers, the district attorney calls and says that he has just received a call from Burt Spence, a city councilman. His cousin, Joan Allen, has just called and told him all about the incident involving Officer Marks. The district attorney says that "Spence wants to know what you are going to do about this pervert," and that if something isn't done right away, everybody in town will hear about this "sexual predator" on your department payroll. And just when you thought that things couldn't get any worse, Marsha Hunt, a reporter for the local newspaper, calls to tell you she is doing a short article about sexual harassment and asks for your comments about this Marks character and his sexual antics with female motorists. It seems that Joan Allen has political pull and is seeking to expose Marks by using every means at her disposal.

Questions for Discussion

1. What should you tell Marsha Hunt?
2. What should you tell the district attorney?
3. What investigative plans should you implement to discover whether or not there is any truth to Joan Allen's allegations and the bases of rumors spread by other officers about Officer Marks?
4. You decide to have a private meeting with Officer Marks. Marks enters your office and sits down. How should you begin the conversation with Marks?
5. During your conversation with Marks, you determine that Marks knows Joan Allen. In fact,

he dated Allen several months ago. When she wanted to "get serious," according to Marks, he broke off all contact with her. He tells you that Allen was very upset with him and left several verbally abusive messages on his answering machine during the next several weeks. It is your distinct impression that Marks is completely innocent, at least in this situation. Fur-

ther, you have reason to suspect that other officers may be jealous of Marks. Under these circumstances, what steps would you take to minimize the damage already caused by Joan Allen?

6. Should you have any further contact with Joan Allen? Why or why not? Explain.

2. THE BROOKSHIRE COUNTY SHERIFF'S DEPARTMENT

The Brookshire County Sheriff's Department (BCSD) is located in a large southern city of 300,000. Under Sheriff Marcia Johnson, who had served two terms as sheriff, the BCSD had an organizational arrangement consisting of 12 different departments or divisions, with six levels of supervision, dealing with everything from juvenile delinquency to major adult crimes. Sheriff Johnson even had a six-member advisory board consisting of several civilians and sheriff's officers to advise her about departmental changes and new program development. Johnson had a prior educational background in business management and had worked for several years as an officer for the Brookshire Police Department, working her way up from patrol officer to sergeant. During her eight years as sheriff, she made lots of changes in the organizational structure of the BCSD and prided herself on attention to small details of the job. However, a new election has replaced Johnson with Gene Dexter, whose background is in the grocery business. Dexter has been a manager of a large grocery store chain in Brookshire County and a member of the Brookshire City Council for several years. He decided to run for sheriff when encouraged to do so by some of his friends. They said that it was time for a change, and that Sheriff Johnson had spent too much on her department. Someone was needed to "economize," as his friends put it.

The first few weeks as sheriff of Brookshire County, Dexter decided to make some major changes in the authority hierarchy of the department. He decided to redistribute existing manpower according to new job definitions and work relationships, and to reassess current departmental policies as they pertain to intraorganizational and interorganizational interactions.

Dexter has decided to modify substantially many of the administrative jobs previously created by Johnson. In fact, he has decided that some jobs are unnecessary and he needs to eliminate them. In a general announcement, Dexter has declared the appointment of a new chief deputy to assist him. The new chief deputy was formerly a sheriff's deputy under Johnson's administration, and he is disliked by many of his fellow deputies. In order to allay anyone's fears about being dismissed, Dexter has said that no one will be fired; however, there will be large-scale reassignments and an elimination of numerous positions. Dexter has drawn up a new organizational chart with only four supervisory levels. This new chart has greatly extended each supervisor's span of control, with more employees under each supervisor.

Dexter has called a meeting of the six existing supervisors and has asked each of them to submit names of persons they believe would be most qualified to perform the chores and responsibilities of the four new supervisory positions he has drawn on the organizational chart. Additionally, Dexter has asked these supervisors to recommend persons who should be transferred to regular deputy duties, in view of each supervisor's impression of his subordinate's work performance. Dexter has emphasized that he expects that the names of those who are recommended should have computer experience, since he is updating the technology of the department with new computers and software for tracking criminal information. Within a week, each of the six supervisors has submitted several names for the new supervisory positions, as well as the names of those recommended for general deputy work. Five out of six supervisors made their recommendations to Dexter without consulting any of the persons they had named for the different positions.

Only one supervisor, Al Langley, the captain in charge of the patrol unit, asked his subordinates what they might like to do under the new administration. Langley, who wanted to be liked by his deputies, had been with the BCSD for 16 years and he believed he had a lot of pull with the new sheriff. He advised his subordinate deputies that "in all likelihood, you'll get the jobs you want." Al Langley was well liked by his men and was known as a nice guy who was willing to go to bat for them in matters concerning their work routine when Johnson was sheriff. In view of his success in getting favors for his subordinates under Johnson, Langley thought he'd be able to do the same thing under Sheriff Dexter. The men he consulted had little reason to believe that they would not be assigned to the new tasks they wanted.

When the transition finally occurred and the new jobs were posted with the names of new appointees and the reassignments on a bulletin board outside of Sheriff Dexter's office, there was some discontentment expressed by most of the deputies and administrative staff about their reassignments and new positions. But the greatest amount of anger was among the deputies previously under Al Langley, who was reassigned to the records division. None of his men received the assignments they had requested. In fact, many of them were shuttled to graveyard duty, which they considered a demotion. When confronted with this announcement and these reassignments, Langley told his deputies, "Look, I've got to do what I'm told like everyone else around here. I'm sorry you didn't get what you wanted, but I did my best. Hey, I didn't get the job I wanted either." Group morale among these deputies sank to an all-time low, particularly when Langley's deputies conversed with deputies in other divisions and departments. These other deputies advised Langley's officers that they had absolutely no say in their subsequent reassignments, but these deputies and supervisory staff seemed more content with the changes Dexter had made.

Questions for Discussion

1. Under what circumstances should subordinates be allowed to participate in decisions affecting their work? Do you think Al Langley acted in accordance with the new sheriff's expectations when he invited the men to express a job preference following the department reorganization? Why or why not? Explain.

2. What are some potential implications of Langley's behavior for his men's attitudes toward their work and toward the BCSD? Elaborate.

3. Langley believed that because he involved the men the way he did, they would respect him more for caring about their personal desires and work aspirations. What general principles can be learned from his behavior under the existing circumstances and in view of the reactions of his subordinates?

4. What interpersonal and individual variables seem most important in the analysis of this scenario? Why?

5. Some persons endorse a seniority system for assigning new jobs to persons undergoing changes in the workplace. In effect, this means that those persons with the most months or years of experience with the department should get the first choice of new jobs. Other persons believe that the new jobs should be assigned on the basis of individual merit, technical competence, and expert qualifications consistent with the bureaucratic model. How do you think that new job assignments should have been made in this company? Defend the method of job selection you have described.

LEADERSHIP IN ORGANIZATIONS

KEY TERMS

Achievement-oriented leadership

Alienative involvement

Authority

Calculative involvement

Chains of command

Charismatic authority

Coercive power

Contingency theory

Delegating style

Directed leadership

Distributed leadership

Employee-maturity theory

Expert power

Flat organizational structure

Great man approach

Horizontal differentiation

Influence

Leader in a particular situation

Leadership

Leadership behavior

Leadership styles

Learned leadership

Legal-rational authority

Legitimate authority

Legitimate power

Moral involvement

Multiple leadership

Normative power

Participating style

Participative leadership

Path-goal theory

Power

Referent power

Remunerative power

Reward power

Selling style

Supportive leadership

Tall organizational structure

Telling style

Traditional authority

Trait approach

Vertical differentiation

CHAPTER OBJECTIVES

The following objectives are intended:

1. To describe and differentiate between power and authority

2. To present three different power schemes, including Max Weber's legitimate types of authority, French and Raven's bases of social power, and Amitai Etzioni's compliance-involvement typology

3. To describe different organizational, interpersonal, and individual variables that impact superior-subordinate relations in various ways

4. To describe five different modes of leadership in organizations, including the great man theory, leadership styles, leadership that can be learned, situational leadership, and multiple or distributed leadership

INTRODUCTION

All organizations, regardless of their size and shape, have patterns of authority that specify functional interrelations between superiors and subordinates. At various authority levels or plateaus in organizations are managers, supervisors, group leaders, work coordinators, bosses, and crew chiefs. Although the list of formal titles by which such persons are designated is vast, at least one common characteristic applies to all persons who perform these roles. This characteristic is the exercise of power, decision making, or influence over the behaviors of lower-level participants in the organization. Those in positions of power can obtain the compliance of subordinates for almost any work-related task.

In any organization, some people give behavioral commands and others receive behavioral commands. Persons in positions of exercising control over others may themselves be subject to orders from persons above them in any hierarchy of authority. Almost always some degree of reciprocal initiation extends from a lower position to a higher one. In any authority relation, the direction of initiating orders is typically from a higher position to a lower one more often than from a lower position to a higher one. Therefore, any organization may be characterized as a pattern of authority relations between individuals at the same or different levels of supervision.

Considerable variation exists among organizations regarding their size, shape, and complexity. On paper, at least, different authority patterns often characterize organizations that perform similar functions (e.g., automobile manufacturing plants, National Guard units, hospitals, legal aid clinics, insurance companies, police departments, and penal institutions). But each position in an organization, whatever it may be, is linked with all other positions. These links are known as **chains of command** and are easily illustrated by the hierarchical relations that exist between different ranks or authority levels in military organizations (e.g., general, colonel, major, captain, lieutenant, sergeant, and private).

The degree to which a formal superior-subordinate arrangement can be maintained in an organization is contingent to a great degree on the nature and severity of sanctions (rewards and punishments) that superiors are capable of imposing. No doubt such variables as organizational size and age contribute substantially to and modify authority arrangements. For instance, a small office of 15 employees would differ in the degree of formality between work roles compared with the superior-subordinate relations in an IBM subsidiary organization of 500 employees. Also, persons who have been with the organization for many years or since its inception, regardless of their rank or position at a later point in time, may believe that they are entitled to violate or bend existing rules governing relations between superiors and subordinates because of their real or imagined personal relationship with the company president or some other high-level figure.

The interests of many organizational researchers regarding authority structures have been twofold: The major focus of attention has been on the impact of general organizational structure (e.g., authority relations, levels of supervision, communication channels) on organizational effectiveness, flexibility, adaptability to change and innovation, and climate; and a second major interest area has been the analysis of the impact of organizational structure on status relations (e.g., relations between superiors and subordinates and among individuals at the same authority levels), styles of supervision and leadership styles, the performance and productivity of employees, and job satisfaction, among other variables.

This chapter begins by describing power and authority. Power is the ability to influence others, whereas authority is vested in persons appointed or selected to perform particular work roles. Several power schemes have been created and described. The work of Max Weber, who developed bureaucratic theory, includes a description of three types of legitimate authority. Weber described charismatic authority, in which particular individuals seemingly have social magnetism or the ability to cause others to follow them because of their greatness. Weber also described traditional authority, which is most evident in fealty and parent-child relations. The third type of legitimate authority described by Weber is legal-rational authority, which he has related to his depiction of bureaucracy. Legal-rational authority adheres in the abstract rules that persons in a bureaucracy are obligated to follow. Legal-rational authority is most evident in governmental appointments and elections, situations in which persons in positions of leadership are vested with the authority to lead or command others (Weber, 1947). Several implications of these types of legitimate authority will be described.

Another power scheme was devised by French and Raven (1959). These researchers emulated the work of Weber to some extent, since their power scheme has several types of power that overlap

Weber's legitimate authority types. For instance, French and Raven described referent power, which closely resembles Weber's depiction of charismatic authority. French and Raven also described expert and legitimate power, which closely resemble legal-rational and traditional authority. But they added two other power dimensions to their scheme. They described reward power and coercive power to denote the ability of superiors to bestow favors on or punish subordinates for their conformity with or deviation from commands. Various implications of each of these power types for organizational personnel are considered in this chapter.

A third power scheme has been described by Amitai Etzioni (1961). This scheme has already been presented as an organizational typology, although it is based on relations between superiors and subordinates in any organization. Etzioni's power scheme is unique in that he speculates about various types of involvement from among the lower-level participants in the organization, or frontline employees. Therefore, his compliance-involvement scheme is used to explain not only why employees comply with directives from higher-ups, but also, the scheme explains some of their behaviors in reaction to being supervised in various ways.

In this chapter we also examine different factors that influence superior-subordinate relations. Factors discussed include organizational size and complexity, the number of supervisory levels, the numbers of persons supervised by any particular supervisor, and organizational technology and change.

Supervisory behavior also may be viewed as leadership behavior. Several theories of leadership have been advanced in criminal justice administration and related fields. The general idea behind these theories is that if certain types of leadership are exercised, then a particular social climate will be created. This social climate will affect individual and group behaviors in various ways. Thus, leadership is viewed as significant in determining the effectiveness of individuals and work groups. Several theories of leadership are examined, including the great man theory, the leader in a particular situation, leadership behavior that can be learned, styles of leadership, and multiple or distributed leadership. Each of these types of leadership is described and explained. The chapter concludes with a retrospective view of how leadership influences employees in various ways, and how leadership itself is impacted by different types of organizations and situations.

POWER IN ORGANIZATIONS

Generally, **power** is the ability of persons to influence other persons to carry out their orders (Parsons, 1951:121). "Ability" is distinguished from the "right" to manage, which adheres in the **authority** vested in particular persons by organizations as the result of their role performance. Both power and authority are types of **influence,** which refers to the capability of modifying one's beliefs and behaviors. Many organizational variables, including interpersonal and individual ones, are linked to power hierarchies in all organizations. Organizational effectiveness is frequently attributed in part to the nature of power relations between various positions within organizations. Likewise, labor turnover, job satisfaction, productivity, group morale, and organizational change are believed to be influenced by the organizational power dimension.

Power is most visible in the behavior of supervisory and managerial personnel in any organization. Supervision over the work of others is a type of power relation. Managerial control over production divisions in a company is also indicative of power relations. In police departments, for instance, the military model is followed closely. Police officer subordinates are under the command and control of higher-ranking officers. These power relations are pervasive throughout organizations, whether we are examining the Illinois State Police, the Royal Canadian Mounted Police, prosecutors and judges, or correctional officers and wardens or superintendents in prisons (Falcone, 1998; Gill, 1998; Hepburn, 1985).

The exercise of power by an individual in an organization is affected by several important factors. Organizational structure may impose constraints on persons who exert power over subordinates. The number of persons over whom one exercises power (e.g., the span of control and whether it is wide or narrow) causes persons in positions of power to modify their modes of supervisory behavior. Logically it can be assumed that someone who supervises 50 subordinates cannot behave toward each of them in the same way that he or she might behave if there were only two or three persons under his or her immediate control. As the number of persons supervised increases, the time a supervisor can devote to directing or criticizing the actions of any specific employee decreases.

Another factor that influences the power exerted by superiors in organizations is one's personality system. A study of gypsum miners shows how subordinate behaviors might change in response to changes in supervisors (Gouldner, 1954). A change in manager-ship in a gypsum mine from the former manager (who in the judgment of other workers was very permissive regarding rule violations) to the new manager (a person who went by the book and was regarded by others as a strict disciplinarian) caused workers to change their attitudes about their work and how they were supervised. One supervisor directly under the new manager's control expressed the general sentiments of his workers by saying, "Vincent [the new manager] is a stickler for running the plant according to the main office. Vincent says that if that's the way they want it, that's the way they get it" (Gouldner, 1954).

Supervisory or managerial behavior is influenced by many factors. A reciprocal relation also exists between that which is affected and that which affects. For instance, organizational structure, the number of subordinates, and personality differentially contribute to the nature of power exercised by a supervisor or manager. At the same time, the supervisory or managerial behavior elicited by these factors affects several crucial organizational variables, including structure, goal attainment, effectiveness, and change.

The Texas Department of Criminal Justice is an example of a large-scale organization that has experienced various reforms and changes, both in its operations and in its mode of managerial control. There are several reasons for these reforms, most of which have resulted from court decrees related to prison overcrowding and insufficient legal services. Inadequate law libraries and legal assistance, a rise in lawsuits stemming from correctional officer-inmate encounters that have resulted in damages and injuries, and a host of other legal claims have caused federal court intervention so that required reforms have been implemented. In the postreform period of Texas prison system reorganization, several major changes have occurred. First, the Texas prison system has become more formalized and centralized. Increased formalization and centralization have been facilitated by the introduction of advanced information processing technologies. Advanced technologies have enabled upper-level prison administrators to centralize decision-making information and then rapidly disseminate that information to prison wardens in the form of preprogrammed decision-making parameters that govern unit-level decisions. Despite increased uncertainty and new fiscal constraints produced by the prison system environment, the Texas prison system has continued to achieve its goals, which have been articulated by several court-ordered reforms (Gorton, 1997).

Before we examine the interplay among authority, power, and organizational structure, several popular classification schemes are described that differentiate the various kinds of power used by management and supervisory personnel at virtually any level within the organizational hierarchy.

SOME POWER CLASSIFICATION SCHEMES

Three power schemes are presented here. In large part, their selection for inclusion is based on their relevance to the origin and development of authority patterns in organizations, their usefulness and explanatory utility relating to organizational behavior, and the frequency with which they are cited in contemporary organizational literature. The schemes presented include (1) Weber's legitimate authority types, (2) French and Raven's bases of social power, and (3) Etzioni's compliance-involvement typology.

Weber's Legitimate Authority Types

Max Weber (1947) has described three types of **legitimate authority** found in all social aggregates. These authority types have established the standard for subsequent authority and power classification schemes. Weber said that legitimate authority has three distinct roots: (1) charismatic, (2) traditional, and (3) legal-rational.

CHARISMATIC AUTHORITY. **Charismatic authority** adheres in the relation of a leader to followers in which the leader possesses the gift of grace or is perceived as having a divine gift. Persons such as Alexander the Great and Napoleon are said to have possessed charismatic authority or charisma. Their commands to subordinates were typically obeyed without question. Followers conformed to a degree paralleling religious zeal or sacred devotion. The inability of social scientists to measure charisma as an indicator of a specific authority pattern has caused this phenomenon to become almost unusable for explaining superior-subordinate relations in organizations.

Nevertheless, in different areas of criminal justice such as policing, some personalities have been considered powerful entities in their own right, perhaps emulating some of the characteristics of charismatic leaders. For instance, during the late 1970s and 1980s, the Los Angeles Police Department was headed by Daryl Gates, a dynamic leader who molded the LAPD according to his own personal style of operation. In the

1990s, Gates resigned in the aftermath of the Rodney King beating, which involved several of his LAPD officers who were subsequently convicted in federal court of violating King's civil rights. Another police chief replaced Gates but was never considered his charismatic equal in reshaping the LAPD and its public image. In the early 2000s, Gates continued to influence LAPD policies with his own radio program in the Los Angeles area. His personal attraction to different community groups has made him a highly desired speaker and fund-raiser. Some would say that Gates has charisma. Police chiefs in general have inspired some writers to characterize them as pivotal entities or important institutional actors at the nexus of police tradition and antagonistic external interests. Historical antecedents to Gates include **O.W. Wilson** and **August Vollmer,** chiefs of police in other cities. They had a dramatic impact on shaping the nature of policing as we know it today. Some of their contributions are noted in Chapter 9. More or less influential individually, police chiefs are primary reference points for organizing the complex processes by which the principles of police legitimacy and models of their expression are constructed socially (Hunt and Magenau, 1993).

In the U.S. Supreme Court, several chief justices, such as Earl Warren, Warren Burger, and William Rhenquist, have achieved a degree of charismatic notoriety with some of the legal decisions they have supported. The Warren court is known for making several important decisions that have seemingly limited the scope of police authority. By the same token, the Burger and Rhenquist courts have become known for expanding police powers. Some people would consider these persons to be charismatic leaders.

TRADITIONAL AUTHORITY. **Traditional authority** is evident in kinship systems in which the rules of descent are patrilineal; that is, the rights of the father at the time of his death pass on to the oldest male child. Kingdoms are usually structured around traditional authority, and power over others is passed on to the next person of royalty in line. Persons living in such social systems support this pattern of authority primarily out of custom or tradition. Some organizations, particularly smaller ones, exhibit characteristics of traditional authority in the same sense. It is expected that the president's (or owner's) son will assume his father's duties when the time comes that the father is unable to discharge them, usually through death, disablement, or retirement.

Despite their bureaucratic and military-like organization and operation, police departments exhibit some amount of traditional authority. Early in their academy training, many new recruits learn that "by the book" procedures and "street justice" are quite different legally. Instructors and field training officers have been known to convey both formal and informal guidelines for on-the-spot decision making in life-threatening situations between police officers and crime perpetrators (Champion and Rush, 1996; Ross, 1993). Furthermore, some officers may lack formal rank but have extensive time in grade as line officers. Younger officers may look to these traditional figures as leaders rather than to less-experienced but higher-ranking officers. Even police corruption may stem from traditional organization of policing in which some amount of police deviance is tolerated and even expected (Sherman, 1974).

LEGAL-RATIONAL AUTHORITY. **Legal-rational authority** is best illustrated by referring to bureaucratic organizations. The authority of superiors in bureaucracies is legitimized by systems of abstract rules and norms. Rights are bestowed on individuals within an authority hierarchy by persons at a higher level and by rules that govern the particular position or role. Governments are run by persons who are elected or appointed, and the positions they hold entitle them to exercise authority over their subordinates.

Law enforcement agencies such as police departments and sheriff's offices operate on the principle of legal-rational authority. There are jurisdictional boundaries to which each department's authority extends. Certainly the legal-rational form of authority defined by Weber is characteristic of most large-scale organizations in contemporary society. Almost every large business or industrial firm, service institution, or philanthropic organization possesses the legal-rational authority pattern described here. Most of these organizations are rationally conceived, have a hierarchical authority arrangement or chain of command, and have explicit rules and norms that govern all roles and interrole relations.

French and Raven's Bases of Social Power

Five different kinds of power have been identified that are present under different interpersonal conditions (French and Raven, 1959). A resulting power scheme fits the perspective of the subordinate toward some superior in an authority relation. The scheme is presented independent of any specific kind of organization, although it will be apparent that several logical connections can be found between the different kinds of power defined and various organizational types. Also, although the power types presented here are arranged so as to appear independent of one another for purposes of conceptual distinctions, it should be apparent that persons in authority positions possess the potential for applying several types of power simultaneously in relation to subordinates. Therefore, the distinctions made do not necessarily rule out the combination of power types in hierarchical relations.

REWARD POWER. According to French and Raven (1959), persons in authority over others are in positions to reward them. Such rewards may include promotions, verbal praise for work well done, more release time for leisure activities off the job without a pay cut, special favors such as relaxing certain rules in the work setting, assignment of easy jobs to perform, and salary increases. Depending on the kind of organization under discussion, rewards may come in many forms. If we were examining the **reward power** of corrections officers in prisons, we might define rewards as overlooking violations of rules such as those prohibiting smoking or providing candy, cigarettes, liquor, and other items to prisoners. Reward power is based on the ability of superiors in a superior-subordinate relation to administer positive valences and to remove or decrease negative valences.

COERCIVE POWER. The ability to administer negative valences or remove or decrease positive valences is defined as the **coercive power** of the superior. In the military, the raw recruit is subject to considerable harassment from noncommissioned officers in boot camp or during the initial training and orientation period.

Supervisors and managers in companies can conveniently overlook an employee for promotion or transfer to a better-paying job if he or she does not dress or behave in a manner that is consistent with the company image. In periods of low employment, when jobs are scarce, rumors circulate about mistreatment of employees by supervisory personnel. The rationale is that the subordinates put up with verbal (and sometimes physical) abuse because of the difficulty in trying to get another job elsewhere.

In prisons, punishments are explicit for particular violations of rules. Visitation privileges may be withdrawn for a prolonged period, or the prisoner may be assigned difficult and unpleasant tasks (e.g., cleaning toilets and handling garbage). The military institution, not altogether dissimilar from the prison, possesses similar types of punishment for those who do not obey the rules. The threat of confinement in brigs, stockades, and other lockups is held over the heads of all recruits as a form of coercion. And the military has many unpleasant jobs to assign stubborn subordinates as well. One of the most severe forms of punishment in the military, apart from being placed in a military prison for disorderly conduct for a specified period, is the dishonorable discharge. Such a discharge will follow the person for the rest of his or her life, exerting a profound impact on their chances for employment and promotion.

EXPERT POWER. **Expert power** is contingent on the amount of knowledge or expertise a superior has (or is believed to have by subordinates). It has often been said that knowledge is power. There is a great deal of support for this statement in the organizational literature. Airlines pilots must master numerous instruments and controls in order to fly aircraft safely. Orders from a pilot to a copilot or other subordinate during a crisis or at any other time during a flight would likely be obeyed without question. Expert power is operating in this instance. The expertise of the pilot is sufficient to bestow on him or her much confidence from subordinates.

REFERENT POWER. **Referent power** is based on the degree of friendship felt by the subordinate toward the superior. Essentially, the subordinate says implicitly, "I will do what you tell me to do because of my friendship with you." A supervisor in one division of an industrial firm may come to the aid of another supervisor in another division because of friendship. This type of power is largely informal and implicit in any superior-subordinate relation.

LEGITIMATE POWER. **Legitimate power** is based on the subordinate's belief that the superior has the right to give orders. Again, we can turn to the military organization for an example. It is an integral feature of the chain of command (i.e., the hierarchy of authority) in any military organization that higher-ranking officers have the right to give commands to any lower-ranking officer. There are exceptions, such as when a lower-ranking officer is given temporary authority by someone who outranks the higher-ranking officer present in the situation. A police officer's command to a crowd to disperse is considered the officer's right and obligation, and such an act is a form of legitimate power, even though some members of the crowd may believe that such an act is coercive, harassing, or in some other way illegitimate behavior.

Some research involving French and Raven's power typology has investigated the implications of using various types of power to elicit compliance from subordinates in different work settings. One of the better studies was conducted by Luthans (1985). Luthans investigated the use of power in various police agencies. He found that whenever coercive power was exercised by administrators or supervisors, subordinates tended to resist change more and had greater dislike for their bosses. As reward power was de-emphasized and used less as a means of affecting officer performance, greater use of coercive power occurred. Furthermore, whenever the use of coercive power intensified, there was greater officer conformity and compliance, although subordinate officers felt greater fear and more frustration with their jobs as well as toward their immediate supervisors. Coercive power use by superiors also tended to induce subordinates to assign blame and punish others for their own mistakes. Actually, the prolonged use of coercive power seemed to cause subordinates to seek revenge against their superiors in various ways.

The most successful types of power in police settings were expert, referent, and legitimate power. These types of power tended to induce a high degree of confidence and trust among subordinates. Reward power was quite influential for subordinates, although their ideas of rewards differed from the perceptions of rewards from superiors. For instance, pay and promotion often were used by management to induce compliance from subordinates, although many subordinates believed they were entitled to increased pay and promotion anyway. Thus, these tangible rewards did not have the desired effect. Other types of less tangible rewards (e.g., remarks from superiors about work well done or administrative support for officers accused of misconduct by citizens) had greater long-term value for improving officer attitudes toward their work and job satisfaction generally (Luthans, 1985:447–458).

Different types of settings (e.g., police agencies, the courtroom, and correctional institutions) do not lend themselves easily to analyses of which types of power are most effective for inducing certain types of compliance. The most successful administrators have learned to adapt to the environmental conditions and strategically apply the type of power that seems most appropriate under the circumstances. Whenever drastic and immediate actions are expected of subordinates, for instance, leaders cannot merely say, "If you do this, we will reward you." Or, "Do this because you like me." Or, "Do this because if you don't, we will fire you." If a correctional institution is being attacked from within by an inmate riot, for instance, subordinates swing into action because of necessity and their training in response to such situations. Sometimes they act in the interests of self-preservation, and whatever supervisors say or do is irrelevant to the immediate actions taken.

Apart from the different factors that influence power and how it is exercised in work settings, an important consideration for managers is what type of involvement they desire or expect from their subordinates. Amitai Etzioni dealt with this type of scenario in his compliance-involvement typology.

Etzioni's Compliance-Involvement Typology

Earlier, Etzioni's compliance-involvement power scheme was introduced as an organizational typology. Etzioni (1961) described three forms of power found in organizations: (1) coercive power, (2) **remunerative power,** and (3) **normative power.** These closely resemble three types of power identified by French and Raven: coercive, reward, and legitimate power. In addition to differentiating between these three types, Etzioni went one step further and postulated that subordinates would become involved in their work activity consistent with the type of power exercised over them. Thus, he described **alienative involvement,** in which persons would become resentful and object to being coerced by superiors to behave in particular ways. **Calculative involvement** was described as the belief a subordinate possessed that if he or she went along with whatever the superior wanted, then rewards of various kinds would be forthcoming (e.g., better working hours, higher pay, better job evaluations). **Moral involvement** would occur if people believed that the power exerted over them was proper and legitimate; therefore, compliance would be motivated by a concern for the moral sense arising from the superior-subordinate relation. Etzioni suggested the following power-involvement associations, which would be congruent with types of power distinguished: (1) coercive-alienative, (2) remunerative-calculative, and (3) normative-moral.

In his discussion of power-involvement congruences, Etzioni used as an example of the first type of power the prison inmate who becomes alienated from the coercive prison organization. Congruencies for the other types might be a salesperson who works harder to make more money and to be promoted more quickly than other salespersons in the organization as an example of remunerative-calculative power, and the political party member who has a high degree of commitment to the party and therefore feels a moral obligation to donate money and time for the ultimate benefit of the party as an example of normative-moral power.

All organizations have hierarchies of authority that involve interactions between subordinates and superiors. The nature and type of interaction between each level of the hierarchy may be prescribed in detail by predetermined organizational rules, such as a highly bureaucratized setting. To some extent, however, the type of organizational arrangement between any pair of levels in the organization may be modified by the personality systems of the respective role occupants, the number of subordinates under any single individual's direct control, interpersonal friendships, built-in control devices such as closed-circuit television cameras that scan entire departments or divisions and are monitored by rule-conscious managerial personnel, and the flexibility of the organization itself.

Theoretically at least, persons react differently according to the various kinds of powder exerted over them. If we accept the assumption that an organization is vitally interested in achieving its goals, remaining competitive, and being effective, then we must also view the nature of authority of managerial personnel as a prime contributor to the success of achieving these organizational aims. In Weber's view, the organization is successful, in part, to the extent that persons within the organization are capable of performing, and in fact do perform, their functions successfully. The concerted action of participants at all levels within the organization, provided that each person functions optimally in the position held, will by implication enable the organization to achieve its goals (Weber, 1947).

What we are discussing is human motivational factors in an organization. What kinds of inputs will motivate individuals to maximize their role performance? The reasoning is as follows: If a particular kind of power is exercised over subordinates, predictable employee behaviors will emerge. Etzioni's compliance-involvement scheme is an excellent example of such thinking. Predictable or congruent behaviors will follow as the result of applying a particular type of power to obtain compliance of subordinates. However,

Etzioni notes that certain incongruent relations between power and involvement may be observed as well and that these may interfere with the congruent schematic representation of things in organizations.

The relation between power exerted and the type of involvement of subordinates (e.g., the degree and nature of motivation, productivity, and morale) is not a simple one. It cannot be viewed in a vacuum, immune from the other external factors impinging on it and modifying it. Power is important, to be sure, but we must grasp and understand the organizational structure within which power is exercised in order to appreciate fully its significance for enhancing organizational effectiveness. Table 6.1 shows a juxtaposition of the three power/authority schemes devised by Weber, French and Raven, and Etzioni.

FACTORS INFLUENCING SUPERIOR-SUBORDINATE RELATIONS

To a great degree, organizational structure determines the nature of power exercised by managers and supervisors over subordinates. Organizational structure may be seen on paper as a work-flow chart or a pattern of authority relations between all positions. Relationships among all persons in the organization may be clearly defined by explicit rules. In addition to the detailed role definitions provided by an organization, other factors contribute to and affect authority relations between superiors and subordinates. These are organizational size, complexity, levels of supervision, span of control, and technology. Different types of factors impinge on supervisor-subordinate relations and must be considered when attempting to understand what is going on and why.

Organizational size is likely to affect the nature of superior-subordinate relations to the extent that greater formality between positions is found in larger organizations compared with smaller ones. Logically, organizations with more members require greater coordination, although it is not difficult to see how easily such a statement is contradicted by organizations in which many individuals perform the same function (e.g., assembly-line work) and are within the full view of a single supervisor. For instance, an entire floor of accountants working at desks in neat rows can be scrutinized by a supervisor fairly easily, and little or no coordination is required among the individual accountants on that particular floor.

TABLE 6.1   A COMPARISON OF THE POWER SCHEMES OF WEBER, FRENCH AND RAVEN, AND ETZIONI

TYPES OF POWER OR AUTHORITY[a]		
WEBER	**FRENCH AND RAVEN**	**ETZIONI**
Charismatic <-------------------------------------->	Referent	
Traditional <-------------------------------------->	Legitimate <-------------------------------------->	Normative
Legal-Rational <-------------------------------------->	Expert	
	Reward <-------------------------------------->	Remunerative
	Coercive <-------------------------------------->	Coercive

[a]The arrows in the table reflect only similarities among the three schemes. They are not intended to portray the influence of one scheme on another. The emergence of three separate yet similar power schemes lends credence to the previously postulated continuity of authority structures in organizations. Certainly such similarities among these classifications mutually validate one another in a sense.

Source: Compiled by author.

In order to make our statement of relation between size and the nature of power relations more plausible, we need to introduce the variable of complexity. Complexity may be defined as the number of different functions an organization performs, regardless of its size. Suppose we have a relatively large organization and furthermore that it is considerably complex, compared with other organizations of the same type. Greater complexity within an organization does require greater coordination among operational units or divisions, and it is very likely that supervisor-subordinate and even supervisor-supervisor interactions will be affected accordingly. One implication of such an arrangement is possible increased formality and adherence to rules on the part of all individuals involved.

Some disagreement exists concerning the relation between flat and tall organizational structures and organizational effectiveness and goal attainment. Flat organizational structures are organizations with few levels of authority, whereas tall organizational structures have many authority levels. A study was conducted of several simulated organizations in which the numbers of supervisory levels were manipulated and varied (Carzo and Yanouzas, 1969). Students at Pennsylvania State University were randomly assigned to two different types of organizations. With 15 work roles assigned to the students in each scenario, one organizational arrangement consisted of four levels of authority, whereas the other organizational arrangement had two levels of authority. Students simulated organizational members and supervisors who were assigned a market-

ing problem. A president was designated to make the overall decision about how the problem should be resolved in each organization, but subordinates at the different levels of authority had input about which problem solutions were best. Those students working under the **tall organizational structure** showed significantly better performance than those students working under the **flat organizational structure.** This result was explained by the fact that the tall structure, with greater numbers of supervisory levels, allowed group members to evaluate decisions more frequently, and that the narrow span of supervision provided for a more orderly decision process (Carzo and Yanouzas, 1969:190–191).

A subsequent study examined 254 government agencies and dealt directly with the problems of authority structure, supervisory practices, and organizational effectiveness (Meyer, 1972). The following hypotheses were tested:

1. Large organizations have more intermediate levels of hierarchy than small ones.
2. Spans of control are quite narrow at intermediate levels.
3. Intermediate supervisors spend considerably more time supervising than first-line supervisors.
4. **Vertical differentiation,** the proliferation of supervisory levels in an organization, is associated with decentralization of authority to make decisions.

5. **Horizontal differentiation,** the proliferation of subunits, is associated with centralization of decision-making authority.

6. Vertical differentiation is associated with formal rules and with rules that partly determine decisions in advance.

Support for each of these hypotheses can be found in Meyer's research, although Meyer said that relationships among variables describing organizations are rarely simple. If there is a general pattern, then it is that variations in organizational structure have multiple and inconsistent effects. The direct effect of increased size is to promote economies of supervision, but the indirect effect is to decrease such economies because of added intermediate supervisory levels. Vertical differentiation leads simultaneously to decentralization and rules that largely determine decisions in advance. Horizontal differentiation has just the opposite effects (Meyer, 1972:104).

In addition to these variables that affect authority relations, we must consider the significant impact of changing organizational technology, or ways of getting things done (whether these changes involve material devices for reducing physical labor in the work setting or simply new ideas about rearranging and processing things).

In the prison setting, the power relation between inmates and correctional officers has been affected according to how administrators have configured inmate involvement in decision making and institutional governance. The Huron Valley Men's Facility at Ypsilanti, Michigan, at one time represented the state of the art concerning prison construction and computer technology in the operation and control of prisoners. Inmates themselves objected to and resisted the coercive control over them exercised by upper-level administration, however. The inmate society was a powerful entity that challenged the prison's formal administration. It was found that greater social stability and control of the prison environment could be accomplished if a more legitimate form of power were utilized by administrators and correctional officers, and if inmate bodies could be included in some of the governance decisions and general decision-making processes of the prison (Stojkovic, 1984).

Organizations are dynamic entities. They are often improving the quality of the product, service, or whatever commodity they distribute. These changes may be defined as changes in technology. Changes in technology not only affect power linkages between supervisors and subordinates, but they often affect the spatial arrangements of personnel. New information-processing systems may enable the organization to make more information available to fewer persons in the higher echelons of the organization. This centralization tends to minimize the effectiveness and decision-making power of middle-level supervisory personnel, not only in terms of organizational function but in the eyes of subordinates as well.

MODES OF LEADERSHIP BEHAVIOR IN ORGANIZATIONS

An organization's effectiveness, climate, and ability to attain goals are influenced by many things. We have already examined various schemes of authority to describe the interaction between organizational structure and manifestations of power in different supervisor-subordinate contexts. Closely related to power characteristics of supervisors and managers is **leadership behavior.**

Leadership in organizations has received considerable attention from theorists and practitioners (e.g., change agents, consultants, organizational researchers). Most of the empirical studies of this aspect of organizations have focused on the impact of various kinds of leadership behavior on motivation, morale, and the work performance of individuals or groups. The findings vary according to the setting studied, including the socioeconomic, personal, and interpersonal attributes of the study targets. In this section, several notions of leadership will be examined. Each notion of leadership is projected into a cause-effect relation such as the following:

Leadership behavior $X \rightarrow$ elicits $\rightarrow$ Social climate X

Then

Social climate $X \rightarrow$ elicits $\rightarrow$ Individual/group behavior X

Five notions of leadership described here include (1) the leader as a great man, (2) the leader in a particular situation, (3) leadership behavior that can be learned, (4) styles of leadership, and (5) multiple leaders who fulfill several organizational functions.

The Notion of the "Great Man"

The **great man approach** to leadership asserts that to become a leader, one must possess certain genetic qualities of leadership. This has been termed the **trait**

BOX 6.1 PERSONALITY HIGHLIGHT

WARREN R. EMMER
Director, Field Services Division, Department of Corrections and Rehabilitation

Statistics: B.S.S.W., University of Wisconsin–Milwaukee; Juvenile Officers' Institute, University of Minnesota

Background: I was born in Milwaukee, Wisconsin. I received an undergraduate degree from the School of Social Welfare at the University of Wisconsin–Milwaukee in 1976. I received further training at the University of Minnesota in their Juvenile Officers' Institute in 1977. Since that time, I have accumulated over 3,000 hours of in-service training. I am also a licensed police officer and social worker in North Dakota.

Work Experience: I began employment in my career field in 1976 when I obtained the job of police liaison officer for the Turtle Mountain band of Chippewa in Belcourt, North Dakota. I worked there for three years servicing problem youth as an employee with the Law and Order Police Agency. In 1979, I was hired as a parole officer by North Dakota and was stationed in Dickinson. In 1981, I became the district supervisor of the Dickinson district office. In 1985, I became the regional supervisor for offices located in Minot, Dickinson, and Williston. In 1990, I was promoted to the position of director of the Parole and Probation Division. In 1998, I became the director of the Department of Corrections, Field Services Division, which not only included the former duties of parole and probation director but also the responsibilities of managing community-placed inmates in the community. Our staff size is about 75 full-time employees and we have a budget of $14 million.

Advice to Students: I moved into this career field because of a desire to help people. I think it is important that anyone interested in working with parole/probation or the corrections field should first have a desire to help other people. It is useful for anyone interested in this field also to work as an intern for a considerable length of time within a corrections agency. Moreover, I think degrees in criminal justice, behavioral science, and/or social work are very beneficial to someone interested in obtaining employment in this field. Our agency is committed to helping people get into this career field. We are willing to assist them in obtaining the appropriate internships to accomplish this goal. I would say that I am now in the middle to late portion of my career, and I have no regrets about my career choice. I still am motivated by a strong desire to help other people.

approach to leadership behavior (Lippitt, 1955). Leaders possess certain traits, and people either have these leadership characteristics or do not have them. It is assumed that such characteristics cannot be transmitted or acquired through learning or specialized training. Although this view is currently regarded as archaic, we still hear about born leaders on occasion. From the standpoint of genetics, there is little support for the idea that leadership qualities are inherent in a person at birth and are destined to emerge at a later date, presumably in adulthood. In some respects, this great man notion parallels Weber's idea of charisma and charismatic leadership.

Great person or trait theories have not been particularly useful in accounting for why some persons are good leaders and others are not. One of the more extensive investigations of leadership traits was conducted by Stogdill (1974), who identified the following traits associated with leadership: (1) good communication skills, (2) decisiveness, (3) persistence, (4) integrity, (5) supportiveness, (6) self-confidence, (7) sincerity, (8) industriousness, (9) flexibility, (10) good interpersonal skills, (11) intuition, (12) intelligence, (13) responsibility, (14) vision, (15) emotional control, and (16) motivation. Many of these traits seem to be to be a function of one's social environment, experience, and training, and thus, some question arises as to whether they are actually in-born traits or learned characteristics. Certainly we can understand in each case why the identified trait might be valuable to someone in a position of leadership.

Subsequent research by others in diverse work settings seems to endorse some or all of the characteristics identified by Stogdill. For instance, Bass (1981) replicated the work of Stogdill and studied leaders under different circumstances. He found that leaders are self-confident, accept responsibility, complete tasks, pursue goals aggressively, deal with interpersonal stresses effectively and have a high tolerance for frustration, take the initiative, demonstrate originality and influence over others, and are good organizers. Another researcher, Stamper (1992), found that leaders are good communicators and organizers, tell the truth and accept responsibility for their own actions, have empathy for others and are good role models and example setters for others who pursue organizational goals, and are aware of their own strengths and weaknesses.

An ambitious study of 2,615 supervisors in different businesses and industries throughout the United States conducted in the late 1980s also found that leaders tended to share the following characteristics: (1) have an ability to motivate others to change and improve, (2) have the vision to perceive others' expectations and needs and encourage participation by subordinates in decisions affecting their work, (3) are role models who recognize both team and individual contributions, and (4) establish trust by collaborating with others and sharing information and power with them (Kouzes and Posner, 1987).

Attempts to investigate leadership traits in criminal justice settings have been inconsistent, such as situations in which some researchers have discovered differences among men and women who possess different sets of previously identified traits. For example, an early study of police administrators by Barbara Price (1974) showed that female police executives seemed to possess more leadership traits than their male counterparts. Women were more likely to be aggressive and self-confident, independent, and intellectually aggressive. However, subsequent research has shown that male and female police chiefs and other police executives and supervisors do not differ substantially on certain leadership traits. A study of 1,665 police chiefs was conducted in 1977 by the National Advisory Commission on Criminal Justice Standards and Goals. The most successful police chiefs had greater ability to communicate with their subordinates effectively. They had greater organizational skills and could develop priorities and organizational objectives. They had good public relations skills and could relate well with community leaders in the development of police-community programs. Further, they were able to improve officer morale and improve general officer effectiveness. Gender differences on these characteristics or traits were not apparent.

The Leader in a Particular Situation

A more plausible explanation of leadership behavior is the concept of the **leader in a particular situation** rather than leadership derived from personal qualities (Standing Bear, 1986). Under certain conditions or situations, persons who lack the inborn qualities of leadership have risen to take command of situations when others (supposedly in possession of such qualities) have failed to do so. Panel members of a jury have been influenced significantly by the logic and cool thinking of persons who, under other circumstances, would be regarded as having little or no influence on anyone. Senior board members of large corporations have been swayed in the direction of opinions expressed by junior board members who happen to have the skills and useful ideas that help to minimize or eliminate certain problems at hand. Under other conditions, junior board members would be considered by almost anyone else as having little or nothing significant to contribute.

In business, industrial, and voluntary organizations, leadership is usually defined by rules and norms. Superior leadership positions are defined and interrelationships among work roles are made explicit by some preestablished pattern. Thus, the situational notion of leadership behavior is not conveniently applicable to such circumstances. It is interesting to note, however, that organizational structure and hierarchies of authority provide avenues for individuals to expose their faults and limitations, especially through promotion.

The situational approach to leadership also has been linked with **contingency theory.** Contingency theory is the view that effective leadership depends on the circumstances and work environment of the leader or administrator. If the work is highly structured and clearly spelled out by rules, such as are specified by the rules of criminal procedure in the courtroom environment, then managers (e.g., judges, court officers, and others) orient themselves toward subordinates in a task-directed fashion. If the work of subordinates is making on-the-spot decisions, even though there are rules to govern subordinate behaviors (e.g., police officers and their interactions with citizens), then managers and administrators may orient themselves toward subordinates in ways that emphasize human relations characteristics. Thus, contingency theory says that the situation governs the type of leadership behavior utilized to gain subordinate compliance.

Contingency theory was advanced originally by Fred Fiedler (1967). Fiedler said that it is easier to change the work environment itself than to change a leader's personality and peculiar methods of leadership. Fiedler said also that organizational leaders can have their authority and responsibilities modified by being given more or less authority and decision-making power or by being assigned to different tasks. Leaders are either task oriented or human relations oriented, depending on organizational requirements. In the probation officer–probationer/client relation, for example, the probation officer is more effective to the extent that he or she develops a sound relationship with each client. Those officers who are rule oriented and enforcement centered seem to be less effective in assisting clients to improve and reduce their rates of recidivism. Correctional officers supervising dangerous inmates are extremely task centered, however, and human relations play a less important role in prison operations. The behavior of an administrator or supervisor is contingent, therefore, on the type of persons to be led and the organizational rules.

Contrasting the great man notion with the situational approach briefly, it seems that there are two distinct issues at odds with one another. The first issue is whether certain traits or abilities are inborn or learned. The second issue is whether any given trait or ability (regardless of its source) almost automatically guarantees leadership regardless of the situation or whether, instead, those traits or abilities or behaviors that are associated with leadership depend on the situation, so that an ability that may result in a person's being chosen or legitimated as a leader in one situation may not have the same result in a different situation (Souryal, 1977).

Leadership Behavior That Can Be Learned

The existence of an ability to internalize various behaviors, to function effectively socially, and to learn different methods of guiding and directing the actions of others has considerable validity, particularly when contrasted with the first two leadership notions pre-

sented earlier. Many works have appeared bearing titles such as *How to Be an Effective Leader* or *The Key to Successful Leadership,* training manuals that specify those characteristics necessary for good leadership (e.g., a good leader must be a good listener, a good follower, a good director, patient, thoughtful, and considerate of the feelings of subordinates). A typical example of this sort of manual is *Training the Supervisor: A Guide on How to Set Up and Conduct a Supervisory Training Program,* published by the U.S. Civil Service Commission. This short monograph contains a checklist questionnaire that has been used in supervisory training (and leadership training as well).

Some researchers have endorsed **learned leadership** (Shanahan, 1978). One analyst lists nine basic leadership skills that are particularly suitable for group discussion situations:

1. The ability to state a problem in such a way that the group does not become defensive but instead approaches the issue in a constructive way

2. The ability to supply essential facts and to clarify the area of freedom without suggesting a solution

3. The ability to draw persons out so that all members will participate

4. The ability to wait out pauses

5. The ability to restate the ideas and feelings expressed accurately but in a more abbreviated, more pointed, and clearer form than when initially expressed by a group member

6. The ability to ask questions that stimulate problem-solving behavior

7. The ability to summarize as the need arises

8. The ability to recognize the need for practicing the skills

9. The ability to deal with deadlock (Maier, 1973:141–142)

It is noted that these skills seem to be essential, although we would contend that persons possessing all of them would be extremely rare. Ideally, such skills would be quite functional for the successful accomplishment of group tasks, particularly if all of them were found in one person.

There is little doubt that programs for developing leadership have been successful in enabling leaders to internalize certain skills and cultivate a better understanding of people. A cursory examination of organizational literature makes it apparent that the quality of leadership at various levels of authority has played a major role in the effectiveness of organizations (Wright et al., 1997). The potential to acquire leadership skills through learning must certainly be counted as a major input affecting organizational behavior.

Styles of Leadership

Some researchers have expressed the belief that supervisors and managers can practice certain **leadership styles.** That is, there are modes of conduct that have been described to emphasize how particular leaders will orient themselves toward subordinates. Leadership styles include laissez-faire, democratic, and autocratic. Under a laissez-faire leadership style, supervisors give their subordinates great latitude in decision making. There is almost no direct input from supervisors concerning what subordinates should do. Under the democratic leadership style, supervisors request subordinate input into decision making. Supervisory decisions are a product of democratic subordinate involvement. Under the autocratic leadership style, supervisors tend to be dictatorial and direct subordinates to do their jobs in particular ways.

Another view of leadership styles emphasizes initiating structure versus showing consideration (Standing Bear, 1986). Supervisors who initiate structure are very much task oriented. They are concerned only with results, and it matters little if subordinates are alienated in the process. Supervisors who show consideration manifest great concern for employee attitudes and involvement in work tasks. The human relations side of management is emphasized, as supervisors attempt to direct subordinates largely on the basis of their feelings and emotional involvement in their work (Goodstein and MacKenzie, 1989).

Initiating structure and showing consideration were two leadership styles described originally by Edwin Fleischman and E.F. Harris in 1962. Fleischman and Harris said that the particular leadership styles they described would be more or less relevant depending on the education and worker independence of subordinates. Less-educated subordinates would require greater initiated structure, whereas more-educated and independent workers might prefer greater consideration from supervisors.

Leadership style has been mistaken for the contingency theory of leadership or situational leadership described earlier. This is because Fred Fiedler used these two leadership styles later but shifted the emphasis from supervisors and their impact on subordinate behavior to subordinate behavior and its impact on supervisory style. Several modifications of Fiedler's work have been presented subsequently. For instance, **path-goal theory** was elaborated by Robert House and T.R. Mitchell (1975). House and Mitchell couched their leadership theory in the context of the goals sought by the organization and the paths by which leaders could most directly influence goal attainment through exercising different styles of leadership over their subordinates. They identified four styles of leadership: **directed leadership, supportive leadership, participative leadership,** and **achievement-oriented leadership.**

Both directed and achievement-oriented leadership are synonymous with Fleischman and Harris's initiating structure and Fiedler's task-oriented leadership. Directed leadership means that leaders spell out exactly what is expected of their subordinates and detail how organizational goals can be achieved by subordinate behaviors. Achievement-oriented leadership involves goal-setting behavior and also reflects task-oriented leadership. Supportive and participative leadership mean greater employee involvement in decision making affecting their work. Administrators consider worker feelings and emotions, together with their knowledge about how to perform the job best. Thus, leaders who practice the supportive leadership style cater to one's emotional needs, whereas those who practice the achievement-oriented leadership style go to a great deal of trouble to acquaint employees with why decisions are made that affect their work and request feedback from these employees in a type of participative decision making.

Several similar schemes depicting virtually identical leadership styles have evolved in later years. Initiating structure has been divided into the **telling style** and the **delegating style,** whereas showing consideration has been divided into the **selling style** and the **participating style** by Hershey and Blanchard (1977). Telling and delegating styles of leadership, according to Hershey and Blanchard, are task oriented and require supervisors to tell subordinates what to do and delegate tasks to those who are emotionally mature enough to perform them. Selling and participating leadership styles emphasize a collaborative relation between supervisors and subordinates, in which subordinates are given emotional consideration and are involved in decision making through feedback solicited from supervisors. These researchers termed their version of leadership style **employee-maturity theory,** clearly emphasizing the emotional and educational maturing of subordinates to be led.

Essentially the same model of leadership styles was elaborated by Blanchard several years later. Blanchard changed the leadership style terms from telling, delegating, selling, and participating to directing, delegating, supporting, and coaching (Blanchard, Zigarmi, and Zigarmi, 1985). Other than the name change, little or nothing was accomplished to advance what we know about the supervisor-subordinate relation beyond the "initiating structure" and "showing consideration" leadership styles articulated 20 years earlier by Fleischman and Harris.

Multiple Leadership to Fulfill Several Organizational Functions

Perhaps the most realistic view of leadership in organizations is considering various group needs and relying on several persons to fulfill leadership roles specifically designed to meet each need rather than depending on a single person to perform such an overwhelming diversification of tasks, a view that is referred to as **multiple leadership.** Leadership in any social aggregate is chiefly the responsibility of the group (Lippitt, 1955). A leadership division of labor of sorts is established, in which some persons are responsible for certain tasks while others see to different tasks. The major point of multiple leadership is that no single person performs or assumes all leadership functions.

The multiple leadership idea has been discussed as **distributed leadership** (Watson, 1966:177). Different persons in a group may have a special facility for calling the group to order, others may be able to quell a troublesome situation, others may be highly respected because of their judgment and character, and still others may be respected because of their expertise and because they have more facts to contribute than any other member.

Researchers also have observed that with respect to small, task-oriented groups, the role of principal facilitator may shift back and forth between two or more persons (Newcomb, Turner, and Converse, 1965:474). It is often impossible, even with respect to one particular kind of contribution, to assert that any single person is the special facilitator. Such considerations suggest that it may be more harmful than helpful to think of leadership as necessarily concentrated in a single person (Newcomb, Turner, and Converse, 1965:474).

It may be fruitful to look at leadership in terms of a teamwork effort, in which the combined input of different experts or specialists can be brought to bear on particular organizational problems. In police departments, bureaucracy is a typical organizational model. This model tends to promote a particular type of work climate that encourages individual efforts from officers, sometimes to the detriment of overall organizational goal attainment. However, police managers may restructure the social psychological processes and patterns of interaction within their departments that would foster shared decision making. The ultimate result would be to increase organizational effectiveness, by which managers manifest a more holistic concern for their officers and encourage greater teamwork in problem solving (Archambeault and Weirman, 1983).

LEADERSHIP IN RETROSPECT: AN ORGANIZATIONAL VIEW

The literature on leadership has been inconclusive regarding attempts to establish continuities in distinguishing leadership traits. However, Gibb (1969: 210–215) has provided an insightful approach to examining leadership behavior, particularly leadership behavior in organizations. The following distinctions have been made among several definitions of leadership and leader:

1. The leader as an individual in a given office (very likely the most appropriate definition for our interests and purposes)
2. The leader as a focus for the behavior of group members
3. The leader defined in terms of sociometric choice (or a function of preference relations among members)
4. The leader as one who exercises influence over others
5. Leadership as headship (as in a university setting) in which the organization confers such recognition on the person rather than the group itself (again, such a view in this context is of interest to us in our consideration of leadership in schools as formal organizations)
6. The leader defined in terms of influence on syntality (or group personality, performance, and behavior)

7. The leader as one who engages in leadership behavior, which places the person in the position of being able to initiate structure
8. Focused versus distributed leadership

Leadership is probably best conceived as a group quality, as a set of functions that must be carried out by the group. This concept of distributed leadership is an important one. If there are leadership functions that must be performed in any group, and if these functions may be focused or distributed, then the leaders will be identifiable both in terms of the frequency and multiplicity or pattern of functions performed (Gibb, 1969:215). Such a conception appears to coincide well with the needs of contemporary research in this area. Heads may be distinguished from leaders in terms of the functions they usually and frequently assume. Similarly, differentiation between all types of influential persons may be possible in terms of the pattern of functional roles characteristic of each (Gibb, 1969:215).

Empirical research about leadership in actual criminal justice settings has been extensive. Police departments have been convenient research targets over the years. One major reason for this research is that police agencies are responsive to many (but not all) suggestions for improving the effectiveness of law enforcement, and most are amenable to experiments that may have successful results for improving organizational effectiveness. In turn, one payoff is greater police-community relations and a favorable enhancement of their public image.

Mitti Southerland (1989, 1990) examined several leadership styles practiced by different police managers and sergeants. She found that the styles most desired by subordinates tended to be task oriented; that is, subordinates were more comfortable being told what to do and how to do it. Similar findings have been reported by Jermier and Burkes (1979) and Kuykendall and Roberg (1988).

Other studies have reported that showing consideration is preferred by selected police subordinates. Investigations of several police departments in the Midwest showed that whenever officers were involved or were permitted to participate in decisions affecting their work, they were more satisfied with their jobs and had greater work effectiveness (Witte, Travis, and Langworthy, 1990; Wycoff and Skogan, 1994). Kuykendall and Roberg (1988), however, found that not all police managers are comfortable sharing decision making with their officer-subordinates, preferring to retain a fairly high degree of control over general pa-

trolling styles and officer decision-making protocol for particular types of police-citizen encounters.

Students of administration cannot omit for consideration the concepts of authority and leadership as important components that contribute to schemes for the prediction and explanation of organizational behavior. Weber placed much emphasis on the idea that organizational effectiveness is highly dependent on the expertise, initiative, loyalty, and quality of the organization's membership, including persons in various leadership roles in the hierarchy of authority. Those persons who are in positions of control over organizational resources and who are responsible for the guidance of their respective institutions toward improvement must be scrutinized as carefully as the structure within which they operate and the complexities and processual arrangements of their functional interrelations.

SUMMARY

All organizations have hierarchies of authority and chains of command. As we have learned from our examination of the bureaucratic model of organizations, persons at all supervisory levels exert some amount of control over their subordinates. The ability of superiors in organizations to influence others is known as power. In contrast, those who hold positions of power or supervisory roles in organizations exercise authority over others. Thus, authority is vested in persons as the result of their performing particular supervisory, managerial, or administrative roles. Both authority and power are types of influence over others.

Several power and authority schemes have been devised by organizational theorists. Max Weber did some pioneering work when he elaborated a model of legitimate authority types. He labeled these types of authority charismatic, traditional, and legal-rational. His view of charismatic authority was that selected persons are endowed with special abilities and serve to attract others. Relatively few persons throughout history have actually manifested charismatic authority as Weber envisioned it, however. Another type of authority was traditional authority. This type of authority derives from early English fealty and kinship systems, in which families passed on their authority from one generation to the next in a patrilineal sense. Traditional authority is informal and is rooted in loyalty to superiors who often have inherited their authoritative positions. Legal-rational authority is a third type of authority described by Weber. This type of authority is closely associated with bureaucratic organizations and is rooted in law. Thus, persons are elected or appointed to authoritative roles, and they exercise influence over others in accordance with abstract rules and legal proclamations.

Subsequently, a power scheme was devised by French and Raven (1959). These researchers described reward power, coercive power, referent power, expert power, and legitimate power. Reward power is exercised through the ability of superiors to offer subordinates incentives for compliance. Coercive power is exercised through force and intimidation. Expert power is exercised in situations in which subordinates follow their superiors because of the special skills and knowledge they possess. Similar to Max Weber's legitimate types of authority, referent power is most like traditional authority and is rooted in custom and friendship relations between supervisors and subordinates. Legitimate power is most like Weber's concept of legal-rational authority. Although there is no direct equivalent in French and Raven's power scheme to charismatic power, it is perhaps most like referent power.

A third scheme has been devised by Amitai Etzioni (1961). We have already seen Etzioni's compliance-involvement scheme depicted in an earlier chapter as an organizational typology. The scheme may be used here, however, to typify the relations between superiors and subordinates. It extends the work of Weber and French and Raven by suggesting that subordinates will react in particular ways or become involved differently in their work depending on the type of compliance used to influence them. Etzioni described remunerative compliance, coercive compliance, and normative compliance as three alternative ways superiors could influence lower-level participants or employees. Respectively, the use of these types of compliance tends to elicit calculative involvement, alienative involvement, or moral involvement from subordinates.

Various organizational, interpersonal, and individual factors influence superior-subordinate relations. These factors include organizational structure, size, and complexity. Superior-subordinate relations also can be affected by such variables as the hierarchy of authority and span of control. As the hierarchy of authority becomes more or less elaborate or complex, the numbers of employees over which a supervisor exerts control change. These changes modify the supervisory methods used by administrators and managers, since their methods for supervising many persons at once are logically different from the methods of supervision they might use to supervise few persons.

Several leadership theories have been described. Leadership behavior is closely associated with authority and power. A prevalent view of leadership is that it influences organizational climate, which in turn influences group and individual behaviors, such as job satisfaction, esprit de corps, work group cohesiveness, and productivity and work effectiveness. Notions of leadership include the great man theory, which is similar to Weber's charismatic view that some persons are born with leadership powers and abilities. This view is difficult to conceptualize empirically, however. More productive and plausible explanations of leadership are that leaders emerge because of the situations in which they find themselves. This view is situational leadership. Another view is that leadership behavior can be learned. Therefore, many writers have attempted to describe what successful leaders must do to lead others and what sorts of characteristics they must acquire to be effective in their leadership roles. Other writers have examined leadership in terms of leadership style. Several styles of leadership have been described, with discussions of the implications of these leadership styles for employee productivity and work group effectiveness. Multiple leadership or distributed leadership also has been described, which surmises that leadership does not adhere in a single person at a given time. Rather, leadership is distributed throughout an organization according to the different abilities and skills of persons who relate well to particular situations that may arise.

QUESTIONS FOR REVIEW

1. What is the difference between power and authority? How does power differ from influence? What are several different meanings of power? How is authority related to the chain of command?

2. Identify and describe four different types of leadership. Which leadership type do you prefer in describing police organizations? Why?

3. Differentiate between the trait and situational approaches to leadership. How valid is the trait approach? Discuss.

4. What are Max Weber's three types of authority? Describe and distinguish between each. Which authority type described by Weber best fits the bureaucratic model of organization? Why?

5. What is the difference between initiating structure and showing consideration? Discuss.

6. What are five types of power noted by French and Raven? Describe each.

7. Relate the work of French and Raven to that of Etzioni. How does the power scheme of French and Raven match up with the compliance-involvement typology devised by Etzioni? What are some general relations between these two schemes and the pioneering work of Max Weber?

8. What is meant by distributed leadership? Which leadership theory do you prefer and why?

9. What is meant by participative leadership? How does participative leadership relate to organizational effectiveness?

10. Distinguish between vertical and horizontal differentiation. What is the difference between flat and tall organizational structures? How do power and authority relate to these types of organizations?

SUGGESTED READINGS

Anderson, Terry D. (2000). *Every Officer Is a Leader: Transforming Leadership in Police, Justice, and Public Safety.* Boca Raton, FL: St. Lucie Press.

Siegel, Michael Eric (2000). "Probation and Pretrial Chiefs Can Learn from the Leadership Styles of American Presidents." *Federal Probation* **64**:27–33.

Vinzant, Janet Coble, and Lane Crothers (1998). *Street Level Leadership.* Washington, DC: Georgetown University Press.

• CASE STUDIES •

1. THE DISPATCHER

Jerry Adams is a 26-year-old dispatcher for the Wrightville Police Department (WPD). Wrightville is a rural community of 40,000 in a northeastern state. The WPD has 46 officers and approximately 20 staff with a variety of office duties. Adams has recently graduated with a B.A. degree in criminal justice from a local college, and he aspires to become a police officer. He has been performing the dispatcher job for the past nine months and has settled into a routine. Not much crime is commited in Wrightville, and therefore, there are not many calls for service. The job of dispatcher can be downright boring at times. But Adams's position is one of those jobs that cannot be ignored. Dispatchers are expected to be on duty should any emergency arise.

The main office of the WPD has two other employees who are not police officers. These employees perform secretarial and filing tasks. According to the chain of command, these office workers take their orders from the chief of police, Gary Flynn. Flynn makes it a point to be away from his office much of the time, with speaking engagements at the Rotary Club, Kiwanis Club, and several other clubs in the greater Wrightville area. He has been with the WPD for 20 years and had been police chief for six of those years. Some people think he should be on the job more fre-

quently, but no one is going to question him about his absences or speaking engagements. Occasionally, Flynn goes to crime scenes to observe his officers in action.

Jerry Adams has made his intentions clear to Flynn about wanting to become a police officer, but the town council has not yet approved a budget appropriation that would justify hiring a new officer. The department has a low turnover rate among existing officers, although a few are reaching retirement age. Adams is just biding his time until the next officer vacancy occurs.

Wayne Hemmingway, the chief's secretary, and Melvin VanDyke, a file clerk, are the two office workers in the WPD office with Adams. Wayne and Melvin love to converse about non–job-related matters while on the job, and "gossip" is their middle name. Melvin is chronically behind in his filing work, largely because he spends so much time with Wayne. Since the chief is away so much, he doesn't notice that Wayne spends relatively little time doing secretarial work in his own office, either

One day, Chief Flynn came into the office and announced that a team of city officials was going to come through the WPD to check things out. He said that the purpose of their visit was to learn more about the WPD and whether or not more funding was necessary. Therefore, he advised, he wanted everyone to look busy and make sure that they were caught up on their paperwork. He announced that they would be having a visit from city officials in two days. Melvin was panicked by this announcement. He knew that there was no way that he could catch up on his filing and sorting of documents and other information before then without some assistance from someone. Wayne was in the same boat. He also had a pile of work to do, but he had ignored it to chat with Melvin.

Melvin had an idea. He saw Adams sitting there doing nothing and approached him. "Jerry," he said, "I understand you want to become a police officer. Did you know that filing and sorting criminal information and documents is a good way to become familiar with police procedures around here?" Adams didn't know that and responded accordingly. "I have some work that you could do if you wanted to learn more about policing," he said. "Come over here and let me show you how it's done." Jerry told him that he was supposed to monitor the dispatch desk, but he said, "Oh, don't worry about that. Wayne will fix that if the chief finds out." Jerry reluctantly left the dispatch desk and went to Melvin's desk, which was in another room. He began to assist Melvin in filing and sorting documents, as Melvin explained where certain files were to be placed. Jerry became so involved in his work with Melvin that he forgot about his dispatch desk. In the meantime, some police officers radioed the dispatcher, requesting backup and assistance on an armed robbery call that was occurring in downtown Wrightville at the Wrightville National Bank. Jerry was far enough away from the dispatch desk that he didn't hear the call for assistance from the officers. There was a terrible shoot-out and one of the officers was critically wounded. The other officer was able to subdue the two bank robbers and take them into custody, however.

When the officer who had called for assistance entered the WPD offices about an hour later, he found Jerry filing documents in Melvin's office. "What the hell's going on," he said. "Didn't you get my message about the bank robbery in progress? We almost lost an officer out there. What the hell do you think you're doing in Melvin's office? You're supposed to have your rear end planted in that dispatcher's chair. If you can't handle this job, I don't think you're going to make it as a police officer. I'm going to report you to Chief Flynn."

Questions for Discussion

1. Who is to blame for Adams's absence from the dispatcher's desk?
2. What type of action should Chief Flynn take against Adams for being absent from his dispatching job?
3. Should the chief say anything to Melvin or Wayne regarding the incident?
4. What should Adams tell Chief Flynn in his own defense? How would you react if you were Jerry Adams? Would you implicate Melvin? Why or why not?

2. ARDMORE PRISON

Ardmore Prison is located in Centerville, in Illinois. It is a maximum security prison, but it is small, holding only 450 inmates. The warden is George Duffy, who has been on the job for four years. Duffy was appointed by the governor, and he runs his prison with an iron hand. Duffy has a zero-tolerance policy about rule infractions. Any inmate who violates a rule, regardless of how petty, gets placed in isolation or solitary confinement for up to two months. The relations between correctional officers and inmates are strained as a result of this policy. Duffy has said that any correctional officer who lets an inmate get away with anything will find himself in deep trouble. He has even instituted a snitch system, through which correctional officers who observe other correctional officers treating inmates in a lenient fashion should report these incidents. Duffy then brings the offending officers into his office, where he chews them out over their lax treatment of inmates and poor discipline. On occasion, he has been known to fire certain correctional officers for failure to follow his policy of strict adherence to rules.

One day in the cafeteria, the inmates were eating lunch. The inmates had a very hostile attitude toward the correctional staff. One inmate activity to pass the time was to pull pranks on correctional officers in ways that the officers would not know who was responsible for the pranks. During lunch, a correctional officer was walking down a row of tables where inmates were eating soup and sandwiches. While the other correctional officers were looking elsewhere, one inmate surreptitiously threw a piece of bread covered in mayonnaise at the back of the officer. The bread struck the officer in the back of his shirt, causing a stain. The officer turned around quickly, attempting to see who had thrown the bread. All inmates appeared to be minding their own business eating. The correctional officer reported the incident to the captain in charge. The captain announced that all inmates were to leave the cafeteria immediately in an orderly manner. All inmates did as they were told and left the cafeteria without finishing their meals.

Later that evening, four inmates were pulled at random from different cells and placed in solitary confinement. The warden announced over the intercom that the four prisoners would be held in solitary confinement for six months or until whoever threw the bread at the officer in the cafeteria confessed. Further, Duffy announced that no dinners would be served to inmates that evening. This was more than the inmates could stand. One inmate set his mattress on fire and threw it out of his cell into the cell block. Other inmates followed suit, setting fire to their mattresses and throwing debris from their cells into the cell hallways. The noise was unsettling. All the inmates began banging various objects on their cell doors, shouting, and making as much noise as they could. Duffy ordered several correctional officers to turn on the fire hoses on each floor and to turn the hoses on those inmates causing the most trouble. The fire hoses put out the mattress fires, but then officers went from cell to cell and hosed down all inmates with a steady stream of cold water. As a punishment, the warden ordered a general lockdown to go into effect immediately. Inmate yard privileges were suspended indefinitely, and inmates would be confined to their cells for 23½ hours a day, with only one-half hour for recreation. They would be permitted to bathe only once a week. They would have

to sleep on the floors of their cells if they had burned their mattresses.

Subsequently, the media heard about the riot and covered the story in the local newspapers and on television. Warden Duffy was interviewed and referred to the riot as a minor incident that "we now have under complete control." The prison is still under general lockdown after six months and inmate morale is at an all-time low. No one ever confessed to the bread-throwing incident.

Questions for Discussion

1. Was Warden Duffy acting responsibly in creating and enforcing strict behavioral standards for these inmates, considering that this is a maximum security prison?

2. What are some alternative ways Duffy could have managed the prison that may have minimized the occurrence of inmate rioting?

3. If you were the correctional officer who had been hit with the bread slice, should you have reported the incident to your supervisor? If you had not reported the incident, and if the other officers did not see the bread being thrown, how do you think this would have been regarded by the prisoners? Did the officer handle the situation properly?

4. Is there anything the correctional officers could have done collectively to meet with Warden Duffy and get him to ease up on his strict disciplinary policies?

5. Is two months in solitary confinement too harsh of a punishment for violating minor institutional rules? What type of power is being exercised here? What type of compliance is to be expected from inmates? Is this compliance predictable? Why or why not?

6. If you were the warden of this prison, what type of leadership would you want to use, both over your officers and over the inmates? What would be your primary objectives as an administrator? Discuss.

CHAPTER
7

FORMAL AND INFORMAL COMMUNICATION NETWORKS IN ORGANIZATIONS

CHAPTER OBJECTIVES

The following objectives are intended:

1. To describe what is meant by formal and informal organizational charts and role arrangements

2. To illustrate the close connection between organizational authority hierarchies and formal communication networks

3. To describe several different types of communication patterns that have been linked with varying degrees of work group effectiveness

4. To describe the functions and dysfunctions of formal communication networks

5. To describe the origins of informal communication networks and their functions and dysfunctions

6. To describe the complementarity between formal and informal communication networks and the implications of communication patterns for organizational effectiveness, interpersonal relations, and employee attitudes

INTRODUCTION

This chapter examines communication in organizations. Communication systems closely parallel authority hierarchies in organizations. Communication systems are networks that are designed to transmit information to and from all positions within an organization. Thus, communication networks officially are defined patterns indicating which persons, or persons in which positions, are supposed to send and receive which kinds of information and messages from which other persons (Freeman, 1999).

Over the years, increased importance has been given to communication networks by business administrators, industrial consultants, and organizational researchers. At one time, communication was regarded as the answer to most problems occurring in organizations. Some writers have said, "Without communication, there can be no organization, and hence, no group productivity, because communication is the only process by which people are tied together in a work group. If there is no communication, there can be no group. Communication is the bridge over which all technical knowledge and human relationships must travel" (Davis and Scott, 1969:255).

The **formal communication network** of any organization is reflected in the chain of command or authority hierarchy, including the horizontal as well as the vertical functional relations among departments in the organization's division of labor. The formally outlined communication pattern most often is related directly to the work-flow sequence among persons performing different roles. This sequence defines the channels through which information and materials must pass in order for the organization to fulfill its overall production objectives. Such objectives can be exclusively material (e.g., assembly of automobiles, manufacturing of furniture, assembly of toys, production of computers), but need not be: An organization may have less tangible goals such as performing services for clients (e.g., hospitals, psychiatric clinics, schools, legal firms, banks, detective agencies). Communication enables organizations to accomplish their objectives, whatever they may be. Thus, the first part of this chapter examines formal communication networks. The advantages and disadvantages of formal communication networks in organizations also are described.

Although formal communication networks are found in every organization, vital information also is disseminated by other means, such as through an **informal communication network.** Grapevines or informal channels of communication usually exist as a normal part of any organizational environment. It is highly unlikely that employees will restrict communications with one another exclusively to job-related matters at all times during the performance of their tasks or at lunch or coffee breaks. It is also naive to believe that communication initiated at any level of authority will follow a perfect downward path commensurate with the organizational chart or the hierarchy of authority. Interdepartmental communications may occur among supervisors with common statuses or among lower-level personnel from one department or division to another. The restriction of information transmission to formal communication channels is virtually impossible. Rumors can be spread throughout an organization by word of mouth on the basis of something overheard or seen by any person. There may be no immediately apparent pattern to such information distributions on an informal basis. Thus, we also must examine the informal nature of organizational communication. Included in this discussion are several advantages and disadvantages of informal communication networks.

Apart from informal and formal communication networks that function to disseminate information to various positions within the organization, other forms of information processing often are used, sometimes simultaneously with these. An organization may publish a newsletter announcing recent organizational changes or developments, promotions among staff members, departmental reorganizations, and anticipated technological changes. Of course, organizations that are housed under a single roof (as opposed to organizations with numerous divisions spatially separated from one another or located in different geographical regions) may convey information to members by assembling them together in a large conference room and making general announcements. The president, administrative officer, or some other high-level functionary may address the entire group directly. Usually, conferences such as these involve the organization at large and do not pertain to a specific unit or department separate from the others. In a general meeting, the warden of a penitentiary may inform all corrections officers about new policies relating to the processing and handling of inmates or new correctional reforms to be implemented.

The last part of this chapter describes the complementarity that exists between formal and informal communication networks. Organizational effectiveness is to a great degree dependent on the effectiveness of the communication system that typifies it. It has been said that informal communication networks always arise from formal communication networks. This phenomenon will be described. The organizational, interpersonal, and individual units of analysis are affected in various ways by these different types of communication networks and patterns.

COMMUNICATION SYSTEMS AND FORMAL COMMUNICATION NETWORKS

Max Weber originally envisioned and outlined a plan for maximizing organizational effectiveness and efficiency (Weber, 1947). His bureaucratic model of organizations made elaborate provisions for the ordering of social relations necessary for the most rapid and perfect means of goal attainment. An apparently crucial component of the ideal bureaucratic organization was impersonal, impartial, and strict obedience to a system of abstract rules by individuals at each level in the hierarchy of authority. Communication between departments within an organization was to be exclusively task related and was essential as a part of the processes leading to success and progress.

But the bureaucratic model revealed that seldom do organizations succeed fully in creating entirely impersonal relations among members of any department or division or at any level of authority. The inevitability of interpersonal associations apart from work-related tasks and simple verbal exchanges between persons on the job is well documented. Informal communication patterns are associated with formal communication patterns. In fact, informal communication is so much a part of our everyday associations with others that we are frequently unaware of it, seeing only occasional glimpses of non–work-related social interactions. However, it is evident that informal associations of persons while performing their formal activities inevitably involves interactions that are incidental to these formal activities (Barnard, 1938:121–122).

The emergence of social groups apart from formal organizational arrangements is such that it reflects the spontaneous efforts of individuals and subgroups to control the conditions of their existence (Selznick, 1966:251). People will resist being treated as mechanical parts in the organizational machinery and will manifest their uniqueness as individuals as opposed to behaving in the expected fashion as automatons.

Keeping in mind the simultaneous existence of informal communication networks adjacent to and a part of formal communication networks in organizations, we will first examine the formal aspects of the communication process. At the outset it should be recognized that because there are many different kinds of organizations, it is unlikely that a particular communication network common to one type of organization, such as a social welfare agency, will necessarily be applicable to all other types of organizations, including jails, prisons, probation and parole departments, or courts. We may conclude that formalized communication networks are essential and important to the perpetuation of *all* organizations, regardless of their types or sizes. Figure 7.1 shows some of the different factors that influence the formal communication networks of most organizations.

Hierarchies of Authority and Formal Communication Patterns

Formal communication patterns and channels are almost always linked directly with the hierarchy of authority in any organization. The hierarchy of author-

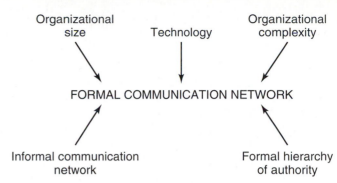

FIGURE 7.1 The Impact of Several Important Variables and Conditions on the Formal Communications Network of an Organization

Source: Compiled by author.

ity is usually depicted through an **organizational chart.** An organizational chart is a diagrammatic portrayal of the vertical and horizontal interrelatedness of all roles in an organization, from the highest level of administration to the lowest level and frontline employees. Each role is represented by a box, and interconnecting lines are drawn to show the superior-subordinate or horizontal relations between boxes (roles). Figures 7.2, 7.3, and 7.4, respectively, show the organizational charts of a small, medium-sized, and large police department.

There are more than a few one- and two-officer police departments throughout the United States, especially in rural areas. Figure 7.2 depicts a two-officer department in the Northeast. In this illustration, there is a captain, who heads the department, and a lieutenant, who also functions as a patrol officer. These officers spell one another and work eight-hour days. The community cannot afford a dispatcher. Not much happens in this community late at night, and thus, the police department is unstaffed during late evening hours. Not much happens during the day, either. In the snowy winters in the Northeast, these officers may have to issue citations to people who use the main street in town for snowmobiling, an activity that is prohibited. Occasionally, these officers break up fights at the local bar in town on weekends or intervene in

Captain

↓

Lieutenant/Patrol officer

FIGURE 7.2 Organization of a Small, Rural Police Department

Source: Compiled by author.

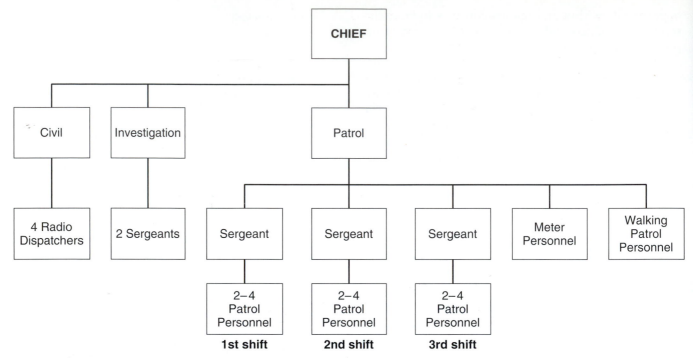

FIGURE 7.3 Organization of a Medium-Sized Police Department
Source: Compiled by author.

domestic violence situations. If crimes are committed and/or emergencies arise requiring police response, either the captain or lieutenant may be reached directly by telephone at their respective homes or by cellular phone or pager. Furthermore, a few county officers in the area may respond if either or both of these other officers cannot be reached by citizens.

Figures 7.3 and 7.4 show increasingly complex organizational charts of larger police departments, with greater numbers of boxes and interconnecting lines. These diagrams of greater complexity are the equivalent of a more detailed division of labor, in which more persons are involved in performing greater numbers of specialized tasks specified by the department. In Figure 7.3, for example, there is a chief who directly oversees a civil administrator, an investigation administrator, and a patrol administrator. The civil administrator oversees four dispatchers who work different shifts in order to staff the police department 24 hours a day. The investigation administrator oversees two sergeants. These sergeants may be detectives with different investigative responsibilities. The patrol supervisor or administrator oversees a number of sergeants, meter personnel, and walking patrol personnel. The

sergeants oversee two to four patrol personnel, and we might assume from this diagram that the three sergeants are responsible for three different work shifts in a 24-hour workday. The number of persons that supervisors have under their direction is called the span of control, which was discussed in Chapter 4. Wide spans of control occur if supervisors have many employees that they must oversee, whereas narrow spans of control involve relatively few subordinates. Someone overseeing the work of 50 employees would be said to have a wide span of control, while someone supervising three or four employees would have a narrow span of control.

Figure 7.4, which is the most complex of the three figures, shows a rather elaborate division of labor and network of interrelated boxes or roles. The interconnecting lines again illustrate the chain of command. In the lower-left corner of Figure 7.4, for example, the lowest-level role is the Motorcycle Unit. The Motorcycle Unit is one of five boxes/units (e.g., Accident Records, Mobile Units, Accident Investigation, School Police, and Motorcycle Unit) that report to the Traffic & Accident box/unit. From the diagram, we might assume that Traffic & Accident is a single person who is

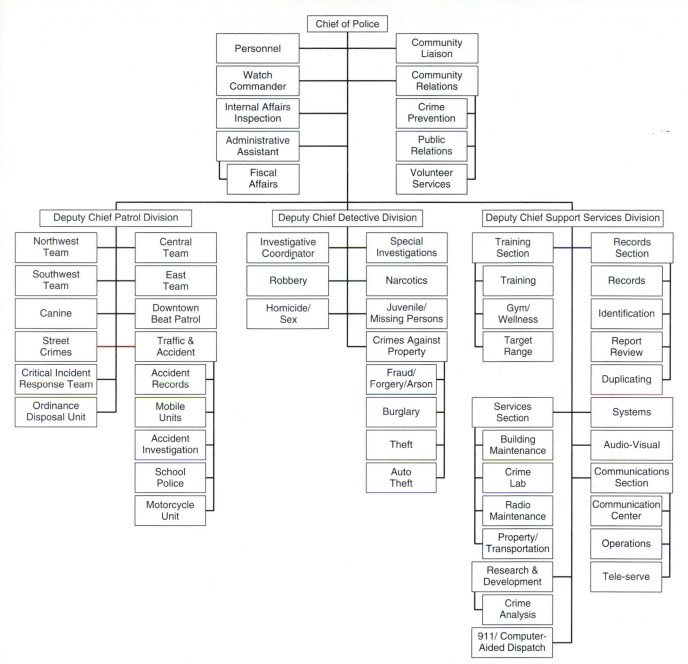

FIGURE 7.4 Organization of a Large Police Department

Source: Compiled by author.

in charge of traffic and accident matters, although more than one person may be in this position at different times during a 24-hour day. Notice that the Traffic & Accident box is connected to the next-higher level, labeled Deputy Chief Patrol Division. Further observe that nine other boxes/units are connected through lines to the Deputy Chief Patrol Division. Although

the boxes in this organizational chart are arranged in a column, the connecting lines are intended to show that each box/unit is a separate entity directly subordinate to the Deputy Chief Patrol Division box/unit.

If we were to describe the organizational chart in Figure 7.4, we would say that this is a police department with a chief who has nine immediately direct subordinates (e.g., Personnel, Watch Commander, Internal Affairs Inspection, Administrative Assistant, Community Liaison, Community Relations, Deputy Chief Patrol Division, Deputy Chief Detective Division, and Deputy Chief Support Services Division). The Community Relations unit/role has three subordinate units/roles, including Crime Prevention, Public Relations, and Volunteer Services. The Administrative Assistant has one subordinate: the Fiscal Affairs unit/role.

The Deputy Chief Patrol Division oversees the Northwest Team, the Southwest Team, the Canine unit, Street Crimes, Critical Incident Response Team, Ordinance Disposal Unit, Central Team, East Team, Downtown Beat Patrol, and Traffic & Accident. The Deputy Chief Detective Division oversees the Investigative Coordinator, Robbery, Homicide/Sex, Special Investigations, Narcotics, Juvenile/Missing Persons, and Crimes Against Property (which is further subdivided into Fraud/Forgery/Arson, Burglary, Theft, and Auto Theft. Finally, the Deputy Chief Support Services Division oversees the Training Section, Records Section, Services Section, Systems, Audio-Visual, Communications Section, Research & Development, and 911/Computer-Aided Dispatch. Some of these sections within the Support Services Division have their own subdivisions as shown.

Hypothetically, if an Operations officer (lower-right corner of Figure 7.4) wants to communicate formally with the Chief of Police, he or she would first communicate with the Communications Section head, who in turn would communicate with the Deputy Chief Support Services Division, who then would communicate with the Chief of Police. This communication follows precisely the lines that have been drawn.

If we further assume that most police departments rigidly follow the military model in which the chain of command is explicitly observed, then the lowly Oper-

ations officer would not attempt to communicate directly with the Chief of Police, but rather, he or she would communicate in an upward manner, through his or her immediate superior, following the prescribed chain of command.

In the real world, when we examine the operations of large police departments, there are hallways, offices, and large work areas with lots of desks. We do not see boxes or separated cubicles connected by white lines drawn on the floors. We see many people, complainants, uniformed officers, and others in street attire, interacting, seated, standing, or moving about in different ways. We would have to sit and observe for many hours in order to detect a pattern resembling whatever is drawn on an organizational chart for that particular police department. Even then, we would fail to capture the full essence of departmental organization, since some offices are located on different floors or even in different buildings in other parts of the community. Therefore, organizational charts only enable us to understand how different roles are interconnected in any organization. In reality, however, ongoing interactions of different persons suggest a more loosely connected social arrangement. Thus, the Operations officer may run into the Chief of Police in a hallway and have a brief conversation. The subject may or may not be work related.

Besides portraying formal communication networks with organizational charts, several simplistic diagrams have been used to represent how information is transmitted between roles or work units. Applewhite (1965) has described five types of communication networks, respectively known as the wheel, chain, "Y," circle, and star. These types of networks are shown in Figure 7.5.

The wheel, chain, and "Y" are essentially the same types of communication networks, although they appear to be different in Figure 7.5. We can rearrange these three diagrams by using boxes, similar to an organizational chart, as shown in Figure 7.6.

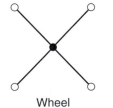   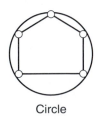 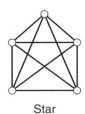

Wheel   Chain   "Y"   Circle   Star

FIGURE 7.5 Group Communication Networks

Source: Roy R. Roberg and Jack Kuykendall, *Police Management,* 2/e.
(Los Angeles, CA: Roxbury Publishing Company, 1997), p. 109.
Reprinted with permission by Roxbury Publishing Corp.

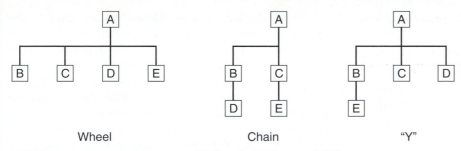

FIGURE 7.6 Rearrangement of Wheel, Chain, and "Y" Communication Networks

Source: Compiled by author.

These diagrams are best appreciated if we envision wallboard partitions between each person. A communication hole is made in each partition between the superior and his or her direct subordinate. Written messages are passed by hand to different persons through these communication holes. In the chain diagram in Figure 7.6, person A can communicate directly with persons B and C, but he or she must rely on B and C to pass messages on to their individual subordinates, D and E. There are no communication holes linking person A with persons D and E. For all practical purposes, the "Y" diagram in Figure 7.6 is the same as the chain diagram in form and function.

The circle and star diagrams in Figure 7.5 portray leaderless situations, in which no central person is designated to coordinate information transmission. The least desirable communication form is the circle, in which communication between persons can only occur between units adjacent to each other in the circle. Communication holes exist only to the left or right of each person. Unless some person is designated in advance as the leader, information exchanges are for the most part unilateral, endless, and possibly pointless.

Theoretically, the most desirable communication/information-sharing form is the star, in which communication holes exist between all persons in the diagram. Although this form of communication maximizes information exchange, no centralizing authority or leader exists to coordinate and assimilate the transmitted information and make a decision about it. In contrast, the wheel, chain, and "Y" have leaders to acquire information, process it, and make decisions about it. From a human relations perspective, however, subordinates in the wheel, chain, "Y," and circle diagrams tend to have less satisfaction with their work

and are not meaningfully involved in decision making. Persons who participate in the star communication network tend to have higher work satisfaction and believe they are more involved in decision making and problem solving.

The idea of using wallboard partitions to separate people from one another and cut-out communication holes to pass through written information may sound silly, but this was actually done experimentally in the 1940s and 1950s to simulate small-group problem solving in business and industry (Argyris, 1960). But the reality of organizational problem solving and interpersonal dynamics of social situations in work settings seriously undermines the scientific value of these simplistic diagrams and their supposed benefits for organizational members. The state of the art relating to organizational communication has gone well beyond the limited descriptive parameters and simplistic experiments of the 1950s. Widespread computerization of work environments and high-speed information access and sharing have caused substantial changes in general management and communication strategies (Sanfilippo, 1969; Souryal, 1995).

Functions of Formal Communication Networks

The necessity for a formalized communication network increases as the organizational membership increases (or as organizational size increases). Herbert Spencer (1898) and Georg Simmel (1903) provide a sociological view that supports this statement. Both theorists argue that an increase in an organization's size requires more complex and formalized communication patterns. What functions, then, do these formalized communication networks serve? Some of the more important functions of formal communication systems follow:

1. Formal communication networks facilitate the coordination of work activity that constitutes the division of labor within an organization. As the organizational membership grows and the tasks performed become increasingly diversified and specialized, communication is necessary to coordinate these various tasks with one another. Consider the potential chaos that would result if formalized communication networks did not exist within a large automobile assembly plant. Departments A, B, C, D . . . N manufacture different automobile components A', B', C', D' . . . N'. How is department A supposed to know how many A's should be produced to accompany the number of items produced by departments B and C? Different departments responsible for ordering bolts and nuts of specific sizes and in sufficient quantities for divisions in which such items are used in each phase of automobile assembly would be in a quandary if any of the bolts and nuts ordered were of the wrong size. In fact, the entire organization could be brought to an absolute standstill if a particular bolt's diameter was off by as little as 1/64 of an inch. Interdepartmental coordination is especially important as precision demands in manufacturing organizations are increased to higher levels. Formal communication channels convey information from one level of authority to another and from one department to another. Each department is presented with a picture of what other departments are doing in relation to it. Accordingly, departmental planning and action are improved considerably.

2. Directly related to the first function listed, formal communication networks provide the feedback necessary to stabilize task performance. Feedback is the assessment by certain departments of the quality and quantity of work performed by other departments. Such assessments are necessary to provide each department with impressions and evaluations of departmental output. If feedback from one department to another indicates that something is amiss, then mechanisms can be brought into play to identify existing problems and develop solutions for them. Bringing to the attention of department A that item A' is 1/64 of an inch too small will enable that department to make the necessary mechanical adjustments to manufacture an item A' that is compatible with the items produced by other departments.

Feedback becomes increasingly important to the extent that departments are interdependent. This means, in essence, that in order for department B to perform its functions satisfactorily, it must wait for the work or information to be passed on from department A. If department A has not done a good job with the product in process, potential frictions will ensue between the two departments. This friction results because department B must either correct the deficiencies of department A (thus slowing down department B's efficiency and possibly getting a low effectiveness rating from higher-ups) or send the product in process back to department A to do over (which results in lost time and drops in efficiency ratings for both departments).

3. Stemming from the first two functions listed, formal communication networks enable an organization to decrease waste or spoilage of product, eliminate unnecessary work operations (duplication of function), and improve its overall efficiency and effectiveness. But despite elaborate formal communication processes, some bureaucracies such as prison systems manage to do wasteful things, such as accrue excessive supplies in their inventories or implement inefficient construction projects (Sharp, 1994). By now it is apparent that perhaps the most important function performed by an effective, formalized communication network is general improvement in organizational effectiveness. And since organizational effectiveness is closely associated with goal attainment, formal communication networks presumably facilitate the achievement of organizational goals. Through feedback and smooth interdepartmental coordination, the primary activities of an organization are completed with little or no difficulty, particularly of an interpersonal nature.

4. Formal communication networks reinforce or lend strong support to the existing organizational structure and hierarchy of power. The transmission of information to all points in an organization is generally characterized as vertical and downward. The typical pattern is for persons in superior positions to dispense information to subordinate personnel, usually under their direct control in the hierarchy of power. In many respects, knowledge is an important medium of power. Members of organizations who possess information about planned changes or decisions about reorganization by higher-ups pertaining to personnel promotions or transfers or to specialized

task requirements are in strategic positions to utilize the information in a manipulative fashion. Deference is afforded to persons with superior knowledge (or even more knowledge) by other persons who have less knowledge and are generally less aware of the internal affairs of the organization. We have already alluded to the existence of employees' grapevines, or informal communication networks that ignore existing formal means of communication for spreading information. Because of such grapevines, it is quite possible for a person with a low formal job status to possess superior knowledge. This particular situation would yield the person involved high returns in terms of informal status. Although an informal employees' communication network is present in most organizations, formal channels of communication still help to solidify a member's formal status in the hierarchy of authority.

Some Dysfunctions of Formal Communication Networks

Although formal communication networks appear to be a vital component of organizations because they provide valuable assistance in the coordination of work activities, convey important information to all sectors of the organization, and enhance smooth relations between departments, there are some inherent limitations and problems associated with these networks. Since the structures of formal communication networks on paper so often parallel the formal authority structures of the organizations within which they are found, it is at times questionable which structure (communication or authority) should be blamed for particular intraorganizational problems. Some of the more important dysfunctions of formal communication networks are outlined in the following paragraphs:

1. Formal communication networks are sometimes criticized for disseminating important information too slowly. Military personnel are quite familiar with the delays encountered in the formalized communication network in bringing to their attention matters such as authorizations for "early outs" (sometimes a branch of the service will permit enlisted personnel to shorten the length of their enlistment by as much as six months or more in order for them to enroll at a university or college by a certain date), transfer to other duties or bases (fields, sites, posts), or promotions. The speed with which information is transmitted becomes crucial to the extent that the information is significant in affecting the roles of various subordinates or total departments.

The speed of the flow of information through formal communication channels can become a critical factor. A hospital situation is a good case in point. In order for a nurse to give a patient a particular kind of medicine or injection (possibly requested by the patient or determined to be necessary by the nurse or attendant), permission must be obtained from the physician assigned to the patient. Frequently, prolonged delays are encountered while various personnel attempt to locate the physician in question. It is possible that during such periods of delay, the patient may die or develop a more serious medical condition.

Slow dissemination of information about the goals of prisons may create confusion among officer ranks concerning which roles and prison functions should be emphasized. In some prison systems, for example, secure custody has been promoted as a primary goal. However, secondary goals have also been emphasized as important, including deterrence and rehabilitation. But if organizational administrators do not prioritize these goals in some official manner, then subordinates will approach their tasks in sometimes confusing and contradictory ways (Coyle, 1991). Even police departments in some jurisdictions have been less effective if the police mission has not been clearly articulated in an efficient manner to the rank-and-file officers (Moore, 1991).

2. Formal communication networks are traditionally conceived as channeling information vertically and downward. This statement follows Max Weber's bureaucratic model, which is popular and specifies the rationality of superior to subordinate communication flow. In instances in which subordinates are in positions of expertise in relation to their superiors, however, formal communication networks are dysfunctional at times. Peter Blau (1968) says that experts who are subordinates are in more strategic positions to know what is going on with respect to their own work than their immediate superiors. Scientific research might be an example of a situation in which communication flow would be more meaningful if it were to emanate from the lower positions (in this case, expert positions) upward toward higher-level supervisors. Blau (1968:458–459) notes the importance of two-way

BOX 7.1 TALK ABOUT A COMMUNICATION BREAKDOWN!

Tulsa, Oklahoma, and the Tulsa County Jail. Michael Chambers was convicted for drunken driving following a fight outside of a bar in Tulsa, Oklahoma, in 1998. He was sentenced to six months in the Tulsa County Jail. After serving only 15 days, however, he was advised by jail authorities that he was to be released. Chambers said the jail staff said that they had his release papers. "I told them that's wrong," Chambers said. But they went ahead and released him anyway. Chambers went directly to his attorney and advised him what had happened. It seems that a private organization, Corrections Corporation of America, recently had taken over the operation and management of the Tulsa County Jail. During the first eight months of operations, Corrections Corporation of America had released at least seven inmates prematurely, based on inaccurate information about their release dates. Chambers and his attorney went back to court and advised District Judge Michael Gassett about the error. Within 15 minutes, Chambers was taken back to jail. He thought that his honesty might get him a reduced sentence. But the judge was not convinced. He allowed the six-month sentence to stand.

How can communications between the courts and corrections be improved? What does this case say about the lack of coordination between jails and courts? What do you think?

Source: Adapted from the Associated Press, "Man Succeeds in Effort to Be Jailed," April 6, 2000.

flows of communication between subordinate experts and their superiors not only because experts tend to be more alienated by one-sided directives but also because they make greater contributions through feedback than persons with poorer qualifications. No doubt the nature of the information being communicated is an important consideration in such instances. If it is assumed that information generated from upper echelons to lower ones is work related and affects the quantity and quality of the final product, then the dysfunctional implications of downward communication flows are quite understandable. However, if the information generated is relatively unimportant with respect to the outcome of the product quantity and quality, then this would not be a meaningful criticism.

Aggressive efforts have been made to professionalize police departments throughout the United States. Programs have been implemented, usually starting at the upper echelons of administration and filtering downward to the rank-and-file officers. More than a few attempts at professionalization have failed, however, since little opportunity exists within a bureaucratic framework for bilateral communication and binding consensual norms (Donahue, 1992). True professionalization of policing, according to some writers at least, emphasizes professional autonomy and self-regulation. Formal communication networks seem to defeat this process to a degree (Donahue, 1992).

3. Formal communication networks are inherently strained. Interdepartmental contacts are inevitable in organizations if effectiveness is to be achieved and maintained. Although feedback from one department to another or from one echelon to another often lessens the potential for friction and strain, a certain amount of intraorganizational strain is consistently observed in most, if not all, organizations, possibly a result of interactions between departments as well. Intraorganizational strain is the incidence of tension or conflict existing between organizational subgroups (Georgopolous and Tannenbaum, 1957:535–540). Organizational effectiveness is the extent to which an organization or social system fulfills its objectives without incapacitating its means and resources and without placing undue strain on its members.

As one important criterion of organizational effectiveness, intraorganizational strain is contingent, in part, on the nature of the formal communication network. The primary argument is that the importance of each unit of an organization is different from that of the other units. One implication of the evident inequality of, and necessity for, intradepartmental contact is that differences in influence between units of equal formal importance will generate strain in communications and that strain will arise in the communications between two units if one of them has to control the other without the control being properly legitimized (Stymne, 1968:82–86). A certain minimum level of intraorganizational strain is probably found in all organizations. Also, too little strain is likely to have a negative effect on the functioning of the organization (Stymne, 1968:96).

In the juvenile justice system in certain jurisdictions, for instance, probation officers have struggled against structured constraints to aid the delinquents in their care. Efforts to break through the bureaucracy are frustrated by institutional gaps in services and responsibilities and agencies working at cross-purposes. Thus, working to overcome official evasion, officers have cultivated reciprocal relations and brokered favors among a network of contacts in other agencies (Jacobs, 1990). A pervasive "no-fault" society mentality characterized by an erosion of individual and institutional accountability has emerged. This situation has created chronic frustration that has in turn spawned morale and accountability problems for probation officers. In short, no clearly articulated juvenile delinquency policy has been communicated to all agencies. Thus, well-intentioned juvenile probation supervision and removal from the home may be ineffective, as well as some court decision making, which is always vulnerable to situational factors (Jacobs, 1990).

Within the framework of the traditional orientation toward organizational structure, as usually depicted by Weber's bureaucratic model, formal communication networks are necessary for several reasons. Attainment of goals, interdepartmental coordination of work activities, and a general reinforcement of the formal authority arrangement are several positive outcomes of the formalized flow of information through specific communication terminals. The ultimate objective is organizational effectiveness. However, some conditions accompanying formal communication networks create difficulties that sometimes prevent the desired degree of organizational effectiveness. Some of the dysfunctional concomitants of formal communication networks are the slowness of information dissemination, the lack of important feedback, especially in the case of experts placed in low-level hierarchical positions, and the inevitable intraorganizational and interdepartmental strains. One of the natural strategies of organizational members, which serves to overcome formal communication dissatisfactions and problems, is the informal communication network.

COMMUNICATION SYSTEMS AND INFORMAL COMMUNICATION NETWORKS

Organizational researchers acknowledge that one of the most important and irritating intervening variables affecting their investigations of relations among organizational phenomena is the presence of an informal group structure distinct from the one that is formally defined. We have already alluded to informal work groups in organizations and to some of the behaviors exhibited by them that place administrators in positions of consternation or conflict. That informal groups exist and exert considerable influence over the affairs of the organization at large is not in question. In this section, we concern ourselves with how they come into being and, more important, with why they appear to persist in virtually every type of organization regardless of size and shape or degree of formality. These are, correspondingly, questions of origin and function. Both questions have been subject to considerable attention in the research literature. In the next section, we are concerned with informal groups insofar as they relate to or interact with formal communication networks and the outcomes and implications of such interactions.

The Origin of Informal Communication Networks

Two factors seem salient in the evolution of informal groups on the job. The first is proximity, and the second factor encompasses similarities or attractiveness in terms of work activities, interests or values shared, complementary personality profiles, and individual social characteristics (social class, status, rank). Considering these factors that perhaps operate simultaneously within the formal organizational environment, persons who work closely with one another and perform similar tasks likely will share certain interests or values. To the extent that persons involved develop a liking for one another and that social class or one's formal position in relation to another is not an overt factor in the social relation, then informal collectivities will emerge and persist (Delbecq, 1968:17–18).

A model of group behavior and interaction has been proposed by George Homans (1950) that appears to coincide with the prominent factors cited previously. The factors cited by Homans as influencing the formation of informal groups include (1) interactions, (2) activities, and (3) sentiments. Although Homans developed more thoroughly the interrelationships among these factors in an elaborate theoretical scheme, a simplified version of their relations and application to the origin of informal groups may be stated as follows: Persons who interact frequently with one another are more likely to develop similar interests and sentiments compared with those who interact less frequently. Persons who perform similar or identical activities are likewise disposed to develop similar outlooks toward things. The reciprocal impact of one factor on each of the others functions to reinforce the social bond that emerges and persists.

Informal groups do not necessarily have to perform the same activities on the job, nor do they have to be of the same socioeconomic level in terms of their occupational affiliations. But the similarities of tasks performed and the frequency of interaction of these individuals on the job daily enhances the solidarity of their informal social bond rather than detracting from it.

Philip Selznick (1966:251–253) says that all organizations are molded by forces tangential to their rationally ordered structures and stated goals. An informal structure will develop within the organization that will reflect the spontaneous efforts of persons and groups to control the conditions of their existence. The informal structure will be indispensable and consequential for the formal system of delegation and control itself.

It is important to recognize the importance that Selznick attaches to the informal group structure as a system of delegation and control through communication and persuasion. This is apart from, but natural and complementary to, channels of formal authority and communication. Informal groupings of persons, then, are common to most, if not all, formal organizations. We are sensitive to the fact that informal groups in any work context perform innumerable functions, as well as dysfunctions, that influence the formal organizational arrangement of things as well as the sentiments and behaviors of members of such informal aggregates. Whenever communities attempt to implement crime prevention strategies or programs, for instance, a formal apparatus often is used to form the infrastructure within a given geographic area. One frequently used approach is termed the *situational approach,* and it encourages a siege mentality that tends to discourage social solidarity and impedes the establishment of social bonds. Another approach is called the *stake-in-conformity approach,* an approach that is impersonal and intrusive. The stake-in-conformity approach emphasizes formal dissemination of strategies to community residents by police officers and administrators. A more effective method of community crime prevention policymaking is through informal control. This approach is rooted in moral involvement and social commitment. Using this approach, community residents can be counted on to form neighborhood watches that are informally regulated and monitored. The values of economic equality and social justice are promoted through informal control, and thus, vigilante justice is not considered as a natural consequence of informal action and regulation (Weiss, 1987).

Functions and Dysfunctions of Informal Communication Networks

The interactions of employees on the job are related to their work tasks for the most part. In many organizations employees are formally reprimanded for exchanging comments with one another about matters unrelated to the job, although under certain conditions, such as in large offices, it is difficult for supervisors to distinguish between contacts that are official and those that are unofficial. Regardless of the rigidity of supervisory control over verbal communication, employees usually are able to get by with informal interactions or communication unrelated to the job. Such informal interactions may occur at coffee breaks, lunch periods, or during actual work activities. Some of the more important functions of informal groups follow:

1. Informal groups provide more rapid means for disseminating information compared with official channels of formal communication. Informal social communication systems are important in making the difference between successful and unsuccessful programs of job change initiated by administrators and passed on to lower-level personnel by formal means (Roethlisberger, 1941). If management fails to understand its entire social structure, including the informal complement, then it does itself and the organization a disservice regarding its overall effectiveness.

Informal groups seem indispensable with respect to performing the communication function. They appear to be not only necessary but also function to promote group cohesiveness and preserve individual integrity (Barnard, 1938). Patrol officers in selected police departments, for instance, exert considerable control over the quality of their work product and enforcement methods despite conflicting demands of

BOX 7.2 PERSONALITY HIGHLIGHT

JAMES R. DAVIS
Adjunct Professor,
St. Peter's College, Jersey
City, New Jersey

Statistics: B.A. (history);
M.A. (sociology); M.S.
(statistics); M.A. (forensic
psychology); M.A. (social
research), Temple
University; Ph.D.
(sociology), Temple
University.

Interests: Corrections and punishment.

Background: I grew up in Philadelphia, where I once made a living selling home improvements and real estate. I moved to New York City in 1968 and was employed as a caseworker for two years, determining eligibility for welfare clients. I became a probation officer in 1970 for the New York City Department of Probation, and I retired from that position in 1993. As a probation officer, I did both presentence investigation reports and supervision of probationers. Now I teach as an adjunct at St. Peter's College, Jersey City, New Jersey, teaching sociology and criminal justice.

I returned to college and obtained a Ph.D. in sociology as well as four master's degrees in sociology, statistics, forensic psychology, and social research. Part of my education was paid for by my union and by the Law Enforcement Education Program. I also use an interdisciplinary perspective in my research and teaching.

Work Experiences: My experiences as a probation officer were significant for my interest in all phases of criminal justice. I have had three books published, and I have had numerous articles and book reviews published in criminal justice journals. My main interests are in corrections and punishment. My books include *Sentencing Dispositions of New York City Lower Court Criminal Judges, The Science of Criminal Justice,* and *Criminal Justice in New York City.*

The most interesting things that have happened to me were interacting with all kinds of probationers. I was very happy to know that some probationers be-

lieved that I had helped them make a successful adjustment to probation. It also made me feel very happy to know that many supervisors believed that I was doing good work. I was fortunate to obtain permission to do research projects for my degrees and for my academic papers that I have presented at various criminal justice meetings. I have found numerous databases in probation that are excellent for research.

I believe that judges, prosecutors, defense attorneys, the public, and academics have great respect for the work of probation officers. Our recommendations, opinions, and reports generally are taken seriously. We have a lot of power in the system. Interacting with various components of the criminal justice system, such as parole, corrections, parents and spouses, program directors, court officers, court clerks, police officers, and so forth, has provided me with valuable experience. The field of probation and parole also offers the possibility of advancement through civil service exams to higher positions in the organization.

Occasionally I supervised offenders who were hostile, threatening, and perhaps even dangerous, both in the office and in jail. A great deal of skill is required to interact with such individuals. At times, probation officers may be in conflict with supervisors or branch chiefs on sentencing recommendations. Supervisors have a great deal more power than probation officers. Probation departments very often impose their own norms on probation officers. For example, in my probation department, there was a strong norm that provided for any offender convicted of a sexual offense to be recommended automatically for jail or prison. This norm was in conflict with some officers' own norms.

Other frustrations in a probation department include deadlines to be met and an enormous amount of paperwork.

The job of probation officer is perceived in different ways by different people who hold the position. For some, it is just a job that needs to be done to make a living. To others, it is a career, and they try to get promoted. Some people believe that it is not a match for their abilities, which can lead to a low self-concept, and even to psychological problems. Probation work inspired me to continue my education and to pursue my interest in writing, research, and teaching. It also gave me a second career after retirement.

Advice to Students: The best advice I can give to students contemplating a career in criminal justice is to remain in school, try to obtain good grades, and possibly advance to graduate work. Good writing skills and the ability to work under pressure are important. Most important, however, is the ability to interact with all kinds of people, especially the rejects of society. Also important, more so than academic ability, is to have a very strong interest in criminal justice.

communities and departmental bureaucracies. The officers control their enforcement patterns largely through a process of mutually accommodating informal roles (Walsh, 1984). The informal nature of role determination and enforcement patterns has contributed greatly to patrol officer work motivation and morale.

2. The informal group is more flexible than the formal organization as a communication medium. If formal communication networks are blocked for one reason or another (e.g., if one person at a higher level fails to pass along information to a subordinate because of forgetfulness or intentional withholding of it), then the informal grapevine usually will become aware of the information some other way. The transmission of information through informal channels of communication may be of benefit to organizational members on many occasions, but sometimes the network of informal interaction functions to their detriment. It has been said that the flow of information in any social group is always imperfect, if we define perfect communication as the transmission of all information to group members with equal speed and without error (Sykes, 1958:87).

In prison settings, for instance, labor turnover among correctional officers has been fairly high. Correctional officer stress often is blamed for high turnover rates. It may seem logical to conclude that the noise and filth of correctional officer surroundings in certain correctional settings may be the bases for such labor-turnover–related stress, although interviews with correctional officers reveal that the primary source of occupational stress often stems from the bureaucratic administration. Training programs have been established in many jurisdictions to enable officers to cope more effectively with stressful situations. However, correctional officers perceive themselves as "buffer workers" caught between superiors and inferiors with conflicting goals. They often consider their correctional roles as ill defined and ambiguous, with tenuous lines of support and with little perceived hope of improvement. Informal communication among officers enables them to acquire better self-definitions and can establish the belief that "somebody up there cares" (Gardner, 1981).

Apart from the fact that the informal group competes with the formal communication network for the transmission of information and possibly for power, at some point in time, a breakdown in communication or some distortion in the transmission of information is inevitable. Some of the important dysfunctions of informal groups on the job are listed in the following paragraphs:

1. Informal communication networks are dysfunctional to the extent that distorted or wrong information is disseminated to group members. Whenever rumors circulate from one person to the next, evidence indicates that because each person interprets the message differently, some transformation of information (rumor) will occur. By the time the original information reaches its intended audience through the informal grapevine, the information quite possibly has undergone some distortion, depending on the nature of the information flow. Virtually all organizational networks have mechanical defects so that messages go astray, lag excessively, are misunderstood, or are distorted, without any intention. Thus, in cybernetic jargon, any message includes a component of noise (Caplow, 1964:252–253).

Distorted rumors transmitted by informal grapevines to organizational members can lead to all kinds of serious outcomes. Misunderstandings between superiors and subordinates (latent or expressed) can foster apathy among employees and deliberate slowdowns or absenteeism. To the extent that distortions of information are perceived as bringing about changes in one's job, employee fears and anxieties are aroused, and the workers lose trust in those above them in the organization. Another concomitant of distortion of information may be resistance to change or new programs introduced by higher-ups. Although subsequent formal channels of communication may provide the organization members with accurate information about changes to be made and how certain jobs will be affected, sufficient damage already may have been done to organizational effectiveness. Some research shows that involving employees in decisions affecting their work and explaining the reasons for organizational changes can do

BOX 7.3 JUDGE IN HOT WATER OVER "TWO TO TANGO" COMMENT

Montgomery County Circuit Court Judge Durke G. Thompson. What does it take to get a judge to apologize for informal, off-the-cuff remarks made in a sentencing hearing? A lot. During a statutory rape case in Rockville, Maryland, against Vladimir Chacon-Bonilla, 23, facts were disclosed that Chacon-Bonilla had raped an 11-year-old girl. It was learned that Chacon-Bonilla had met the 11-year-old over the Internet in a chat room. Eventually, the two got together, and when it was too late to turn back, the 11-year-old was overpowered by Chacon-Bonilla and raped. Or so it seemed. Additional information provided by Chacon-Bonilla's defense counsel suggested that the 11-year-old was a more-than-willing participant in the sexual encounter. Following the presentation of evidence against Chacon-Bonilla, Montgomery County Circuit Court Judge Durke G. Thompson found Chacon-Bonilla guilty of a second-degree sex offense. At the sentencing hearing, Judge Thompson angered child advocates and prosecutors when he told the 11-year-old girl's parents that "it takes two to tango." He made these remarks as he sentenced Vladimir Chacon-Bonilla to an 18-month prison term. Later when interviewed by members of the press, Judge Thompson said, "I regret those words have caused concern and confusion over the seriousness and gravity with which I treated this matter. Nevertheless, I still think that the girl was partly to blame for being sexually molested by Chacon-Bonilla because of her Internet use and deceptive communications."

What do you think the judge meant by the "it takes two to tango" remark? This remark was made during the sentencing hearing for the offender. To what extent should judges make such informal remarks about the incidents over which they preside? If the judge had adhered strictly to formal communication principles, would these types of remarks ever have been made? What do you think?

Source: Adapted from the Associated Press, "Judge Apologizes for Comments," January 9, 2000.

much to create greater levels of social stability and job satisfaction (Jermier, 1979).

2. An alternative communication network in relation to the formal communication network can be a deterrent to effective norm enforcement and supervisory authority. The informal communication network may be viewed as a parallel set of power relations, in which knowledge of organizational events is a tool of manipulation over others. Formally authorized or legitimized officials are placed in awkward and humiliating positions when they discover that information about organizational affairs, particularly knowledge common only to their levels of authority and supposedly confined within their office boundaries, has become available to lower-level participants or subordinates without their realization. Under such circumstances, supervisors and other functionaries likely will believe that their authority has been undermined, and the importance of their official position in the eyes of their subordinates decreases substantially.

Relations between the police and prosecutors can become strained and in conflict whenever either aggregate perceives that the other has established unwritten rules or policies about how laws should be enforced or crimes should be prosecuted. Plea bargaining may undermine police confidence in the prosecutor's office, in instances in which officer safety has been placed in jeopardy to effect certain types of drug arrests. Plea bargaining may be regarded as defeating the rigorous law enforcement efforts of police officers, who make every effort to enforce the law. When prosecutors are seen as being soft on certain types of criminals in terms of their proffered leniency toward particular offenders, this situation creates an unhealthy ambiguity that can be detrimental to a community's law enforcement efforts as well as to officer morale (Littrell, 1979). However, police officers may not understand the need for case prioritizing if prosecutors' offices are understaffed and prosecutors are overworked because of massive caseloads (Heumann, 1978).

FORMAL AND INFORMAL COMMUNICATION NETWORKS: COMPLEMENTARITY

A generally accepted phenomenon is that formal organizations always are accompanied by informal groupings of employees. Both formal and informal organizational structures tend to generate parallel communication networks, authority patterns, and reward systems. Problems are encountered whenever information is transmitted too slowly through official formal channels or when the information disseminated by either the formal or informal communication network becomes distorted as it is passed on from one person to the next, from position to position, and from level to level.

Communication is vital to the organization. A sound communication system may help significantly to promote organizational effectiveness, whereas a communication network with several defects and limitations will tend to deter the organization from achieving its goals satisfactorily. For many years, managers of large firms and business administrators have analyzed the problems of communication in organizations from diverse viewpoints. For instance, the presence and significance of informal groups in organizations must be considered as equally important with the formal arrangement of the hierarchy of authority and the communication network. The inevitability that both kinds of organization will exist under one roof simultaneously makes it mandatory that we take into account the theoretical and substantive complementarity of these structures in our organizational research.

Formal organizational structures are dynamic entities, as are their dimensions and attributes (Schneider, 1991). As one significant attribute, the communication network of an organization is impermanent and transitory. It is a malleable dimension responsive to changes in many organizational variables (Levi, 1977). We must consider the nature and effectiveness of it within the context of change.

SUMMARY

Communication systems are networks designed to disseminate information throughout an organization to all persons and departments. Communication patterns in organizations have captured the attention of researchers who believe that organizational effectiveness is highly dependent on the nature of communication. Within a bureaucratic context, an authority hierarchy exists in all organizations. Formal communication networks tend to follow these authority hierarchies closely. Thus, communication is directed most often downward from supervisors to subordinates.

The bureaucratic model provides that abstract rules are known to all organizational members, and that information is transmitted frequently to them that will improve their work effectiveness. Formal, impersonal relations exist between work units, according to the bureaucratic model. It is unrealistic to expect that all organizations are totally dependent upon their formal communication networks for information, however. Arising out of every formal organization are groups of employees who form informal networks characterized as grapevines. Thus, all organizations have both formal and informal communication systems. These different kinds of communication systems or networks complement one another in various ways.

Several advantages of formal communication networks are that they facilitate the coordination of work activity that makes up the division of labor in any organization. Formal communication networks channel valuable information to all employees and also provide valuable information to employees about their work performance in the form of feedback from higher-ups. Formal communication networks also enable organizations to eliminate the duplication of different functions and to improve overall organizational effectiveness. A further function of formal communication networks is that they reinforce the existing organizational structure and power relations among positions.

Among the disadvantages and dysfunctions of formal communication networks are that frequently, they disseminate important information too slowly. The vertical and downward nature of information transmission means that seldom do lower-level participants have an opportunity to communicate information to their supervisors or administrators. Further, formal communication networks are inherently strained.

Out of all formal organizations and communication networks evolve informal communication networks and work groups. These informal work groups and the communication channels that characterize them are functional to the extent that they transmit information about organizational events more rapidly than formal communication channels. This information may be distorted or inaccurate on occasion, however. Yet a positive aspect of informal communication channels is that they are more flexible than formal communication networks. Another dysfunction of informal communication networks is that sometimes organizational rule enforcement and supervisory authority are undermined. Despite the dysfunctional aspects of informal communication networks, effective communication, either formal or informal, is indispensable to all organizations. Sound communication systems enable organizations to improve their overall effectiveness. Both formal and informal communication networks are complementary with one another, and organizational, interpersonal, and individual units are affected in various ways by these networks.

QUESTIONS FOR REVIEW

1. What is meant by the formal communication network? How is it related to the chain of command or hierarchy of authority?

2. What is an organizational chart? What is it intended to depict? How do organizational charts differ from real-world action occurring in organizational settings? Discuss.

3. How does communication become increasingly important as an organization becomes larger?

4. What are the wheel, chain, star, and "Y" communication experiments? Which communication pattern is associated with the highest amount of worker satisfaction? Which communication pattern is associated with the lowest amount of worker satisfaction? Why?

5. What are three important functions of formal communication networks?

6. What are three important dysfunctions of formal communication networks?

7. What is the difference between the formal and informal communication network? What are some functions of each?

8. In what sense does a formal organization spontaneously create informal organizational networks? What are some implications of informal communication networks for affecting organizational effectiveness?

9. Are formal communication networks always good? Why or why not? Are informal communication networks always bad? Why or why not?

10. What are several important factors that have influenced the evolution of informal groups in the work setting?

SUGGESTED READINGS

MacDonald, S. Scott, and Cynthia Hart-Baroody (1999). "Communication Between Probation Officers and Judges: An Innovative Model." *Federal Probation* **63**:42–50.

McCamey, William P., and Gayle Tronvig Carper (1998). "Social Skills and Police: An Initial Study." *Journal of Crime and Justice* **21**:95–102.

Schneider, Stephen R. (1999). "Overcoming Barriers to Communication Between Police and Socially Disadvantaged Neighborhoods: A Critical Theory of Community Policing." *Crime, Law, and Social Change* **30**:347–377.

• CASE STUDIES •

1. THE OVERWORKED POLICE CHIEF

You are Chief Richard Jenkins, the 46-year-old head of a medium-sized police department in a midwestern city. You find that your days are busier than you anticipated when you first took on this job five years ago. You are frequently invited to speak at schools and civic luncheons. You have been asked to join various boards and clubs. City councilmen and the mayor are continually calling you for favors, either for themselves or their constituents. During a particular week, you are asked to preside at the opening ceremonies of a new indoor target range established for city and county law enforcement officers. The ceremonies are scheduled for the following Monday, August 26. You accept and the planners of the ceremonies prepare a program with your name as a keynote speaker. Late on August 23,

your secretary advises you that a progress report on your departmental activities is due to the mayor and city council by 5:00 P.M. on Monday, August 26.

After a hectic weekend that included preparing for the speech you plan to present at the opening ceremonies for the shooting range, you arrive at your office at 8:30 A.M. on Monday. A detective has arranged to see you at 9:00 A.M. to advise that one of your police officers, Officer Ben Smith, has been arrested over the weekend on a drunken-driving charge in another county, but that the state highway patrol officer who made the arrest wants to talk with you about it before filing his arrest report. The highway patrol officer is waiting outside in the hallway. Your recollection of Ben Smith is that he is a fairly reliable officer with 19 years' experience with the department. His career is without blemish. He has an excellent driving record. Smith is one of the most popular officers in the department, and he is well liked by virtually every other officer. Many of them look up to him because he has received several citations for bravery in the line of duty during his years with the department. But you also know that his only daughter was recently killed in a plane crash and that he has been deeply depressed since that event. As you are thinking about Ben Smith, you receive a telephone call from your son at home. A water pipe has burst in your home basement and the basement is beginning to flood. Your son says that if you don't come home in a big hurry, your extensive rifle and pistol collection in a large gun case on the basement floor will be ruined. With your mind on the opening ceremonies and the progress report you planned to polish up later that afternoon, how are you going to arrange your schedule to accomplish these tasks?

Questions for Discussion

1. What priority should you give to each of these events? (A) the opening ceremonies for the shooting range; (B) the flood in your home basement and possible loss of thousands of dollars worth of firearms; (C) the detective and the highway patrol officer who are there to see you about Officer Ben Smith; (D) the report due to the mayor and city council by 5:00 P.M. that very afternoon.

2. What should you do when the highway patrol officer comes into your office? You anticipate that he might want to feel you out concerning the arrest of Ben Smith. How should you communicate your feelings about this situation? Should you disclose to the highway patrol officer Ben Smith's private matters? Why or why not?

3. How should you handle the matter of Ben Smith himself? You plan to have a conversation with Smith concerning his drunk-driving arrest later. What should you say to Smith to bring up the subject? What would you accept as a defense of Smith's actions?

4. Should you put off your speaking engagement in view of these urgent departmental developments? Should you ask the city council and mayor for more time in presenting your departmental report? Why or why not? How do you think such a delay would be interpreted by the councilmen and the mayor?

5. Should you use your position as chief to intervene in Smith's drunken-driving charge and ask the highway patrolman to downgrade the charge to reckless driving? Why or why not? What message would this send to the highway patrol about your view of law enforcement?

2. SERGEANT JOE BRIGGS

You are Daniel Wells, the chief investigator of the drug unit of a large metropolitan police department. An officer, Sgt. Joe Briggs, has been with the police department for 21 years. During that time, Briggs has received six citations and commendations for actions taken in the line of duty to prevent crimes from occurring or to save the lives of crime victims. Briggs has a bachelor's degree in police science. Complaints from citizens against him have been minimal, especially when compared with other officers in the department. During the past year, however, Briggs's wife left him and his three children for someone else in another state. Briggs received divorce papers and the divorce

occurred three months ago. He appeared not to take the divorce too hard, but rearing three children on his own has placed Briggs under a great deal of stress. Briggs began showing up late for work. Several citizens filed complaints against him for his overbearing attitude when they were stopped for traffic violations. Briggs's partner, Fred Jones, has told others informally that he senses that Briggs occasionally seems "high," as though he were on something.

In a recent bust of alleged drug dealers, investigating detectives discovered Briggs rummaging through a bedroom closet in the house where the drug suspects lived. Subsequently, when the alleged drug suspects were charged and arraigned, it was disclosed that 18 ounces of cocaine had been confiscated. One of the suspects blurted out in court, "There was a kilo of coke in our closet! Somebody ripped us off." No one seemed to pay much attention to this statement, but Jones suspected that Briggs had taken some of the cocaine. Within a few days following the drug bust, a reliable informant advised Jones that his partner, Briggs, had caught the informant selling cocaine six weeks earlier. According to the informant, Briggs had demanded all of the drugs in exchange for keeping quiet about the incident. Jones told the detectives what his informant had told him about Briggs.

The following Friday evening, Jones and other officers were invited to Briggs's house to watch a football game. At one point, Jones asked if he could use the bathroom. Briggs told him, "Use mine in the bedroom down the hall, 'cause it's cleaner and the kids are using the guest bathroom." Jones used the bedroom bathroom, and when he flushed the toilet, the water continued to run. He jiggled the handle but the toilet kept running. Jones lifted the water basin lid to fix the problem and noticed two plastic bags taped to the inner basin that contained a white substance. Jones pulled off one of the bags and examined the contents. It was cocaine. He replaced the cocaine in the toilet water basin and went back to join the others watching the game. The next morning, Jones calls for an urgent appointment with you and tells you what he found at Briggs's house. Further, he tells you the stories of the missing cocaine from a recent drug bust and the alleged shakedown of one of his reliable informants. You advise Jones that you will look into it.

Questions for Discussion

1. Which other personnel should you communicate with in your attempt to learn more about Briggs's conduct?

2. Should you have a meeting with Briggs directly, or should you have other detectives question him about the missing drugs?

3. Since you were the person Fred Jones chose to contact, how much responsibility should you bear for assigning others to investigate Briggs? Should you report Briggs's activities to the chief of police or others at this point? Why or why not?

4. What influence, if any, should Briggs's commendations and citations in past years have on whether you pursue the investigation against him vigorously?

5. Knowing that Briggs is rearing three children on his own and is recently divorced, should any special provisions be made for referring his case to private counseling and therapy?

CHAPTER
8

MOTIVATION, SATISFACTION, AND MORALE
OF EMPLOYEES

KEY TERMS

Achievement motivation theory   Dual-factor theory of motivation   Job enrichment

Burnout   Equity theory   Satisfiers

Dissatisfiers   Expectancy theory   Stress

CHAPTER OBJECTIVES

The following objectives are intended:

1. To describe several important need schemes that relate to personal motivation and work satisfaction

2. To relate job satisfaction with specific organizational, interpersonal, and individual variables

3. To show how various motivational models influence work group and employee effectiveness

4. To examine several critical factors that influence job satisfaction

5. To describe the relation of job satisfaction, motivation, and morale of employees to stress and burnout, job prestige and status, the nature of the organizational reward structure, and participation in decision making

INTRODUCTION

This chapter is about the motivation, satisfaction, and morale of criminal justice employees and their supervisors. Organizational effectiveness is greatly dependent on the work orientations of members and the successful performance of their tasks—whether they are hourly workers, salaried, or voluntary personnel (Hanna, 1987). The nature and complexity of the authority hierarchy and the complementarity between formal and in-

formal communication networks in the organization are primary considerations as well (Stewart et al., 1995). Consistent with this view, this chapter examines the importance of the job satisfaction, motivation, and morale of criminal justice workers as each supposedly functions in relation to overall organizational effectiveness. Our major focus of attention is some of the more crucial factors in organizations that elicit predictable changes in these variables. Of necessity we include the individual and individuals' attitudes that influence work orientations and job performance. But it also must be acknowledged that worker attitudes and motivations have been associated with negative outcomes, including job stress and suicide (Schmidtke, Fricke, and Lester, 1999).

It is difficult if not impossible to gain adequate knowledge of intraorganizational activity without considering the psychological attributes and attitudinal perceptions of organizational members (Aldag and Brief, 1978). This does not mean that sociological factors in organizations will be ignored. Rather, the intent is to investigate the interplay of sociological and psychological variables and how they contribute to the effectiveness of organizations. This chapter examines some of the salient literature on worker motivation, job satisfaction, and morale in a variety of criminal justice organizations. It also delineates and discusses some of the more important interrelations among specific organizational, interpersonal, and individual variables and their conjoint action on personal satisfaction with tasks performed, motivation toward work, and group morale.

THE LOGIC OF CONSIDERING PERSONAL MOTIVATIONS IN ORGANIZATIONAL RESEARCH

Although there are certain problems with conceptualizing organizational effectiveness, this variable is the overwhelming preoccupation of organizational leadership. The bulk of the existing literature about organizational behavior is directly or indirectly stimulated by a generalized concern for organizational effectiveness and its diverse concomitants (Weston, 1978). Some people believe that virtually all literature about organizational behavior is designed to provide management with new and more effective means of manipulating lower-level employees for some kind of personal gain (Hanna, 1987; Stewart et al., 1995). Although it is true that various benefits accrue to management as the result of much organizational research, it also must be acknowledged that commensurate benefits are obtained by the lower-level membership as well. Strong arguments may be formulated for each view, but it is not our intention to discuss the goodness or badness of organizational research and its implications for the deliberate manipulation of organizational behavior. Rather, our attention will be directed toward describing the presence or absence of variables (organizational, interpersonal, and individual) that correlate highly with the motivations and satisfactions of employees.

A number of factors associated with organizational effectiveness are identified as individual attitudes and orientations toward the work performed and strong attachments to small work groups. Figure 8.1 shows a common approach to organizational effectiveness based on personal and interpersonal considerations. It is not difficult to follow the logic underlying the relationships portrayed in the diagram. The individual is considered by this logic to be the central figure in all functional organizational operations. If

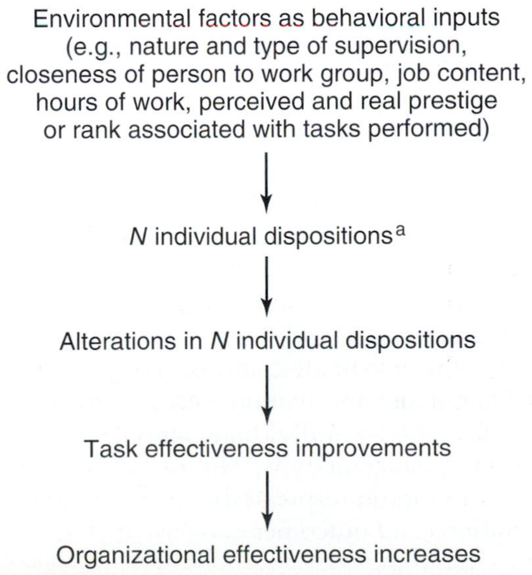

Environmental factors as behavioral inputs
(e.g., nature and type of supervision,
closeness of person to work group, job content,
hours of work, perceived and real prestige
or rank associated with tasks performed)

↓

N individual dispositions[a]

↓

Alterations in N individual dispositions

↓

Task effectiveness improvements

↓

Organizational effectiveness increases

FIGURE 8.1 The Individual and Organizational Effectiveness

[a]N individual dispositions refers to the multiplicity of personality or attitudinal attributes that are directed toward what one does within the definition of the work role in an organization. No single attribute or characteristic or individual sentiment or orientation is believed to be a direct causal factor in relation to task effectiveness. Rather, many of these sentiments operating conjointly make up a profile of an individual disposed to improve quality or quantity of performance or both.

Source: Compiled by author.

certain key factors are introduced, eliminated, or altered in the life space of the individual (i.e., the person's external environment), then it is argued that changes in the individual's psychological disposition will occur. The resulting dispositions will lead to noticeable increases or decreases in individual effectiveness in task performance. Improvements in task performance of most persons in the organization will generally improve overall organizational effectiveness. Therefore, we find ourselves turning to a fundamental question pertaining to intraorganizational behavior: What motivates a person to perform tasks with maximum effectiveness? Almost all criminal justice organizational research can be seen as providing potential partial answers to this question.

Max Weber's conception of the ideal type of bureaucratic organization incorporated elements similar to those we will discuss. In addition to prescribing the duties and responsibilities of organizational officials in a formal authority hierarchy with abstract rules, Weber outlined certain dispositions that officials should have toward the tasks they perform (e.g., they should view their work as a career or a predominant life activity and manifest strong loyalty toward their employing organization). In Weber's view, the end result of such dispositions would be the maximization of organizational effectiveness and efficiency (supposedly achieved by hiring loyal personnel who are experts in specialized spheres of competence and are highly committed to the goals of the organization). This view has some merit and deserves consideration. But it also may be an oversimplification of the relation between employee sentiment and overall organizational effectiveness. It seems more productive to regard individual motivation and satisfaction as contributing to rather than determining the effectiveness of organizations.

JOB SATISFACTION AND THE MOTIVATION OF EMPLOYEES

What is the relation between job satisfaction and motivation to produce in criminal justice organizations? This question is inevitably asked because a prevailing belief exists that a satisfied employee is a more productive one. Thus far, the evidence supporting this belief is inconsistent, inconclusive, and often contradictory. The formalized search for variables leading to increased job satisfaction (i.e., contentment of employ-

ees with a variety of work dimensions) and presumably greater productivity is generally acknowledged to have commenced with the Hawthorne studies, which were examined in Chapter 3. These studies focused on the manipulation of environmental factors, such as the frequency and length of rest pauses and the amount of illumination, and how they were associated with improvements in work performance by industrial laborers in a division of the Western Electric Company in Chicago (Roethlisberger and Dickson, 1939). One of the more important implications of these studies was that worker satisfaction was more a function of the humane treatment shown by supervisors and the cohesive relations among workers than a function of any specific financial incentives or physical conditions (e.g., rest pauses, temperatures of workrooms, or illumination of work environment). Although many statements have been made for and against these studies, the findings (regardless of their validity) prompted numerous investigations of similar relations among variables in a variety of work settings (Hilgendorf and Irving, 1969:415).

It is discouraging to report that the accumulation of information about worker satisfaction with various job dimensions and motivation to produce during the most recent 30-year period has been largely descriptive and speculative. This is true despite the fact that much of the research has been experimental.

The following motivational schemes have been used to relate work quantity and quality with employee motivation: (1) Abraham Maslow (1954) sees motivation as a function of the degree to which an organization can meet certain needs that he has postulated to exist in a hierarchy (needs of physiology, safety, belonging, esteem, and self-fulfillment or self-actualization); (2) Frederick Herzberg (1966; Herzberg et al., 1959) advances a dual-factor theory of worker motivation, a theory that specifies that different factors account for satisfaction ("satisfier" factors such as characteristics of job content) as opposed to "dissatisfiers" or those factors that stimulate job dissatisfaction (e.g., "preventative" factors, including environmental conditions; company policy and administration; status; technical supervision; and interpersonal relations among superiors, subordinates, and peers); (3) Victor Vroom (1964:6) defines motivation as a process governing choices, made by individuals among alternative forms of voluntary activity. His research views satisfaction with work in terms of the relationship between expectations and outcomes.

FIGURE 8.2 Maslow's Hierarchy of Needs

Source: Abraham Maslow, *Motivation and Personality* (New York: Harper), p. 124.

Maslow's Hierarchy of Needs

Maslow (1954) investigated the needs of various types of persons in diverse work environments. His efforts led to the establishment of a hierarchy of needs, illustrated in Figure 8.2.

The hierarchy of needs is a pyramid with physiological needs at its base. Self-actualization needs are shown at the top of the pyramid. Between the physiological needs at the base and self-actualization needs at the top, other needs are identified, including safety needs, belongingness needs, and esteem needs. Maslow considered the lowest needs at the base of the pyramid to be the most basic needs of human beings. Physiological needs are associated with hunger and thirst. As an individual achieves or satisfies these lower needs, other higher needs emerge as important. Safety needs concern one's desire for security from danger. Having a roof over one's head or a safe place to stay satisfies the safety need. Once people know they will eat and have a roof over their heads, they concern themselves with belonging or bonding with others, according to Maslow. Belongingness needs involve the need for friendship, social associations, and love. If the belongingness need is satisfied, then persons seek es-

teem. Esteem needs include recognition and the desire for self-respect. Theoretically, at least, once the esteem need is satisfied, then an individual will attempt to fulfill his or her self-actualization need, which is the development of a person's ultimate potential.

Related to work experiences in probation and parole work, for instance, Maslow's need scheme could be applied as follows: A probation officer has a guaranteed salary and fringe benefits. This enables the officer to satisfy the physiological and safety needs. Next, the officer seeks to establish good social relations with colleagues and/or probationer/parolee-clients. The probation officer next seeks promotion or some type of pay increase, advancement, or other form of recognition. Perhaps the esteem need is fulfilled if the officer has a low recidivism rate associated with his or her client-probationers. The officer may seek to publish articles in professional journals about probation work and ways for improving probation officer effectiveness or may become an officer in a probation or parole association. These events satisfy one's need for esteem. Subsequently, the officer may attempt to satisfy self-actualization needs by accepting more challenging work assignments or supervising more difficult clients. Some officers may take additional training or coursework to certify themselves as experts in particular client problems, such as drug or alcohol dependencies or psychological disturbances. This advanced training may be regarded as moving toward developing one's ultimate potential.

Therefore, Maslow's scheme provides a framework within which to view employee motivation to work harder or to become more effective. The hierarchy of needs to be fulfilled is a convenient way of explaining why some employees work harder than others. It also provides a way for managers to manipulate employees in different ways to inspire them to perform well and succeed in their jobs. Thus, it is not unusual for managers to say, "If you do these sorts of things over time, eventually you can become an administrator or supervisor." In police work, many line officers aspire to become detectives and perform plainclothes work. And so they are motivated by a desire for advancement to jobs associated with greater prestige and recognition, powerful driving forces to inspire workers.

Maslow's scheme places all worker motivation to perform in a positive context. The scheme assumes that persons are motivated by a desire to become upwardly mobile, continually seeking new challenges, new positions, new responsibilities, and greater esteem and recognition. Therefore, Maslow is at a loss to explain why more than a few people working in different criminal justice organizations do not want to be promoted. They prefer to remain in their present positions, performing work they know how to do. They may be afraid of new challenges and responsibilities. They turn down opportunities for promotion and never apply for higher-ranking positions in their departments. Some security can be found in the performance of repetitive work. Furthermore, Maslow's scheme fails to account for persons who engage in acts of corruption or misconduct. Why do some police officers jeopardize their jobs by committing perjury on the witness stand or by stealing from victims? Why do some officers accept illegal gratuities from drug dealers and others engaged in illegal enterprises in exchange for looking the other way? Maslow's hierarchy of needs does not explain this kind of motivation. We cannot explain it either.

Vroom's Dual-Factor Theory of Motivation

Victor Vroom (1964) draws heavily on the work of Maslow, although Vroom has divided different motivating factors into two categories, satisfiers and dissatisfiers. **Satisfiers** are those factors related directly to job content, such as the intrinsic interest in work performed, the potential for advancement and recognition, and the responsibility of the tasks. **Dissatisfiers** have to do with working conditions, such as the nature of supervision, the supervisor-subordinate relation, salary, and work stress. Vroom called his view the **dual-factor theory of motivation.**

The significance of distinguishing between satisfiers and dissatisfiers is that different factors account for one's satisfaction and dissatisfaction. For instance, we might increase the diversity of work performed by an individual, and this in turn might cause a person's satisfaction with work to increase. However, if we were to simplify an employee's work tasks, this would not necessarily cause the employee's satisfaction to decrease. As another example, we might increase a police officer's work stress by changing from two-person patrol units to one-person patrol units, thus making patrols more risky and life threatening. This might cause an officer's dissatisfaction with the job to increase. However, if we were to increase the safety conditions of patrols, this would not necessarily lessen a particular officer's dissatisfaction with the work, since police

work is stressful generally. Also, the fact that police officer salaries are typically low compared with other jobs in the private sector may be a strong source of job dissatisfaction. If we were to increase officers' salaries, this change may have no impact whatsoever on the level of dissatisfaction, since the officers may believe they are entitled to the pay increase anyway.

Vroom's Expectancy Theory

Vroom (1964) also described **expectancy theory,** which casts a worker's motivation to perform into a performance-outcome framework. Employees are taught by their organizations that hard work and following the rules will lead to desirable outcomes, such as promotion, advancement, and greater recognition. This is similar to the carrot-stick philosophy, meaning that specific rewards are held out as incentives to conform with the rules, and through hard work, the rewards eventually will be realized or achieved.

In fact, Vroom's expectancy theory is a derivative of the descriptive work of Max Weber, who set forth several predictable outcomes of officeholders in a bureaucracy. Efficient and effective job performance should lead to promotion; the best performers are advanced to higher positions with greater rewards. These rewards are articulated in advance, and thus, workers are motivated to achieve them. They have sufficient expertise to know how to perform their jobs well, and there is strong organizational support for those seeking to advance up the hierarchy of authority toward greater recognition and responsibility.

Other Motivational Theories

Several other theories have been described that parallel closely the works of Maslow and Vroom. One Maslow offshoot is **achievement motivation theory,** elaborated by David McClelland (1985). McClelland says that persons engage in goal-setting behaviors, in which the goals involve challenging work. Through aggressive action toward goal attainment, and through a problem-solving process, people obtain important feedback from others, such as supervisors and other workers, about the quality of their work performance. The ultimate payoff for high achievers is the attainment of desired goals, such as promotions, advancements, and tangible recognition and rewards. Sometimes, **job enrichment** has been used to describe the process of vesting particular work tasks and responsibilities with more intrinsically interesting functions. Job enrichment is not simply giving people more to do in their present jobs. Job enrichment implies infusing tasks with problem-solving activities and more complex and challenging duties that require thinking and creativity. Job enrichment seems to work for those employees with greater amounts of education (Carlan, 1999; Hoath, Schneider, and Starr, 1998). But for those with lesser amounts of education, job enrichment may be threatening and not desired (Dantzker, 1994, 1997).

Another view of motivation is **equity theory.** Equity theory posits that workers desire equitable treatment when performing their jobs. They compare themselves with others who perform similar work tasks. They believe that their work output is a product of their job input, and that the rewards as outcomes should be equivalent to the rewards of others who expend similar energy to reach the same goals. Workers are content to the extent that they perceive that equity exists among all employees who perform similar work and are rewarded by the system equally (Harris and Baldwin, 1999). However, if perceptions of some workers suggest inequities in rewards given for similar work, then tension is created (Winfree and Newbold, 1999).

Frankly, almost everyone who performs work in any criminal justice agency wants to be treated equitably or equally with others who do similar work. The fact is that not everyone sees their work as exactly equivalent to the work performed by others, even if administrators consider the different work tasks to be similar or even identical. Male police officers, for instance, may resent the intrusion of female police officers into a traditionally male work environment. That female officers are paid at the same rate as male officers may cause some male officers to feel that they are being treated unfairly, particularly if they believe that males are doing a better law enforcement job compared with females.

As another example, court clerks and court reporters may view one another as essentially on the same level in terms of the importance of work performed. But court clerks may be resentful of court reporters, who may receive higher pay for their courtroom activities. But many court reporters must complete much of their courtroom work at home at night in order to keep up with the cases on which they are working, a fact that may be ignored by resentful clerks. These unseen intangibles create the appearance of inequity, which may have the same demoralizing effect as if inequity actually existed.

In probation and parole work, some probation officers may resent other officers who are perceived to have lighter work schedules. Some probation officers supervise fewer clients compared with other officers, but these fewer numbers of clients may be under more intensive probation supervision. This more intensive supervision may require a probation officer to spend a great deal of time in the field conducting surveillance and writing reports. Those with higher caseloads may not have as much paper detail and surveillance responsibility, although they may perceive the difference in caseloads as a major inequity.

Most of these theoretical schemes about worker motivation are linked closely with Max Weber's bureaucratic model and how officerholders are supposed to orient themselves toward their work. Weber's ideal description of a bureaucratic setting set forth equity as a major requirement. Each person would have a particular sphere of competence and expertise. Each person would be paid according to the relative importance of work performed. But as we have already seen, Weber's ideal plans are flawed and frustrated by organizational reality and personality systems.

Most attempts to summarize the job satisfaction literature have noted the difficulty of trying to compare different studies because of the diversity of methodological approaches used and variations in definitions of key concepts (Cordner, 1978). Several factors seem associated with job satisfaction, such as individual differences, age, education and intelligence, gender, immediate supervision, social environment, communication, security, monotony, and pay. Work performance, absenteeism, and labor turnover are alternative consequences of job satisfaction (Fournet, Distefano, and Pryer, 1966; Weston, 1978).

Another summary of job satisfaction findings suggests that a more appropriate way of defining satisfaction is in terms of the degree of fit between organizational demands and individual needs, and that the employee's satisfaction with the job and the employer's satisfaction with work quality and performance will only be high when this fit is a good one (Farkas, 1999; Mumford, 1970:72). The general nature of one's work environment is also an important source of job satisfaction (Zhao, Thurman, and He, 1999).

FACTORS RELATED TO JOB SATISFACTION

Job satisfaction is the positive orientation of an individual toward the work role that is presently being performed, which can be restated as an individual liking more aspects of the work than aspects disliked

(Vroom, 1964:99). Social scientists believe that the most important factor related to job success is motivation, and that at the heart of motivation is work satisfaction (Arkin, 1975; Brief, Aldag, and Wallden, 1978). Some of the more significant factors affecting job satisfaction that are a part of intraorganizational behavior and that have been investigated as independent variables in relation to this term are (1) style of supervision or leadership; (2) the intrinsic interest of the job; (3) the cohesiveness or cohesion of work groups (possibly interpersonal conflict or harmony); (4) workload and pressure; (5) the prestige or status of the job in relation to other jobs (possibly involving perceived opportunities for advancement or enlargement of the job); (6) the type of reward structure (e.g., payment on an hourly, daily, weekly, monthly, or annual basis); and (7) participation in decision making.

Style of Leadership or Supervision

Research on job satisfaction has devoted considerable attention to delineating particular styles of leadership or supervisory behaviors that function to alter one's attitude toward the task performed. Some evidence indicates that job satisfaction is affected by certain styles of leadership in predictable ways. An early study by James Worthy (1950) examined flat (those with few supervisory levels and wide spans of control) versus tall (those with many supervisory levels and narrow spans of control) organizational structures in Sears, Roebuck and Company. The argument was that supervisors with narrow spans of control supervised their subordinates closely, whereas in flat structures, supervisors were forced to spend their time coordinating work activity rather than concentrating their attention on the performance of any given employee. The general implications of Worthy's research appeared to be that the more persons supervised, the more general the supervision, and the more the employees working under these conditions liked their jobs. Other studies have lent support to the contention that styles of leadership or supervision that allow subordinates a high degree of freedom of movement or autonomy will engender greater job satisfaction among those subordinates (Reisig, 1996).

For instance, supervisors who exhibit interest in their subordinates and support them in the tasks they perform are significantly more likely to stimulate increased job satisfaction among lower-level personnel (Zander, 1961). However, some researchers caution that simply being employee centered and showing consideration or permissiveness will not automatically lead to increased job satisfaction among employees. A critical factor in determining whether an employee would be favorably responsive to a supervisor's consideration was the amount of influence the supervisor had up the line with superiors (Pelz, 1952). Supervisors who had more influence with their own superiors and who also were permissive toward subordinates elicited higher job satisfaction from them, whereas those supervisors with little or no influence up the line generated job dissatisfaction among their subordinates, even though these supervisors were supportive of their employees.

Certainly factors in addition to supervisory behavior must be considered as possible intervening variables affecting the results of these investigations. For instance, blanket generalizations cannot be made about which style of leadership will lead to higher job satisfaction among employees. Obvious variations in the socioeconomic status of subordinates, their age, educational achievement, seniority in the organization, and many other factors are likely to interact with the styles of leadership exhibited at a given time and place. There does appear to be consensus among researchers that humanistic, permissive leadership is an effective means of managing subordinates. At least, few researchers fail to condone permissive leadership practices in relation to the satisfaction and productivity of workers.

The Intrinsic Interest of the Job and Job Content

Job satisfaction is frequently viewed from the position that jobs that offer challenges and contain intrinsically satisfying characteristics, as opposed to more simplistic tasks, are inherently more rewarding to the employee (Buzawa, Austin, and Bannon, 1994; Dantzker, 1994). For instance, Faunce (1958) found job satisfaction to be highly correlated with employees' perceptions of their work experiences in nonautomated engine plants compared with subsequent experiences in automated ones. Workers with more education found automated tasks less satisfying than workers with less education did. One implication here is that the more education a person has, the more challenging one's expectations about the job to be performed in order for it to be satisfying and rewarding.

A study of job satisfaction and motivation of employees at Texas Instruments Inc. has revealed that a challenging job is one that allows a feeling of achievement, responsibility, growth, advancement, enjoyment of the work itself, and earned recognition (Myers, 1964). It also was found that certain job dissatisfiers existed, including conditions external to the job being performed (e.g., seniority rights, fringe benefits, and coffee breaks). It may be that job enrichment may lead to increased satisfaction with tasks and can be obtained if employees exhibiting certain abilities and skills are matched with challenging jobs commensurate with such skills (Herzberg, 1968).

Some of the early research on the influence of responsibility and challenge on satisfaction reveals findings essentially consistent with contemporary investigations. For instance, a study of drill-press operators in the parts-manufacturing department of an IBM plant found that the job operators initially performed boring and repetitive activities (Walker, 1950). During a subsequent 10-year period, various changes occurred in the plant that upgraded the jobs by raising the level of skill required and instituting more complex operations. The end result of the change was job enlargement. Job enlargement was accompanied by a substantial rise in efficiency and job satisfaction. More interest, variety, and responsibility were perceived by workers to be integral aspects of their changed jobs. But other research has shown that job enlargement and redesign also have yielded negligible effects on one's job satisfaction level in certain organizations, such as police departments (Lund, 1988).

A close connection can be found between job satisfaction and individual needs, including those outlined by Abraham Maslow. Some support for the scheme's validity can be found if Maslow's need scheme is applied to the work setting. For instance, a sample of Catholic priests was studied to determine some of the reasons for variations in satisfaction among them (Carey, 1972). The study showed that those priests who felt that their positions allowed them greater opportunity for self-expression were significantly more satisfied with their work than those who did not.

Satisfaction of needs and a feeling of doing work that is important are two important factors for increasing job satisfaction. For instance, a survey of 2,680 skilled female workers in 48 sections of a large company revealed that during a four-month period, there were 169 resignations. Those who resigned were interviewed and completed questionnaires, and their responses were compared with those who remained on the job (Ross and Zander, 1957). Based on a survey of those who quit compared with those who remained on the job, those who quit had perceived lower degrees of recognition, had more dissatisfaction with recognition, were dissatisfied with their personal achievements, perceived considerably less autonomy, and were more dissatisfied with their autonomy.

Some investigators do not believe that we should place too much emphasis on job enlargement and challenge as a means of promoting greater job satisfaction. Sometimes the factors that account for differences in job satisfaction levels are prior work experiences and cultural differences among workers (Hulin and Blood, 1968). It may be, for instance, that two persons who perform identical functions in the same organization and who receive equal pay may not assess their job in the same way or to the same degree. The explanation may be that the workers have different work values that are suggestive of different cultural backgrounds and individual aspirations, and that have a latent effect (Homans, 1961:271).

Those who perform scientific jobs have been studied to determine their job satisfaction. For instance, a large military research and development laboratory with 82 scientists was investigated (Friedlander and Walton, 1964). These workers were asked, "What would you say are the most important factors that are operating to keep you here with this organization?" The scientists said that among the prime satisfiers that attracted them to their positions was their interest in the work and their technical freedom.

Some support for this view also can be found in the police literature. Based on questionnaires administered to 162 police officers in four New Mexico police departments, the effects of service, gender, and work activities were studied by Winfree, Guiterman, and Mays (1997). Generally, officers' job satisfaction levels were related more closely to what they did than to who they were. Job satisfaction levels of officers in the junior ranks with fewer years of on-the-job experience were generally lower than officers with more years of experience and those in their mid-career or late-career stages. These findings suggest that as officers acquire greater experience and responsibility, their job satisfaction levels increase accordingly. Career growth potential and greater organizational commitment among police officers over time seemed to enhance job satisfaction levels of a sample of officers studied in the Los Angeles Police Department as well (Lasley and Hooper, 1998). Gender and ethnicity among police officers have not been significantly related with job satisfaction (Felkenes and Lasley, 1992).

Another factor to consider is that in many criminal justice organizations, including police agencies, increasing numbers of new recruits have greater amounts of education. Thus, better-trained and more highly educated recruits are entering the police officer workforce annually and are expecting greater job challenges. For instance, Mark Dantzker and his associates (Dantzker and Surrette, 1996) have studied 2,611 police officers in 12 urban agencies located in seven states. These officers responded to 23 job-specific and three global job satisfaction items. Although the officers generally were satisfied with their work, it was clear that these officers had anticipated that their work should be more intrinsically challenging in order to meet their previous work expectations. In some of the departments Dantzker studied, he found that those officers who said they were dissatisfied with their jobs believed that the jobs simply did not measure up to their personal expectations and were not considered challenging. Dantzker concluded that the failure of police organizations to respond to this change in the profile of entering recruits could lead to increasingly dissatisfied officers. A logical consequence to be expected is that greater labor turnover might occur as dissatisfaction with work increases.

Some distinction has been made between factors as either positive or negative motivators to elicit, respectively, job satisfaction or job dissatisfaction. Positive motivators are often linked with factors intrinsic to the job itself, whereas negative motivators, or those factors that can cause dissatisfaction with work, are extrinsic in nature. The following factors have been identified as intrinsic and positive: (1) recognition, (2) achievement, (3) the work itself, (4) advancement, and (5) responsibility. The factors considered as extrinsic and negative are (1) salary, (2) company policies, (3) the technical competence of the respondent's supervisor, (4) interpersonal relations, and (5) working conditions (Biggam and Power, 1996; Wernimont, 1966).

Opportunities for advancement and promotion have been found to affect a worker's level of satisfaction positively. Furthermore, community support for the work police officers perform as well as recognition for greater work effectiveness appeared to increase job satisfaction level for police officers studied in several different countries (Bennett, 1997).

Intrinsic work factors also may pertain to whether or not employees believe that they are making a difference in the lives of those they assist or supervise (Graves, 1996). For instance, in a Prison Social Climate Survey of 2,979 correctional officers in the U.S. Bureau of Prisons, those correctional officers who believed that their interpersonal interactions with inmates in institutional settings were significant exhibited greater job satisfaction levels than officers who did not perceive their interactions and interventions with inmates as significant (Britton, 1997). And in two separate studies of Canadian correctional institutions, a study of 658 employees within the federal correctional jurisdiction and a sample of 213 officers with postsecondary educational credentials showed that those officers with the lowest degrees of organizational commitment and who were the least positive about their influence in rehabilitating offenders had the lowest levels of job satisfaction. Also, they were least involved in their jobs and had the poorest work habits. By comparison, officers who had greater organizational commitment and believed they made a positive difference in offenders' lives had much higher levels of work satisfaction and job performance (Robinson, Porporino, and Simourd, 1996, 1997).

In probation work, an officer's job satisfaction also has been found to be highly dependent on client success experiences. If a probation officer's clients have been successful and have refrained from committing new offenses, officer satisfaction levels are particularly high (Shillingstad et al., 1995).

Job satisfaction clearly is a multifaceted variable, dependent on many things besides intrinsic job factors associated with job content (Henderson, 1981; Sullivan, 1977). Thus, the presence of certain factors (e.g., salary, good interpersonal relations) may not necessarily increase satisfaction, but their absence may cause dissatisfaction. Persons who are well paid, for instance, may accept their salaries as commensurate with their abilities and skills: "It's good they're paying me this high salary because I'm worth it." But if these same persons are underpaid, it could be a sore point: "I'm good and ought to be paid much more than they are currently paying me." There is not necessarily a one-to-one relation between variations, either increases or decreases, of particular variables and changes in satisfaction.

Work Group Cohesiveness

The argument relating work group cohesion to job satisfaction is as follows: An employee who has good relationships with the work group and is well integrated into it will be a happier employee than one who is not solidly integrated into a work group. This argument has some merit. Certainly a factor contributing to whether or not a person will like or dislike the job is the nature of the relationship achieved with coworkers (Morris, 1971; Williams, Rodeheaver, and Huggins, 1999). Few people will argue that having to work around coworkers one dislikes will have a negative effect on job satisfaction (Davis, 1984).

An investigation of the practices in production planning in two textile mills in India has shown that managerial techniques within the mills differed markedly from one another (Chowdhry and Pal, 1957). Findings dealing with workers' satisfaction and the stability of membership in work groups included evidence that as the stability of the groups increased, so did satisfaction within the groups. A general positive relation between the cohesiveness of work groups and job satisfaction has been reported by others also (Britton, 1997; Stohr et al., 1995; Viteles, 1953).

Several researchers have endorsed the notion that cohesiveness or identification with a work group is a positive factor in increased satisfaction with the general work environment (Trumbo, 1961; Zaleznik et al., 1958). Generally, we may say that social attachments to work groups are important to members of organizations (Schmidtke, Fricke, and Lester, 1999; Triplett and Mullings, 1999). However, some individuals prefer to work by themselves and to have little or nothing to do with others, although such isolates are probably more the exception than the rule. Group cohesiveness serves several functions, among which is increasing the satisfactions of the members of groups (Biggam et al., 1997; Lennings, 1997). However, the interactions of informal groups and the satisfactions derived from them constitute only a single dimension of intraorganizational behavior (Lancefield, Lennings, and Thomson, 1997). It should not be concluded too quickly that a happy employee in a highly cohesive work group is necessarily a high producer. In some instances, highly cohesive groups can operate effectively to restrict the production of members, thus making a dysfunctional contribution to the organization. The attraction of the group for the individual is like a double-edged sword: It is a source of satisfaction on the one hand, but it also can operate to restrict employee productivity.

Work group cohesiveness has been studied in many types of settings, including correctional institutions. A study of 641 correctional executives who responded to the 1995 National Corrections Executive Survey revealed that although job satisfaction levels among corrections executives had declined during the 1980s, levels of job satisfaction remained high or increased for those executives who perceived that they

had strong social support from other administrators in their institutions as well as support from their subordinates (Flanagan, Johnson, and Bennett, 1996).

The quality of working relationships with others also has been cited as a major source of job satisfaction for corrections employees (Pelletier, Coutu, and Lamonde, 1996). A study by Stephen Walters (1996) investigated 339 Canadian and 229 American corrections officers in five different correctional institutions. The highest levels of work satisfaction were found among those officers who perceived that they enjoyed high-quality working relationships with other staff. Satisfying working relationships were linked closely with reducing officer stress levels arising from correctional work. Also contributing to closer quality interactions with other officers was length of service; more senior officers reported higher levels of satisfaction compared with junior officers. This might be explained by the fact that those with longer time in grade had more opportunity to cultivate satisfying interpersonal relationships and group cohesiveness.

In police agencies, group cohesiveness has been linked directly to higher levels of job satisfaction. Studies of 500 English and Welsh police officers focused on organizational structure and climate. Coworker cohesion was considered a primary determinant of greater levels of job satisfaction for the senior officers studied (Brown, Cooper, and Kirkcaldy, 1996). Similar findings have been reported in a survey of over 4,000 police officers in South Australia, Queensland, and New South Wales (McConkey, Huon, and Frank, 1996). And in an examination of 159 Canadian police managers and supervisors, group cohesiveness or social nearness was reported to generate higher levels of job satisfaction despite the perceived stress of the job and the nature of supervision from higher-level administrators (Perrott and Taylor, 1995).

Looking at sources of job satisfaction from the standpoint of organizational constraints, situations that inhibit meaningful discourse and interpersonal relations have been linked with decreases in work satisfaction under certain conditions (Tewksbury and Vannostrand, 1996). Perceptions of role conflict and a lack of support from one's work group and the administration also has been found to contribute to higher rates of labor turnover (Stohr et al., 1995).

The importance of peer support cannot be overstated, nor are these studies limited to corrections and police work. For instance, a survey of 424 defense attorneys was conducted in New York, Massachusetts, Connecticut, and Pennsylvania in 1987. Although the study focused primarily on male-female differences and how they related to career orientations and job prestige, some evidence showed that peer support and work group cohesiveness contributed directly to higher job satisfaction levels among attorneys (Hall, 1995).

An interesting scenario that illustrates the importance of work group cohesiveness and its impact on job satisfaction is found among individuals who perform undercover work in drug interdiction in state and local police agencies. Working in an undercover capacity is an especially stressful duty for any police officer. If an officer's cover is blown and his or her true identity is discovered, the possibility exists that the drug dealers will kill the officer. Thus, investigations of teams of undercover agents have revealed that although these persons feel isolated and stressed in their work, this isolation and stress is mitigated by group solidarity and loyalty. These officers have learned to function under stressful and dangerous circumstances as a team, and the quality and depth of team interaction is an integral part of an agent's job satisfaction, ultimately contributing to their ability to perform their long-term covert assignments (Mericle, 1994).

Workload and Pressure: Stress and Burnout

Workload and pressure often are associated with the amount of challenge or intrinsic interest associated with various tasks. Workload and pressure refer to the amount of work assigned and the existence of deadlines or schedules to which one must adhere (Alexander and Walker, 1996; Violanti and Paton, 1999). Job enlargement differs in that it pertains to a greater diversification of work assignments or variety in routine. The challenge of the job pits the skills and talents of the worker against the requirements of the work itself (Hendricks and Byers, 1996; Hurst and Hurst, 1997).

Some observers have described employees whose entire personality has to be interested in their work and who need to become absorbed by it (Friedmann, 1955). When their thought and attention are not absorbed by their work, they feel a growing discomfort or tedium. For others, distraction in monotonous work may serve as a diversion. Yet others may completely automatize their processes of work. The mind, wholly independent, may wander at will without the performance of physical movements being any less certain (Friedmann, 1955:139).

We cannot specify the precise amount of work persons should be assigned as their optimum workload (Thomas, 1987). Neither can we determine precisely the influence of deadlines on specific personalities. Different people plausibly work differently under various workloads and deadlines. This relation has not yet been sufficiently explored for a more definitive statement on the subject. We know that deadlines create anxiety and that they can lead to dissatisfaction with the job, including burnout (Cannizzo and Liu, 1995; Lindquist and Whitehead, 1986a). However, more and more organizational members today are becoming accustomed to working with deadlines and pressures as jobs become increasingly demanding and stressful (Cornelius, 1994; Morton, 1991). In some respects, reductions in stress-related emotional states have been attributed to workers acquiring better coping skills, through which they learn about stressors and ways of dealing with stress reduction (Kirkcaldy, Copper, and Brown, 1995).

STRESS. **Stress** is a nonspecific response to a perceived threat to an individual's well-being or self-esteem (Selye, 1976). Stress responses are not specific, since each person reacts differently to similar situations that cause stress. Several factors, including one's previous experiences with the event, constitutional factors, and personality, may function to mediate the stress and one's reaction to the event. Some stress is good. A moderate amount of stress enhances the learning and creative processes, whereas too little stress may induce boredom or apathy (Burke and Kirchmeyer, 1990a). Stress can vary according to the types of inmates supervised by correctional officers (Wiggins, 1989). For example, some correctional officers who supervise sex offenders perceive these offenders as more dangerous, harmful, violent, tense, bad, unpredictable, mysterious, unchangeable, aggressive, irrational, and afraid (Weekes, Pelletier, and Beaudette, 1995). These perceptions of certain inmates can lead corrections officers to believe they are more difficult to supervise and can thus raise the level of stress in the job.

SOURCES OF STRESS. Stress among police officers, corrections officers, and others arises from several sources (Cooper, 1986; Lindquist and Whitehead, 1986a). Stress researchers have targeted the following factors as the chief sources of stress among POs: (1) job dissatisfaction, (2) role conflict, (3) role ambiguity, (4) officer-client interactions, (5) excessive paperwork and performance pressures, (6) low self-esteem and public

BOX 8.1 PERSONALITY HIGHLIGHT

HOWARD ABADINSKY
Professor, Saint Xavier
University–Chicago

Statistics: B.A. (political
science), Queens College,
NY; M.S.W., Fordham
University School of Social
Services, NY; Ph.D.
(sociology), New York
University

Interests: Set on law school and a legal career, in my senior year at Queens College I took a criminology course that exposed me to the work of parole officers. Intrigued by what I read, I telephoned the New York State Division of Parole and made an appointment for information. The agency was in need of parole officers and I could qualify with one year of graduate education in social work. That ended my career in law—a decision I have never regretted. After one year of social work school, I was sworn in as a New York State parole officer. Several years later the agency sent me back to complete the second year of graduate school to earn an M.S.W. While still a parole officer, I would later return to school to earn a Ph.D., courtesy of the federal Law Enforcement Education Program.

Work Experience: With only a minimum of training—that has since changed, and training now is extensive—equipped with a badge, handcuffs, and a .38 special revolver, I was assigned to the waterfront section of South Brooklyn known as Redhook. In those days, Redhook was dominated by a faction of one of New York City's five organized crime families. Prior to my arrival, this faction had been involved in a conflict

with the rest of the crime families, and Redhook had been the scene of a great deal of violence; a tentative truce was in effect. It was an exciting experience and led to an interest in and insight into organized crime, a topic about which I have written several books (e.g., *Organized Crime* 6/e, 1998).

Work as a parole officer in New York City was a mixture of exhilaration and depression, excitement and boredom. Being able to assist men (male parole officers supervised only male offenders then) who had little or no employment experience or skills, often with a history of substance abuse, provided an unequaled sense of fulfillment. My colleagues and I enabled these men to enter job training and education programs; we reached out to employers to find them jobs; and our close monitoring provided the ego strength for avoiding a return to drug or alcohol abuse. Of course, there were failures—clients who were arrested for new, sometimes serious, crimes; others who returned to prison for drug use or absconding from supervision.

Early in the A.M., I rousted parolees out of bed: "Get up. Get dressed. Here's a list of job leads I want you to follow up on. Be in my office first thing in the morning tomorrow to discuss the results." I visited the homes of clients in the afternoons in order to experience their environment and talk with others living in the residence. Conditions were frequently depressing and I had to ask myself, "How would I behave if I had to live under these conditions?" The answer was unsettling.

Advice to Students: Although I retired from the New York Division of Parole more than 20 years ago, the experience remains vivid, reinforced by continuing contact with former colleagues, some also retired, others now executives in the field. If I had the chance to do it over again, would I become a parole officer? Would I recommend a career in parole to others? Absolutely!

---

image, and (7) job risks and liabilities (Stohr et al., 1994; Wiggins, 1989). One important and negative consequence of stress is burnout (Cheek and Miller, 1982; Maslach, 1982a).

BURNOUT.   **Burnout** is one result of stress (Daviss, 1982). Maslach (1982b:30–31) has identified at least 15

different connotations of the term including the following:

1. A syndrome of emotional exhaustion, depersonalization, and reduced personal accomplishment that can occur among individuals who do "people work" of some kind

2. A progressive loss of idealism, energy, and purpose experienced by people in the helping professions as a result of the conditions of their work

3. A state of physical, emotional, and mental exhaustion marked by physical depletion and chronic fatigue, feelings of helplessness and hopelessness, and the development of a negative self-concept and negative attitudes toward work, life, and other people

4. A syndrome of inappropriate attitudes toward clients and self, often associated with uncomfortable physical and emotional symptoms

5. A state of exhaustion, irritability, and fatigue that markedly decreases the worker's effectiveness and capability

6. To deplete oneself, exhaust one's physical and mental resources, or wear oneself out by excessively striving to reach some unrealistic expectations imposed by oneself or by the values of society

7. To wear oneself out doing what one has to do; an inability to cope adequately with the stresses of work or personal life

8. A malaise of the spirit, a loss of will, or an inability to mobilize interests and capabilities

9. To become debilitated and weakened because of extreme demands on one's physical and/or mental energy

10. An accumulation of intense negative feelings that is so debilitating that a person withdraws from the situation in which those feelings are generated

11. A pervasive mood of anxiety giving way to depression and despair

12. A process in which a professional's attitudes and behavior change in negative ways in response to job strain

13. An inadequate coping mechanism used consistently by an individual to reduce stress

14. A condition produced by working too hard for too long in a high-pressure environment

15. A debilitating psychological condition resulting from work-related frustrations, which results in lower employee productivity and morale

Burnout usually causes a reduction in the quality or effectiveness of one's job performance (Burke and Deszca, 1986; Farmer, 1988). In the field of criminal justice, debilitating reductions in effectiveness often are accompanied by higher recidivism rates among probationers and parolees, more legal problems and case filings from officer-inmate interactions, and greater labor turnover among correctional officers (Robinson, Porporino, and Simourd, 1997). Gender, age, amount and type of education, length of job-related experience, self-esteem, marital status, and the degree of autonomy and job satisfaction function as intervening variables (Wright et al., 1997). The social support system is made up of others who perform similar tasks as well as the frequency of contact with these people for the purpose of sharing the frustrations of work (Fishkin, 1987). Stress is manifested by physiological, psychological, and/or emotional indicators (American Federation of State, County, and Municipal Employees, 1982). Burnout may result (Burke, 1987; Thomas, 1988). One important consequence of burnout may be labor turnover (Stevenson, 1988).

MITIGATING STRESS AND BURNOUT.   Stress and burnout may be mitigated by giving employees greater say in organizational decision making (Dufford, 1986). In corrections, correctional officers may use their knowledge of prison culture to establish more secure inmate policies and correctional officer safety (Walters, 1996). This is often accomplished through participative management. Participative management is the philosophy of organizational administration in which substantial input is solicited from the work staff and used for decision-making purposes for situations that might affect one's work. Generally, a lack of participation in decision making is a key source of stress and burnout (Burke and Kirchmeyer, 1990b).

Supervisors have a substantial impact on the stress of their subordinates (Brown, 1987). In corrections, for instance, some correctional officers have reported that their supervisors only provide criticisms of work improperly done and leave unrewarded work of good quality. The morale of personnel suffers greatly in this type of environment (Flanagan, Johnson, and Bennett, 1996; Whitehead and Lindquist, 1985, 1986). In most organizations, supervisors play key roles in reducing employee stress (O'Brien, 1985). Shapiro (1982) describes several ways that supervisors can help to reduce the stress levels of their subordinates:

1. Leadership that provides support, structure, and information

2. Communication that is timely, appropriate, and accurate

3. An environment that is efficient and orderly
4. Rules and policies that are explicit
5. Workers who have freedom to be self-sufficient and make their own decisions
6. Room for staff creativity and innovation
7. Support and nurturing from supervisory staff
8. Manageable job pressure
9. Peer networks of friendship and support among staff

Studies of probation officers have given us some insight about the function of work pressure in relation to job retention or quitting behavior. A survey of 186 officers who resigned from various Florida probation departments attempted to link job stress and dissatisfaction with one's inclination to quit. Job stress, workload, and pressure seemed only moderately related to one's inclination to quit (Simmons, Cochran, and Blount, 1997). Interestingly, some of those who quit had fairly high levels of job satisfaction. This finding suggests that factors other than job satisfaction were responsible for causing some of these officers to quit their jobs. Some officers said they wanted to enter more challenging work and would probably remain in correctional work, but at the federal level. Others complained about the relatively low pay and long working hours as primary motivators that caused them to quit.

Sometimes workload and pressure are affected by the extent to which employees experience role conflicts about how they should perform their roles or whether their roles are ambiguously defined. Role conflict is the degree of incongruity of expectations associated with a role, whereas role ambiguity is the lack of clarity of role expectations and the degree of uncertainty regarding the outcomes of one's role performance (Golembiewski and Byong, 1990; More, 1992; Nay, 1990). Workload and pressure are aggravated to the extent that role conflict and ambiguity exist, and such pressure can lead to absenteeism, turnover, and low performance effectiveness (Aldag and Brief, 1978).

The Prestige and Status of the Job

It seems logical that persons who occupy positions with high prestige and status should be more satisfied with their work than those individuals who perform more menial and demeaning tasks (Adamson and Deszca, 1990; Brewer and Wilson, 1995; Wright et al., 1997). For instance, a study of 545 manual workers in automobile and metal fabrication found support for the notion that job satisfaction varies directly with oc-

cupational level (Form and Geschwender, 1962). Researchers reported that workers with 10 or more years of tenure were significantly more satisfied with their jobs than those without tenure. Further, workers earning a better rate of pay were significantly more satisfied than those earning less. Also, those in higher occupational prestige categories (sales, clerical, foremen) were significantly more satisfied than those in lower prestige categories. Thus, the higher one's occupational level, the more likely one was to be tenured, receive more pay, and enjoy greater prestige. These three variables were highly correlated (Form and Geschwender, 1962:235).

Another study investigated the relationship between bureaucracy and alienation (Bonjean and Grimes, 1970). Alienation as a negative motivator was found to exist to a lesser degree among managerial personnel than among lower-level personnel, although the differences were slight. These researchers offer one possible explanation for this difference by stating that managers and businesspeople may have better developed means of coping with bureaucratization than hourly paid workers. Their higher education, social status, and income may provide them with a better rationale and more opportunities to experience feelings of integration both on and off the job.

Job prestige and status are invariably linked with community perceptions of how various criminal justice work roles are defined and how individuals perform in the roles (Buzawa, 1984; Hall, 1995; Meagher and Yentes, 1986). For example, a study was conducted to assess the impact of the Beat Policing Pilot Project in Toowoomba, Australia. The objective of the project was to deliver higher-quality police services to urban communities with higher crime rates. Another objective was to heighten community awareness of police presence and to create positive perceptions of police and their community interventions. Subsequently, residents reported perceptions of greater safety in their communities and they attributed these perceptions to the actions of the police. In these communities, at least, police earned a great deal of respect from community residents. Their prestige was elevated to a much higher level following implementation of the Beat Policing Pilot Project (Queensland Criminal Justice Commission, 1995).

Media portrayals of police officers are also an important source of job prestige and status. A study of 66 Florida public information officers revealed that positive media reports about the quality of work performed by these officers did much to enhance their

BOX 8.2 POLICE PERSONALITY AND EFFECTIVENESS

What Makes a Successful Police Officer? This argument never ends. What qualities should be stressed or which traits are desired in potential police officers who are selected for training academies? What sort of training should they receive once they are in these places of training? The public's expectation of police officers is that they can make arrests, conduct high-speed chases safely, and fire their weapons in a competent manner. The ability to solve crimes would be desirable as well. Most police departments put new police recruits through a standard course of training, emphasizing both physical and cognitive skills. In fact, a 1993 survey disclosed that 83 percent of all large city police departments test applicants for cognitive skills, including reading, writing, and reasoning. More recent tests stress achievement motivation and openness to experience. Lobbyists and vested interest groups have launched a strong attack against the use of such tests and selection procedures, however, labeling them as racist and irrelevant. Their claim is that these selection procedures keep out large numbers of minority applicants. They believe that more minority applicants are needed, in part, to fulfill civil rights expectations and obligations and to create a more level playing field for law enforcement and the general public.

The Department of Justice entered the debate about how police officers should be selected by siding with those groups filing lawsuits critical of including cognitive skills on selection tests. Results have been mixed. In Long Island's Nassau County, orders were given to administer a federally approved selection test. After the test was administered to numerous minority applicants, the Department of Justice threw out most of the test sections because they had too much of an adverse impact on minorities. Of the nine sections remaining on the federally approved test, eight sections tested personality. The remaining cognitive section

was a reading test. In order to pass, applicants merely had to score as well as the bottom 1 percent of currently employed police officers. At the other end of the continuum of critical opinion, it is argued that if police forces cannot test for basic intellectual skills, they will end up with recruits who cannot learn the rules from the police academy, who cannot follow the rules once they are on the street, who cannot write crime reports that will hold up in court, and who cannot keep their facts straight when confronted by defense attorneys in court.

In New York, former Mayor Rudolph Giuliani has said that "It requires a problem-solving approach. There's a lot more expected of the officer. That means you need police with the right stuff." New York City police commissioner William Bratton said in 1997 that what the "right stuff" means is that new police recruits should have at least two years of college. He adds that what community policing is all about is people being empowered to make decisions. But if you are going to empower them, you also have a responsibility to make sure they are equipped to exercise that power. Bratton says that to use the lowest 1 percent standard as the primary selection criterion for police officer recruitment is foolish. He says, "That's like saying the least talented person . . . becomes the base on which we're now going to build. The whole idea is to raise standards." The Department of Justice makes a good point; however, police departments need to recruit larger numbers of minorities. But the solution should not be to water down standards; rather, an aggressive attempt should be made to attract more qualified minority applicants.

What methods would you use to hire new police officers? What do you believe are the most important skills a police officer should possess in order to do a good job? What do you think?

Source: Adapted from David A. Price, "Police Need Brains, Not Personality." *USA Today,* July 30, 1997:A13.

self-images and feelings of prestige (Surette and Richard, 1995).

It is important to recognize that the existence of other factors may affect the direct association between prestige and job satisfaction. For instance, job content, workload, and pressure play important roles in deter-

mining job satisfaction in many instances (Hepburn and Knepper, 1993; Sullivan, 1977; Tewksbury, 1994). Examples can be cited of persons who have qualifications for higher-prestige jobs but who prefer lower-level jobs because of their intrinsic interest. Some persons also avoid higher-prestige positions because they fear the additional responsibility associated with such jobs. Thus, some persons might turn down promotions in order to avoid additional duties and greater job pressures.

The Type of Reward Structure

In much of the early work on motivation and the satisfaction of organizational members, continual references can be found to the potential importance of monetary rewards as influences on these variables. The argument is that the more a person is paid, the greater the job satisfaction level and job effectiveness. The ultimate result, according to this argument, is greater productivity among organization members and greater organizational effectiveness (Harrison and Pelletier, 1987; Lombardo, 1976). Maier (1965: 443–444) says that money in itself has no incentive value. Since our economic structure has made it a medium of exchange, however, it can be used to obtain the real incentives. Money is sought after in our society because of what it represents. Maier adds that money reflects the satisfaction of various kinds of worker needs. If monetary rewards are seen within a need framework, then it becomes easier to understand the underpinnings of the "money leads to job satisfaction" argument. Organizational researchers see the importance of monetary rewards in a different light, however.

In most organizations in which volunteers are not an integral feature of the intraorganizational structure, several types of payment systems operate. A person may be paid hourly, weekly, monthly, or annually. An employee may be paid according to the number of units of product produced per day, or some other standard. This is the piece-rate system. Salespersons often are on a quota system and earn commissions on excess sales above a certain quota. Given the diversification of payment systems in existence, it is not surprising to see the emergence of invidious distinctions between each method of payment. For instance, payment "by the hour" may not have as much prestige as someone paid on a monthly or annual basis.

Before considering some of the implications of varying payment methods for satisfaction, we should be aware of the following facts: Money is essential for the survival of most persons. Money constitutes a means to multiple ends. Money is an intermediate reward for services or work performed. In turn, it can be exchanged for other things people want. As it is a variable common to all organizations of the type we are discussing, we must inevitably raise certain questions about money as a potential significant input to job satisfaction (Weston, 1978). Is there a relationship between the method of payment and job satisfaction? If so, what is the nature of this relationship?

Some persons argue that little or no relationship exists between money and job satisfaction. One reason is that many persons bring to their jobs particular expectations about salary requirements. The employer-employee relation is a bargaining one. Once an agreement has been reached, employees perform their functions, receive sums they have agreed on from the organization, and feel satisfied to the extent that the organization has lived up to its part of the bargain. Future salary increments or raises are viewed by the employee as expected or deserved. Under such circumstances, employee job satisfaction levels are unlikely to rise significantly, if at all. However, if a person assumes additional duties and responsibilities with little or no increase in financial rewards, he or she may become dissatisfied with that particular arrangement.

Some investigators think that too much attention is given to pay. Pay does not always have the intended effect of increasing employee work satisfaction. Pay is often confounded by other factors, such as age, occupational level, and education (Herzberg et al., 1957; Troxell, 1954).

Probably the most visible example of the influence of method of pay on job satisfaction is the piece-rate system found in many factories. Workers are encouraged to work harder to produce more in order to earn more. They are assigned quotas, and any excess units of product above their quotas will result in bonuses or additional pay. Although the piece-rate system is primarily a device to increase one's incentive to work, theoretically it does have some merit for increasing a worker's satisfaction. In reality, however, the piece-rate system generally fails to achieve the desired expectations of management (Roy, 1960).

In sum, methods of payment appear to be only moderately influential in relation to job satisfaction. The operation of informal work group norms is sufficient to act against the potential satisfactions derived from exceeding quotas under a piece-rate system. Job expectations, including commensurate salary requirements, make it difficult to determine the precise impact of pay on the level of satisfaction. Receiving remuneration below one's expectations is more likely to produce dissatisfaction than receiving payments above the quality of one's work is to produce satisfaction. Thus, pay is more likely to be associated with negative motivators than positive motivators.

Participation in Decision Making

Probably no other variable has received so much attention as a prerequisite and determinant of job satisfaction as participation (Jermier, 1979; Rousch and Steelman, 1981). The concept of the psychology of participation is that the more persons participate in decisions affecting their work, the more likely they are to stick with that work and enjoy it (Brewer and Wilson, 1995; Wilson and Beck, 1995). A more recent phrase that expresses this notion is *participative management.* In some research, job enrichment also has been equated with greater involvement in decision making affecting one's work (Cordner, 1978; Greene, 1989). In parole work, for instance, parole officers who have been given greater decision-making responsibilities in relation to parolee-clients have reported higher levels of job satisfaction and that their work is more meaningful and important (Lindquist and Whitehead, 1986b). Information flow about decisions affecting one's work is especially important (Perryman, 1981). If certain employees, such as police officers, feel uninvolved in the information flow in their police agencies, this condition creates high levels of job dissatisfaction (Hochstedler and Dunning, 1983).

Perhaps the formalized origin of employees' participation in decision making and other work-related matters was the Hawthorne studies (introduced in Chapter 3), which were conducted at a plant of the Western Electric Company during the period 1927 to 1932. Elton Mayo and Roethlisberger and Dickson gave the principle of participation considerable importance in their later writings, which have been examined elsewhere. Subsequent research on the relationship between participation in decision making and job satisfaction has revealed a positive association for the most part.

Impressive evidence has been offered to support the relation between participation and job satisfaction (Brief, Aldag, and Wallden, 1978). For instance, Holter (1965) studied 591 blue-collar and 461 white-collar employees in insurance companies, industrial firms, and factories. All employees were nonsupervisory personnel. Holter asked these employees, "Do you believe that employees in general participate sufficiently in decisions that concern the management of the establishment as a whole?" Most employees said "No"

when answering this question. However, Holter asked a crucial follow-up question: "Do you believe that you personally participate sufficiently in decisions made at your place of work, or do you want to participate more in them?" Again, a majority said either that they would like to participate more in decisions that directly concern their own work and working conditions, or that they would like to participate more in decisions that concern the management of the enterprise. Holter concluded that on the basis of her interviews with these workers, fairly wide support could be found for the idea of greater participation in decision making.

Some investigators believe that not all employees want to be included in organizational decision making. Given the many individual differences that exist among personnel of any organization, it is likely that greater participation in decision making and job satisfaction may, in fact, be inversely related (Conley, 1979). At the very least, we should allow for the possibility that some workers prefer the safety of not being required to make decisions (Hulin and Blood, 1968). Vroom (1960) also says that it has been demonstrated that not all workers are satisfied when they are allowed to take part in the decision-making process about their jobs, and significant individual differences exist between workers who respond positively to the opportunity to make decisions and those who do not. Although not exactly to the point, these data at least indicate that some workers prefer routine, repetition, and specified work methods to change, variety, and decision making.

Given the significant amount of evidence produced thus far, the relationships between participation and job satisfaction are clearly dependent on a number of factors at the social and psychological levels. We know that most of the organizations with which we are familiar follow a bureaucratic format not only in structure but in intraorganization relationships (i.e., impersonality, selection by test, specialization of task performance, rigid adherence to a body of abstract rules). Hierarchies of authority exist that are based on the false assumption that persons at higher levels in the hierarchy are more educated or more knowledgeable than members at the lower levels. On the surface, at least, it would appear that increased involvement in decision making at all levels is in direct contradiction to bureaucracy.

Some studies have investigated the relationship between an organization's size and the level of job satisfaction of individuals in the organization. Fourteen law enforcement agencies were studied in seven different states, involving 2,733 officers. Police departments were divided into large and small departments, with small departments defined as those having 100 or fewer sworn personnel. Regardless of the area of the country studied, those officers in smaller police departments tended to have higher job satisfaction levels compared with officers in larger police departments. This difference may be a function of the fact that smaller departments are able to involve their subordinate officers in the decision-making process to a greater degree (Dantzker, 1997).

The notions of needs and need fulfillment have been introduced at various points and juxtaposed with particular organizational forms, supervisory styles, job content and challenge, and participation in decision making. No doubt the needs of the individual employee are integral factors that are responsive to various kinds of intraorganizational conditions and interpersonal relations. The ability of an organization to satisfy employees' needs is likely to exert a direct impact on levels of satisfaction. The list of variables that has been explored in this section is certainly not exhaustive. Many additional inputs into employees' satisfaction in the organization can be examined, but we have selected what are believed to be some of the more salient variables.

We also might conclude that job satisfaction is a direct contributor to employee morale. Morale is not so much an individual variable as it is an interpersonal one. It generally refers to a property of groups wherein the members share common values, interests, and goals. The impact of group morale on productivity is similar to that of job satisfaction.

More than a few writers believe that the general relationship among job satisfaction, morale, and productivity is vague. According to Warren Bennis (1966), we are not all clear today about the relationship of morale to productivity, nor are we sure that there is any interdependence between them. Too many instances of high morale with low productivity and low productivity with low morale can be cited. If there is a relationship among job satisfaction, morale, and productivity, it has not yet been delineated and demonstrated empirically.

SUMMARY

An almost universalistic concern exists among administrators and managers about what factors influence

their subordinates to work harder and become more effective when performing their jobs. Some reasearchers believe that a direct relationship exists between employee motivation to work and organizational effectiveness. If employee motivation can be enhanced or improved, then organizational effectiveness will increase. Not everyone agrees with this view, however.

Studies of employee motivation have focused on those factors that increase an employee's job satisfaction. Job satisfaction is the product of numerous factors, and it is sometimes difficult to explain. Several theories have been advanced to account for worker motivation to achieve. One popular view was devised by Abraham Maslow (1954). Maslow described a hierarchy of needs to explain why people are motivated to behave in various ways. His motivational scheme includes needs such as safety, security, belongingness, esteem, and self-actualization. Worker behavior therefore is conceptualized as a type of need-fulfilling behavior, according to Maslow's view. An alternative motivational scheme was devised by Vroom (1964), who developed a dual-factor theory of worker motivation, envisioning different factors that account for increases in one's job satisfaction compared with other factors that decrease one's job satisfaction. He termed these factors satisfiers and dissatisfiers.

A third theory of employee motivation was Victor Vroom's expectancy theory, which casts worker motivation in a performance-outcome scenario. Thus, promotion, advancement, and other organizational rewards are instilled within workers by their organizations as desirable outcomes for them to achieve. Several other theories include David McClelland's (1985) achievement motivation theory, in which employees engage in goal-setting behaviors that involve challenging work. Equity theory, described by Harris and Baldwin (1999), focuses on perceived equity between organizational positions; employees compare their work and rewards with the work performed and rewards received by others.

Properly motivated employees will tend to become more satisfied with their jobs. Job satisfaction is a complex variable, however, and is related to numerous job dimensions and organizational factors. For instance, job satisfaction seems to vary according to the style of leadership employees receive. Authoritative supervisors who supervise their subordinates closely are likely to produce job dissatisfaction, whereas supervisors who show their employees consideration and give them greater work autonomy generate higher amounts of work satisfaction. Also important is the intrinsic interest of the job itself. Is the work repetitive, or does it involve complex, problem-solving effort from employees? This factor seems to make a difference, although employees with different amounts of education and training respond differently to similar work challenges.

Employees who have formed close ties with others in their work settings seem to be more contented with their jobs. Thus, work group cohesiveness is viewed as contributory to greater levels of job satisfaction. Those employees who do not involve themselves in close-knit work groups may not be as satisfied with their work. Also, the sheer workload and pressure of the jobs performed may cause employee job satisfaction to vary in different ways. Different personality systems respond in a variety of ways to the same organizational stimuli. Although we do not know exactly what personality characteristics are closely related with differing degrees of job satisfaction, some employees obviously respond better or worse to work-related stresses and pressures. Some people thrive on stress, whereas others are devastated by it.

A concomitant of stress is burnout. Some persons in stressful occupations and professions, such as police work, may become emotionally exhausted and become less effective in their job performance. Stress and burnout are mitigated to a degree by enabling subordinates to become more involved in the decision-making process. In a sense, this is the participation hypothesis, which suggests that the more persons become involved in decisions affecting their work, the more actively they become involved with and like their jobs. Also, the prestige and status of the work performed makes a significant difference to many employees. In some respects, this prestige and status reflects Maslow's and Vroom's thinking about worker motivation to attain esteem and recognition. Involving employees in decisions affecting their work is presumed by employers to be a positive factor that promotes greater amounts of job satisfaction. Some employees are content to merely perform their jobs and not seek involvement in decision making, however. This is because of the responsibilities that generally accompany decision making. Some people do not want such responsibilities, because they do not want to be blamed by anyone if something goes wrong.

No discussion of job satisfaction would be complete without some mention of the rewards associated with the work performed. Usually, rewards are measured by pay or salary levels and salary increments over time, although there are less tangible rewards. These might include satisfying interpersonal relations in the workplace, a more congenial work environment, and supervisory practices that do not intimidate or threaten subordinates.

QUESTIONS FOR REVIEW

1. Describe the hierarchy of needs outlined by Abraham Maslow. How does need fulfillment relate to one's work?

2. What is stress? What job-related factors seem to cause stress? How can stress be reduced?

3. What is burnout? What are some consequences of burnout for employees in different organizations? Is there anything administrators can do to alleviate or mitigate burnout in the workplace? What kinds of things can be done to reduce burnout among employees?

4. What is Vroom's dual-factor theory of motivation? Describe this theory and its significance for employees.

5. What is expectancy theory? How does it relate to job satisfaction?

6. Distinguish between satisfiers and dissatisfiers as factors affecting job satisfaction. How do these factors influence one's work satisfaction level, if at all?

7. How does participating in the decision-making process influence one's level of satisfaction? Do all persons want to be involved in decision making affecting their work? Why or why not?

8. What is job enrichment? How do administrators use job enrichment as a means of affecting an employee's productivity or effectiveness in the work setting?

9. What is meant by work group cohesiveness? Is group cohesion good or bad as a source of job satisfaction? Is a cohesive group necessarily a productive or effective group in the work setting? Explain.

10. What is the relationship between the type of reward structure used by an organization for its employees and employee effectiveness and work productivity? How does the prestige or status of the job influence one's work satisfaction? Explain.

SUGGESTED READINGS

Beito, Linda Royster (1999). *Leadership Effectiveness in Community Policing.* Bristol, IN: Wyndam Hall Press.

Josi, Don A., and Dale K. Sechrest (1998). *The Changing Career of the Correctional Officer: Policy Implications for the 21st Century.* Boston: Butterworth-Heinemann.

Quinsey, Vernon L., et al. (1998). *Violent Offenders: Appraising and Managing Risk.* Washington, DC: American Psychological Association.

• CASE STUDIES •

1. THE TACTLESS SERGEANT

At roll call today, you sit attentively while the shift sergeant lists the usual priorities for the officers getting ready for patrol duties. "We've got what looks like a serial rapist operating in the Regency Park area, mostly going after women who are short, with long, dark hair. A witness said that the perp looks Oriental, probably in his early twenties, last seen wearing a green shirt, black pants, and sneakers. Keep an eye out for someone like that." Then the sergeant launched into a tirade about citizen complaints. "Some of you officers haven't been very polite to our citizens. Some of you have been downright ugly when somebody asks you to help them. One of our citizens reported that an officer she contacted, who was sitting in his cruiser at a deli, said he was busy eating lunch, and told her to take a hike when she told him she had just been beaten by her boyfriend. We can't have that kind of publicity. She got the number of the cruiser and I know who you are. So let's get with the program, people, and try to make a difference helping our citizens."

The sergeant added, "By the way, the mayor says that crime is up and we haven't been doing a good job out on the streets. So let's keep our eyes open. The chief agrees. He thinks the department is lazy. I know some of you work hard to do a good job, but I also know that some of you goof off and make it bad for the rest of us. So let's try to get some good PR going for us for a change." The sergeant made several announcements and gave the group of officers additional information. All in all, it was a pretty depressing episode. As the officers filed out of the meeting room, overall morale was not particularly high. You decide that just to spite the sergeant and the whole department, you will ignore all traffic violators today and will be conveniently absent from your vehicle "on business" whenever calls for service are directed to you.

Questions for Discussion

1. Imagine yourself as a police officer at roll call. How would you feel after getting reprimanded by the sergeant?
2. How motivated would you be to go out and "serve and protect" the citizens who apparently have been complaining about police officers generally?
3. How motivated are you to go to work, knowing the mayor and chief of police probably think you are lazy and not doing a good job?
4. Can the sergeant bring up these incidents in alternative ways that will not alienate the officers? Discuss.
5. What effect do you think the sergeant's remarks have had on departmental morale?

2. THE NEW KID ON THE "BLOCK"

As the new correctional officer walked along a corridor of a cell block one afternoon, he heard some screaming coming from one of the cells. As he approached, he saw a prisoner lying on the cell floor, apparently in pain. He stepped up to the cell bars and asked if he could do anything. Suddenly, the inmate got up and threw a handful of feces at the officer, spattering his face and uniform with human excrement. "I've got AIDS," the prisoner shouted. "I hope to hell I've just given it to you." The officer took out a handkerchief and wiped off his face and headed for the bathroom, where he washed his face and hands thoroughly. He got out of his uniform quickly and stepped into a shower stall, washing himself thoroughly. Later he found out that the prisoner did not have AIDS but that he was psychologically disturbed. It was the officer's first day on the job. He was shocked that an inmate would throw feces at him. Later in the day, other officers took him aside and told him what they had experienced. One officer said, "Listen, they despise us guards. It's them against us. That's the way it is around here, 24/7. Just go with the flow and don't take anything from any of them. You just have to show 'em who's boss." Three months later, the officer quit and decided to go into a different occupation outside prison walls.

Questions for Discussion

1. Imagine that you are the correctional officer who was just assaulted with feces thrown by an inmate. This filthy incident is certainly not what you had envisioned for your first day on the job as a correctional officer. And when you heard the horror stories of what happened to other officers working at the prison, including physical assaults and verbal taunts from prisoners, how motivated would you be to continue working there?

2. What kind of work satisfaction will you experience if you are despised by inmates and are treated in ways that are demeaning?

3. What sort of preparation do you believe correctional officers who are going to work around dangerous inmates should have?

4. If you were the correctional officer in charge, what would you say or do to assist the new correctional officer in coping with the humiliating incident?

CHAPTER
9

POLICE AND SHERIFFS' DEPARTMENTS

KEY TERMS

Accreditation

Affirmative action

August Vollmer

Beat patrolling

Bobbies

Bow Street Runners

California Personality Inventory (CPI)

Calls for service

Chancellors

Civilian complaint review boards

Code of ethics

Constables

Day watch

Debtors' prisons

Decertification

Detroit Police Ministation Program

Field training officers (FTOs)

Frankpledge

Frumentarii

Gaols

Henry Fielding

Hue and cry

Indentured servant system

Justices of the peace

Law Enforcement Assistance
   Administration (LEAA)

Legalistic model

Line personnel

Metropolitan Police Act of 1829

Metropolitan Police of London

Ministations

Minnesota Multiphasic Personality
   Inventory (MMPI)

Night watch

Night watchman

O.W. Wilson

Patrick Colquhoun

Peace officers

Peace Officer Standards and Training
   (POST)

Police

Police-community relations

Police discretion

Police misconduct

Police professionalization

Polygraph tests

Probationary employees

Professionalization movement

Psychological screening

Rattle watchmen

Reeves

Schouts and rattles

Service model

Sheriff

Shires

Sir John Fielding

Sir Robert Peel

Staff personnel

Stare decisis

Thief-takers

Watchman model

Watchmen

Wickersham Commission

CHAPTER OBJECTIVES

The following objectives are intended:

1. To describe the history of policing and the role of police in society
2. To describe contemporary police departments, their organization, and operations
3. To describe the goals, functions, and division of labor of modern police departments
4. To examine the recruitment process used to select new officers, including the hiring of women and minorities
5. To describe police department administration
6. To describe the goals and functions of sheriffs' departments, including their recruitment procedures and operations
7. To examine several key law enforcement issues, including officer training and professionalism
8. To examine police-community relations and methods to improve such relations
9. To describe various forms of police misconduct and how such misconduct is dealt with by internal affairs bureaus and citizens' complaint review boards

INTRODUCTION

This chapter is about the history, organization, and operation of police and sheriffs' departments, and how this history has influenced contemporary police agencies and procedures. Policing has been an essential part of virtually every society for many centuries. Modern U.S. law enforcement practices are grounded to some extent in certain historical precedents from different countries. The first part of this chapter explores the history and role of police in society generally. A brief synopsis of key events leading up to modern-day policing is presented. This synopsis includes a description of the Metropolitan Police of London, a model on which many contemporary police agencies are organized.

Local law enforcement agencies are typically divided into police and sheriffs' departments, with police departments having primary jurisdiction over cities. Sheriffs' departments have primary jurisdiction over counties. Obviously some overlap of jurisdiction exists, since almost every city is located in a county. Despite overlapping jurisdiction, police departments tend to be organized somewhat differently from sheriffs' departments, although both types of law enforcement agencies have similar functions. These differences in organization and functions are described.

The organization of law enforcement also is examined. This includes a description of both simple and complex police and sheriffs' organizations. All departments have divisions of labor. These divisions of labor are identified, and key roles and responsibilities are described. A key element in any law enforcement organization concerns the recruitment and selection process for new officers, which we examine also.

The latter part of this chapter examines several important issues of relevance to local police and sheriffs' departments. These issues pertain to law enforcement officer training and quality control; measuring police performance and effectiveness; police professionalization; police-community relations; officer misconduct, corruption, and internal affairs; citizens' complaint and review boards; and liaisons between police and sheriffs' departments and federal organizations and agencies.

THE HISTORY AND ROLE OF POLICE IN SOCIETY

The word **police** comes from the Greek word *polis*, meaning "city," and it has been applied historically to the exercise of civil or collective authority (Manning, 1977:39). The new and modern policing concept is neither new nor modern (Inkster, 1992; Tonry and Morris, 1992). Early records indicate the existence of police forces in ancient Egypt and Mesopotamia by about 1500 B.C. (Adamson, 1991). While the functions of these forces in Egypt and Mesopotamia have not been carefully documented, it is clear that some of these police officers interacted with the public they served in various ways, sometimes adversely. Nevertheless, their presence seems to have been order maintenance and crime control through neighborhood patrolling and response to community interests.

Ancient and Medieval Law Enforcement

Ancient Egypt and Mesopotamia had police forces charged with order maintenance and resolving community disputes (Adamson, 1991). These were principally civilian forces organized and administered by civilian authorities. Adamson says that these police officers sometimes had bad reputations for molesting or beating prisoners in custody, although their testimony in court was considered generally trustworthy. In early Roman times, from about 100 B.C. to A.D. 200, centurions were used as either military or paramilitary units for policing purposes. Centurions usually commanded units of 100 men and were used for both policing and combat. Evidence shows that around A.D. 100, the Romans established the first professional criminal investigative units in Western history, known as *frumentarii.* The *frumentarii* had three principal duties: (1) to supervise grain distribution to Rome's needy, (2) to oversee the personal delivery of messages among government officials, and (3) to detect crime and prosecute offenders (Kelly, 1987). *Frumentarii* reenacted crime scenes, conducted custodial interrogations of criminal suspects, compared statements made to different interrogators, and offered immunity to various criminal accomplices in exchange for incriminating testimony against their confederates.

Descriptions of policing in different parts of the world during the period A.D. 100 to about 800 are fragmented (Bailey, 1986). American policing activities were influenced significantly by events in early England at the time of the Norman Conquest in 1066. English jurisdictions were divided into **shires,** the equivalent of present-day counties. The chief law enforcement officers in shires were called **reeves.** Thus, each shire had a reeve. The combined use of *shire* and *reeve* eventually generated the term **sheriff,** used to describe the chief law enforcement officer of American counties. In England, shire-reeves were agents of the king and collected taxes besides maintaining the peace. The king also utilized **chancellors** as his agents to settle disputes between neighbors, such as property boundary issues, trespass allegations, and child misconduct. An early equivalent of the chancellor with similar duties and responsibilities were **justices of the peace,** dating back to about A.D. 1200. Together with the chancellors and/or justices of the peace, reeves would maintain order in their respective jurisdictions or shires.

Policing functions during this period were shared among community residents. The Norman Conquest had ushered in the **frankpledge** system, which required loyalty to the king of England and shared law and order responsibilities among the public. The frankpledge system directed that neighbors should form into small groups to assist and protect one another if they were to be victimized by criminals. The neighborhood groups were commanded by **constables** appointed by favored noblemen of the king. These constables were the forerunners of modern-day police officers. Over the next 200 years, some degree of specialization in law enforcement duties occurred. In the seventeenth century, citizens were obligated to perform **day watch** duties or **night watch** duties on a rotating basis. Day and night watches were comparable to modern-day shift work. These **watchmen** would be expected to yell out a **"hue and cry"** in the event they detected crimes in progress or any other community disturbance, such as a fire or other emergency situation. The modern-day position of **night watchman** derives from this early practice.

The English system of the administration of justice and law enforcement was at best informal. Laws were uncodified, emphasizing the importance of individual and interjurisdictional judicial proclamations and precedents under the principle of *stare decisis* (legal precedent). Reeves were often corrupt. Bribing officials was commonplace, and reeves accepted bribes from relatives of those incarcerated in makeshift jails called **gaols. Debtors' prisons** were increasingly common. And so was life imprisonment for minor offending, since those imprisoned for any crime could not be released unless or until they could make restitution or pay the fine imposed. Since inmates were not permitted to perform labor to earn money to pay their fines, many of them died in prison. Subsequently, reeves were able to exploit those confined by allocating their manual labor to merchants and businesspersons looking for cheap help.

Under the debtors' prison concept, it was only a matter of time before English prisons burgeoned with inmates. When the American colonies were settled, English prisons were opened and many inmates were transported to the colonies to perform manual labor for England under an **indentured servant system.** Indentured servants were ordinarily obligated to give free labor to their benefactors for a period of seven years. Following this indentured servitude, such individuals would be freed to pursue their own ambitions, with obviously limited resources. The benefactors were not always affiliated with the government of England. Many merchants used indentured servants in exchange for small commissions paid to government officials.

Of significance is the fact that the American colonists perpetuated the system of law enforcement and jurisprudence with which they were most familiar—the English system. Besides reeves, constables were used for maintaining law and order in colonial communities. The duties of constables included collecting fees for highway usage, tax collecting, and presiding over minor legal issues. Subsequently, the position of sheriff was created, and sheriffs became principal law enforcement officers in various counties throughout the colonies.

Policing in the American Colonies

Differences in law enforcement and judicial practices began to appear in the American colonies because of the great distance from England. Colonists generated systems in which sheriffs became elected or appointed officials who could hire deputies to assist them in law and order tasks and other miscellaneous county endeavors. Nevertheless, certain practices of law enforcement begun in early England were continued in many colonial jurisdictions. The watchman style of policing was continued during daytime and nighttime hours.

Most colonial communities were rural. Therefore, formal policing was unnecessary. Informal policing arrangements were most practical under those conditions. The watchman style of policing was quite popular, since between 1630 and 1790, there were only eight communities with populations of 8,000 or more (Hageman, 1985:16). Trojanowicz and Bucqueroux (1990:46) indicate that some jurisdictions, such as the colony of New York, used **schouts and rattles,** persons who were equipped with actual noisemaking rattles and who were expected to shout and rattle their rattles if they observed crimes in progress or saw fleeing suspects. **Rattle watchmen** were also paid 48 cents per 24-hour shift. Furthermore, offenders were sentenced to rattle watches as their punishment for a crime (Trojanowicz and Bucqueroux, 1990:46).

In the early 1700s, jurisdictions such as Philadelphia created patrol areas supervised by constables who commanded squads of volunteers, drawn largely from the citizenry. These semiorganized policing methods were copied by other colonies throughout the

1700s. During this same time period in England, **Henry Fielding** (1707–1754), an author turned politician, developed some interesting ideas about law enforcement. In 1748, he was appointed chief magistrate of Bow Street Court in London (Peak, 1993:9). He organized small groups of citizens to pursue criminals. These persons were known as **thief-takers** and were selected primarily because they could run fast. Thief-takers received rewards from victims whenever they returned stolen merchandise taken from captured criminals. When Henry Fielding died in 1754, his half brother **Sir John Fielding** (1721–1780) succeeded him and converted the thief-takers into the **Bow Street Runners,** a small group of paid police officers who were also quite successful at apprehending criminals. These activities did not go unnoticed in the colonies. Eventually, the Revolutionary War effectively separated and resolved English and American political and legal policies, although English influence on subsequent policing methods continues to the present.

Law Enforcement from 1800 to the Present

EARLY DEVELOPMENTS IN POLICING IN ENGLAND. The development of police in England can be understood best by examining certain societal structural changes, including various reforms of the country's political-legal system (Manning, 1977:52–71). Between 1750 and 1820, the population of London doubled, from 676,000 to 1.3 million. In fact, between 1801 and 1831, England's population grew from 8.9 million to 13.9 million. These population changes resulted in part from growing birthrates, a sharp reduction in the death rate, and extensive citizen migration from rural areas to densely populated cities. Simultaneously, several significant occupational changes occurred, including the shift of many persons from agricultural to nonagricultural employment, growing numbers of skilled workers and artisans, and the formation of a middle class.

During the first years of the nineteenth century, the Napoleonic Wars eroded England's economic situation to a critical level (Manning, 1977:57–59). Prices of goods and wares skyrocketed, and postwar unemployment levels were extraordinarily high, with large numbers of former soldiers and sailors looking for work. These persons committed fraud and petty crime to support themselves. Also, struggles for power and competition for political domination between various British classes were prevalent between 1770 and 1828. At night in the late 1700s, London was a "hell of a place" according to some observers (Pringle, 1955:29). There was almost no street lighting or police presence. "Burglary, robbery, and other violent crimes were widespread, and the roads on the outskirts of London were infested with highwaymen" (Pringle, 1955:29–30). It was in the context of great social, economic, and political changes that several significant events related to policing were about to occur.

THE METROPOLITAN POLICE OF LONDON.   The most significant event of the early 1800s was the establishment of the **Metropolitan Police of London** in 1829 by **Sir Robert Peel** (1788–1850), the British Home Secretary. This organization was established during an era of police reform. Earlier, in 1792, an influential London magistrate, **Patrick Colquhoun** (1745–1820), originated some unique ideas about the functions of police. Colquhoun was a legal reformist. He believed that police should be used to establish and maintain order, control and prevent crime, and set an example of good conduct and moral sense for the citizenry. He also believed that existing enforcement methods, at least in London, were outmoded and improper. He wanted to inculcate his officers with some professionalism, and he believed that his officers should be funded by the particular jurisdiction they served (Lee, 1901). Colquhoun died before he could realize these reforms. However, Sir Robert Peel was successful in his efforts to establish the first official law enforcement organization in England, through the **Metropolitan Police Act of 1829.** Initial hirings included 6,000 officers whose primary qualifications included the ability to read and write, good moral character, and physical fitness (Trojanowicz and Bucqueroux, 1990). Members of the London police force became known as **bobbies,** after Sir Robert Peel, and this name has been used to refer to these officers informally to the present day.

POLICING DEVELOPMENTS IN THE EARLY UNITED STATES.   During that same period, some of the larger cities in America, such as Boston and New York, were experiencing similar problems of rapid population growth and urban density from migration and industrialization. Formal police departments were created first in Boston in 1838, next in New York in 1845, and successively in Chicago, 1851, Cincinnati and New Orleans, 1852, Philadelphia, 1854, and Newark and Baltimore, 1857 (Manning, 1977:123). Especially in Boston, widespread thievery, drunkenness and crime, vagabondage, lewd and lascivious behavior, assault and battery, and many other forms of unruly conduct caused citizens to create an agency for law enforcement. New York City faced a similar crime problem; the city's streets were called "pathways of danger" (Richardson, 1970:25).

Policing in the United States was not unknown prior to 1838, however. In 1643, New Amsterdam (later New York) had a burgher watch. Constables, marshals, and watches (i.e., guards or lookouts on duty) were appointed or elected in every settlement (Bayley, 1985:32). Under the new and emerging government of the United States, specialized federal marshals were introduced in 1789.

Increasing numbers of law enforcement agencies in the United States during the early 1800s were influenced significantly by the newly established Metropolitan Police of London and the organization's policing methods. The New York City Police Department modeled its own organization after its London counterpart in 1844. By the late 1850s, many other cities had patterned their law enforcement organizations after London's Metropolitan Police, including Chicago, Boston, Baltimore, Philadelphia, New Orleans, and Newark. The objectives of these police departments were similar—Boston and New York City police officers had responsibilities for keeping the peace and were therefore known as **peace officers.** They maintained the peace by being visible deterrents to criminals by patrolling the streets. Their effectiveness as deterrents to crime was measured by the absence of crime in their jurisdictions (Fosdick, 1920).

Over the next several decades, industrialization and urbanization changed the nature of law enforcement, particularly in large cities. Police organizations in larger cities became bigger and more bureaucratic, with increasing numbers of specialized divisions and departments. Eventually state and federal law enforcement organizations emerged with new jurisdictional boundaries.

AUGUST VOLLMER AND POLICE TRAINING.   In 1908, **August Vollmer** (1876–1955), the chief of police of Berkeley, California, demanded and incorporated greater formal professional and educational training for the police officers under his command. Vollmer pioneered an academic regimen of police training, including investigative techniques, photography, fingerprinting, and anatomy, among other academic subject areas. He used various forensics technologists to assist in some of this training. By 1917, he persuaded the

University of California–Berkeley to try his new criminology and law enforcement curriculum for the purpose of assisting his new recruits in acquiring more formal academic training. These academic foundations of police training were most instrumental in the eventual development of **Peace Officer Standards and Training (POST)**, which are fairly common training programs throughout most U.S. jurisdictions.

Vollmer's innovations are widely documented. He established the first fully motorized police force to develop more effective patrolling activities for his officers. Motorizing the police force decreased the use of **beat patrolling.** Inadvertently, Vollmer generated greater social isolation between police officers in cruisers and neighborhood residents. At the time, however, mobilizing the police force was considered a major innovation that meant more rapid response to calls for service by police whenever crimes were committed and reported.

Vollmer was responsible for introducing the two-way radio in police automobiles. This innovation greatly enhanced law enforcement effectiveness and the apprehension of fleeing suspects. His police selection methods resulted in officer appointments based on emotional, educational, and physical fitness through selection by test. He interviewed prospective recruits and also employed psychologists to screen recruits. In many respects, Vollmer is considered the father of **police professionalization.** Some scholars have termed this period the **professionalization movement** (Walker, 1992:12). One of Vollmer's students was **O.W. Wilson** (1900–1972), a former police chief in Wichita, Kansas, and Chicago, Illinois. Wilson subsequently became the first dean of the School of Criminology at the University of California–Berkeley in 1950. Also, Wilson centralized police administration and introduced command decision making in Berkeley and in several other cities during the 1950s and 1960s (Wilson and McLaren, 1977).

CRIMINAL STATISTICS AND NEW TECHNOLOGY. The Prohibition era of the 1920s and 1930s was a turning point in police organization in the United States (Manning, 1977:96–98). Three major changes occurred in the 1930s that had a profound effect on the nature of the police role: (1) the development of a systematic collecting, gathering, and publishing of crime statistics through the *Uniform Crime Reports* distributed by the FBI, commencing in 1930; (2) the linking of criminal statistics published in such reports to the notion of professionalism among the police; and (3) the police

use of radios and automobiles and their dispatch/control/supervision systems, which permitted more mechanized and immediate response whenever crime incidents were reported.

THE WICKERSHAM COMMISSION. In 1931, the first study of the U.S. criminal justice system of national magnitude was conducted under the auspices of the federal government. In 1929, President Herbert Hoover appointed a National Commission on Law Observance and Enforcement, known subsequently as the **Wickersham Commission.** After a two-year investigation, the Wickersham Commission issued a critical 15-volume report that referred to police lawlessness and abuse of authority. Another criticism was that little consistency could be found pertaining to the selection, training, and administration of police recruits throughout the United States. Substantial changes in existing recruitment and training practices for police officers were recommended. These ideas for change were strongly endorsed by both Vollmer and Wilson. Over the next several decades, more sophisticated police selection and training methods were established in many jurisdictions and have been reasonably successful in improving the quality of officers in police departments generally.

THE LAW ENFORCEMENT ASSISTANCE ADMINISTRATION (LEAA). The next major stage of police reform and innovations in policing occurred in 1968 with the creation of the **Law Enforcement Assistance Administration (LEAA).** The LEAA was one outgrowth of the President's Crime Commission during the period from 1965 to 1967, a time of great social unrest and civil disobedience. Racial and political tensions were exceptionally high. Racial segregation was being dismembered in various parts of the country, the Vietnam War was escalating along with protests against the war, delinquency was increasing, and the level of criminality was uncomfortably high. The police were commanding a more prominent role in controlling community events and maintaining law and order. The LEAA allocated millions of dollars to researchers and police departments over the next decade for various purposes. Many experiments were conducted with these monies, many of which led to innovative patrolling strategies in different communities. It is beyond the scope of this chapter to describe these innovations. Rather, it is important to recognize the influence of the LEAA in giving greater attention to policing methods nationally. Particularly, the LEAA underscores the emergence, importance, and/or rediscovery of community policing as a viable method of community crime control.

In 1977, the National Advisory Commission on Criminal Justice Standards and Goals promulgated several important goals for police departments in order to clarify their policing functions. These goals are as follows:

1. Maintenance of order
2. Enforcement of the law
3. Prevention of criminal activity
4. Detection of criminal activity
5. Apprehension of criminals
6. Participation in court proceedings
7. Protection of constitutional guarantees
8. Assistance to those who cannot care for themselves or who are in danger of physical harm
9. Control of traffic
10. Resolution of day-to-day conflicts among family, friends, and neighbors
11. Creation and maintenance of a feeling of security in the community
12. Promotion and preservation of civil order (National Advisory Commission on Criminal Justice Standards and Goals, 1977:104–105)

POLICE DEPARTMENTS: ORGANIZATIONAL SIZE AND OPERATIONS

Considerable consistency can be found concerning the structural features of police organization and administration in the United States over time (Barker, 1986). Many early organizational models of police departments were patterned after the Metropolitan Police of London, and many U.S. police departments retain many similarities to their 1829 counterpart in England (Becker and Whitehouse, 1980:34–36). In recent years, however, public demand for greater police efficiency in reducing crime, together with internal administrative concerns for organizational effectiveness and the elimination of corruption, has resulted in significant changes and reforms.

The organization of police departments is divided into line, staff, and auxiliary functions (Souryal, 1995). Line functions are patrol, traffic, juvenile, and detective work. Staff functions are performed by both civilians and police officers. These persons may work as

clerks or in public relations jobs, and they are responsible for improving police-community relations. They are professionally trained to coordinate internal organizational activities and law enforcement assignments among different police divisions. Auxiliary personnel include maintenance employees, jail guards, and other supporting workers (Becker and Whitehouse, 1980:38–40).

In most cities, police departments are municipal agencies under the direct control of the chief executive such as the mayor or city manager (Coleman, 1995). In Chicago, the police superintendent is appointed by the mayor. In Los Angeles, however, the commissioner of police is appointed by a Board of Police Commissioners (Ruchelman, 1973:6). And in Indianapolis, Indiana, the mayor appoints a public safety director who in turn appoints a police chief, with the mayor's approval, and who serves at the director's (and mayor's) pleasure (Hudnut, 1985:21).

As we have seen, there is considerable variation in the size of police departments throughout the United States. Some of the smallest departments have one or two officers, whereas some of the largest departments have between 2,000 and 36,000 officers. Figure 9.1 shows the organization of a small midwestern police department. This type of police department is fairly

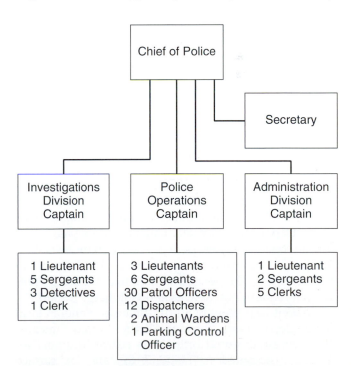

FIGURE 9.1 Small Police Department Chain of Command

typical of departments throughout the nation, inasmuch as about 85 percent of the 13,578 police agencies in 1996 had 99 or fewer full-time sworn personnel (Reaves and Goldberg, 1998:5). In the same year, 62 percent of these police agencies had fewer than 10 full-time officers.

The police department organizational chart is deceptively simple. Three basic divisions each are headed by a captain: the investigations division, police operations, and the administrative division. Within the investigation division, there are 10 investigative personnel, including three detectives, five sergeants, a lieutenant, and a clerk. The operations division (the most visible division) consists of three lieutenants, six sergeants, 30 patrol officers, 12 dispatchers, two animal control wardens, and one parking control officer.

On the average for the nation, there were about 15 officers per 10,000 residents in 1996. The District of Columbia had 66 officers per 10,000 residents, the highest number of officers of all jurisdictions. By contrast, New York had 30 officers per 10,000 residents. California, which is one of the most populated states, only had 11 officers per 10,000 residents. Again by contrast, a sparsely populated state, North Dakota, had 9 officers per 10,000 residents, not altogether different from the 11 officers per 10,000 residents in California. Variations in the numbers of officers in different states are influenced by many variables, including the crime rate, law enforcement budget, and the general need for law enforcement services.

Among the 50 largest local police departments in 1996, the New York Police Department was the largest, with 36,813 full-time sworn personnel. Between 1992 and 1996, the number of personnel increased by 27.8 percent, indicating substantial hiring during that period. The Chicago Police Department had the next largest number of full-time sworn officers, with 13,237 officers. The Chicago Police Department saw an increase of 5 percent in personnel between 1992 and 1996. Some departments, such as the Washington (DC) Police Department, actually had a personnel reduction during the 1992 to 1996 period. Although the Washington Police Department had a force of 3,587 officers in 1996, this was 26.6 percent smaller than the force of officers it had in 1992 (Reaves and Goldberg, 1998:6).

About 70 percent of all full-time personnel in local police departments throughout the United States in 1996 were uniformed officers on patrol or otherwise regularly assigned to respond to calls for service (Reaves and Goldberg, 1998:6). Sixteen percent of all full-time sworn personnel performed investigative functions, such as detective work and crime scene investigation. Only 2 percent of these officers were assigned to jail operations or court functions. A major reason for this is that in most jurisdictions, such work is the primary responsibility of sheriffs' departments. Also, jails are most frequently operated by sheriffs' departments. Relatively few cities have jail facilities independent of county jail facilities.

Increasing priority is being given to police-community interaction (Dantzker, Lurigio, and Hartnett, 1995a, 1995b). Many communities are moving away from the traditional view of police toward a more service-oriented police role (Weisheit, Wells, and Falcone, 1994). These reforms are concerned with (1) improving police-public communication, (2) emphasizing the service functions of the police and rewarding officers for doing well in that area, and (3) democratizing police departments by involving rank-and-file police officers in policy making to a greater degree (Walker, 1979:168).

Goals and Functions of Police Departments

THE POLICE MISSION.   What is the true mission of modern police departments and the officers who must interact with citizens throughout the diverse communities in the United States? What roles are expected of these police departments and personnel as an integral part of our social fabric? If police departments cannot achieve consensus about their general mission and objectives, it is equally difficult for them to impart to their police officers what they should do and how they should do it. Furthermore, many police officers indicate that they often experience conflicts between what they ideally ought to do and what they actually do when performing their jobs.

For instance, Burton and his colleagues (1993) investigated the legal codes of all 50 states and identified legislatively mandated police functions divided into three major categories: law enforcement functions, peacekeeping functions, and service functions. Most states had codes mandating law enforcement and peacekeeping functions, but few states had service-mandated codes. Among the states, little agreement could be found about which tasks were most important. Thus, police officers themselves must merge their own role expectations according to what is prescribed and what is preferred. The officers' enacted roles are a blend of legislatively prescribed and preferred role expectations. Police officers are plagued with role conflict, as neighborhood residents have conflicting expectations of police and what laws they should enforce, in the context of state legislature–mandated roles for police. The absence of service-mandated roles for police causes local governments to establish service priorities for police officers to follow in many jurisdictions. These service functions are often diffuse and unclear, so that police officers experience some degree of role conflict when performing their role expectations.

THE GOALS AND FUNCTIONS OF POLICE DEPARTMENTS.   The goals and functions of police departments are fairly uniform throughout jurisdictions and include

1. Preventing crime
2. Enforcing the laws
3. Preserving the peace
4. Protecting civil rights and liberties
5. Providing services

MODELS OF POLICE STYLES FOR ORGANIZATIONAL GOAL ATTAINMENT.   Three basic styles or models of policing have been described. These include the (1) legalistic model, (2) the service model, and (3) the watchman model (Wilson, 1968).

The **legalistic model** is the one most consistent with urban policing, because it limits the discretionary power of employees and allows for the greatest amount of control by police supervisors. It includes the following characteristics:

1. Highly specialized with great division of labor and a centralized style of command
2. Strict rules, policies, procedures, and compliance
3. Emphasis on crime suppression and apprehension of criminals
4. Impersonal attitude toward the public and its problems
5. Selection of personnel based solely on achievement and criteria, tests, education, and past accomplishments
6. Influence of authority for task completion
7. Narrowly defined employee work roles
8. Exemplary conduct of employees based on threat, external control, and enforcement of rules

9. Traditional methods related to narrow job descriptions used for evaluation purposes
10. Intradepartmental or intraregional training

The **service model** has the following characteristics:

1. Generalized approach with less division of labor and a decentralized style of management
2. Stress on individual discretion and trust of individual decision making
3. Emphasis on prevention and crime deterrence
4. Personal involvement with the public and its problems
5. Selection of personnel based on tests, achievement, and ascriptive criteria with voluntary recognition of need to recruit culturally diverse people
6. Stress on influence of persuasion with subtle use of authority to accomplish tasks
7. Expanded role of employees toward greater decentralization
8. Exemplary conduct of employees based on training, self-control, individual responsibility, and peer pressure
9. Evaluation according to a holistic instrument to fully assess the totality of the individual and relationship to the community
10. Training at national level and use of private-sector courses
11. Encouragement of networking, planning, research, and publication

The **watchman model** has the following characteristics:

1. Stress on order maintenance
2. Keeping the peace
3. Neither proactive nor reactive
4. Order maintained through physical presence and crime deterrence

It is apparent that the legalistic and service models emulate Weber's bureaucratic model in several close respects, with emphases on adherence to abstract rules, selection of personnel according to test, use of authority to achieve tasks and administer decision making, and independent training and expertise. The watchman style is outmoded, tending to reflect nineteenth-century style policing, with little or no emphasis on officer professionalism or proactive involvement in crime detection, criminal apprehension, or community safety.

The Division of Labor: Line and Staff Duties and Responsibilities

Like most other organizations, police departments have a division of labor and hierarchy of authority. Throughout the organization, regardless of its size, are personnel identified as either **line personnel** or **staff personnel.** Generally, line personnel are considered operational personnel who carry out the primary goals of the organization. In an automobile assembly plant, for instance, line personnel would be workers who operate machines at different points along the automobile assembly process and ensure that the automobiles are assembled properly. In police agencies, line personnel consist of full-time or part-time sworn officers who respond to calls for service. **Calls for service** are reports of crime from citizens or requests for any other type of police assistance within the scope of police authority, duties, and responsibilities.

The Recruitment and Selection Process

Police officer recruitment practices have improved greatly since the days of the Metropolitan Police of London in 1829 and the Boston and New York City police departments of the 1830s and 1840s. Original selection criteria included physical size, gender, age, and the ability to read and write. Little progress occurred in developing better police selection criteria until the establishment of the first police training school in the United States in 1908 by Berkeley (California) Chief of Police August Vollmer. In 1916, Vollmer and Professor Alexander M. Kidd developed the first criminology curriculum in the United States at the University of California at Berkeley. This program became a division of the Department of Political Science in 1939, and in 1963, a Doctor of Criminology degree program was established (Becker and Whitehouse, 1980:49–51). Other institutions such as the University of Southern California, the University of Chicago, and Michigan State University developed similar programs during the late 1920s and 1930s. In 1979, there were over 700 academic degree programs in law enforcement offered in community colleges and universities throughout the United States (Becker and Whitehouse, 1980:51). No one knows for sure how many degree programs in criminal justice exist today, because so many of these

programs are intertwined with the programs of departments of political science, public administration, sociology, and other behavioral sciences. Estimates of the total number of programs range from 1,000 to 1,500.

Considerable variation can be found in police recruitment programs among police departments (Ash, Slora, and Britton, 1990). In rural areas with small police departments, no formal selection criteria may exist. Applicants might be hired as police officers with only a cursory check of their background. Usually in such remote areas, there is not a great deal of competition for these jobs. In most of the larger municipal police departments, in which numerous applicants compete for positions, however, the selection process is more formal. It may include completing numerous personal data forms, submitting college transcripts or records of university work completed, taking several psychological personality and abilities tests, and submitting to a polygraph or lie detector test (Kornfeld, 1995).

The primary objective of these screening procedures is to select candidates who will make the best police officers. Some of the psychological tests are designed to identify well-adjusted officers or those who can handle stressful situations. Since the prospective police officer inevitably will be exposed to stressful situations while enforcing the law, those recruits who demonstrate a better ability to handle stress might make better police officers than those who have a low capacity for stress.

Two selection tests administered to police recruits in various jurisdictions are the **Minnesota Multiphasic Personality Inventory (MMPI)** and the **California Personality Inventory (CPI)** (Scogin, Schumacher, and Gardner, 1995). These instruments purportedly measure personality dimensions such as anxiety, sociability, personal adjustment, and social adjustment. Precisely how such personality dimensions relate to making good choices in police officer selections is unknown. The current state of the art in psychological testing for police recruitment is such that the test results are useful, but to a limited degree. The results of these tests should be cautiously interpreted by any agency using them for selecting new police recruits. Some agreement can be found among police departments about certain desirable qualities for police officer roles: honesty, reliability, emotional stability, patience, and good character (Hogue, Black, and Sigler, 1994).

Currently, about 99 percent of all police departments use criminal record checks to screen potential police officer applicants. Background investigations, driving record checks, and medical examinations are conducted for over 98 percent of all new police recruits. Another 91 percent of all recruits are subjected to psychological screening tests, whereas 84 percent of all applicants are screened according to various aptitude tests. Nearly 80 percent of all potential officers are further screened with tests of physical agility (Bureau of Justice Statistics, 1999b:1).

EDUCATIONAL REQUIREMENTS FOR POLICE OFFICERS. The educational standards for new police recruits are not particularly rigorous. In 1997, only 1 percent of all police departments in the United States required their officers to have four-year college degrees, and only 8 percent of these departments required two-year associate degrees. About 14 percent of all police departments that employ 31 percent of all new recruits required their future officers to have some college completed, however (Bureau of Justice Statistics, 1999b:1). Field and classroom training requirements for new officer recruits averaged about 1,000 hours in 1997, and about seven in eight departments required officers to complete some in-service training, with an average annual requirement of 29 hours. Starting salaries for local police officers averaged about $28,400 in 1997, ranging from an average of $18,800 in the smallest jurisdictions to $30,600 in the largest jurisdictions (Bureau of Justice Statistics, 1999b:1).

In recent years, an employment shortage of qualified candidates has occurred in some of the larger police departments, such as Chicago and New York. Advertising firms have been enlisted by some of these police agencies in order to devise better recruitment strategies to attract and retain qualified recruits.

Minority Hiring Practices

In 1968, the National Advisory Commission issued its Report on Civil Disorders, noting that among the causes of civil disorders was discrimination directed by police officers against racial minorities. The commission said that despite the fact that blacks made up at least 12 percent of the U.S. population, their proportionate representation among police officers was less than 5 percent. Several reasons were cited for this low minority representation.

Prior to 1948, blacks were not allowed to be members of the Atlanta (Georgia) Police Department (Kuykendall and Burns, 1983:64). And when some of them were hired in 1948, they were initially not per-

mitted to wear uniforms similar to those worn by white officers. By 1981, black police officers in the Atlanta Police Department made up 46 percent of all city police officers compared with an Atlanta black population of 67 percent (Stroup, 1985). This underrepresentation of minorities has not been limited to southern cities. Every major municipal jurisdiction in the United States has had the same problem for decades. In 1981, the Los Angeles Police Department had a black police officer membership of 9 percent even though 17 percent of the city consisted of blacks. And even in Washington, DC, where the proportion of blacks in the population is 70 percent, the police department in 1982 had only 50 percent black membership. Among the 50 largest cities in the United States in 1982, only Toledo, Ohio, had a proportion of black police officers (18 percent) commensurate with the proportion of blacks in that city generally (17 percent). In the other 49 cities, the proportionate discrepancy was sizable (Walker, 1983:5). By 1997, the proportionate representation of racial and ethnic minorities in law enforcement had changed dramatically. Racial and ethnic minorities comprised 21.5 percent of all full-time sworn officers in local police departments. This compares with 19.1 percent in 1993, 17 percent in 1990, and 14.6 percent in 1987 (Bureau of Justice Statistics, 1999b:1).

WOMEN IN LAW ENFORCEMENT. There is a growing number of women in law enforcement. Before 1967, there was only a negligible percentage of female police officers performing patrol work in most U.S. jurisdictions. Many female police officers had duties exclusively related to issuing parking tickets or performing routine clerical tasks (Segrave, 1995). By 1981, affirmative action caused an increase in the employment of women to 6 percent of all U.S. law enforcement officers. By 1993, women comprised 8.8 percent of all full-time local police officers (Reaves, 1996:1). In 1998, female officers made up nearly 11 percent of all full-time sworn police officers in the United States (Maguire and Pastore, 2000).

One major limitation restricting the influx of women into police roles is that police departments find it difficult to attract, hire, and retain women. An investigation of the motivation of women for entering police work reveals that little is known (Thomann, Pilant, and Kay, 1994). Women are initially attracted to police work because of salary and an opportunity to help others (Morash and Haarr, 1995). Affirmative action policies have influenced greatly the proportion of minorities and women in police departments throughout the nation (Felkenes and Unsinger, 1992). Ample legal justification exists for using quotas in establishing appropriate racial/ethnic/gender balances in police agencies, particularly if there is a compelling state interest in rectifying past discrimination. Most police executives are complying with the general principles of affirmative action in their hiring practices (Carter and Sapp, 1991). However, although a proportion of minority recruits possesses similar educational backgrounds compared with white recruits, the requirement of a college education continues to function as a discriminatory barrier and thus disadvantages minorities who want to pursue law enforcement careers (Felkenes and Unsinger, 1992).

The Administration of Police Departments

Police departments in the United States are political organizations and extensions of municipal political authority (Souryal, 1995). Because political systems in cities developed at about the same time as police agencies, a close relation has always existed between the two bodies. A study of 493 police chiefs was conducted during the period from 1982 to 1983 that described the training and background of chief executives of police (Witham, 1985). Police chiefs tended to be about 49 years old, were police chiefs for about five years, and had an average of 24 years of experience as law enforcement officers. Fifty percent had bachelor's degrees and most had experience working in at least one other law enforcement agency.

Compared with the professional training of administrators of corporations employing similar numbers of persons, the credentials of police chiefs have not been particularly impressive (Witham, 1985). Over 80 percent of the administrators in the private sector had bachelor's degrees, for example, compared with only 50 percent for police chiefs. Chiefs tended to define their roles too narrowly and were not involved directly in formulating policies affecting their department officers. Critics have contended that police chiefs are no more than 50-year-old police officers.

In recent years, however, police chiefs have acquired additional education and experience, and more than a few have added business management to their skills and backgrounds (Cox and Moore, 1992). This training is designed to enhance police administrators' effectiveness in job performance so that they become familiar with a variety of managerial strategies. Public

concerns for administrative reform were contained in an earlier 1967 report of the President's Crime Commission. This report reflected a traditional approach to police reform: (1) greater administrative efficiency, (2) more expert leadership, and (3) higher qualifications for police officers. In more recent years, studies have suggested that in order to be more successful in their work performance, police chiefs are going to have to alter their approaches to leadership and redesign their organizations to fit the more diverse needs of contemporary society (Bennett, 1992:257–258).

SHERIFFS' DEPARTMENTS

In mid-1996, there were 3,088 sheriffs' departments in the United States (Reaves and Goldberg, 1998:1). By mid-June 1997, 263,427 full-time employees worked in sheriffs' departments, including 175,000 sworn personnel. Since 1993, employment in sheriffs' departments has increased about 4.4 percent per year (Bureau of Justice Statistics, 1999c:1).

Eighty percent of all sheriffs' departments are relatively small, employing fewer than 50 full-time sworn personnel in a survey in 1996. Less than 10 percent of all sheriffs' departments have 100 or more full-time sworn personnel (Reaves and Goldberg, 1998:8). Texas has the most sheriffs' departments with 254, followed by Georgia (159), and Virginia (125). The average number of full-time sworn officers per 10,000 residents in 1996 was 6. Louisiana had the largest number of sheriffs' deputies, 20 per 10,000 residents, followed by Wyoming (11), Florida (10), and Virginia (10) (Reaves and Goldberg, 1998:10). Between 1992 and 1996, a 12 percent increase was seen in the number of full-time sworn sheriffs' personnel in U.S. sheriffs' departments (Reaves and Goldberg, 1998:8).

Goals and Functions of Sheriffs' Departments

The goals and functions of sheriffs' departments are similar to the goals and functions of local police departments. Sheriffs' departments have the primary responsibility of enforcing county laws, and for the most part, the jurisdiction of sheriffs' deputies is restricted to the counties in which they are hired. In 1996, about 42 percent of all full-time sworn sheriffs' personnel were patrol and other uniformed officers whose regularly assigned duties included responding to calls for service. Besides these patrol duties, sheriffs' deputies are responsible for operating one or more jails and

BOX 9.1 PERSONALITY HIGHLIGHT

DEBORAH K. NESS
Chief of Police, Bismarck
Police Department, North
Dakota

Statistics: B.A. (business
administration), Minot
State University; M.S.
(administration), Central
Michigan University; FBI
National Academy;
Backsters School of Lie
Detection; National Crime
Prevention Institute

Presently I am chief of police of the Bismarck (North Dakota) Police Department. Prior to this position, I was a captain with the Minot Police Department for 23 years, in charge of investigations. I have been an instructor for the Department of Criminal Justice at Minot State University as well as the IACP Community Policing Consortium for several years.

Background: I grew up on a farm in Edgeley, North Dakota, with eight brothers and sisters. After escaping farm life, I attended Minot State University, earning an associate of arts degree in criminal justice. In 1974, I was one of three women hired as the first female patrol officers for the Minot Police Department.

My career in law enforcement started on a bet. While in high school, a representative from Minot State University came to our school to speak to the "men" in our class about the Criminal Justice Program. I decided to sneak into the back of the auditorium to hear the presentation. It was all very interesting. After the presentation, I went to the school counselor's office to discuss law enforcement as a possible career field. The counselor had been stressing how important it was to select a career field before graduation. Well, the counselor didn't feel that police work would be appropriate for a girl and strongly suggested I look at other possibilities. It was after this discussion that I made a bet with my school counselor that not only was I going to major in criminal justice, but that I had every intention of seeking a job as a police officer once I finished my education. Guess what?

It is now almost 30 years later and I'm still loving my career choice.

Interesting Experiences: Throughout my career I have had an opportunity to be involved in many interesting events. It does not matter which section or division you are assigned. The possibility always exists that the most insignificant calls will turn into something interesting. For instance, I remember a time just before Christmas, and everyone was busy doing their last-minute shopping. I was dispatched to the JCPenney store located on Main Street to pick up a shoplifter. I parked my squad car in front of the store and started to prepare to go in. As I put on my hat, which at the time it was mandatory to wear, a very grandmotherly looking woman jumps into the rear seat of my car. Needless to say I was surprised by her willingness to leave the store unescorted and get into my squad car without even being arrested. I turned toward the back seat and asked her, "Are you my shoplifter?" She said, "Of course not, aren't you my car driver?" Obviously, we had surprised each other!

Insights: Police work can be both exciting and frustrating. But that's what makes the job fascinating and challenging. The profession of law enforcement finds us

1. Working strange hours, weekends, and holidays
2. Being either utterly bored because nothing is going on or faced with sheer chaos because everything is going on
3. Always on guard since any given minute you could be faced with a life-threatening situation, either your own or someone else's
4. Writing traffic tickets, which everyone hates, and they all let us know how much they hate them
5. Responding to fatality accidents, homicides, suicides, and unattended deaths
6. Comforting those who find themselves faced with a tragic situation
7. Breaking up bar fights, family fights, school yard fights, and neighborhood disputes

8. Cautiously entering buildings that have been burglarized

9. Dealing with people who have had too much to drink or are under the influence of drugs

10. Photographing crime scenes, attending autopsies, interviewing suspects, witnesses, and victims

11. Arresting the bad guys and seeing them successfully prosecuted in court

12. Helping a child find their lost bike

13. Calming the fears of a senior citizen who heard strange noises in the night

These are just a few things officers are called on to do every single day. It takes a special person to be willing to attend to the needs of the public and to do it in a kind, caring, and compassionate manner, no matter how badly the person on the last call may have treated you.

As a police officer and a detective, I have had the opportunity to work many major cases. It is surprising, however, that solving the big case does not necessarily give the most satisfaction in this profession. I have found that many times, it is the little everyday things we do for people that is the most rewarding.

Advice to Students: The best advice I could give any student is that if you are truly interested in a career in law enforcement, do not be afraid to pursue it and never say you can't. If this is where your passion lies, then make your dream come true. I promise you, you will not be disappointed.

---

fulfilling court-related responsibilities, such as serving process and court security. In 1996, about 30 percent of all sheriffs' officers performed jail duties (Reaves and Goldberg, 1998:9). For a majority of the larger sheriffs' departments, jail operations accounts for the largest amount of officer resources. In Cook County (Chicago, Illinois), for instance, 58 percent of all sheriffs' officers were assigned to jail duties, and another 32 percent were assigned to court-related functions. These figures highlight at least one important difference between sheriffs' agencies and police departments. Sheriffs' departments have a substantially higher involvement in jail-related duty rather than patrol compared with local police officers.

Generally, the goals and functions of sheriffs' departments are to

1. Investigate crimes and enforce county laws

2. Patrol county roads and prevent crime

3. Staff and maintain county jails

4. Serve warrants, restraining orders, and liens

5. Collect delinquent taxes and conduct real estate sales for nonpayment of taxes

6. Serve as court bailiffs

7. Assist local and state police in law enforcement and traffic functions

8. Enforce drug laws and cooperate with multi-agency drug task forces

9. Work as school resource officers

The Division of Labor

The chief executive officer of sheriffs' departments is the county sheriff. This is most often an elected position. No special qualifications exist for those who aspire to be sheriffs in most jurisdictions. Sheriffs may or may not have previous law enforcement experience. Because these posts are filled most often by elected officials, some of these persons may be ex-police officers, ex-sheriffs' deputies, ex-restaurant managers, or even ex-school superintendents. Although the National Sheriffs' Association disseminates information to its membership about jails and jail problems, there is not much more to foster national sheriff professionalism, unity, or consistency of performance (Senese, 1991).

Sheriffs are responsible for appointing staff and officers for different office functions, including jail operations and patrolling. Sheriffs usually appoint chief deputies who oversee different aspects of county sheriff operations. These chief deputies are usually selected from among the officer ranks and thus have the most extensive law enforcement experience (Bureau of Justice Statistics, 1999c).

Recruiting Sheriffs' Deputies and Ancillary Personnel

Compared with police officers, sheriffs' deputies are among the lowest-paid law enforcement personnel in the United States. For example, the mean starting

BOX 9.2 PERSONALITY HIGHLIGHT

MARY ROGERS
Program Coordinator,
Minot State University
Minot, North Dakota

Statistics: B.S. (criminal justice major, psychology minor), Minot State University; M.S. (criminal justice), Minot State University; licensed addiction counselor, North Dakota (October 2000).

As the Program Coordinator for the criminal justice department of Minot State University, my role involves coordination of two degree programs, advising over 100 students, teaching, and the management of the internship program. Our programs are located in Bismarck, North Dakota, at the Bismarck State College campus and are considered an extended degree program in which students can complete the degree requirements for the B.S. in criminal justice or management. My current plans for continued professional development include the doctoral program at the University of Minnesota.

Background: My career in law enforcement began after trying several other areas of interest to me. I was a real estate agent, day-care facility owner, emergency medical technician, and reserve police officer in a small town in South Dakota, all at the same time! I chose law enforcement quite frankly because of the opportunity to be involved with people in a meaningful way and the excitement guaranteed by the nature of the job. I was employed as a deputy sheriff with the Pennington County Sheriffs' Department in Rapid City, South Dakota. During my employment, some of the experiences, I can tell you, were more exciting than I had expected or in some instances wanted. It was a good decision, however, and one that has led the way to new and challenging opportunities for me.

I completed my education after making the decision to leave law enforcement. Interestingly enough, I changed my majors three times before I realized that my interest was in criminal justice. During the time I completed my degree requirements through Minot State University, I was offered an opportunity to teach a course, and I knew then what direction I would take with my career. I have been in my current position since 1995 and am always afforded opportunities through the university for professional development.

Interesting Experiences: Some of my more interesting "war stories" that I have shared with many students as they relate to course content include responding in full riot gear to Sturgis, South Dakota, during the Sturgis Rally when biker gangs attempted to have one of their own released from the hospital following a stabbing/shooting incident; working with the Secret Service and FBI agents in South Dakota providing security for President George Bush and his wife while they were fishing for trout and later meeting the president at a picnic; wrestling with a senior citizen after I told him I was placing him under arrest for DUI; taking another senior citizen home after stopping him as a DUI suspect, and finding out that he couldn't see to drive (we had to stop for milk and bread before "going home"); being involved in a hostage situation in which shots fired at four of us could have ended my life as well as those of fellow officers; and as a D.A.R.E. officer, working with kids to educate them and learn from them about the dynamics of growing up today. As you can imagine, I had many more experiences, but the others you should know about are those times working with other officers and developing a sense of trust, friendship, respect, and humor to carry me through some very difficult situations. I am still in touch with the department and continue to maintain friendships with those I worked with.

My role with the university is diverse, and my past experiences and work history allow me to help students explore future career goals, with a realistic approach. As an advisor, I always ask the new students to tell me two things: their career goals and how much money it will take to make them happy. Most students are surprised by this approach; however, I have found that all too often, students are provided information about education and career goals but not given encouragement, support, or the realities of the choices they are making.

Advice to Students: While completing your degree, expose yourself to as many work and career opportunities as possible. If an internship program exists, it can provide you with more than experience. Successful interns develop a networking system that is beneficial for future employment, providing recommendation letters for the extra edge over other potential job candidates. Volunteer with community organizations with a commitment for hours you can realistically serve. Finally, be patient while working toward the career goal. I was rewarded last fall with a call from a former advisee who told me that everything paid off and that he realized his goal of becoming a DEA agent.

salary for entry-level municipal police officers in 1997 was $29,859 compared with a mean starting salary for sheriffs' deputies of $25,994. Explaining this salary differential is a $5,000 difference in the median total operating expenditure per employee between city police and county sheriffs' officers ($54,000 for city police and $49,200 for sheriffs' deputies) (Bureau of Justice Statistics, 1999a:4).

In 1997, about 1 percent of all sheriffs' departments required new deputy recruits to have a four-year degree and 7 percent required a two-year associate's degree. Overall, 11 percent of all sheriffs' departments required new deputies to have completed at least some college work, compared with 14 percent of all police departments. Sheriffs' deputies averaged about 800 hours of field and classroom training, compared with an average of 1,000 hours required for city police officers. In-service training obligations for deputies averaged 20 hours per year, compared with 29 hours per year for city police. All of these differentials suggest that on the average, sheriffs' deputies are not as educated, nor are they as well trained, as their city police counterparts. Low salaries and slow promotion rates within sheriffs' department ranks fail to attract and retain the most qualified personnel for sheriffs' department work (Bureau of Justice Statistics, 1999a, 1999b, 1999c).

Nevertheless, nearly all officers worked for departments that used criminal record checks, background investigations, driving record checks, and medical exams to screen applicants. Psychological, aptitude, and physical agility tests were also widely used in the sheriffs' officer recruitment process (Bureau of Justice Statistics, 1999c:1). Minority recruitment within sheriffs' departments has increased over the years. Racial and ethnic minorities comprised about 19 percent of all full-time sworn sheriffs' officers in 1997. This compares with 16.9 percent in 1993, 15.5 percent in 1990, and 13.4 percent in 1987. Compared with local police departments, sheriffs' departments have proportionately 3 percent lower minority employees who are full-time sworn officers, although these numbers over the period from 1987 to 1997 are encouraging for increasing the numbers of minority officers in sheriffs' officer ranks (Bureau of Justice Statistics, 1999c:1).

LAW ENFORCEMENT ISSUES

Several issues are discussed in this section concerning law enforcement officers, their training, and their conduct. These issues are (1) law enforcement officer training and quality control, (2) accreditation, (3) measuring police performance, (4) police professionalism, (5) police-community relations, (6) officer misconduct and internal affairs, and (7) citizen complaint review boards and other sanctions.

Law Enforcement Officer Training and Quality Control

August Vollmer wanted to do at least four things for improving the quality of police selection and services. He wanted to (1) eliminate political influence from police administration, (2) secure expert leadership in police management, (3) modernize the organizational structure of police departments, and (4) raise the quality of the rank-and-file police officers (Walker, 1979:164). It is highly unlikely that political influence will ever be removed from the affairs of police administration. It is unlikely also that major changes will be made in the organizational structures of most police departments. However, indications can be seen that police leadership is being upgraded and improved through hiring more competent personnel in administrative positions, with both police experience and political skills, to network with community leaders and agencies. Furthermore, strong indications also show that the quality of police training is improving annually.

Improving the quality of police officers means several things. Most large police departments use psychological screening devices to select their police recruits (Kornfeld, 1995). Many of these departments also use professional psychologists as members of their oral screening boards to assist in candidate interviews and selections (Pollock and Becker, 1995). Minimum educational requirements have been established as prerequisites for employment in many municipal police departments. Stringent physical standards are upheld. All candidates must pass a thorough investigation and background check.

One consequence of having larger numbers of college-educated police officers communicating more effectively with the public is improved police-community relations. However, on-the-job training is perhaps the most important component of police training programs. In White Plains, New York, for instance, a 40-hour in-service training program is required of all personnel and is designed to increase job proficiency and enhance an officer's self-image and motivation (Bradley, 1986). Human relations training is also an important component of a recruit's learning experience (Das, 1986). The human relations approach says much about the sorts of tasks and problems confronting police officers daily (Bohm, 1986). Because urban police officers are confronting an increasingly culturally diverse citizenry, cultural sensitivity training is emphasized to a greater degree in large city police departments (Barlow and Barlow, 1994).

THE RECRUITMENT PROCESS. The recruitment process begins with advertising. Advertisements are placed by police agencies in professional publications, newspapers, and newsletters. Letters are sent to departments of criminal justice and other social science departments expressing the desire to communicate with interested students about their future career plans. Two important requirements for consideration for entry into most police and sheriffs' departments in the United States are evidence of U.S. citizenship and a high school diploma or its equivalent.

Prospective applicants submit letters of interest, indicating their desire to pursue law enforcement careers. These applicants usually have an initial interview and are subjected to preliminary screening. Subsequently, those who pass these preliminary interviews must pass various written and oral tests. Most of the larger jurisdictions, such as New York, Los Angeles, Philadelphia, Miami, and Detroit, require applicants to take civil service examinations. These standardized tests help to objectify the selection process by providing testers with a fairly clear appraisal of an applicant's verbal and written skills. Additionally, physical agility is assessed during scheduled physical exercise ses-

sions. In most of the larger jurisdictions, prospective recruits are subjected to intensive background checks of their records. Any officer with a criminal record for any serious misdemeanor or felony will be disqualified and no further consideration will be given to their application. Some departments administer **polygraph tests** or lie detector tests designed to determine their truthfulness in response to oral questions about their personal habits and histories.

One vital component in selecting police officers is the **psychological screening.** Psychological screening usually is accomplished through both written and oral assessments of prospective recruits. Law enforcement agencies do not want to select recruits with emotional problems that could interfere with their work with the public. For instance, several factors have been associated with disturbed personality systems. Trompetter (1993) has listed the following as indicators of problem officers who might use excessive force or abuse their discretionary powers: (1) childhood history of fire-setting, runaway behavior, school suspensions, vandalism, cruelty to animals, attention deficit disorders, and/or foster home placements; (2) gang affiliation; (3) home environment in which violence was used to enforce house rules; (4) use of violence to overcome low self-esteem; (5) history of paranoia; (6) history of aggressive behaviors in response to stress; (7) bullying behavior; (8) exploitation or manipulation of others; (9) self-centeredness and narcissism; (10) history of arrests for aggressive or assaultive behavior; (11) family history of antisocial conduct; (12) history of drug and/or alcohol abuse; (13) interpersonal irresponsibility; (14) history of rebellious, defiant attitudes toward authority or social conventions; (15) history of authoritarianism and close-mindedness and social intolerance; (16) history of one or more major mental disorders; (17) history of abnormal sexual behaviors; and (18) unstable work history.

Provided that officer candidates pass the oral and written tests and screens, they then must attend a training academy. Many states have Law Enforcement Training Academies (LETA) that are conducted for new recruits for 15 to 17 weeks. These LETAs include physical exercise; educational coursework; training in driving, accident investigation, criminal and traffic law, use of radar, and intoxilyzer testing; radios and weapons training; and CPR certification.

Many law enforcement agencies regard their new recruits as **probationary employees.** Probationary officers remain in this status for varying periods, usually up to one year. They are under the supervision of a senior officer. In some jurisdictions, these officers in charge of new recruits are **field training officers (FTOs).** FTOs are usually selected on the basis of their own good records and prior experience. They are in a position to pass along their experiences to new officers and to train them in areas unaddressed or underaddressed at their training academy. These experiences include making discretionary judgments in volatile situations as well as the application of sound ethical practices (Kleinig, 1996). FTOs observe their subordinates in action, and they are able to provide critical feedback and potentially life-saving information that will prove useful in future encounters with dangerous subjects or volatile situations. Also, in an effort to professionalize police services, many law enforcement agencies are seeking recognition and accreditation from national police organizations.

Training and Accreditation

Accreditation is certification by an officially recognized body or agency to ensure that a particular training program complies with national standards and requirements (Bizzack, 1993). Officially, accreditation of law enforcement programs was established by four law enforcement agencies in 1979. These were the Police Executive Research Forum, the National Organizational of Black Law Enforcement Executives, the International Association of Chiefs of Police, and the National Sheriffs' Association. These four organizations created the Commission on Accreditation for Law Enforcement Agencies (CALEA). The program was designed to establish national standards by which police and sheriffs' departments could evaluate themselves. It is strictly voluntary, although the cost of accrediting a department is fairly high. For instance, the cost of accrediting a small or medium-sized police department is about $6,000, whereas accrediting a large police department can cost as much as $25,000 (International Association of Chiefs of Police, 1995).

MEASURING POLICE PERFORMANCE

How do we know if police officers are effective at whatever they are supposed to do? What measures determine if officers are performing their jobs responsibly and in accordance with department policies? One way of evaluating an officer's or an agency's performance is to consider the number of complaints filed by citizens against the officer or agency. Those officers who receive more complaints than others might be considered less effective, whereas those officers receiving fewer or no complaints might be considered more effective. Agencies receiving large numbers of citizen complaints also might be considered less effective and poorer performers compared with agencies that receive fewer complaints. We do not know this for sure, however.

The relationship between an officer's educational level and his or her ability to handle stressful situations also can be determined. It has been found in some police departments that having a college degree, compared with not having one, is positively related to patrol effectiveness (Dantzker, 1989). Better-educated officers seem to handle stressful situations more effectively than lesser-educated officers. Thus, requiring officers to have college degrees might be one way of ensuring that more competent officers are hired, and that their performance levels generally will be higher also.

POLICE PROFESSIONALISM

Police professionalism is an elusive concept. It is used frequently in the law enforcement literature, but few attempts have been made to define it or give it a precise and consistent interpretation (Skolnick, 1994; Virginia State Crime Commission, 1994). Despite its lack of precise meaning, the concept has been used to explain victim satisfaction with police services and responses to calls, police discipline, conduct and corruption, and general policing effectiveness (Brandl and Horvath, 1991; Woods, 1993).

Professionalism signifies the achievement of at least five objectives. These are (1) a clearly defined body of knowledge; (2) a code of ethics; (3) ongoing education; (4) uniform standards of excellence for selection, education, and performance; and (5) an unequivocal service orientation (Shigley, 1987).

A Clearly Defined Body of Knowledge

Great diversity can be found among police departments, both large and small, concerning how much information is transmitted to officers in their training programs. It is difficult to define a body of knowledge applicable to all police officers in all jurisdictions.

Ongoing Education

More police departments are requiring their officers to acquire more education and in-service training. In many jurisdictions, however, educational courses for police officers usually are recommended but not required. Although greater amounts of educational training are associated with greater professionalism, the precise type and amount of education and training are most often unspecified. One incentive for police officers to acquire additional education is that in order for them to advance to higher ranks, they must take and pass qualifying examinations. These examinations are based on additional educational study. But it is not a mandatory expectation of all police officers that they aspire to higher ranks or different law enforcement duties. Many officers are content simply to perform their daily work routines. For more than a few officers, a great deal of job satisfaction can be derived from such routinization of job performance.

A Code of Ethics

One important step toward greater police professionalization has been the development of a law enforcement **code of ethics.** A code of ethics binds the membership to comply with certain behavioral requirements of propriety and obligates them to behave appropriately at all times. The existence of an ethical code enables law enforcement administrators to sanction those members who violate one or more of the code's provisions. Since the code of ethics is tacitly adopted by those entering law enforcement in most jurisdictions, the enforcement potential and existence of sanctions are quite important for inducing conformity among the membership.

Uniform Standards of Excellence for Selection, Education, and Performance

Standardization of selection, education, and performance criteria has been only partially achieved. Less than half of all police departments have been accredited by any nationally recognized organization. A majority of law enforcement agencies have not attempted to become accredited. POST programs are operative in most jurisdictions, although great variation can be found in their format and content. The Law Enforcement Training Academy in North Dakota offers a curriculum and coursework similar to that offered in Topeka, Kansas, although there are substantial differences between the two training programs. We cannot say, for instance, that officers graduating from the two academies will have the same degree of educational and legal sophistication and training if they were somehow compared.

An Unequivocal Service Orientation

Most law enforcement agencies and their most stringent critics probably would agree that the service orientation among the corps of police officers is strong. Printed on many cruisers in a majority of jurisdictions throughout the United States is the motto "To Serve and Protect." Service is a key function of police officers. In fact, most police departments keep meticulous records of "calls for service" when reporting on the activities of their officers. Enforcing the laws and catching criminals are clearly service activities performed by police officers for their citizens.

POLICE-COMMUNITY RELATIONS

The concept of **police-community relations** originated in the St. Louis (Missouri) Police Department in 1957 (Geary, 1985:211). Since then, community relations have been popularized among many police departments throughout the nation. Community policing is both a law enforcement and crime prevention strategy through which some community residents work cooperatively with local law enforcement agencies to manage community crime through detection and investigation, identification of possible perpetrators, and expanding communication and dialogue with neighborhood police officers.

Many terms have been used interchangeably to refer to essentially the same thing. More or less synonymous with community policing are police-community relations, the back-to-the-community movement, problem-oriented policing, community-based policing, proactive policing, neighborhood policing, community-oriented policing, community crime and drug prevention, community-based crime prevention, citizen coproduction of community safety, the new blue line, team policing, order maintenance policing, ombudsman policing, community wellness, grass-roots policing, and crime control policing. Many of these terms or phrases connote a cooperative or symbiotic relation between law enforcement and the community (Das, 1986). Whichever term is used to describe community policing, the following priorities are emphasized: (1) the improvement of human relations between police officers and community residents, (2) heightened community safety through improved crime control strategies, (3) maximization of crime prevention techniques, (4) a general reaffirmation of the concept of "community," and (5) greater use of citizens in quasi-policing roles.

BOX 9.3 THE LAW ENFORCEMENT CODE OF ETHICS

The Code of Ethics. All law enforcement officers must be fully aware of the ethical responsibilities of their position and must strive constantly to live up to the highest possible standards of professional policing. The International Association of Chiefs of Police believes it is important that police officers have clear advice and counsel available to assist them in performing their duties consistent with these standards, and has adopted the following ethical mandates as guidelines to meet these ends.

PRIMARY RESPONSIBILITIES OF A POLICE OFFICER. A police officer acts as an official representative of government who is required and trusted to work within the law. The officer's powers and duties are conferred by statute. The fundamental duties of a police officer include serving the community, safeguarding lives and property, protecting the innocent, keeping the peace, and ensuring the rights of all to liberty, equality, and justice.

PERFORMANCE OF THE DUTIES OF A POLICE OFFICER. A police officer shall perform all duties impartially, without favor or affection or ill will and without regard to status, sex, race, religion, political belief, or aspiration. All citizens will be treated equally with courtesy, consideration, and dignity. Officers will never allow personal feelings, animosities, or friendships to influence official conduct. Laws will be enforced appropriately and courteously, and in carrying out their responsibilities, officers will strive to obtain maximum cooperation from the public. They will conduct themselves in appearance and deportment in such a manner as to inspire confidence and respect for the position of public trust they hold.

DISCRETION. A police officer will use responsibly the discretion vested in the position and exercise it within the law. The principle of reasonableness will guide the officer's determinations, and the officer will consider all surrounding circumstances in determining if any legal action shall be taken. Consistent and wise use of discretion, based on professional policing competence, will do much to preserve good relationships and retain the confidence of the public. There can be difficulty in choosing between conflicting courses of action. It is important to remember that a timely word of advice rather than arrest—which may be correct in appropriate circumstances—can be a more effective means of achieving a desired end.

USE OF FORCE. A police officer will never employ unnecessary force or violence and will use only such force in the discharge of duty as is reasonable in all circumstances. Force should be used only with the greatest restraint and only after discussion, negotiation, and persuasion have been found to be inappropriate or ineffective. Although the use of force is occasionally unavoidable, every police officer will refrain from applying the unnecessary infliction of pain or suffering and will never engage in cruel, degrading, or inhuman treatment of any person.

CONFIDENTIALITY. Whatever a police officer sees, hears, or learns of, which is of a confidential nature, will be kept secret unless the performance of duty or legal provision requires otherwise. Members of the public have a right to security and privacy, and information obtained about them must not be improperly divulged.

INTEGRITY. A police officer will not engage in acts of corruption or bribery, nor will an officer condone such acts by other police officers. The public demands that the integrity of police officers be above reproach. Police officers must, therefore, avoid any conduct that might compromise integrity and thus undercut the public confidence in a law enforcement agency. An officer will refuse to accept any gifts, presents, subscriptions, favors, gratuities, or promises that could be interpreted as seeking to cause the officer to refrain from performing official responsibilities honestly and within the law. Police officers must not receive private or special advantage from their official status. Respect from the public cannot be bought; it can only be earned and cultivated.

COOPERATION WITH OTHER OFFICERS AND AGENCIES. Police officers will cooperate with all legally authorized agencies and their representatives in the pursuit of justice. An officer or agency may be one among many organizations that may provide law enforcement services to a jurisdiction. It is imperative that a police officer assist colleagues fully and completely with respect and consideration at all times.

PERSONAL/PROFESSIONAL CAPABILITIES. Police officers will be responsible for their own standard of professional performance and will take every reasonable opportunity to enhance and improve their level of knowledge and competence. Through study and experience, a police officer can acquire the high level of knowledge and competence that is essential for the efficient and effective performance of duty. The acquisition of knowledge is a never-ending process of personal and professional development that should be pursued constantly.

PRIVATE LIFE. Police officers will behave in a manner that does not bring discredit to their agencies or themselves. A police officer's character and conduct while off duty must always be exemplary, thus maintaining a position of respect in the community in which he or she lives and serves. The officer's personal behavior must be beyond reproach.

Source: Adapted from the Executive Committee of the International Association of Chiefs of Police, *Code of Ethics* (Louisville, KY: Annual Meeting of the International Association of Chiefs of Police, October 1989).

Detroit was one of the first experimental programs to offer direct community policing services to residents. This experiment was called the **Detroit Police Ministation Program** (Detroit Police Department, 1983). This program placed police officers in neighborhood **ministations,** or smaller versions of police precincts. These ministations were staffed by officers 24 hours a day, and they provided all of the regular services a regular precinct provides except detention facilities. In order to build better police-community relations, the police department has encouraged citizen participation and involvement in staffing these ministations. Nearly 40 ministations serve the neighborhood needs of Detroit residents. As community residents have perceived police officer interest in these ministations as genuine, citizen participation has been heightened.

Many urban police training programs are emphasizing greater communication skills. Police officers are increasingly an integral part of a multilingual society in which verbal and nonverbal communication is critical in influencing police-community resident interactions and outcomes (Brown and Warner, 1992). Training courses and experiences that produce larger numbers of police officers more inclined to use reason rather than force in police-citizen encounters are stressed. One outcome of this training is the selection of larger numbers of minority officers with college educations who are more professional in their relationships with community residents (U.S. Department of Justice, 1987).

A primary goal of community policing programs that emphasize acquisition of greater human relations skills is to improve community acceptance of and support for police officers and to promote more positive attitudes toward them (International Association of Chiefs of Police, 1988). Creating greater awareness among police officers of ethnic and racial differences among community residents is an important step in promoting acceptance and support.

OFFICER MISCONDUCT AND INTERNAL AFFAIRS

One of the greater issues police administrators must confront and deal with is abuse of discretion and misconduct. **Police discretion** is autonomy in decision making or how police decide to enforce the law (Stenning and Shearing, 1991). Police discretion is the balancing mechanism between justice that is deserved by an individual and justice as equal treatment (Cohen, 1985). Ideally, police discretion is professional individual and/or collective judgments that preserve and promote community and citizen safety, respect for the law, and citizen rights to due process and equal treatment under the law. This definition recognizes citizen rights to privacy and equal treatment as set forth by the Fourteenth Amendment as well as the right of communities to ensure that their safety and security are not compromised. The use of "professional" in this definition recognizes the formal training officers receive through police training academies and other educational experiences.

Police misconduct applies to officers who commit a crime and/or who do not follow police department policy guidelines and regulations in the course of their duties. Herman Goldstein (1967) was one of the first of the modern-day law enforcement experts to note the complex nature of the police function. He called for police departments to outline all forms of police misconduct as well as to identify the factors contributing to such misconduct. He was among the first to promote the use of officer training programs for the purpose of instilling officers with a commitment to their professional responsibilities that would minimize and eventually eliminate misconduct. Further, he called for the integration of both internal and external review mechanisms as means of controlling and guiding officer discretion that may involve misconduct. Radelet and Carter (1994:236–237) provide a list of behaviors that are examples of police misconduct:

1. Accessing police records for personal use
2. Abuse of sick leave
3. Lying to supervisors and managers
4. Perjury on reports and in court
5. Commission of a crime
6. Falsifying overtime records
7. Excessive use of force
8. On-duty drinking
9. Off-duty firearms incidents
10. Failing to complete police reports
11. Accepting gratuities
12. Providing recommendations for an attorney, towing service, or bail-bond service
13. Failure to report misconduct of a fellow officer
14. Failure to inventory recovered property or evidence
15. Sleeping on duty
16. Cheating on a promotional examination
17. Sexual harassment or improprieties

Although all of these forms of police misconduct are serious in their own right, some of these behaviors are more important to citizens than others. For instance, citizens are perhaps more concerned about the possible use of excessive force when police officers make arrests. Also, perjury in court and sexual harassment are considered serious police misconduct. Acts such as lying to superiors about overtime records or other matters, cheating on promotional exams, sleeping on duty, and failing to inventory recovered evi-

dence may be deemed less important, since they are farther removed from those events that directly affect citizens.

Various types of police misconduct can be identified. Criminologists and others have attempted to establish typologies or classifications that depict varieties of such behavior. For instance, David Carter (1986:150–152) established a fourfold typology of police misconduct according to the following designations: (1) physical abuse/excessive force, (2) verbal/psychological abuse, (3) legal abuse/violations of civil rights, and (4) police sexual violence toward women.

1. *Physical abuse/excessive force.* Physical abuse and/or excessive force mean applying considerably more force than is necessary to effect an arrest. When officers injure suspects they arrest, especially when there is little or no need for the use of such force, citizens label such behavior as physical abuse or excessive force. It is difficult to define clearly what is and is not excessive. Excessiveness varies by degree, as on a continuum. How much force is needed to effect an arrest depends on the particular situation. There are almost always two opinions concerning whether too much force has been applied—the officer's opinion and the arrestee's opinion. If some arrestees believe that they have been unnecessarily physically abused, they might bring a lawsuit against arresting officers. If we see officers slam an arrestee's head down on the hood of a car and twist his arm to handcuff him, we may believe that this force is excessive. However, the force may be "standard" and in accordance with what is otherwise prescribed by the officer's training when making arrests of suspects who resist. We do not see the amount or degree of resistance by arrestees. Usually, only officers making the actual arrest know how much resistance is being used to prevent the arrest. A more overwhelming force is required to offset an arrestee's resistance force.

2. *Verbal/psychological abuse.* Verbal/psychological abuse takes the form of taunting or ridicule. When police officers are arresting a citizen, they may make insulting remarks or engage in taunting. When police officers interrogate suspects or transport prisoners from one site to another, they may engage in verbally abusive behaviors. Often, these behaviors occur in settings in which the actual events cannot be corroborated. In one-on-one interactions between officers and various citizens, the courts clearly side with the testimony of officers, whether it is true or false.

3. *Legal abuse/violations of civil rights.* Title 42, Section 1983 of the U.S. Code contains provisions protecting one's civil rights. Whenever police officers act in ways that may infringe one's civil rights, affected citizens may file Section 1983 actions. In a Hawaiian case, Scott Sabey was stopped by military police in Waikiki for having beer cans in his automobile. The police officers involved, DeCoito and Tagalicod, placed Sabey in handcuffs and ordered him to a drainage ditch nearby. After beating Sabey, the officers urinated on him and made him "bob" for toads at gunpoint in the muddy waters of the ditch. Subsequently, Sabey sued these officers and the city of Honolulu. After protracted Section 1983 litigation, the city of Honolulu was ordered to pay Sabey $100,000 in damages for the officers' misconduct. The judge was incensed by the officers' behavior and hoped that this settlement would send a message to other officers in this and other jurisdictions (*Crime Control Digest,* 1989:9–10).

4. *Police Sexual Violence Toward Women.* One of the more appalling aspects of police misconduct is sexual violence by male officers toward women. Female motorists are regarded as fair game and are preyed on by certain police officers in various jurisdictions. It is unknown how much police sexual violence toward women goes on or how prevalent it is. However, many laypersons and others believe that if it occurs at all, it is too much, especially when perpetrated against women by a relatively elite corps of officers sworn to uphold the law. Police sexual violence toward women (PSV) includes those situations in which a female citizen experiences a sexually degrading, humiliating, violating, damaging, or threatening act committed by a police officer through the use of force or police authority (Kraska and Kappeler, 1995:93). In one case of PSV, two female motorists were made to strip and allow themselves to be searched in the backseat of a police cruiser. They were ordered to place themselves in the cruiser backseat on their hands and knees, with their legs spread. In this position and in plain view of onlooking male officers, female officers searched these women's vaginas with their fingers, probing for drug contraband. Their justification for this body-cavity search was that one of their relatives was suspected of dealing in drugs. Thus, in order to get to their relative,

the police resorted to PSV in their case. These two women were threatened with future searches if they did not give police incriminating evidence about their relative (*Timberlake v. Benton,* 1992).

Nonviolent misconduct by police officers is most often associated with varying degrees of graft or corruption. Officers who accept gratuities in exchange for special favors to citizens exhibit one type of misconduct. They profit through illicit social exchanges. Some officers give false testimony in court against suspects in order to enhance the case against them and heighten the chances of a conviction.

Incidents of corruption among police officers include everything from minor favors, such as courtesies to waive tickets for speeding or DWI for fellow officers, to bribery and extortion. Barker (1986:12–13) says that police work is ideal for engaging in patterns of deviance and corruption, because many officers are socialized to engage in corruption and these same officers condone it over time. Barker studied police corruption in one department and identified 10 types of corrupt behavior. He asked officers the extent to which each would not report to other police officers the actions listed. The corrupt patterns included the following:

1. Corruption of authority (free meals, services or discounts, liquor)
2. Kickbacks (money, goods, and services)
3. Opportunistic threats (victims, burglary, or unlocked buildings)
4. Shakedowns (criminals)
5. Protection of illegal activities (vice operators, businessmen)
6. Traffic fixes
7. Misdemeanor fixes
8. Felony fixes
9. Direct criminal activities (burglary, robbery)
10. Internal payoffs (off days, work assignments)

In every case, a substantial number of officers questioned said that they would rarely or never report these types of conduct to other officers. Based on this and other studies, Barker has concluded that police deviance is not a peculiar form of deviant conduct. Further, the police peer group indoctrinates and socializes rookies into patterns of acceptable corrupt activities, discourages deviations outside these boundaries, and censures officers who do not engage in any corrupt acts (Barker, 1986:19).

A primary goal of police accountability is to attain a balance between competing publics, interests, and mechanisms, on the one hand, and responsiveness and legality, on the other (Shadmi, 1994). Internal affairs divisions of police departments are investigative mechanisms staffed by senior police officials and whose function it is to determine if officers are guilty of any type of misconduct. Every large police agency has an internal affairs division. These divisions are viewed with some disdain by most line officers. Investigations by internal affairs personnel often are clandestine, and frequently, police officer–snitches are used to obtain evidence against fellow officers (Heck, 1992). Some persons question whether police agencies can effectively police themselves through internal affairs, however. They believe that outside sanctioning mechanisms should be established, such as civilian complaint review boards.

CIVILIAN COMPLAINT REVIEW BOARDS AND OTHER SANCTIONS

Many municipalities have created **civilian complaint review boards** or simply complaint review boards. These boards are independent of the police department and members are civilians from the community often appointed by the mayor or other officials (Kerstetter and Rasinski, 1994). One reason for the establishment of independent citizen complaint review boards is that many citizens distrust internal police mechanisms for policing their own. Citizens suspect collusion between officers who are members of internal affairs divisions and regular line officers who have charges of misconduct filed against them. It is not unusual, therefore, to find citizen review boards that are comprised of *both* officers and citizens to review the decisions of internal affairs, when complaints against officers are investigated. The history of investigating complaints against officers by both internal and external review mechanisms continues to be debated (St. Clair et al., 1992). Proponents of civilian complaint review boards say that

1. Police agencies cannot be objective when investigating and sanctioning their own officers in response to allegations of misconduct; police agencies are biased in favor of their own officers whenever allegations of misconduct are raised.

2. Independent citizen boards *are* objective in this regard and can impose necessary sanctions, if warranted and needed.

3. Public trust in police generally is enhanced through establishing independent civilian boards without police agency vested interests.

4. Citizens are more responsive to community-oriented policing when police officers are subject to independent accountability mechanisms.

5. Civilian boards can clear officers of excessive force or misconduct charges just as easily as they can find compelling evidence against them.

Opponents of civilian complaint review boards contend that

1. Civilians cannot empathize with police officers and the high level of risk associated with their work.

2. Civilians do not understand the necessity for police to use force in subduing suspects.

3. The authority of police agencies to sanction their own officers is undermined by a parallel civilian sanctioning mechanism.

4. Civilians are biased against police officers whenever police misconduct is alleged.

5. Civilians are simply not qualified to judge the performance and behaviors of police officers; thus, civilian review boards are meaningless.

Police response to civilian complaint review boards is that police officers are accountable and responsible only to the chief of police. Civilian review boards are perceived by police officers as infringing on police authority and involving "lay people with little knowledge" of police work (Fyfe, 1985). Since these citizen review boards have little or no independent investigative capabilities, they ordinarily rely on what police tell them anyway.

An alternative to citizen review boards is to improve the mechanisms for the receipt, investigation, and review of citizen complaints against police officers. A thorough documentation of complaints is required, including the involvement of several officers at different administrative levels in the review process. Most important, citizens must be provided with meaningful feedback about what has been done about their complaints (Fyfe, 1985). Major citizen complaints have to do with the fact that they file allegations and no action is taken regarding these allegations. Establishing a feedback system would increase police credibility and ensure greater fairness for both citizens and officers.

One immediate remedy against police misconduct is **decertification.** Decertification is a process by which a police agency revokes certificates or licenses of police officers. In at least 31 states, Peace Officer Standards and Training Boards implement decertification proceedings against officers who have been found guilty of misconduct, including unconstitutionally obtaining evidence against citizen/suspects or abuse conduct. Officers who have been decertified by these boards cannot work as police officers again until such time as they are recertified (Goldman and Puro, 1987). Schmidt (1985) describes some of the more common methods used by police departments to minimize or prevent the hiring of officers who are unfit for police work and who likely will engage in misconduct in the future. Some of these methods include (1) administering psychological tests to ferret out sadists, depressives, and other unqualified police applicants; (2) use of training programs that go well beyond state-mandated levels; (3) better firearms training and awareness; and (4) hiring police legal advisors.

SUMMARY

Police forces existed as early as 1500 B.C. The word "police" derives from *polis,* which means "city." In ancient Egypt, police forces existed to maintain order and resolve disputes among citizens. In Roman times, formal police investigative units known as *frumentarii* were created. These persons oversaw grain distribution, delivered messages to others from government officials, and detected crime and prosecuted offenders. In fifteenth-century England, shires or English counties appointed reeves to maintain order. Thus, each shire had a reeve. Subsequently, these words were combined to form the word "sheriff." Sheriffs are modern-day chief law enforcement officers in most U.S. counties.

Policing in early colonial times in the Americas was performed by citizens who used rattles to warn others about the presence of criminals. In the mid-1700s, an author and politician named Henry Fielding established organized patrols of law enforcement officers known as thief-takers. These persons were fast runners and could be relied on to chase down thieves and other criminals. A small group of paid thief-takers known as the Bow Street Runners was estab-

lished in London in 1754. The next major development in police history was the establishment of the Metropolitan Police of London in 1829 under the direction of Sir Robert Peel, the British Home Secretary. This organization promulgated a code of conduct, ethical standards, and a mission statement that has served as a guide to contemporary police agencies in the United States.

The Metropolitan Police of London had a subsequent impact on police organization and operations in the United States, as police departments were established in Boston, New York, Chicago, Philadelphia, and other large cities during the 1830s through the 1850s. In 1908, August Vollmer became the chief of police in Berkeley, California. He did much to professionalize policing operations. His work related to police professionalization led to the creation of Peace Officer Standards and Training (POST) programs, which have been widely used to train new police recruits. One of Vollmer's students, O.W. Wilson, contributed to the work of Vollmer by centralizing police organization and command and control functions. Both Vollmer and Wilson modeled their police organizations after the military model. This model presently is used by almost every police department in the United States, regardless of its size.

The goals of contemporary police and sheriffs' departments are to prevent crime, enforce laws, preserve the peace, protect civil rights, and provide services to civilians. Several policing styles have been used over the years to accomplish these objectives. These styles include the legalistic model, the service model, and the watchman model. Each model stresses different policing objectives. As police organizations have developed, the sophistication of the recruitment process has increased dramatically. Educational requirements for prospective police officers have been raised in most jurisdictions. Increasing numbers of minorities and women have been recruited into police officer and sheriff's deputy roles.

Several law enforcement issues were examined in this chapter. These issues relate to law enforcement officer recruitment, training, and quality control; accreditation of police training programs; measuring police performance; improving police professionalism; improving police-community relations; regulating and minimizing police misconduct and corruption; and establishing citizen complaint review boards as independent investigative bodies to handle citizen complaints if police misconduct of any kind is alleged.

The recruitment process includes the administration of polygraph tests and personality inventories to screen candidates for police officer and sheriff's deputy positions. Rigorous physical and educational training programs are utilized to train prospective officers. Police performance is measured several different ways. Field training officers are used in the early stages of one's policing career to evaluate officer conduct and performance. Uniform standards are advocated for dealing fairly with the public and assuring that their constitutional rights are not violated. Greater emphasis has been placed on police-community relations as police departments seek to improve their public image as service agencies.

Internal affairs divisions and citizen complaint review boards have been established in virtually every large jurisdiction to investigate citizen complaints lodged against individual officers. Procedures have been created for punishing those officers found guilty of misconduct. One punishment is decertification, a process in which one's arrest authority is revoked by a city or state agency. Police officers are increasingly aware of their diverse responsibilities to the citizens they serve. A majority of police departments have incentive programs calculated to improve officer performance and effectiveness as well as reduce the numbers of lawsuits against individual officers and departments.

QUESTIONS FOR REVIEW

1. What are civilian complaint review boards? What are some positive and negative implications for police officers as the result of using civilian complaint review boards? Discuss.
2. Who were the Metropolitan Police of London? What is the significance of the Metropolitan Police of London for modern-day law enforcement?
3. Describe briefly the contributions of the following persons to policing: (a) Henry Fielding, (b) Sir Robert Peel, (c) Patrick Colquhoun, (d) O.W. Wilson.
4. What was the Wickersham Commission and how did it change modern-day law enforcement?
5. What is meant by police professionalism? What are some key characteristics used to describe police professionals?
6. How do sheriffs' departments differ from police departments? In what ways are they similar?
7. What are several different forms of police misconduct? Distinguish between violent and nonviolent police misconduct.
8. What are three models of police styles that have been used during the past century? Describe each.
9. What are three key law enforcement issues? Describe each.
10. What methods exist for combating police corruption and misconduct? Discuss each.

SUGGESTED READINGS

Cordner, Gary W., and Robert Sheehan (1999). *Police Administration* (4/e). Cincinnati, OH: Anderson Publishing Company.

Skogan, Wesley G., et al. (1999). *On the Beat: Police and Community Problem Solving*. Boulder, CO: Westview Press.

Zhao, Jihong (1996). *Why Police Organizations Change: A Study of Community-Oriented Policing*. Washington, DC: Police Executive Research Forum.

• CASE STUDIES •

---

1. THE JUNIPER SPEED TRAP

In Juniper, Colorado, a small town of 15,000 people, the police department consists of 13 officers, a police chief, and her assistant. Chief Joanna Mason has been on the job for the past 15 years. She started out as a rookie and worked her way up through the ranks.

Up until the last five years, the town of Juniper was on a major state highway and received a lot of business from out-of-state travelers. At that time, a major interstate highway was constructed about two miles from the state highway, and community business subsequently declined by over 50 percent. Several solutions to the declining Juniper economy have been proposed, including large billboards placed at two off-ramps from the interstate highway. These billboards would advertise local attractions, as well as restaurants, gas stations, and motels, but Juniper is located between two much larger Colorado cities and attracts little attention from motorists. At one of the town meetings, someone suggested that the Juniper Police Department might start ticketing speeders more frequently on the interstate highway, since a portion of the highway crosses the Juniper town limits for about three miles.

Chief Mason, therefore, has directed her officers to be creative and more aggressive at detecting and citing speeding interstate highway travelers. During the past two years, the revenues generated from more aggressive policing on the interstate highway have greatly improved the Juniper economy. In fact, the Juniper area has acquired some notoriety as a speed trap for motorists. Thus, as many motorists approach the town limits of Juniper, they deliberately reduce their speed and proceed through that area without incident.

In response to this change in motorist driving patterns, Chief Mason has encouraged her officers to be on the lookout for suspicious-looking vehicles and travelers. Furthermore, she has asked her officers to begin to question those stopped for traffic infractions about whether they have weapons or drugs in their vehicles. Almost everyone stopped denies that weapons or drugs are in their automobiles. However, Juniper police officers then ask these persons if they wouldn't mind if their vehicles are searched. Almost every motorist has been compliant with such requests. Often, these searches yield nothing. On some occasions, however, police officers have discovered drugs or drug paraphernalia, even some firearms, which have been secreted away in the trunk or glove compartment or under the car seats. Some motorists have carried substantial sums of money as well. In these instances, the motorists have been arrested and their drugs, guns, and/or money have been seized. The pretext for seizing the money is that it is suspected of being connected with drug revenue and thus is illegal.

One development resulting from these stops and seizures is that Juniper has benefitted substantially from asset forfeiture, or simply seizing assets (e.g., automobiles and money). The motorists are routinely advised that if they want their money back, they will have to prove where they obtained it. For some travelers, at least, this is difficult to do. Furthermore, the Juniper Police Department has acquired some forensics laboratory equipment and is able to examine the money seized. Interestingly, about 75 percent of all currency seized from passing motorists has some cocaine residue. This fact has provided Juniper officials with ample justification for keeping the money as illicit drug money. But the truth is that a national scientific investigation of most currency in circulation shows that it has some drug residue merely from being in contact with currency that has been involved in illicit drug use. Most citizens, therefore, are likely to possess drug-tainted currency, regardless of whether or not they have ever used drugs.

Two Juniper police officers, Mitch Bryant and Kevin Miller, have been especially adept at stopping motorists and seizing large amounts of cash or property. But it has come to the attention of Chief Mason that Bryant and Miller have been stopping mostly minority motorists, including blacks and Hispanics. In fact, her department has received a number of complaints from national civil rights organizations about the conduct of her officers and the policies of her department related to stopping motorists who travel through Juniper. Some complaints from motorists and these civil rights organizations allege that money and property have been seized but that the Juniper Police Department has no record of such seizures. It may be that officers such as Bryant and Miller may be pocketing some of this money and converting some seized property rather than turning it in to the department for inventorying and safekeeping. Mason is now fearful that the actions of at least some of her officers may lead to civil lawsuits and that her own job might be in jeopardy as the result of inappropriate and discriminatory officer conduct.

Questions for Discussion

1. While enforcing traffic laws is not illegal, is it wrong for police departments such as the Juniper Police Department to conduct searches of vehicles that have been stopped for simple traffic violations? What is wrong with this law enforcement, if anything?

2. How can Chief Mason determine whether or not her officers, Bryant and Miller, are deliberately

keeping seized money and property for their own use? What are some means she can employ to discover whether they are engaging in misconduct?

3. Is it proper for police departments such as the Juniper Police Department to seize large sums of money from passing motorists who have been stopped for traffic violations? What alternatives do motorists have for retrieving their property and money short of filing a lawsuit?

4. Is Mason an out-of-control police chief, or is she simply responding the best way she can to community directives to generate greater revenue for her town?

5. What organizational variables are influencing policing policy in this case? Should the situation be changed? If so, how would you go about changing the way policing is done in Juniper?

2. THE COUSIN AND THE BRIBE

Today is Monday, March 11. As police chief, you have been asked to award citations to a local boys' group later this afternoon. You arrive at your office and the first person waiting to see you is Fred Burke, the fire marshal. You invite Burke into your office and he relates a story concerning Bill Beal, a local businessman who owns several restaurants in your community. It seems that Beal offered Burke $2,500 to overlook some fire code violations at several of his restaurants when they were inspected last month. The renovations needed to bring the restaurants into compliance with the fire code would cost about $30,000, and Beal doesn't feel that the expenditure is justified by what he considers to be minor violations. You listen to Burke, and when he is finished, you tell him you will get back to him later that day with an opinion.

Since this appears to you to be bribery of a public officer, you ask one of your detectives to look into it. The detective you select is Joe Johannsen. Johannsen is an honest detective. He has been with the police department for 17 years. He is known by others as "squeaky clean." Unknown to you, however, is the fact that Johannsen is Bill Beal's first cousin. Johannsen raises his eyebrows a little when you mention Beal's name and the alleged bribe, but Johannsen says he will look into it. While you are making this request of Johannsen, your secretary is placing some papers in your filing cabinet nearby. When Johannsen leaves, your secretary approaches you and says, "I couldn't help but overhear your conversation with Detective Johannsen. Did you ask him to investigate Bill Beal?"

"Yes, I did," you reply. "Well, you might be interested to know that Johannsen is Beal's cousin. He might not be the best person to assign to investigate this alleged bribe." At this point, you know your day is not going to get any better.

About 10 minutes later, the secretary enters your office and hands you a note. Your son has been reprimanded for an unknown offense at school and school officials have decided to call a parent-teacher-principal meeting with you, your wife, and your son present. The meeting is scheduled for the next day, March 12, Tuesday, at 1:00 P.M. Suddenly your telephone rings and it is your wife. She has just heard from school officials about your son and the meeting scheduled at school for Tuesday. She is very upset and has had to cancel a business meeting the next afternoon to make the appointment at school. She is so upset, in fact, that she insists that you leave immediately and meet her at the school, where your son is being held by school officials. It seems that the school principal just called again and wants you to come and take your son home immediately. You have no idea what it is that your son did, but you are becoming upset yourself as your wife continues to insist that you meet her. You assure your wife that you are on your way out the door and headed to the school. You tell your secretary to apologize for you to the boys' group, but something important has come up that requires your immediate attention. As you move through the main office of the department and head for the exit, Joe Johannsen is putting on his jacket and headed for the exit door also.

• CASE STUDIES •

Questions for Discussion

1. How should you deal with the matter of Beal and his alleged offer of a bribe to Fire Marshal Burke? What should you as police chief tell Burke about what you plan to do?

2. How would you prioritize your day today as well as Tuesday, March 12, regarding the meeting at school concerning your son?

3. How should you handle the matter of your secretary advising you about Beal and his familial relation with Johannsen? Is it proper for secre-

taries to suggest alternative actions to their bosses? Why or why not? What compelling circumstances create an exception here?

4. Should you say anything to Johannsen as you encounter him leaving the building? Should you confront him about being Beal's cousin and not mentioning that fact to you? Why or why not?

5. Can you trust Johannsen to conduct a thorough and objective investigation of his cousin, Beal? Why or why not?

CHAPTER
10

COURT ORGANIZATION AND ADMINISTRATION

KEY TERMS

Aggravating circumstances

Alternative dispute resolution (ADR)

Assistant United States attorneys
  (AUSAs)

Bailiffs

Bench trials

Chancery courts

Charge reduction bargaining

Circuit courts

Circuit courts of appeal

Circuit riders

Court clerks

Court of civil appeals

Court of criminal appeals

Court of last resort

Court reporter

Courts of common pleas

Courts of record

Creative sentencing

Determinate sentencing

Diversion

Evarts Act

Exclusive jurisdiction

Family courts

Federal district courts

Finders of fact

General jurisdiction

Guidelines-based sentencing

Harmful error

Implicit plea bargaining

Indeterminate sentences

Judicial plea bargaining

Judicial review

Judiciary Act of 1789

Jury trials

Juvenile courts

Kales Plan

Lifetime appointments

Limited jurisdiction

Malicious prosecution

Mandatory minimum sentencing

Missouri Plan

Mitigating circumstances

Original jurisdiction

Petitioners

Petit juries

Plain errors

Plea bargaining

Presumptive sentencing guidelines

Prosecutor

Prosecutorial misconduct

Randolph Plan

Restorative justice

Reversible error

Rule of fours

Sentence recommendation bargaining

Sentencing hearings

Special jurisdiction

Supreme court

Texas model

Traditional model

United States attorneys

U.S. Supreme Court

Venire

Veniremen

Veniremen lists

Virginia Plan

Voluntary sentencing guidelines

Writ of mandamus

Writs of *certiorari*

CHAPTER OBJECTIVES

The following objectives are intended:

1. To compare and contrast state and federal court organization
2. To describe the functions of state and federal courts
3. To describe the duties of judges, prosecutors, and other courtroom work group members
4. To describe the trial process, including bench and jury trials
5. To examine and discuss several critical issues, including plea bargaining and judicial and prosecutorial selection and conduct
6. To examine court caseloads and reasons for delays

INTRODUCTION

Besides law enforcement, which is visible to virtually all citizens 24 hours a day, the next most visible component of the criminal justice system is the courts. Anyone who reads a newspaper or watches a cable television network cannot escape exposure to the courts. Several popular television programs highlight and portray what goes on in different types of courts. Courts are fictionalized in television programs such as *Law and Order, The Practice,* and *Judging Amy.*

For instance, in *Law and Order* episodes, which are probably the most realistic portrayals of what goes on in the criminal justice system, the first half hour of the hour-long show is a scenario featuring a crime and its investigation by police. The show's formula usually has a suspect identified following the crime. Evidence is gathered and delivered to the prosecutor's office. The last half hour is mostly courtroom drama, in which witnesses testify both for and against the accused. The prosecution usually wins, but not always. Sometimes cases are appealed to higher courts. We are treated to short segments of these appellate sessions and the dialogue of appeals. On rare occasions, a *Law and Order* case reaches the U.S. Supreme Court.

In contrast, *Judging Amy* is about a young divorced woman who is a family court judge. Each week, she decides child custody cases and determines if evidence of parental neglect exists. She also determines the fate of certain juveniles who appear before her. Cases such as these actually constitute the bulk of court business; high-profile criminal cases may receive more publicity but are not as prevalent as the television shows involving them might suggest.

Some television programs are about lawyers and only incidentally involve the police. *The Practice* pro-vides an in-depth view of criminal defense attorneys defending unsavory clients and their interactions with prosecutors and judges. Although all of these weekly television programs are fictional, they are liberally laced with fact and frequently are based on actual cases that have been decided in the real world.

At the other end of the spectrum, reality-based television shows featuring the courts include *Court TV, Judge Judy, Judge Mills Lane,* and *Divorce Court.* These programs feature real participants. In addition, most students of college age will remember seeing the O.J. Simpson double-murder trial in California in 1995. *Court TV* is unique in that it insinuates itself directly into courtrooms and enables viewers to see courts in action. Murder trials are of greatest interest to viewers, or at least this is what we gather on the basis of the trials *Court TV* decides to cover. But entertaining courtroom dramas are also found on shows such as *Judge Judy,* featuring a former family court judge. All of the cases appearing before Judge Judy are civil, not criminal. Her jurisdiction is limited to civil cases, and she can enter maximum monetary judgments of up to $5,000 for either the plaintiff or the defendant.

For the casual viewer, therefore, a court is a court is a court. Judges always sit at the front of the courtroom, and almost always they are attired in black robes and bang gavels on their desks. They are decision makers, ruling on motions, deciding the admissibility of certain kinds of evidence, and often determining a defendant's guilt or innocence.

This chapter is about courts, their organization, and operations. Every town, city, municipality, county, and state has a court system. Some towns have only one court, whereas others have numerous courts. Each state has a more or less elaborate court organization, from the highest court, usually the state supreme court, to the lowest court, perhaps a justice of the peace. And great variation can be found among the states regarding their court systems and how they are organized. A virtual Tower of Babel is created when we understand that city, county, and state courts not only differ by state, but they also differ in how each court is designated or labeled.

Additional complexity occurs when we understand that a separate federal court system exists apart from state court organization. Not only are there many federal courts, but there are many different types of federal courts. Therefore, in order for us to understand court organization, we must examine court apparatuses for both the federal and state systems.

The first part of this chapter describes federal and state court organization. Included are descriptions of the different levels of courts within the federal and state systems. In order to simplify the task of describing these courts, we focus primarily on those courts whose jurisdiction is related to criminal behavior. Thus, the descriptions of courts in this chapter primarily cover events that might be relevant for the courts featured on *Law and Order* rather than *Judging Amy* and *Judge Judy*.

All criminal courts, regardless of their level or complexity, have several important actors. These include all court officers, such as the judge, prosecutor, defense counsel, court reporter, and bailiff. Following our examination of federal and state court organization, we describe the different court officers and their functions. Three key actors are featured in this description: judges, prosecutors, and defense attorneys. Some attention is given to how these persons are selected and qualify for the roles they play. These roles are described as well as the formal and interpersonal dynamics that exist among them.

Next, we focus on two different types of trials available to criminal defendants: bench trials and jury trials. Bench trials are relatively simple affairs in which judges decide a defendant's guilt or innocence. In contrast, jury trials are more complex and lengthy. The jury trial process also is examined in detail.

This chapter concludes with an examination of several important issues relevant to court processes. These issues include the ethics and importance of plea bargaining and negotiated guilty pleas, forms of judicial and prosecutorial misconduct and how such misconduct is sanctioned, and court caseloads and delays.

COURT ORGANIZATION

Despite the diversity among state court organizations and operations, several common features are applicable to all of these systems. Figure 10.1 is a side-by-side comparison of the federal and state court systems. The two systems are completely separate and self-sustaining systems.

The federal courts have jurisdiction over all federal laws, whereas the state courts have jurisdiction over state and local statutes and ordinances (National Center for State Courts, 1995). Despite the individuality and separateness of the federal and state court systems, some degree of interplay or interrelatedness exists between them. State court cases may eventually enter the federal appellate process at some point.

Federal Court Organization

Most major courts in the United States originated from the actions of delegates to the Constitutional Convention in the 1780s. Prior to the final vote on the Bill of Rights, convention delegates passed the **Judiciary Act of 1789,** which was influenced by the **Virginia Plan** (sometimes called the **Randolph Plan**) (Carp and Stidham, 1993).

The Virginia Plan consisted of superior and inferior courts, with the former having considerable appellate authority over the latter (Goebel, 1971). The Virginia Plan evolved from England's royal court system. When the new court system was created through the Judiciary Act of 1789, it retained the Virginia Plan's provisions for lifetime appointment of federal judges. Royal judges in England had served "at the King's pleasure during good behavior," or the equivalent of **lifetime appointments.** This practice is still followed in all federal district and appellate courts, and in some states also, judges are appointed for life or until they decide to retire.

The Judiciary Act of 1789 provided for three levels of courts: (1) thirteen **federal district courts,** each presided over by a district judge; (2) three higher **circuit courts of appeal,** each comprising two justices of the Supreme Court and one district judge; and (3) a **supreme court,** consisting of a chief justice and five associate justices (Carp and Stidham, 1993).

The federal district courts were given jurisdiction in all civil and criminal cases. The circuit courts review decisions of federal district courts, although they have some limited original jurisdiction (Flango, 1994b). The Supreme Court was given jurisdiction in interpreting

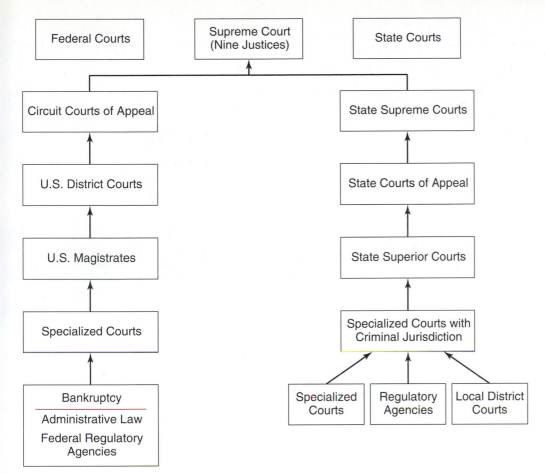

FIGURE 10.1 The Federal and State Court System

Source: Compiled by author.

federal legislation and balancing the interests of the states and nation through the maintenance of the rights and duties of citizens (Hughes, 1966:1). Figure 10.2 shows the structure of the federal judicial system.

The United States Supreme Court

At the very top of the federal court system is the **U.S. Supreme Court.** This is sometimes referred to as the **court of last resort** and is the most powerful court in the nation. This is because all appeals from both lower federal and state courts eventually are directed to the U.S. Supreme Court. The U.S. Supreme Court has both original jurisdiction and exclusive jurisdiction over all actions or proceedings against ambassadors or public ministers of foreign states and all controversies between two or more states. **Original jurisdiction** means the court may recognize a case at its inception, hear that case, and try it without consultation with other courts or authorities. **Exclusive jurisdiction** means

that no other court can decide certain kinds of cases except the court having exclusive jurisdiction. A juvenile court has exclusive jurisdiction over juvenile matters, for example. Adult criminal courts have no jurisdiction over juveniles, unless certain juveniles have been waived or transferred to criminal court or have been certified as adults for purposes of a criminal prosecution.

The U.S. Supreme Court is directly instrumental in shaping diverse policies, including abortion and the death penalty. Abortion reforms have been attempted on numerous occasions following the U.S. Supreme Court decision in *Roe v. Wade* (1973), although reformists have been unsuccessful thus far in changing *Roe v. Wade* policy (Farr, 1993). Besides abortion reform, the U.S. Supreme Court has influenced how death penalty cases are decided and procedurally how death sentences should be imposed (*Gregg v. Georgia*, 1976), how greater racial equity can be preserved in the jury selection process (*Batson v. Kentucky*, 1986),

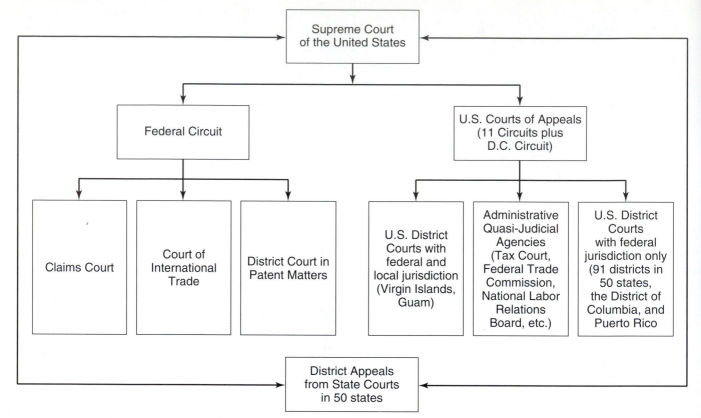

FIGURE 10.2 The Federal Judicial System
Source: Compiled by author.

and how due process can be preserved in prison disciplinary hearings (Palmer, 1996).

The Supreme Court is the ultimate reviewing body regarding decisions made by lower appellate courts or state supreme courts. The Supreme Court is primarily an appellate court, since most of its time is devoted to reviewing decisions of lower courts (Carp and Stidham, 1993). It is the final arbiter of lower court decisions unless Congress declares otherwise. Congress may change existing constitutional amendments or other acts.

The U.S. Supreme Court meets 36 weeks annually, from the first Monday in October until the end of June. In the 120th term of the U.S. Supreme Court in 2001, several landmark decisions were rendered. For instance, the high court ruled on the constitutionality of prayer at public school athletic events, child custody matters relating to immigration and naturalization, and the constitutionality of the *Miranda* warning when police make arrests and interrogate criminal suspects.

THE CASE OF *MARBURY V. MADISON* (1803). The review powers of the U.S. Supreme Court were established in the case of *Marbury v. Madison* (1803). This case involved a political conflict between the Federalists and the anti-Federalists. Exiting president John Adams made several new circuit court appointments and signed commissions for their appointment on his last day of office. However, Secretary of State James Madison withheld processing these commissions, anticipating that the new president, Thomas Jefferson, (of a different political party) would make appointments within his own party. This was a blatant attempt to create additional judicial appointments for certain party members who were favorable to the new president. One of Adams's appointments was William Marbury, who petitioned the U.S. Supreme Court to compel Secretary of State Madison to issue his new appointment as a circuit judge. Chief Justice John Marshall and the U.S. Supreme Court ruled in Marbury's favor and issued a **writ of *mandamus*** compelling the secretary of state to issue the commissions that had been authorized by former president John Adams. Thus, the right of **judicial review** was established. This is the power of the U.S. Supreme Court to review and determine the constitutionality of acts of Congress as well as the executive branch. The judicial review power of the U.S. Supreme Court also was extended to state governments in 1810 in the case of *Fletcher v. Peck.*

U.S. SUPREME COURT APPOINTMENTS. U.S. Supreme Court justiceships are lifetime appointments by the president of the United States, subject to congressional approval. The composition of the U.S. Supreme Court is considered crucial in affecting interpretations of the U.S. Constitution and important amendments relevant to citizens. In 1999, the salary of the chief justice was $175,400, and the salary of associate justices was $167,900 (Administrative Office of the U.S. Courts, 2000).

Since the president of the United States appoints justices subject to congressional approval, these appointments influence Supreme Court decision making in favor of liberal or conservative interests. It is the responsibility of justices to be objective in their appraisal and resolution of any constitutional issue, but the personal views of individual justices have been evident frequently as dissenting opinions. The rationales underlying such dissenting opinions are often equally as persuasive as the rationales accompanying majority opinions. Thus, the composition of the U.S. Supreme Court cannot be regarded lightly, as it is the primary force in interpreting the U.S. Constitution and affecting the rights of all U.S. citizens. Table 10.1 shows the U.S. Supreme Court composition in 2000, the years when each justice was appointed, and the U.S. presidents who appointed them.

CASELOAD OF THE U.S. SUPREME COURT AND GAINING ACCESS. The caseload of the U.S. Supreme Court has grown considerably since the early 1960s. In 1963, the Supreme Court was presented with 2,294 case filings. In 1973, these filings had grown to 5,079 cases, or an increase of 121 percent. In 1997, the number of cases on the docket was 7,692. The fact that a case appears on the U.S. Supreme Court docket is no guarantee that it will be heard. Although the figures vary from year to year, about 10 to 15 percent of all cases filed are never heard. In 1997, for instance, 933 cases (12 percent) remained on the docket when the Supreme Court's term ended. Full-text opinions are written in less than 2 percent of all cases filed annually (Carp and Stidham, 1993). Table 10.2 shows the number of cases granted review by the U.S. Supreme Court and the actual number of full opinions written by the justices from 1976 through 1997.

Cases reach the U.S. Supreme Court one of two ways. Cases are appealed directly from the individual state supreme courts or from the various federal circuit courts of appeal. Writs of *certiorari* are filed by **petitioners. Writs of *certiorari*** are requests for the U.S. Supreme Court to hear particular cases. These writs are certifications of lower court records in which the lower court's decision is presented, together with a statement of the legal issues or questions involved, as well as a brief rationale for why the U.S. Supreme Court should hear and decide the case. Some sentences are appealed automatically. *All* death sentences are appealed automatically, for example.

In order for the U.S. Supreme Court to hear a case, at least four justices must agree that the case is meritorious and deserves to be heard (Kadish, 1994). Justice Scalia or Justice O'Connor cannot thrust his or her will

TABLE 10.1 U.S. SUPREME COURT COMPOSITION IN 2000

SUPREME COURT JUSTICE	YEAR OF APPOINTMENT	U.S. PRESIDENT APPOINTING JUSTICE
Chief Justice William H. Rehnquist	1986	Ronald Reagan
Justice David H. Souter	1990	George Bush
Justice Clarence Thomas	1991	George Bush
Justice Atonin Scalia	1986	Ronald Reagan
Justice John Paul Stevens	1975	Gerald Ford
Justice Ruth Bader Ginsburg	1993	Bill Clinton
Justice Sandra Day O'Connor	1981	Ronald Reagan
Justice Stephen G. Breyer	1994	Bill Clinton
Justice Anthony M. Kennedy	1988	Ronald Reagan

TABLE 10.2 CASES FILED WITH THE U.S. SUPREME COURT COMPARED WITH CASES WITH FULL OPINIONS WRITTEN, 1976–1997

YEAR	NUMBER OF CASES FILED	NUMBER OF FULL-TEXT OPINIONS	PERCENTAGE
1976	4,730	176	3.7%
1977	4,704	172	3.6
1978	4,731	168	3.5
1979	4,781	156	3.2
1980	5,144	154	3.0
1981	5,311	184	3.4
1982	5,079	163	3.2
1983	5,100	184	3.6
1984	5,006	175	3.5
1985	5,158	172	3.3
1986	5,134	175	3.4
1987	5,268	167	3.2
1988	5,657	170	3.0
1989	5,746	146	2.5
1990	6,316	125	2.0
1991	6,770	127	1.9
1992	7,245	116	1.6
1993	7,786	99	1.3
1994	8,100	91	2.4
1995	7,565	87	1.2
1996	7,602	87	1.1
1997	7,692	93	1.2

Source: Administrative Office of the U.S. Courts, 2000.

on the Court and force it to hear a case. The **rule of fours** is invoked, meaning that four or more justices must agree to hear the case. This means simply that the case is scheduled for a hearing. Once the case is scheduled for a hearing, there is no guarantee that it will eventually be heard. As mentioned earlier, in 1997, about 12 percent of all filed cases remained on the docket. These are not the first cases to be handled during the following term. They must be redocketed together with newly appealed cases.

Circuit Courts of Appeal

In the early history of the United States, three circuit courts of the United States existed without any permanent personnel (Goebel, 1971). Two Supreme Court justices and a federal district judge comprised the transient judiciary of the circuit courts. These judges were called **circuit riders,** and they held 28 courts per year. This created considerable hardship, because transportation was poor and it was difficult to travel great distances. Furthermore, since federal district judges were a part of the original circuit judiciary, they were placed in the prejudicial position of reviewing their own decisions (Goebel, 1971).

Over the next two centuries, numerous changes occurred in circuit court structure. Several reforms such as the Judiciary Act of 1891 or the **Evarts Act** were introduced to create the current scheme for federal appellate review. In 2000, there were 13 federal judicial circuits (including the District of Columbia Circuit and the Federal Circuit) with 179 circuit court judges (U.S. Code, Title 28, Sec. 41, 2001). A list of the circuits is shown in Table 10.3. These circuit court geographical boundaries also are shown in Figure 10.3 (p. 212).

The circuit courts of appeal have appellate jurisdiction for all federal district courts in each circuit. For instance, the Eleventh Circuit Court of Appeals includes Alabama, Florida, and Georgia. These states are divided into several divisions, each containing one or more federal district courts. When decisions are appealed from any federal district court within

■ **TABLE 10.3** THE THIRTEEN JUDICIAL CIRCUITS, COMPOSITION, AND NUMBERS OF CIRCUIT JUDGES, 2000

CIRCUITS	COMPOSITION	NUMBER OF CIRCUIT JUDGES
District of Columbia	District of Columbia	12
First	Maine, Massachusetts, New Hampshire, Puerto Rico, Rhode Island	6
Second	Connecticut, New York, Vermont	13
Third	Delaware, New Jersey, Pennsylvania, Virgin Islands	14
Fourth	Maryland, North Carolina, South Carolina, Virginia, West Virginia	15
Fifth	Canal Zone, Louisiana, Mississippi, Texas	17
Sixth	Kentucky, Michigan, Ohio, Tennessee	16
Seventh	Illinois, Indiana, Wisconsin	11
Eighth	Arkansas, Iowa, Minnesota, Missouri, Nebraska, North Dakota, South Dakota	11
Ninth	Alaska, Arizona, California, Idaho, Montana, Nevada, Guam, Oregon, Washington, Hawaii	28
Tenth	Colorado, Kansas, New Mexico, Oklahoma, Utah, Wyoming	12
Eleventh	Alabama, Florida, Georgia	12
Federal	All Federal Judicial Districts	12
Total		179

Source: U.S. Code, Title 28, Sec. 44, 2001.

Alabama, Florida, or Georgia, the appeal goes to the Eleventh Circuit Court of Appeals, not to the Sixth or Seventh Circuit. The appeals of Stacey Koon and Laurence Powell, ex-police officers who were convicted in a Los Angeles, California, U.S. district court of beating motorist Rodney King in 1993, were directed to the Ninth Circuit Court of Appeals, the appellate court with jurisdiction over all federal district courts located in California as well as several other states.

All circuit courts of appeal have appellate jurisdiction for all final decisions from federal district courts. Panels of three circuit court judges must convene at regular intervals to hear appeals from the different federal district courts in their respective circuits. If the appellant disagrees with the decision of a circuit court, then the U.S. Supreme Court is the court of last resort for all final appeals. The caseload for the U.S. circuit courts of appeal has increased substantially from the 1980s through 1990s. In 1982, for instance, 27,948 cases were filed in the U.S. circuit courts of appeal. In 1998, 53,805 cases were filed, a 92 percent increase (Administrative Office of the U.S. Courts, 2000).

CIRCUIT COURT OF APPEALS JUDICIAL APPOINTMENTS AND SALARIES. The president of the United States makes lifetime appointments of judges to various circuit courts of appeal. Nominations by the president must be approved by Congress. The Senate Judiciary Committee hears arguments both for and against these presidential appointees and either approves or rejects them. In 1999, circuit court judges' annual salaries were $145,000 (Administrative Office of the U.S. Courts, 2000).

U.S. District Courts

In 1999, 647 federal district judges practiced in the United States within the various circuits (U.S. Code, Title 28, Sec. 133, 2001). Federal district judges are appointed for life by the president of the United States, with the approval of Congress. Annual salaries of federal district court judges in 1999 were $136,700. Federal district judges who serve 10 or more years with good behavior may retire anytime thereafter and receive their annual salary for life. Federal district courts are the basic trial courts for the U.S. government. All violations of federal criminal laws are tried in the

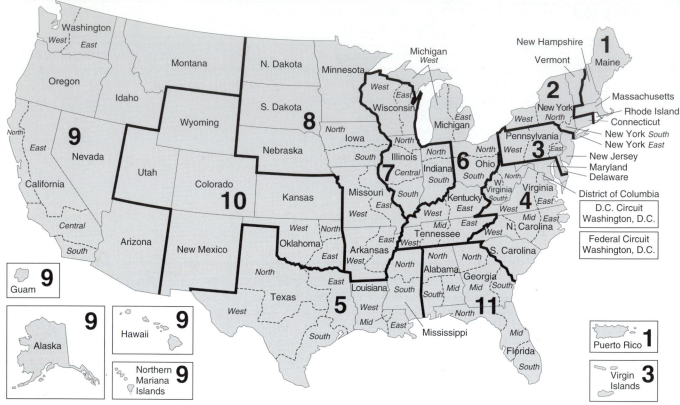

FIGURE 10.3 District and Appellate Court Boundaries, 2000

Source: Administrative Office of the U.S. Courts, 2000.

district court. Besides hearing criminal cases, federal district courts have the following jurisdictional authority:

1. To hear all civil actions in which the matter exceeds $10,000 and arises under the laws, Constitution, or treaties of the United States
2. To try diversity of citizenship matters, determine amounts in controversy, and costs
3. To entertain bankruptcy matters and proceedings
4. To hear interpleaders or third-party complaints
5. To enforce ICC orders
6. To hear commerce and antitrust suits
7. To hear cases involving patents, copyrights, trademarks, and charges of unfair commercial competition
8. To hear Internal Revenue cases and customs duty matters
9. To judge tax matters by states
10. To hear civil rights cases
11. To hear matters in which the United States is a plaintiff or defendant

Criminal cases heard in these district courts begin in the same way as cases start in local and state courts. Federal law enforcement officers arrest suspects directly, or federal grand juries or federal prosecutors issue indictments, presentments, or criminal information against defendants. These defendants appear before magistrates to have their bonds established, or else they are released on their own recognizance. Arraignments are conducted in district courts by federal judges. Like the higher appellate federal courts, the caseloads for U.S. district courts have increased substantially over the past several decades. In 1963, 95,376 civil and criminal cases were filed in U.S. district courts. Of these, 31,746 (48.5 percent) were criminal cases. In 1973, 140,994 cases were commenced, and 42,434 (30 percent) of these were criminal cases. In 1983, the caseload had nearly doubled to 277,714 cases. Of these, only 35,872 (12.9 percent) were criminal cases. In 1998, the number of criminal cases filed in U.S. district courts was 57,023. This was 15 percent of the combined civil and criminal cases filed in U.S. district courts (Administrative Office of the U.S. Courts, 2000).

Other Federal Courts

Some of the other federal courts include the U.S. magistrate court, bankruptcy court, the court of international trade, and the court of federal claims. U.S. magistrates are appointed judicial officers within each of the U.S. district courts. These judges originated through the 1968 Federal Magistrate's Act, which authorized fewer powers for these judges compared with U.S. district court judges. U.S. magistrates set bail bond for federal defendants and hear numerous minor cases, mostly involving federal misdemeanors. Driving recklessly in a national park or building a campfire in a federally protected area may result in the issuance of a citation by a park ranger. Defendants must appear before a U.S. magistrate, who will decide the case. U.S. magistrates hear both civil and criminal cases. Criminal cases heard by U.S. magistrates are bench trials and do not involve juries. The judge decides the case. Appeals from decisions of U.S. magistrates are directed to the U.S. district court. About 100,000 cases are heard annually by U.S. magistrates.

STATE COURTS

Great diversity can be found among state court organization. One reason for this diversity is the number of reforms that have occurred within state court systems (Flango, 1994a). This section describes the organization and operation of state courts. Figure 10.4 is a general diagram of the state judicial system. The diagram shows the state supreme court to which all appeals from lower courts are directed. The supreme court is at the top of the diagram; also shown are intermediate courts of appeal, a superior court, and lesser courts including probate, county, municipal, magistrate, and domestic relations courts.

Not all states follow the model shown in Figure 10.4. There is considerable variation in court structure among the states. Some states do not have justices of the peace. And although the same kinds of courts exist in most states, they often are designated by different names. Some states have courts of equity or chancery, **chancery courts,** in which civil matters and child custody cases are litigated. Some of these same matters are litigated in **juvenile courts** or **family courts.** Other states refer to these courts as **courts of common pleas,** or **circuit courts.**

The highest courts are called supreme courts in most states, but there are exceptions. In Massachusetts, the highest court is called the Supreme Judicial Court. In New York, the highest court is called the Court of Appeals. And in West Virginia, this court is called the Supreme Court of Appeals (Harvard Law Review Association, 1994).

Beneath the state supreme court usually are intermediate appellate courts; over two-thirds of the states have intermediate appellate courts. These appellate courts hear appeals directly from city and county trial courts. For example, Tennessee has a Court of Appeals and a Court of Criminal Appeals, which function, respectively, as the civil and criminal routes through which trial court cases must pass as they are ultimately appealed to the Tennessee Supreme Court. If the Tennessee Supreme Court rejects an appeal, then the appellant may appeal directly to the U.S. Supreme Court.

A superior court is shown in Figure 10.4. This is sometimes known as a circuit court or court of common pleas. New York calls this court a supreme court to add confusion to an already confusing nomenclature. At the lower levels of court organization are probate courts, county courts, municipal courts, and domestic relations courts. Sometimes these are known as courts of **limited jurisdiction.** Limited or **special jurisdiction** means that the court is restricted to handling certain types of cases, such as probating wills or adjudicating juvenile offenders. Criminal courts exclusively process criminal offenders. Frequently, the amount of money in controversy also limits a court's jurisdiction. Thus, courts of domestic relations do not conduct murder trials, and lawsuits for negligence demanding $35 million in compensatory damages do not fall within the jurisdiction of a justice of the peace or city municipal judge. In 1999, there were over 14,300 courts of limited jurisdiction in the United States (Maguire and Pastore, 2000).

Another common classification is a court of **general jurisdiction.** Trial courts are courts of general jurisdiction in many states, because they are not restricted to certain kinds of cases (Black, 1990:684). Some states have both civil and criminal trial courts, or even more elaborate court systems to perform a wide variety of jurisdictional functions. When applied to jurisdiction, the terms *general* and *limited* indicate the difference between a legal authority including an entire subject and one limited to a part of it. As mentioned previously, limited jurisdiction is also called *special jurisdiction* (Black, 1990:927–928). In 1999, there were 5,200 courts of general jurisdiction in the United States (Maguire and Pastore, 2000).

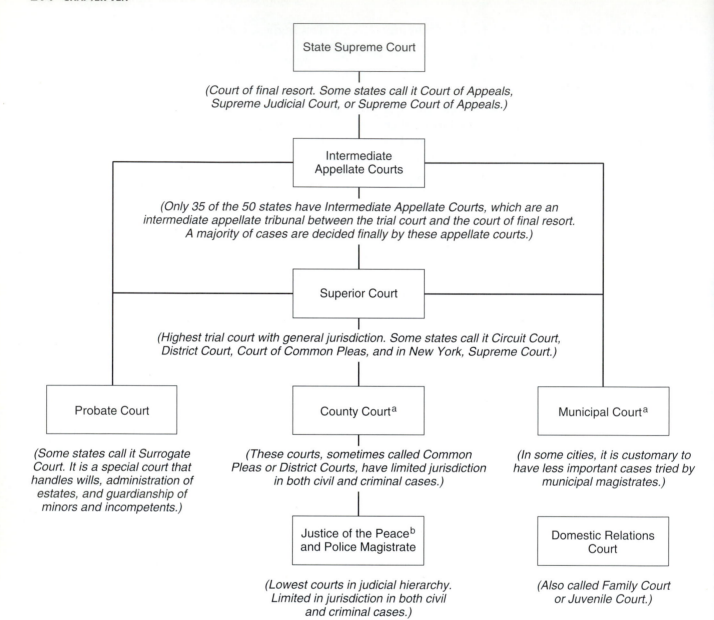

FIGURE 10.4 The State Judicial System

[a]Courts of special jurisdiction, such as probate, family, or juvenile courts, and the so-called inferior courts, such as common pleas or municipal courts, may be separate courts or part of the trial court of general jurisdiction.

[b]Justices of the peace do not exist in all states. Where they do exist, their jurisdictions vary greatly from state to state.

Source: Compiled by author.

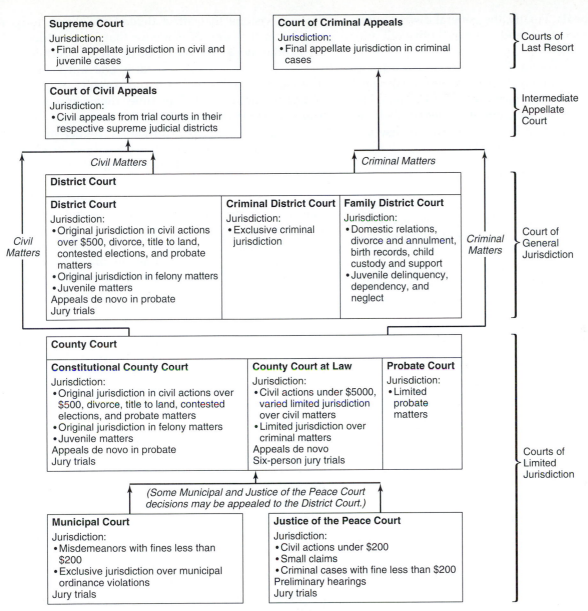

FIGURE 10.5 The Traditional Court Model (Texas Model)
Source: Compiled by author.

The most popular model of state court organization is the **traditional model,** or the **Texas model.** The Texas model is shown in Figure 10.5. The Texas model includes two courts of last resort, the supreme court, which hears cases of a civil nature and juvenile matters, and the court of criminal appeals, which has final appellate jurisdiction in criminal cases. Both courts at this level have nine judges, just as there are nine judges in the U.S. Supreme Court.

Between the basic trial courts and the supreme court, a **court of civil appeals** is shown in the diagram of the model. This court hears all civil appeals from lower trial courts. These trial courts are designated as district courts, and each is assigned a jurisdiction. The family district court oversees matters having to do with child custody questions, juvenile delinquency, and child abuse cases. The criminal district court has exclusive criminal jurisdiction. Appeals from criminal district courts are directed to the **court**

of criminal appeals. Finally, the general district court has general jurisdiction, and it hears both civil and criminal cases.

The lower levels of the Texas court system include county courts and municipal courts. There are also justice of the peace courts, which are in Texas. These are courts of limited jurisdiction, and the extent of their jurisdictions varies greatly in other states that use the traditional model for their court system.

Functions of State and Local Courts

The functions of state and local courts are directly associated with their jurisdictions. The American Bar Association has described the standards relating to trial courts and their administration (American Bar Association, 1975). Although these standards are not binding on specific trial courts, judges often abide by them because of their objectivity and clarity. Trial courts perform three primary functions: (1) decide conflicting contentions of law and disputed issues of fact, (2) formulate sanctions and remedial orders, and (3) require supervision of the activity of persons subject to the authority of the court.

The Texas model shown in Figure 10.5 illustrates the diverse functions performed by various courts of limited jurisdiction. At the county court level in Texas, the constitutional county court has jurisdiction over civil actions involving amounts between $200 and $1,000. This court also hears probate matters involving wills and estates. It conducts six-person jury trials and can also grant requests for new trials to appeal jury verdicts.

The county court at law has jurisdiction over civil actions in which the amount is less than $5,000. It may conduct six-person jury trials and grant appeals for new trials. It also has jurisdiction over certain types of criminal matters. The probate court deals exclusively with probate matters such as wills and estates. Finally, the municipal and justice of the peace courts make up the largest number of Texas courts. They have jurisdiction over misdemeanors involving fines of less than $200, traffic offenses, and violations of municipal ordinances. Small claims in civil actions are settled in these courts, and they also may conduct preliminary hearings to determine probable cause.

COURT ADMINISTRATORS AND OFFICERS

Judges

DUTIES AND RESPONSIBILITIES. The most important person in any courtroom is the judge. Judges make decisions that affect defendants' lives. Judges decide on the type of evidence that is introduced at trial and may decide to include or exclude certain evidence. The judge decides what is relevant testimony. The judge controls the pace and conduct of the trial. Judges are not perfect. Sometimes they commit errors. **Harmful error** or **reversible error** may result in judicial decisions being overturned by higher appellate courts. Harmful errors are often prejudicial to a defendant's case, and juries might render guilty verdicts because of such judicial errors. The same is true about reversible error. Reversible error is considered by appellate courts when reviewing transcripts of lower court proceedings. If judges have committed reversible errors, their judgments are ordered reversed by higher courts. But not all errors are detected in a trial. Some errors may be **plain errors** and may not affect the trial outcome. Also, not all guilty verdicts are appealed, and not all appeals are heard on their merits by higher courts.

JUDICIAL QUALIFICATIONS: HOW ARE JUDGES SELECTED? One misconception among citizens is that all judges are lawyers and know the finer points of the law (Provine, 1986). In many jurisdictions throughout the United States, many judges have no legal training and are not former lawyers. Judges are either appointed or elected (Dubois, 1990). Five methods of judicial selection as basic variations on appointments or elections are (1) popular election by partisan ballot, (2) gubernatorial (or presidential) appointment, (3) popular election by nonpartisan ballot, (4) appointment by legislative election, and (5) selection through the merit plan (Alfini, 1981:253).

At the federal level, the president nominates judges for district, circuit, and U.S. Supreme Court judgeships, with congressional approval (Solomon, 1984). In most states, governors appoint judges to court posts. In many other jurisdictions, persons campaign for judgeships, since they are political offices. In fact, politics is the primary reason for such large numbers of nonlawyers in positions such as municipal judges, justices of the peace, and county court judges. Despite the great variation in judicial selection methods, no single method of selecting judges has been found superior to the others (Dubois, 1990).

Politically appointed or elected judges raise several important issues, however. Are the most qualified persons selected for the judgeship? Elected officials are popular with their constituents, but they may not be the best persons for the job. In a purely bureaucratic

BOX 10.1 PERSONALITY HIGHLIGHT

ROBERT O. WEFALD
District Court Judge,
South Central Judicial
District, Bismarck, North
Dakota

Statistics: B.A. (social
science, honors program),
University of North
Dakota, 1964; J.D.,
University of Michigan
Law School, 1970

All eight judges of the South Central Judicial District travel to all 12 counties to handle cases. All of North Dakota's 42 district court judges sit as courts of general jurisdiction handling all civil and criminal cases. The North Dakota Supreme Court is the only appellate court and handles all appeals.

Experience: After graduation from the University of North Dakota, I joined the Navy and was commissioned at Officers' Candidate School in October 1964. My three years of active duty included 28 months on board the USS Lynde McCormick (DDG-8) with one six-month tour off the coast of Vietnam in 1966 as the gunnery officer. After my release from active duty, I attended law school and actively participated in the Naval Reserve for the next 24 years, retiring as a captain in 1991.

After graduation from law school, I became a law clerk for the North Dakota Supreme Court and was admitted to the practice of law in 1970. I entered private practice in July 1971 and helped to create a general practice law firm in Bismarck. I was elected as attorney general of North Dakota in 1980 and served from 1981 to 1984. In 1985, I returned to private practice as a solo practitioner until 1998, when I was elected as a district court judge, taking office on January 1, 1999.

On Becoming a Judge: Although I ran a close but unsuccessful race for a seat on the North Dakota Supreme Court in 1992, I had never thought of becoming a trial judge. My goal early in my adult life was to be successful in politics, and that goal was partially achieved. Being a lawyer gave me a wide variety of options and allowed me to provide for my family in North Dakota, the place where I grew up and where I wanted to live and pursue a political career. I loved being a lawyer and working for people. I particularly enjoyed my four years as attorney general, serving as the people's lawyer representing their government. It was a great job. To get there, I not only had to be successful as a lawyer, but I had to work diligently at all levels of party politics until I had an opportunity to earn my party's endorsement for the office. I have run three state-wide campaigns and one limited to 12 counties, and I have loved them all. They certainly were a lot of hard work, but I thoroughly enjoyed traveling all across North Dakota, from one corner to the other, and I loved meeting all kinds of people. Those campaigns were wonderful experiences.

After the 1992 campaign, I was all set to scale down my efforts in politics and simply enjoy my remaining years of private practice until I eventually decided to retire. But early in 1998, it became apparent that one of our judges who was up for reelection was not going to be able to run because of a serious illness. I wanted my fellow lawyers to let him run for reelection without opposition, so that when he ultimately had to step down because of his illness, the governor could simply appoint his successor. But when it became clear that he would not even be able to finish his term, several lawyers expressed an interest in running for his seat on the bench. Until that moment, I had never thought about being a trial judge, although I had years of experience in handling trials of all kinds.

Quite frankly, I had always thought that being a judge was not a particularly good job, because judges I knew often would complain about their work. It just did not sound like it would be any fun, and I wanted to continue enjoying my work as a lawyer. But at a meeting of the local bar association, several lawyers encouraged me to seek this job, and I agreed, as I thought being a judge might be a nice change of pace after 28 years of practice. I received overwhelming support from my fellow attorneys in particular and from the people in general and I was elected by a substantial margin. Curiously enough, closing my law practice in less than two months was one of the most intensely busy times I have ever had as an attorney.

On Being a Judge: I am so grateful that I was encouraged to run and that I won, because this is absolutely the best job I have ever had. I simply cannot understand why those other judges were complaining. Being a judge is a wonderful experience. No doubt the fact that I had more than 28 years of legal experience equipped me for this job. Although I have been handling a greater variety of cases, I have not yet run into anything that I felt I was unable to handle. The great bulk of my time actually in court is spent on criminal cases, and I enjoy them. Many of the civil cases ultimately wind up being settled before trial.

I love traveling to all 12 of the courthouses in the counties of the South Central Judicial District, as getting out on the open prairies is just good for my soul. I never tire of the travel. My only source of minor frustration so far is that I do not remember every detail of everyone's case. In private practice, I would maybe have 100 open files and I would work rather intensely on six or seven of those in an average week. But as a judge, I sometimes get more than 100 cases a week in which I have to take action. Sometimes they come so quickly, one after the other, that I find myself totally concentrating on the case before me, putting the case I just handled out of my mind and not thinking about the case coming up. My focus is so intent on the present case that I often have to be reminded about what happened with a particular case when someone later asks me about it.

I enjoy the cases I handle, since in criminal matters I am convinced I am doing justice for the people and to each defendant, and in civil matters I know I am getting things resolved for the litigants so that they can get on with the rest of their lives. When it comes to being a judge, experience counts. I did a little research and discovered that when I was elected at age 56, all of the other judges then on the bench had taken office at an earlier age and with less experience.

Advice to Students: Study hard in the chosen subjects you enjoy, as there is no one undergraduate field that is any better preparation for law school than any other. What really counts is being a conscientious and hardworking student. Go to the best law school you can afford. Choose a place where you want to live and work, because to build a practice, you have to stay in one community where your reputation can grow in the community and among your fellow attorneys. Become active in a service club, a church, and various community organizations, such as the Boy Scouts or Girl Scouts, and volunteer to raise money so you can get to know a lot of people. Most clients come from referrals from other attorneys or from other clients.

Get as much experience as possible in as many areas as possible. Try as many cases as you can, because there is no better experience for being a judge than to have tried lots of cases. Besides, it is fun trying cases, and that is why you will enjoy being a lawyer. Don't worry about becoming a judge, but keep yourself prepared so that you will be ready to try for a judgeship if the opportunity presents itself. When you do become a judge, never forget where you came from and how you wanted to be treated by the judges when you were appearing before them. And be sure to have fun, because it is a great job.

context, Max Weber would say that judges should be appointed on the basis of merit and their expertise. But clearly this is seldom the case, especially in state courts.

Another issue is whether or not political appointments contribute to corruption among the judiciary (Blankenship, Spargar, and Janikowski, 1994). Because of their powerful positions, judges can and do influence trial outcomes, dismiss cases, find innocent defendants guilty, and declare guilty defendants not guilty. Judges also control the severity of penalties imposed when defendants are convicted. All states have judicial sanctioning boards. These boards usually are operated through state bar associations, and provisions are in place to question and sanction inappropriate judicial conduct. However, studies comparing the qualities of judges who are elected as opposed to those who are appointed show almost no difference in judicial performance or quality (Blankenship, Spargar, and Janikowski, 1994).

Just about every bar association at the state and federal levels has attempted to identify those qualities that good judges should possess. For instance, the Report of the Committee on Qualification Guidelines for Judicial Candidates indicated nine criteria for judicial selection: (1) age, (2) communication skills, (3) health, (4) industry, (5) integrity, (6) judicial temperament, (7) justice (impartiality, fairness, objectivity), (8) professional skills, and (9) social consciousness (American Judicature Society, 1983). But this general list is used only in the primary screening phases of judicial nominations. Furthermore, no guidance has been suggested as to which of these characteristics should have priority over the other characteristics. No one knows for sure what the qualities of good judges are or should be.

Several states have adopted the Missouri Plan. Originally proposed in 1940, the **Missouri Plan** is a method of judicial selection using the merit system for appointments to judgeships (President's Commission on Law Enforcement, 1967:66–67). The features of the Missouri Plan include (1) a nominating committee consisting of lawyers and nonlawyers appointed by the governor and chaired by a judge, (2) a listing of qualified candidates who are nominated by the committee for each judicial vacancy, (3) a procedure through which each judicial vacancy is filled by the governor by referring to the list of candidates nominated by the committee, and (4) a declaration that any appointed judge seeking reelection will run only on the issue of whether or not he or she should be retained on the basis of merit.

The Missouri Plan is a variation of the much earlier Kales Plan (Kales, 1914). The **Kales Plan** required a nonpartisan aggregate of lawyers, judges, and nonjudicial personnel to make a list of the most qualified candidates on the basis of their records and expertise, which was then submitted to the governor for use in making appointments. Vacancies because of death, retirement, or removal because of incompetence or any other reason could be filled without reference to any political affiliations or associations. Ideally, any choice a governor made from the list provided by nonpartisans would, by definition, be a good choice. The important point is that the influence of politics is minimized in the selection process. The Kales Plan, therefore, comports well with Weber's bureaucratic model and how persons are selected for their respective positions. Despite the Missouri Plan or any other merit plan currently in use, some critics question if politics can ever be eliminated entirely from the judicial selection process (Blankenship, Spargar, and Janikowski, 1994).

Because of the unevenness in quality among judges at both the state and federal levels, several training schools for judges have been established to socialize anyone about to perform the judicial role. These schools seek to train judges in common court procedures. One such school is the National Judicial College (NJC) in Reno, Nevada (Chereb, 1996). Both federal and state court judges attend the NJC. Instructors include established members of both the state and federal judiciary. The NJC offers an array of courses that run from two days to three weeks. It may seem like a whirlwind experience to expect a judge to learn all there is to know about "judging" in three weeks, but these intensive sessions at least equip judges with the fundamentals they need to perform their judicial chores.

For instance, both the federal and state trial courts operate according to rules of procedure, whether these rules are criminal or civil. Furthermore, both federal and state courts have rules of evidence that apply and govern the admissibility or nonadmissibility of certain evidentiary materials and testimony. Judges tailor their curriculum to fit whatever their specialty is, and they attempt to learn as much as they can before they take the bench. But because not everything that judges should know can be taught in any specific curriculum, even by the NJC, this means that almost all judges will commit errors when presiding over trials. A major reason for the many state and federal appeals that are filed annually is alleged errors committed by judges when ruling on motions or the admissibility of evidence for either the accused or prosecution.

The rules of criminal procedure as well as the rules of evidence are cumbersome compendiums of material that must be mastered over time. And there are numerous exceptions to the rules. A three-week crash course, even if offered by the Harvard Law School, will not prepare judges adequately for applying all of these rules. Judges gradually acquire a working familiarity with these rules and attempt to apply them fairly. Almost every criminal court judge has one or more legal assistants or clerks to investigate the latest technicalities and exceptions to the rules of evidence. When case law is cited by either side, the prosecution or defense, the judge is either familiar with the case or will soon become familiar with it, with the assistance of these legal aides. This is one reason why judges will reserve ruling on certain motions for several hours or days, in order to allow themselves time to do the necessary research on the technicalities of motions or evidentiary issues.

EVALUATING THE EFFECTIVENESS OF JUDGES. How do we know if judges are doing good jobs? Several methods exist for determining judicial effectiveness. First, if judges are elected officials, their reelection is considered an overt indicator that the public, at least, is satisfied with their performance. This does not mean that they are good or effective judges, however. Almost every state has one or more judicial conduct organizations whose job it is to ferret out bad judges

(Maguire and Pastore, 2000:74). Also, local bar associations and private organizations maintain files of complaints against particular judges. These complaints are investigated and may eventually lead to recalls of judges from their judgeships. However, only a small fraction of complaints against judges results in any formal sanction from either the local or national bar association or any other authoritative board (Maguire and Pastore, 2000:450–451).

Various polls have been conducted to determine the amount of confidence the public has in the judiciary. Over the years, the confidence expressed by the public toward the judiciary has eroded. In 1997, for instance, about 40 percent of the public had low or very low confidence in the honesty and integrity of the judiciary (Maguire and Pastore, 2000). Lawyers generally were categorized similarly by the public, with 41 percent of the public having low or very low confidence in the honesty and integrity of lawyers.

A third and perhaps the best indicator of judicial effectiveness is the number of court decisions that are appealed and result in trial verdicts being overturned. Over 99 percent of all appealed trial court verdicts at either the state or federal level are upheld on appeal (Maguire and Pastore, 2000). One reason for this low appeal success rate is that higher appellate courts assume from the outset that whatever was decided by the lower court must be true or correct. Therefore, appellants who launch their appeals to higher courts must overcome the incredible burden of showing that whatever the trial court judge did was not only wrong but materially changed the trial outcome. Most appeals by criminal defendants who allege judicial misconduct or errors in decision making are lost simply because the appellate court finds that even if there were errors committed, they are harmless errors and the trial outcome would not have been affected if they had not occurred. Thus, it is a rare event to have a judge's decision overturned by an appellate court, and such a reversal is clearly indicative of a substantial and serious error.

Considerable variation can be found among both the federal and state judiciary about the rate of trial verdicts that are overturned. Some judges have much higher rates of decisions being overturned than others. This is tangible evidence that can be used to evaluate judicial effectiveness. Reviewing bodies and/or the electorate may consider this evidence and seek to remove certain judges from their offices.

ETHICAL CONSIDERATIONS. Judges are bound to observe an ethical code of conduct. They must be impartial and not favor either side. Judges are human beings and are subject to the weaknesses of human beings, however. They have their biases and prejudices. Some of these biases and prejudices are difficult to detect. Many judges who are biased or prejudiced in different ways are skillful at hiding these biases from others. These biases may be directed toward persons of particular races or ethnicities or may pertain to particular types of criminal offenses, such as child sexual abuse or rape.

Age, gender, and socioeconomic status play important parts in affecting judicial decision making as well. Some judges are more lenient when sentencing elderly offenders. In certain parts of the country, however, elderly offenders receive harsher sentences than younger offenders convicted of the same or similar offenses (Champion, 1988b). Sometimes, judges are influenced by whether defendants are represented by private counsels or public defenders (Champion, 1988a).

Ideally, *who* represents a criminal defendant should not make a difference to the judge hearing the case. But the fact is that public defenders generally do not fare as well in earning acquittals for their clients or securing more lenient treatment for their clients in the sentencing process (Lehtinen and Smith, 1974). One explanation for this differential in the lesser effectiveness of public defenders is that the indigent clients who are represented are often convicted of street crimes, and strong evidence can be provided against them. Another reason is that public defenders are generally less experienced compared with privately retained counsel. Public defenders are not paid much for their services either. This means that they might not expend the same degree of effort in a case compared with privately retained counsel. Despite these performance differences, however, judicial impartiality should be unaffected, regardless of who represents the criminal defendant. If it is true that judges are biased in favor of private counsel and allow this bias to influence their decision making, then this raises some serious ethical questions about judicial conduct. But as we have already seen, formal sanctions against judges at all levels have had an impotent effect thus far (Maguire and Pastore, 2000).

Prosecutors: Federal, State, and Local Government

The next most important figure in any court proceeding is the **prosecutor**. At the federal level, each of the U.S. districts has a **United States attorney** appointed by the president of the United States, with the advice and consent of the Senate. These attorneys are appointed for four-year terms and are subject to removal by the president. The attorney general of the United States appoints one or more **assistant United States attorneys (AUSAs)** as required, depending on the caseload of any particular district. These AUSAs are subject to removal by the attorney general. Following are the duties of the United States attorney for any given district:

1. To prosecute for all offenses against the United States
2. To prosecute or defend for the government all actions, suits, or proceedings in which the United States is concerned
3. To appear on behalf of the defendants in civil actions and suits or proceedings pending in his or her district against collectors or other officers of the revenue or customs for any act done by them or for the recovery of any money exacted by or paid to these officers
4. To institute and prosecute proceedings for the collection of fines, penalties, and forfeitures incurred for violation of any revenue law
5. To make such reports as the attorney general may direct (U.S. Code, 2001)

At the state and local levels, the prosecutor may be called the district attorney, state's attorney, city attorney, commonwealth attorney, county attorney, or simply the prosecuting attorney (DeFrances and Steadman, 1998:2). District attorneys (DAs) at both the federal and state levels decide which cases to prosecute, and they represent the government in all civil and criminal matters. DAs initiate prosecutions of defendants and seek indictments from grand juries against prospective criminal defendants, or they may issue criminal informations. They appoint assistant district attorneys according to their respective caseloads and city or county budgets. They are also pretrial intermediaries between judges and criminal defendants. These prosecutors may negotiate plea agreements. In the courtroom, these prosecutors present evidence against defendants and seek convictions for crimes alleged.

PROSECUTORIAL ROLES AND RESPONSIBILITIES. Local, state, and federal prosecutors always represent the government's interests whenever criminal laws violations are alleged. The U.S. Attorney's Office decides which cases should be prosecuted. At the state and local levels, city and county attorneys make similar decisions about filing criminal charges against defendants.

Considerable variation exists among jurisdictions concerning how prosecutors are selected. In some states, the state supreme court appoints a state attorney general for a specified term. In Tennessee, the supreme court appoints an attorney general for a term of eight years. In New Mexico, the state attorney general is elected through a partisan election and serves one four-year term. In other states, the attorney general may be appointed by the governor. In city and county government, the position of district attorney is often an elected position.

FUNCTIONS OF PROSECUTORS. The functions of prosecutors at the local, state, and federal levels include, but are not limited to, the following: (1) deciding or screening cases slotted for prosecution, (2) representing the government in cases against suspects before the grand jury, (3) conferring with police participating in the initial arrest and ensuring the suspect's right to due process, (4) evaluating the sufficiency of evidence against the accused, (5) conferring with defense attorneys in pretrial conferences in an effort to avoid a trial proceeding, and (6) presenting the case against the defendant in court.

Screening Cases. Prosecutors examine each case in terms of how it would appear to a judge and jury if it were to come to trial. Prosecutors may view each case differently compared with the arresting officers who bring the case to their attention initially. Each case has different prosecutorial merit. Because of the sheer volume of cases, or the caseload, prosecutors cannot possibly prosecute every case presented to them. Therefore, they must prioritize cases on the basis of which ones are the most important and which ones have the most prosecutive merit. This issue is covered in more detail later in this chapter.

Presenting Cases Before the Grand Jury. Prosecutors present cases to grand juries in those jurisdictions with grand jury systems. About half of all states use grand juries to indict criminal defendants. Prosecutors must convince grand jurors that probable cause exists to believe that the person(s) they prosecute have committed one or more crimes.

Conferring with Police About a Defendant's Right to Due Process. Part of the screening process of a criminal case is consulting with arresting officers and determining the circumstances surrounding the arrest. The prosecutor will ask questions about whether or not the accused were informed of their constitutional rights, and if the police gave the suspects the *Miranda* warning.

Evaluating the Sufficiency of Evidence Against the Accused. Is there sufficient evidence against persons accused of a crime that a conviction is likely? Prosecutors must evaluate the evidence presented to them by police officers and make a determination in this matter. Sometimes, the evidence against someone is overwhelming and compelling. At other times, the evidence is merely circumstantial. Cases against criminal suspects in which only circumstantial evidence exists to show guilt are more difficult to prove. Prosecutors must weigh the advantages and disadvantages of proceeding against suspects on the basis of the evidence collected against them. This is one way prosecutors prioritize their cases to be prosecuted.

Conferring with Defense Counsel. Prosecutors usually meet with defense counsel who represent criminal defendants. The result of these conferences is often an accommodation of sorts, and some kind of deal frequently is worked out. This deal is known as a *plea bargain agreement,* which allows the defendant to plead guilty to one or more criminal charges in exchange for some type of prosecutorial leniency. Over 90 percent of all guilty pleas in U.S. courts are obtained through plea bargaining. Thus, this particular prosecutorial function is quite important.

Presenting the Case Against the Defendant in Court. The prosecutor presents the government's case against the accused in court. This responsibility includes calling witnesses who can give incriminating testimony supporting the accused's guilt. It also involves coordinating the presentation of other relevant evidence with detectives, police officers, and laboratory experts. This particular function of prosecutors is best known to many people, since we are exposed to courtroom dramas on television and in the media daily.

WHO ARE PROSECUTORS AND HOW ARE THEY SELECTED?

In 1996, a survey of state court prosecutors revealed that 2,343 prosecutors' offices employed over 71,000 persons (DeFrances and Steadman, 1998:1). About 37 percent of all these personnel, or 26,270 persons, were either chief or assistant prosecutors in these offices. About 24,000 of these prosecutors were assistant prosecutors. The median length of service of chief prosecutors in 1996 was six years, but some prosecutors had served in their positions for as long as 32 years. Over 95 percent of all state prosecutors are elected locally (DeFrances and Steadman, 1998:1). The remainder are appointed, usually by a city mayor, city council, or state governor.

EVALUATING THE EFFECTIVENESS OF PROSECUTORS: PLEA BARGAINING AND CONVICTION RATES.

The effectiveness of prosecutors is usually measured by the number of convictions they obtain on an annual basis. In 1996, for instance, all state prosecutors averaged an 88 percent conviction rate for both felons and misdemeanants (DeFrances and Steadman, 1998:5). Generally, prosecutors in cities of 1,000,000 or larger had a 76 percent conviction rate, whereas prosecutors in cities of 250,000 or smaller had an 87 percent conviction rate. Since no explanation has officially been provided to account for these different rates of conviction between larger and smaller cities, we can only speculate and say that perhaps those prosecutors in smaller cities are less overworked compared with prosecutors in larger cities. Regardless of the different rates of conviction between larger and smaller cities, over 90 percent of all misdemeanor and felony convictions were obtained through plea bargaining (Maguire and Pastore, 2000).

ETHICAL CONSIDERATIONS.

Like judges, prosecutors do not always adhere to the highest standards they are expected to observe. Occasionally they engage in various forms of **prosecutorial misconduct** or immoral, unethical, or illegal acts associated with their prosecutorial duties. It is unethical for a prosecutor to pursue a case against a defendant if the prosecutor knows the defendant is innocent. **Malicious prosecution** is any prosecution begun in malice without probable cause to believe that the criminal charges will ever be sustained (Black, 1990:958). It is also unethical for prosecutors to threaten certain defendants with prosecution for very serious offenses for which little evidence is available, if any, unless these defendants plead guilty to lesser charges. In more than a few cases, defendants have pleaded guilty to offenses in which no evidence existed against them. Their motive is a simple one: They wish to avoid a prosecution on more serious, yet groundless, charges, because there is a chance that a jury might find them guilty. The public seldom hears about such prosecutions or guilty pleas entered by innocent defendants.

Another type of prosecutorial misconduct is to encourage witnesses to slant their versions of events when testifying during trials. FBI agents, DEA agents, local and state police officers, and a host of other witnesses sometimes are rehearsed in particular versions of cases to fit a certain prosecutorial scenario. The testimony given by these persons may or may not be factually accurate. But the prosecutors succeed in getting their witnesses to tell the story *their* (the prosecutor's) *way.* A particular spin on a witness's version of events may prejudice juries against defendants.

Defense Counsel

Defense counsel are attorneys who represent people charged with crimes. Defense attorneys are obligated to do everything that is ethically and legally possible to defend their clients. All criminal defendants are entitled to an attorney as a matter of right. Many defense counsel are retained privately by those able to afford them. In many cases, defense counsels are appointed by the courts to represent indigent defendants.

The functions of defense counsel are to (1) represent their clients faithfully, (2) attack the prosecution's case vigorously, (3) discuss with the defendant the best course of action in the case, (4) negotiate with prosecutors for a case resolution most favorable to their client, (5) vigorously cross-examine prosecution witnesses to attack and undermine their credibility in front of jurors, and (6) use all legal means to defeat the government's case.

Court Reporters

Another crucial court officer is the **court reporter.** In all **courts of record,** a written or tape-recorded record of all court proceedings is maintained. The trial court is a court of record. At the federal level, U.S. district courts are courts of record. Court reporters are appointed, and they make verbatim or word-for-word transcriptions of court proceedings. In all criminal trials, transcriptions of what transpires are important, especially if either side decides to appeal the verdict to a higher court. A defendant's guilt or innocence may rest on evidence that was presented in court for the jury's consideration or that was excluded. Judges decide what evidence may be included or excluded. Judges also overrule motions made by the defense or sustain objections made by the prosecution. If the admissibility of evidence is at issue, or if questions arise about the integrity of judges' rulings on motions or objections, a guilty verdict sometimes may be overturned by a higher court. Judges must follow certain rules of procedure in their courts, and their failure to do so may result in reversals of their decisions. The court reporter provides a record of the proceedings that can be reviewed if verdicts are appealed.

Court Clerks

Court clerks are elected officials. In federal district courts, the court clerk is often the judge's secretary or personal aide. The court clerk is a court officer who may file pleadings, motions, or judgments, issue process, and keep general records of court proceedings. In U.S. district courts, each district court may appoint a clerk who may, in turn, appoint deputies, clerical assistants, and employees. These court clerks keep records of court dockets for federal judges and may advise them concerning the scheduling of cases for trial.

Bailiffs

Bailiffs are also court officers. They are in charge of maintaining order while the court is in session. All trial courts have bailiffs. The bailiff often is placed in custody of the jury in a trial proceeding, and sometimes the bailiff has custody of prisoners while they are in the courtroom. If certain persons in the courtroom are not behaving properly, the bailiff is empowered to remove them from the courtroom.

Known also as criers and messengers in federal district courts, bailiffs may be given additional duties by federal judges, including the duties of law clerks. These criers call the court to order, attend to the needs of jury members while deliberations are taking place, and generally serve the interests of the federal judge (U.S. Code, Title 28, Sec. 751-755, 2001).

THE TRIAL PROCESS

The two types of trials, bench trials and jury trials, are discussed in detail in the following subsections. An examination of the sentencing process is also included, as it is an integral part of the trial process.

Bench Trials

Bench trials, also known as trials by the court or trials by the judge, are conducted either if petty offenses are involved and a jury is not permitted, or in cases in which defendants waive their right to a jury trial. A judge presides, hears the evidence, and then decides the case, relying on rational principles of law.

Some of the advantages of bench trials are that they are more efficient than jury trials. Juries do not have to be selected for a bench trial, and judges hear the evidence and decide the defendant's guilt or innocence. Some of the disadvantages of bench trials are that some judges are influenced by extralegal factors, such as race, class, ethnicity, and/or gender (Williams, 1995a, 1995b). Judges also are influenced by their personal feelings about the types of offenses charged. Greater susceptibility to corruption also exists if the judge is the sole arbiter of the fate of defendants. Briefly summarizing, the major advantages of bench trials are

1. Case processing is expedited.
2. Cases are usually decided on the merits of the case rather than on emotionally charged appeals in the case of heinous offenses.
3. The appearance of a defendant may be undesirable to jurors, but judges usually can be dissuaded from considering such extralegal factors.
4. In complex cases, judges are often in a better position to evaluate the sufficiency of evidence against the accused and make fairer judgments.
5. Judges are less persuaded by media attention given to high-profile cases in which juries might be influenced unduly against defendants.
6. Bench trials are usually cheaper than jury trials, since they do not take as long to complete and require less attorney time.

Some of the major disadvantages of bench trials are

1. Judges may impose more severe punishments on certain defendants, depending on the crimes they have committed.
2. Judges are more susceptible to corruption when left to their own decision making.
3. Defendants waive their right to a jury trial, in which the defendant's situation, appearance, and emotional appeal may work to the defendant's benefit.

Jury Trials

Persons charged with felonies are guaranteed the right to **jury trials** in the United States. This guarantee also applies to each state. The landmark case of *Duncan v. Louisiana* (1968) limits the right to a jury trial to those offenses for which imprisonment for more than six months can be imposed. This standard has been upheld in related cases, including *Baldwin v. New York* (1970) and *Blanton v. City of North Las Vegas* (1989). The only exception to this provision for a jury trial is if the judge declares to the defendant that he or she does not intend to impose incarcerative punishment longer

than six months if the defendant is subsequently convicted. Thus, unless otherwise provided by state law, persons are only entitled to a jury trial if they are in jeopardy of receiving incarceration greater than six months as a punishment.

In the last few decades, the number of trials by jury has increased for both major crimes as well as for lesser offenses or misdemeanors (Maguire and Pastore, 2000). Juries are comprised of a defendant's peers. These peers are intended to represent a cross section of the community within which the defendant resides. Juries that are selected and whose job it is to determine a defendant's guilt or innocence are **finders of fact** and are known as **petit juries.**

For both federal and state courts, jurors are selected in similar ways, although the source or pool of individuals eligible for jury duty may differ. A **venire** or list of eligible persons is prepared from which a jury will be selected. Individuals selected as potential jurors are **veniremen.** These potential jurors' names are drawn from voting registration lists, tax assessors' records, lists of persons with drivers' licenses, or any other public documents listing citizens who reside within a given federal district (Knowles and Hickman, 1984). These lists are **veniremen lists.**

THE FUNCTIONS OF JURIES. Juries perform the following functions: (1) preventing government oppression, (2) determining guilt or innocence of an accused, (3) representing diverse community interests, and (4) acting as a buffer between the accuser and the accused.

THE NUMBERS OF JURORS AND JURY VOTING. Federal courts conduct jury trials with 12 jurors. Usually several alternate jurors are chosen in the event that one or more of the original 12 jurors become ill or cannot attend the full trial. Technically, a federal jury size of 11 can proceed with judicial approval if juror attrition causes this jury size reduction.

State juries can range from 6 jurors to 12 jurors. There is nothing sacred about the number 12 as a jury size. It is a historical accident. The U.S. Supreme Court has never declared an upper limit for the size of either a federal or a state jury. A lower limit for jury size has been established, however. The minimum number of jurors in state courts is six persons. Any jury size smaller than six is unconstitutional.

Jury voting and the requirement of unanimity of voting varies among the states. In federal district courts, jury voting must be unanimous, either for a vote of guilty or not guilty. In state courts, however, unless otherwise provided by legislative proclamations, jury voting does not have to be unanimous. The U.S. Supreme Court has ruled in certain state cases that jury voting of 9 to 3 or 10 to 2 or 11 to 1 is constitutional. For instance, in the cases of *Apodaca v. Oregon* (1972) and *Johnson v. Louisiana* (1972), the respective defendants were convicted by a majority of jurors, but there was no unanimity of agreement. Six-member juries must be unanimous in their verdict (*Burch v. Louisiana*, 1979).

THE VERDICT AND SENTENCING. Juries render verdicts as directed by the rules of criminal procedure in their respective jurisdictions. Typical verdicts are either guilty or not guilty. No state or the federal system has an "innocent" verdict. This is because under due process, the presumption of a defendant's innocence exists unless the prosecution can prove his or her guilt beyond a reasonable doubt. If the defendant's guilt is not established and the jury votes "not guilty," then the innocence presumption continues. If the jury returns a guilty verdict, however, the judge must impose a sentence.

Sentencing

THE INFLUENCE OF PROSECUTORS AND JUDGES ON SENTENCING DECISIONS. Although judges make the final sentencing decision, prosecutors are key players in the nature and severity of sanctions that will be imposed subsequently on convicted offenders. Prosecutors decide which charges should be pursued against criminal defendants. In over 90 percent of the cases, prosecutors can forecast with a high degree of accuracy the actual criminal penalties that judges will impose. This is because of the plea bargaining that precedes negotiated guilty pleas, in which defense attorneys, their clients, and prosecutors reach an accord about what it will take for a guilty plea to be elicited. This means that both prosecutors and defendants make concessions. Prosecutors make it more attractive to defendants to plead guilty by reducing charges against them or promising a more lenient disposition compared with what defendants would face if they were convicted through a trial. This give-and-take plea bargaining arrangement is quite typical of the American system of justice.

FUNCTIONS AND PURPOSES OF SENTENCING. The functions of sentencing are (1) to reflect the seriousness of the offense, (2) to promote respect for the law, (3) to provide just punishment for the offense, (4)

to deter the defendant from future criminal conduct, (5) to protect the public from the convicted defendant, and (6) to provide the convicted defendant with education and/or vocational training or other rehabilitative relief. The purposes of sentencing include punishment or retribution, deterrence, custodial monitoring or incapacitation, and rehabilitation.

TYPES OF SENTENCING SYSTEMS. There are five different kinds of sentencing systems that vary from one state to the next, and jurisdictional variations can be found within each state. The sentencing systems include (1) indeterminate sentencing, (2) determinate sentencing, (3) mandatory minimum sentencing, (4) presumptive sentencing guidelines, and (5) voluntary sentencing guidelines (Bureau of Justice Assistance, 1998:1–2).

Indeterminate Sentencing. **Indeterminate sentences** are sentences of imprisonment by the court for either specified or unspecified durations, with the final release date determined by a parole board (Black, 1990:771). Indeterminate sentencing provides sentencing judges with maximum flexibility in the discretion they can exercise in any offender's case. In 1996, 37 states had indeterminate sentencing.

Determinate Sentencing. **Determinate sentencing** involves a fixed term of incarceration that may be reduced by good time or earned time. Explicit standards specify the amount of punishment and a set release date with no review by an administrative agency, such as a parole board. Postincarcerative supervision may be imposed as a part of the sentence (Bureau of Justice Assistance, 1998:1). Good time credits that may reduce an inmate's sentence are provided by statute, such as 30 days off the maximum sentence for every 30 days served. Earned good time may be accumulated by participating in prison vocational/educational programs or counseling. Meritorious good time may be earned for inmate acts of heroism, such as breaking up fights between other inmates or rescuing correctional officers from inmate assaults. The nature and amount of good time credits awarded to inmates vary among the states with little uniformity. Fourteen states had determinate sentencing provisions in 1996 (Bureau of Justice Assistance, 1998:4–5).

Mandatory Minimum Sentencing. **Mandatory minimum sentencing** is a fixed sentence an inmate must serve before discretionary release can occur. Habitual offender laws reflect mandatory minimum sentencing. In some states, such as Kentucky, if offenders are convicted of three or more felonies, the third or fourth conviction makes them eligible for prosecution as a habitual offender. If they are convicted of being a habitual offender, they will receive a sentence of life imprisonment. This is a mandatory sentence. All 50 states and the District of Columbia have mandatory minimum sentencing statutes and provisions (Bureau of Justice Assistance, 1998:4–5).

Presumptive Sentencing Guidelines or Guidelines-Based Sentencing. **Presumptive sentencing guidelines,** also known as **guidelines-based sentencing,** are sentences that meet all of the following conditions: (1) The appropriate sentence for an offender in a specific case is presumed to fall within a range of sentences authorized by sentencing guidelines that are adopted by a legislatively created sentencing body, usually a sentencing commission; (2) sentencing judges are expected to sentence within the range or provide written justification for departure; and (3) the guidelines provide for some review, usually appellate, of the departure. Presumptive guidelines may employ determinate or indeterminate sentencing structures. In 1996, 17 states used presumptive sentencing (Bureau of Justice Assistance, 1998:2). Federal district courts have used presumptive sentencing guidelines since 1987.

Voluntary Sentencing Guidelines. **Voluntary sentencing guidelines** are recommended sentencing policies that are not required by law. They serve as a guide and are based on past sentencing practices, but the legislature has not mandated their use. Voluntary/advisory guidelines may use either indeterminate or determinate sentencing structures. There were seven states using voluntary sentencing guidelines in 1996 (Bureau of Justice Assistance, 1998:2).

AGGRAVATING AND MITIGATING CIRCUMSTANCES. Judicial decisions at the time of sentencing convicted offenders are affected by aggravating and mitigating circumstances. **Aggravating circumstances** are those that may lessen the severity of punishment. Aggravating circumstances include but are not limited to the following: (1) if the crime involved death or serious bodily injury to one or more victims; (2) if the crime was committed while the offender was out on bail facing other criminal charges; (3) if the offender was on probation, parole, or work release at the time the crime was committed; (4) if the offender was a recidivist and had committed several previous offenses for which he or she had been punished; (5) if the offender was the leader in the commission of the offense involving two or more offenders; (6) if the offense involved more than one victim and/or was a violent or nonviolent crime; (7) if the offender treated the victim(s) with extreme cruelty during the commission of the offense; and (8) if the offender used a dangerous weapon in the commission of the crime and the risk to human life was high.

Mitigating circumstances are factors associated with the commission of the criminal offense that tend to lessen the crime's severity. These include but are not limited to the following: (1) The offender did not cause serious bodily injury by his or her conduct during the commission of the crime, (2) the convicted defendant did not contemplate that his or her criminal conduct would inflict serious bodily injury on anyone, (3) the offender acted under duress or extreme provocation, (4) the offender's conduct was possibly justified under the circumstances, (5) the offender was suffering from mental incapacitation or physical condition that significantly reduced his or her culpability in the offense, (6) the offender cooperated with authorities in apprehending other participants in the crime or in making restitution to the victims for losses suffered, (7) the offender committed the crime through motivation to provide necessities for himself or herself or his or her family, and (8) the offender did not have a previous criminal record.

THE SENTENCING HEARING. For cases in which individuals have been convicted of serious crimes, **sentencing hearings** are usually conducted. A sentencing hearing is held so that defendants, their attorneys, prosecutors, and victims or their families can make statements to influence the sentencing decision. Judges are supposed to consider mitigating and aggravating circumstances surrounding the offense; the age, psychological and physical condition, and social/educational background of the offender; and the minimum and maximum statutory penalties of incarceration and/or fines accompanying the crime in arriving at a decision. Following the presentation of evidence and commentaries from the various interested parties, including the defendant, the judge imposes the sentence. The judge must resolve certain issues, including whether or not the contemplated sentence is fair. Also, the judge must determine the anticipated future dangerousness of the offender if leniency, such as probation, is considered.

The judge also has at his or her disposal several sentencing options, which may be creative sentences. **Creative sentencing,** or alternative sentencing, offers offenders, especially those who have committed relatively minor or nonviolent offenses, an opportunity to serve their sentences outside of the prison setting. Usually, alternative sentencing involves some form of community service, some degree of restitution to victims of crimes, becoming actively involved in educational or vocational training programs, or performing some other worthwhile service. The goals of alternative sentencing are twofold. First, it is designed to help offenders avoid imprisonment. Imprisonment is not always the best option for certain criminals, largely because of the likelihood that if imprisoned with other offenders, they may become more criminalized through their prisonization experience. Second, alternative sentencing is considered a reasonable means of reducing prison overcrowding and minimizing the high cost of incarceration.

THE ORGANIZATIONAL MILIEU OF PROSECUTORS AND JUDGES

The organizational milieu of prosecutors and judges is highly bureaucratized, particularly in more urban jurisdictions. This is because a fixed protocol and procedures govern prosecutors' offices and how criminal processing is conducted. Furthermore, judges are bound to observe the rules of criminal procedure that are rather precisely outlined for their particular jurisdictions. When conducting trials or sentencing convicted offenders, both judges and prosecutors must follow rules that have been proscribed by legislative mandate. If either prosecutors or judges depart from these rules to any significant degree, then their decisions are subject to question, usually in the form of appeals to higher courts. The appeals are usually grounded in technicalities (e.g., a judge or prosecutor violated one or more of the rules governing his or her conduct before, during, or after a criminal trial). This does not mean that prosecutors and judges are completely lacking in wiggle room for individualized decision making or applying their personal styles at different points in criminal processing, however.

The idea that the law is either black or white, although technically correct, is a fiction. A great deal of gray area exists between how the law should be applied and how it is actually applied. Prosecutors and the judiciary are constantly having to make judgment calls in the performance of their duties. These judgment calls are not easy to make under all conditions. For instance, prosecutors gain prominence and assure their continued performance as prosecutors by securing large numbers of convictions against criminal defendants. Prosecutors do not like to lose cases. More than a few prosecutors will engage in questionable actions and make ethically inappropriate decisions to influence case outcomes in their favor (Jonakait, 1987).

The mere fact that the court and its actors operate within a fixed bureaucratic context but with widely variable and diffuse personalized standards throughout the entire set of events associated with offender processing means that inappropriate behaviors for both judges and prosecutors are difficult to define and detect. Although public and private agencies have been established to function as sanctioning bodies to follow up on grievances filed by individuals who believe they have been somehow wronged by the criminal justice process, the fact is that only a small fraction of allegations against judges and prosecutors are ever sustained (Cominsky, Patterson, and Taylor, 1987; Kiel et al., 1994; Klein, 1984).

SELECTED ISSUES INVOLVING THE JUDICIARY AND PROSECUTORS

Plea Bargaining

Plea bargaining is a preconviction agreement between prosecutors and defense counsel involving a guilty plea from a defendant in exchange for some type of sentencing leniency. Plea bargaining originated in the 1830s in Boston, Massachusetts (Vogel, 1999). It arose as a part of political stabilization and an effort to legitimate institutions of self-rule. These were vital to the Whig Party's efforts to reconsolidate the political power of Boston's social and economic elite. To this end, the tradition of episodic leniency from British common law was recrafted into a new cultural form—plea bargaining—that drew conflicts into courts while maintaining elite discretion over sentencing policy (Vogel, 1999). Plea bargaining is commonplace in the United States, and it is also used in Canada and other countries. The primary objective of plea bargaining in countries in which it is used is expediency, not necessarily due process (Nasheri, 1998).

The four types of plea bargaining are (1) implicit plea bargaining, (2) judicial plea bargaining, (3) sentence recommendation bargaining, and (4) charge reduction bargaining. **Implicit plea bargaining** refers to the "going rates" or prevailing punishments for particular offenses in certain jurisdictions. For instance, it may be customary to impose a two-year sentence of incarceration for someone with a prior record who has committed aggravated assault. The actual maximum incarcerative penalty for aggravated assault may be 10 years in prison, but because of prison/jail overcrowding and other factors, maximum sentences for different offenses are seldom imposed. Thus, a mutual understanding can be reached between the prosecution and defense that the client likely will be offered a two-year sentence in exchange for a plea of guilty to the aggravated assault charge. It would be unrealistic of the defense counsel to expect to obtain probation for his or her client under these implicit circumstances; the defense attorney tries to make the best bargain under the circumstances.

Judicial plea bargaining is a sentence recommendation that is proposed by the judge in exchange for a plea of guilty from the defendant. More often than not, this occurs for misdemeanor cases that carry minimum penalties. Judges simply may offer defendants the opportunity to plead guilty to a lesser criminal charge in exchange for a fine instead of jail or prison time. The judge also may offer some alternative sentence, such as community service or victim restitution (Boland, 1997).

Sentence recommendation bargaining is initiated by prosecutors. Prosecutors have the direct charging responsibility after criminal charges have been filed against defendants. In effect, prosecutors promise defense counsels that they will recommend specific sentences to the sentencing judge if the defense counsel's client pleads guilty to a specific charge. The sentence recommendation, which may be probation, is considered significantly more lenient than the probable outcome of a trial and the actual sentence the judge might impose under those different circumstances.

Charge reduction bargaining is initiated by prosecutors as well. They may offer defendants the opportunity to plead guilty to less serious offenses than those for which they were originally charged. For example, a prosecutor may offer a second-degree murder charge to a defendant originally charged with first-degree murder and facing the death penalty, in exchange for a guilty plea. Charge reduction bargaining always involves downgrading original charges to less serious offenses in exchange for guilty pleas. The potential consequences for defendants who persist in their right to a trial, even a jury trial, are that they might be convicted of the more serious charges and be sentenced to death or lengthy imprisonment.

We have noted that plea bargaining accounts for over 90 percent of all misdemeanor and felony convictions. This means that protracted trials are avoided in all of these plea-bargained cases. It is difficult to envision the court system operating efficiently or effectively without some form of plea bargaining. Despite the fact that less than 10 percent of all criminals go to trial, court delays and crowded court dockets are commonplace.

Prosecutorial and Judicial Misconduct

In 1969, the American Bar Association formulated the Canons of Judicial Ethics (American Bar Association, 1972). The code represents the standards that judges should observe. It consists of statements of norms called canons, the accompanying text setting forth specific rules, and commentary. Unless otherwise indicated, the canons and text establish mandatory standards. Unfortunately, no procedures were enacted to ensure that judges would comply with these standards or ethical practices in their everyday court affairs (American Judicature Society, 1973).

Prosecutors also have evolved ethical standards by which to conduct themselves in prosecuting cases. Similar to judicial ethical standards, prosecutorial ethics have been clearly articulated by the American Bar Association and other professional societies. But again, no clear sanctioning mechanisms exist for prosecutors who abuse their offices or authority. This does not mean that judges and prosecutors are immune from criticism or can completely escape punishment or sanctions if they engage in misconduct of any kind. It means, however, that the methods currently in place to deal with misconduct of any kind are simply ineffective (Noonan and Winston, 1993; Pollock-Byrne, 1989).

One questionable prosecutorial practice is the use of subpoenas to compel defense counsels to appear before grand juries to provide testimony concerning certain clients they represent (Suny, 1987). These subpoenas have sought information relating to financial and business transactions of clients, client identity, and the source, amount, and method of payment of the attorney's fee. Such subpoenas are destructive of the attorney-client relationship and the adversary system and should be permitted only in exceptional circumstances (Suny, 1987).

Judges are not exempt from the subjectivity of questionable judgment calls in their decision making, either. When a judge denies a defense motion to introduce certain exculpatory evidence, this may seriously influence the trial outcome and increase the likelihood that a defendant will be convicted (Territo, Halsted,

COURT ORGANIZATION AND ADMINISTRATION

and Bromley, 1998). Judicial rulings are often reflections of a judge's own subjectivity about the case and what he or she believes to be true. A judge's ruling can allow or disallow the prosecution or defense the latitude to make or break a case against the accused. Subtle rulings at critical points during a trial may have profound effects on jury decision making. And the likelihood that a judge's rulings will be overturned on appeal is somewhat remote in most jurisdictions. In most jurisdictions in which judges are elected, incumbent judges are often reelected regardless of whether they are good or bad judges. Their popularity with the public is more critical than their ethical conduct and decision-making quality in trial proceedings (Kiel et al., 1994; Noonan and Winston, 1993).

Court Caseloads and Delays

ENTER PLEA BARGAINING.   With plea bargaining accounting for over 90 percent of all felony and misdemeanor convictions in the United States annually, it is difficult to imagine that our courts would have overcrowded dockets and suffer lengthy trial delays. The Speedy Trial Act of 1974 was supposed to speed up the process by which offenders were processed, from the time of their arrest to the time of trial. In federal district courts, there is a 100-day time line from the time someone is charged with a federal crime to the date of a trial. Many states copy the federal speedy trial provisions and use the 100-day time line. One of the lengthiest time lines is in New Mexico, which has a 180-day span from the time charges are filed against criminal suspects to their trial dates. But these time lines for both federal and state jurisdictions do not give us a true picture of how cases are actually processed and over what time intervals.

SPEEDY TRIALS?   Case delays occur that frequently violate speedy trial time lines. However, these delays are both normal and constitutional. Criminal defendants can ask for and usually get extensions in order for their defense counsels to prepare for trials. Witnesses must be interviewed and scheduled. Psychiatric examinations may need to be worked in and time must be allowed for them. Trial preparation for both prosecutors and defense counsels is a time-consuming process. Also, if the judge's court docket is clogged or glutted and it is impossible for a trial to proceed within the prescribed time interval from when someone is indicted and arraigned, this is a constitutional

circumstance that is beyond the judge's control and is considered an acceptable reason for a delay of a trial.

North Carolina is one of many states concerned with speedy trials and their application. In the late 1980s, a report was issued by the state's Speedy Trial Act Study Committee (1989). This report indicated that North Carolina's speedy trial provisions were actually interfering with case processing effectiveness by increasing the workload of the already overloaded staff of the courts (Speedy Trial Act Study Committee, 1989). The committee observed that many North Carolina trial judges were merely granting continuances of cases rather than concluding them with speedy trials. This meant more paperwork and precise tracking of cases for court personnel, particularly if certain suspects were being held in pretrial detention. One recommendation made by the committee was that judges should consider releasing offenders who are not brought to trial within a reasonable time period or within suggested guidelines developed by the state legislature.

NUMBERS AND LENGTHS OF CRIMINAL TRIALS. Just how many trials are there? In 1996, 997,973 felony convictions were recorded in state courts (Maguire and Pastore, 2000:432). Of these, 91 percent (905,957) were plea bargained. There were 92,015 actual trials, with 37,541 jury trials and 54,474 bench trials. In federal district courts, 48,532 felony cases were prosecuted, with 93.1 percent (45,207) plea bargained. This means that 3,325 felony trials were held in U.S. district courts in 1996.

The actual average length of time between an arrest for a felony and a convicted defendant's sentencing was 219 days in 1996. Jury trials in state courts for those charged with felonies averaged 355 days from arrest to sentencing. Bench trials in state courts averaged 202 days from arrest to sentencing. Even for cases in which guilty pleas were entered, the average was 235 days from arrest to sentencing. By specific offense, murder cases tried by juries in state courts averaged 447 days from arrest to sentencing. Even bench trials in murder cases in state courts averaged 268 days from arrest to sentencing (Maguire and Pastore, 2000:434). In U.S. district courts, justice is seemingly more swiftly dispensed, but the time from arrest to conviction for federal felonies actually averaged 10.4 months (Maguire and Pastore, 2000:429). About a third of all felony jury trials in federal courts lasted 20 days or longer. To say that U.S. courts are incredibly overworked and consumed with offender processing is an understatement. Incredibly, a study conducted of urban trial courts and speedy trial provisions in 1987, and the statistics cited, found that the American Bar Association had developed a "reasonable" standard as a gauge of measuring whether or not courts were functioning efficiently in case processing. The standard created was processing a case within *one year* from the time of an arrest (Goerdt et al., 1989). Not much changed in either state or federal case processing time during the 1990s, at least.

Court delays are not restricted to the United States. Similar delays have been reported in England, Canada, South Africa, and New South Wales (Frazer, 1993; McCoy, 1997; Weatherburn and Lind, 1996). Interestingly, organizational strategies have been attempted in each of these countries and elsewhere in an effort to streamline the trial process. Centralizing case processing was attempted in England, for example. The result was the increased production of waste, inefficiency, and more court delay than existed before centralization (Frazer, 1993).

OBSTACLES TO SPEEDY JUSTICE. At least 315 ideas for dealing with court congestion and delay have been generated by judges and court administrators in the past few decades. A majority of these ideas have been deemed unworkable, and most of the other ideas were submitted to various interested committees and organizations for further study (Snellenburg and Dickey, 1989). The Correctional Association of New York studied court delay and found several significant structural obstacles. These included issues relating to the discovery process, inadequate judicial training in efficient case management, inadequate motivation for judicial productivity, a lack of coordinated scheduling during a case, and an absence of a uniform case-tracking system (Correctional Association of New York, 1993). The commission recommended that court delays could be reduced by improving court leaders' commitment to change, accompanied by management changes and the designation of a strong central administrator with leadership capacity and authority. The commission suggested implementation of a formal, organized case management system that incorporated early and complete disclosure, a true revised speedy trial law, case management training for judges, an organized case-tracking system, realistic timetables, a case monitoring system with built-in accountability, and an integrated, computerized calendaring system.

But articulating what is needed and actually doing something about it are two different things.

DIVERTING INCREASING NUMBERS OF DRUG CASES TO SPECIAL DRUG COURTS AND OTHER EFFORTS TO SPEED UP CASE PROCESSING. Because of the increased importance attached to drug cases, a general movement began during the 1990s to create special drug courts to process drug offenders (Ostrom and Kauder, 1999). After all, drug cases require a substantial amount of court time. The thinking was that specialized drug courts would eliminate these sorts of cases from state and federal court dockets and court time can be better spent with other types of felonies. As of July 1998, there were 430 drug courts. Of these, 140 were operating for two years or less. About another 166 drug courts were being planned as of 1998 (Maguire and Pastore, 2000:77). These courts may make a considerable difference in the absolute volume of state and federal cases, since over a third of all offenses and criminal trials in 1996 were drug felonies, both for possession and trafficking (Maguire and Pastore, 2000:432). But even if 600 or more drug courts had been operating from 2000 to 2001, each of these courts would have had to process an average of 670 cases per year. That is a lot of cases to process. Undoubtedly, it will take more time and more drug courts to reduce existing court delays in future years.

COMPUTERS AND COURTROOMS. In our increasingly technical world, it would seem that computer use in courtrooms might speed things along. But even with state-of-the-art technology at our fingertips, only an imperceptible change has been seen in the speed of case processing (Polansky, 1993).

Other suggestions for speeding up the trial process include actually reducing the number of trials or their average duration and making more effective use of trial court capacity by eliminating court vacations and hiring more judges (Weatherburn, 1993). Unfortunately, shortening trials is easier said than done, since this would mean eliminating important testimony and evidence, which tends to protract trial proceedings. The unconstitutionality of such court time reductions and the subsequent unfairness to criminal defendants are obvious. Everyone charged with a crime is entitled to his or her day in court (or weeks or months as the individual case dictates). This issue has been addressed by more than a few researchers concerned with defendant rights (Martin and Maron, 1991). In the general case, court delays have been defined as a management problem and they continue to be so. Although court managers at different levels support the abstract concept of efficiency irrespective of the caseloads of their courts, insurmountable differences exist between judges, attorneys, clerks, and administrators that make practical problem solving impractical (Mays and Taggart, 1986).

One increasingly important consideration as courts move to computerize their recordkeeping and data-retrieval systems is the matter of public access to confidential records (SEARCH Group Inc., 1990). As efforts to computerize courtrooms and court operations progress, we must be increasingly sensitive to who should have access to increasingly sensitive courtroom information. Some recordkeeping is rather routine. However, psychiatric reports and other types of examinations that are considered confidential or perhaps not subject to discovery may be placed in computer systems and made available to persons who are not ordinarily authorized to have access to such information. A similar issue has emerged relating to the confidentiality of juvenile records in various jurisdictions (Virginia Commission on Youth, 1993).

CARROT-STICK TECHNIQUES FOR IMPROVING CASE PROCESSING. Even monetary incentives have been suggested to speed up case processing. In New York City, the Speedy Disposition Program was established in 1984 as a means of providing monetary incentives to district attorneys' offices to expedite cases more quickly. It was suggested that their attention should be directed to the oldest felony cases, thereby relieving the pressure on the city's overcrowded pretrial detention facilities. But the program failed because the prosecutors' offices lacked the managerial capacity to deal with the sheer volume of cases (Church and Heumann, 1989).

THE GROWING MOUNTAIN OF CIVIL LITIGATION. In U.S. district courts, a major problem is the rapidly increasing number of civil lawsuits that are being filed. About 85 percent of all federal court action is civil; only 15 percent is criminal. But even the small percentage of criminal cases that are heard in federal district courts are time consuming, as we have seen.

It has been recommended that federal prosecutors should not bring any narcotics cases into federal courts if they can file charges in state courts. But this merely complicates state court docketing and results in transferring court delay problems from one jurisdiction (federal) to another (state) (U.S. Federal Courts Study Committee, 1990).

PREEMPTIVE STRIKES BY JUDGES AND SUMMARY JUDGMENTS. How easy would it be for judges in federal and state courts to merely entertain and grant motions for dismissals of cases or summary judgments? Certainly this would speed up case processing time by eliminating protracted litigation. Sound bases must exist for granting motions to dismiss or summary judgments, however (Freedman, 1989). In criminal court actions, there are motions for summary judgment and dismissals granted frequently. In most of these instances, however, the bases for these judgments have been frivolity. Many lawsuits filed by state and federal inmates are considered frivolous by judges and a waste of valuable court time.

DIVERSION AND MEDIATION. It has been suggested that less serious cases should be diverted to mediation for resolution under civil rather than criminal circumstances (Cook, 1995). Pretrial diversion is a procedure through which criminal defendants are diverted to either a community-based agency for treatment or assigned to a counselor for social and/or psychiatric assistance. **Diversion** is an official halting or suspension of legal proceedings against a criminal defendant and a referral of that person to a treatment or care program administered by a nonjustice agency or private agency. Diversion is used primarily for first offenders who have not committed serious crimes. All divertees must comply with minimal behavioral requirements, such as remaining law abiding and reporting to the court regularly for a specified period, perhaps one year. Each diversion case is considered on its own merits.

Another increasingly used option for speeding up the trial process is **alternative dispute resolution (ADR).** ADR is a community-based, informal dispute settlement between offenders and their victims. Misdemeanants are most often targeted for participation in these programs. Increasing numbers of ADR programs are being implemented throughout the United States and world (Palumbo, Musheno, and Hallett,

1994). With early roots in the Midwest, victim/offender mediation or ADR programs now exist in over 100 U.S. jurisdictions, 54 in Norway, 40 in France, 26 in Canada, 25 in Germany, 18 in England, 20 in Finland, and eight in Belgium (Umbreit, 1994:25). Umbreit (1994:25) says that in most victim-offender programs, the process consists of four phases: (1) case intake from referral sources; (2) preparation for mediation, during which the mediator meets separately with the offender and the victim; (3) the mediation session, which consists of a discussion of what occurred and how people felt about it, followed by negotiation of a restitution agreement; and (4) follow-up activities such as monitoring restitution completion. Examples of the volume of referrals in specific mediation agencies are 591 mediations in 1991 in Albuquerque, New Mexico; 903 mediations in Minneapolis, Minnesota, in 1991; 541 mediations in Oakland, California, in 1991; and 1,107 mediations in 1991 in Austin, Texas (Umbreit, 1994:28).

ADR is also known as **restorative justice** (Bazemore, 1998). ADR involves the direct participation of the victim and offender, with the aim of mutual accommodation for both parties. The emphasis of ADR is on restitution rather than punishment, and the costs associated with it are small contrasted with trials (Axon and Hann, 1995). However, it is sometimes difficult to decide which cases are best arbitrated through ADR and which should be formally resolved through trial (Glensor and Stern, 1995). Alternative dispute resolution (ADR) is a relatively new phenomenon, but it is recognized increasingly as a means by which differences between criminals and their victims can be resolved through a conciliation, mediation, or arbitration process (Krapac, 1996).

THE MIDTOWN COMMUNITY COURT PROJECT. In selected jurisdictions, some communities are experimenting with problem-solving approaches to quality-of-life offenses. One project located in Manhattan, New York, was the Midtown Community Court Project (Sviridoff et al., 1997). The project included several departures from normal procedures in the city's criminal courts such as a coordinating team to foster collaboration with the community and other criminal justice agencies, an assessment team to determine if defendants have mental health or substance abuse problems or require shelter, a resource coordinator to match defendants with treatment facilities, community service projects intended to pay back the community harmed by crime, a community advisory board, court-based

mediation, and a court-based research unit. Increased use was made of community services over a three-year period of the project's duration. Arrest-to-arraignment time averaged 18 hours, substantially faster than in comparison to criminal courts. Sentencing produced more than double the frequency of intermediate sanctions than in other criminal courts, and increased use was made of community service and social service sentences. Compliance rates averaged about 75 percent compared with 50 percent compliance in comparison criminal courts. Although there was substantial evidence that the project contributed to improvements in the quality of life for the local area and that it succeeded in pulling together staff members from different agencies who worked as a team, the higher cost of the project compared with traditional offender processing suggested that it may be unworkable on a larger scale in this and other jurisdictions in future years, however.

SUMMARY

Courtrooms are the centerpiece of the criminal justice system. A defendant's guilt or innocence is determined through courtroom procedures. Courts are highly regulated organizations, adhering to a set of abstract rules and procedures set forth in either civil or criminal rules of procedure. These rules regulate virtually every stage of offender processing from the time persons are arrested and booked through how trials are conducted and the nature of sentencing if a defendant is convicted. In this respect, courts are highly bureaucratic entities with many of the characteristics set forth by Max Weber.

The United States has a dual court system consisting of federal courts and state courts. Within both the federal and state court systems, different levels of courts have a particular type of jurisdiction over certain matters and issues. In the federal system, the court structure is dominated by the U.S. Supreme Court, which is often termed the court of last resort. This is because this court hears and determines the outcome of all state and federal appeals. Below the U.S. Supreme Court are 13 circuit courts of appeal and over 500 U.S. district courts, which are basic federal trial courts. The lowest level of federal courts are the courts of U.S. magistrates, in which minor crimes are processed. State courts are structured similarly, with supreme courts that function to resolve all matters relevant to each state. All states have appellate courts and basic trial courts that are known by different names, depending on the jurisdiction. These court levels are similar to Weber's hierarchy of authority in an organization, because lower courts are answerable to higher, appellate courts. The rule of law dictates all aspects of what transpires in these courts.

All federal and state trial courts have courtroom work groups consisting of judges, prosecutors, defense counsel, court reporters, bailiffs, and court clerks. Judges and prosecutors in state courts are either elected or appointed, whereas judges and prosecutors in federal courts are appointed. Judges, prosecutors, and defense counsel are expected to adhere to codes of ethics that regulate their conduct to avoid the appearance of impropriety. Both the federal and state court systems are adversarial. A primary objective of prosecutors is to obtain convictions against defendants, whereas defense counsel attempt to win acquittals for their clients.

The trial process itself is tightly regulated. Trials are either bench trials, in which judges decide the case facts, or jury trials, in which jurors or finders of fact deliberate and decide a defendant's guilt or innocence. Jurors are selected from veniremen lists, and they are expected to take their jury duties seriously. In most jurisdictions, juries must be unanimous in their finding of the guilt or innocence of the accused.

When defendants are found guilty, they are sentenced, usually at the conclusion of a sentencing hearing. Sentencing hearings are proceedings that enable judges and others to hear aggravating and mitigating circumstances that might enhance or lessen the harshness of the sentence to be imposed. Several sentencing schemes have been described. These include indeterminate sentencing, determinate sentencing, presumptive or guidelines-based sentencing, and mandatory sentencing. Depending on the jurisdiction, judges must abide by the particular sentencing scheme that has been approved by the legislature.

One important issue of relevance to defendants and courts generally is plea bargaining. Plea bargaining is a preconviction agreement worked out between a prosecutor and defense counsel in which a guilty plea to a criminal charge is entered in exchange for some form of leniency in sentencing. Four types of plea bargaining include implicit plea bargaining, judicial plea bargaining, sentence recommendation bargaining, and charge reduction bargaining. Plea bargaining is controversial, since it involves a waiver of certain constitutional rights by defendants who forgo their right to a trial. Despite the controversy surrounding plea bargaining, it accounts for over 90 percent of all criminal convictions in the United States annually.

Other issues include judicial and prosecutorial misconduct and how to minimize or prevent it. Considering the number of state and federal judges and prosecutors, the amount of judicial and prosecutorial misconduct is not especially extensive. Various sanctioning mechanisms have been established for recalling judges who are incompetent or corrupt. However, the rate of judicial recall is quite low. Similarly, few prosecutors are removed from their positions, since it is often difficult to prove misconduct even when such behavior occurs and is detected.

Judicial and prosecutorial interests are focused on speeding up case processing and avoiding trial delays. Several alternative court options have been examined to facilitate and expedite the application of justice in American courts. Diversion and alternative dispute resolution also have been suggested as options to the trial process itself.

QUESTIONS FOR REVIEW

1. How are U.S. federal judges appointed and how does their appointment influence courtroom procedure?

2. What are writs of *certiorari* and what are their uses? How can cases get scheduled for hearing before the U.S. Supreme Court? What is the rule of fours?

3. Differentiate between courts of limited and general jurisdiction. What are circuit courts and their functions?

4. What are two popular judicial selection methods? Compare and contrast the weaknesses and strengths of the two methods.

5. What are the functions and roles of prosecutors for both the state and federal government?

6. Identify four different kinds of court officers. Describe their functions.

7. What is the difference between bench and jury trials? Must all jury trials be unanimous when jurors vote on the guilt or innocence of defendants? Why or why not? Explain.

8. What are the functions of juries?

9. What are four types of sentencing systems? What are their weaknesses and strengths?

10. What is plea bargaining? What are four different forms of plea bargaining?

SUGGESTED READINGS

Abraham, Henry J. (1998). *The Judicial Process: An Introductory Analysis of the Courts of the United States, England, and France* (7/e). New York: Oxford University Press.

Cole, David (1999). *No Equal Justice: Race and Class in the American Criminal Justice System.* New York: New Press.

Ostrom, Brian J., and Roger A. Hanson (1999). *Efficiency, Timeliness, and Quality: A New Perspective from Nine State Criminal Trial Courts.* Williamsburg, VA: National Center for State Courts.

• CASE STUDIES •

---

1. THE DATING JUDGE

Molly McGinnis, a rape victim, testified in the case against her rapist, William Franks. Franks was charged with multiple counts of rape, oral copulation, and attempted murder. Following a jury trial in which Franks was found guilty, Lincoln County Superior Court Judge Benjamin Sadler sentenced Franks to two life sentences plus 105 years to life for the various rape and attempted murder counts. Then something strange happened.

Following the conviction and sentencing, Judge Sadler, 56, who has been married for 25 years and has two grown children, invited the prosecutor, Kim Wesley, and the victim, Molly McGinnis, to his office. He complimented the victim on her trial testimony and invited both the prosecutor and McGinnis to join him and his family for an upcoming holiday at a local restaurant. About an hour later, Judge Sadler called Wesley's office and advised her that because of a conflict in his schedule, he would have to cancel the proposed dinner plans at the restaurant. But when McGinnis called Judge Sadler's office to accept the invitation, Judge Sadler said that his wife was ill and that he and McGinnis should go ahead and meet at a restaurant anyway. Also, he said that Kim Wesley would not be joining them because of previous commitments. He referred to his dinner plans with McGinnis as a "date." Subsequently, McGinnis began to have doubts about the dinner with the judge without his family present. She called and cancelled the dinner plans. Later she brought the matter to the attention of Kim Wesley, and an investigation of Judge Sadler's actions was commenced.

The prosecutor's office subsequently alleged that Judge Sadler had violated judicial ethics by suggesting that the victim meet him at local restaurant for a date, according to Assistant District Attorney Michael Spandau. Spandau said in a letter that "it is our opinion that Judge Sadler's conduct might have created an appearance of impropriety and might constitute a violation of the judicial ethics code. Judicial ethics rules ban a judge from using the prestige of his office to advance personal interests."

In response to these allegations, Judge Sadler's lawyer, Bruce Black, said that his client had done nothing wrong. "Judge Sadler denies everything, absolutely and adamantly, that there is an impropriety or an ethical violation. I think he was trying to comfort her," Black said. Subsequently, after the allegations had been made, Judge Sadler was transferred from the Criminal Courts Building in the city to a civil court in Brockton, a suburban community. Defense lawyer Erin Erickson, who represented the convicted rapist, Franks, said she would ask the appellate court for a new trial for her client based on Sadler's conduct.

Questions for Discussion

1. Should judges ask victims to dinner following rape and attempted murder trials, even if it is an innocent-appearing family event?
2. Was the judge wrong to invite Ms. McGinnis to dinner by himself at the restaurant and to refer to their dinner as a date? Why or why not?
3. What sanctions would you impose on the judge, if indeed this is a true case of an ethical violation? What do you think?
4. What should the relationships be among the judge, defendant, and other courtroom actors?
5. Should Franks get a new trial because of the judge's alleged impropriety? What do you think?

• CASE STUDIES •

2. THE UNDERSTAFFED PROSECUTOR'S OFFICE

You are the state's attorney and have just met with the city manager who has advised you that for the next fiscal year, you will have to operate with a budget cut of 20 percent. This is a sizable cut, but it is necessary because city revenue was down by at least 20 percent the previous year. Thus, all departments and divisions are experiencing budget cuts. You quickly assess the state's attorney's office and your needs mentally. You do not really need new assistant state's attorneys, since you hired four new prosecutors during the past year. Your case flow is moderate, but the number of drug cases coming to your attention has increased dramatically in recent months. You wonder if the need to hire more prosecutors to handle the anticipated greater case volume may arise. But the bottom line is that the budget cut means that you must make some hard decisions about your staff. In order to remain within the budget, the 20 percent cut means that at least two prosecutors are in jeopardy of losing their jobs. It is your position as state's attorney to recommend which two prosecutors you must release.

You have eight prosecutors who work on a large number of cases. Four of these persons have been with the state's attorney's office for five years or more. One prosecutor, Richard Jefferies, 53, has been with the office for 20 years. As mentioned previously, four of the prosecutors were hired recently. Two of the new prosecutors are married, and one has a family, including a newborn baby. The other married prosecutor was recently married and is living in a low-priced condominium west of town. The two new single prosecutors have previous city work experience and are somewhat older. One is the brother-in-law of a city council member, and the other is the nephew of the mayor. You must decide which of the prosecutors in your office should be terminated to get your budget within the new figure given you by the city manager.

You agonize for several days over this matter and attempt to think of alternative ways of cutting the budget back without having to terminate employees. One day while you are thinking about the problem, one of your long-term prosecutors, Carla McFate, comes to you with a grievance about another prosecutor. The other prosecutor, Richard Jefferies, was caught drinking on the job. Jefferies has had an alcohol problem in the past, but he seemed to be over it, through counseling and self-control. But Jefferies has recently divorced and is taking it hard. Several other prosecutors will back up McFate's report of Jefferies's drinking. In your office, drinking on the job or abusing drugs is punishable by suspension or termination or both. But Jefferies has a good prosecution record over the years. There is no indication that his drinking problem has affected his ability to prosecute and win cases.

Questions for Discussion

1. What should you say to McFate about how you plan to handle the report about Jefferies? Should anyone else be consulted concerning this matter?

2. What kinds of budget cutting can you think of that does not involve the termination of one or more of your prosecutors?

3. Would you want to discuss the matter of Jefferies's drinking directly with Jefferies? Why or why not?

4. If you chose to discuss the incident with Jefferies, what would you ask him? Do you think that Jefferies is a good possibility for termination or early retirement? Why or why not?

5. Should terminations be based on one's seniority, or should greater weight be given to one's effectiveness in prosecuting cases? What criteria would you use to decide who to terminate?

CHAPTER
11

JAIL AND PRISON ORGANIZATION AND ADMINISTRATION

KEY TERMS

Admin max

Auburn State Penitentiary

Auburn system

Authoritarian model

Bridewell Workhouse

Bureaucratic-lawful model

Congregate system

Human services approach

Inmate control model

Jail

Jailhouse lawyers

John Howard

Maxi-maxi prison

Maximum-security prisons

Medium-security prisons

Megajails

Minimum-security prisons

Negligence

Negligent assignment

Negligent entrustment

Negligent retention

Negligent training

Penitentiary Act of 1779

Pennsylvania system

Philadelphia Society for Alleviating the
  Miseries of Public Prisons

Prison

Prison overcrowding

Privatization

Professionalization

Shared-powers model

Solitary confinement

Superintendents

Tiers

Tier system

Wardens

Workhouses

CHAPTER OBJECTIVES

The following objectives are intended:

1. To differentiate between jails and prisons and describe their important characteristics

2. To describe the history of jails, including their goals and functions

3. To describe the characteristics of jail personnel, their selection, and training

4. To examine selected jail issues, including overcrowding, inmate classification, jail architecture, and privatization

5. To describe the history of prisons in the United States, including major prison functions and goals

6. To describe the characteristics of prison administrators and alternative management styles

7. To describe types of prison inmates and how they are classified

8. To examine selected prison issues, including overcrowding, jailhouse lawyers and litigation, and the legal liabilities of prison employees

INTRODUCTION

When we think of corrections, large prisons such as Alcatraz, Sing Sing, or San Quentin may come to mind. *Corrections* is a large umbrella term that encompasses a wide variety of agencies and institutions designed to manage convicted offenders. In fact, a portion of the managed correctional population of offenders happens to be unconvicted. Traditional categorizations for corrections usually consist of (1) jails, (2) prisons or penitentiaries, and (3) community corrections. In this chapter, we examine the organization and administration of jails and prisons. In the following chapter, we give close attention to the organization and operations of community corrections, a growing feature of American society.

This chapter is organized as follows: First, we distinguish between jails and prisons. Each type of organization, regardless of its elaborateness, is designed to perform specific functions. Great variation can be found among jails and prisons concerning their respective functions. Thus, it is important to examine first what is meant by jails, how they originated, and what were their intended uses. Over the years, jail functions have changed. These changes in functions and jail operations are described. Subsequently, we examine prisons, their origins, and past and present functions. Similarly, prisons or penitentiaries have undergone a metamorphosis of sorts. Although their general functions have remained fairly constant, several significant events have occurred that have caused important changes in how prisons are managed and operated.

Attention is given next to the recruitment of both jail and prison administrators and officers. Those who work in such correctional environments are to some extent at risk, since the inmate populations supervised are potentially volatile and dangerous. For jail officers especially, the daily changing inmate populations of their organizations have large numbers of mentally ill offenders who pose unusual supervisory problems as well as risks. Attention is given to the training received by correctional officers of both jails and prisons. Several important issues are examined that are relevant for both aggregates of employees, including their legal liabilities in relation to supervised inmates.

Next, we discuss several management models that typify prison wardens and superintendents; these management models also might be applicable to those in charge of jails, especially large ones. One pervasive problem of jail and prison management is overcrowding. Rising crime rates and jail and prison construction programs that have failed to keep pace with the numbers of convicted offenders entering corrections daily underscore the importance of learning how to manage growing populations of inmates effectively. One negative consequence of chronic overcrowding is increasing inmate litigation filed against jail and prison systems. Jailhouse lawyers, inmates who have acquired some legal expertise, have been instrumental in bringing successful lawsuits against many jails and prisons. Sometimes the results of these suits have been jail and prison improvements. Some of these lawsuit issues are examined.

As inmate populations have increased, the need for more prisons has become critical. The private sector has responded to this need by delving into inmate management for both adult and juvenile inmate populations. Several private corporations have entered the correctional field and presently operate numerous facilities in many states. Some controversy exists about whether or not private interests should become involved in corrections, and this privatization controversy is described. The chapter concludes with an examination of the legal liabilities of jail and prison officials and officers.

JAILS AND PRISONS: CATALOGING THE DIFFERENCES

Prisons are intended and designed to house long-term offenders who usually are convicted of more serious offenses compared with those housed in jails. Generally, **jails** are intended and designed to house less serious offenders for shorter incarcerative periods. Exceptions to these generalizations can be found, however. Before we consider these exceptions, let us review some of the major differences between jails and prisons. Following are some of the characteristics of jails as compared to prisons:

- Jails have a greater diversity of inmates, including (1) witnesses for trials, (2) suspects or pretrial detainees, (3) defendants awaiting trial who are unable to post bail or whose bail was denied, (4) juveniles awaiting transfer to juvenile facilities or detention, (5) persons serving short-term sentences for public drunkenness, driving while intoxicated, or city ordinance violations, (6) mentally ill or disturbed persons awaiting hospitalization, and (7) overflow from state and federal prison populations (Cornelius, 1997).

- Jails do not have vocational, technical, or educational programs or facilities associated with long-term incarceration, and most jails do not have industries such as are found in prisons, recreation yards, psychological or social counseling, or therapy.

- Jail personnel have less training hours. Many jail personnel are untrained, undertrained, or otherwise less qualified to supervise inmates.

- Jails are not elaborately divided into maximum-, medium-, or minimum-security areas; they also lack guard towers with armed correctional officers who patrol regularly.

- Jails are not surrounded by barbed perimeter wire or razor wire, nor are they equipped with underground sound-detection equipment and other exotic electronic devices to detect prisoners digging or otherwise attempting to escape.

- Jail inmate culture is less pronounced and persistent; this is ensured by a high degree of inmate turnover on a daily basis.

- The physical plant of jails is substandard, with many jails under court order to improve their physical facilities to comply with minimum health and safety standards. (Cornelius, 1997)

One of the most significant differences between prisons and jails is their respective admission rates. In 1998, about 1.4 million state and federal inmates were in prison custody. The average daily population of inmates in U.S. jails in 1998 was about 600,000 (Maguire and Pastore, 2000:481). There are about 550,000 new state and federal prison admissions and about 360,000 releases from state and federal prisons annually (Maguire and Pastore, 2000:496–497). But there are between 10 and 13 *million* jail admissions and releases annually (Maguire and Pastore, 2000). This means that it takes about three years for the nation's prison population to turn over just once, but the jail population turns over 20 to 25 times each year (Maguire and Pastore, 2000).

JAILS: SMALL AND LARGE JAIL SYSTEMS

The word *jail* originated from an old English term, *gaol* (also pronounced "jail"), which was used as early as A.D. 1166 in a declaration by Henry II of England. Henry II established gaols as a part of the Assize or Constitution of Clarendon (Roberts, 1997). Gaols were locally administered and operated, housing many of society's misfits, including paupers and vagrants, drunkards, thieves, murderers, debtors, highwaymen, trespassers, orphan children, and prostitutes. Many religious dissidents were housed in these gaols as a punishment for not following the precepts of the powerful Church of England.

Jails and Local Political Control

One feature common to most jails that originated in England and persists today in most U.S. jurisdictions is local political control over the administration and operation of jails by sheriffs. Sheriffs are elected officials, and thus, political influence on jails and jail conditions is considerable. We might suspect that changing jail conditions from one administration to the next are largely a reflection of local political control changes that occur through elections and new administrative appointments.

The gaols of England were originally designed as holding facilities for law violators. Accused law violators were held for trial until their guilt or innocence could be determined. Such persons would be termed pretrial detainees today, and these people make up a significant proportion of the present U.S. jail population. In England, however, these persons often were held for extended periods, for one year or longer, before their cases were ever heard. In the meantime, they were subject to inhumane conditions characterized by filth and squalor. In the sixteenth century, many gaols were transformed into **workhouses,** which were established because of merchant demands for cheap labor. One of these was the **Bridewell Workhouse,** which was established in 1557.

It is important to recognize this type of facility and why it was perpetuated for so many years. First, Bridewell Workhouse accommodated many of the city's vagrants and general riffraff. The jail and workhouse sheriffs were quick to cash in on the cheap labor these facilities generated, and they profited greatly as a result of this exploitation of forced labor. In short, sheriffs hired out their inmates to the highest bidders. These inmates performed skilled and semiskilled tasks for interested merchants. Although the manifest functions of workhouses and prisoner labor were to improve their moral and social fiber, the real reason for their prolonged detention was labor exploitation and profiteering among sheriffs and sheriffs' deputies. Most of the monies collected from inmate labor were pocketed by corrupt jail and workhouse officials. This system of inmate labor exploitation continued in the

American colonies during the 1600s and 1700s. Early colonial jails housed orphans, prostitutes, drunkards, thieves, and robbers. These persons were most frequently crowded into large, dormitory-style rooms with hay and blankets for beds. No regard for inmate health or rehabilitation was evident among sheriffs and other officials.

THE PHILADELPHIA SOCIETY FOR ALLEVIATING THE MISERIES OF PUBLIC PRISONS. But William Penn, the founder of Pennsylvania, and members of the Quaker faith made substantial changes and reforms in the nature and operations of jails, especially after the Revolutionary War. For instance, the Quakers were able to incorporate several of William Penn's earlier correctional philosophies through the creation in 1787 of the **Philadelphia Society for Alleviating the Miseries of Public Prisons.** This society consisted of many prominent Philadelphia citizens, philanthropists, and religious reformers. They believed prison and jail conditions should be changed and that more comfortable living conditions should be provided for inmates. Members of this Society visited each jail and prison in the city daily, bringing food, clothing, and religious instruction to inmates. Some of these members were educators who sought to assist prisoners in acquiring basic skills such as reading and writing. Subsequently, the deplorable conditions of jails were brought to the attention of politicians who decided that jail operations ought to be changed. One fact that helped influence these politicians to change jail conditions was that men, women, and children were being held in common areas. One can only imagine the sexual exploitation by the strong of the weak in such conditions.

In 1790, the Pennsylvania legislature authorized the renovation of a facility originally constructed on Walnut Street in 1776, a two-acre structure initially designed to house the overflow resulting from overcrowding of the High Street Jail. The Walnut Street Jail was both a workhouse and a place of incarceration for all types of offenders. But this 1790 renovation was quite innovative because (1) it separated the most serious prisoners from others in 16 large solitary cells, (2) it separated other prisoners according to the seriousness of their offense, and (3) it separated prisoners according to gender. Also, inmates were assigned to various kinds of productive labor depending on their gender. Women made clothing and performed washing and mending chores. Skilled inmates worked as carpenters and shoemakers and in other occupations.

Unskilled prisoners beat hemp or jute for ship caulking. Prisoners received daily wages for their work that were used to offset their daily maintenance costs.

JAIL INFORMATION AND INMATE POPULATION GROWTH, 1880–1998. Information about the early growth of jails in the United States is limited. The U.S. Census Bureau began to compile information about jails in 1880 (Cahalan, 1986:73). At 10-year intervals since 1880, jail information was obtained according to inmate race, place of birth, gender, and age. Originally, the U.S. Census Bureau presented data separately for county jails, city prisons, workhouses, houses of correction, and leased county prisoners. In 1923, however, figures were combined to reflect more accurately what we now describe as jail statistics. The jail inmate population in 1880 was 18,686, and it grew to 592,462 in 1998 (Maguire and Pastore, 2000).

Over the years, U.S. jail conditions have been reported as unfavorable: (1) Most of the U.S. jails were built before 1970, and many were built five decades or more before that; (2) local control of jails often results in erratic policies that shift with each political election, thus forcing jail guards and other personnel to adapt to constantly changing conditions and jail operations; and (3) jail funding has low priority in budgeting in most jurisdictions; thus, with limited operating funds, the quality of jail services and personnel is considerably lower than state and federal prison standards and personnel.

Currently, no one knows for sure the exact number of jails in the United States at any given time. Between 1950 and 1998, the jail population grew by 600 percent. A substantial decrease in the number of jails in the United States was seen between 1970 and 1997, with 4,037 jails reported in 1970 and 3,328 jails reported in 1998 (Maguire and Pastore, 2000). How can fewer existing jails accommodate greater jail inmate populations? One reason is that many old jails have been demolished, remodeled, and/or expanded. Many new and larger jails have been constructed to replace smaller, older ones.

ACCREDITING JAILS AND JAIL PERSONNEL. Because many jails are small, it has been difficult to stimulate interest among local officials to accredit them through certification from any national organization. The American Correctional Association Division of Standards and Accreditation reports that often, hesitancy on the part of jail officials and sheriffs to apply for accreditation is due to a lack of funds (Thompson and Mays, 1991). The primary benefits of accreditation include (1) protecting the life, safety, and health of both jail staffs and inmates; (2) assessing the strengths and weaknesses of jails to maximize their resources and implement necessary changes; (3) minimizing the potential for costly, time-consuming litigation through negligence and other liability; (4) enhancing the jail's credibility with courts and the public; (5) achieving professional and public recognition of good performance; and (6) improving staff and inmate morale (Washington, 1987:15).

Most county jails throughout the United States have sought accreditation from organizations such as the American Jail Association and the American Correctional Association. The El Paso County (Colorado) sheriffs' office, for instance, is devising policies and procedures to enhance inmate programs and officer safety in compliance with nationally accepted standards evolved from the ACA (Hilte, 1998:33–34). Recommendations are solicited from both the private sector and from corrections agencies to improve jail officer effectiveness with various forms of jail training in jurisdictions such as Alameda County, California (Ryan and Plummer, 1999).

Administering Jail Systems

In the majority of jurisdictions, jails are county operated and funded from local sources. Most large cities in the United States also have jails. These city jails are staffed by the local police department. As much diversity exists in jail operations as there are jails in the United States. Traditionally, the chief executive officer in charge of jail operations is the county sheriff, an elected position. No special qualifications exist for those who aspire to be sheriffs. Because these posts are filled most often by elected officials, some sheriffs may be ex-police officers, ex-sheriffs' deputies, ex-restaurant managers, or even ex-school superintendents. A National Sheriffs' Association exists to disseminate information to its membership about jails and jail problems. Except for this organization, however, there is a distinct lack of resources to foster a unified approach to promotion of national sheriff professionalism or consistency of performance in managing jail operations (Senese, 1991).

JAIL MANAGEMENT AND OPERATIONS. Most jails in the United States are locally operated by sheriffs' departments. Sheriffs appoint chief jailers and jail staff. They also administer and monitor the health and safety of jail inmates. Other duties of sheriffs include protecting their counties from criminals and ensuring public safety, as described in more detail in Chapter 9.

The Functions and Goals of Jails

Jails are administered to fulfill some specific functions and/or attain certain goals, including the following:

1. Hold pretrial detainees
2. House offenders sentenced to short terms of incarceration
3. Hold witnesses in protective custody
4. Hold convicted offenders who are awaiting sentencing
5. Temporarily house juvenile offenders
6. Confine misdemeanants, drunks, and derelicts
7. House the mentally ill
8. Hold prisoners wanted by other jurisdictions on detainer warrants
9. Hold probation and parole violators
10. Accommodate state and federal prison inmate overflow

Jail Personnel, Recruitment, and Selection

Jail officers frequently have little or no formal training in law enforcement (Poole and Pogrebin, 1997). Sheriffs' deputies tend to receive lower pay and have lower prestige compared with officers employed by large cities. There are exceptions, such as California and Nevada, where deputy sheriffs receive higher average salaries than in other jurisdictions. One indication of the low status and prestige of jail correctional officers is that some sheriffs assign their regular deputies to jailer duty as a punishment for violating one or more department rules or disciplinary infractions.

Stringent minimal educational requirements are lacking, since these requirements would decrease greatly the available job pool of applicants for jail officer positions. High school diplomas or GED certificates are required as educational minimums in many jurisdictions. Jail staff often are untrained in subjects such as search and seizure and how visitations should be supervised. A primary reason it is difficult for jails to recruit and retain high-quality jail personnel is low pay. In 1998, for example, the average starting salary for jail officers nationwide was $24,706, ranging from a low annual salary of $17,000 in McCracken, Kentucky, to $32,856 in Ramsey, Minnesota (Camp and Camp,

1999a:288). The average turnover rate was 13.1 percent, with the largest jails having the lowest turnover at 8.9 percent and the smaller jails having the greatest turnover at 16.4 percent. The differences in labor turnover rates are likely attributable to better pay and working conditions in the larger jails compared with the smaller ones.

The average jail administrator's salary is $71,014, with a low annual salary of $48,000 in Broome, New York, to a high of $104,104 in San Luis Obispo, California. Average starting lieutenants' annual salaries were $49,470. Titles for jail administrators vary among jurisdictions. For example, 52 percent of all jail systems in the United States are administered by sheriffs, 19 percent by directors, 10 percent by superintendents, and the rest by wardens, captains, superintendents, and chief deputies (Camp and Camp, 1999a).

A distribution of selected sociodemographic characteristics for U.S. jail staff for 1998 is shown in Table 11.1. Approximately 190,000 jail personnel were employed in 1998, with about 70 percent of these performing roles as jail officers (Maguire and Pastore, 2000). In 1998, about 72 percent of all jail officers were male and 70 percent were white (Camp and Camp, 1999a:265). Statistics for newly hired jail officers in 1997 indicated that over 68 percent were male and 66 percent were white. Additionally, 71 percent of all jail officers have been in their positions for two years or less. Approximately 33 percent of all officers are over age 30. About 42 percent of all jail officers have had some college experience.

Correctional supervision encompasses a much wider area compared with the vast majority of government agencies and businesses operating today (Kerle, 1995:5). Line officers in jails are supposed to supervise and manage inmates. But competent inmate management and supervision is acquired only through an effective training program in which various skills are transmitted. Jail managers and staff should receive more training relative to ethics and responsibility, human relations skills, progressive staff discipline, and jail management techniques. All too often, jail supervision of inmates is nothing more than monitoring cell blocks every half hour or so. Giving staff more responsibilities for managing inmates means greater participatory management. Empowering more staff to act on their own, especially when accompanied by more effective human relations training, can do much to improve staff effectiveness and make jail organization and operation run more smoothly.

The nature of training jail supervisors and staff receive has been described in literature examining the criminal justice system (Cornelius, 1995:62). Jail staff have been encouraged to adopt a **human services approach** during their periods of inmate supervision. First, jail staff must recognize that there is considerable inmate diversity, and that this diversity goes well beyond ethnic, racial, and gender differences. Many jail inmates cannot handle being confined, some constantly complain, and some anger easily. Coupled with overcrowding, budget constraints, manipulative inmates, and lawsuits, these different dimensions of jail supervision and inmate diversity make inmate management more complicated than it might appear (Cornelius, 1995:62).

Three essential components in jail inmate control are (1) effective planning, (2) close cooperation with other criminal justice system components, and (3) the development of an array of intermediate sentencing options and alternatives to pretrial incarceration. Planning is crucial to maximizing a jail's effectiveness. Good jail managers can anticipate future jail growth and potential problem areas. Good supervisors need to be thoroughly familiar with jail operations as well as have exceptional interpersonal skills. The right kinds of supervisors can make all the difference in the world whether a jail is effective or ineffective. Poor supervision leads to employee dissatisfaction and poor security (Sigurdson, 1996:9–11).

JAIL OFFICER ATTITUDES AND WORK PERFORMANCE. Many morale problems can be found in jails throughout the United States. Ken Kerle has studied the morale and training of jail officers. One of his findings is that jail officers often are poorly trained. Furthermore, jail policies are frequently absent. Pervasive inequality also exists among male and female officers regarding wages. These are clear impediments to overall efficiency in jails and to personal job satisfaction. Kerle says that opportunities for promotion often are thwarted primarily by relegation of female officers to work only with female inmates. Kerle thinks that more jail administrators will have to give up their former stereotypes of female officers in order for significant change to occur. Strong leadership is crucial to the advancement of all qualified jail personnel, according to Kerle (1998).

For example, the Mecklenberg County Jail in North Carolina has implemented new awareness programs designed to improve communications among all jail staff. In 1994, Sheriff Jim Pendergraph became

■ **TABLE 11.1** JAIL OFFICER AND ADMINISTRATOR CHARACTERISTICS, 1998

CHARACTERISTIC	OFFICERS (%)	STAFF/ADMINISTRATORS (%)
Gender		
Male	71.6	68.4
Female	28.4	31.6
Race/Ethnicity		
White	69.7	74.3
Black	28.4	18.7
Other	1.9	7.0
1997 Hires		
Male	68.4	74.6
Female	31.6	25.4
White	66.3	68.7
Black	29.9	27.6
Other	3.8	3.7
Education		
High school or less	18.0	8.0
Some college	42.0	36.0
College graduate+	40.0	56.0
Length of Time in Jail Corrections		
Less than 1 year	34.0	28.0
1–2 years	37.0	35.0
3–4 years	19.0	21.0
5 or more years	10.0	16.0
Age		
21 or younger	16.0	4.0
22–25	22.0	21.0
26–30	29.0	33.0
31–40	25.0	26.0
40+	8.0	16.0

Sources: Compiled by author from data provided by Camp and Camp, 1999a and Maguire and Pastore, 2000.

the new administrator of a 614-bed, direct-supervision facility and outfitted it with the most up-to-date, state-of-the-art security equipment, a massive kitchen designed to feed 10,000 persons, and a centralized agency training facility (Emerick, 1996:53). Initially, low morale was apparent among the jail staff and labor turnover among the jail staff was high. Pendergraph found that many jail staff did not know what was expected of them. They were unaware of avenues by which they could be promoted, or even whom to report to for advice and information. Most of his jail officers performed their 12-hour shifts and left.

Pendergraph knew that changes had to be made. In December 1995, he organized small focus groups within his jail. Fifty officers were selected at random and divided into five groups of 10 each. These groups met one hour a week for a month. During these meetings, they shared information about their work, their personal feelings, and their personal interests when not working at the jail. Later meetings encouraged complaints, grievances, and concerns. The sheriff met with each group and encouraged all officers to say whatever was on their minds. Each group devised a list of problems and possible solutions for them. Later, he involved all jail personnel in decision making that affected their own areas and gave each officer responsibility for making changes in their work routines. Most of the group's suggestions were implemented, and Pendergraph distributed memos to inform all jail officers of the changes generated through these focus groups. In short, Pendergraph gave all officers significant input in influencing jail affairs. By 1996, Pendergraph and his officers were working together on other strategic ideas for improving communications within the jail (Emerick, 1996:58). Pendergraph believes that he has created more positive attitudes among his staff and that employee morale has improved markedly. One indication of this is that labor turnover has decreased greatly.

FORMAL JAIL OFFICER TRAINING PROGRAMS. The actual amount of formal training received by jail officers varies greatly among jurisdictions (Koren, 1995:43–44). Prior to the 1970s, jail officer education and training was almost nonexistent. Later, correspondence courses were offered in jail management. By the 1980s, state and local training services were established in Michigan and other jurisdictions. In Michigan, for example, prospective jail officers were given 160-hour basic training courses and experiences through the Michigan Corrections Officers Training Council (Durkee, 1996:60). At Lansing Community College in Michigan, courses are offered in prisoner behavior, first aid, stress management, sexual harassment, ethics, correctional law, booking/intake, cultural diversity, defensive tactics, prevention of inmate suicides, and custody/security. All of this formal training is designed to professionalize jail staff and provide them with a better understanding of jail clientele (Durkee, 1996:59–60).

Such certification provides entry-level skills for the person who wants to enter the job market as a corrections officer at a jail or local lockup after two semesters of study. Besides this academic preparation, a 160-hour Local Corrections Basic Training program was developed in Michigan in the late 1980s (Durkee, 1996:58). This training provided useful skills for officers who were already employed at one of the local county jails or city police lockups. The training was an important step and signified a substantial upgrading of skills for participating officers. Similar programs

have been incorporated into the curricula at participating colleges and universities in other jurisdictions, such as Washburn University in Topeka, Kansas (Heim, 1993:18–19).

Considerable effort has been made in recent years to upgrade and improve the quality of jail correctional officers and other correctional personnel generally (Tartaglini and Safran, 1996). Additional education and training for jail personnel is good practice, and jail officer **professionalization** has been significantly improved as a result (Koren, 1995:43). Further, additional training will make these officers more effective in dealing with culturally diverse inmates. Formerly, the selection of correctional officers emphasized physical attributes rather than behavioral and educational attributes. Contemporary jail officer training programs focus on personal skills, such as human relations and effective writing (Blowers, 1995). In fact, increasing numbers of jails are seeking various types of accreditation from organizations such as the American Jail Association and American Correctional Association (Ryan and Plummer, 1999). Further, the National Institute of Corrections Jails Division provides direct services to jail staff, including technical assistance, training, and information. Issues addressed by the institute include new jail planning, operations, and management (Hutchinson, 1999:15).

IMPROVED JAIL STANDARDS AND MANAGEMENT. By 1995, 25 states developed and implemented jail standards that provide mandatory minimum training (Koren, 1995:45). Most of these states make it mandatory for all jail personnel to participate in annual in-service training. Much of this training is tactical or inmate control oriented, although efforts have been made to provide personnel with a more formal or academic set of skills, such as communication, crisis intervention, and interpersonal problem solving. Not only is jail officer training targeted as a key priority, but substantive concerns relating to inmate mental health also are viewed as critical areas for improvement (Walsh, 1998). Today's jail supervisor may have to perform one or all of the following responsibilities: (1) setting and maintaining jail standards, (2) keeping up with changes in modern jail operations, (3) conducting routine jail inspections, (4) assisting jail administrators with policy changes, (5) providing proactive risk management to reduce liability, and (6) training and mentoring line staff (Hansen, 1995:37).

One way of equipping jail staff with useful skills that will improve their supervisory effectiveness is to establish jail officer training programs. Often, local universities may be the ideal sites for such training programs. At Winona State University in Minnesota, a training program established for jail officers was the first higher education program certified by the International Association of Correctional Officers (IACO). The program focused on applied or practical experiences as well as theory (Flynt and Ellenbecker, 1995:57–58).

Another jail officer training program is the one operated at Stephen F. Austin State University in Nacogdoches, Texas. It is one of the most comprehensive jail training programs ever established in the United States (Boyd and Tiefenwerth, 1995:59). This program provides a 40-hour annual jail officer certification, including courses covering verbal and nonverbal communication skills and the proper use of force. Topics include handling mentally ill inmates/confinees, procedures for HIV/AIDS inmates, cultural sensitivity, security procedures, correctional officer stress recognition and reduction, and other relevant areas.

Jail Inmates and Their Characteristics

Some general characteristics of jail inmates are shown in Table 11.2, which includes distributions of selected sociodemographic characteristics of jail inmates compared for the years 1983, 1989, and 1996.

Approximately 90 percent of all jail inmates are males. The proportion of female inmates is growing, however, increasing from 7.1 percent in 1983 to 10.2 percent in 1996. A disproportionate number of blacks can be found in jails compared with their proportionate distribution in the population (Harlow, 1998). In 1996, blacks accounted for 41 percent of all jail inmates, up from 37 percent in 1983. In contrast, whites made up only 37 percent of the 1996 jail inmate population, down from 46 percent in 1983. The proportion of Hispanic jail inmates rose from 14 percent in 1983 to 18 percent in 1996. About half of all jail inmates had been convicted of a crime previously.

Statistics for 1996 also show that a growing number of jail inmates had used drugs regularly within a month prior to their instant offense, and a third of them had used drugs during the commission of their offense. The average age of jail inmates has remained constant over the years, although the proportionate distributions of those 17 and younger have increased (from 1.3 percent in 1983 to 2.3 percent in 1996), whereas the proportionate distributions of those age 55 and older have decreased (from 2.4 percent in 1983

to 1.5 percent in 1996). Table 11.2 compares jail inmates for the years 1983, 1989, and 1996 according to the most serious offenses charged. Although proportionate decreases occurred among those charged with violent offenses, from 31 percent in 1983 to 26 percent in 1996, and among those charged with property offenses, from 39 percent in 1983 to 26 percent in 1996, the greatest proportionate change occurred among those charged with drug offenses. Only 9 percent of all jail inmates in 1983 were charged with drug offenses, but 22 percent were charged with drug offenses in 1996 (Harlow, 1998:4).

Selected Jail Issues

Several issues regarding jail operations have been targeted by critics in the professional literature. These include (1) overcrowding, (2) the creation of megajails, (3) inmate classification, (4) jail architecture and older jails, and (5) the privatization of jails and contracting.

JAIL OVERCROWDING. Overcrowding is perhaps the major cause of inmate lawsuits in federal and state courts (Pontell and Welsh, 1994). In 79 percent of the cases involving county jails in California during 1975 to 1989, for instance, overcrowding was the most frequently cited problem to be rectified by court action. Other issues were related to inadequate medical care, sanitation problems, hygiene, access to courts, food services, and ventilation (Welch and Gunther, 1997a, 1997b). No matter how much planning jail officials can do, optimum jail capacities simply are not predictable. Thus, daily fluctuations in jail inmate populations cause unanticipated problems for jail staff.

THE CREATION OF MEGAJAILS. **Megajails** are jails with 1,000 or more beds (Cornelius, 1997:19). In 1995, the nation's 25 largest jails housed 30 percent of all jail inmates. When jails equal or exceed 1,000 or more beds, more complex logistical problems are created that must be dealt with on a daily basis. The following breakdown of jail sizes gives us some perspective about how jail capacities are defined (Cornelius, 1997:19):

Megajails = 1,000 or more beds
Large jails = 250–999 beds
Medium jails = 50–249 beds
Small jails = 49 or fewer beds

TABLE 11.2 MOST SERIOUS OFFENSES OF JAIL INMATES, 1996, 1989, 1983

MOST SERIOUS OFFENSES	PERCENTAGE OF JAIL INMATES				
	1996			1989	1983
	Total	Convicted	Unconvicted		
Violent offenses	26.3	21.8	36.6	22.5	30.7
Murder[a]	2.8	1.2	6.0	2.8	4.1
Negligent manslaughter	0.4	0.3	0.5	0.5	0.6
Kidnapping	0.5	0.5	0.6	0.8	1.3
Rape	0.5	0.3	0.8	0.8	1.5
Other sexual assault	2.7	2.7	2.9	2.6	2.0
Robbery	6.5	5.6	8.8	6.7	11.2
Assault	11.6	10.0	15.4	7.2	8.6
Other violent[b]	1.3	1.2	1.5	1.1	1.3
Property offenses	26.9	28.6	25.5	30.0	38.6
Burglary	7.6	8.0	7.7	10.7	14.3
Larceny/theft	8.0	9.5	5.7	7.9	11.7
Motor vehicle theft	2.6	2.3	3.3	2.8	2.3
Arson	0.4	0.3	0.6	0.7	0.8
Fraud	4.6	4.8	4.3	4.0	5.0
Stolen property	2.1	2.4	1.9	2.4	2.5
Other property[c]	1.6	1.4	2.2	1.6	1.9
Drug offenses	22.0	23.7	20.2	23.0	9.3
Possession	11.5	12.6	10.0	9.7	4.7
Trafficking	9.2	9.5	9.2	12.0	4.0
Other drug	1.3	1.5	1.0	1.3	0.6
Public-order offenses	24.3	25.5	17.4	22.8	20.6
Weapons	2.3	2.4	2.2	1.9	2.3
Obstruction of justice	4.8	3.3	4.0	2.8	2.0
Traffic violations	3.2	3.8	1.7	2.7	2.2
Driving while intoxicated[d]	7.4	9.5	3.6	8.8	7.0
Drunkenness/morals[e]	2.0	1.9	2.4	1.7	3.4
Violation of parole/probation[f]	2.6	2.7	1.7	3.0	2.3
Other public order[g]	2.0	1.8	1.8	1.8	1.6
Other offenses[h]	0.5	0.4	0.3	1.6	0.8
Number of jail inmates	496,609	315,442	166,295	380,160	219,573

Note: Excludes inmates for whom offense was unknown.

[a]Includes nonnegligent manslaughter.

[b]Includes blackmail, extortion, hit-and-run driving with bodily injury, child abuse, and criminal endangerment.

[c]Includes destruction of property, vandalism, hit-and-run driving without bodily injury, trespassing, and possession of burglary tools.

[d]Includes driving while intoxicated and driving under the influence of drugs or alcohol.

[e]Includes drunkenness, vagrancy, disorderly conduct, unlawful assembly, morals, and commercialized vice.

[f]Includes parole or probation violations, escape, AWOL, and flight to avoid prosecution.

[g]Includes rioting, abandonment, nonsupport, immigration violations, invasion of privacy, liquor law violations, tax evasion, and bribery.

[h]Includes juvenile offenses and other unspecified offenses.

Source: Caroline Wolf Harlow, *Profile of Jail Inmates 1996* (Washington, DC: U.S. Department of Justice, 1998), p. 4.

Megajails require greater coordination among the individual components and divisions. Greater formality between jail officers and inmates is expected. Inmate control becomes an increasingly important problem as well. Megajails operate similar to prison systems. These jails are large enough to hire full-time medical and support staff to be on call for jail inmate emergencies. Greater segregation among prisoners is achieved with more massive jail size. Some of these megajails have their own commissaries, where prisoners may purchase personal items, articles of clothing, and snacks. These jails also are equipped with weight rooms, small tracks, and other amenities usually found in large prison systems. But despite these amenities, megajails can be overcrowded as well, with all of the problems accompanying overcrowding. Some of the issues associated with megajails are (1) epidemics of AIDS and tuberculosis, (2) expansion of jail industries, (3) diminishing revenues with which to fund jail operations, (4) privatization, (5) increase in inmate programs, (6) continuing searches for alternatives to incarceration, (7) employee incentives, and (8) inmate populations becoming more institutionalized and sophisticated (Cornelius, 1997).

CLASSIFYING JAIL INMATES. Because jails are designed to house offenders for short terms, not much attention has been given to classifying them for segregation purposes (Kennedy, 1999). More jails are accommodating more diverse types of offenders for longer periods (one or more years), however. Thus, in situations in which inmates are housed in jails for lengthy periods, classification procedures become increasingly important and should be implemented to promote better jail operations and inmate control. In the mid-1980s, for instance, Michigan jail officials established a Jail Inmate Classification System (JICS) for use as a decision tree for screening incoming inmates. The screening instrument was designed to identify potential medical and suicide risks and to justify special accommodations, such as temporary cell assignments and observation. Subsequently, computerized and automated versions of these screening procedures were created. The JICS instruments have been used successfully throughout Michigan to improve jail organization and planning. Several important reasons for jail inmate classification are (1) to provide greater inmate safety; (2) to provide greater staff safety; (3) to provide greater public safety; (4) to provide for greater equity, consistency, and fairness among inmates with regard to their placement; (5) to provide for more orderly processing and discipline; (6) to protect the agency against liability; and (7) to provide data for planning, resource allocation, and greater jail efficiency (Brennan and Wells, 1992).

JAIL ARCHITECTURE AND OLDER JAILS. Many jails in the United States are over 50 years old. Furthermore, these jails are chronically overcrowded. One method of improving jail architecture is to eliminate old jails and replace them with modular facilities that provide safer custodial environments for staff and inmates. For instance, the Pinellas County Jail in Florida houses 192 inmates in three interconnected, octagonally shaped buildings of a modular design. Made of precast concrete, the Pinellas Jail is an example of how new jail construction may be implemented at relatively low cost to taxpayers. The structure eventually will reach a height of five stories, the first modularly constructed jail in the nation to achieve that height. With various components of these jails prefabricated and assembled off-site, these jails can be completed in less than a year, some in about eight months. The initial unit costs range from $16,000 (one-person cells) to $29,000 (two-person cells). Statistics show that in other jurisdictions, prison and jail construction using more traditional building concepts have ranged from $40,000 to $100,000 per one-person cell (Camp and Camp, 1999a).

PRIVATIZING JAIL SERVICES AND CONTRACTING. One controversial proposal is the **privatization** of jail and prison management (Pollock, 1997). From a constitutional standpoint, nothing bars private interests from operating jails under the theory of agency. For example, contracts were awarded to the Nashville-based Corrections Corporation of America (CCA) and the St. Louis–based Correctional Development Corporation (CDC) to develop and operate a detention site for the U.S. Marshal's Office. The new facility was believed by the U.S. Marshal's Office to save the government considerable money during its operation as well as ease jail overcrowding. Reasons for and against privatization are listed here for consideration (Ethridge and Liebowitz, 1994:56).

FOR PRIVATIZATION

1. Relieve overcrowding
2. Save taxpayers money
3. Relieve county of liability
4. Boost local economy—add new jobs
5. Provide better care for inmates

6. Provide better classification and evaluation

7. Provide better rehabilitation

AGAINST PRIVATIZATION

1. Private companies should not have control of inmates.

2. Cost will be too expensive for the county.

3. They will not relieve the county from liability.

4. Inmates will be abused.

5. Security risks may occur.

6. Government agencies are more efficient and effective.

7. Private companies are only interested in making money.

8. Danger exists of company declaring bankruptcy.

In addition to privatization, more jail systems in the United States are renting their jail cell space to state and federal prisoners in other jurisdictions. For example, the Albany County Jail in New York has an average daily inmate population of 783 and a capacity of 834 (Szostak, 1996:22–24). The jail began to receive prisoners from other jurisdictions in the mid-1970s. The outside inmate population grew steadily each year. But the jail has had to become increasingly diverse in its approach to managing inmate problems and dealing with controversial inmate issues. For one thing, the level of inmate dangerousness has escalated. As these jails have taken in new inmates from federal and state penitentiaries, they have had to adapt to a new and more dangerous class of offender. This means that they must learn even more about offender management, especially that aspect of offender management relating to rioting, fighting, and other potentially deadly disruptions that may occur with the influx of so many additional dangerous persons to their jail inmate populations.

PRISON SYSTEMS: THE DIVISION OF LABOR

Brief History of Prisons

Prison creation and growth was influenced originally by English and Scottish penal methods (Hughes, 1987). **John Howard** (1726–1790), a prison reformer in England, criticized the manner and circumstances under which prisoners were administered and housed. In order to get new and better ideas about prison operations, Howard visited several countries, such as France and Italy. The Maison de Force (House of Enforcement) of Ghent was impressive to Howard, since prisoners were well fed, adequately clothed, and humanely lodged separately during evening hours. His observations were duly reported to the British House of Commons and resulted in the passage of the **Penitentiary Act of 1779.**

This act provided that new facilities should be created, in which prisoners could work productively at hard labor rather than suffer the usual punishment of banishment. Prisoners were to be well fed, clothed, and housed in isolated sanitary cells. They were to be given opportunities to learn useful skills and trades. Fees for their maintenance were abolished, rigorous inspections were conducted regularly, and balanced diets and improved hygiene were to be strictly observed. Through their hard and productive labor, prisoners could reflect on their crimes and repent. A new term, *penitentiary,* was coined that was equated with reform and punishment.

THE FIRST STATE PRISON AND THE PENNSYLVANIA SYSTEM. An underground prison in a converted copper mine in Simsbury, Connecticut, was used first in 1773. Later, in 1790, a permanent prison was made of it (American Correctional Association, 1995). In the meantime, the Walnut Street Jail in Philadelphia (mentioned in the section about jails in this chapter) was considered by historians to be the first true American prison. The purposes of punishment were to reform offenders, to prevent them from committing future crimes, and to remove them from society temporarily until they developed a repentant attitude. The pattern of discipline and offender treatment practiced at the Walnut Street Jail eventually was known as the **Pennsylvania system** (Rogers, 1993). Prisoners were encouraged to exercise regularly and eat wholesome foods. Prisoners were permitted to grow their own gardens and manufacture some of their own clothing and other useful items. Some of these prisoner-produced goods were sold directly to the public for a profit, to help defray the costs of incarcerating offenders. Thus, the first prison industry was created at the Walnut Street Jail under the Pennsylvania system.

THE AUBURN SYSTEM. In 1816, the **Auburn State Penitentiary** was built in New York and designed with **tiers,** in which inmates were housed on several different levels. The **tier system** became a common feature of subsequent U.S. prison construction, and today, most prisons are architecturally structured according to tiers. The Auburn State Penitentiary copied several features of the Walnut Street Jail, such as **solitary confinement.** Prisoners were housed in solitary cells during evening hours. Solitary confinement also was used as a punishment for the most dangerous and unruly inmates. Today, solitary confinement is an administrative segregation procedure in every major U.S. prison (Rogers, 1993). Another aspect of Auburn State Penitentiary, however, was that prisoners were allowed to work together and eat their meals with one another during daylight hours. This was known as the **congregate system,** because of the opportunity for inmates to congregate with one another.

Auburn State Penitentiary also separated prisoners according to their offenses. Violent offenders were housed on one tier, whereas property and nonviolent offenders were housed on other tiers. These divisions at the Auburn State Penitentiary were the forerunners of minimum-, medium-, and maximum-security designations used by modern prisons. The **Auburn system** became popular with prison authorities and was widely copied. Another feature of the Auburn system that was adopted from the Walnut Street Jail was a system that allowed inmates to help defray their housing and food costs through manual labor. Prison officials contracted with various manufacturers and retailers for purchases of prison goods.

THE ELMIRA REFORMATORY.   The next significant event in American correctional history was the creation of the American Correctional Association (ACA) in 1870. The original goals of the ACA were to formulate a national correctional philosophy, to develop sound correctional policies and standards, to offer expertise to all interested jurisdictions in the design and operation of correctional facilities, and to assist in the training of correctional officers. The ACA was originally called the National Prison Association, then the American Prison Association, and finally and more generally, the American Correctional Association.

The United States was undergoing considerable correctional reform at the time the association was founded, and subsequently, the Elmira State Reformatory in Elmira, New York, was established in 1876. The Elmira Reformatory experimented with new rehabilitative philosophies and was touted as an example of the new penology because the latest, state-of-the-art scientific advancements in correctional methods were used there. Elmira was truly a reformatory. Prisoners pursued education and vocational trades, and their good behavior and productivity could earn them re-

ductions of their full sentences. But Elmira was not as successful as its founders wanted it to be. Many prisoners left Elmira Reformatory unreformed and became recidivists.

THE FAILURE OF REHABILITATION.   Rehabilitation is not a bad concept theoretically. In fact, it is one of correction's continuing goals (Waite, 1993). But prison inmates from the time of Elmira Reformatory to the present day have had very high rates of recidivism. More than 65 to 70 percent of all releasees will commit new crimes and be reincarcerated within a few years (Maguire and Pastore, 2000). This figure has remained fairly constant over the years and suggests that rehabilitation occurs only for a minority of jail and prison inmates. Among the factors accounting for high rates of recidivism among prison inmates are (1) pervasive inmate idleness; (2) not enough prison industry jobs for all inmates to be employed; (3) few incentives for inmates to improve themselves educationally or vocationally; (4) extensive overcrowding; and (5) insufficient, inadequate, and understaffed programs offered to inmates (Johnson, 1996; Sharbaro and Keller, 1995).

Functions of Prisons

The functions served by prisons are closely connected with the overall goals of corrections. Broadly stated, correctional goals include deterrence, rehabilitation, societal protection, offender reintegration, just deserts, justice and due process, and retribution or punishment. The goals of prisons are described in the following paragraphs.

PROVIDING SOCIETAL PROTECTION.   Locking up dangerous offenders or those who are persistent nonviolent offenders means that society will be protected from them for variable time periods. But at present, all offenders who deserve to be incarcerated cannot possibly be locked up. Space limitations are such that we would require at least four or five times the number of existing prisons to incarcerate all convicted felons and misdemeanants.

PUNISHING OFFENDERS.   Restricting one's freedoms, confining inmates in cells, and obligating them to follow rigid behavioral codes while confined is regarded as punishment for criminal conduct. The fact of incarceration is a punishment compared with the greater freedoms enjoyed by probationers and parolees.

REHABILITATING OFFENDERS.   Little support exists for the view that imprisonment rehabilitates offenders. However, many prisons have vocational and educational programs, psychological counselors, and an array of services available to inmates in order that they might improve their skills, education, and self-concepts.

REINTEGRATING OFFENDERS.   Many prisons have prerelease programs that offer inmates an opportunity to work at jobs outside of prison shortly before they are to be released. These programs are referred to by different names, such as work or educational release, and furloughs. The purpose of these programs is to enable inmates to reenter society and make a smooth transition from the heavily regimented prison life to which they have become accustomed. This is especially true for offenders who have served lengthy sentences.

Administering Prison Systems

STATE PRISON SYSTEMS AND DEPARTMENTS OF CORRECTIONS.   Wide variation exists among states in their correctional organizations and operations. Examples of two states with similar numbers of correctional officers and probation/parole officers are Utah and Oregon. In 1998, Oregon had 2,088 personnel in their adult correctional system, with 1,091 correctional officers. In contrast, Utah had 1,810 personnel and 938 correctional officers (American Correctional Association, 1999). Despite these correctional personnel similarities, significant differences can be found between the two states regarding numbers of parolees, probationers, and inmates in their correctional facilities.

In 1998, Utah had about half as many prison inmates (4,284) compared with Oregon (7,999). Utah had about a fourth as many convicted offenders on probation compared with Oregon (9,306 compared with 42,292) (American Correctional Association, 1999). However, Utah had about one fifth of the parolees (2,920) compared with Oregon's parolee population (15,800). One explanation is that Utah has a statute restricting the length of probation terms and limits the use of probation to less serious types of crimes (Maguire and Pastore, 2000). Yet overall, there were 66,091 Oregon inmates, probationers, and parolees under the supervision of 1,198 correctional officers, compared with about a fourth as many inmates, probationers, and parolees (16,510) under the supervision of 558 correctional officers in Utah in 1998 (Camp and Camp, 1999a:134). In 1998, the Utah correctional operating budget was $155 million compared with an Oregon correctional operating budget of $652 million. According to their respective per-inmate costs, both states are similar in their operating monies.

There is much variation between Utah and Oregon concerning their correctional organization. Oregon has a Department of Corrections that provides correctional services through Institutions. The Department of Human Resources provides juvenile correctional services through the Oregon Youth Authority. Oregon's correctional institutions include 11 correctional facilities: a penitentiary, six correctional institutions, a women's correctional center, two correctional facilities, and a camp. Juvenile Services has two training schools and five correctional camps.

Utah has a Department of Corrections that administers five correctional facilities and a women's facility. There are six regional field offices and six community corrections centers. The department of human services is divided according to a division of youth corrections and a youth parole authority. The division of youth corrections is further subdivided into three regions managing 13 youth centers and three assessment units. Utah has a youth parole board, but Oregon does not have one. But there are nearly four times as many wardens and superintendents of adult correctional facilities in Utah compared with Oregon.

Oregon has a three-member Board of Parole and Postprison Supervision; members of the board are full-time employees appointed by and answerable to the governor for parole decisions. Utah has a Board of Pardons and Parole consisting of five full-time board members who have full parole, pardon, and commutation authority over all sentenced prisoners. The decision-making authority of Utah board members is autonomous and uninfluenced (American Correctional Association, 1999). Considerable autonomy and responsibility is given to individual counties for administering detention centers, holdover facilities, and community corrections programs in both jurisdictions. These responsibilities also include the construction and operation of prisons to house a variety of offenders.

Because local and state correctional agencies and organizations are so fragmented, their operations of programs and services usually suffer. Many state and local correctional agencies make little if any effort to coordinate their activities. An absence of effective and efficient planning is more the rule than the exception. In the Oregon-Utah example of correctional organizations, Utah has a more decentralized system, whereas Oregon's correctional agencies are more centralized.

BOX 11.1 PERSONALITY HIGHLIGHT

ELAINE LITTLE
Director, North Dakota Department of Corrections and Rehabilitation

Statistics: B.S., Business Administration (major), Accounting (minor), Dickinson State University

Work History and Experiences: I graduated from Dickinson State University in 1975 with a degree in business administration and a minor in accounting. I began employment following college with the Legislative Council of North Dakota as a fiscal analyst and remained there until 1981. From 1981 to 1983, I was a budget analyst for the Office of Management and Budget. I analyzed many institution budgets both at the Legislative Council and the Office of Management and Budget. While working with the institutions in North Dakota, I became very familiar not only with their budgets but also with various program areas. I chaired a committee in 1987 to 1989 to explore the feasibility and support for the creation of a Department of Corrections for the state. In 1989, the North Dakota Legislature passed legislation that created the North Dakota Department of Corrections and Rehabilitation and I was appointed as its director.

While I was employed as the director, I had many opportunities to get involved in the penitentiary and state industrial school's operations. I saw how disjointed correctional services were in the state and saw the creation of a department of corrections as a real opportunity to establish a single philosophy and shape a coordinated system of corrections for North Dakota. Both adult correctional services and juvenile correctional services were provided by a number of different state agencies, and I believed that the only way to have a coordinated system was to have all correctional services provided by a single state agency.

Work Experiences: Some of my most interesting experiences have been from direct involvement with various offenders. My opinion of corrections and of the criminal justice system has been formed over the years through conversations with offenders, observations of what programming works or does not work with offenders, visiting and studying other state corrections systems, and analysis of research done in the corrections area. My term as president of the Association of State Correctional Administrators (1994–1996) also brought with it some very interesting experiences. Having the opportunity to speak on behalf of all state corrections directors was both exciting and humbling.

Most experiences during my tenure as director of the department have been positive. Even though the public and the legislature does not like to spend tax dollars on corrections, the support the Department of Corrections has received from both has been gratifying. Also positive is that the employees of the Department of Corrections are exceptional. They are bright, innovative, hardworking, and, I believe, the best in the business. It takes a special person to work with offenders.

Some of the negative experiences I have had through the years usually involved politics. I do not believe that decisions made in corrections should ever be made for political reasons. Another disappointment has been that often correctional research has been ignored when policy makers have made decisions and adopted legislation that have affected corrections and the criminal justice system for the long term. An example of this is that even though research has shown that mandatory sentencing creates more problems for a system than it resolves, the legislature has passed several pieces of mandatory sentencing legislation in the past few years.

Advice to Students: Anyone who wants to enter the corrections profession must like to work with people and have compassion for them. Corrections is not a field that will be rewarding in a monetary sense. If a person is interested in making a difference in people's lives and believes that people can change if given the opportunity, however, then corrections can be very rewarding. Students should be aware that there are many areas in corrections to consider, including juvenile or adult corrections, counseling, corrections officer work in institutions, parole and probation officer work, or juvenile community case management. We most often encourage students to pursue a criminal justice or social work degree if they are interested in working in corrections.

The Utah Board of Pardons and Parole can make decisions independent of others, including the governor. Oregon's governor can intercede and override Oregon Board of Parole decisions about particular inmates, however. This power relation is influenced by the fact that the governor appoints and terminates parole board members at will. Generally, the greater the decentralization of power relative to offender management, the more difficult it is for effective coordination between organizations to occur.

Wyoming has the greatest correctional centralization, with four major administrative organizations to oversee all correctional operations. The Wyoming Department of Corrections is responsible for the management of all penal institutions. A Division of Field Services operates all probation and parole activities. The Board of Parole recommends sentence commutations to the governor and controls good-time awards. Fi-

nally, the Department of Family Services oversees all juvenile functions (American Correctional Association, 1999). Most of the other states have decentralized systems, since so many different boards and departments have jurisdictional authority over various facets of their corrections operations.

Figure 11.1 shows a fairly simple organizational chart for a state department of corrections and rehabilitation. At the top of the chart is a director who administers four separate divisions, including Jail Inspections, the Division of Adult Services, the Central Office, and the Division of Juvenile Services. The Division of Adult Services oversees the state penitentiary, two correctional centers, and Rough Rider Industries. This division also oversees adult probation and parole programs. Under Juvenile Services, a Youth Correctional Center and Community Services for juveniles are supervised. Figure 11.2 is an organizational chart of the

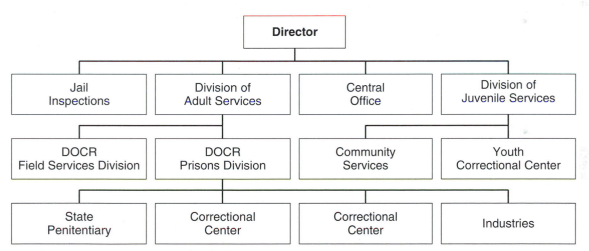

FIGURE 11.1 Department of Corrections and Rehabilitation Organizational Chart

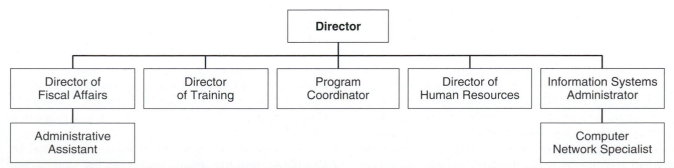

FIGURE 11.2 DOCR Central Office Organizational Chart

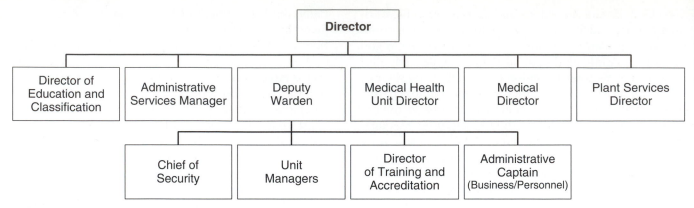

FIGURE 11.3 DOCR State Penitentiary Organizational Chart

Central Office, whose primary responsibilities include program coordination, fiscal affairs, training, human resources, and information systems.

Figure 11.3 is an organizational chart of the state penitentiary. This penitentiary had an original design capacity of 670, although because of sentencing structural changes by the state legislature in 1994 influenced by President Bill Clinton's Crime Bill, the state inmate population had risen to well over 1,000 inmates by September 2000. The explanation for this rapid inmate population increase is simple. Prior to 1994, prisoners were paroled after serving approximately 35 to 40 percent of their sentences. Following truth-in-sentencing legislation and the acceptance of federal monies for correctional grants and other forms of assistance, the state legislature revised the criminal laws to provide that inmates would be eligible for parole after serving at least 85 percent of their maximum sentences. This sentencing change had a dramatic effect on increasing the prison inmate population over the next several years. Some of this inmate overflow has been shifted to some of the larger jails in the state, and other inmates have been accommodated with new prison construction at the penitentiary site.

For the state penitentiary shown in Figure 11.3, there is a warden, a deputy warden, and directors in charge of education and classification, medical health, and plant services. An administrative services manager and a medical director also report directly to the warden. The chief of security, several unit managers, a director of training and accreditation, and an administrative captain report to the deputy warden. This is not a particularly large prison. In fact, it is the smallest prison system of all state prison systems. But despite its small size, the state penitentiary is facing unprecedented inmate population growth and has acquired an administrative nightmare as one result of the state's sentencing law changes.

FEDERAL CORRECTIONS ORGANIZATION: THE FEDERAL BUREAU OF PRISONS. Several federal correctional facilities were constructed during the 1790s and early 1800s, although no central authority system existed to administer these facilities until Congress established the Federal Bureau of Prisons (BOP) in 1930 (American Correctional Association, 1999). By 1998, the BOP operated 101 correctional institutions arranged according to level of custody from maximum-security penitentiaries such as the one at Marion, Illinois, to minimum-security prison camps like Allenwood Federal Prison Camp at Montgomery, Pennsylvania (American Correctional Association, 1999).

Under the direction of the attorney general of the United States, the Bureau of Prisons was established to manage and regulate all federal penal and correctional institutions, to provide suitable quarters, subsistence, and discipline for all persons charged with or convicted of federal crimes, and to provide technical assistance to state and local governments in the improvement of their own correctional facilities (18 U.S. Code, Sec. 4041–4042, 2001). A director oversees six U.S. regions in which all federal correctional institutions are located. Regional directors are headquartered in Atlanta, Dallas, Kansas City, Philadelphia, San Francisco, and Dublin, California. The director of the Federal Bureau of Prisons in 1998 was Dr. Kathleen M. Hawk Sawyer (American Correctional Association, 1999:581).

In 1998, there were 101 federal correctional institutions, ranging from penitentiaries and prison camps to detention centers, medical centers, and low-security facilities (American Correctional Association, 1999:508–550). The construction of new federal prisons was sluggish until 1985. Between 1985 and 1998, 54 new federal prisons were constructed. The oldest U.S. penitentiary still operating is in Atlanta and was constructed in 1902. The smallest U.S. penitentiary is in Florence, Colorado, with a rated capacity of 490, whereas the largest is the one in Atlanta, with a rated capacity of 2,117.

These penitentiaries confine the most serious federal offenders and those serving the longest sentences. Federal penitentiaries designated as **admin max** house inmates with serious and persistent misconduct problems. Their average stay is 36 months (American Correctional Association, 1999). The federal correctional institutions have different security levels. Metropolitan correctional centers and camps are designed to house short-term and low-risk federal offenders at all security levels. Federal medical centers are designed for federal prisoners who require medical, surgical, or psychiatric care. Federal prison camps are minimum-security institutions with no fences, with dormitory housing and low staff-inmate ratios. They are program oriented and focused on work. Finally, federal detention centers are designed to house pretrial detainees and criminal aliens awaiting deportation hearings (American Correctional Association, 1999).

Tactical policies and procedures have been established by the U.S. Federal Bureau of Prisons to respond to emergency situations, including riots and other inmate disturbances (U.S. Federal Bureau of Prisons, 1994). Six strategic goals have been realized, including (1) more effective population management, (2) human resource management, (3) security and facility management, (4) correctional leadership and effective public administration, (5) inmate programs and services, and (6) building partnerships. A 1995 study determined that among 46 different state departments of corrections, 94 percent of these departments had established similar emergency plans and tactical response teams for countering inmate disturbances (Bryan, 1995).

Typically, federal prisoners are housed in federal facilities, state prisoners are housed in state facilities, and local criminals are incarcerated in local facilities. For many decades, however, some federal and state prisoners have been housed in local correctional facilities, largely because of overcrowding in federal institutions. Under Title 18, Section 4082 of the U.S. Code (2001), the attorney general "may designate as a place of confinement any available, suitable, and appropriate institution or facility, whether maintained by the federal government or otherwise, and whether within or without the judicial district in which the person was convicted, and may at any time transfer a person from one place of confinement to another." Also, if space is unavailable in particular localities where federal prisoners are to be housed, the attorney general is authorized to cause to be erected in the area a house of detention, workhouse, jail, camp, or other place of confinement that can be used to house those convicted of federal crimes (18 U.S.Code, Sec. 4003, 1999).

In 1995, the Federal Bureau of Prisons had a budget of $3 billion, with $1.8 billion in salaries and $459 million in administration/operations (American Correctional Association, 1999). There were 112,973 federal inmates in 1997, with 34,202 federal probationers and 56,591 federal parolees (U.S. Department of Justice, 1999). In 1997, a total of 25,515 Federal Bureau of Prisons personnel were employed, and 10,248 of these were corrections officers (American Correctional Association, 1999).

Prison Administrators and Their Characteristics

BACKGROUNDS OF PRISON ADMINISTRATORS. Although prison organization varies greatly among state and federal jurisdictions, some common elements are associated with most prison systems. All state prisons as well as comparable federal facilities have **wardens** or **superintendents** who oversee prison operations. These people have various administrative responsibilities, including hiring and firing corrections personnel, implementing new correctional policies, ensuring the safety of all prisoners as well as prison staff, and establishing internal sanctioning systems for dealing effectively with rule infractions by staff or inmates.

Prison administrators come from diverse backgrounds. Most prison officials lack legal training. Frequently, former correctional personnel are appointed to warden positions after many years of service in other correctional capacities. Because of increased prisoner litigation during the past several decades, prison administrators have devised various defensive policies and educated their staffs about strategies that will reduce the number of lawsuits filed by inmates or their families. In many prisons, inmate grievance committees have been established to head off many minor prison problems that might otherwise develop into major litigation issues in court (Gorton, 1997).

BOX 11.2 FEDERAL PRISON ORGANIZATION: ORGANIZATION OF THE FEDERAL BUREAU OF PRISONS IN 2001

Director, Dr. Kathleen M. Hawk Sawyer

Administration Division

Budget development, execution, capacity planning, design and construction, facilities management, finance, management support, procurement and property, site selection and environmental review, trust fund

Community Corrections and Detention Division

Community corrections, detention services, National Office of Citizen Participation

Correctional Programs Division

Correctional services, chaplaincy services, psychology services, correctional programs, inmate systems management

General Counsel and Review

Office of general counsel, legislative and correctional issues, commercial branch, equal employment opportunity, freedom of information/privacy, ethics, rules, administrative remedies, National Legal Training Center, Staff Training Academy-Glynco

Health Services Division

Office of medical director; systems, policy, planning, and evaluation; health services program

Human Resource Management Division

Labor-management relations, affirmative action, national recruiting office, examining, conference coordinator, security and background investigation, training operations, field training services, employee relations, human resources management information system, human resource research and development, policy and professional development, pay and position management, staffing

Industries, Education, and Vocational Training

Corporate management, ombudsman, management information systems, management control system, project group, human resources, plans and policy, products, marketing, procurement, engineering, financial management education, training and recreation, inmate work programs, competition, activation

Support Divisions

Information, Policy, and Public Affairs Division

Public affairs, security technology, national policy review, archives, external liaison, documents control, research and evaluation information systems

National Institute of Corrections

Technical assistance, grants, National Academy of Corrections, National Jail Center, information clearinghouse

Program Review Division

Office of assistant director, program review branch, program analysis branch, internal control branch, competition advocacy program, office of strategic planning

Regional Offices

Mid-Atlantic (Annapolis Junction, MD)

North Central (Kansas City)

Northeast (Philadelphia)

South Central (Dallas)

Southeast (Atlanta)

Western (Dublin, CA)

A majority of prison administrators are men. In 1998, about 26 percent of all administrative prison staff were women (Camp and Camp, 1999a). Once persons are appointed to be prison wardens or administrators, they do not stay on the job for particularly long periods. The average length of service for prison wardens in 1998 was about three years (Camp and Camp, 1999a). Those wardens with the longest tenure in their posts have served an average of 13.5 years, with one warden in Kentucky serving for 26 years (Camp and Camp, 1999a:129). The minimum served by any warden was 2.5 years in Maine.

Professional improvisation among prison administrators is frequently required. Furthermore, it is clear that the types of inmates that administrators must supervise influence the nature of supervision practiced. Fixed and limited correctional budgets impose serious constraints that prevent administrators from being fully effective in the performance of their tasks. No single administrative style describes the typical prison warden or superintendent. No uniformity exists among the states or even within them about how each prison facility should be managed and what sort of correctional officer conduct is to be prescribed.

One of the most common problems among correctional officers is their relations with prison administration (Wright, 1998). Since many prison administrative personnel come largely from professional backgrounds unrelated to corrections, gaps can occur in communication between administrators and officers about how best to perform correctional work. It is likely, however, that administrators quickly become attuned to their settings and make necessary adjustments to acquire the required skills to facilitate communication between themselves and their employees as well as the inmates.

CENTRALIZING OR DECENTRALIZING THE DECISION-MAKING PROCESS. No particular administrative style fits all prison administrators, wardens, managers, or superintendents. Each administrator develops a style individualized to fit the setting, staff, and inmate culture. But since administrators are in key power positions, they may choose to consolidate this power or distribute it among several staff members. Prison administrators may either centralize or decentralize the decision-making process within their institutions, and they may conduct their administrative affairs according to the power scheme they have fashioned. If certain correctional officers are working in a prison in which the administrative philosophy is based on centralization of decision making, these officers may feel powerless in influencing prison operations. But officers who work in settings in which decentralization is used for administration will probably be involved to a greater degree in the decision-making process. As we have seen in an earlier chapter, if employees are permitted greater participation in decision making that affects their work, they may be more satisfied with their jobs, possibly more loyal to the organization, and potentially more effective workers. In contrast, officers who are less involved in decisions affecting their work may be less satisfied and effective (French, Israel, and Aos, 1960).

The participation hypothesis also applies to inmates. In recent years, most prisons have established inmate councils or committees that hear inmate grievances and have limited input about the operations of their institutions. These grievance committees are often helpful in heading off much formal court litigation that might arise over petty matters. Some grievance committees and inmate councils permit limited prisoner input into how the prisons ought to be operated.

Looking at officer recruitment and job performance from a purely bureaucratic approach, this view suggests that those most capable of performing their roles would be hired initially, and that they would relate to and perform their work professionally. They would perform their jobs according to *a priori* job specifications, and they would maintain impersonal relations between themselves, other correctional officers, and inmates. But in the real world of prison life, this ideal scenario seldom occurs. Interpersonal relations cannot be eliminated from any people-processing institution, especially prisons. Because of this fact, the human relations model has considerable relevance in analyses of correctional officer–prisoner interactions as well as administrator–correctional officer encounters.

The human relations approach in correctional officer–inmate interactions has been affected by computer technology in all types of penal institutions (Elchardus et al., 1994). Locking or unlocking doors, inmate recognition, and other forms of prisoner control are being relegated to a few computer functions, with minimal direct staff involvement or contact with prisoners. Whether or not this will seriously influence the nature of officer-prisoner relationships in the future cannot be determined now, but computerized prison settings will no doubt have impacts similar to the depersonalizing effects associated with technological change observed to occur in business or service organizations (Vogel, 1995a, 1995b).

Alternative Prison Management Styles

Barak-Glantz (1986) identifies four prison management styles that typify how most prisons are administered by wardens and superintendents. These include (1) the authoritarian model, (2) the bureaucratic-lawful model, (3) the shared-powers model, and (4) the inmate control model. These models are best viewed as ideal types in much the same way as Max Weber conceived bureaucracy as an ideal type of organizational model.

THE AUTHORITARIAN MODEL. The **authoritarian model** has a high degree of centralization of authority and decision making. Wardens limit the amount of authority to a few trusted subordinates. Inmates have virtually no say or input regarding prison operations. This model typified early twentieth-century prisons, although many prisons in the United States today have a similar centralized scheme. Because prisoners have been excluded from any type of decision-making power in this system, it has been attacked repeatedly by civil rights groups. Eventually, lawsuits filed by inmates led to the establishment of administrative grievance procedures in all prisons through which prisoners may register complaints about their conditions and treatment.

THE BUREAUCRATIC-LAWFUL MODEL. Departments of corrections in various jurisdictions have contributed to the bureaucratization of prisons and to the establishment of elaborate chains of command linking prison administrators with their subordinates. This is the **bureaucratic-lawful model.** Barak-Glantz notes that the evolution and growing importance of civil service and accompanying recruitment regulations have further bureaucratized prison settings. Control is the key to maintaining order in the prison. The courts also have contributed to the orderly and bureaucratic administration of prisons through decisions that acknowledge certain inmate rights.

THE SHARED-POWERS MODEL. An increasingly popular scheme is the **shared-powers model,** in which some degree of decision-making power is extended to inmates as well as to correctional officers and administrators. Reflecting the ideology of rehabilitation, the shared-powers model is apparent in those prisons with strong inmate councils that hear and decide inmate grievances and disputes. Prison officials acknowledge certain inmates as leaders, possessing the skills and influence to persuade other prisoners to comply with prison policies and rules. This perspective is viewed by some as democratizing prisons (Toch, 1995a).

THE INMATE CONTROL MODEL. Under the **inmate control model,** prisoners form inmate government councils and establish organizations such as the California Union, a prisoner union patterned after those established by Scandinavian prisons (Barak-

Glantz, 1986:50). Although the idea of inmate unions is not a novel one, it has encouraged prisoners to act collectively to ensure that their constitutional rights are observed by prison staff. Greater weight is attached to lawsuits filed by an inmate collective, in which rights violations of various kinds are alleged. Inmate unions have lobbied successfully in some jurisdictions for the abolition of the indeterminate sentence, the establishment of certain worker rights for prisoners including the recognition of minimum wages for work performed, and the right to bargain collectively.

All of these models are found in different U.S. prisons. The model most frequently observed is the bureaucratic-lawful model, although increasingly, the shared-powers model is gaining in popularity. A high degree of inmate participation in decision making is instrumental in achieving and maintaining internal social control. Although some administrators do not particularly like or accept this model, they cannot deny that it is somewhat effective for maintaining order and ensuring inmate compliance with most prison regulations.

WARDEN LEADERSHIP STYLES. Profiles of 283 prison managers from various jurisdictions have been described to establish the first national database in correctional management (Mactavish, 1992:162–164). Mactavish has used the Myers-Briggs Type Indicator (MBIT) as a means of typifying correctional management behaviors and orientations. These wardens and administrators participated in a 10-day program sponsored by the National Institute of Corrections' Correctional Leadership Development Program.

Sixteen personality types have been described by Mactavish, which are grouped into the following four categories: (1) people who are driven either by extroversion, the outer world of actions, objects, and people, or by introversion, the world of concepts and ideas; (2) people who either rely on their five senses to sense the immediate, real, and practical facts, or use intuition to consider possibilities and follow their hunches; (3) people who either make decisions by thinking objectively and impersonally, or by weighing subjective values and feelings; and (4) people who live mostly either by judgment, in a decisive, planned, and orderly way, or by perception, in a spontaneous and flexible way (Mactavish, 1992:164).

From responses of the 182 wardens and prison superintendents, sensing, thinking, and judgment characterize the preferences of correctional managers. Those profiles most common to prison wardens describe these individuals as analytical managers who like facts and details; as fact-minded, practical organizers; as intuitive, innovative organizers; and as logical, critical innovators (Mactavish, 1992:164). Mactavish says that most correctional managers prefer to use their senses over their intuition as a means of acquiring information. They prefer to work with facts, enjoy routines, and like to use skills they already have rather than learning new skills. They generally dislike new problems unless they can use standard procedures for solving them. They prefer to maintain the status quo, and when change is necessary, they must be convinced of the necessity for change by facts. Thus, most prison administrators, at least those studied by Mactavish, follow the bureaucratic model of structuring their own lives as prison managers as well as the lives of the inmates they manage.

PRISON ADMINISTRATOR SELECTION AND TRAINING

Wardens, superintendents, and other prison managers are typically hired or appointed (Camp and Camp, 1999a:129). In 1999, the average length of service for prison wardens was 13.5 years. States with the longest warden longevity were Kentucky (26.1 years), Arizona (25.1 years), and Missouri (23.9 years). Wardens' minimum salaries averaged $50,732, and their maximum salaries averaged $77,216 (Camp and Camp, 1999a:129). The lowest minimum warden's salary, in Arizona, was $34,290. The highest maximum salary was in the Federal Bureau of Prisons, at $115,311.

Of the 1,531 wardens, superintendents, or prison managers reported by alternative sources in 1998, 74 percent were male and 21 percent were black (Camp and Camp, 1999b). Actually, the percentage of black wardens is up from 16 percent in 1995. Some insight into the backgrounds of prison wardens and superintendents may be gleaned from a study of Pennsylvania wardens by Whitmore (1995). Whitmore conducted both a survey and interviews with 55 Pennsylvania prison administrators. Whitmore found that most respondents, 82 percent, had completed some college, with only 14 percent possessing advanced degrees. Most respondents (96 percent) were white. The field of undergraduate study most common to these administrators was criminal justice. He noted that 42 percent of these managers had their first corrections position in security, followed by treatment (34.5 percent). The most frequent ages of these wardens, by category, were 41 to 45 years old (24 percent) and over 56 (24

percent). The mean length of service of these administrators in corrections was about 17 years, with the range of service for all survey participants ranging from three years to 36 years (Whitmore, 1995:54–55). The administrators indicated that they regularly performed a total of 272 tasks, and the following tasks were the most common (Whitmore, 1995:57):

1. Managing change within the institution
2. Providing leadership for the organization
3. Managing organizational performance
4. Conducting inspections and tours
5. Managing liability exposure and risk management
6. Maintaining professional staff

This description is not necessarily typical of administrators in other state jurisdictions, but the Pennsylvania study does give us an idea of the range of backgrounds represented as well as some of the principal duties performed by these managers.

TYPES OF PRISONS AND INMATE CLASSIFICATION

All prisons in the United States today have classification schemes of one type or another for differentiating among prisoners and assigning them to particular accommodations (Champion, 1994). The use of such schemes has varying utility depending on the purpose of the initial classification, such as identifying those likely to engage in assaultive or aggressive disciplinary infractions (Van Voorhis, 1993). But regardless of the type of classification scheme employed by corrections officials in screening their inmates, prisoners are eventually channeled into one of several fixed custody levels. These are minimum-, medium-, and maximum-security.

Minimum-Security Prisons

Minimum-security prisons are facilities designed to house low-risk, nonviolent first offenders. These institutions also are established to accommodate those serving short-term sentences. Sometimes, minimum-security institutions function as intermediate housing for those prisoners leaving more heavily monitored facilities on their way toward parole or eventual freedom. Minimum-security housing often has dormitory-like quality, with grounds and physical plant features resembling a university campus rather than a prison.

Medium-Security Prisons

About 35 percent of all state and federal prisons in the United States are **medium-security prisons** and minimum-security institutions (Camp and Camp, 1999a:19). The Federal Bureau of Prisons uses a six-level scale ranging from Level 1 to Level 6, with Level 1 being a minimum-security facility such as the Federal Prison Camp in Big Spring, Texas, and a Level 6 being a maximum-security facility such as the Marion (Illinois) Penitentiary. Medium-security facilities are really a catchall type of prison, because often, both extremely violent and nonviolent offenders are placed in common living areas (Wooldredge, 1998). Visitation privileges are more closely regulated, and privileges, freedom of movement, and access to various educational, vocational, and/or therapeutic programs are greatly restricted.

Maximum-Security Prisons and Maxi-Maxi Prisons

Approximately 31 percent of all U.S. prisons are **maximum-security prisons,** classified either as "maximum" or "close/hi" (Camp and Camp, 1999a:19). Ordinarily, those sentenced to serve time in maximum-security facilities are considered among the most dangerous, high-risk offenders.

The very worst and most dangerous prisoners are sent to prisons such as the United States Penitentiary in Florence, Colorado. This facility is one of the newer federal penitentiaries. It was built in 1994 and can hold 490 inmates (American Correctional Association, 2000). The federal penitentiary at Florence is considered a **maxi-maxi prison,** or admin max, with restrictions so severe and pervasive as to be unparalleled by almost any other prison in the United States. Maxi-maxi prisons make up about 5 percent of all U.S. penitentiaries (Camp and Camp, 1999a).

PRISON ISSUES

Several prison issues are discussed in this last section. Wardens and prison superintendents must deal with these issues on a continuing basis. No immediate or broadly applicable solutions exist for the problems generated by particular issues. But they are at the heart of many management headaches shared by prison administrators everywhere. These issues include (1) prison overcrowding, (2) jailhouse lawyers, (3) privatization of prison services, and (4) the legal liabilities of corrections administrators and officers.

Prison Overcrowding

Many problems associated with prison operations and management involve **prison overcrowding.** In 1998, prisons in 51 U.S. agencies were operating at an average of 15 percent over their rated capacities (Camp and Camp, 1999a). Overall, state prisons were operating at between 90 and 170 percent of their capacities in 1998, and the federal prison system was operating at 125 percent of its rated capacity (Camp and Camp, 1999a).

Overcrowding in prisons has been linked with violent deaths, suicides, psychiatric commitments, disciplinary infractions, and increased litigation by inmates (Call, 1995a, 1995b). With the increasing threat of various communicable diseases in prison and jail settings, overcrowding is quickly emerging as a most critical issue (Tonry and Hatlestad, 1997).

Jailhouse Lawyers

Jailhouse lawyers are inmates who have acquired some degree of legal expertise and assist both themselves and others in filing petitions and suits against their institutions (Belbot, 1995). Many of these suits are frivolous and seldom result in monetary damages awarded to petitioning inmates. But jailhouse lawyers and lawyering will continue to influence jail and prison reforms.

Jailhouse lawyers have had a sketchy batting average with the U.S. Supreme Court and other appellate courts in which they have directed their cases. In some instances, monetary damages have been awarded. In other cases, inmate litigation has been the catalyst for substantial changes in entire prison systems. The Texas Department of Corrections, for example, fell under a court order to improve its legal assistance to inmates as the result of court action by jailhouse lawyers. Inmates also have been successful in suits involving their meals, hair length, religious rituals, and general treatment by correctional officers. Native American inmates in various prisons have sued prison officials and departments of corrections specifically for rights pertaining to possession of religious artifacts used in religious rituals. In Missouri, for example, the Department of Corrections prohibited ceremonial pipes, medicine bags, eagle claws, and altar stones because of increased security risks. The courts declared that such prohibitions did not violate Native American inmate religious rights under the First Amendment (*Bettis v. Delo*, 1994). However, other jurisdictions have permitted certain Native American religious items, such as ceremonial pipes (*Sample v. Borg*, 1987).

Privatization of Prison Services

No state or federal statutes prohibit private enterprise from operating prisons in any jurisdiction. Privatization is delegated power to act on behalf of the state. Also, since many prison administrators have backgrounds unrelated to corrections and a majority have no previous experience as prison correctional officers, this raises serious questions about the suitability of anyone for correctional administrative work. A majority of correctional administrators have business or social science backgrounds, most are educated with the minimum of a bachelor's degree, and most have some managerial experience. Thus, a considerable amount of private sector involvement in prison management already exists.

Twenty percent of all U.S. prisons were under court order in 1996 to reduce their inmate populations (Blakely and Bumphus, 1996:49). Prison overcrowding has been one of the most important reasons for the privatization of prisons. Privatization of prisons is the financing and/or operation of prisons and other correction institutions by private, for-profit organizations. Privatization of prisons is growing in the United States and is found in other countries, such as Japan, Germany, and China (Hagemann, 1995; Johnson, 1994; Seymour and Anderson, 1998).

Privatization is not new. Private business enterprises have been contracting with prisons on a regular basis for several decades for the provision of various goods, services, and prison work programs. Private enterprise operations in corrections have been particularly noticeable in the juvenile justice system, in which minimum-security detention facilities are often privately organized and managed. Since a private state prison system was established in late 1980s, at least 21 states have subsequently established private prisons or passed legislation for their creation (Blakely and Bumphus, 1996:49). These states include Alaska, Arizona, Arkansas, California, Florida, Indiana, Kansas, Kentucky, Louisiana, Montana, Minnesota, Nebraska, Nevada, New Hampshire, New Mexico, North Dakota, Oklahoma, Tennessee, Texas, Utah, and West Virginia.

Legal Liabilities of Correctional Administrators and Officers

About a third of all jails in the United States are currently being sued or are involved in some type of legal action. Increased filings of lawsuits are crippling both prison and jail systems (Hunter and Sexton, 1997).

Many of these lawsuits are initiated as the result of insensitive jail officers who do not know how to relate with prisoners in humane ways. Many jail officers simply fail to work within their job description and fail to follow established policies and procedures. Other officers have personal biases and prejudices that affect their relations with inmates, especially minorities. Jail lawsuits can be minimized by (1) hiring the right staff; (2) providing staff training with greater emphasis on development and self-understanding; and (3) using participatory management, in which jail officers are involved more in decision making that affects their work. Professionalizing the jail workforce can do much to reduce the incidence of jail lawsuits (Koren, 1995).

One way of professionalizing the jail officer workforce is to compel it to seek greater formalized training. In Texas, jail officers must enroll in and successfully pass POST (Peace Officer Standards and Training) curricula. Further, they are required to attend annual in-service training as a part of their growing professionalism. The thrust of this training is to professionalize jail staff and make them sensitive to inmate needs. All jail inmates should receive proper care and be supervised by a well-trained staff cognizant of correctional law. One positive outcome of such training is the minimization of lawsuits filed by inmates against jail officers or supervisors for different kinds of misconduct (Etter and Birzer, 1997:67).

More sophisticated jail officer training exposes these persons to diverse employee-inmate encounters that may be unanticipated. For instance, certain inmates have challenged jail policies that limit their religious practices. Even jail telephone systems have been the subject of certain lawsuits (Cohn, 1998; Townsend and Eichor, 1995). Older inmates may need special handling. Some inmates require special religious artifacts to perform their rituals, whereas others may want special diets if their health or their beliefs forbid them from eating certain kinds of foods. It is quite important that jail officers receive some training in the rights of inmates under their control (Cohn, 1998; Potter, 1991).

Jail officers also need to know how much force to apply when moving prisoners from place to place within their jails. Some lawsuits allege that jail administrators have failed to properly train their officers in the proper use of force. Some jail inmates who suffer physical injuries may not receive immediate treatment because some jail officers may choose to neglect these injuries or regard them as unimportant. Since many of these lawsuits are successful, this emphasizes the importance of adequately training jail staff and equipping them with a variety of interpersonal, physical, and psychological skills (Drapkin and Klugiewicz, 1994a, 1994b). Critical contact points between jail officers and inmates include (1) stabilizing inmates with handcuffs or other restraint devices, (2) monitoring inmates and debriefing them, (3) searching inmates, (4) escorting inmates, (5) transporting inmates (e.g., to hospitals or schools), and (6) turnover (e.g., turning inmates over to other authorities, such as state corrections officials for movement to other facilities) (Drapkin and Klugiewicz, 1994b).

Jail and prison overcrowding have contributed significantly to inmate violence as well as to substandard health and safety conditions. It is not difficult to understand why more than a few judges have held prison officials accountable and obligated to remedy prison conditions to make them more fit for human inhabitation (Cole and Call, 1992). When inmates are sexually assaulted by other prisoners in small cells containing four inmates but designed to accommodate only two inmates, should the prison administrator be held accountable (Maahs and del Carmen, 1996)? Through court litigation, cases are decided every day concerning whether or not one or more parties in a jail or prison are negligent.

Negligence refers to a duty of one person to another to act as a reasonable person might be expected to act, or the failure to act when action is appropriate. Legally, negligence is the failure to exercise reasonable care toward another (Black, 1990:1033–1034). Different kinds of negligence can be determined, as well as different degrees of negligence. State and federal governments may be liable if their prison correctional officers fail to perform according to certain standards of training. Under theories of **negligent training** (an officer is simply improperly trained or untrained), **negligent assignment** (an officer is assigned a position for which he or she is unqualified), **negligent entrustment** (administrators fail to monitor those officers entrusted with items they are unfamiliar with using, such as giving firearms to prison correctional officers without first exposing them to firearms training), or **negligent retention** (officers determined to be unfit for their jobs are kept in those jobs anyway), inmates may have grounds to sue the government or their administrative representatives (Josi and Sechrest, 1998).

Degrees of negligence include slight, ordinary, and gross, although the courts regard as significant degrees of care rather than degrees of negligence (Black, 1990:1033–1034). Gross negligence includes willful, wanton, and reckless negligence, in which acts are performed that are totally unreasonable and without regard for their consequences. A civil standard exists for establishing negligence of officials or officers. This is the *preponderance of evidence* standard. Thus, whether the plaintiff (usually the inmate) or defendant (usually administrators of a prison or jail or their agents, correctional officers or other officers) prevails is contingent on whether the preponderance of evidence is in the plaintiff's favor or the defendant's favor.

If the government is negligent or if any agent or agency of the government is negligent in its treatment of prisoners, liability is incurred and damages may be sought by inmates for relief. But establishing negligence is difficult. Several cases are worth describing. In one case, an inmate was placed in a District of Columbia prison in a cell with another inmate who had active tuberculosis (*Sypert v. United States,* 1983). The plaintiff sued prison administrators alleging negligence, because he was placed in a cell with a tubercular inmate, and because subsequent skin tests showed the presence of tubercle bacilli in his body. But since he never developed active tuberculosis, the court said that he had not been physically injured and dismissed his case.

In an Oregon case, an inmate was stabbed by another inmate (*Walker v. United States,* 1977). The injured inmate sued Oregon officials, alleging that they were negligent because they failed to search other inmates for contraband, knives, or other dangerous weapons. But the preponderance of evidence presented in court by the inmate was insufficient to show that the correctional officers or warden were negligent.

In two other cases in which inmates were seriously injured or killed, evidence was presented of administrative knowledge of gang presence in the prison as a threat to prisoner safety. In one case, a lawsuit alleged administrative negligence in the classification of the plaintiff to a higher level of security and interaction with more dangerous prisoners. The inmate was subsequently killed by other violent inmates and his relatives brought suit against the administrator of corrections (*Quinones v. Nettleship,* 1985). General jail safety conditions were challenged, including where the correctional officers were or should have been stationed, and what measures should have been taken by administrators to protect other inmates from gang violence. But again, insufficient evidence was presented to show administrators or correctional staff were at fault.

In a Texas case, an inmate was being held in the Dallas County Jail. He became a snitch for the government and informed them about certain illegal activities of another inmate. The incident was reported in the local newspaper, which was distributed to other jail inmates. When the other inmates found out about him and learned how he had helped the government in their case against another jail inmate, he was beaten severely. He sued the U.S. government and jail employees, alleging that they failed to protect him from danger. The court ruled that the government had no duty to foresee such acts and absolved jail officials of blame in the incident (*Hackett v. United States*, 1978).

SUMMARY

There are over 3,300 jails in the United States. These are conventionally regarded as short-term confinement facilities for less serious offenders and are locally operated and funded in most jurisdictions. Contemporary jails are patterned after jail architecture pioneered during the 1800s. Jails in the American colonies were deplorable, and it was not until the creation of the Walnut Street Jail in Philadelphia in the 1790s that jail operations and organization became more sophisticated and humane.

Jails usually are administered by county sheriffs who oversee jail staff. Jails are intended to hold pretrial detainees, witnesses in protective custody, those held on detainer warrants and who are wanted in other jurisdictions, probation and parole violators, and misdemeanants. Increasingly, some of the larger jails are accommodating inmate overflows from state prisons. Until the past few decades, little attention was devoted to jail officer training and professionalization. Many improvements have been made recently, however, and educational and training programs have been established to professionalize these officers. One result has been a general improvement in jail standards and inmate treatment. Several jail issues of interest to administrators are jail overcrowding, inmate classification, the emergence and presence of gangs, jail architecture and aging jails, and jail privatization.

In contrast, prisons are self-contained institutions designed to hold more serious inmates for longer periods. The first state prison was established in a former copper mine in Connecticut in the 1770s. In the early 1800s, the construction of prisons increased dramatically, particularly in Pennsylvania and New York. The Auburn Penitentiary was constructed in 1816 and ush-

ered in several innovations that were widely copied by other prisons. A tier system was used to segregate prisoners according to their offense seriousness. In 1876, the Elmira Reformatory was built in New York as a commitment to the rehabilitative ideal. The American Correctional Association was founded during that same time period, and considerable attention was focused on prisons as rehabilitative institutions. High rates of recidivism among offenders released from these institutions suggested that rehabilitation was not occurring, however. Although the rehabilitative ideal has not been abandoned, the general orientation of prisons today is punishment and incapacitation.

Several prison functions include providing societal protection, punishing offenders, rehabilitation, incapacitation, and reintegration. Most prisons have work programs involving a portion of their inmate populations, and some inmates may participate in educational and other vocational opportunities as well. Prisons also offer a full range of individual and group counseling services for dealing with drug and alcohol dependencies. It is uncertain if these programs are successful in effecting offender treatment and recovery, however.

Administration of prisons is largely political; wardens and superintendents often are appointed by governors and other high-level government officials. Prison superintendents and wardens show a great deal of diversity in their backgrounds and qualifications for correctional administration. Many of these administrators do not have extensive experience in the correctional field. More than a few administrators have business administration backgrounds, and their management of prison affairs reflects their academic backgrounds and credentials. Several management styles typify prison management. These include the authoritarian model, the bureaucratic-lawful model, the shared-powers model, and the inmate control model.

Several important prison issues include inmate classification, overcrowding, litigation, legal liabilities, and prison privatization. Prisons must accommodate all types of offenders. Most prisons are chronically overcrowded, and such overcrowding is a detriment to the quality of vocational and educational programs that are offered to prisoners. Prison officials and correctional officers are constantly exposed to possible liabilities arising from their actions. Numerous lawsuits are filed each year by jail and prison inmates against officers, administrative staff, and entire prison systems. Some of these lawsuits are successful and have resulted in substantial changes in how prisoners are treated. Another issue is the rapid of growth of privatization in jail and prison operations. Private corporations have increasingly intruded into corrections at all levels. Their involvement in corrections generally is controversial, although no constitutional prohibitions exist against private enterprises operating correctional services. Additionally, both jail and prison administrators are increasingly sensitive to their legal liabilities. Often, lawsuits are filed by inmates that allege negligence. Negligence theories include negligent training, negligent assignment, negligent entrustment, and negligent retention. Administrators continually strive to hire more qualified personnel and to ensure that their subsequent training will minimize the incidence of lawsuits from prisoners.

QUESTIONS FOR REVIEW

1. Distinguish between prisons and jails. What are some key functions of jails?

2. What are four primary classification methods for distinguishing between different types of prison inmates? Describe each.

3. What are four prison management models? Which one do you prefer and why?

4. What qualifications exist for jail personnel? What is meant by certification?

5. What are some common types of subjects taught in jail certification courses? Why do you think they are important?

6. How can jail officers minimize lawsuits from inmates? What is the human services approach? Describe it.

7. What are three major jail issues? Discuss each issue briefly and explain why it is important.

8. What are three major prison issues? Why is privatization of corrections controversial?

9. What are the academic backgrounds of a majority of wardens and superintendents in the United States? How do these credentials qualify them for their posts?

10. Who are jailhouse lawyers and what have they accomplished relating to prison reforms? Are monetary rewards often won by jailhouse lawyers? What are two important cases prisoners have lost concerning prison overcrowding? Describe each.

SUGGESTED READINGS

Bartol, Curt R. (ed.) (2000). "Standards for Psychology Services in Jails, Prisons, Correctional Facilities, and Agencies." *Criminal Justice and Behavior* **27**:427–494.

Henderson, Martha, et al. (2000). "Race, Rights, and Order in Prison: A National Survey of Wardens on the Racial Integration of Prison Cells." *Prison Journal* **80**:295–308.

Tonry, Michael, and Joan Petersilia (eds.) (1999). *Prisons.* Chicago: University of Chicago Press.

• CASE STUDIES •

1. THE SNITCH

At Cookeville Prison, a seemingly endless supply of drugs was available to the 1,400 inmates. The warden, John Sharpton, had been on the job about six months and was constantly receiving reports that drugs had been found during cell shakedowns, which were conducted randomly by different correctional officers. No one seemed to know how the prisoners were getting the drugs. Inmates were allowed personal visits each week from their family members, but correctional officers subjected these persons to extensive searches. K-9 units with dogs also were used for the purpose of detecting drugs. But no drugs were found being brought in by prisoners' families.

Warden Sharpton suspected that one or more correctional officers were smuggling illegal drugs into the prison, although he could not prove it. The correctional officers had a union that prohibited them from being subject to body cavity searches. Furthermore, they could bring in lunch boxes and suitcases that were not subjected to routine inspections. The union was even strong enough to prevent the use of K-9 units to check correctional officers when they entered the prison to report for work.

• CASE STUDIES •

One afternoon, Bill Brehm, a new correctional officer, asked to see Warden Sharpton. Brehm had been a former police officer. He was older than the other correctional officers. In fact, at age 48, he was the oldest correctional officer in the prison. The younger correctional officers did not relate to him well, mostly because of the age difference. When Brehm entered Sharpton's office, he closed the door and asked Warden Sharpton if there was any way that they could be overheard by anyone. Sharpton reassured him that his office was secure and reasonably soundproof. Besides, his secretary in the outer office was taking his lunch break.

Brehm proceeded to describe what he had seen over the last few weeks. He said that six correctional officers routinely gathered at a bar in town called the Lucky Strike when they were off duty. Brehm happened to go by there one evening and saw the officers together at a table drinking beer and talking loudly. He entered the bar and noticed that they were tipping the waitress exceptionally well, giving her a $20 bill for an $8 pitcher of beer and telling her to keep the change. He sat unobserved at a table in another section of the bar, but he could overhear some of their conversation. He was able to hear enough to make him suspect that these officers were involved in a scheme to smuggle drugs into the prison. Later, he told Warden Sharpton, he was in the officers' dressing area one morning preparing for work. The other officers had already left and he was alone in the locker room. Using prior knowledge acquired as a police officer and a lock-picking kit, he picked the locks of three lockers belonging to the officers he had overheard earlier at the bar. Surreptitiously, he opened the three lockers and examined briefcases that the officers had brought into the prison. One briefcase contained a large amount of money, probably as much as $30,000. Another briefcase contained probably a kilo of cocaine or heroin. Brehm was not sure, because he did not want to take the time to make a more thorough inspection. In the third locker, he found two bags of marijuana, at least a pound or more, as well as another large sum of money. He estimated that the $100 bills totaled more than $10,000. He locked the lockers again so that no one would know that they had been opened.

He took out a typed piece of paper and gave Warden Sharpton a list of the six officers he had overheard at the bar. He put asterisks beside the names of those officers whose lockers he had searched. He said that he had not been observed by anyone while examining their lockers, and that as far as he knew, no one suspected what he had discovered.

Questions for Discussion

1. If you were Warden Sharpton, what would you advise Brehm to do? Would you want Brehm to continue his informal surveillance of these men, or would you want him to try to get close to them and gain their confidence?
2. As a warden, is there any way that you can manufacture a reason to conduct a search of the correctional officer locker room without tipping off these officers that you know about the drugs and money?
3. Is there anything you can say to correctional officer union officials about the incident and what you have learned that will encourage them to let you take aggressive action against the officers who are dealing in drugs?
4. Should you notify the state or federal authorities about the drug problem and your correctional officers' involvement in it? Why or why not?
5. Did Brehm act properly by searching the officers' lockers without their knowledge or permission, based on what he heard them say at the bar? Why or why not?

2. A Case of Negligence?

Sheriffs' deputies Joan Arthur and Alvin Smith pulled over an out-of-state car that was weaving late at night on a county highway. The deputies approached the car and found a middle-aged man slumped over the driver's wheel. The man was babbling incoherently. Arthur and Smith believed the man was drunk. They lifted him from the car, handcuffed him, and manhandled him into the back of their cruiser. When they got to the county jail, the man was passed out. They searched him and removed his wallet. They determined from his ID that he was MacArthur Sims, 58 years old, and that he was from a nearby state. He was carrying $425 in his wallet and appeared to be well dressed. The officers had some jail officers help them carry him into one of the drunk tanks where they placed him on a cot. There were 12 other men in the drunk tank being held on various drinking-related charges. Arthur told Smith and the jail officers, "This guy's too tanked to book. Let's put him in the drunk tank where he can sleep it off." No one administered any type of blood test to determine Sims's intoxication level. The next morning, a jail officer opened the drunk tank and found Sims lying on the cot asleep. He awakened Sims, who seemed in a daze. Sims asked where he was, and the officer said, "You were pulled over for drunk driving last night and you're in our county jail." Sims was indignant and said, "I wasn't drinking last night. I was driving from my cousin's house where they had a wedding reception for my niece. I'm a lawyer and I had no alcoholic beverages last night. I remember getting dizzy and having chest pains while driving and then there were some flashing lights in my rearview mirror. But after that, it's all a blank. By the way, where's my wallet, watch, and rings?" The jail officer said, "What watch and rings? The deputies that brought you in here took your wallet with over $400 in it. We have it in a bag for you. We put you in the tank to sleep it off. You can post $250 bond and leave now if you want. But you'll have to appear before Judge Brown tomorrow on drunk-driving charges or forfeit the bond." Sims removed $250 from his wallet, which the jail officer returned to him, obtained a receipt, and left the jail.

Shortly thereafter, Sims went to a nearby hospital and was examined by a physician, Dr. Lauren Wilson. Dr. Wilson performed some tests and determined that Sims had had a mild heart attack the previous evening and that this brought on the dizziness. Absolutely no evidence was found that he had been drinking the night before, and no alcohol or drugs were found in his blood when it was tested. Sims contacted one of his lawyer friends in the community, Jeff Arlington, who met him back at the county jail. The men entered the jail and Arlington asked to speak with Sheriff Abe

Giles. The sheriff invited the men into his office. "Abe," said Arlington, "You guys really screwed up last night. You pulled over my attorney friend here, Mac Sims, who had suffered a mild heart attack. He was thrown into one of your deputies' cars and taken to your jail. Then he was tossed into the drunk tank. Sometime between the time he was arrested, taken to the drunk tank, and let out this morning, he lost his expensive watch and some valuable rings he was wearing. I want to know where that property is. Where are the deputies who made this arrest, anyway? I understand from the paperwork that they were Arthur and Smith. I'd like to talk to them right away. They have some explaining to do."

Questions for Discussion

1. If you were Sheriff Giles and this was the first you had heard of the incident, how would you respond to Arlington?

2. Should you attempt to provide an explanation for the missing watch and jewelry? You strongly suspect that the officers who put Sims in the drunk tank were not particularly careful in removing Sims's personal effects. Thus, you surmise that one or more of the drunk tank occupants probably stole those items from Sims while he was passed out and disabled. Who should be held accountable for the missing items?

3. What responsibilities do Arthur and Smith have when making arrests of suspects who appear to be intoxicated? Should they have obtained a blood alcohol check of Sims before putting him in the drunk tank? Why or why not?

4. Were the jail officers who assisted Arthur and Smith negligent in failing to book Sims properly before confining him in an unconscious state in a cell with others? Why or why not?

5. If you were Sheriff Giles, what policies would you enact to prevent such an occurrence in the future?

6. Who is liable for what happened and why?

CHAPTER 12

COMMUNITY CORRECTIONS ORGANIZATIONS

KEY TERMS

Absolute immunity
Client
Community corrections
Community corrections act (CCA)
Community residential centers
Community service orders
Creaming
Day fine
Day fine programs
Day reporting
Day reporting centers

Electronic monitoring
False negatives
False positives
Financial/community service model
Fines
Furlough
Halfway house
Home confinement
House arrest
Paraprofessional
Parolee

Parole officer (PO)
POs
Probationer
Probation officer (PO)
Quasi-judicial immunity
Restitution
Victim/offender mediation model
Victim/reparations model
Volunteer
Work/study release

CHAPTER OBJECTIVES

The following objectives are intended:

1. To define and describe community corrections and community corrections acts

2. To describe conventional probation and parole services available to clients

3. To describe the functions and goals of probation and parole agencies

4. To describe the recruitment process for probation and parole officers, including the criteria used for officer selection and training

5. To examine several community corrections programs, including home confinement and electronic monitoring

6. To describe several prerelease programs for prison and jail inmates, including work release, study release, and furloughs

7. To describe several programs for parolees, including halfway houses, community residential centers, and day reporting programs

8. To discuss several important issues associated with community corrections, including the rights of clients who are supervised, the legal liabilities of those who work in community corrections agencies, and the use of volunteers and paraprofessionals

INTRODUCTION

This chapter examines community corrections, an umbrella term that encompasses everything from pretrial diversion to intermediate punishments, including probation, parole, home confinement, electronic monitoring, day fine programs, work release, furloughs, and any other nonincarcerative option available to those convicted of crimes or facing conviction. Since a majority of community programs involve either probationers or parolees, attention will be given to their management by different state and federal agencies and organizations. Even persons who are unconvicted, such as pretrial divertees, usually are supervised under the auspices of probation departments in communities.

The first part of this chapter provides a general overview of community corrections, including its goals and functions. These goals and functions direct the work of probation and parole officers (POs) who supervise various types of clients. A client is any person, unconvicted or convicted of a crime, who is under the direct supervision of a community corrections agency, whether it is a probation or parole office or a community services organization. A brief profile of community corrections clients is presented to illustrate the diversity and nature of clients supervised.

Probation and parole services are examined next, including the organization and administration of these departments. The goals and functions of probation and parole services are discussed, including the recruitment, selection, and training of POs and other types of client supervisors. Probation and parole programs vary in the intensity of the degree of supervision over clients, and these different forms of supervision intensity are considered. PO work is dangerous, and therefore, one aspect of this section will be to examine the use of firearms as well as firearms training for POs who interact with an increasingly dangerous client aggregate.

The next section broadly surveys several types of community programs that fit either probationers or parolees. For probationers, these programs include home confinement, electronic monitoring, and intensive supervised probation. For parolees, these programs include work/study release, furloughs, and halfway houses. Of course, more than a few parolees are subject to home confinement and electronic monitoring as well, as a part of their parole programs. Many offenders also are involved in different types of restitution programs to compensate victims and the state for

their wrongs and for damages they have inflicted that have caused property loss or physical impairments. Day reporting centers, fines, community service, and various forms of restitution and restorative justice are discussed.

The last section of this chapter examines several issues relevant to community corrections, including the rights of clients and the legal liabilities of persons who supervise them. Some of these people are volunteers, and others are paraprofessionals. These distinctions will be briefly highlighted as a part of the discussion of related community corrections issues.

AN OVERVIEW OF COMMUNITY CORRECTIONS

Community-based programs vary among communities but share these characteristics:

1. One or more large homes or buildings located within the residential section of the community with space to accommodate between 20 and 30 residents are provided within walking distance of work settings and social services.
2. A professional and paraprofessional staff is on call for medical, social, or psychological emergencies.
3. A system is in place for heightening staff accountability to the court concerning offender progress.
4. Community-based program administrators have the authority to oversee offender behaviors and enforce compliance with their probation conditions.
5. These programs have job referral and placement services available in which paraprofessionals or others act as liaisons with various community agencies and organizations to facilitate offender job placement.
6. Administrators of these programs are available on the premises on a 24-hour basis for emergency situations and spontaneous assistance for offenders who may need help.

Community Corrections Acts

A **community corrections act (CCA)** is the enabling medium by which jurisdictions establish local community corrections agencies, facilities, and programs. It is administered on a statewide basis and distributes funds to local governments for the purpose of planning, developing, and delivering correctional sanctions and services. Community corrections acts are intended to divert prison-bound offenders into local, city, or county programs in which they can receive treatment and assistance. The philosophy of community corrections is to provide offenders with rehabilitation and permit reintegration into their communities. **Community corrections** encompasses probation and parole services, halfway houses, work/study release, home confinement and electronic monitoring programs, **day fine** and **day fine programs,** restitution and restorative justice, and work/study release.

Functions and Goals of Community Corrections

The goals of community corrections programs include (1) facilitating offender reintegration, (2) fostering offender rehabilitation, (3) providing offender punishment, (4) heightening offender accountability, (5) monitoring and supervising clients, (6) providing employment assistance, (7) alleviating prison and jail overcrowding, (8) facilitating vocational and educational training, and (9) ensuring public safety.

Community corrections programs aim to allow offenders to remain in their communities and maintain contact with their families. This residential objective is regarded as a significant attempt to rehabilitate offenders and encourage them to become law-abiding citizens. A certain element of trust is given to offenders who become eligible for such programs. At the same time, restrictions govern these programs in the form of behavioral requirements. These restrictions or conditions must be complied with explicitly. If clients fail to observe these requirements and obligations, they may be in jeopardy of being terminated from their programs and sent to jail or prison. Thus, this is a punishment function that is often overlooked by a critical public who may see community corrections as coddling offenders rather than helping them in various positive ways.

Restitution, community service, drug/alcohol checks, curfews, and reporting requirements are typical of many of these programs. In fact, some convicted offenders have chosen jail or prison rather than subject themselves to the rigors of community corrections program requirements. This may sound strange, but these clients may be rousted by POs at anytime during the day or evening hours for no reason other than to search their premises for illegal contraband or anything that might demonstrate to investigating POs that clients are not complying with program requirements.

Most community corrections clients are supervised more or less closely. They are obligated to check in regularly to a central location or be subjected to random visits by POs or others. This periodic checking ensures program compliance. Employment assistance is offered as well, since many clients are unfamiliar with filling out job application forms or may not know who to contact for jobs. Community corrections organizations maintain lists of employers who are willing to hire ex-offenders. These are valuable contacts for clients that they would not have if they were merely released into communities without supervision following confinement in jail or prison.

A variety of educational and vocational services is offered to these clients, often at a nominal charge. Sometimes, fees for these services are waived. Improving the educational and vocational training qualifications of these clients reduces their need to commit crimes to support themselves when living in the community. The direct benefits of reducing jail and prison overcrowding by allowing a substantial portion of offenders to remain in their communities are apparent. Currently, we would need at least five times as much existing prison and jail space to lock up everyone who deserved to be incarcerated if community corrections programs were not available. Thus, community agencies who supervise these clients perform a valuable service by keeping the numbers of jail and prison inmates lower than they would be if they were confined, even for short incarcerative periods.

Public safety can never be guaranteed. Risks are involved whenever criminals are released into communities. However, attempts are made at every level, including judicial and parole board decision making, to release only those persons who pose the greatest chance of being successful in their programs. Screening devices of various kinds have been designed to measure an offender's dangerousness or the risk posed to community residents. No instrument has ever been devised to be completely foolproof, however. Thus, some offenders always will slip through the cracks. False positives and false negatives are most disturbing to our judicial and parole board decision makers. **False positives** are those individuals predicted to be dangerous who turn out not to be dangerous. We overpenalize them by denying them access to these community programs. **False negatives** are those predicted not to be dangerous but who turn out to be

BOX 12.1 PERSONALITY HIGHLIGHT

TIM BREHM
Community Corrections Manager, Department of Corrections and Rehabilitation, Division of Field Services, North Dakota

Statistics: A.A. (criminal justice), Minot State University; B.S. (human resources administration and management), Valley City State College

Work Experience: Captain, U.S. Army Reserves; Battalion Operations and Training Officer for the 439th Engineer Battalion, Bismarck, North Dakota; Logistics Staff Officer, HHD Commander Intelligence Staff Officer; Commanding Officer of the 793rd Engineer Unit, Minot, North Dakota.

Awards and Honors: Bismarck AMVETS Color and Honor Guard; 1997 recipient of Governor's Award for Excellence; 1996 recipient of Bismarck/Mandan Chamber of Commerce Golden Eagle Award; one of North Dakota's Ten Community Heroes to carry torch in U.S. Olympic relay event; first North Dakota military soldier to receive the Military Outstanding Volunteerism Award; Infantry and Airborne Ranger.

Interests and Background: I currently have a B.S. degree with a major in human resources administration and management. I began my criminal justice career in 1976 with the Jamestown Police Department, North Dakota, just two months following an honorable discharge from the U.S. Army. I served as a sergeant for the Stutsman County Sheriff's Department in Jamestown, and in 1985, I began my employment with the North Dakota Division of Parole and Probation, where I am presently employed as a community corrections program manager.

I initially became interested in police work because I enjoy working with people, and I am very community minded. I identified this position as an opportunity not only to make a difference with individuals but also within the larger community. Subsequently, I selected corrections as the criminal justice field for my work because I believed I could make an even bigger difference in the lives of those individuals on probation or parole.

Interesting Work Experiences: My most memorable experiences in 23 years include the following:

1. A standoff with a murderer
2. My involvement in the Gordon Kahl incident in Medina, North Dakota, and arresting the wife of Gordon Kahl
3. Development and implementation of 11 community service/restitution programs in North Dakota
4. Responsibility for the first victim/offender mediation gang-related murder case in Minot, North Dakota

Over the years, I have had an opportunity to observe the increased professionalism and quality of young people who are applying for positions with our agency. We are receiving very qualified and excellent applicants for our parole and probation officer positions.

I find it hard to cite frustrating things about my work. A combination of really enjoying this profession as well as working with wonderful people on a regular basis may account for this. Probably the most frustrating item I can single out is having to advise employees that they are discharged from employment as they did not meet the required expectations of our department.

Advice to Students: I would advise students who went to enter the criminal justice field to (1) treat others as you would want to be treated in a similar situation; in other words, think about how it might feel to be in another person's shoes before you make your final decision; (2) always, always treat others with the utmost respect; and (3) have patience with others, be courteous, and most of all, be honest.

dangerous and who commit additional crimes that harm community residents when participating in a parole or probation program.

Profiling Community Corrections Clients

In 1998, there were 1.7 million offenders in state community corrections programs (Maguire and Pastore, 2000). About 85 percent of these offenders were required to pay supervision fees, court costs, and fines. A third had to pay restitution to victims, and 25 percent had to perform community service. Nearly half of these offenders were required to participate in substance abuse treatment programs and counseling. They also were subject to random drug and alcohol checks. Less than 5 percent of these clients were restricted in their movements around the community, with only 4 percent placed on electronic monitoring and/or house arrest with curfews.

PROBATION AND PAROLE SERVICES

Different departments and agencies in each state administer probation and parole departments. Most states have departments of corrections that supervise both incarcerated and nonincarcerated offenders. These tasks sometimes are overseen in other jurisdictions by departments of human services, departments of youth services, or some other umbrella agency.

Functions and Goals of Probation and Parole Services

The functions and goals of probation and parole services are as follows: (1) to supervise offenders; (2) to ensure offender-client compliance with program conditions by conducting random searches of offender premises, maintaining contact with offender-client employers, and otherwise maintaining occasional face-to-face spot checks; (3) to conduct routine and random drug/alcohol checks; (4) to provide networking services for employment assistance; (5) to direct offender-clients to proper treatment, counseling, and other forms of requested assistance; (6) to protect the community and its residents by detecting program infractions and reporting infractions to judges and parole boards; (7) to assist offenders in becoming reintegrated into their communities; and (8) to engage in any

rehabilitative action that will improve offender-client skills and law-abiding behavior.

Organization and Administration of Probation and Parole Departments

Each state and large city has its own organization for administering and supervising probationers and parolees. A **probationer** is someone who has been convicted of a crime but has been sentenced to terms in his or her own community rather than being incarcerated. A **parolee** is someone who has been convicted of a crime, sentenced to prison or jail, and released short of serving his or her maximum sentence. A probationer or parolee under supervision in his or her community is referred to as a **client.** A **probation officer** typically supervises probationer/clients, whereas a **parole officer** supervises parolees. A further distinction is that probationers are under the jurisdiction of their original sentencing judges; but parolees are generally under the jurisdiction of parole boards. In some jurisdictions, probation and parole supervisory responsibilities are combined into a single agency. Probation and parole officers are simply referred to collectively as **POs.**

The volume of offenders makes a significant difference in how departments are managed and the sizes of caseloads POs have. In some areas of the country, such as New York City, PO caseloads for supervising probationers are as high as 400. In other parts of the country, caseloads for POs may be as low as 10. Obviously, in those areas in which PO caseloads are sizeable, the supervision exercised over these offenders is different from the supervision received by clients in jurisdictions in which client caseloads are under 25.

Some jurisdictions have established drive-in windows in shopping centers so that clients may drive up to a window as if they are going to withdraw cash from an automated teller machine. Instead of withdrawing cash, however, they place their hands on a surface that reads their palm prints and verifies their whereabouts. In other locations, such as Long Beach, California, large numbers of probationers and some parolees report to a central office monthly to verify that they are employed and are remaining law abiding. These check-ins mean that numerous offenders can be supervised. The quality of this type of supervision is questionable, however. Without frequent, random, and direct face-to-face contact with offender-clients, POs have no way of knowing whether these clients are law abiding or

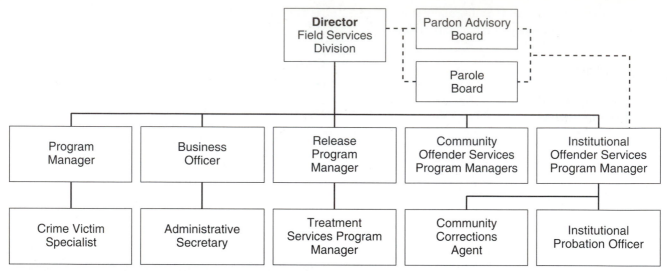

FIGURE 12.1 A Field Services Division Central Office Organizational Chart

engaging in some illicit behavior. Only those who do something to attract the attention of police come to the attention of POs. Also, POs may detect probation or parole program violations during random visits to offender-clients' premises at odd hours.

Most states and the federal government attempt to divide clients according to the seriousness of their prior offending. Some offenders are deemed at greater risk of reoffending than others. Therefore, they are targeted for more intensive supervision. Lower-risk offenders are less likely to reoffend, and therefore their supervision does not need to be as intense. An example of a typical probation and parole agency is the field services division central office of a midwestern state; Figure 12.1 shows a diagram of this office. There is a director, a program manager, a business officer, a release program manager, three community offender services program managers, and an institutional offender services manager.

One good feature of this field services division organizational chart is that it is relatively simple. There are not that many people on probation or parole in a typical midwestern state. For example, in 1998, 2,600 probationers and 100 parolees were being supervised in one midwestern state (Maguire and Pastore, 2000). Despite these low numbers, even the state probation and parole field services division can be fairly complex. Figure 12.2 (p. 272) shows a diagram of the division of labor for a typical parole and probation field services division.

The organizational chart in Figure 12.2 shows a general manager over each of four major regions of the state, along with a manager who supervises an intensive program for offenders who need to be more closely monitored. In this example, the state is large geographically, so it is imperative to divide it according to quadrants, with a west region supervisor, a central region supervisor, a south region supervisor, and a north region supervisor. Notice that there are 14 correctional centers in the areas served by these four regions. Under the intensive program, there also are four regional supervisors and support staff to supervise offenders.

The general mission of the field services division overseeing probationers, parolees, and other community-based clients is to protect society by ensuring that the community-placed offenders are provided responsible supervision that requires them to be an active participant in their rehabilitation. Supervising offenders requires proactive intervention and case management strategies. The field services division continuously reviews and modifies programs it provides to address community safety issues, prison overcrowding, and offender needs. The intensive supervision program typifies programming designed to facilitate the supervision of those offenders posing the greatest risks and needs. Halfway houses, home confinement programs, and curfews are some of the intermediate sanctions used to verify compliance with supervision sanctions. Electronic monitoring and on-site drug testing also are tools used regularly by POs to supervise offenders.

BOX 12.2 PERSONALITY HIGHLIGHT

JACKIE C. JENSEN
Chief Officer, Division of Parole and Probation, Minot, ND District, North Dakota Department of Corrections and Rehabilitation

Statistics: B.S.S.W. (social work), Criminal Justice and Psychology (minors), University of North Dakota; Licensed Social Worker, North Dakota

Background and Training: I grew up in Grand Forks, North Dakota, and so, of course, I had to attend the University of North Dakota. I graduated with a bachelor of science degree in social work in 1985. I had minors in criminal justice and psychology. I was licensed as a social worker for North Dakota in 1985 also. I completed the North Dakota Law Enforcement Training Academy in 1987, and I am currently a licensed law enforcement officer for North Dakota. In the past few years, I have participated in nearly 1,300 hours of training involving various law enforcement and social work topics.

Work Experience: My first professional job out of college was for the Adams County Social Service Board as a social worker in Hettinger, North Dakota. I held this position from May 1985 to June 1986. It was at this point that a deputy sheriff position opened up in Adams County and I entered the field of law enforcement. I was a deputy in this county until October 1989, when I was hired by the North Dakota Department of Corrections and Rehabilitation, Division of Parole and Probation. My initial post was in the Bottineau, North Dakota, area, and I transferred to Minot, North Dakota, in February 1991. I am currently the lead officer in the Minot district.

For as long as I can remember, I have always been interested in criminal justice. I was basically a rebel when I was growing up and found that life to be exciting. I also saw how destructive risk-taking behavior could be, and so I walked a fine line, which means I rarely got caught. I never wanted to be an actual police officer and patrol the streets, but I knew that in order to be employed by the department of parole and probation, I needed this kind of experience. In order to work with people who have gotten themselves into trouble, you need to know where they came from and how they grew up.

When you work as a patrolman, you see the best and the worst of people in many situations. I majored in social work in order to learn about behaviors, different societies, and lots of interviewing techniques. I do not think that I would have gotten as much practice dealing one-on-one with people and learning how to conduct interviews if I had majored in criminal justice. The biggest problem I had with social work is that it is basically nonconfrontive and my nature is to be up front and to get right to the point of matters. I also strongly believe that people in general need to be accountable for their behavior and need to be responsible. I believe that as a parole officer, you need to care about what the end results are, care about what happens to people, and that most people do not like to confront their weaknesses, but when they do, they become better people.

Interesting and Frustrating Experiences: Early in my career, one of my clients was continuing to deal drugs, and so I was involved in a series of searches one night with other law enforcement agencies that netted over four pounds of marijuana, more than $32,000 in cash, and numerous firearms. Other searches have resulted in removing pounds of marijuana off the streets of our community, which is very rewarding. It feels great to have a good cooperative relationship with other law enforcement agencies working for the same goal. It is also interesting when old clients that were not very cooperative during supervision come back to you years later and tell you how you affected their lives.

My biggest frustration is with the whole court process. In our area, we are involved in completing presentence investigations that often result in uncovering long histories of criminal behavior. Even before the prosecuting attorney gets this report, he has plea-bargained with the defense attorney for a sentence that, in my opinion, is not appropriate and that sends out a message to the defendant that his behavior is not that bad. I do not believe that many defendants are held accountable. I am not against giving defendants a chance, but if they are placed on probation and violate that order, I really believe that there need to be consequences or else we are just enabling that defendant to continue his or her criminal behavior. We also need appropriate conditions ordered by the court to supervise defendants. It is sad when drug offenders do not have a urinalysis clause or a search clause in their probation or parole agreements. It is also scary when sex offenders are not prohibited from having contact with children under the age of 18.

Advice to Students: For anybody who wants to enter the field of probation and parole, I would suggest that they get out in the world and get experience working with a wide range of people. We not only work with defendants but with their families, attorneys, judges, treatment staff, child support, social services, and lots of law enforcement personnel. I strongly encourage students to participate in an internship during their education. Our department hires many interns because they have the work experience. I would also suggest that students take any class they can that focuses on and practices interviewing. It is also important to get involved in other activities totally unrelated to this field so that they do not get pessimistic and think that all people are bad and worthless. You need to feel good about yourself and about what you are doing.

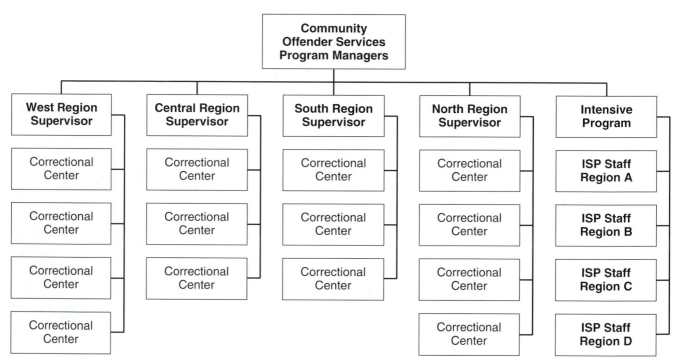

FIGURE 12.2 Parole and Probation Field Services Organizational Chart

Intensive Supervision Program

A prototype of an intensive supervision program for community-based correctional services has been established by the American Probation and Parole Association. Figure 12.3 shows a diagram of this prototypical intensive supervision program.

The program development process begins with the offender-client population to be served by different community agencies. These agencies devise mission statements that articulate clearly their goals and policies. Relations with local law enforcement agencies, parole boards, judges, and courts are lumped under "Other CJS Components." The community in which the agency is based is considered as another significant input that influences agency policy and protocol. One of the primary goals of these community-based agencies is to reduce offender recidivism. This goal is achieved in part through shifting from a custodial, incapacitative, and punitive mode to a more integrated approach of interventions and risk-control

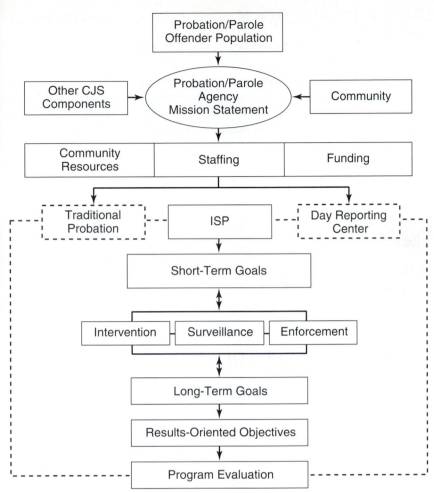

FIGURE 12.3 Intensive Supervision Program Development Process

Source: Betsy Fulton, Paul Gendreau, and Mario Paparozzi, "APPA's Prototypical Intensive Supervision Program: ISP As It Was Meant to Be," 1995, *APPA Perspectives* **19**:25–41. Reprinted with the permission of the American Probation and Parole Association.

strategies. A balanced approach to offender supervision is stressed, in which individual offender needs are prioritized and met. Prior agency goals were short-term ones; under future agency planning, goals are projected as long-range ones. Better risk control is both a short-term and long-term goal sought by all community-based agencies. Such risk control is achieved to a greater degree when agencies provide a greater range of assistance and offender services that meet offender needs, particularly in the areas of employment and substance abuse. The prototype also encourages focusing on results of programs rather than program activities. The two primary missions of pro-

bation and parole are to protect society and rehabilitate offenders.

Critical factors in effective program development include (1) needs assessment; (2) adequate staffing; (3) proper and ample funding; (4) engagement of stakeholders, including establishment of working task forces and creation of more effective public relations; (5) development of a network with community service providers; (6) close program monitoring and evaluation; (7) need to target greater numbers of high-risk/need offenders for program involvement and treatment; and (8) development of better selection instruments for the inclusion of program participants

(Fulton, Gendreau, and Paparozzi, 1995:27–30). Several ambitious goals have been outlined for the ideal community-based ISP agency: (1) increased public safety, (2) rehabilitation of offenders, (3) provision of intermediate punishments, (4) reduction in prison/jail overcrowding, and (5) reduction in operating costs. ISP objectives should be specific, measurable, achieved within a limited time, and identified with an actual result (Fulton, Gendreau, and Paparozzi, 1995:31). Critical elements for successful program implementation include smaller PO caseloads, a greater range of correctional interventions, a more objectives-based management system, systematic case review, a system of positive reinforcement for clients, a system of control and accountability, victim restitution, community involvement, and aftercare. Successful community-based ISP programs include New Jersey's ISP program devised in 1983; the Massachusetts Intensive Probation Supervision Program, implemented in 1985; and the Colorado Judicial Department's Specialized Drug Offender Program (SDOP), which was created in the early 1990s.

Selection Requirements for POs

Minimum educational requirements for those individuals entering the field of probation and parole in 1998 were fairly high. About 80 percent of the jurisdictions required a GED or high school diploma for an entry-level PO position, whereas 25 percent required either a community college (two-year) diploma or a bachelor's degree. The examination process for PO recruitment used in most jurisdictions has been described by the American Correctional Association (1995). Over 80 percent of the jurisdictions required a written examination, and about 40 percent subject recruits to psychological screening. The Minnesota Multiphasic Personality Inventory (MMPI) and Inwald Personality Inventory seem to be most popularly given, if such tests are used. Very few jurisdictions had recruitment processes that required physical examinations, medical checks, or FBI inquiries.

Training for recruits places considerable emphasis on the legal liabilities of POs and other types of corrections officers. The cultivation of skills in the management and supervision of offender-clients also is stressed. Programs also are offered for managing stress, crisis intervention and hostage negotiations, proposal and report writing, legal issues training, managing community corrections facilities, dealing with the mentally ill offender, and suicide prevention.

In 1998, POs averaged 243 introductory training hours, with an average of 37 hours of in-service training (Camp and Camp, 1999a:201; Maguire and Pastore, 2000). Several probation and parole agencies require bachelor's degrees or equivalent experience, with an emphasis on a social science major. At least two states lack strenuous entry requirements. For instance, Minnesota requires applicants to pass a basic reading comprehension examination and a structured oral interview. In Nevada, POs must possess a high school diploma and have four years' experience, although the type of experience is unspecified. Nevada offers prospective recruits the option of possessing a bachelor's degree in lieu of four years' experience, however.

Characteristics of Probation and Parole Officers

Relatively little detailed information about POs exists, although several surveys have been conducted that describe their characteristics. These surveys indicate a gradual move toward greater PO professionalization. One indication of greater professionalization has been the movement toward accreditation and the establishment of accreditation programs through the American Correctional Association (ACA) and the American Probation and Parole Association (APPA). About 50 percent of all POs are male and about 24 percent are nonwhite. Many POs possess bachelor's degrees and have 9 to 12 years of on-the-job experience. Thus, the labor turnover among POs is not as great as it is among correctional officers.

The average PO annual salary in 1998 for entry-level work was $25,821, ranging from a high entry-level salary of $34,075 in Connecticut to a low of $20,004 in West Virginia (Camp and Camp, 1999a:202; Maguire and Pastore, 2000). The average salary of POs in 1998 was $33,316. The highest salaries for POs ranged from a low of $32,760 in Wyoming to a high of $83,000 in Alaska. Probation work pays a little better than parole work when departments of probation and departments of parole are compared, although the salary differences are not substantial. The federal system pays significantly higher salaries than most state systems at different grade levels, and thus, many POs start out in state PO work and eventually transfer to federal jobs when they are available. Most

POs in the sample studied had a bachelor's degree as the median educational level attained. Currently, many state systems require a bachelor's degree as the minimum educational level for entry-level parole officer positions. In many states, however, the general entry-level requirements for PO positions are less stringent.

PO Duties

POs perform many functions, including supervision, surveillance, investigating cases, assisting in rehabilitation, developing and discussing probation conditions, counseling, home visiting and working with clients, making arrests, making referrals, writing PSI reports, keeping records, performing court duties, collecting fines, supervising restitution, serving warrants, maintaining contracts with courts, recommending sentences, developing community service programs, assisting law enforcement officers and agencies, assisting courts in transferring cases, enforcing criminal laws, locating employment for clients, and initiating program revocations (Rogers, 1998).

Criticisms of Probation/Parole Programs

Historically, rehabilitation was believed to be possible for all types of offenders under most circumstances. Offenders sentenced to probation and those granted parole release were targeted for involvement in various types of community programs geared to improve their self-concept, skills, and job potential. But over time, rehabilitation occurred less frequently than recidivism, despite the best efforts of POs or the programs offered to offender-clients. Regardless of the true causes of recidivism among probationers and parolees, POs are often blamed and labeled as inadequate or ineffective. Some of the major criticisms of probation and parole programs and personnel are as follows:

1. Only one state required a college education of probation or parole officer applicants prior to 1980; some states only required that POs have the ability to read and write so that they could fill out PSI reports.

2. Past selection procedures for probation and parole officers have focused on physical attributes and security considerations.

3. Probation and parole officer training often has been based on the military model used for police training.

4. Probation and parole programs historically have been fragmented and independent of other criminal justice organizations and agencies.

5. The general field of corrections has lacked professionalization associated with established fields with specialized bodies of knowledge.

6. Most jurisdictions have lacked licensing mechanisms through which officers can become certified through proper in-service training and education.

ADMINISTERING WORK RELEASE, STUDY RELEASE, AND FURLOUGH PROGRAMS

Work/Study Release

Work/study release is any program in which inmates in jails or prisons are permitted to work in their communities with minimal restrictions and supervision, are compensated at the prevailing minimum wage, and must serve their nonworking hours housed in a secure facility (Camp and Camp, 1999a). In 1998, there were 17,000 work releasees in the United States under federal or state jurisdiction. New York led all states with 2,404 inmates involved in work release programs. Other states with large numbers of work releasees included Florida (1,657) and Illinois (1,397) (American Correctional Association, 1999:xxviii–xxix).

The first use of work release occurred in Vermont in 1906 when sheriffs assigned inmates to work outside jails in the community. By 1975, all states and the federal system had initiated some form of work release program. Work release is also known as day pass, day parole, temporary release, and work or education furloughs (Marlette, 1990).

Some types of work release are labeled as study release, since high school or college courses often are taken by eligible inmates. Many prisons lack educational facilities, and thus, study release enables prison administrators to supplement their existing resources. Only minimum-security offenders are allowed into work or study release programs (Marlette, 1990). Offenders who work outside prisons under some form of work or study release have greater employment opportunities because they can network with employers and earn their trust and respect.

The Goals and Entry Requirements of Work/Study Release

The goals of work release programs are to (1) reintegrate offenders into the community, (2) give offenders an opportunity to learn and/or practice new skills, (3) provide offenders with the means to make restitution to victims of crimes, (4) give offenders a chance to assist in supporting themselves and their families, (5) help authorities to more effectively predict the likelihood of offender success if paroled, and (6) foster improvements in self-image or self-concept through working in a nonincarcerative environment and assuming full responsibility for one's conduct.

In order for offenders to become eligible for work release, they must meet the following criteria:

1. Inmates must have served a minimum of 10 percent of their sentences.
2. Inmates must have attained minimum custody by the date they are to begin participating in work release.
3. Inmates must not have had an escape attempt within six months of the approval.
4. Inmates must not have had a major infraction of prison rules within three months of approval.
5. If inmates are serving a sentence for a serious sexual or assaultive crime or have such a history, the approving authority for minimum custody is the director's review committee (Witte, 1973).

Work release programs are more successful when client eligibility standards are enforced. Typically, these programs have low recidivism rates compared with standard parole recidivism figures. One appeal of these programs is that they offer motivated offenders a chance to become reintegrated into their communities and acquire skills and educational backgrounds that will enhance their employment opportunities. Maintaining employment is a key factor in probation and parole program effectiveness and is associated with significant reductions in recidivism. Some amount of trust is created between the inmate and community. Completing a work or study release program without incident will increase an inmate's parole chances considerably.

Furloughs

A **furlough** is an authorized, unescorted leave from confinement granted for specific purposes and for designated time periods. Furloughs originated in 1918 in Mississippi. By 1970, about half the states had furlough programs (Marley, 1973). In 1998, there were only 5,500 furloughees in the United States (American Correctional Association, 1999:xxviii–xxix). One reason for this low number is that in the recent past, several furloughees who were not considered dangerous committed serious crimes, including rape and murder. When it became known that these persons were on furloughs and roamed throughout their communities freely, the public was irate and called for the complete suspension of furlough programs.

The Goals and Functions of Furlough Programs

Furloughs are beneficial to both prisoners and their families, because they permit family members to get used to the presence of the offender after a long incarcerative absence. Furloughs also enable some inmates to work at different jobs and to prove themselves to employers. Furthermore, parole board members have an opportunity to evaluate offenders and determine how they adapt to living with others in their community.

The functions of furloughs include (1) offender rehabilitation and reintegration, (2) the development of self-esteem and self-worth, (3) opportunities to pursue vocational/educational programs, and (4) aiding parole boards in determining when inmates are ready to be released.

HOME CONFINEMENT PROGRAMS

House arrest or **home confinement** is an intermediate punishment consisting of confining offenders to their residences for mandatory incarceration during evening hours after a specified curfew and on weekends (Jones and Ross, 1997a). In 1998, more than 20,000 offenders were under house arrest and supervision by probation officers in the United States (Maguire and Pastore, 2000:471). House arrest is an increasingly used sentencing option for low-risk first-offenders (Courtright, Berg, and Mutchnick, 1997).

Goals and Eligibility Requirements of Home Confinement

The goals of home confinement programs include the following: (1) to continue punishment while permitting offenders to be confined to their personal residences, (2) to enable offenders the freedom to hold jobs and earn a living while caring for their families and/or making restitution to victims, (3) to reduce jail and prison overcrowding, (4) to provide a means for ostracism while ensuring public safety, (5) to reduce the costs of offender supervision, and (6) to foster rehabilitation and reintegration by maintaining the controlled presence of offenders within the community.

Probationers and parolees placed in home confinement usually share the following characteristics:

1. Clients tend to be first offenders.
2. Clients tend to be nonviolent and/or have been convicted of nonviolent property offenses.
3. Clients tend to be those with fairly strong family ties, who are married and live with their spouses in structured living arrangements.
4. Clients do not have drug or alcohol dependencies.
5. Clients have jobs or good prospects of becoming employed and maintaining their employment over time.
6. Clients tend to have higher amounts of education and vocational skills.
7. Clients tend to be older, age 30 and over.

The positive aspects of home confinement include the following: (1) It is cost-effective, (2) it has social benefits, (3) it is responsive to local citizen and offender needs, and (4) it is easily implemented and is timely in view of jail and prison overcrowding. The negative aspects of home confinement include that (1) house arrest may actually widen the net of social control, (2) or it may narrow the net of social control by not being a sufficiently severe sentence, (3) it focuses primarily on offender surveillance, (4) it is intrusive and possibly illegal, (5) race and class bias may enter into participant selection, and (6) it may compromise public safety.

ELECTRONIC MONITORING PROGRAMS

Electronic monitoring is the use of telemetry devices to verify that offenders are at specified locations during particular times (Payne and Gainey, 1998). Electronic devices such as wristlets or anklets are fastened to offenders and must not be removed during the duration of their parole or probation. In 1998, over 75,000 offenders, both juvenile and adult, were on some form of electronic monitoring (Maguire and Pastore, 2000).

The four types of electronic monitoring used for client surveillance include (1) continuous signalling devices that emit a constant signal that can be intercepted by telephonic communication from a central dialing location such as a probation office or police station; (2) programmed contact devices, with which telephonic contact is made at random times and by which the offender's voice is verified electronically by computer; (3) cellular telephone devices that are worn by offenders and that transmit a signal that can be intercepted by local area monitors; and (4) continuous signalling transmitters that also are worn by offenders and that emit continuous signals that may be intercepted by probation officers with portable receiving units. These units save POs a great deal of time, since they only have to drive by the offenders' residences to verify their presence (Virginia Department of Criminal Justice Services, 1998). Face-to-face visits are not ordinarily required, unless the PO suspects the offender is not at home or where he or she is supposed to be at any given time.

For administrators interested in establishing electronic monitoring in their jurisdictions, the initial costs are quite high, ranging from $25,000 to $50,000 or more, depending on the sophistication of the electronic monitoring system and how many clients are to be monitored. However, once the system is in place, electronic monitoring is a cheap means of verifying an offender's whereabouts. Costs for monitoring one client per day range from $3.00 in Arkansas to $28.60 in Maryland (Camp and Camp, 1999a:184–185). It costs an average of $9.32 per day per client for electronic monitoring in the United States. By comparison, it costs an average of $55.50 per day per inmate for incarceration in federal or state prisons (Camp and Camp, 1999a:91).

Electronic monitoring has the following advantages:

1. Assists offenders in avoiding criminogenic atmosphere of prisons or jails and helps reintegrate them into their communities (e.g., avoids labeling as criminals)
2. Permits offenders to retain jobs and support families
3. Assists probation officers in their monitoring activities and has potential for easing their caseload responsibilities

4. Gives judges and other officials considerable flexibility in sentencing offenders (e.g., placement in halfway houses or on work release)

5. Has potential of reducing recidivism rate more than existing probationary alternatives

6. Potentially useful for decreasing jail and prison populations

7. More cost-effective in relation to incarceration

8. Allows for pretrial release monitoring as well as for special treatment cases such as substance abusers, the mentally retarded, women who are pregnant, and juveniles

Electronic monitoring has the following disadvantages:

1. Some possibility exists for racial, ethnic, or socioeconomic bias by requiring offenders to have telephones or to pay for expensive monitoring equipment and/or fees.

2. Public safety may be compromised through the failure of these programs to guarantee that offenders will go straight and not endanger citizens by committing new offenses while free in the community.

3. Electronic monitoring may be too coercive, and it may be unrealistic for officials to expect full offender compliance with such a stringent system.

4. Little consistent information exists about the impact of electronic monitoring on recidivism rates compared with other probationary alternatives.

5. Persons frequently selected for participation are persons who probably do not need to be monitored anyway.

6. Technological problems exist that make electronic monitoring somewhat unreliable.

7. Electronic monitoring may result in widening the net by being prescribed for offenders who otherwise would receive less costly standard probation.

8. It raises right to privacy, civil liberties, and other constitutional issues such as Fourth Amendment search and seizure concerns.

9. Many people interpret this option as going easy on offenders and perceive electronic monitoring as a nonpunitive alternative.

10. The costs of electronic monitoring may be more than published estimates.

11. Clients can access the Internet and may come into contact with other convicts and/or engage in illegal activities or acquire illegal contraband without violating the terms of the electronic monitoring arrangement.

HALFWAY HOUSES AND OTHER COMMUNITY SERVICES

Halfway Houses

A **halfway house** is a transitional residence for inmates who are released from prison (Twill et al., 1998). These residences offer temporary housing, food, and clothing for parolees recently released from prison. These homes offer services to offenders on a voluntary basis. They assist inmates in making the transition from rigid prison life to community living. In 1998, there were over 15,000 clients in public or private halfway houses in the United States (American Correctional Association, 1999:xxviii–xxix).

The major functions of halfway houses overlap some of those associated with other programs for parolees. These include (1) parolee rehabilitation and reintegration into the community; (2) provisions for food and shelter; (3) job placement, vocational guidance, and employment assistance; (4) client-specific treatments; (5) alleviating jail and prison overcrowding; (6) supplementing supervisory functions of probation and parole agencies; and (7) monitoring probationers, work/study releasees, and others with special program conditions.

Some of the major advantages and disadvantages of halfway house programs are

1. Halfway houses are more effective in preventing criminal behavior in the community than other alternatives that involve community release.

2. The placement of halfway houses in communities neither increases nor decreases property values.

3. Halfway houses assist their clients in locating employment but not necessarily maintaining it.

4. Halfway houses are able to provide for the basic needs of their clients as well as other forms of release.

5. At full capacity, halfway houses cost no more, and probably less, than incarceration, although they cost more than straight parole or outright release from correctional systems. (Carlson et al., 1977)

Community Residential and Day Reporting Centers

Community residential centers and **day reporting centers** are transitional agencies located in neighborhoods. Offenders may obtain employment counseling, food and shelter, and limited supervision pertaining to one or more conditions of probation or parole at these centers. Day reporting centers are operated primarily during daytime hours for the purpose of providing diverse services to offenders and their families. **Day reporting** is a highly structured nonresidential program utilizing supervision, sanctions, and services coordinated from a central focus. Offenders live at home and report to these centers regularly, usually daily (Diggs and Pieper, 1994:9).

Fines

In an increasing number of cases, judges are imposing **fines** as a punishment together with incarceration or some type of community-based supervision. Over 14 million persons are arrested each year in the United States, and most of these are fined following their convictions for minor offenses (Maguire and Pastore, 2000). Ordinarily, state and federal criminal statutes provide for various incarcerative lengths on conviction. Fines are imposed at the discretion of judges. Every state and federal criminal statute has a specific fine and maximum penalty. Judges must remain within a statute's parameters when sentencing criminal offenders.

Community Service Orders and Restitution

Under the Victim and Witness Protection Act of 1982 (18 U.S. Code, Sec. 3579–3580, 2001), restitution to victims was incorporated as an option in addition to incarceration at the federal level. Community service differs from restitution in that usually, although not always, offenders perform services for the state or community. The nature of community service to be performed is discretionary with the sentencing judge or paroling authority through the issuance of **community service orders.** In some jurisdictions, prisoners must perform a specified number of hours of community service such as lawn maintenance, plumbing and other similar repairs, or services that fit their particular skills (Tonry, 1999).

Community service orders are symbolic restitution, involving redress for victims, less severe sanctions for offenders, offender rehabilitation, reduction of demands on the criminal justice system, a reduction of the need for vengeance in a society, or a combination of these factors. Some of the chief benefits of community service include the following: (1) The community benefits because some form of restitution is paid, (2) offenders benefit because they are given an opportunity to rejoin their communities in law-abiding responsible roles, and (3) the courts benefit because sentencing alternatives are provided (Donnelly, 1980). Offenders sentenced to community service should have individualized sentences so that their skills and interests can be maximized for community benefit. On the average, between 50 and 200 hours of community service might be required for any particular convicted offender (Byrne, Lurigio, and Petersilia, 1992).

Restitution Programs for Victims

Another important component of many probation programs is **restitution.** Restitution is the practice of requiring offenders to compensate crime victims for damages offenders may have inflicted. Several models of restitution have been described by Patel and Soderland (1994). These include (1) the financial/community service model, (2) the victim/offender mediation model, and (3) the victim/reparations model. The **financial/community service model** stresses the offender's financial accountability and community service to pay for damages inflicted on victims and to defray a portion of the expenses of court prosecutions. The **victim/offender mediation model** focuses on victim-offender reconciliation. Alternative dispute resolution is used as a mediating ground for resolving differences or disputes between victims and perpetrators. The **victim/reparations model** stresses that offenders should compensate their victims directly for their offenses.

SELECTED COMMUNITY CORRECTIONS ISSUES

Administrators must deal with several important issues on a regular basis during the normal course of operating community-based corrections agencies. This list is not exhaustive, but some of the more important issues include (1) the rights of clients supervised by community corrections, (2) the legal liabilities of community corrections agencies and employees, (3) the use of volunteers and paraprofessionals, and (4) the privatization of community-based corrections.

The Rights of Clients Supervised by Community Corrections

A major issue about community corrections is public safety. Citizens are opposed to having convicted felons roam freely among them. Officials attempt to minimize this fear by selecting low-risk inmates for placement in community programs. Citizens seldom are concerned about the ultimate program objectives, which are largely reintegrative and rehabilitative. Although prisoners do not have an absolute right to rehabilitation, it is in the community's best interests for some offenders about to be released to be gradually eased into society through work/study release or furlough. These transitional programs involve clients who have been carefully screened and selected so that their recidivism is minimized. But there are always exceptions.

Whenever inmate-clients participate in community programs, their chances for success and making it in the community on their own increase substantially. Some amount of trust must be given to these inmates. Most of these offenders will be released eventually anyway. The transitional nature of community-based programs is such that inmates have an opportunity to adjust to the shock of sudden freedom. Thus, the rights of community residents must be balanced against the interests of the state and programming that is considered fundamental to an inmate's successful community reintegration.

Legal Liabilities of Community Corrections Agencies and Employees

PO and community-based correctional work involves more or less continuous contact with a wide variety of probationers and parolees. These clients vary greatly in their conviction offenses. Thus, POs have somewhat different expectations about property offenders compared with violent offenders generally. We might anticipate, for instance, that violent offenders who are placed on probation or parole are comparatively more dangerous than property offenders. Interestingly, regardless of their original conviction offenses, probationers and parolees under some form of PO supervision risk having their programs revoked if they misbehave in any way or do not otherwise conform to program requirements. Therefore, a built-in incentive exists for these offender-clients to behave well. Furthermore, some property offenders may turn out to pose greater risks and be more dangerous than certain violent offenders. Also, some violent offenders may never harm others again. Predictions about which offenders pose the most risk are seriously flawed, and POs have to adjust their supervisory tactics accordingly.

POs and other community workers must have some degree of interaction with their clients in client dwellings. Sometimes danger arises from neighborhoods and neighborhood gangs where clients live, but the clients themselves are not responsible for the neighborhood circumstances and where they can afford to live. The fact is that PO work is dangerous.

POs are in the business not only of supervising and monitoring offender conduct, but also of assisting these clients in finding jobs and keeping them. POs perform a wide variety of informal services, including counseling and other therapeutic treatments. POs may offer advice and counsel to certain clients who use these POs as sympathetic listeners. Sometimes POs give their clients bad advice, although this is seldom intentional. If certain clients suffer damages because of what they have been told or advised by their supervising POs, then these clients may resort to lawsuits.

Increasing numbers of lawsuits are being filed against POs. Many of these lawsuits are frivolous, but they consume much time and cause many job prospects to turn away from PO work (Morgan, Belbot, and Clark, 1997). But POs who act on behalf of the state or federal government have various types of immunity to protect them from legal actions by their clients against them. There are three types of immunity: (1) **absolute immunity,** meaning that those acting on behalf of the state can suffer no liability from their actions taken while performing their state tasks (e.g., judges, prosecutors, and legislators); (2) qualified immunity, such as that enjoyed by probation officers if they are performing their tasks in good faith; and (3) **quasi-judicial immunity,** which generally refers to PO preparation of PSI reports at judicial request (Jones and del Carmen, 1992:36–37).

Generally, POs enjoy only qualified immunity. This means that they are immune only when their actions were made in good faith. Jones and del Carmen (1992) acknowledge that the rules governing qualified immunity as applied to POs are vague and undefined. However, they have clarified at least two different conditions that seem to favor POs in the performance of their tasks and the immunity they derive from such conditions: Probation officers are considered officers of the court and perform a valuable court function, namely the preparation of PSI reports; and probation officers perform work intimately associated with court process, such as sentencing offenders.

Specific types of problems applicable to POs in their relations with clients include the following:

1. Some types of information about a PO's clients may be subject to public disclosure, whereas other types of information are protected from public scrutiny. If POs disclose protected information about their clients to employers or others, the POs may be liable.

2. PO use of firearms may lead to personal injuries to clients or others.

3. POs may be negligent in how their clients are supervised.

4. POs may prepare PSI reports that reflect unfavorably on their clients. This information may influence subsequent probation program conditions and their severity. Causes of legal action may result from certain types of PSI report preparation.

5. If PO agencies have failed to train their POs properly, PO actions in relation to their clients may be ineffective or even counterproductive. Lawsuits may arise based on negligent training, negligent retention, and deliberate indifference to client needs.

Usually, POs can defend themselves against various types of lawsuits filed against them by probationers and parolees by claiming one or more of the following:

1. POs were acting in good faith while performing their roles.

2. POs have official immunity, since they are working for and on behalf of the state, which enjoys sovereign immunity.

3. POs may not have a special relationship with their clients. Thus, if their clients commit future offenses that result in injuries or deaths to themselves or others, POs are not liable to others for client actions.

Use of Volunteers and Paraprofessionals in Community-Based Programs

Many community-based corrections agencies at both the state and federal levels use volunteers and paraprofessionals to assist POs and community agency personnel in their daily tasks. Some of these volunteers and paraprofessionals work directly with offender-clients. A **volunteer** is any unpaid person who performs auxiliary, supplemental, augmentative, or any other work or services for any law enforcement, court, or corrections agency. Corrections volunteers vary greatly in their characteristics and abilities, in their ages, and in their functions. Some volunteers may be retired judges or lawyers who work with jail and prison inmates to assist them with legal matters. Other volunteers may be men or women who are involved in community service work. They are uncompensated and enjoy the fact that they are helping others to succeed.

At any given time, we do not know how many volunteers work in U.S. institutional or community corrections. On the basis of state and federal estimates, probably 500,000 or more volunteers are working in different communities at any given time. For instance, there were 3,000 volunteers working in various capacities with the Pennsylvania Department of Corrections in 1992 (Lehman, 1993:84). The Federal Bureau of Prisons (BOP) used at least 4,000 volunteers in different ways for institutional and community corrections services in 1996 (Walsh, 1997).

Arnold (1993:120–122) lists some of the following functions performed by volunteers for community-based corrections: (1) serving as tutors at the skill training center and handling most GED preparation; (2) providing transportation to parenting sessions at residential centers; (3) teaching people skills such as carpentry, knitting, sewing, and dressmaking; (4) teaching computer and job search skills at the skill training center; and (5) providing gifts or food for families at holidays.

From an administrative standpoint, it is difficult to control the behavior of volunteers in their relations with offender-clients, unless they are closely monitored by POs or other trained professionals who know how to act around criminals. Volunteers cannot be fired. They cannot be offered raises or promotions as incentives to do good work. In short, they are loose cannons and highly unpredictable. They may unwittingly violate client confidences with other clients. They may give poor advice and counsel. Despite their best efforts, they may do more harm than good for the community agency.

Several criticisms of volunteers include that (1) they are naive, (2) they sometimes make long-term and close commitments with offender-clients, (3) they sometimes work independently of trained PO supervisors, (4) they lack experience and are easily manipulated by clients, (5) they may disclose confidential information that is harmful to the client and/or agency, (6) they may threaten the job security of paid professionals, (7) they are not as motivated as permanent POs, and (8) they may contribute to criminal activity. Several safeguards have been recommended. Ogburn (1993:66) suggests the following safeguards to screen volunteers: (1) evaluating the need for volunteers, (2) developing goals and job descriptions for volunteers, (3) involving staff together with volunteers as teams, (4) recruiting volunteers more selectively, (5) educating volunteers about inmates and how volunteers might be manipulated, (6) explaining security needs to volunteers, (7) giving volunteers the big picture of where they fit in and how they can best fulfill the organizational mission, (8) evaluating program effectiveness, and (9) recognizing the volunteers' contributions (Ogburn, 1993:66).

However, if POs and community agencies must spend a great deal of time with volunteers to prepare them for their working relations with offender-clients, then they may be more trouble than they are worth. PO time spent supervising volunteers to make sure they do not make mistakes is perhaps better spent supervising more clients.

A step up from a volunteer is a paraprofessional. A **paraprofessional** is anyone who possesses some formal training in a given correctional area, is salaried, works specified hours, has formal duties and responsibilities, is accountable to higher-level supervisors for work quality, and has limited immunity under the theory of agency. *Agency* is the special relation between an employer and an employee through which the employee acts as an agent of the employer, able to make decisions and take actions on the employer's behalf (Black, 1990:62). Black (1990:1112) also defines a paraprofessional as "one who assists a professional person though not a member of the profession himself."

Paraprofessionals have some degree of training and require less supervision compared with volunteers. No accurate profile of the education and training of paraprofessionals has ever been undertaken (Dembo et al., 1999). One major difference between volunteers and paraprofessionals is that paraprofessionals are paid by community agencies for their services. This means that the community agency has greater control over paraprofessionals who work for them compared with volunteers. Paraprofessionals do not assume the same tasks and responsibilities as regular POs or community agency workers, however, although they do incur similar liabilities when working with offender-clients.

The Privatization of Community-Based Programs

The issue of privatization of American corrections in both prison and jail operations has already been examined in earlier chapters. Applied to community-based correctional services and agencies, privatization is just as controversial as it is in relation to institutional corrections for both adults and juveniles (Archambeault and Deis, 1996). Ironically and from a historical view, crime control was almost always entirely private and community based until the past few centuries. Government police forces, prosecutors, courts, and prisons are all relatively recent historical developments (Benson, 1998). Thus, privatization is arguably not new. Furthermore, privatization is a worldwide phenomenon and not localized to the United States (Colson et al., 1989; Peach, 1999).

No reliable or precise figures exist to indicate the extensiveness of privatization throughout communities in the United States. However, a 1999 survey by the Criminal Justice Institute, Inc., located in Middletown, Connecticut, provides some descriptive information derived from 90 privately operated reporting facilities representing 49,027 prisoners (Camp and Camp, 1999b:19). About 5.4 percent of these prisoners, or about 2,647 clients, were being supervised under privately operated community-based correctional programs in 1999.

Although no one seems to know why, privately operated community-based agencies have lower client recidivism rates compared with publicly operated agencies. One explanation is that privately operated agencies are especially sensitive to client needs and seek to avoid criticisms leveled against them by those opposed to privatization generally. Another explanation is that privately operated agencies may engage in **creaming,** a situation in which only the lowest-risk clients are accepted into private community programs. It is debatable whether privately operated community-based agencies have greater control over who is admitted to their programs and who is not admitted to them, however. Interestingly, creaming may be perpetrated by the public system itself. Correctional institutions and the courts may assign the lowest-risk probationers and certain parolees to private community agencies simply because it is believed that private interests are in a better position to manage low-risk offenders compared with more dangerous, high-risk offenders. No systematic or concrete evidence exists to support this explanation, however. More evaluative research is needed in order to determine the true impact of privatization of community-based corrections on recidivism rates, rehabilitation, and other important variables.

In Wisconsin, for instance, there were approximately 68,000 offenders in community corrections programs in 1997 (Mitchell, 1999). Wisconsin authorities reported approximately 196,000 crimes committed annually by some of these community-based offenders. Since most of Wisconsin's community programs were publicly operated in 1997, a new approach was recommended for future years to privatize community corrections or at least a portion of it. This proposal was made in light of the fact that many probationers and parolees presently supervised by private corporations have significantly lower rates of recidivism (Mitchell, 1999). Wisconsin researchers believe that community programs in that state have been ineffectively managed, which is possibly attributable to a significant lack of funding appropriated for community services and client supervisory tasks.

By 1996, only 21 state legislatures had passed enabling legislation for the purpose of authorizing private correctional initiatives (Blakely and Bumphus, 1996). Four broad areas relating to privatization of corrections were identified: contractor qualifications, operational services, treatment services, and limits of authority. Few states had made significant progress toward privatization.

SUMMARY

Community corrections encompasses everything from pretrial diversion to intermediate punishments, including probation, parole, home confinement, electronic monitoring, day fine programs, work release, furloughs, and any other nonincarcerative option available to those convicted of crimes. Most clients who are supervised by community corrections programs are probationers and parolees. Probationers are those who have been convicted of crimes but are serving their sentences within their communities. They are under the jurisdiction of the original sentencing judge. Parolees also have been convicted of one or more crimes, but they have served some jail or prison time and have been released short of serving their full sentences. Usually these offenders are under the supervision of parole boards. In some jurisdictions, probationers and parolees, also

known as clients, are supervised by the same agency, although in most jurisdictions, separate probation and parole agencies and services provide supervision.

Probation and parole departments are organized according to the number of clients they must supervise. The number of clients supervised by any particular agency varies considerably. Also, great client diversity can exist with regard to the nature of their offenses and any special problems they might have, such as drug or alcohol dependencies. Probation and parole officers are required to have a minimum of a high school education, with some college preferred. Many recruits are selected on the basis of objective tests and personality assessments. Many receive several hundred introductory hours of training as well as some in-service, on-the-job training. The duties of probation and parole officers, usually designated as POs, are to supervise, conduct surveillance, investigate cases, assist in offender rehabilitation, counsel offenders, make arrests, make referrals, and supervise offender compliance with all program requirements.

Community corrections programs are intended to facilitate offender reintegration within their communities by monitoring clients, providing them with employment assistance, and heightening their accountability. Thus, community corrections oversees community service, restitution, drug/alcohol checks, curfews, and reporting requirements required by judges or parole boards. Various educational and vocational services often are provided for clients.

Home confinement involves the use of one's home or dwelling as a place of confinement. Offenders sentenced to home confinement must observe curfews and only leave their residences for work and emergencies. Sometimes offenders are placed under electronic monitoring supervision as a supplement to home confinement. For parolees, transitional residences known as halfway houses are operated within communities. These are supportive facilities in which clients can receive employment assistance and other forms of aid and support. While incarcerated, some inmates may be permitted to participate in furlough programs, which involve unescorted leaves from prisons, usually for weekends. Other inmates are allowed brief periods of absence from prison to participate in work release or study release programs offered in their communities. Often, these clients are within a few months of being released anyway, and thus these programs are viewed as transitional in nature. Other program requirements may include making restitution to victims, performing community service, and paying fines.

Numerous volunteers and paraprofessionals work with clients in community corrections programs. These are persons who have either no training or minimal training to assist probation and parole officers in their supervisory chores. Volunteers are useful in teaching clients how to read or fill out employment applications. Volunteers receive no monetary compensation for their services. Paraprofessionals have some training and are salaried.

Increasingly, community corrections programs are being operated by private interests. Privatization enables different governmental agencies to supervise and monitor larger numbers of offenders. Different views provide arguments about whether or not privatization is an acceptable alternative to government supervision of probationers and parolees. One important issue is agency liability. All persons working with offender-clients incur some degree of liability in these relationships, in the event that some clients are injured or suffer other difficulties. Various types of immunity are provided to those who supervise offenders, although in most cases, such immunity is limited or qualified.

QUESTIONS FOR REVIEW

1. What is community corrections? What are community corrections acts? Describe their purposes.

2. What are some general goals of probation and parole services? From your reading, what seems to be the general mission of certain probation services?

3. What are some general selection requirements for probation officers? What are some characteristics of probation officers? Describe some of their general duties.

4. What are some criticisms of probation programs?

5. What is meant by work/study release? What are some of the major goals of work/study release programs? Who qualifies for work/study release?

6. Distinguish between furloughs and work/study release. What are some general goals and functions of furlough programs?

7. What is meant by home confinement? Do all offenders qualify for home confinement? Why or why not? Explain.

8. What are electronic monitoring programs? What are different types of electronic monitoring devices? How effective is electronic monitoring for controlling offender behavior? Explain.

9. Distinguish between halfway houses and community residential and day reporting centers. What are some general functions of halfway houses? Identify those primarily served by halfway houses.

10. What are the primary objectives of (a) fines, (b) community service orders, (c) restitution, and (d) victim compensation programs?

SUGGESTED READINGS

Cromwell, Paul, and Rolando V. del Carmen (1999). *Community-Based Corrections* (4/e). Belmont, CA: West/Wadsworth.

Harris, Patricia M. (ed.) (1999). *Research to Results: Effective Community Corrections.* Lanham, MD: American Correctional Association.

Latessa, Edward J., and Harry E. Allen (1999). *Corrections in the Community* (2/e). Cincinnati, OH: Anderson Publishing Company.

• CASE STUDIES •

---

1. THE VOLUNTEER

Jane is a volunteer, a member of a religious faith that encourages its followers to visit prisons and counsel inmates who are serving long prison terms or who are on death row. She enjoys her volunteer work, because she meets various prisoners, brings them religious in- struction, and offers them counsel and a shoulder to lean on in their times of despair and need. Jane is unmarried, 45, and does not have a lot of friends. One of the inmates she visits, Joe, purports to be a convert to her religion and says he wants to learn more about it. Jane brings him religious periodicals every time she

• CASE STUDIES •

visits. He discusses his personal life with her and talks a lot about his boyhood and the things that got him into trouble. Joe says he was physically and sexually abused by both his mother and father, and he blames his home life and circumstances on his current state of imprisonment. Joe says that he is innocent of the charges against him, but he never tells Jane what his crimes were. Jane becomes quite attached to the young prisoner. After a few months of weekly visits, Joe asks Jane if she will do him a favor. Joe asks Jane to mail some letters for him. This is against prison rules, but Jane has grown to like Joe and is willing to do this small favor. Over the next few months, Joe mails quite a few letters through Jane.

One afternoon, Jane is approached by the prison warden, who asks Jane to come to his office. When Jane enters the warden's office, the warden brings out a large box containing numerous envelopes. These are letters written by different persons to Joe. It seems the warden has inspected these letters and has determined that Jane is the one who has been secretly mailing letters for Joe. He shows the letters to Jane. She opens the first letter and a photo of a young girl falls out onto the warden's desk. The girl is nude. On the photo the girl has written, "All my love to you, Joe . . . Phyllis." The letter itself is very sexually explicit. Jane is shocked, but she opens several other letters, finding that most of them contain nude photos of young girls like Phyllis. It seems that Joe has placed ads in newspapers and has portrayed himself as a 14-year-old male looking for a teenage girl companion. Over 50 letters from different girls have been received and are in the box on the warden's desk. The warden tells Jane that Joe is a convicted pedophile and is suspected in the deaths of five young girls, although only circumstantial evidence exists of his guilt. He is in prison because he was convicted of raping six girls under age 16. He has a long history of rape and is a serious murder suspect. The warden chides Jane for being so gullible and for violating prison rules. He then politely informs her that she and other members of her church are no longer welcome at the prison. Jane feels utterly stupid and used. She trusted Joe and actually liked him. But now she realizes Joe tricked her. Worst of all, he lied and caused her to violate prison rules.

Questions for Discussion

1. Imagine yourself as Jane, the religious volunteer. You have been duped by an inmate, lied to, and deceived. The inmate took you into his confidence and got you to violate prison rules. You had enjoyed your volunteer work for the church, and you really believed that you were making a difference in assisting prisoners with their personal lives. Now you are not so sure. You are depressed and despondent. If this prisoner, Joe, fooled you, what about all of the other prisoners you have counseled and assisted? Have they been deceiving you as well? Will you ever be able to trust anyone again? You were so sure about Joe and believed that he was sincere. Should you quit your job as a volunteer? Why or why not?

2. As a volunteer, would you continue working with Joe despite the fact that he tricked you into mailing illicit materials to others? Why or why not? Discuss.

3. What does this scenario say about the potential hazards and liabilities of volunteer work generally?

4. What would you, as Jane, encourage other volunteers to do when dealing with inmates in the future?

2. THE NEW PROBATION OFFICER

You are Jonathan Walters, a new probation officer. You have a master's degree in social work and an undergraduate degree in psychological counseling, and you have always wanted to work with probationers. You have had 160 hours of in-service training, and you are interested in working with offenders who have problems with alcohol or drugs. In your particular probation agency, there are 22 probation officers with more than 1,800 clients. The agency uses the specialized caseloads model, and two other probation officers have been assigned to special-needs offenders who have drug and alcohol problems. Presently, no need exists for additional POs for special-needs offenders.

• CASE STUDIES •

Your agency chief, Al Green, has told you that as soon as a vacancy becomes available, he will consider you for it. In the meantime, you have been given a caseload of 65 nonserious probationers to supervise. Your task is to visit each of these clients monthly and make a brief report of your face-to-face visit. This caseload seems to be the standard caseload other POs in your agency are assigned.

During the process of visiting your clients, you visit the apartment of Cleo Little, who is a 24-year-old unwed mother. Little was convicted of prostitution and fraud, but because she had a small child, the judge was lenient and sentenced her only to probation for three years. She has been on probation for about a month, and therefore, both of you are fairly new to the process of face-to-face visits. During these visits, you are required to inspect the premises of your clients and administer drug tests on a random basis. Because this is your first visit with Little, you tell her that you are going to test her for cocaine and marijuana. She acts somewhat uncomfortable about this test, and she says, "Why do you have to give me those tests? My convictions were for prostitution and fraud." You explain simply that you are doing your job, and that it is nothing personal. You are obligated to perform the tests. After conducting the on-the-spot tests, you determine that Little has tested positive for cocaine. You confront her with this information. "Look, Cleo, you've just tested positive for cocaine. When was the last time you used it?" Little looks at you sheepishly and says, "I guess I used it a little at a birthday party for a girlfriend of mine the other night. Someone else brought it, and everyone did it. I knew I shouldn't have done it, but everybody else said, 'Go ahead,' and so I did. I just shouldn't have done it. You're not going to report me, are you? I could go to prison and lose my baby!"

You decide to practice some of your social work skills and counseling training that you learned in school with Little. You have a conversation with her about how much she has used drugs in the past. She explains that she had never used drugs up until that birthday party, and that was just a one-time thing. You tell her that you will get back to her. Later at the office, you look up Little's record and there is no indication that she was using drugs at the time of her arrest and booking. She was soliciting for prostitution and she

had written some bad checks, and that is all the record shows. There was a presentence investigation report in her information packet, but you ignored it, focusing primarily on the original police report of her arrest and booking. Later in the week, you drop in on Little and have another conversation with her. You tell her that you are not going to report the violation this time, but that she is going to have to stay clean from drugs as long as you are supervising her. You administer another drug test to her, and this time, only trace amounts of cocaine are disclosed by the test. You accept this factual evidence as an indication that she has not used drugs since your last visit. Further, you decide not to report the incident at the agency, since you believe that Little needs a break. You think that if you can supervise her effectively, that you will prove yourself capable of supervising others who have drug dependencies.

About two weeks later, you drive by Little's apartment and are surprised to see an ambulance and police cars outside. A crowd has gathered. You exit your vehicle and approach the officers. After identifying yourself, you ask what has happened. "Some girl died from an overdose of cocaine," one of the officers says. "Who was she?" you ask. "Her wallet and personal effects says she's Cleo Little," answers the officer. "Looks like she was on probation. Whoever was supervising her didn't do a very good job of testing her for cocaine use. We found over three ounces of cocaine in her dresser drawer."

You retreat back to your vehicle. You sit there and ponder what you have done. You counseled and tested Little just a few weeks ago. She tested positive for cocaine use, but you chose not to report it. Now she is dead because of a cocaine overdose. You drive back to the agency, where you seek out Al Green. "Al," you say, "there's something I need to talk with you about." Green invites you into his office. You relate the story about your encounter with Cleo Little, testing her for drugs, finding that she tested positive for cocaine, and not reporting it. You explain to Green why you did what you did. Then you break the news that you just discovered that she died of an overdose of cocaine.

Green asks you to wait for a moment and he retrieves Cleo Little's file from a secretary. He comes back in the office and takes a few minutes to thumb

• **CASE STUDIES** •

through the information. You notice that he is carefully reading the presentence investigation report that you had previously ignored. All of a sudden, Green looks up from the report and says, "My God, Jonathan, didn't you read this presentence investigation report?" You advise him that you only looked at the original arrest report and that it said nothing about cocaine use. Green says, "Why, right here it shows that the PO who did the PSI for her noted that she had some serious psychiatric problems and chemical dependencies. She had been diagnosed as a schizophrenic by a psychiatrist a year ago, prior to her arrest and conviction. She had been going to Alcoholics Anonymous at the time of her arrest and was otherwise clean. But her history shows some serious drug abuse. What about that?"

Questions for Discussion

1. How much did Jonathan Walters contribute to the death of Cleo Little, if at all? Explain.
2. Should Walters have reported the positive cocaine test in his initial encounter with Little? Why or why not?

3. As a new PO with advanced training in psychological counseling and social work, do you think Walters was justified in taking independent action in Little's case? What do you think he was trying to accomplish by not reporting Little to the agency and filing a report with the sentencing judge?
4. What action, if any, should be taken by Al Green to punish Walters for his obviously sloppy work in supervising Cleo Little? Should Walters be fired over this incident? Why or why not?
5. What did Walters fail to do in performing his job as a new PO properly? Outline his mistakes. Should his in-service training program have covered these sorts of problems with clients who might be chemically dependent? Since Cleo Little was not under special-needs offender supervision, should the agency itself take any responsibility for failing to see that she was properly supervised? Was Jonathan Walters the best choice to supervise Little, or was this a misclassification problem on the part of the agency? What do you think?

CHAPTER 13

JUVENILE JUSTICE ORGANIZATIONS AND THEIR ADMINISTRATION

KEY TERMS

Adjudication
Adjudicatory hearing
Adultification
Age of majority
Blended sentencing statutes
Certification
Child savers
Common law
Conditional dispositions
Criminal-exclusive blend
Criminal-inclusive blend
Curfew violators
Custodial dispositions
Delinquency
Demand waiver
Dependent and/or neglected children
Direct file
Discretionary waivers
Dispositions

Houses of refuge
Intake
Intake hearings
Intake officers
Intake screenings
Intermediate punishments
Judicial waivers
Juvenile delinquency
Juvenile delinquent
Juvenile-contiguous blend
Juvenile-exclusive blend
Juvenile-inclusive blend
Juvenile justice system
Juveniles
Mandatory waivers
Mission statements
New York House of Refuge
Nominal dispositions
Nonsecure custody

Once an adult/always an adult provision
Petitions
Poor Laws
Presumptive waivers
Probation
Referrals
Reform schools
Reverse waiver
Runaways
Secure custody
Station house adjustments
Status offenders
Status offenses
Statutory exclusion
Transfer
Truants
Waivers
Walnut Street Jail

CHAPTER OBJECTIVES

The following objectives are intended:

1. To provide a brief historical background for the emergence of contemporary juvenile courts

2. To describe the major U.S. Supreme Court cases that have affected directly the rights of juveniles

3. To describe the juvenile justice system and how juvenile offenders are processed from arrest, through intake, adjudication, and disposition

4. To describe how the juvenile justice system is administered

5. To describe the different dispositional options for juvenile offenders

6. To describe the processes by which juveniles are placed under the jurisdiction of criminal courts, including waivers, transfers, and certifications

7. To discuss blended sentencing statutes and their implications for juveniles

8. To examine several important issues in juvenile justice, including heightened offender accountability and greater parental involvement in juvenile justice outcomes

9. To describe the variety of community-based interventions available to juvenile offenders

INTRODUCTION

Paralleling the criminal justice system with its own sequence of youthful offender processing is the juvenile justice system. The **juvenile justice system** is a more or less integrated network of agencies, institutions, organizations, and personnel that processes juvenile offenders. This network consists of law enforcement agencies; prosecutors and courts; corrections, probation, and parole services; and public and private community-based treatment programs that provide youths with diverse services.

The juvenile justice system is in many respects a different world from that of the criminal justice system. In fact, some observers have said that "the juvenile court and the juvenile justice system is a mystery to the general population" (Wicklund, 1997:13). First, the juvenile justice system is a civil system, not a criminal one. Adults who are tried and convicted of criminal offenses acquire criminal records. Juveniles found guilty by juvenile court judges are declared delinquent. Juveniles in most jurisdictions are extended an extraordinary number of protections under the law that insulate them from their adult counterparts. Access to juvenile records by *anyone* (including law enforcement authorities) is strictly prohibited in a majority of jurisdictions, except under court order or special circumstances. Second, people must acquire a new language when referring to different dimensions of the juvenile justice system. For instance, adults are arrested; juveniles are *taken into custody.* Adults are booked, have initial appearances, and are arraigned; juveniles are processed through *intake.* Adults are convicted; juveniles are *adjudicated.* Adults are sentenced; juveniles are *disposed.* The first part of this chapter, therefore, briefly describes the evolution of the juvenile court. In order to understand why juveniles are treated as they are today, we must first become acquainted with how they were treated in past decades and centuries. This description depicts some of the major events and occurrences that have changed how juveniles are conceptualized, including who should bear the responsibility for their conduct and the nature and types of punishment to be imposed for different types of juvenile offending.

Although the juvenile justice system is distinct and separate from the criminal justice system, some people believe that juveniles should be treated just like adults whenever they commit adultlike crimes, such as murder, rape, robbery, or aggravated assault. The second part of this chapter classifies and categorizes juveniles according to the seriousness of their offense. Especially for youths who commit very serious offenses, mechanisms exist for changing the jurisdiction of youths from the juvenile courtroom to the criminal courtroom where adults cases are heard. These mechanisms are waivers or transfers, and their use, though limited, is very controversial. Whether or not it is warranted by accurate data, a prevailing perception exists among the general public that juveniles are committing more serious and violent offenses annually. Thus, more drastic measures to deal with these increasingly violent juveniles are demanded, especially when the public thinks the juvenile court has been too lenient in its treatment of youthful offenders. If a juvenile has his or her case changed to the jurisdiction of a criminal court, he or she is exposed to a far greater range of punishments than would be imposed on the juvenile if the case had remained with the juvenile court. This process is described in some detail, since it is important to understand precisely where the criminal justice system interfaces with the juvenile justice system as a youth is processed.

Regardless of *where* a juvenile's case is eventually heard, whether in juvenile or criminal court, juveniles have approximately the same general range of punishments available as adult offenders (Lyons and Turpin, 1997). A major difference is that juveniles under the age of 16 cannot be subjected to the death penalty. Even life-without-parole options are seldom used for juveniles. However, juveniles may be placed on diversion, probation, intensive supervised probation, home confinement, electronic monitoring, and parole. These dispositional options are a major part of community corrections for juveniles.

Juveniles also may be incarcerated in juvenile facilities, usually referred to as industrial schools, which are the functional equivalent of adult prisons or penitentiaries and are called *secure facilities*. Since these *are* juvenile offenders, and since much of the language used to refer to their processing is different from the language used to describe what happens to adult offenders convicted of crimes, there is no such thing as a *juvenile prison* or *juvenile penitentiary*. Also, since juveniles eventually become adults when they turn either 18 or 21, the juvenile justice system loses its jurisdiction over them at that point. Thus, a juvenile's period of confinement in these secure facilities is of relatively short duration. A short period of confinement for a juvenile averages about 30 days, whereas long-term juvenile confinement in secure facilities averages about 180 days. It is unusual for *any* juvenile to serve an incarcerative term of two or more years. Even the average length of time a juvenile might be incarcerated in a juvenile facility for rape or murder averages about three years nationally.

The next section of this chapter examines various dispositional options available to juveniles, ranging from probation and community corrections to institutional placement and supervision. These alternative punishments are administered either by separate juvenile justice agencies or by subunits of state agencies or corrections departments.

Consideration is given to transferring the more serious juvenile offenders to criminal courts for processing. These juveniles are then prosecuted as adult criminal offenders. At this point, juveniles interface with the criminal justice system in significant ways. This section describes the transfer or waiver process. Several types of actions that result in the imposition of adult criminal penalties on juveniles who have been convicted of crimes in criminal courts are also discussed.

The chapter concludes by examining some important issues associated with administering juvenile justice programs, such as juvenile justice reform and the confidentiality of juvenile records, changing the nature and severity of optional sanctions available to juvenile courts, creating greater accountability among juvenile court judges, revisiting policies relating to both parental and juvenile accountability for criminal actions of youths, and rethinking both institutional and community correctional programming for juveniles.

A BRIEF HISTORY OF THE JUVENILE COURT

Juvenile courts were established in the United States in 1899. Laws pertaining to juveniles could be found in different countries many centuries earlier, however. Under Roman law in biblical times, for instance, parents were given the exclusive responsibility for disciplining their children. Roman law determined the age of seven as the age used to separate infants from older children who were held accountable under the law for their actions. English **common law** under the existing monarchy in the Middle Ages followed the same standard and used the age of seven as the beginning of juvenile accountability. Some states follow this practice today.

Between the 1500s and 1700s in England, youthful offenders age seven or older were treated like adult criminals and placed in stocks and pillories, chained to whipping posts, branded, and subjected to other forms of corporal punishment. More than a few youths were placed in jails for lengthy periods, and no attempt was made to separate them from either male or female adult offenders. Many juveniles were confined to workhouses, which were primarily confinement facilities with no amenities. Persons incarcerated in workhouses were exploited for their labor potential by greedy merchants. Jailers who operated these workhouses profited by farming out both adult and juvenile inmates to wealthy merchants who paid minimal wages. Today such practices would be prohibited, and violators would be subject to harsh criminal and civil penalties for violating child labor laws and exploiting children. But in the 1700s, incarcerated children had no legal voice. They were essentially an unprotected class with no rights.

Most adult offenders were incarcerated in these workhouses as well and also were exploited. Some of these facilities were called *debtors' prisons.* Persons incarcerated in debtors' prisons were placed there because they owed others money and could not pay their debts. They got out of these debtors' prisons either by having someone pay their way out or by working off whatever they owed to creditors. But their wages were minimal, and some persons died in these prisons. Often many of those in prisons, such as the disabled or elderly, were unable to work. These types of facilities were created and operated under **Poor Laws** that were directed at the poor or socioeconomically disadvantaged. In 1601, some statutes were passed that provided constructive work for youths determined by chancellors to be vagrant, incorrigible, truant, or simply neglected.

During this time, many youths also became apprenticed to master craftsmen under a system of involuntary servitude. A common agreement was eventually established between various craftsmen and their apprentices by which apprentices would provide their free labor for a seven-year period. At the end of seven years, the craftsmen would release these apprentices and pay their debts. Servitude for juveniles essentially lasted until youths attained the age of 21. During the colonial period, English influence on penal practices in America was strong, and familiar traditions for administering laws and sanctioning offenders were relied on by colonists. The legal status of juveniles was never given any priority during that period, however.

England and the colonies were not unique in their lack of provisions for youths and their treatment of youthful offenders. In Italy, the Hospital of Saint Michael was established in 1704 in Rome at the request of the pope to provide for unruly youths and other young people who violated criminal laws. The Hospital of Saint Michael was more like a workhouse than a hospital. Youths were exploited for their labor potential just like in English workhouses. Apprenticeships similar to those in England and the American colonies were also common in Italy for youthful offenders who could eventually earn their freedom through mandatory servitude.

The Revolutionary War and religious interests did much to improve the condition of juveniles in trouble with the law in America. The Quakers in Pennsylvania established the Philadelphia Society for Alleviating the Miseries of the Public Prisons in 1787. This philanthropic society was made up of prominent citizens, religious leaders, and philanthropists who visited local jails in Philadelphia regularly and brought food, clothing, and religious instruction to adult and juvenile inmates. By 1790, an old Philadelphia jail facility was renovated and renamed the **Walnut Street Jail.** As described in Chapter 11, this facility was the first to classify and segregate offenders according to age, gender, and crime seriousness. This was particularly significant for females and children, who previously had been sexually assaulted and exploited by more powerful adult male inmates. Rehabilitation also was promoted at the Philadelphia jail. Inmates were trained for different types of labor, such as sewing, shoemaking, and carpentry. Furthermore, decent wages were paid to both juveniles and adults in the jail for their skilled or unskilled labor.

Many families moved to large cities such as New York, Philadelphia, and Boston during the early 1800s to find work. These families brought their children with them, but child care was not a viable option for most of these families in which both parents worked long shifts at manufacturing plants. Many unsupervised youths vandalized businesses and committed assorted street crimes. Others simply roamed the streets during daytime hours. Subsequently, various citizens banded together to protect these children from themselves and from being exploited on the city streets. These persons became known as **child savers** and provided various forms of assistance to youths. Groups of child savers also were formed in Scotland and England during the 1850s. The **New York House of Refuge** was established in New York City in 1825 by the Society for the Prevention of Pauperism. Eventually, **houses of refuge** were established in many other cities, and their activities were focused on providing various forms of assistance to runaways and incorrigible children. These houses of refuge were not always benevolent toward children. Some of these homes were headed by sadistic administrators who sought to force children into hard labor and adhered to rigid discipline. The Western House of Refuge (WHR) located in Rochester, New York, during the 1880s was operated more like a prison than anything else, and it housed children who were orphaned, abused, or neglected.

Until the late 1830s, no clear-cut division of labor existed between parental, religious, and state authority regarding child supervision and responsibility for their care and treatment. Churches attempted to provide assistance as well as religious instruction to youths. In some communities, regulations were passed seeking to institutionalize youths and make education and vocational training compulsory. The state began its formal encroachment into parental rights over child-rearing and other child responsibilities in 1839, when *Ex parte Crouse* was decided. This case involved a father who attempted to secure the release of his daughter, Mary Ann Crouse, from the Philadelphia House of Refuge. Without any sort of hearing or trial, the girl had been committed to the Philadelphia facility by the court because she was considered unmanageable. Her commitment was made arbitrarily by a judge. The father's claim that parental control of children is exclusive, natural, and proper was declared invalid by a higher court, and it ruled in favor of the state to exercise necessary reforms and restraints in the interests of children. Thus, children in Pennsylvania and a growing number of other states were effectively denied any legal standing concerning their own welfare, and parental rights were superseded by state-controlled organizations and agencies.

Throughout much of the nineteenth century, various institutions were created to supervise errant juveniles. **Reform schools** were opened in all state jurisdictions by the 1890s. These institutions had prisonlike characteristics and were distinguished by the strict discipline and control they had over juveniles. The Civil War was responsible in part for the creation of these reform schools, since many children were left orphaned and unsupervised as the result of the deaths of one or both parents. Many children of dead Civil War soldiers were placed in reform schools, often just to rid the streets of them. At the same time, increasing numbers of jurisdictions also were establishing schools so that youths could learn how to read and write. School attendance became compulsory for all children. A new class of juveniles was created as the result of these compulsory school laws. They were known as **truants.**

Actually, truants were "invented" in Massachusetts in 1852, where the first compulsory school attendance statute was passed. All other states developed similar statutes by 1918. Colorado is credited with passing the first Compulsory School Act in 1899, the same year that the first juvenile court was established in Illinois. Colorado wanted to prevent truancy, and the act specifically mentioned youths who were habitually absent from school, wandered about the streets during school hours, and had no obvious business or occupation.

Few successful legal challenges of state authority were made by parents during the late 1800s, largely because of the immense power of the state and its jurisdiction over all juvenile matters. In 1899, the Illinois legislature passed the Act to Regulate the Treatment and Control of Dependent, Neglected, and Delinquent Children, or the Illinois Juvenile Court Act. This act provided for limited courts of record. The jurisdiction of these courts included all juveniles under the age of 16 who violated any state law. Provisions also were included for the care of **dependent and/or neglected children.** No minimum age was specified to limit the jurisdiction of juvenile court judges. The act empowered judges to impose secure confinement on juveniles 10 years of age or over in state-operated reform schools.

It is important to note that children in the 1800s and early 1900s were regarded as wards of the state and under the powerful jurisdiction of the government. This was a continuation of how youths were treated in early English history, when children were considered as chattel or farm property and lumped together with the cows, pigs, and horses when censuses were conducted by government officials. Well into the 1900s, children continued to be treated as objects without rights in most juvenile courts. Juvenile court judges presided over juvenile matters under the traditional authority of *parens patriae*, which symbolically conveyed that the king [of England] was the father of the country, including its children. Continued in the United States to the present day, this doctrine has influenced juvenile court judicial decision making and adjudicatory outcomes.

In effect, the juvenile court evolved from an informal welfare agency into a scaled-down, second-class criminal court as a result of a series of reforms that diverted less serious offenders from juvenile court and moved more serious offenders to criminal courts for processing (Feld, 1993b). Quite simply, it became more convenient to establish special courts to hear and decide juvenile matters. As juvenile court systems became more numerous, it became apparent that these proceedings were quite different from criminal court proceedings. Typically, early juvenile court proceedings were one-sided and accusatory. Complainants, most often adults, gave incriminating testimony against youths and judges decided the guilt or innocence of the accused youths. More often than not, judges sided with adults, simply because they were deemed more responsible and trustworthy compared with juveniles. Juveniles were not provided with defense counsel, nor were they permitted to offer testimony in their own defense. They were not allowed to cross-examine their accusers. All of these prohibitions were entirely proper, since juveniles did not have any rights anyway. Without rights, juveniles had no need for defense counsels.

Furthermore, juvenile courts were closed to the general public. The reason given to justify these closed proceedings was to protect the identities of youths being processed. But in fact, juvenile court judges were ruling with a heavy hand and making decisions based on whims of the moment rather than clearly evaluating and deciding based on the facts presented. Despite all of the juvenile court reforms that have occurred since the 1960s, most juvenile court judges continue to rule their courts without a great deal of accountability to others. One explanation for little or no juvenile court judicial accountability is public complacency or apathy about juvenile matters. Even today, despite rising juvenile violence, juvenile cases are considered relatively unimportant and trivial by both police and the public. Furthermore, many persons continue to believe that juvenile court judges know what is best for juveniles and will prescribe the most appropriate punishments. In the mid-1960s and early 1970s, the juvenile courts were substantially transformed, however.

The Court Cases That Bureaucratized Juvenile Courts

In the 1960s, several important juvenile cases came before the U.S. Supreme Court that drastically changed the nature of juvenile court proceedings. The first major juvenile rights case decided in the 1960s was *Kent v. United States* (1966). Kent was a 14-year-old on probation in 1959 who was charged with burglary and rape in the District of Columbia. The juvenile court judge shifted jurisdiction over Kent to the criminal court where he believed tougher sanctions could be imposed. Kent's attorney opposed the waiver but it was done anyway and Kent was subsequently convicted. The U.S. Supreme Court eventually heard Kent's case in 1966 and overturned his conviction because he had not been entitled to a hearing before being waived to the jurisdiction of the criminal court. Among other things, the *Kent* case established the precedent of requiring waiver hearings before juveniles can be transferred to the jurisdiction of a criminal court.

The following year, the U.S. Supreme Court decided the case of *In re Gault*. Gault was a 15-year-old living in Arizona in 1964. He was subsequently taken into custody by police officers and charged with making obscene telephone calls to an adult female neighbor. On uncorroborated and circumstantial evidence at best, Gault was declared delinquent and ordered to the Arizona State Industrial School until age 21. Thus, he received nearly a six-year sentence for allegedly making an obscene telephone call. An adult convicted of the same offense may have been fined $50 and probably would not have served any time in jail or prison. During his juvenile court hearing, Gault was denied the opportunity to cross-examine his accuser, the female recipient of the obscene telephone calls. Further, he was denied the opportunity to testify in his own behalf. The only testimony presented came from a juvenile court officer who was generally familiar with what had happened. In 1967, the U.S. Supreme Court heard his appeal and reversed the juvenile court. The high court said that Gault had been denied several important rights, including the right against self-incrimination, the right to cross-examine his accuser, the right to a list of charges, and the right to counsel.

In 1970, the U.S. Supreme Court heard the case of *In re Winship.* Winship was a 12-year-old boy living in New York City with his parents. He was charged with stealing a woman's pocketbook. During his family court hearing, the juvenile court judge determined that he was guilty on the basis of the preponderance of the evidence. Winship was ordered to the state industrial school (comparable to a juvenile prison) for 18 months, subject to 18-month renewals of confinement, until his eighteenth birthday. The U.S. Supreme Court heard his appeal and overturned the court ruling, holding that because his freedom had been jeopardized, the standard used to prove his guilt should have been the same criminal standard used in criminal courts: beyond a reasonable doubt. The family court in Winship's case had applied the civil standard, that of the preponderance of the evidence.

Thus, in four short years, the juvenile court had been transformed into a criminal court–like apparatus, and juvenile rights had been expanded considerably. The *Kent, Gault,* and *Winship* cases have been referred to as the "big three" in juvenile justice literature, largely because of their constitutional significance for juveniles. But they have not been the sole cases on which juvenile rights have been based.

In 1971, the U.S. Supreme Court decided the case of *McKeiver v. Pennsylvania.* McKeiver was a juvenile who demanded a jury trial from the juvenile court judge. The judge declared that the trial would be conducted without benefit of a jury. McKeiver was subsequently declared delinquent and appealed. The U.S.

Supreme Court declared in *McKeiver* that juveniles are not entitled to a jury trial as a matter of right. In 2001, only 11 states had provisions entitling juveniles to jury trials in juvenile courts, under special circumstances. In all other states, jury trials for juveniles were left to the discretion of juvenile court or family court judges.

In 1975, the U.S. Supreme Court decided the case of *Breed v. Jones.* Jones was a 17-year-old in California who was charged with robbery in 1971. A juvenile court declared him delinquent and then transferred him to criminal court where he was convicted of the same charge. In 1975, the U.S. Supreme Court overturned his criminal conviction, holding that this conviction amounted to double jeopardy, since he had already been adjudicated delinquent in juvenile court. Thus, juveniles may not be adjudicated delinquent on a specific charge in juvenile court and be tried for that same offense later in criminal court, since this violates their Fifth Amendment right against double jeopardy.

The net result of these U.S. Supreme Court rulings has been the increased criminalization of the juvenile courts. Because of the increasing similarities between juvenile and criminal courts, some thought has been given to blending them into one unified court system, although court unification of any kind in any jurisdiction presently is not feasible for various logistical reasons. One important reason is that the juvenile court continues to reflect a strong rehabilitative orientation, whereas the criminal court has all but abandoned rehabilitation as a primary aim and currently concentrates on punishing offenders and incapacitating them. Another factor is that juvenile court judges are unwilling to relinquish their power over juvenile offenders. A third reason is that blending both court systems would effectively remove the civil element from juvenile courts.

Despite the reluctance of different court systems to merge into one unified court, the juvenile court itself has evolved into a largely bureaucratic organization with many bureaucratic attributes. Individuality of judicial decision making has been gradually replaced with impersonality. The large number of youthful offenders entering the juvenile justice system annually has caused juvenile courts to adopt more streamlined methods of case processing, similar to those used by criminal courts. More juveniles today have attorneys representing them in juvenile court matters than at any other time in U.S. history.

These and other events have created and exacerbated a continuing conflict over who should be held accountable for youthful offending, which jurisdiction should punish these offenders, and what should be the nature and severity of the punishment. These are administrative questions worth addressing. Before we deal with these questions, however, different types of juvenile offenders need to be described.

TYPES OF JUVENILE OFFENDERS

Juvenile Court Age Jurisdiction for Juveniles

About a fifth of all states define the upper age limit for juveniles at either 15 or 16. In most other states, the upper jurisdictional age limit for juveniles is 17, except for Wyoming, where it is 18. A general definition for the jurisdiction of juvenile courts includes all juveniles between the ages of seven and 18 (Black, 1990:867). Federal law defines **juveniles** as any persons who have not attained their eighteenth birthday (18 U.S. Code, Sec. 5031, 2001).

Although upper age limits for juveniles have been established in all U.S. jurisdictions, little uniformity exists concerning lower age limits. Under English common law, any juveniles under the age of seven are presumed incapable of formulating criminal intent. Thus, those children under age seven fell outside the jurisdiction of criminal courts. In the United States today, some juvenile courts have no minimum-age limits for their jurisdiction over juveniles. Generally, juvenile courts in the United States have broad discretionary powers over most persons under the age of 18. There are three broad classes of juveniles who fall within the scope of juvenile court jurisdiction: (1) juvenile delinquents, (2) status offenders, and (3) children in need of supervision.

Juvenile Delinquents

Federal law says that **juvenile delinquency** is the violation of a law of the United States by a person prior to his eighteenth birthday, which would have been a crime if committed by an adult (18 U.S. Code, Sec. 5031, 2001). A **juvenile delinquent** is anyone who is determined by a juvenile court to have committed a delinquent act. A broader definition of juvenile delinquency is the violation of any state or local law or ordinance by anyone who has not yet achieved the age of majority (Black, 1990:428). Black (1990:428) defines a juvenile delinquent as a delinquent child. The **age of majority** depends on the defining jurisdiction. The most liberal definition of juvenile delinquency is whatever the juvenile court believes should be brought within its jurisdiction.

Status Offenders

When juveniles commit offenses that are not crimes but nevertheless bring these youths to the attention of the juvenile courts, they may be considered **status offenders. Status offenses** are any acts committed by juveniles that would bring the juveniles to the attention of juvenile courts and would not be crimes if committed by adults. Examples of status offenses include running away from home, truancy, and curfew violations. Adults would not be arrested for running away from home, being truant from school, or walking the streets after a given evening curfew time for juveniles. If juveniles engage in these activities, however, they may be taken into custody by police officers and brought to the attention of the juvenile court.

Runaways are those youths who leave their homes without permission or their parents' knowledge and who remain away from home for prolonged periods ranging from several days to several years. About 101,000 children were arrested as runaways in 1999 (Maguire and Pastore, 2000). Other types of status offenders are truants and curfew and liquor law violators. Truants are those who absent themselves from school without either school or parental permission. In 1999, about 100,000 youths were arrested for truancy in the United States (Maguire and Pastore, 2000). **Curfew violators** are those youths who remain on city streets after specified evening hours when they are prohibited from loitering or not being in the company of a parent or guardian. In 1999, about 40,000 youths were arrested for curfew violation in the United States (Maguire and Pastore, 2000).

ARRESTING AND PROCESSING JUVENILE OFFENDERS

Referrals and Arrests

Referrals are notifications made to juvenile court authorities that a juvenile requires the court's attention. Referrals may be made by anyone, such as concerned parents, school principals, teachers, neighbors, and others. More than 90 percent of all referrals to juvenile court are made by law enforcement officers. Police have broad discretionary powers in their encounters with the public and dealing with street crime. Other

ways that juveniles can enter the juvenile justice system include referrals from or complaints by parents, neighbors, victims, and others, such as social workers and probation officers.

Following referrals or direct contact with juveniles on the streets, police officers usually take youths into custody. Depending on the offenses alleged, juveniles are held in different processing areas of local jails or detention facilities. Any youth taken into custody must be classified by police and jail officers. Many youths are suspected of committing crimes and are considered delinquents. They are placed in particular jail areas for a period of time until it can be determined if they should be processed further into the system. Other youths are status offenders. These juveniles are usually held in less secure areas of jails or police offices. Very often, the intent of their short-term custody is to reunite them with parents or guardians. Some youths who are taken into custody require special care, are needy or dependent, or are otherwise unsupervised by adults or guardians. Frequently, they are transported to social welfare agencies or human service organizations where they can be supervised temporarily until parents or guardians can be notified or until they can be placed in foster care.

It is important for proper classifications of juveniles to be made at all stages of juvenile justice processing. Juveniles differ considerably in terms of type of offense, likelihood of reoffending, emotional needs, educational levels, vocational skills, honesty, and other factors. About 10 percent of all youths arrested by law enforcement officers have committed serious crimes, and their preventive detention is anticipated. The next step in their processing is intake.

Intake

Intake is a screening procedure conducted by a court officer or a probation officer, in which one or several courses of action are recommended. Intake varies considerably among jurisdictions. Some jurisdictions conduct **intake hearings** or **intake screenings,** during which comments and opinions are solicited from significant others such as the police, parents, neighbors, or victims. Other jurisdictions have informal intake proceedings, usually consisting of a brief meeting between the juvenile and **intake officers.** Intake proceedings are a critical stage in juvenile offender processing. Important decisions are made at the intake stage about whether or not further processing is necessary. Intake officers who conduct these screenings are either court-appointed officials who hear complaints against juveniles and informally resolve the least serious cases, or more often, they are juvenile probation officers who perform intake as a special assignment. In many smaller jurisdictions, juvenile probation officers may perform diverse functions, including intake, enforcement of truancy statutes, and juvenile placements.

Intake officers consider the youth's attitude, demeanor, age, offense seriousness, and a host of other factors: Has the juvenile had frequent prior contact with the juvenile justice system? If the offenses alleged are serious, what evidence exists against the offender? Should the offender be referred to certain community social service agencies, receive psychological counseling, receive vocational counseling and guidance, acquire educational or technical training and skills, be issued a verbal reprimand, be placed on some type of diversionary status, or be returned to parental custody? Interviews with parents and neighbors may be conducted as a part of an intake officer's information gathering.

Intake usually results in one of the following actions: (1) dismissal of the case; (2) remand of the youth to the custody of his or her parents; (3) remand of the youth to the custody of his or her parents, with a referral to counseling or special services; (4) diversion of the youth to an alternative dispute resolution program if available; or (5) referral of the youth to the juvenile prosecutor for further action.

Prosecution

The most serious juvenile cases are referred to juvenile prosecutors. These prosecutors have broad discretionary powers that may include dropping the charges or downgrading them. Some of these cases may be referred by the prosecutor to the jurisdiction of the criminal court. Prosecutors either file **petitions** or act on petitions filed by others. Petitions are official documents filed in juvenile courts on the juvenile's behalf, specifying reasons for the youth's court appearance. Filing a petition is the official action that brings the juvenile before the juvenile court judge. Some juveniles may come before juvenile court judges in less formal ways as nonpetitioned cases. About 45 percent of the cases brought before the juvenile court each year are nonpetitioned cases. Of all cases brought before the juvenile court, less than 1 percent of these cases result in out-of-home placements, 30 percent receive probation,

50 percent are dismissed, and the remainder are diverted, downgraded, or result in verbal warnings (Bilchik, 1998).

Juvenile Courts and the Adjudicatory Process

Increasingly, juvenile courts are more like criminal courts in many respects, although considerable diversity still exists among jurisdictions about how juveniles are processed. In many juvenile courts, the physical trappings of criminal courts are present, including the judge's bench, tables for the prosecution and defense, and a witness stand. A time and date for an adjudicatory hearing are specified. An **adjudicatory hearing** for a juvenile is like a trial for an adult charged with a crime. The prosecutor presents the case against the juvenile, in which the allegations are outlined. Witnesses may be called on to give testimony against the juvenile. A defense attorney furnishes exculpatory evidence, if any, and defense witnesses may be called. Following the presentation of evidence, the judge makes a determination of whether or not the facts as alleged by the prosecutor are true on the basis of the evidence. This determination is called an **adjudication.** If a petition has been filed against the juvenile, the judge decides whether the allegations raised in the petition are true or false. The juvenile court judge has the absolute power of determining the adjudicatory outcome in nearly 80 percent of all states. As noted earlier, juveniles may or may not be entitled to a jury trial as a matter of right. These jury trials usually are reserved for the most serious offenders and are prescribed by state statutes. Otherwise, the judge decides whether or not to grant a jury trial to a juvenile if one is requested.

The power of juvenile court judges is extensive, and it encompasses what kinds of evidence will be permitted and who will be permitted to offer testimony. Juveniles are afforded certain constitutional rights, and these rights must be observed. An increasing number of juvenile cases involve defense counsel, and these attorneys are instrumental in ensuring that a youth's rights are safeguarded. Many juvenile court judges are not known for their attention to important constitutional details. Sometimes it takes the presence of a defense attorney to heighten court awareness of the full range of a juvenile's rights.

Depending on what allegations are lodged against particular juvenile defendants, the judge will make one of several different optional determinations. If the petition alleges **delinquency** on the part of a juvenile, the judge determines whether the juvenile is or is not delinquent. If the petition alleges that the juvenile involved is dependent, neglected, or otherwise in need of care by agencies or others, the judge decides the matter. If the adjudicatory hearing fails to yield supporting facts for the petition filed, then the case is dismissed and the youth exits the juvenile justice system. If the adjudicatory hearing supports the allegations in the petition, then the judge must dispose the juvenile according to a range of punishments. **Dispositions** are the equivalent of sentences for convicted adult offenders. When adult offenders are convicted of crimes, they are sentenced. When juveniles are adjudicated delinquent, they are *disposed.*

Optional Dispositions for Juvenile Court Judges

At least 12 dispositions or punishments are available to juvenile court judges, if the facts alleged in petitions are upheld. These dispositions are broken down into three major categories of sanctions: (1) nominal, (2) conditional, or (3) custodial options.

NOMINAL DISPOSITIONS. **Nominal dispositions** are either verbal warnings or stern reprimands and are the least punitive dispositional options. The nature of such verbal warnings or reprimands is a matter of judicial discretion. Release to the custody of parents or legal guardians completes the juvenile court action against the youth. Usually, juvenile court judges impose these nominal sanctions on first offenders who are considered low risk.

CONDITIONAL DISPOSITIONS. **Conditional dispositions** include all forms of probation. Probation is the most frequently imposed disposition. Youths who are placed on **probation** are required to abide by certain conditions for a probationary period, which may range from a few months to one or more years. These dispositions usually require offenders to do something as a condition of probation. If youths have problems with alcohol or drugs, they may be required to attend individual or group counseling. Property offenders may have to make restitution to victims or to compensate them in some way for their property losses. Offenders with pronounced behavioral disorders may require more intensive probation supervision. They may be required to submit to electronic monitoring and house arrest for a period of time. In 1999, more than 300,000 juveniles were on probation in various state ju-

risdictions (American Correctional Association, 1999). Juveniles also may be placed in community-based residential programs or exposed to various therapies and treatments or training.

CUSTODIAL DISPOSITIONS. **Custodial dispositions** are designated as either nonsecure custody or secure custody. **Nonsecure custody** involves some type of out-of-home placement, such as in foster care. Some jurisdictions place youths in group homes or have them attend special camps where they can receive individualized attention from supervisors and youth workers.

Secure custody means placement in some type of juvenile incarcerative facility for a period of time. Secure custody is often considered as the worst punishment and a last resort for serious juvenile offenders. Judges refrain from placing youths in secure custody because they fear the adverse effects of labeling. They do not want juveniles to identify with adult criminals and their treatment. Being placed in a secure juvenile facility is tantamount to imprisonment in a penitentiary or prison, even though the amount of time spent by juveniles in these facilities is relatively short. As stated previously, short-term incarceration for juveniles averages about 30 days nationally, whereas long-term incarceration averages about 180 days or six months. Fewer than 10 percent of all juveniles processed by juvenile courts annually are subsequently placed in either nonsecure or secure facilities. In 1999, 52,700 juveniles were in residential and nonresidential correctional programs other than probation (American Correctional Association, 1999:xxxvi–xxxvii).

Juveniles also may be placed on parole. After juveniles have served a portion of their incarcerative terms, they may be paroled by a juvenile paroling authority to the supervision of an appropriate state or community agency. In 1999, 75,000 juveniles were on parole in various state jurisdictions (Camp and Camp, 1999b).

NONSECURE AND SECURE DISPOSITIONS FOR JUVENILE OFFENDERS

Nonsecure Dispositions

Many juveniles never make it as far as the juvenile court. Police officers have the discretion to make **station house adjustments,** which are on-the-spot decisions to release the juvenile to the custody of parents or guardians following his or her apprehension, usually for a minor offense. But as we have seen, many juveniles are moved forward into the juvenile justice system through intake, followed by an appearance before a juvenile court judge. By far the most frequently applied sanction for juvenile offenders is probation. But other dispositions of a nonsecure nature include nominal sanctions, such as verbal warnings or reprimands. Other sanctions include alternative dispute resolution, diversion, and other intermediate punishments.

ALTERNATIVE DISPUTE RESOLUTION. Juvenile court judges are admonished by their jurisdictions to exercise minimum use of incarceration or detention except in the most serious cases. This is one of the important reasons why the public views the juvenile justice system as overly lenient with youthful offenders. If verbal warnings will suffice, then judges will use them. Interestingly, nominal warnings are effective in many juvenile cases. The mere appearance of a juvenile before a juvenile court judge may be sufficiently frightening that the juvenile will not reoffend. If the juvenile stays in the jurisdiction, a further appearance before the same juvenile court will be noted, since the court maintains records of juvenile arrests and previous dispositional information. Often, this known fact is a sufficient deterrent.

Sometimes the judge will direct the juvenile and his or her parents to meet with the victim(s) and work out an agreement for the juvenile to make restitution to the victim or pay for damages to property or to reimburse lost wages. Suppose the juvenile stole a neighbor's car and was eventually stopped by police for joyriding. The car was damaged when the youth collided with another automobile. If no one was injured in the accident, the youth may be directed by the judge to make restitution so that the neighbor can repair her car. Frequently, the process used to determine the amount or type of restitution is known as *alternative dispute resolution*. This is an informal mechanism by which the victim and youthful offender meet and reach an agreement about an appropriate remedy. Usually, alternative dispute resolution is supervised by a judicial official, perhaps a retired judge or a lawyer. Sometimes, a community citizen may act as the unofficial arbiter in this process. A satisfactory arrangement must be reached by both parties. If not, then the case will proceed to juvenile court where the judge will decide. Thus, alternative dispute resolution is a way of keeping the case out of juvenile court.

DIVERSION. Another option available to juvenile court judges is to use diversion. *Diversion* is the temporary cessation of proceedings against the juvenile offender and the imposition of conditional sanctions, usually involving some form of victim compensation, restitution, or community service. The juvenile's case is temporarily suspended, usually with the approval and/or recommendation of the juvenile prosecutor. Diversion may include other conditions, such as attending individual or group counseling, or participating in a drug/alcohol counseling program. Whatever the conditions imposed by the court, the juvenile is obligated to comply with them. Failure to do so will result in the youth being formally adjudicated by the judge in court. The period of diversion may range from three months to a year or longer.

What happens if the juvenile successfully completes the diversion conditions? In most cases, the original charges against the juvenile are dropped and the record of the offense is expunged or deleted from court records. Thus, a strong incentive is built into the system for complying with diversion program conditions.

Diversion is not new. It is a form of deferred prosecution with which offenders, especially low-risk ones, can have a chance to prove themselves as law-abiding persons. For juveniles, diversion was originated by Conrad Printzlien, New York's first chief probation officer. Printzlien was concerned that many youths were stigmatized by rapid prosecution and conviction, and thus he set out to find an alternative to unnecessary and unwarranted incarceration of juveniles (Rackmill, 1996). Printzlien formulated the Brooklyn Plan, a deferred prosecution program that provided a way to distinguish situational offenders from more serious chronic and persistent juvenile delinquents. Between 1936 and 1946, 250 youths were handled as divertees. The program was deemed successful at decreasing recidivism among divertees in New York and was used in other jurisdictions with similarly positive outcomes.

PROBATION AND OTHER INTERMEDIATE PUNISHMENTS. Probation for juveniles is routine for most juvenile courts. Several types of probation programs exist. Probation may be unconditional or conditional, although this is largely a semantic distinction. *Any* probationary disposition involves conditions. The fact is that standard probation involves minimal contact with the juvenile probation authorities and no special requirements other than to remain law abiding and stay out of trouble. Juvenile probation is pretty much the same as it is for adult offenders who are convicted of crimes. Juveniles on probation usually have complete freedom to move about in their communities. They may have to turn in periodic reports of good conduct to their probation officers, perhaps on a monthly basis. These are usually forms that are completed by elementary or high school officials attesting to the fact that these juveniles are in school and doing passable work. Little standardization or individualization exists for juvenile probation.

For more serious offenders, juvenile court judges can impose one or more conditions for a juvenile's probation program. These conditions might include a certain number of hours of public or community service, providing restitution to victims, payment of fines, employment, and/or participation in specific vocational, educational, or therapeutic programs. A standard probation agreement applicable to juveniles is shown in Figure 13.1.

As a part of one's probation, the juvenile court judge can impose home confinement or electronic monitoring, or the judge can direct that certain juveniles should be closely supervised by their probation officers. These alternative punishments are collectively termed **intermediate punishments,** which means that the punishments range somewhere between standard probation and incarceration or secure confinement. Intermediate punishment programs presently are operated in all states for both juvenile and adult offenders. Sometimes these programs are known as creative sentencing. In some jurisdictions, such as Tennessee, electronic monitoring and house arrest are considered last resorts before a particular juvenile is incarcerated in a secure facility. Such intermediate punishment procedures are not especially expensive to operate, but valuable time is expended by juvenile probation officers who are in charge of seeing that probation program conditions are enforced.

Under intensive probation supervision (IPS) or intensive supervised probation (ISP), juvenile probation officers merely visit their youthful clients frequently. This compares with almost no visits under standard probation. "Frequently" might be a face-to-face visit between the juvenile client and the probation officer once or more per week. It might even mean once a month.

Recidivism figures relating to juveniles on probation are somewhat unreliable. Thus, it is difficult to evaluate the success of any given juvenile probation program. One reason recidivism is hard to track is that many youths simply grow out of delinquency, as they move from age 15, to 16, to 17, and to 18. In ad-

dition, many youths move to other jurisdictions where they become first offenders once again. Juvenile recordkeeping and information sharing among jurisdictions is inadequate at present, although several jurisdictions are making needed improvements. Once a youth moves away from the jurisdiction where he or she was originally adjudicated, there is almost no way that youth can be tracked successfully. Many of these youths move away with their families in the middle of their probation programs. The ability of the juvenile court to stretch its arms over city and state boundaries is severely limited. Furthermore, because of the confidentiality of juvenile court records, it is often impossible for interested researchers to evaluate any juvenile community program and its success at reducing recidivism, unless the study is conducted over a relatively short period of time.

Secure Dispositions

By the end of the year 1999, 130,000 juveniles were under some form of correctional supervision in 51 jurisdictions in the United States (Maguire and Pastore, 2000). Approximately 2.1 million admissions and discharges of juveniles from secure confinement facilities were made during 1997. Minority youths made up about 60 percent of those confined.

Juvenile corrections is one of the most important components of the juvenile justice system. Juvenile corrections encompasses all personnel, agencies, and institutions that supervise youthful offenders. Secure custodial sanctions usually are administered to youthful offenders who have been adjudicated delinquent and considered sufficiently serious or dangerous to deserve secure confinement. The goals of juvenile corrections are (1) deterrence, (2) rehabilitation and reintegration, (3) prevention, (4) punishment and retribution, and (5) isolation and control.

Secure custodial facilities are the juvenile equivalent of adult prisons or penitentiaries. Such institutions are known by different names among the states. These long-term facilities might be called youth centers or youth facilities, juvenile institutions, schools, schools for boys, training schools or centers, youth development centers, youth services centers, secure centers, industry schools, and/or youth development centers. In previous decades dating back to the 1950s and 1960s, these facilities were known as reform schools. The term, *reform school* is no longer applied to any secure juvenile facility in the United States, however.

INSTRUCTIONS:
1. Original to Probation Files
2. Pink to Parents
3. Blue to Minor
4. Goldenrod to Division Officer

**ORANGE COUNTY PROBATION DEPARTMENT
INFORMAL PROBATION AGREEMENT**

The authority for undertaking a plan of informal probation which may include the use of a crisis resolution home or shelter-care facility is contained in Section 654 of the Welfare and Institutions Code, which is printed in full on the reverse side of this form. Before signing this agreement, please read it and resolve any questions about it with the deputy probation officer.

GENERAL RULES AND REQUIREMENTS

Minor's Initials

_____ 1. You are to report in person and submit written reports to your probation officer as directed.

_____ 2. You are to obey all laws, including traffic rules and regulations. You are not to operate a motor vehicle in any street or highway until properly licensed and insured. You are to report to your probation officer any arrests or law violations immediately.

_____ 3. You are to obey the curfew law of the city or county in which you live or any special curfew imposed by the Court or the probation officer; specifically: _____

_____ 4. You are not to leave the state of California or change your residence without first getting permission from your probation officer. Prior to change of residence, you are to notify your probation officer of the new address. You are not to live with anyone except your parents or approved guardian without specific permission of your probation officer.

_____ 5. You are to attend school every day, every class, as prescribed by law, and obey all school regulations. Suspension from school and/or truancies/tardiness could result in action being taken by the Probation Department. Your are to notify your probation officer by 10:00 a.m. on any school day that you are absent from school. If you are home from school because of illness or suspension, you are not to leave your home that day or night except to keep a doctor's appointment.

_____ 6. You are not to use or possess any intoxicants, alcohol, narcotics, other controlled substances, related paraphernalia, poisons, or illegal drugs, including marijuana. You are not to be with anyone who is using or possessing any illegal intoxicants, narcotics, or drugs. Do not inhale or attempt to inhale or consume any substance of any type or nature, such as paint, glue, plant material, or any aerosol product. You are not to inject anything into your body unless directed to do so by a medical doctor.

_____ 7. You are not to frequent any places of business disapproved by your probation officer, parents, or guardian, specifically: _____

_____ 8. You are not to associate with individuals disapproved by your probation officer, parents, or guardians, specifically: _____

_____ 9. You may be required to participate in any program outlined in Section 654 W&I Code.

_____ 10. You are to seek and maintain counseling if and as directed by the probation officer.

_____ 11. You are not to have any weapons of any description, including firearms, numchucks or martial arts weaponry, and knives of any kind, in your possession while you are on probation, or involve self in activities in which weapons are used, i.e., hunting, target shooting.

_____ 12. You are ordered to obey the following additional terms of probation: _____
_____

Probation will expire on _____ unless you fail to abide by the above terms and conditions of your probation resulting in court action.

I have personally initialed, read and understand the above rules and requirements of informal probation that apply in my particular case as explained to me by the probation officer. I understand that my failure to comply with the initialed items could result in the petition, that is pending in my case, being filed with the District Attorney.

SIGNED: _____ DATE: _____
(minor)

SIGNED: _____ DATE: _____
(parent)

SIGNED: _____ DATE: _____
(parent)

MICHAEL SCHUMACHER
Chief Probation Officer

BY: _____ DATE: _____
(Deputy Probation Officer)

**FIGURE 13.1 Orange County Probation Department Informal
Probation Agreement**

INTERFACING JUVENILES WITH THE CRIMINAL JUSTICE SYSTEM

Suppose an 11-year-old male deliberately kills six persons with a high-powered rifle and threatens to kill additional people. The juvenile court judge believes that the case deserves to be heard in criminal court rather than in juvenile court. In another case, suppose a 13-year-old boy rapes and murders a 12-year-old girl from school. He is apprehended while throwing her mutilated body into a river. The juvenile court judge believes that his case ought to be heard in criminal court. In yet another case, suppose a 12-year-old hit man and Detroit gang member who has 24 confirmed kills to his credit is caught murdering a 14-year-old rival gang member in an alley. The juvenile court judge believes that the 12-year-old ought to appear before a criminal court judge rather than have the case heard in juvenile court.

These cases are based on actual incidents that have occurred and that will continue to occur annually. There are 11-year-old mass murderers and serial killers. There are 13-year-old murderer-rapists. There are 11-year-old hit men. We do not like to admit it, but they are out there in society. They are children. They are young. They are delicate and fragile beings. They are immature. They are not fully formed adults. They are questionably accountable for their actions. Sometimes they do not know what they have done or the seriousness of the consequences of their actions. They deserve individualized counseling and treatment. They need special care (Steinberg and Cauffman, 1999). *But* they have committed heinous crimes. Should their crimes be forgiven outright, and should they be permitted to rejoin their families and remain free in society? A substantial portion of juvenile court officers think so. And so do many academics who study juvenile justice and the problems and causes of juvenile offending. Unfortunately, no one has conclusively demonstrated that maturity instantly occurs at any particular age. Thus, gauging whether or not a nonadult is suitable for treatment as an adult is very difficult, and the use of specific age limits to effect transfers to criminal courts or to bar such transfers assumes an overnight transition to adulthood on a particular birthday. Developmental psychologists and others would agree that the onset of maturity occurs over time. Indeed, maturity occurs at different times for different persons. Some persons never reach a socially acceptable level of maturity, regardless of their age.

Currently, only a fraction of all juvenile offenders fit into the category of chronic, serious, and violent juvenile offenders. Some indication even exists that the amount of violent juvenile offending decreased slightly during the last half of the 1990s. Sufficient numbers of serious and violent juvenile offenders are still out there, however, so many members of society are clearly disturbed about these juveniles and believe that drastic measures should be applied to punish them and control their conduct.

Several procedures have been in place for many decades to make it possible for serious and violent juvenile offenders to suffer more severe consequences for their actions by being treated and punished as though they were adult offenders. These procedures are known as transfers, waivers, or certifications.

Transfers, Waivers, or Certifications

A **transfer** refers to changing the jurisdiction over certain juvenile offenders from the juvenile court to the criminal court. Transfers are also known as **waivers**, signifying the waiver of jurisdiction over a juvenile by the juvenile court judge to the jurisdiction of a criminal court judge. Some jurisdictions such as Utah move selected juveniles to the jurisdiction of criminal courts simply by declaring them adults for the purposes of a criminal prosecution. This process is known as **certification.** Between 10,000 and 13,000 juvenile offenders are sent to criminal court through the transfer or waiver process each year (Maguire and Pastore, 2000). This represents less than 1 percent of all juvenile offenders who come to the attention of the juvenile courts.

The primary reason for using transfers or waivers is to ensure that the most serious juvenile offenders will be sent to criminal courts where the harshest punishments, including capital punishment, will be imposed. Juvenile courts have limited jurisdiction. The worst punishment they can impose is placement in secure facilities until these youths reach adulthood. Additional reasons for using transfers, waivers, or certifications include (1) to provide just deserts and proportionately severe punishments for those juveniles who deserve such punishments by their more violent actions, (2) to foster fairness in administering punishments according to more serious offending, (3) to hold serious or violent offenders more accountable for what they have done, (4) to show other juveniles who contemplate committing serious offenses that harsh punishments can be expected if serious offenses are committed, (5) to provide a deterrent to decrease juvenile violence, (6) to overcome the traditional leniency of juvenile courts and provide more realistic sanctions, and (7) to make youths realize the seriousness of their offending and induce remorse and acceptance of responsibility.

Since the clear intent of transfers of juveniles is to make it possible for the worst offenders to receive the harshest punishments from criminal courts, then it makes sense that only the worst offenders would and should be transferred each year to criminal court for processing. Probably we would agree that the worst juvenile offenders would be those who have been charged with murder, rape, robbery, or aggravated assault. We would not necessarily consider shoplifters or status offenders as targets of transfers, nor would we lump 13-year-old petty thieves and 14-year-old small-time burglars together with murderers, rapists, and robbers. We might want to include some 12-year-old drug dealers who move 10 or 20 kilos of cocaine a year, however. But again, we are designating only the worst types of juvenile offenders for transfer to criminal courts.

Assuming most of us agree that only the most serious juveniles should be transferred to the jurisdiction of criminal courts, the next logical question is, Does this actually happen? The answer is no, it does not. In 1994, for instance, 12,400 youths were transferred to criminal court.

Most juveniles transferred were male; only 600 females (0.5 percent) were waived (Butts and Snyder, 1997). About 6,800 (55 percent) of all transferred juveniles were black or other minority, despite the fact that white juveniles comprised about 64 percent of all cases referred to juvenile court. Furthermore, those charged with violent offenses and waived to criminal court in 1994 made up only *42 percent* of those transferred. About *46 percent* of those waived to criminal courts were charged with property or public order offenses, and about 10 percent of those waived were charged with low-level drug offenses (Bilchik, 1996:13). In 1999, the proportion of the 12,000 or so transferred youths who were charged with violent offenses was about 48 percent. Property and drug offenders made up more than half of all transferred youths (Maguire and Pastore, 2000).

Even more remarkable is what happens to transferred youths once they reach criminal courts. Although these figures vary slightly from year to year, they are disturbingly similar. About 50 percent of all transferred youths, regardless of their offense, either have the charges against them dropped or dismissed, or criminal court judges downgrade them to nonserious levels. Another 40 percent receive probation from criminal court judges. About 10 percent actually do time in prison or jail (Maguire and Pastore, 2000).

Clearly the waiver process is seriously flawed. The major reason it is flawed is that juvenile court judges have almost absolute power to determine who is or is not waived. Further, there are no clear-cut standards for guiding judges about who should be waived to criminal courts in most states. Considerable variation can be found among states about how old juveniles should be before they can be transferred. Juvenile

court judges have their own opinions about these decisions as well, regardless of what the statutes say or provide.

In 1997, 18 states and all federal districts indicated no specified age for transferring juveniles to criminal courts for processing. Two states, Vermont and Wisconsin, specified age 10 as the minimum age at which a juvenile could be waived. Colorado, Missouri, Montana, and Oregon established age 12 as the earliest age for a juvenile waiver. Eighteen states used age 14 as the youngest transfer age, and the District of Columbia set the minimum transfer age at 15. One state, Hawaii, used the minimum transfer age of 16. But just because states provide these ages as minimum transfer limits, this does not mean that juvenile court judges are obligated to transfer youths who are otherwise transferrable.

Because of the discretionary nature of the waiver process, large numbers of the wrong types of juveniles are transferred to criminal courts. They are the wrong types of juveniles because they are not those originally targeted by juvenile justice professionals and reformers to be the primary candidates for transfers. Interested citizens want to know why juvenile courts send property offenders or public order offenders to criminal courts for processing each year.

What possible reasons could a juvenile court judge give for transferring such low-risk offenders to criminal court for processing as an adult? Some information is available about why this situation occurs. More than a few juvenile court judges are tired of seeing the same petty offenders in their courts on a monthly basis. They believe that if such persistent offenders are sent to criminal courts, this will be a significant deterrent to their future offending (Champion and Mays, 1991). Some juvenile court judges abhor drug dealing or drug use of any kind and they have a "hit list" of youths to target for the harshest punishments as a means of discouraging them from future offending. Therefore, any juvenile who uses or sells drugs and appears before one of these judges who has an antidrug agenda can count on being transferred to criminal court. Additional factors cited by juvenile court judges that result in the transfer of nonserious property, public order, or drug offenders to criminal court are that

1. Certain property offenders, although not serious or violent, appear in juvenile court so frequently as to be bothersome, and the judge wants to teach them a lesson.
2. Some jurisdictions require that certain offenders should be transferred to criminal court if

they have been adjudicated delinquent a certain number of times, regardless of the seriousness or nonseriousness of their offending.

3. Individual differences among juvenile court judges dictate which juveniles are transferred, despite the seriousness of their offense, so if the judge simply does not like a particular youth's attitude, the youth will be transferred.

4. What is a serious or violent offense in one juvenile court jurisdiction may not be considered serious or violent in another jurisdiction, so different standards are applied to the same types of juveniles in different jurisdictions.

5. In some jurisdictions where gang presence is strong, local task forces have targeted gang members for harsher treatment, including the greater likelihood of being transferred to criminal court.

Types of Waivers

There are four main types of waiver actions: (1) judicial waivers, (2) direct file, (3) statutory exclusion, and (4) demand waivers.

JUDICIAL WAIVERS. The largest numbers of waivers from juvenile to criminal court annually are **judicial waivers,** which means that the juvenile court judge decides whether or not to send forward a juvenile's case to criminal court. Three kinds of judicial waivers include (1) **discretionary waivers,** which means the judge can waive the juvenile to the jurisdiction of a criminal court; (2) **mandatory waivers,** which means the juvenile court judge *must* waive the juvenile to criminal court if the judge determines that probable cause exists that the juvenile committed the offense; and (3) **presumptive waivers,** which means the burden of proof shifts from the state to the juvenile concerning whether or not the juvenile should be transferred. Also, under the presumptive waiver scenario, juveniles must convince the juvenile court judge that they are good candidates for rehabilitation.

DIRECT FILE. Under **direct file,** the prosecutor has the sole authority to determine where the juvenile's case will be heard, either in criminal court or juvenile court.

STATUTORY EXCLUSION. **Statutory exclusion** means that certain juvenile offenders are automatically excluded from the juvenile court's original jurisdiction

because of the crimes they have committed. In 1997, 16 states had statutory exclusion provisions and excluded certain types of offenders from juvenile court jurisdiction. These waivers also are known as *automatic waivers* or *legislative waivers,* since legislatures created them.

DEMAND WAIVERS. Sometimes, juveniles may submit motions for **demand waiver** actions. Demand waivers are requests by juveniles to have their cases transferred from juvenile courts to criminal courts. One reason is that criminal courts are traditionally lenient with juvenile offenders. Another reason is that all serious juvenile offenders would be entitled to a jury trial in criminal court, whereas if their case remained in juvenile court, they may not necessarily receive a jury trial.

Other Types of Waivers

REVERSE WAIVERS. A **reverse waiver** is an action by a criminal court to transfer direct file or statutory exclusion cases from criminal court back to juvenile court, usually at the recommendation of the prosecutor (Bilchik, 1996).

ONCE AN ADULT/ALWAYS AN ADULT. The **once an adult/always an adult provision** is perhaps the most serious and long lasting for affected juvenile offenders. This provision means that once a juvenile has been convicted in criminal court, he or she is forever after considered an adult for the purpose of criminal prosecutions.

Blended Sentencing Statutes

Because of the controversial nature of waivers or transfers and the often protracted hearings and court debates that occur, the legislatures of a growing number of states have vested both juvenile and criminal court judges with the power to impose both juvenile and adult penalties on adjudicated or convicted youthful offenders. These are known as **blended sentencing statutes.** Blended sentencing refers to the imposition of juvenile and/or adult correctional sanctions on serious and violent juvenile offenders who have been adjudicated in juvenile court or convicted in criminal court (Torbet and Szymanski, 1998:6).

There are five blended sentencing models: (1) juvenile-exclusive blend, (2) juvenile-inclusive blend,

(3) juvenile-contiguous blend, (4) criminal-exclusive blend, and (5) criminal-inclusive blend.

THE JUVENILE-EXCLUSIVE BLEND.   The **juvenile-exclusive blend** involves a disposition by the juvenile court judge that is either a disposition to the juvenile correctional system or to the adult correctional system, but not both. New Mexico provides such a sentencing option for its juvenile court judges.

THE JUVENILE-INCLUSIVE BLEND.   The **juvenile-inclusive blend** involves a disposition by the juvenile court judge that is both a juvenile correctional sanction and an adult correctional sanction.

THE JUVENILE-CONTIGUOUS BLEND.   The **juvenile-contiguous blend** involves a disposition by a juvenile court judge that may extend beyond the jurisdictional age limit of the offender. When the age limit of the juvenile court jurisdiction is reached, various procedures may be invoked to transfer the case to the jurisdiction of adult corrections. States with this juvenile-contiguous blend include Colorado, Massachusetts, Rhode Island, South Carolina, and Texas.

THE CRIMINAL-EXCLUSIVE BLEND.   The **criminal-exclusive blend** involves a decision by a criminal court judge to impose either a juvenile court sanction or a criminal court sanction, but not both.

THE CRIMINAL-INCLUSIVE BLEND.   The **criminal-inclusive blend** involves a decision by a criminal court judge to impose both a juvenile penalty and a criminal sentence simultaneously.

One of the positive benefits of blended sentencing statutes is that they are intended to provide both juvenile and criminal court judges with a greater range of dispositional and/or sentencing options. In the 1980s and earlier, juvenile courts were notoriously lenient on juvenile offenders. Dispositions of juvenile court judges were mostly nominal or conditional, which usually meant verbal warnings and/or probation. Although juvenile courts continue to overuse probation, many states have vested their juvenile and criminal court judges with greater sanctioning powers. Thus, in some states, such as Colorado, Arkansas, and Missouri, juvenile court judges now can impose sanctions that extend well beyond their original jurisdictional authority. Juvenile court judges in New Mexico can place certain juveniles in either adult or juvenile correctional facilities. Criminal court judges in Florida,

Idaho, Michigan, or Missouri also can place those convicted of crimes in either juvenile or adult correctional facilities, depending on the jurisdiction.

But just because juvenile court judges have blended sentencing statutory power, this does not mean that they will exercise it effectively. A good example of poor judicial decision making involved a Michigan 11-year-old, Nathaniel Abraham. Abraham obtained a rifle and practiced with it on cardboard targets that resembled people. When he had perfected his aim, he waited for a particular 18-year-old boy to appear and then carefully shot him in the head, killing him instantly. Michigan had just implemented a blended sentencing statute, and thus, the juvenile court judge did not have to worry about transferring Abraham to adult court for processing. The judge could impose both juvenile and adult sanctions on Abraham for his premeditated murder. Abraham's case came before the juvenile court judge in 1999, when Abraham was 13. The judge adjudicated Abraham delinquent and imposed only a juvenile incarcerative term. Abraham would be free when he turned age 21. Was this judicial decision appropriate? The judge thought so.

A close inspection of the Abraham case reveals certain flaws inherent in the juvenile justice system. Essentially, juvenile court judges, at least in Michigan, can do pretty much whatever they want. The judge in Abraham's case not only undersentenced Abraham to a relatively short term, but he also deprived Abraham of any sort of incentive to take advantage of counseling or learning programs available to him and other delinquents in Michigan's secure facilities for juveniles. If the judge *had* imposed an adult sentence in addition to Abraham's juvenile incarcerative term, what would the implications for Abraham have been? Would he necessarily have to serve the adult term once he had finished serving the juvenile portion of his sentence? No. In Abraham's case, and in *all* cases involving persons sentenced under blended sentencing statutes, a mandatory hearing is required before these juveniles reach adulthood. These hearings usually are held six months before the juvenile becomes an adult. Thus, in Abraham's case, he would have had a mandatory hearing six months before he turned 21. The purpose of the mandatory hearing is to determine whether the adult portion of the sentence earlier imposed by the judge should be imposed or suspended. Much depends on the offender's prior institutional conduct: Was it good or bad? In Abraham's case, a board would have reviewed Abraham's prior institutional conduct.

Was he a compliant juvenile inmate? Did he take advantage of self-help programs, earn his GED, participate in therapeutic individual or group counseling, take anger management courses, and learn to be law abiding? Or did he continually violate institutional rules, get into fights with others, and generally cause problems for staff? Unfortunately, Abraham is now in a situation in which he lacks the incentive to participate in any sort of program aimed at assisting him in becoming a better citizen. Abraham can merely "do time," and when he is through doing time, he can walk out of the juvenile facility a free man. This is what the Michigan juvenile court judge did for Nathaniel Abraham. The judge even chided the Michigan state legislature for passing this law in the first place (referring to the blended sentencing statute).

Fortunately, not all juvenile court judges have responded to these blended sentencing statutes as did the Michigan judge. For the most part, these statutes have proved workable thus far in jurisdictions in which they exist. Many improvements have been made in juvenile justice administration, particularly in the area of juvenile corrections. We are no longer warehousing juvenile offenders and mistreating them. No longer are most of these facilities depriving juveniles of needed counseling, vocational-technical training, educational opportunities, and other positive experiences. In the following section, we examine juvenile justice administration.

ADMINISTERING JUVENILE JUSTICE SYSTEMS

How does the juvenile justice system manage adjudicated juveniles once they have been processed by the juvenile court? Virtually every state has evolved an intricate process for dealing with juveniles who have come to the attention of juvenile courts. Considerable variety exists among states pertaining to the types of programs that have been established for juvenile offenders and how they should be supervised and treated. Several elaborate programs and detailed organizational charts have been created for juvenile services in states such as New York, California, Massachusetts, and Illinois. One example of a state system designed for juveniles requiring supervision and treatment is illustrated in Figure 13.2.

In this midwestern state, a division of juvenile services has been established. This division was established in 1989, and therefore, it is a fairly recently developed apparatus. With few exceptions, this state is predominantly rural. The chart in Figure 13.2 shows a director who oversees two community services divisions, as well as a youth correctional center, an interstate compact coordinator, and a training director.

A detailed diagram of the community services for juveniles in the state is shown in Figure 13.3. On average, fewer than 500 juvenile delinquents are in the state at any given time. Despite these low numbers of delinquents, the division of juvenile services has established eight regional offices, making available a variety of services and placement options for juveniles. The regional offices replaced a more archaic system in which children and youths determined to be at risk, unruly, deprived, or delinquent were provided services by a variety of state, regional, and county agencies. Currently, the division of juvenile services is a fairly elaborate bureaucracy, complete with systemwide planning and assessment tools, including a treatment and rehabilitation plan, classification and risk assessment, and strategies for juvenile supervision. Each of these instruments contributes to individualizing and defining the treatment needs, legal history, risk to self and others, appropriate placement, and therapeutic approaches indicated for each juvenile. Figure 13.4 shows a diagram of the state youth correctional center. The juvenile division services and organizations in the state

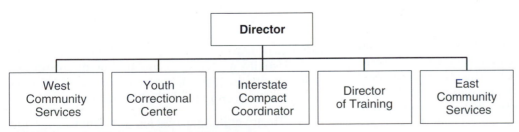

FIGURE 13.2 Division of Juvenile Services Organizational Chart

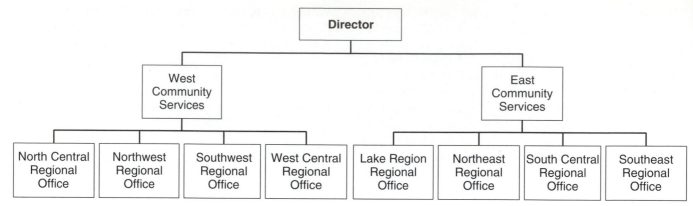

FIGURE 13.3 Organization of Community Services for Juveniles

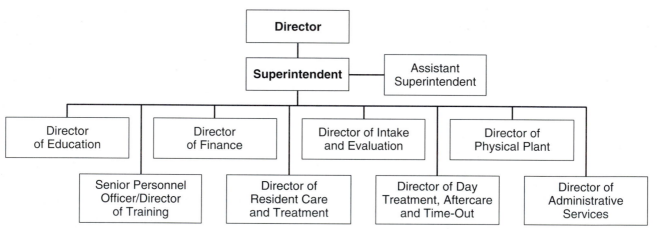

FIGURE 13.4. Youth Correctional Center Organizational Chart

supervise a wide range of youths, some of whom are placed in the community under supervision and some of whom are placed in secure confinement.

Mission Statements

Most bureaucratic organizations in both the criminal and juvenile justice systems have established **mission statements** to articulate an agency's goals or mission. Mission statements for juvenile services organizations are designed to provide a continuum of services to juvenile delinquents and unruly youth in the state and to protect society from those juveniles who are a danger to themselves and others. This is accomplished through the development of a treatment and rehabilitation plan for each juvenile and through the provision of an array of services by a dedicated staff that ensures that the juvenile receives these services in the least restrictive environment.

Juvenile Services: Organization and Staff Training

Most states have juvenile or family courts, and it is common practice in many states for the juvenile courts to notify juvenile services of any impending hearing, whether it is a custody hearing or transfer hearing. A division of juvenile services representative attends the hearing and accepts the juvenile as a part of his or her caseload. Each juvenile is assessed and classified at the time of admission to someone's caseload, and an individualized treatment and rehabilitation plan is developed. Usually, a plan is formulated as the result of a meeting with the juvenile's parents or guardians. Consideration is given to the following factors:

1. The juvenile's current legal situation
2. Family, education, recreation, work, medical, and legal histories

BOX 13.1 PERSONALITY HIGHLIGHT

ALTON LICK
Director, Division
of Juvenile Services,
North Dakota Department
of Corrections and
Rehabilitation

Statistics: B.S. (elementary
education), Dickinson
State University; M.P.A.
in progress (public
administration),
University of North
Dakota

Background: I obtained a bachelor of science degree in elementary education from Dickinson State University in 1965. I have completed extensive work on a master's of public administration from the University of North Dakota. I have been employed as a teacher and a budget analyst but have spent the majority of my career in public administration at various levels.

I think that part of my interest in juvenile services was a carryover from my teaching days. I also was interested in creating a balanced juvenile corrections system that could serve troubled adolescents at both an institutional and community level, a system in which troubled adolescents would be held accountable for their behavior but also would have available good treatment and education programs.

Work Experience: While working in the field, I have met some very, very interesting people from North Dakota and around the nation. These people, along with observing both excellent and mediocre systems and programs, have allowed me to develop what is in my mind an "ideal" juvenile corrections service delivery system. North Dakota is not there yet, but we continue to work toward that goal.

The good certainly has outweighed the bad. North Dakota is lucky in that it has, for the most part, hard-working, caring people who are attempting to help troubled adolescents, and I appreciate working side by side with them. I enjoy watching the young people in our care and custody mature and grow as they pass through the many different levels of care. They often begin as scared, angry adolescents struggling in school, at home, and with alcohol usage. They leave feeling that they can control their lives and deal with their anger, and they recognize the importance of an education for the future.

One of the frustrations in my years in juvenile corrections has been watching it become the repository for all of the troubled adolescents other systems do not want to serve. A prime example is the large increase of adolescents who are struggling with mental health issues. If those issues would be identified and addressed early in their development, they would not have to commit a crime to receive services.

Advice to Students: First, you need to inventory your interests and skills and see if you have some of the qualities and skills listed here:

- A sincere, honest interest in troubled adolescents and a willingness to help them
- Compassion, understanding, fairness, and an ability to be firm
- An ability to keep your wits about you when everyone else is losing theirs
- Sound judgment skills
- A desire to deal with dysfunctional families
- A good, balanced personal lifestyle

If these interests and abilities apply to you, you are a good candidate to work in juvenile corrections. You may not be able to change the world, but you can put a dent in it. The rewards will be many, but I would warn you that you also will experience frustrations.

3. Current and past involvement with drugs or other controlled substances

4. Assessment of risk to self and others

5. Strategies for supervision including goals, objectives, and a projected date for termination of services

The individualized treatment plan is reviewed every 90 days and modified accordingly. Juvenile cases are under constant informal observation, and correctional specialists are required to have a minimum of two contacts per month with juveniles who are under supervision in the community.

Michigan is one of several states with a juvenile services division that has been accredited by the American Correctional Association. Staff training is an integral part of the accreditation process. All staff members are required to undergo at least 40 hours of supervised training in community case management prior to assuming direct responsibility for cases. Regular three-day sessions are conducted at certain intervals to ensure that all staff are adequately trained to give the best assistance to juveniles. The recidivism rate among Michigan juveniles is about 20 percent, well below the national average. Approximately 420 juveniles are under some form of community supervision annually. The most commonly used community resources include drug screenings, monitoring home detention, and electronic monitoring. Juveniles receive an average of 49 hours of individualized service, at an average cost of $15 per hour. Placement in foster care costs between $66 to $189 per day, and detention costs average about $120 per day.

The state Youth Correctional Center is used for the most serious juvenile offenders. The average number of youths actually placed in the correctional center averages about 70 per year. The average stay in the center is about 18 months for female offenders and 21 months for male offenders. Juveniles who are placed in the state Youth Correctional Center are exposed to state-of-the-art educational and treatment experiences. Drug and alcohol programs are mandatory for those with drug or alcohol dependencies. Child psychiatric services are made available to those in need as well. Certain juveniles are sex offenders, and they are exposed to a pretreatment program for sex offenders. A special management program exists to help especially unruly youths. Gang activity and identity are strictly prohibited. A zero-tolerance policy exists relative to gangs in the correctional center. A fairly elaborate educational program exists to assist youths in obtaining their high school diplomas. Excellent physical education facilities also are provided.

Michigan has a fairly effective apparatus for dealing with juvenile delinquents. The type of organization that characterizes Michigan's juvenile justice division and that administers programs for adjudicated offenders is not especially unique. More complex systems can be found in other more populous states. Nevertheless, this example gives us a good picture of how many state programs for juveniles operate.

ISSUES IN JUVENILE JUSTICE ADMINISTRATION

Administrators throughout the juvenile justice system increasingly are confronted with pressures to change their procedures and operations in an effort to decrease the frequency of delinquency, reduce juvenile recidivism, and provide effective programming for youths at all levels throughout the nation. Although the following list of issues is not exhaustive, it exposes us to some of the primary concerns of both citizens and juvenile justice professionals that deserve addressing:

1. Reforming juvenile justice and the confidentiality of juvenile recordkeeping

2. Changing the nature and severity of optional sanctions available to juvenile courts

3. Creating greater accountability among juvenile court judges

4. Revisiting policies relating to both parental and juvenile accountability for criminal actions of youths

5. Rethinking both institutional and community correctional programming for juveniles

6. Establishing more effective community-based interventions involving collaboration with parents and juvenile authorities

Juvenile Justice Reform and the Confidentiality of Juvenile Recordkeeping

Some investigators have observed that as the juvenile justice system has expanded the rights of juveniles and made juvenile court proceedings similar to criminal court proceedings, what has occurred is the **adultification** of the juvenile justice system (Altschuler, 1999). But many of the original juvenile justice trappings and procedures have persisted to the present day. Despite the expansion of juvenile rights and the application of due process in juvenile court proceedings, juvenile court judges continue to make decisions in the best interests of children, or at least decisions that these judges think are in the child's best interests. Even the U.S. Supreme Court has made seemingly contradictory or inconsistent rulings concerning what should or should not be juvenile rights. Thus, a somewhat schizophrenic quality can be found in the juvenile court's direction during the most recent two decades (Shepherd, 1999:19). Indeed, the late Roscoe Pound, dean of the Harvard Law School, once wrote that "the juvenile court has become like the illegitimate issue of an illicit relationship between the legal profession and the social work profession, and now no one wants to claim the little bastard" (Reader, 1996:482).

Should juvenile justice remain individualized and rehabilitation centered, or should it be concerned principally with dispensing due process and justice to adjudicated juveniles? As we have seen, the public expects the juvenile court to deal more harshly with juvenile offenders, especially serious and violent ones. But at the same time, we have seen that serious and violent juveniles account for only a fraction of the total number of juvenile offenders who appear before juvenile court judges annually. Many juvenile court judges want to appease both sides in this important issue: There are those who favor a get-tough approach with juvenile offenders and those who would prefer to see a more rehabilitation-centered approach, favoring treatment over punishment.

One major juvenile justice reform has been the establishment of blended sentencing statutes. It will take some time before a sufficient number of cases are processed in different jurisdictions under these statutes. Therefore, a proper evaluation of the effectiveness of blended sentencing provisions will not be forthcoming for at least a decade or more, well into the twenty-first century. Evaluation research requires a long-term backward examination of how particular policies have affected juveniles and recidivism rates. Are juveniles sentenced under blended sentencing statutes being helped or harmed? We do not know yet. But evaluation research, when it is conducted in the future, may tell us.

One policy change that has occurred since the mid-1980s has been more open accessibility to previously confidential juvenile court records. Since juvenile courts are civil in nature, there is a strong vested interest on the part of court officials to protect the identities of adjudicated juveniles. It was very common in past years to read about juvenile violence in the newspapers or see reports of juvenile crime on television, but the names of involved juveniles were not reported. Increasing numbers of citizens wanted to know if some of these youths were their neighbors. Were they some of the kids their own children were playing with at school?

But beyond the sheer curiosity of persons wanting to know juvenile offenders' identities, a more compelling reason arose for pressuring juvenile court disclosure of this confidential information. Actually, this reasoning reaches back to colonial times, when thieves were branded in conspicuous places and adulterers or adulteresses were forced to wear the letter "A" on their clothing. The primary objective of such early punishments was public shaming of offenders. Since everyone would know who these offenders were, they could be shunned or avoided socially. This social exclusion functioned as a strong deterrent to crime of any kind. Hardly anyone wanted to be branded a thief, and certainly no one wanted to walk around with an "A" on their clothing. Essentially the same principle applies to youths. The argument is as follows: If the identities of youths, and often their parents, are made known to the public, they will lose their anonymity and their offenses will become known to other citizens. The affected juveniles might not be shamed and shunned, but the mere fact that they and their actions would become known to others, especially to their neighbors and school peers, might serve as a deterrent. The power of this social pressure cannot be overestimated. We might surmise that parents themselves would be sufficiently embarrassed to keep better track of their youths' activities. The youths themselves would be under a social microscope, so that any suspicious actions on their part might be reported to authorities by others.

More than a few jurisdictions have taken steps to remove the cloak of anonymity from juveniles and their offending behaviors. By 1997, for instance, 30 states had provisions for open hearings in juvenile or family court proceedings. Only eight states did not provide for the release of the names of those juveniles charged with serious offenses. Only two states did not permit court records to be released to news services or other interested parties. In fact, all states currently make juvenile court records available to any party showing and/or having a legitimate interest in the case. In these situations, the requested information is obtained through a court order. Fingerprinting and photographing of juveniles are now conducted routinely in most states. Half of the states require registration of all juvenile offenders when they enter new jurisdictions. Also, most states presently have state repositories of juvenile records and other relevant information about juvenile offending. Seventeen states prohibit sealing or expunging juvenile court records after a juvenile becomes an adult (Bilchik, 1996:37–38). Therefore, juveniles today are considerably more likely to have their offenses known to the public.

Is this necessarily a good policy? One clear intent of the policy is to heighten offender accountability. Presently, in jurisdictions that still protect the identity of juvenile offenders, no visibility among one's peers means no social or psychological sanctions other than those imposed by juvenile courts. Greater visibility will heighten a youth's accountability, simply by exposing their otherwise hidden actions to significant others. Some persons fear that exposure of juvenile records to public scrutiny will cause these children to become labeled as delinquents, and that they will be discriminated against unfairly at school and other places. These children *are* delinquents. They have committed crimes. Often they have harmed others. Should we hide their crimes from public view and act as if they had never offended? Where is the accountability in that mode of thinking? Maybe greater social awareness of their actions might prompt them to alter their behaviors and, more importantly, their thinking.

Pervasive problems with the juvenile justice system that have been highlighted in recent years include the following:

1. Moderately to severely crowded juvenile detention and corrections facilities
2. Insufficient services for youths who have significant emotional and educational needs, warning signs for potential future delinquency
3. Overrepresentation of minority youth at most of the major decision points in the juvenile justice process, stemming from complex cultural, societal, and system factors
4. Excessive reliance on incarceration

Cross-agency efforts designed to bring about positive changes within the juvenile justice system occur whenever participating agencies do the following:

1. Agree on goals
2. Clearly articulate the system problems to be addressed

3. Avoid placing blame
4. Identify a connection between planned changes and desired outcomes
5. Coordinate changes across agencies and communities being served
6. Obtain feedback about the consequences of the changes and alter efforts accordingly (Hsia and Beyer, 2000:3–4)

Changing the Nature and Severity of Optional Sanctions Available to Juvenile Courts

Should we be concerned with juvenile violence and how it is being punished? After all, juvenile justice professionals and researchers report that during the latter half of the 1990s, juvenile violence declined. The National Center for Juvenile Justice in Pittsburgh, Pennsylvania, reports that juveniles accounted for 17 percent of all violent crime arrests in 1998 (Snyder, 1999b:1). And although juvenile violent crime arrests declined by 19 percent between 1994 and 1998, the juvenile arrest level was still 15 percent above the juvenile Violent Crime Index arrests in 1988. Looking at these figures in terms of raw juvenile arrest numbers, about 98,000 juvenile arrests were made in 1988 for violent crimes, but this figure had risen to 112,200 arrests in 1998 (Snyder, 1999b:1).

Presently, the juvenile court has several powerful sanctioning options for adjudicated juveniles. The most severe dispositional option is placement of the adjudicated juvenile in a secure facility for a period of time. According to the national average, less than 20 percent of all adjudicated delinquent offenders are placed in secure confinement, since a majority of juvenile court judges continue to believe that secure confinement should be the last resort after other interventions and punishments have been imposed with little or no positive effect (Maguire and Pastore, 2000). Of course, for the serious and violent few, blended sentencing statutes also may be invoked in nearly half of all states.

But what many juvenile courts attempt to do is adopt a balanced approach that is aimed at protecting society, heightening juvenile offender accountability, and reducing juvenile recidivism by individualizing treatment through the application of creative sanctions. States such as Virginia are attempting to use this balanced approach in combatting delinquency. Restitution and community service are expected of all adjudicated juveniles in Virginia. In those few serious and violent juvenile offense cases, the more hard-core juvenile offenders may be sent to boot camps for fixed periods. Further, adult treatments may be extended to more advanced juvenile offenders who have been adjudicated for violent felonies. The Virginia budget has been increased to provide for net increases in commitment to juvenile facilities in extreme cases (Lyons and Turpin, 1997:104). In fact, Virginia has expanded its adult penitentiaries to provide special facilities on prison grounds to accommodate youths sentenced as adults for serious crimes.

Before juvenile court judges can impose the most appropriate punishments for adjudicated juveniles, however, effective classification systems should be in place for their use and consultation. Unfortunately, juvenile classification is only beginning to near the state of the art (Champion, 1994). In 1994, less than half of all states had any sort of juvenile classification system to separate youths into different categories for punishment and/or treatment. By 1996, several states had enacted legislation to *begin* the process of devising such classification schemes. These states include Michigan, Ohio, Pennsylvania, South Dakota, Alabama, and Oklahoma (Lyons and Turpin, 1997:104).

Apart from devising more effective schemes for classifying juvenile offenders, some states such as Arizona have taken aggressive action to change the sanctioning powers of juvenile courts. Arizona has adopted a get-tough strategy to deal particularly with serious and violent juvenile offending. In 1996, Proposition 102 was passed, which was aimed at decreasing juvenile violence by increasing punishments for juvenile offenders. Proponents of Proposition 102 believed that passage of this legislation would "end the coddling of violent and repeat juvenile offenders. More importantly, it would remove discretion from the judiciary who they alleged had abused their power. The initiative wanted to put more authority in the hands of elected officials who proponents felt would better exercise discretion. The initiative [also wanted to] empower county attorneys to establish diversion programs, rather than the juvenile court, for less serious offenders" (Wicklund, 1997:12). The legislation passed in December 1996. The influence of the legislation was far-reaching. Arizona governor Fife Symington appointed a 10-member advisory committee to make recommendations for the implementation of Proposition 102. Within a month after this committee convened, it issued the following stringent recommendations:

1. Dramatically expand criminal prosecution of juveniles as adults beyond the specific crimes of murder, armed robbery, and sexual assault
2. Create a "three strikes and you are in the adult system" proposal
3. Require mandatory incarceration in the juvenile system for the second felony
4. Require mandatory incarceration in the adult system for the third felony—which exceeds the consequences many adults currently receive
5. Eliminate the appointment of legal representation for juveniles accused of misdemeanor offenses when detention or incarceration is not a possible sanction

If some or all of these recommendations are implemented by the Arizona legislature, Arizona juveniles who contemplate committing crimes would have much to consider before doing so. But merely proposing such changes and seeing these changes actually incorporated into law are two different things. At least these recommendations give the appearance of getting tough on juvenile criminals. It remains to be seen if such policies will be adopted and how effective their implementation would be on decreasing juvenile offending.

Creating Greater Accountability Among Juvenile Court Judges

Collectively, juvenile court judges have broad discretionary powers over large numbers of juveniles. When called on to comment or write articles about the present state of juvenile justice and the integrity of juvenile courts, at least some of these judges are notoriously self-serving and whitewash their actions, whatever they might be. They skillfully shift our attention from what goes on in their courtrooms to what is happening in one's own school, church, neighborhood, or family (Lewis, 1999:12). Rhetoric such as "the approach to delinquency must be a multidisciplinary one" or "adult, not juvenile, violence is our nation's number one crime problem" is also espoused by some of these judges (Lederman, 1999:22–23; Lewis, 1999:6–9).

The Arizona experience reported in the previous section specifically targeted the juvenile court judiciary who allegedly had engaged in a pattern of coddling offenders and abusing their own power (Wicklund, 1997:12). Several of the recommendations of an Arizona committee appointed by Governor Fife Symington involved mandatory penalties for persistent and serious juvenile recidivists. It is not difficult to understand why these mandatory penalties were recommended in view of the track record of Arizona juvenile court judges. In many cases, serious juveniles *were* being coddled, in the sense that it was taking five or more adjudications of delinquency before these judges would order the affected juveniles to secure confinement (Snyder, 1988).

Barry Feld (1998:93–94) says that the fundamental shortcomings of the juvenile court are that it conceives itself as a social welfare agency with penal social control. Thus, attempting to combine social welfare and penal social control functions within one agency assures that the court will do both badly. Feld says that providing for child welfare is a societal responsibility, not a judicial one. He adds that juvenile courts fail to define eligibility for services or create an enforceable right or entitlement based on young people's lack of access to decent education, lack of adequate housing or nutrition, unmet health needs, or impoverished families. In the long range, according to Feld, recent changes in juvenile court waiver and sentencing policies emphasizing punishment, accountability, and personal responsibility further reinforce juvenile courts' penal foundations and reduce the legitimacy of youths' claims to compassion or humanitarian assistance.

Why do juvenile court judges have the reputation, deserved or undeserved, of being lenient on juvenile offenders, regardless of the seriousness of their offenses? One obvious reason is that in many jurisdictions, such as South Dakota, the juvenile correctional system is overcrowded to the point that juvenile court judges in that state have no place to send the most violent juveniles once they are adjudicated. Thus, overcrowding might explain some of this leniency. Another explanation might be that juvenile court judges everywhere are encouraged to be lenient or to use the least restrictive punishments when serious juvenile offenders are adjudicated. Yet another explanation for juvenile court leniency is the lack of sufficient resources to make appropriate decisions in all juvenile cases. In Illinois, for example, it has been estimated that it would take 1.5 hours of judicial time per case to adequately listen to and decide particular juvenile cases. At this rate, each juvenile court judge in Illinois could handle about 1,000 cases per year. This would require a minimum of 10 juvenile court judges in Cook County (Chicago) alone in order to handle the 10,200 cases these courts process annually. But in 1999, there were only five juvenile court judges to do the job (Hurst, 1999:2).

We accept the validity of many of these arguments. The juvenile correctional system *is* overcrowded. Juvenile court judges *are* encouraged to be lenient. Juvenile courts *are* underfunded and/or understaffed and juvenile court judges *are* overworked. But what about juvenile court judges who simply do not perform their jobs, even given these limitations and constraints? Why are only about 40 percent of all juveniles who are transferred to criminal courts for processing each year violent offenders, and the remainder, the vast majority of transferees, are property offenders, public order offenders, and low-level drug offenders? Since the same statistics are seen annually without much variation, no trend can be identified. Those responsible for this situation are, for the most part, juvenile court judges. How can these judges be held to account for sending a 14-year-old property offender to criminal court, where this case will eventually be dismissed or downgraded anyway? Arizona has indicated a willingness to clean up this problem by imposing mandatory dispositions for juvenile court judges to follow. Whether their efforts will be successful or not remains to be seen. But the problem of heightening juvenile court judge accountability is a national one, not one confined just to Arizona. Currently, no effective sanctioning mechanisms exist to hold these judges accountable for their actions. It is still business as usual in most of our juvenile courts.

Revisiting Policies Relating to Both Parental and Juvenile Accountability for Criminal Actions of Youths

Twenty-two state legislatures had enacted legislation in 1996 addressing the victims of juvenile crime. This state legislation addresses the role of victims in various ways, such as (1) including victims of juvenile crime in the victim's bill of rights, (2) notifying the victim of the release of the offender from custody, (3) increasing opportunities for victims to be heard in juvenile court proceedings, (4) expanding victim services to victims of juvenile crime, (5) establishing the authority for victims to be notified of significant hearings, (6) providing for release of the name and address of the offender and the offender's parents to the victim on request, and (7) enhancing sentences if the victim is elderly or handicapped (Torbet et al., 1996:48). States enacting such legislation include Alabama, Alaska, Arizona, California, Connecticut, Florida, Georgia, Idaho, Iowa, Louisiana, Minnesota, Montana, New Mexico, North Dakota, Pennsylvania, South Dakota, Texas, Utah, Virginia, and Wyoming (Lyons and Turpin, 1997).

When enacting this legislation, a major consideration was the matter of restitution to victims. Restitution is increasingly regarded as an essential component of fairness in meting out dispositions for juvenile offenders. Offender accountability is heightened as restitution is incorporated into the disposition, especially if there was some type of property loss, damage, physical injury, or death. In reality, however, many states continue to haggle over how reparations will be imposed on either the youths or their families or both. Some states have incorporated into their juvenile statutes high dollar limits relating to parental liability when children destroy the property of others or cause serious physical injuries. The theory is that if parents are held accountable, they will hold their own children accountable (Hurst, 1999). Thus, assessing reparations against parents for the wrongdoing of their children is an indirect way of preventing delinquency, or so some state legislatures have contemplated (Yee and Turpin, 1999).

Rethinking Both Institutional and Community Correctional Programming for Juveniles

States such as Kansas are presently rethinking their strategies for dealing with juvenile offenders (Musser, 1999). Local solutions to local problems are being sought by Kansas juvenile justice officials. Community planning is a grassroots team effort involving representatives from at least 20 different entities, including mental health providers, business and community leaders, and public schools (Musser, 1999:152). Furthermore, local citizens are being included as a part of 29 state planning teams across the state in a Communities That Care program. These community teams are encouraged to identify risk factors that contribute to juvenile crime and to devise strategies that keep juveniles on a path toward productive growth.

In the Kansas Communities That Care Program, some of the benefits accruing to Kansas residents include (1) creating a system according to community norms and values, in which community sanctions, in-

terventions, and prevention services can be devised according to their own norms; (2) creating data-driven plans, in which youth attitude surveys are used, including data such as arrest statistics and other community information; and (3) allowing community ownership of the plan, because the plans are locally recreated with diverse representation on the team (Musser, 1999:153).

Musser (1999:153) notes that patience and time to allow the planning process to work are necessary. Furthermore, a cultural shift for local government to accept a community-based system as opposed to a state-operated system is a challenge. Finally, it should be recognized that there has been a history of a lack of community-based services. Thus, plans have to be devised to expand the state's capacity to handle out-of-home placements, sex offender treatment programs, and substance abuse treatment centers.

Establishing More Effective Community-Based Interventions Involving Collaboration with Parents and Juvenile Authorities

It is one thing for the government to propose and implement various interventions to curtail juvenile offending. It is quite another thing to obtain community involvement in these programs in order to ensure their acceptance and continuation. For instance, in 1991, it was recognized in New Mexico that serious, violent juvenile offending was reaching dramatic proportions and that something needed to be done about it. Bills were passed and new laws were created to make it possible to impose harsher punishments on juvenile offenders. This legislation was believed to be strong enough to deter those intent on committing juvenile crimes. New Mexico juvenile offending continued unabated, however. By 1993, it was evident that more needed to be done. The New Mexico Council on Crime and Delinquency was created, and a committee subsequently was appointed to study the delinquency problem (Utton, 1994).

The composition of the committee reflected a concerted effort to diversify community representation and involve persons from all sectors. The panel consisted of three children's court judges; a district attorney; two attorneys specializing in child and family law; a child psychiatrist; the judge for a Native American pueblo; a public schools representative; a law professor expert in juvenile issues; representatives from the state's departments of health, human services, and youth authority; and the director of a large youth service organization. Ex officio members included the chairman of the council and a retired attorney and legislator who was instrumental in passing an earlier 1972 children's code in New Mexico (Utton, 1994:6). Judge Ann Kass, the task force chair, noted that "We sought members who would provide varied ethnic, gender, geographical, political, and philosophical viewpoints. We accomplished that goal, particularly the philosophical diversity" (Utton, 1994:6). Furthermore, 5,000 questionnaires were distributed to various individuals, groups, and agencies throughout the state. A series of town meetings were held in communities, and over 300 committee volunteers analyzed, discussed, argued, agonized, and eventually presented their opinions to the committee concerning what should be done about juvenile crime. The critically important aspect of this effort was the concerted involvement of so many persons in solving a common delinquency problem.

Some jurisdictions have done a lot more than build new juvenile secure facilities to accommodate growing numbers of delinquents for either long-term or short-term confinement. In Virginia, for instance, numerous community programs have been established that rely heavily on citizen involvement in juvenile offender management and treatment. Networking with helping agencies also has been carried out in Alaska, Nebraska, and Washington (Lyons and Turpin, 1997:104–105).

Citizen involvement in juvenile delinquency intervention programs is considered crucial in Missouri. Missouri's Division of Youth Services (DYS), for example, has two training schools for boys and girls, the Boonville Training School for Boys and the Chillicothe Training School for Girls (Steward, 1997:90). These facilities combine to house over 800 juvenile offenders that the juvenile justice system deems worthy of secure confinement. But what about the other youths throughout Missouri who are treated in the community? What kinds of programs and supervision are available to them? Missouri juvenile authorities believe that strong community relations are vital to any program operated by the DYS. In order to facilitate greater dialogue between the community and the DYS, youths at many DYS sites have volunteered to work with local service organizations, including homeless shelters, senior centers, hospitals, and children's mental health facilities. Many DYS youths have joined scout troops and other local organizations, including

antidrug programs in schools. Furthermore, others have become significantly involved with the American Red Cross, Big Brothers–Big Sisters, the Junior Optimist Club, Easter Seals, and the American Cancer Society (Steward, 1997:91). One positive outcome of these youth–community organization interactions is that involved youths are provided with opportunities to practice the skills they have been learning in DYS institutions to acquire a more positive outlook toward authority and adults. By the same token, adults working with these youths have become more tolerant and appreciative of their efforts to reform.

In Philadelphia, Pennsylvania, a community-based program has been established to assist at-risk youths in avoiding delinquent behavior. A project was developed in Philadelphia called the Friends for the Love of Reading Project (Howell, 1999). This project is an adopt-a-school program to work with a portion of the city's low-income families who have children well below the national reading level. Consistent with the primary goal of promoting and advocating for a juvenile justice system with a full range of services responsive to the needs of the community, family, and youths, this proactive partnership addresses delinquency prevention on the front end (Howell, 1999:27). "Friends" are provided to children with reading difficulties. These friends are members of the Division of Juvenile Justice Services who work on a one-to-one basis with particular juveniles. Eventually, the program attracted the attention of a growing number of community volunteers—more than 20,000 parents and other individuals who became mentors for children with reading difficulties over a two-year period. Reading levels among children assisted by these friends have improved substantially.

One of the contributing factors that place children at risk is that they often drop out of school for various reasons. Perhaps they do not read as well as others, or they may not assimilate into school culture like others. In many cities during the mid-1990s, a federal government-sponsored project was implemented called Communities in Schools (CIS). CIS is a network of local, state, and national partnerships working together to bring at-risk children four basics every child needs and deserves: (1) a personal one-on-one relation with a caring adult, (2) a safe place to learn and grow, (3) a marketable skill to use after graduation, and (4) a chance to give back to peers and community (Cantelon and LeBoeuf, 1997:2). The CIS program is based on the idea that dropping out of school is a problem for which the entire community must take responsibility.

Thus, CIS brings together businesses and public and private agencies in communities—welfare and health professionals, employment counselors, social workers and recreational leaders, the clergy, and members of community groups. These people provide a support system of caring adults to build a child's self-worth and equip him or her with the skills needed to embark on a more productive and constructive life (Cantelon and LeBoeuf, 1997:2). Students who have participated in the CIS program have reported overwhelmingly that they want to stay in school, have better self-concepts, and are less inclined toward delinquency. Thus, it is apparent that a close, collaborative relation must be developed between official government programming and communities in order to maximize the effectiveness of just about any delinquency intervention strategy attempted.

SUMMARY

Similar to the criminal justice system for adults, a parallel justice system for juveniles exists. It is known as the juvenile justice system. A formal juvenile court was created in Illinois in 1899, and all states had juvenile courts by the 1940s.

In early England, juveniles were regarded as chattel and counted as farm property together with various farm animals. They had no rights, and matters involving juveniles were settled by chancellors who were appointed by the king to make decisions for him. During the 1600s through the 1800s, juveniles were governed according to English common law, which presumed that any youth under the age of seven was incapable of formulating criminal intent. Subsequently, various religious and philanthropic interests become involved in juvenile matters, and groups such as the child savers came into prominence. Following the Civil War, there were many homeless children or children in families that had both parents working in large cities. These youths roamed the streets unsupervised. Various homes and shelters were established to care for them.

Early juvenile courts were intended as social welfare agencies, and the interests of children were considered primary. During the first half of the twentieth century, classifications for juvenile offenders were formalized. Delinquents are youths who have committed offenses that would be crimes if committed by adults. Status offenders are youths who commit offenses that would not be crimes if adults committed them. Delinquency includes traditional crimes such as burglary, larceny, homicide, vehicular theft, rape, and aggravated assault. Status offenses include truancy, runaway behavior, and curfew violation.

During the 1960s and 1970s, the U.S. Supreme Court decided several important cases that bestowed various rights on juveniles, including the right to an attorney, the right to notice of charges, the right against self-incrimination, and the right against double jeopardy. Juveniles also became entitled to the criminal standard of proof, which is beyond a reasonable doubt. Juvenile courts are traditionally civil in nature, and juveniles who are adjudicated delinquent in such courts do not acquire criminal records. Juveniles are brought before juvenile courts through referrals from different sources, such as police officers, school authorities, parents, and neighbors. Petitions are filed and juvenile court judges act on these petitions. Juveniles brought into the juvenile justice system are screened in a process known as intake.

During the 1970s, the Juvenile Justice and Delinquency Prevention Act was passed. This act encouraged the separation of juvenile delinquents and status offenders and promoted the removal of status offenders from secure juvenile institutions. Today, most states make provisions for differentiating between status offenders and delinquent offenders and how they are processed.

Usually only the most serious juveniles are petitioned to juvenile court. Judges deliberate and decide these cases in bench trials. As a general rule, juveniles are not entitled to a jury trial as a matter of right, except in a few states. An adjudicatory hearing is held, which is similar to a trial for an adult. The judge adjudicates the juvenile as delinquent or nondelinquent and then imposes a punishment or disposition. Three types of dispositions are nominal (e.g., verbal warnings), conditional (probation), and custodial (incarceration in a juvenile facility). Placing youths in secure confinement or custody is a last resort for most juvenile court judges. Nonsecure dispositions include group home placements or foster care, camps, and ranches.

The most serious juveniles are transferred or waived to the jurisdiction of criminal courts where they can receive harsher adult punishments. Sometimes transfers or waivers are called certifications. Juveniles are entitled to hearings before being transferred to criminal court. About half of all juveniles transferred to criminal court are accused of committing violent offenses. Only about 10 percent of all transferred youths annually actually are sentenced to confinement in an institution, however. Most other youths have their charges downgraded or dismissed, or they are placed on probation. In recent years, various states have passed blended sentencing statutes, which enable juvenile court or criminal court judges to sentence convicted youths to dual penalties, one penalty as a juvenile and one penalty as an adult. These blended sentencing statutes are a part of the growing get-tough movement that is one response to rising juvenile violence.

Administering juvenile justice systems is similar to administering various dimensions of the criminal justice system. Persons who administer agencies and institutions designed for youths, however, must be more sensitive to the confidentiality of information disclosed about juveniles. Greater attention is given to policies about how juveniles convicted of crimes or adjudicated as delinquent should be punished. Most juvenile justice programs presently are aimed at heightening offender accountability and offering more sophisticated programming to assist juveniles to become rehabilitated. Great controversy exists about how much punishment juveniles should endure at the hands of the state. Currently, two extreme views are held: One is that juveniles should be held to account for law violations and punished accordingly, and the other is a traditional, softer view encouraging leniency and rehabilitation. Many juvenile justice reforms are in progress, and the nature and direction of juvenile courts and juvenile processing are changing dramatically.

QUESTIONS FOR REVIEW

1. What were the provisions under common law concerning the age of accountability for juveniles? How were juveniles treated before juvenile courts were established for them in the late 1800s and early 1900s?

2. What were the Poor Laws? How did they affect juveniles? How did offenders get out of prison if they were sentenced to long terms under the Poor Laws?

3. What was the Walnut Street Jail? Why was it significant in the evolution of the treatment of juvenile offenders?

4. Why was the juvenile court considered an informal welfare agency during the early 1900s? In what ways did this perception change with the advent of legal rights for juveniles in the mid-1960s?

5. What was the significance of *Kent v. United States* in 1966? How did *In re Gault* and *In re Winship* modify juvenile rights in 1967 and 1970, respectively?

6. Distinguish between juvenile delinquents and status offenders. Which ones are more serious and why?

7. What is intake? What are some of its functions? Who conducts intake proceedings?

8. What is a petition? Who can file petitions? What are the results of petition filings?

9. What is meant by a station house adjustment? How can station house adjustments benefit affected juveniles in terms of their acquisition of juvenile records?

10. Distinguish between alternative dispute resolution and diversion. What are the respective implications for juvenile offenders?

SUGGESTED READINGS

Elrod, Preston, and R. Scott Ryder (1999). *Juvenile Justice: A Social, Historical, and Legal Perspective.* Gaithersburg, MD: Aspen.

Feld, Barry C. (1999). *Bad Kids: Race and the Transformation of the Juvenile Court.* New York: Oxford University Press.

Latessa, Edward J., Dana Jones, and Betsy Fulton (1999). *An Evaluation of Selected Juvenile Justice Programs in Ohio Using the Correctional Program Assessment Inventory.* Cincinnati, OH: Division of Criminal Justice, University of Cincinnati.

1. THE UNTRAINED INTERN AND THE DELINQUENT

Alice Graham, a senior undergraduate college student majoring in criminal justice, was finishing an internship of 100 hours in a criminal justice agency. Graham was interested in working with juveniles, and she expressed an interest in an internship opening at the state secure juvenile facility about two hours from her college. She consulted with her faculty advisor, Dr. Pat Forbes. Dr. Forbes knew that all criminal justice majors were required to take seven core or required criminal justice courses before they signed up for an internship. The reason was that exposure to the core curriculum would better prepare students for their internship programs. Dr. Forbes noticed on Graham's course transcript that she had taken only five out of the seven required courses. One of the courses she had not completed was juvenile justice. But Graham was an older student, 35 years of age, and she seemed mature enough to handle the job. Dr. Forbes had had Graham in several of her courses and she was a straight-"A" student. Therefore, with some confidence, Dr. Forbes approved Graham's internship with the juvenile institution.

Graham reported to the institution for work the following week. Dr. Forbes assumed everything was going smoothly. Then, after about two weeks, Dr. Forbes received a call from Helga Smedley, the director of the juvenile facility. "Dr. Forbes," Smedley said over the telephone in an angry tone, "what sort of students are you producing there at your school?" Dr. Forbes was taken by surprise and asked Ms. Smedley what she meant. "What I mean is that you have sent us this Alice Graham, a complete idiot, to work with dangerous juveniles. I'm sending her back to your school and I want you to fail her. She has done nothing but cause problems since she arrived."

Curious, Dr. Forbes asked what Graham had done. "What has she done?" exclaimed Smedley. "Where should I start? To begin with, she has taken a particular liking to one of our 16-year-old boys. She's been giving him money, which is against the rules. She allows him out of his recreational area at odd times, and she gives him an inordinate amount of attention. Frankly, I think she has a crush on this kid. And what really bugs me is that this kid is one of our worst offenders. He's in here for rape of a 12-year-old girl. He's

got a record a mile long, beginning when he was nine. He is a master manipulator and he has Graham wrapped around his little finger. Her special treatment of this monster has upset the entire facility. Other kids are complaining that they aren't getting money from the other supervisors or interns, and that they aren't receiving the same kind of treatment as this kid. This Graham person needs to get some education about working around juveniles. Don't you people have courses on delinquency? Obviously, she is a few cards short of a deck here, and I think she is in bad need of a crash course on juvenile delinquency. You really dropped the ball with this student. Why did you send her to us in the first place?"

Dr. Forbes listened attentively and then said, "Ms. Smedley, let me talk with Alice later this week when I can schedule an appointment with her. I'd like to hear her side and try to determine how she got herself in this mess." After conversing with Smedley, Forbes had the departmental secretary call Graham's apartment and leave a message on Graham's answering machine to contact her. The next morning, Graham called Dr. Forbes. She sounded upset: "I didn't do anything wrong. They just didn't like me. They had it in for me. Why did they tell me to leave? Is there anything you can do, Dr. Forbes?" Forbes asked Graham to visit with her the next day at a mutually convenient time. She advised Graham to get some rest and try not to think about what happened. The next day Graham showed up at her office. It was obvious she had been crying and was very upset. She related the following story to Forbes.

When Graham came to the juvenile facility, she was placed in an advising position over 12 youths. One of these was Tommy Walker, the 16-year-old Smedley had mentioned. Graham said that Walker was very polite and went out of his way to do nice things for her the first week she was there. During lunch breaks, Walker sought out Graham and told her that he needed to talk with her. In those conversations, Walker told Graham about his home life, that his mother had been a prostitute and his dad had been a drunk. He was beaten all the time, he said. He added that the rape he was supposed to have committed against a 12-year-old was not really a rape. He said he had been staying with his uncle and aunt and their 12-year-old daughter. One night he was going to his bedroom and passed the bathroom. The bathroom door was open and the girl was getting out of the bath-tub. She was naked. She turned and looked at Walker, who was staring at her. She screamed and Walker ran to his bedroom. A few minutes later, Walker's uncle came into his room and grabbed him by his neck. "I'll teach you to mess with my daughter," he said. Then he slammed Walker against the wall, bruising his arm and shoulder. About 15 minutes later, the police arrived and took Walker into custody. The girl claimed that Walker came into the bathroom and tried to rape her. Graham said that the boy seemed very sincere and even cried a little when he told her that story. Later, on another after-noon, Walker approached her and said that he only had 50 cents for a cola, and he needed another quarter to get a drink from the soft drink machine. "Don't worry about it," Graham said. "Here's a quarter. Get your soda."

The next day, she continued, several other boys asked Graham if she had a lot of quarters, since they were all thirsty and wanted sodas. Graham said that she did not know what they were talking about, but she suspected that Walker had told others about get-ting money from her. "That's the only thing I did. I just tried to be a good listener and help Walker out. He seemed like such a nice kid." Dr. Forbes asked Graham if she had done anything around the youth that might be misconstrued as affection. "I gave him a hug before he went to his dormitory one night," she said. "I've given him a kiss on the cheek once in a while when he has brought me small gifts. That's all." It was clear to Dr. Forbes that Graham had been easily manipulated

by Walker. It was also clear that she had gone out of her way to do special favors for him and not for the other boys, who must have complained loudly to Smedley and others.

Questions for Discussion

1. What should Dr. Forbes do in this incident? Should she fail Alice Graham in the internship course? Why or why not?

2. Should Dr. Forbes offer Graham another intern-ship option to make up for the mess she had caused at the juvenile facility? What would you do or say to Graham about this matter?

3. Should Dr. Forbes have granted Graham's in-ternship request in the first place, given the criminal justice major requirements? What do you think?

4. Do you believe that Graham had a crush on Walker at the juvenile facility, or was she just trying to be helpful in rehabilitating him?

5. How can Dr. Forbes smooth out things between her, the school, and Ms. Smedley so that they might be receptive to the idea of receiving other interns from the school in the future? How can Smedley be approached and what should Dr. Forbes tell her? Should Dr. Forbes apologize to Smedley for sending Graham to the juvenile facility?

2. The Essay

One afternoon in Norman, Oklahoma, a high school English teacher gave his students an assignment. He wanted them to write an original essay or story. One 13-year-old boy, Mitch Reagan, wrote a Halloween horror story for his English class. The school assign-ment described a high school shooting in which a teacher and two classmates were killed. The English teacher, Gerald Tanner, thought the boy did such a good job that he gave him an "A" for the paper, plus extra credit for reading the paper aloud in class. The paper was written in the first person. The story told about a 13-year-old ninth grader, "Mitch," who be-comes angry in school after being made fun of by two

classmates, goes home and gets his father's semiauto-matic pistol, returns to school, and shoots the two classmates and a teacher who attempts to prevent the shooting. The boy actually used the English teacher's name, Gerald Tanner, as the teacher-victim in the shooting. Two other students were named in the essay as being the shooting victims who died as the result of their wounds. The essay was strongly patterned after the shooting that occurred at Columbine High School in Colorado in April 2000. After Mitch Reagan read the essay to the class, several students became worried. After school, they went home and told their parents that they had been mentioned as murder victims in a paper written by Mitch Reagan in their English class.

• CASE STUDIES •

The parents immediately contacted the police. Police officers were called to investigate, and the paper was retrieved from the teacher, Mr. Tanner. A subsequent investigation led to the 13-year-old's arrest and detention in the city jail for five days. A representative of the police department said, "We're dealing with real people, named specifically in the classroom, and that's a real problem." School superintendent Joan Archambeault said that the outcome might have been different had the boy used fictitious names instead of real names. She declared that Mitch would be suspended from school indefinitely until he underwent a psychological examination. Mitch said, "I was supposed to write a horror story. I don't think I did anything wrong." Mitch's parents were very upset over the whole experience. Mitch's father, who owns a Colt .45 semiautomatic pistol, said, "I think they made far too much out of this incident. Are they going to arrest you now for your thoughts?"

Questions for Discussion

1. In view of the increase in violence occurring on middle school and high school campuses throughout the United States, do you think that the students and parents overreacted in this incident? Why or why not?

2. Did Mitch Reagan commit any crime by writing the essay? Should Mitch be admitted back into school without any penalty? Why or why not? Discuss.

3. Were police and the superintendent of schools justified in taking the action they did by investigating the incident? Why or why not?

4. Was Mitch's detention for five days in the city jail justified under the circumstances? Why or why not?

5. What protocol would you devise in order to protect students from verbal threats from other students? Under what circumstances should essays such as the one written by Mitch Reagan attract police interest? Are the recent school shootings sufficient bases for the actions taken by various officials in this incident?

CHAPTER 14

EVALUATING ORGANIZATIONAL EFFECTIVENESS

CHAPTER OBJECTIVES

The following objectives are intended:

1. To describe what is meant by evaluation research and provide several examples of replication investigations

2. To examine how organizational effectiveness is measured or determined for law enforcement, the courts, corrections, and the juvenile justice system

3. To describe several important assumptions about and expectations of law enforcement, and how law enforcement effectiveness can be improved

4. To describe assumptions about and expectations of prosecutors and the courts,

and how the effectiveness of prosecutors and the judiciary can be improved

5. To describe assumptions about and expectations of corrections, and how the effectiveness of corrections can be increased

6. To describe assumptions about and expectations of the juvenile justice system, and how juvenile justice system effectiveness can be improved

7. To describe codes of ethics and professional responsibilities of key actors in criminal justice system organizations

INTRODUCTION

When administrators make decisions affecting their employees and the organization, they want those decisions to be good ones. Administrators have a vested interest in quality decision making, since organizational effectiveness is enhanced as one result of how well administrators do their jobs. When police officers arrest criminal suspects, they want to ensure that they have

complied with the technical requirements of arrest procedures and that subsequent cases will not be thrown out because of sloppy police work. When police chiefs implement new policies designed to reduce citizen complaints concerning police misconduct or excessive force, they expect that the new policies actually will have some positive impact and reduce the amount of litigation against their officers. When prosecutors prosecute particular cases, they want convictions. When judges sentence convicted offenders, they want to make sure that their sentences are appropriate, given the nature of the offense, the prior record of the offender, and other important factors. When correctional administrators implement new policies relating to correctional officer treatment of inmates, they are hopeful that the changes will be positively received and that inmate disruptions and discontent will decrease. When parole boards release offenders short of serving their full sentences, they want to make sure that they have made the right decision and paroled the most eligible offenders who are most likely to succeed.

This chapter is about how decision making at different points throughout the criminal justice system changes the system, in the hope of improving it. We cannot be absolutely certain at any given time that the decisions we make will have totally predictable results. Despite our best intentions, some decisions are disastrous ones and have adverse consequences for the organization. At other times, some of our decisions are only partially implemented or effective. We are (or should be) sensitive to the particular impact of each and every decision made, however, as well as the implications of these decisions for the future of the system. In order to know which strategies are most effective or efficient or produce the best short-range or long-range results, research often is conducted to assess these results as well as the strategies used to attain them. This is known as evaluation research.

The first part of this chapter examines what is meant by evaluation research. Several examples of evaluation research are presented from literature in the field to acquaint us with the general idea of how the results of decision making are evaluated or assessed. Examples are presented in each of three key areas: (1) law enforcement, (2) prosecution and the courts, and (3) corrections.

The second part of this chapter considers separately each of these three major components of the criminal justice system. Several questions are addressed in each subsection. These questions pertain to the expectations we have of each component. For instance, what is expected of law enforcement agencies? How do we know when law enforcement agencies are fulfilling their objectives? If these objectives are not being fulfilled the way we expect them to be, what can we do to heighten goal attainment and promote conditions that will enable law enforcement agencies to maximize their effectiveness? The same questions are asked about prosecutors, the judiciary, and the court system generally. What are our expectations of these

actors in the system? Are the courts achieving their objectives? What are some of the ways the system can be improved so that these objectives can be achieved more effectively? The questions also are asked about corrections, both institutional and community-based organizations. What do we expect of corrections? Are the goals of corrections being realized? What can be done to improve corrections and heighten the effectiveness of different types of corrections organizations? In each of these cases, various strategies are proposed that are designed to improve overall organizational effectiveness.

The chapter concludes with an examination of three basic solutions and recommendations directed at both actors within their respective organizations and the organizations themselves. These recommendations pertain to (1) heightening actor accountability at all levels in any criminal justice organization, (2) developing codes of ethics and standards of professional responsibility to promote personal and organizational integrity, and (3) integrating or synthesizing community interests with each and every criminal justice agency to foster greater mutual understanding and respect.

EVALUATION RESEARCH

Evaluation research is any investigation that attempts to answer practical and applied questions. It refers to any investigation designed to test the efficacy of a strategy or intervention in relation to some event, such as delinquency or criminality. When students who study criminal justice or criminology gather information for papers required for their classes, they often do library research. This research consists in part of working the stacks, scanning books and periodicals collected by their university library or information online that may contain valuable information of use in writing a research paper. University or college libraries particularly are repositories of more or less extensive information from diverse sources, including government agencies, private organizations, and numerous publishing companies. Some of these publications are journals, which feature research articles written by professors and other professionals who study crime and delinquency. A portion of these articles contains descriptions of research experiments, in which investigators studied the impact of certain variables on other variables and reported their research results. The Internet is increasingly used. Its various search engines facilitate research on virtually every topic imaginable.

Information about criminal justice systems is also available on CDs that categorize research articles according to a wide variety of topics. Most of this experimental research might be considered evaluation research, since these investigators were interested in observing particular outcomes and describing them. Interestingly, much of the experimental research reported in professional journals is *successful* research; that is, positive and/or predictable outcomes are attained. Perhaps a vast amount of experimental research exists that remains unpublished, largely because it is *unsuccessful*. Success or lack of success almost always depends on whether or not the predicted outcomes of the research project were realized.

It should be recognized that whenever program interventions are attempted and experiments conducted, the results, whether favorable or unfavorable, successful or unsuccessful, do not necessarily mean that the interventions are good or bad, worthless or worthwhile. Patricia Van Voorhis, Frank Cullen, and Brandon Applegate (1995:19) advise that program outcomes vary in their significance depending on the relevance of factors involved in the intervention in relation to those targeted for intervention. For instance, they suggest that three different types of scenarios are entirely possible: (1) A good program fails because it is targeted to individuals who cannot benefit from the program; (2) a good program works with some and not with others, and the successes are cancelled out by the failures, so the program looks bad even though it really *did* work with some offenders; and (3) the program was a true failure because planners did not provide a service that targeted a factor that is related to the client (Van Voorhis, Cullen, Applegate, 1995:19).

When do we know the difference between a good program and a bad one? We do not recognize the difference when the program is introduced initially. Only time will tell. This is where replication research becomes relevant. **Replication research** involves repeating the experiment under sufficiently similar conditions paralleling the original research conducted. It takes a lot of time in order for sufficient research to be generated on any particular topic before we acquire a level of confidence to inspire policy changes in any organizational activity or intervention. Therefore, no single study, regardless of its magnitude, is the definitive study for any topic studied. Scientific research accumulates slowly, and our knowledge accrues as fast as the research is conducted and reported. It may take decades before we know, with some degree of certainty, if certain interventions are worthwhile and other interventions are not.

Some Examples of Evaluation Research

THE ORIGINS OF EVALUATION RESEARCH AND REQUESTS FOR PROPOSALS.   The origins of evaluation research are vast and diverse. It is customary, for example, for government agencies to distribute **requests for proposals (RFPs).** These are solicitations from either public or private organizations to submit research plans for investigating particular topics of interest to these organizations. Various persons submit research plans and these are either accepted and funded or rejected. Subsequently, some of the funded research is submitted to the agency as a report that is eventually published. These publications may be articles in professional journals or they may appear as research reports in government documents.

An example of an RFP comes from the American Probation and Parole Association (APPA), which received a grant from the U.S. Department of Justice, Bureau of Justice Assistance (BJA) (Dunlap, 2000:17). The grant was intended to assist probation, parole, and community corrections professionals in exploring and embracing their place in primary crime prevention initiatives. Dunlap (2000:17) says that "the major product of this project will be a primary crime prevention curriculum that introduces the overarching concept of community justice and will explore how crime prevention activities are a natural fit in this proactive agenda. The project will build upon and enhance the content and training methods of a curriculum initially developed by the APPA Prevention Committee. . . . After the curriculum is developed, a pilot training program will be conducted and the curriculum tested. Following final revisions and review, master copies of the curriculum will be disseminated for use by [various government agencies]."

Dunlap notes that a part of a probation or parole officer's responsibility is to develop community programs that provide intervention and advocacy and assistance for the offender and the offender's family. But Dunlap says that traditionally, probation and parole officers, together with community corrections agency professionals, all too often are reactive instead of proactive. That is, when an offender commits a new offense, these officers and agencies react or intervene.

EVALUATING ORGANIZATIONAL EFFECTIVENESS **323**

But a crime prevention model anticipates the conditions under which new crimes are committed. Probation and parole officers have unique capacities to assess their offender-clients, and with their knowledge of crime and community conditions, they have the power to intervene in several ways. Thus, the grant proposed by the APPA is intended to establish a training curriculum that will increase the crime prevention and intervention effectiveness of probation and parole officers as well as community-based organizational members. Exposure to this newly developed curriculum is intended to decrease client propensity to recidivate, because these officer-supervisors will be able to anticipate potential problem areas with certain clients and take aggressive interventions to prevent new crimes.

EXAMPLES OF EVALUATION RESEARCH FROM LAW ENFORCEMENT. Following are three examples of evaluation research in the field of law enforcement.

Study by Robert J. Kane. A study of police officers in Philadelphia, Pennsylvania, was conducted by Robert Kane (2000). Kane observed that in Philadelphia, as in many other large cities, the *beats* or patrols of police officers in different precincts were changed, usually at fixed intervals, such as every four or six weeks. Some of the reasons for changing officer beats were to give the officers some variety in their work, expose them to new geographical territory, and make it less likely for officers to cultivate routines in repetitive relations over time with different businesspersons and citizens on long-term beats. Such long-term police-citizen contacts have been associated with occasional officer corruption, such as accepting illegal gratuities from businesspersons in exchange for not giving their customers parking tickets when parking meter times expired. Kane studied the impact of *permanent beat assignments* as a part of a new community policing model Philadelphia had adopted. Kane predicted that one result of assigning officers to permanent beats would be to heighten their interest in the public housing sites that they patrolled. After a sufficient time interval, Kane assessed the impact of the change to permanent beat assignments for involved officers compared with a sample of officers not involved in permanent beat assignments. Indeed, one outcome observed by Kane was a significant increase in self-initiated field investigations of public housing sites by those officers assigned permanent beats compared with a sample of officers not assigned to permanent beats (Kane,

2000:273). Kane's evaluation research demonstrated at least for the Philadelphia officers studied that permanent beat assignments improved officer interest in the housing projects involved in their patrols and significantly increased the level of police-initiated investigative activity.

Study by Stephen D. Mastrofski and Colleagues. Another study of police officers was conducted by Stephen D. Mastrofski and his colleagues (1999). Mastrofski and his associates studied the St. Petersburg (Florida) Police Department. St. Petersburg had implemented community-oriented policing (COP) during the early 1990s, and public officials wanted to know both citizen and officer reactions to COP over time. Thus, in 1997, Mastrofski observed and/or interviewed 277 officers and police supervisors, together with a random sample of 1,900 St. Petersburg residents selected from the most recent telephone directory. In this after-only study, it was found that COP officers spent about 66 percent of their time with citizens compared with other officers who responded only to 911 calls for service and spent about 45 percent of their time with citizens (Mastrofski et al., 1999:1). Eighty-five percent of the citizens who were interviewed said they were very satisfied with their neighborhood police services in neighborhoods where COP was implemented. Mastrofski's evaluation research showed that community policing clearly made inroads in the outlook of St. Peterburg's officers and that the strength of these effects is related to whether an officer has a specialized community policing assignment or serves as a general patrol officer (p. 2).

Study by Gregory D. Russell and Susan MacLachlan. Gregory D. Russell and Susan MacLachlan (1999) conducted a relatively simple study of police officer job satisfaction as affected by their subsequent participation in a community-oriented policing (COP) program. These researchers hypothesized that officer satisfaction would increase as the result of participation in a COP program in their police department. The study was carried out in a medium-sized law enforcement agency in northern California in late 1995 and early 1996. Three years before the study was conducted, the police department had changed from a traditionally organized and operated agency to a COP agency, in which substantial decentralization and greater officer decision-making power were introduced. The researchers used survey questions and probed 53 employee perceptions of general employee satisfaction, collaborative decision making, and the change in both over a five-year interval before and after COP had been implemented. The evaluation research conducted by these investigators showed that at least for the present sample of 53 officers studied, the change to community policing significantly improved employee satisfaction in the law enforcement agency. We can only infer that, based on improved employee satisfaction, the participating officers also improved their work effectiveness, although this factor was not investigated.

EXAMPLES OF EVALUATION RESEARCH FROM THE COURTS.   The following two studies are examples of the application of evaluation research to aspects of the court system.

Don M. Gottfredson's Research.   Don Gottfredson (1999) investigated 962 felony offenders in Essex County, New York, who were sentenced for crimes in 1976 and 1977. He also studied 18 judges who had originally imposed these sentences. Gottfredson tracked these offenders for 20 years and sought to determine the degree to which judicial sentencing decisions affected the subsequent criminal careers of the sentenced offenders. It should be noted that this type of research is relatively rare, since such an extensive time interval is spanned. Furthermore, numerous variables were included over which Gottfredson exerted little or no control. Despite these limitations, Gottfredson was able to draw several interesting tentative conclusions about these offenders and the diverse sentences they received. Regarding recidivism rates, 70 percent of the offenders who were not originally sentenced to incarceration were rearrested for new offenses during the 20-year period, whereas 82 percent of those sentenced to incarceration were rearrested during the same time interval. Additionally, offender survival in the community over time without being rearrested was about the same for nonincarcerated offenders as for those offenders who had been incarcerated for a period of time. Gottfredson also found that judicial sentencing policies varied widely, although these sentencing policy differences exerted little or no effect on offender recidivism. Also, additional jail time served did not provide any deterrent to an offender's future recidivism. Interestingly, the Gottfredson study offers little support for the idea that changing sentencing practices as a matter of punishment policy has any significant effect on offender recidivism. Thus, the evaluation research conducted by Gottfredson showed that apart from sheer incapacitation, the sentencing variations examined along with offender behavior over the 20-year period of the investigation showed no effect on crime control, rehabilitation, or deterrence. Needless to say, Gottfredson's evaluation of sentencing variations and recidivism rates was negatively received by vested political interests who believed that changing sentencing patterns would lead to greater deterrence, rehabilitation, and general crime control.

Study by Michael B. Blankenship and Colleagues. Michael B. Blankenship and his colleagues (1997) were interested in studying juror understanding of judicial instructions given following the conclusion of death penalty cases. They solicited the assistance of 495 persons who had been summoned for jury duty in Shelby County (Memphis), Tennessee. By using various measures to gauge juror comprehension of sentencing instructions, Blankenship and his colleagues compared several sets of jurors according to 17 different death penalty case scenarios. All of these persons were given Tennessee's death penalty jury instructions. After familiarizing themselves with these instructions, they responded to a questionnaire in which they were asked to disclose their obligation under the law, according to the jury instructions they had read. Blankenship and his colleagues found that the jurors exhibited widely different understanding of the law relating to death penalty cases. When faced with clear and concise instructions, jurors had greater comprehension of their responsibilities under the law and how to treat aggravating and mitigating circumstances. When jury instructions were poorly worded or vague, or when serious omissions regarding the law existed, jurors' comprehension was severely limited. This evaluation research concluded that, at least for the jurors studied, inherent defects exist in death penalty jury instructions in Tennessee as well as in other states, where wording similarities exist. Therefore, it is likely that under certain circumstances, some capital defendants may have been given the death penalty erroneously, at least within the context of information generated by this research sample.

EXAMPLES OF EVALUATION RESEARCH FROM CORRECTIONS.   In the following three examples, researchers used evaluation research techniques to study corrections organizations.

A Study by Markey, Ariessohn, and Mudd.   Vicki Markey, Sunny Ariessohn, and Margaret Mudd (1997) were concerned with pregnant probationers who had serious drug and alcohol dependencies. They wanted to know what programs or interventions might decrease the painful and costly consequences of prenatal drug and alcohol abuse, which included increased likelihood of premature births, higher incidence of congenital irregularities, and mental and physical handicaps manifested through learning disabilities and emotional and neuro-behavioral difficulties (p. 21). In 1992, the San Diego County Probation Department redesigned its adult supervision efforts and developed several performance-based outcomes. One of these new supervision models was the Women and Their Children Program (WATCh). Prior to the implementation of WATCh, pregnant probationers received little or no specialized supervision, and the officers who supervised them had almost no specialized training, as well as caseloads of 50 clients per officer. Thus, many of the pregnant offenders continued to use drugs and alcohol. Many babies were born with birth defects attributable to the toxicity levels in the bodies of these drug-abusing women. Estimates placed the cost to taxpayers at $400,000 per toxic baby in medical, foster care, and special education costs. In an effort to decrease these costs and reduce the incidence of toxicity among newborns, the WATCh Program massed all pregnant probationers into groups of 35 women each, and each group lived in a single unit of residence under the supervision of one officer with special drug and alcohol training. The period of supervision included prenatal and postnatal care up to six months. Pregnant clients were subjected to at least two drug/alcohol tests per week under a zero-tolerance policy imposed by the judge. Probation officers were trained in subjects such as relapse prevention and recovery and the use of perinatal networking among community-based organizations. During the period of the study, from October 1991 to September 1994, 84 offenders gave birth to 90 infants. Eighty-three percent of the births were substance-free babies. The resulting savings to taxpayers was estimated at $33,200,000. The results of this evaluation research were regarded as positive and cost-effective, with an estimated $400,000 saved per baby against an estimated $2,500 per year per probationer in traditional intensive supervision costs. Besides the monetary savings of this program, the female clients clearly benefitted from their experience, since many of them did not recidivate in subsequent follow-up investigations.

Jeff Nossaman's Study. Some evaluation research is directed almost exclusively at ways of saving money for cities, counties, states, and/or the federal government rather than inmate rehabilitation, reintegration, crime control, or crime prevention. In 1991, Jeff Nossaman studied a new generation jail, the Corrections Center of Northwest Ohio (CCNO) (Nossaman, 1996). The CCNO was the first regional corrections center of its type in Ohio and in the United States. The CCNO established a community public works program (CPWP) at that time in an effort to reduce inmate idleness by permitting inmates to work outside of the CCNO and give back to their communities to some extent through an organized community service program. Inmates considered for CPWP employment are screened with a classification instrument that purports to measure whether or not particular inmates pose serious risks to community residents. The inmates who pose the least serious risk are selected for participation in CPWP. Initially, the CPWP began with eight inmates, and by 1996, 65 inmates were involved in various community service activities. The CPWP estimates that over 18,000 inmate worker days have been accumulated, providing over 14,000 hours of community service. At a cost of $4.35 per hour, the program has saved area communities over $600,000 since 1991. Nossaman (1996:76) has indicated that the CPWP has benefitted the inmates, jail officials, and the community by supplying free inmate labor in the form of community service. Although the actual benefits accruing to inmates were unspecified in the research reported by Nossaman, we might infer that at least for the inmate-participants, their idleness was definitely reduced. The evaluation research showed a considerable cost benefit from the free inmate labor provided through the CCNO and its sponsored CPWP.

Study by Bayens, Williams, and Smykla. During the period from 1965 to 1985, numerous lawsuits were filed by both state and federal inmates against various jails citing Eighth Amendment violations. Besides lawsuits, there also were large numbers of inmate incidents, fighting, rioting, and general disruptions that resulted in injuries and/or deaths to various inmates and jail personnel. One result of these numerous lawsuits was a radical change in jail design, specifically the creation of podular jail units known as new generation jails. In 1988, a new generation jail was constructed to house 220 inmates and was staffed with 50 jail officers. Gerald J. Bayens, Jimmy J. Williams, and John Ortiz Smykla (1997) were interested in studying the impact of direct supervision management and the new generation architectural design philosophy on disruptive inmate behavior, and whether or not such changes in jail design would decrease inmate assaults, contraband weapons, disorders, escapes, fires, and vandalism. These researchers gathered pre–new generation jail data from 1983 and kept meticulous track of infractions and inmate disruptions for a 10-year period, through 1993. Their records included 70 infraction categories, such as the frequency of assaults, arson, sex offenses, suicides/attempts, escapes, and other disruptive behavior. The results of their evaluation research were favorable. Bayens, Williams, and Smykla reported that negative inmate behavior decreased during the 10-year period in 51 out of the 70 categories, particularly aggressive behavior. These researchers said that "podular design coupled with a proactive inmate behavior management orientation reduced the number of staff reports of incidents involving inmate aggressive behavior and helped alleviate many of the deficiencies which were associated with the traditional jail" (p. 60). Thus, their evaluation showed that direct supervision facilities produce a number of benefits, including a reduction in violent inmate behavior. And to highlight the importance of replication research, these researchers added a most critical phrase as a part of their study conclusion: "We hope that this research has contributed to the *growing literature* on the new generation philosophy and its impact on staff reports of negative behavior" (p. 61) [italics added].

AN EXAMPLE OF EVALUATION RESEARCH FROM JUVENILE JUSTICE. The following example illustrates the use of evaluation research to study the juvenile justice system.

The Kammer, Minor, and Wells Study. Not all evaluation research has a storybook ending with positive results. For example, James J. Kammer, Kevin I. Minor, and James B. Wells (1999) were interested in studying the effects of a relatively new diversion program for juvenile offenders that was being implemented in Fayette County, Kentucky, in 1991. Diversion is a method of removing a juvenile from the juvenile justice system temporarily and subjecting him or her to various program conditions. After successful completion of the diversion program, the offender has his or her record either expunged or the charges are downgraded in seriousness with minimally severe dispositions in juvenile court. A key objective of diversion is to minimize the stigma or labeling resulting from formal delinquency processing in a criminal-like juvenile court. Among other objectives, these researchers wanted to know whether a sample of divertees in the

Fayette County, Kentucky, program would subsequently have lower recidivism rates resulting from their diversion compared with nondiverted juveniles. The program was called the Diversion Plus Program (DPP). There were 94 juveniles assigned to the DPP from July 1991 through November 1992, the term of the investigative period. Youths ranged in age from 11 to 17. These investigators found that of the original 94 juveniles who entered the DPP, 81 (86.2 percent) graduated or successfully completed the diversion requirements. Kammer, Minor, and Wells studied these juveniles during a one-year follow-up after their graduation from the DPP. They discovered that about two thirds of all DPP graduates recidivated within the one-year follow-up period. Clearly, these researchers were disappointed by their research results. It would seem from their findings that the results of the DPP program were about the same as if the affected juveniles had never participated in the DPP and had been supervised under standard probation.

Some Conclusions About Evaluation Research

We have seen samples of evaluation research from several key areas of criminal justice. Much of this research is limited to short time frames, such as one to three years. The samples sizes vary considerably, from 15 or 20 to several thousand persons involved in the study. The interventions assessed and treated as experimental variables are never 100 percent successful. Some interventions seem worthless, and we might question why they were ever used. But evaluation research includes a strong exploratory element, meaning that we are unsure about the true effects of an experimental variable when we begin to study it.

Wide-ranging differences can be found among the samples selected for study. Often, these samples are convenient and located near where the researchers who conduct the research are headquartered. Much variation exists from one sample to the next, even if the same kinds of evaluations are made of the same programs. Thus, we may be dealing with the same program, such as the Diversion Plus Program, but we may study it in Fayette County, Kentucky, or San Bernadino, California, or Chicago, Illinois, or Omaha, Nebraska. There is absolutely no reason to expect that the samples of adults or juveniles in each of these locations will be the same. Therefore, even if the same intervention is applied, different and even contradictory results might be anticipated that are often attributable to differences among the samples of clients themselves.

Replication research is fundamental to evaluation research. We need to investigate the same types of programs under different study conditions in diverse jurisdictions. Only after repeated study on different research samples will we begin to see the emergence of patterns or trends. More successful interventions or strategies will have better success records, whereas ineffective strategies or interventions will tend to exhibit substantially fewer successful results. Over time, the better strategies are incorporated into policy statements for different criminal justice organizations. Indeed, these more successful strategies will find their way into training programs for personnel who work with adult and juvenile clients.

HOW DO WE KNOW ORGANIZATIONS ARE EFFECTIVE?

Determining organizational effectiveness is a continuous process. Provided that we can define the criteria by which an organization's effectiveness can be judged, we can pronounce an organization effective today. But what about tomorrow, next week, or next year? Will the organization continue to be effective? The following list of considerations, although not exhaustive, provides some guidance about whether or not organizations are effective:

1. Does the organization have a mission statement?
2. Does the organization have clearly articulated goals for its membership?
3. Do the subunits and membership of the organization understand the organizational goals?
4. What are the individual and group goals?
5. Are the individual and group goals consistent with the overall organizational goals?
6. Are the organizational goals realistic and attainable?
7. To what extent are the organizational goals achieved?

The integrating elements of these questions are goals and goal attainment. We may presume that all organizations have goals. We also may presume that to the extent that these organizational goals are achieved, organizational effectiveness is achieved. But is evaluating organizational effectiveness really that simple? Consider the following hypothetical scenarios from

law enforcement, prosecution and the courts, corrections, and juvenile justice.

LAW ENFORCEMENT

1. The mayor of Philadelphia says that crime is going to be reduced significantly in the city next year because he has established new goals for the Philadelphia Police Department. The police are going to strictly enforce all laws and double the number of arrests over previous years.

2. The New Orleans Police Department was recently investigated by the FBI for corruption and illegal payoffs to numerous police officers who were taking money from known criminals in exchange for protection. Twenty-two officers were arrested by FBI agents and charged with federal crimes. Unidentified sources said that they had only scratched the surface of corruption in the New Orleans Police Department and much more work needed to be done to root out corruption at all levels.

3. During 1999, the number of rapes in Los Angeles increased by 212 percent over the number of rapes in 1998. The murder rate increased between 1998 and 1999 by 21 percent, and the amount of burglary and larceny increased by 18 percent during that same period.

4. In Baltimore, Maryland, a sample of residents gave police officers a very favorable review when questioned by researchers following the implementation of a "back-to-the-people" community policing movement established during the past few years. Fear of police by citizens in Baltimore has declined by 75 percent.

5. The number of civil lawsuits against police officers in Detroit, Michigan, has declined by 42 percent during the period from 1996 to 1999, following the establishment of anger management and police-citizen courses at the Michigan Law Enforcement Training Academy. All sworn police officers in the state of Michigan are required to be certified in police-community relations and anger management as of September 1, 1998, and thereafter, by the issuance of certifications showing that particular courses were completed at the training academy.

PROSECUTION AND THE COURTS

1. In a recent FBI sting operation called Operation Overlord, 56 state and federal judges were arrested for accepting illegal gratuities and bribes in civil cases. FBI agents posed as respondents in civil actions in which it

BOX 14.1 PERSONALITY HIGHLIGHT

JOAN M. "JONI" BRUNNER
Program Coordinator, Community Service Program, Rehab Services, Inc., Minot, North Dakota

Statistics: B.S. (criminal justice), Minot State University

Prior Work Experience: I graduated from Minot State University in December 1996 with a major in criminal justice and minor in gerontology. I decided to go to college after having lost the job I held for 13½ years at Interstate Brands, Inc. (Sweetheart Bakery) in Minot. I grew up in Minot with my dad, who is a retired sergeant of the Minot Police Department and have lived in Minot all my life.

Interests: While taking classes at Minot State University, I had the opportunity to take an independent study course. I chose court monitoring for the Domestic Violence Crisis Center in Minot. My responsibilities included attending municipal court and monitoring how judges handled cases of domestic violence and simple assault. The resulting statistics were then sent to Bismarck where they were compiled for the entire state. While in the courtroom I met the Minot community service coordinator. She asked me if I would be interested in volunteering in her office. I volunteered in her office for nine months, until April 1997 when the program was transferred to Rehab Services, Inc. In June 1997, when I heard that the community service coordinator position was open, I applied and was hired for that position.

Background and Responsibilities: The community service program is responsible for Ward and Renville Counties. We receive referrals from juvenile court, municipal court, district court, and parole and probation. Often, judges will allow offenders to work off their court fines and fees with required community service hours, or community service may be required in addition to fines and fees. In 1998, the program had over 12,000 hours of community service completed.

In addition to the community service coordinator position, I am also the coordinator for the PRODD (Progressive Restructuring of Offenders Daily Duties) program, which is better known as the Day Reporting Program. Through this program, I receive referrals from our local probation and parole office and the parole board at the North Dakota State Penitentiary in Bismarck. A referral from the local probation office is generally an intermediate sanction resulting from a probation or parole violation. Usually, clients are in need of employment, are lacking education, have recent alcohol or drug violations, or need closer supervision. At times, day reporting is used as a wake-up call, as an alternative to sending a client to jail or prison, or as a part of a parole board order as a condition of their release. Clients may be ordered to remain on the program for 30, 60, or 90 days, or until they get a job.

Day reporting clients must meet with me on a daily basis and submit a daily itinerary. I contact them by telephone throughout the work day, ensuring that they are where they are supposed to be according to the itinerary. They are to contact me with any changes they make in their itinerary. In addition, we do random home and work site visits to make sure clients are following program requirements. After business hours, on weekends and on holidays, Recovery House staff (a Rehab Services, Inc. residential treatment program for alcohol and drug addition) makes the contact calls for day reporting.

My first experience on a home visit was quite interesting. Our secretary took me to check on a client who did not have a telephone. The only other person I had heard of with this particular client's name was a professional football player who once played for the Minnesota Vikings and who was a huge African American man. I soon discovered that I was guilty of stereotyping. When I knocked on the client's door, I was surprised. My client did not have on a shirt and his pants were only half zipped. He was barely 5'4" tall, had long hair, had tattoos everywhere, his nipples were pierced—and he was white.

While working in the criminal justice system, one is able to make contacts with several other departments, and other job opportunities can arise. For instance, during community service intakes at juvenile court, I was asked to conduct curfew and electronic monitoring surveillance during the evening hours. I signed a contract to be hired temporarily for curfew monitoring. I have had up to 25 juveniles to telephone every evening, with time and frequency of calls established by the juvenile probation officer. I have made calls beginning at 7:00 P.M. and continuing until 1:00 A.M. I record whether or not the client was at home on time, and of course, I do callbacks to ensure that they do not leave home after I have recently spoken with them. I am able to do this job from my home and use a cellular telephone when I am out of town. The youths do not realize the number of times I have made contact calls from hundreds of miles away. Also, I have had several juveniles put under house arrest. If that does not get their attention, then they are placed on electronic monitoring.

One of the most frustrating parts of my job is how judgmental people can be regarding others. Many people assume that those who are doing community service are bad people. I tell my clients that there is not one of us who could not end up doing community service or one of us who does not know someone who is required to do community service. Community service is a means for change and moving forward.

Advice to Students: My advice to anyone interested in criminal justice as a profession is to work internships, volunteer, job shadow in an agency, or ask to do a ride-along. Many different job opportunities can be found in the criminal justice field. You just have to be willing to explore the businesses in your area. If you find yourself getting burned out or becoming judgmental regarding the people with whom you are working, however, it is time to find another job. It only takes one bad news release concerning a criminal justice employee to give all criminal justice careers a black eye.

was alleged that they were negligent in their business practices. All 56 judges were indicted and temporarily suspended from their positions pending subsequent trials.

2. State prosecutors in the Miami-Dade (Florida) area have achieved a 97 percent conviction rate against persons charged with drug use and sales during 2000.

3. The Georgia State Bar Association has suspended the licenses of 102 practicing lawyers for unethical behavior and has initiated proceedings to disbar these attorneys permanently from practicing law.

4. Four prosecutors recently were removed from office when it was determined that they had engaged in prosecutorial misconduct by filing false and unsupportable charges against 116 defendants, 102 of whom were convicted. Those cases in which convictions were obtained are currently under independent review.

CORRECTIONS

1. Fourteen jail officers in South Carolina were suspended with pay pending an investigation that they sexually assaulted different female inmates on at least 65 occasions. A class action suit was filed against the jail officers by 22 females who claimed that they were forcibly raped at different times, and that two or more of these jail officers were present during some of these sexual assaults. Criminal charges also were pending.

2. The rate of imprisonment in the United States rose by 4.2 percent from 1999 to 2000. The U.S. attorney general cited more professional law enforcement, more aggressive prosecutions, and greater adherence to the truth-in-sentencing provisions enacted by various state legislatures during the 1990s as responsible for confining more criminals behind bars.

3. In 2000, 36 jail and prison systems were under federal court order to bring their physical plants up to state and federal standards in compliance with the equal protection clause of the Fourteenth Amendment.

4. Prison inmate rioting and the frequency of disruptive behavior among prisoners has declined for the period from 1995 to 1999. Authorities have commended prison administrators for managing their institutions in ways that minimize inmate discontent and aggressiveness.

5. The U.S. Department of Justice reported in 2000 that during the period from 1996 to 1999, probation and parole revocations increased by 22 percent. Also, probationers and parolees had a combined recidivism rate of 66 percent within two years of commencing their respective programs.

JUVENILE JUSTICE

1. For the fourth straight year, violent juvenile offending in the United States has declined. Between

1995 and 1999, the rate of juvenile violence has dropped by 17 percent, although the rate of juvenile violence is still 33 percent above the 1987 level. Credit for the decreasing juvenile violence has been given to various types of intervention programs, such as boot camps and intensive supervised probation, electronic monitoring, and home confinement.

2. The rate of secure confinement for juveniles in the United States has increased by 4 percent during the years 1994 to 1999. Many of these incarcerated juveniles are property offenders, but they often have been incarcerated because of chronic offending.

3. In 1999, the number of juveniles transferred to criminal courts increased by 3,000, from 11,000 in 1995 to 14,000 in 1999. Unnamed sources say that this is proof that the get-tough movement is working.

4. Female juvenile violence increased in Minnesota for the third straight year, outpacing male juvenile violence by 16 percent. Minnesota authorities are concerned about this new female juvenile crime wave, which is largely due to the growing presence of female gangs.

5. Recent findings concerning the effectiveness of boot camps, based on a study of 40 boot camp programs operating in 34 different states, reveal a recidivism rate among boot camp graduates of 64 percent. This compares with a 62 percent recidivism rate of standard juvenile probationers and a 68 percent recidivism rate among juvenile parolees during the same period. Some observers claim that boot camps are failures and should be discontinued, since they do not significantly decrease juvenile recidivism.

What sense are we to make of all of these statements, even if they were actually true? Are organizations effective or ineffective because someone, named or unnamed, says so? Consider the law enforcement scenarios. Although the mayor of Philadelphia may be an important person, he is actually far removed from the front lines of law enforcement. Who has he consulted to establish new goals for the Philadelphia Police Department? Have the police officers themselves adopted these goals as their own? Are they eager to enforce all laws and double their records of arrest? What about the New Orleans Police Department? Is it really as corrupt as FBI agents claim it is? Who are these unidentified sources? What about considering whether or not federal prosecutors will obtain convictions against the accused officers?

In Los Angeles, does a rise in rates in different crime categories mean that the Los Angeles Police Department is not doing a good job of enforcing the law? What about other crime categories? Has crime increased for all crime categories? Besides law enforcement, what factors might be alternative explanations for rising crime? And does a sample of Baltimore, Maryland, residents giving their police department a favorable rating necessarily mean that the "back-to-the-people" movement of community policing is responsible? Or are more professional police officers being hired? What about neighborhood crime prevention programs that may have been established? What are the real causes of reductions in the fear of police by the citizens interviewed? And are the citizens interviewed representative of all Baltimore residents?

In the prosecution and courts scenarios, some of these findings are indeed alarming. We do not like dishonest judges. Operation Overlord resulted in the arrest of 56 state and federal judges. How much dishonesty can be found among judges generally? There are thousands of judges in the United States—what proportion of judges does this sample of arrested judges represent? Will they be convicted? And in Miami-Dade, what does a 97 percent conviction rate mean? It may mean that the prosecutors chose to pursue only the most solid cases against low-level drug dealers or users. What about their conviction rates or prosecutions against drug suppliers or drug lords further up the narcotics chain?

What does it mean that the Georgia State Bar Association has suspended the licenses of 102 attorneys? What were the charges? Will these charges be sustained on subsequent review? What about the prosecutors who were removed from office? Again, what percent of the prosecutors does this small number represent? Were they convicted or simply charged? What evidence was compiled to show that they had filed false charges against certain criminal defendants?

In the corrections scenarios, we can raise similar questions. A few jail officers suspended for allegedly sexually assaulting some female jail inmates do not represent jail officers everywhere, even within that particular jurisdiction. Will the criminal charges, if filed, be sustained? Also, will the civil litigation result in awards to the plaintiffs? What about the rate of imprisonment? Might that have anything to do with the growing amount of U.S. prison construction? Is there a rising wave of crime? We simply do not know, at least from this information. And what about the jail and prison systems under court order to improve their physical plants? Are there roaches and rats in inmate cells? Are rodent droppings found in inmate food? Are the cells too hot in the summer and too cold in the winter? Why have these systems been placed under court order to improve? What does this mean?

Can we draw any definitive conclusions about the reduction in inmate rioting in U.S. prisons during a five-year period? What is causing decreased rioting? Is changing prison architecture to reduce the number of blind areas in which correctional officers cannot see really what is going on? Are jail and prison supervisory improvements and better celling arrangements in any way connected to decreased inmate discontent? Also, because probation and parole revocations are increasing, does this necessarily mean that probation and parole are not working effectively as rehabilitative programs? Or are probation and parole officers turning up the intensity of their supervision of clients and catching them in more technical program infractions? What are the reasons for these increased numbers of program infractions?

In the area of juvenile justice, we know that numerically, there were more adjudicated delinquents in 2000 compared with those adjudicated delinquent in 1995. But what about decreased juvenile violence? Is this a true trend, or will it begin to rise again over the next few years? What about other types of juvenile offending that actually have increased rather than decreased for the same period? Should the same programs that are given credit for decreased juvenile violence also be given credit for rising public order offending, burglary, and larceny? Furthermore, does incarcerating more juvenile offenders necessarily mean that juvenile crime is increasing? Does the increased use of transfers of juveniles to criminal court mean anything significant concerning changes in juvenile crime? If juvenile violence is decreasing, and if the most serious juvenile cases are supposed to be transferred to criminal court, then why has research not shown a corresponding decrease in juvenile transfers compared with decreasing juvenile violence?

Crime waves instigated by female offenders may or may not be real. We know that there are more female juvenile gangs today than 10 years ago, but are these gangs the major reason for increased female juvenile violence? Or are police arresting more female juveniles today than in past years, when many female juveniles were not arrested but returned to the custody of their parents or guardians? And should we abandon boot camps because of some similarities in recidivism

figures between a sample of boot camps studied and a sample of juvenile probationers and parolees?

Therefore, in order to answer the question of whether organizations are effective, we need to determine which organizations we are examining. We also need to know the perspectives of those defining what is or is not effective. There are many dimensions of law enforcement agencies, prosecution and the courts, corrections, and juvenile justice. Which dimensions are being evaluated, and according to which criteria?

Unfortunately, criticisms of organizations often are made in the abstract, and specific institutions are blamed. Churches are to blame for crime and delinquency, according to this type of thinking, because they are not instilling proper moral values in children in their formative years. Or the family is to blame, because parents are more concerned with their jobs than their families. The schools are to blame, because their students are receiving inadequate or poor instruction. Law enforcement is to blame, because too many crooked or unconcerned officers do more to harm citizens than to protect them. Correctional institutions, probation and parole departments, and community-based correctional services are to blame, because they fail to deter their clients from committing new crimes. How can these institutions be attacked? Who can be blamed for program failure, rising crime, or children out of control?

In order for meaningful criticisms to be leveled against any agency, institution, department, program, subunit of an organization, or a person or persons in charge, we must have both goals and role clarity. With goals in place, organizations and programs can be assessed according to the degree or level of goal attainment. With role clarity, individuals can be expected to have an understanding of what it is they are expected to do and how to do it.

For example, the New Orleans Police Department (NOPD) has a mission and several important goals. One of the chief goals of the NOPD is law enforcement. If officer corruption is uncovered as the result of an FBI investigation or information developed from informants, who or what is to blame? The *who* part of this question relates to individuals in positions of authority who have the responsibility to ensure officer integrity and work effectiveness. When this effectiveness and integrity are challenged by the discovery of corruption, specific individuals are singled out for criticism, for failing to do their own jobs effectively. The solution often is to replace these individuals with others who are considered more responsible. Quite often, the responsible person is the chief of police, who is replaceable. Replacing the chief of police is considered the solution to the problem. But the chief of police may have little or nothing to do with front-line officer graft and corruption. Those more responsible than chiefs of police may be sergeants, lieutenants, and captains, who may themselves be corrupt. Their positions enable them to protect corrupt officers and perpetuate corruption and misconduct, despite replacing the chief of police. The act of replacing the police chief is more symbolic than anything else. The new police chief enters the department, makes a few speeches about departmental improvements, shuffles officers around, fires a few, retires others, and believes the problem has been solved. But the corruption continues. Subsequently, new allegations of corruption arise, and the most recent chief of police is targeted for termination and replacement.

The answer to the *what* part of the question is that the system itself may create the conditions that condone and perpetuate corruption. There may be weak or nonexistent accountability policies. Ineffective monitoring of officer conduct may occur. Police officers themselves may remain tight-lipped about the misconduct or corruption of their fellow officers, largely because of the strongly influential and routinized police subculture and police personality. One police officer will find it difficult to report another for misconduct or corruption. At least, that is what *we* think. But many police officers remain silent about the affairs of their fellow officers because it is the accepted practice. If that practice were somehow violated, then those violating this practice would be ostracized and shunned by other officers and condemned for airing their dirty laundry in public. Therefore, it is safer to keep quiet about the misconduct or corruption of other officers than it is to report the misconduct or corruption. It may even be life saving, since more than a few officers' lives have been jeopardized when they have come forward to report the misconduct or corruption of their fellow officers. The other officers could make and even carry out threats against those who "rat out" their fellow officers and report them to internal affairs investigators or their immediate superiors.

Therefore, blame may accrue to one or more specific persons, usually those performing the most visible and prestigious roles in the organization. Or blame may accrue to the system itself and how it operates. Both the *who* and the *what* must be dealt with in order to ascertain why an organization does not appear to be effective to others. In the following sections, we examine the criteria used to assess the effectiveness of (1) law enforcement, (2) the prosecution and the courts, and (3) corrections. In each instance, we examine what is conventionally expected of these organizations and what can and/or should be done to improve their effectiveness.

MEASURING THE EFFECTIVENESS OF LAW ENFORCEMENT

How do we know that law enforcement is effective? Each year, a publication called the *Uniform Crime Reports* is produced. The *National Crime Victimization Survey* also is published annually. Besides these information sources about crime, we also have the *Sourcebook of Criminal Justice Statistics,* which is published by the Hindelang Criminal Justice Research Center in Albany, New York. This massive undertaking is not only available in a 650-page book, it also is available in a CD-ROM format. Annually, the National Institute of Justice, Department of Justice Statistics, Office of Juvenile Justice and Delinquency Prevention, and a host of other agencies publish documents about crime statistics. Much of this information is free or available at nominal expense to interested persons who want to study crime and different aspects of it. The fact is, we have an enormous output of statistical information available to us, and not just from official federal government sources. Cities, counties, and states each produce their own compendiums of statistical information about how much crime exists, and comparisons are made for almost every imaginable time period. Thus, more than adequate information is available about how much crime there is now, how much there was in the past, and projected crime in future years.

We have intricate breakdowns of crime according to cities and towns of different sizes. Crime categories are listed, and trends are noted over designated time periods. For almost any city in the United States, we can determine at any given time different rates of crime, numbers of police officers, numbers of arrests, numbers of prosecutions, numbers and rates of conviction, and a host of other statistical information. We are on information overload concerning crime.

Therefore, when we want to know if law enforcement is effective, we can examine all sorts of crime trends for different parts of the country and determine whether crime generally has increased or decreased, or whether it has increased or decreased according to particular categories. We can correlate this information with different law enforcement programs in experimental research and generate research findings that are indicative of whether or not law enforcement agencies are doing their jobs.

We can take one specific example of one specific law enforcement agency—the Border Patrol. Suppose the Border Patrol seized 25 million tons of marijuana, 6 million kilos of cocaine, 2 million tons of uncut heroin, and 5 billion bottles of illegal prescription drugs in 2000. Suppose the Border Patrol seized $28.8 billion in cash that same year from illegal drug transactions. Suppose the Border Patrol acquired through asset forfeiture a whopping $500 billion in assets seized from those engaging in illegal trafficking. Suppose the Border Patrol apprehended 600,000 illegal immigrants at U.S. borders and returned them to their countries of origin. We probably would think that if a Border Patrol representative presented this information in a formal annual report to the U.S. Congress, the Congress would be most impressed. Does this mean that the Border Patrol is effective? We might think so.

But wait a minute! Many more tons of marijuana, cocaine, heroin, and other illegal substances get smuggled into the United States each year. Hundreds of thousands of undetected illegal aliens are living and working in the United States each year. What about all of the *unseized* money and assets that *could have been seized* if the Border Patrol and other federal agencies were aware of their existence initially?

Some apologists might say that these organizations cannot possibly be expected to catch *everyone* committing an illegal act *all of the time.* This is true, but since we also cannot possibly know exactly *how much* illegal activity transpires across U.S. borders at any given time, how do we *really know* that the Border Patrol is effective? We do not know. The simple fact is that effectiveness is a very elusive term. It means different things to different people at different points in time. In simple terms, law enforcement effectiveness means whatever we want it to mean.

Consider the very real possibility that we always will have crime. Law enforcement agencies always will be necessary to pursue criminals who commit crime. These law enforcement agencies will be more or less aggressive in their pursuit of criminals and investigations of criminal activities. Therefore, it is perhaps more realistic to consider what can be measured and

used to gauge how much crime is reported and investigated, how many criminals are actually apprehended for these crimes, and how many are actually convicted and punished. But beyond these considerations, we must accept other assumptions about the real world of law enforcement. Although the following list of assumptions is certainly not exhaustive, it does provide us with a sense of reality for appreciating why it is difficult to measure the effectiveness of law enforcement:

SOME ASSUMPTIONS ABOUT LAW ENFORCEMENT AND CRIME FIGHTING

1. Many different law enforcement agencies exist at the local, state, and federal levels.
2. Organizational effectiveness is measured according to different criteria, depending on the particular agency we are examining.
3. Crime trends, either upward or downward, are only one indication of a law enforcement organization's effectiveness.
4. Law enforcement may or may not be related to reducing crime.
5. Crime fluctuates for a variety of reasons that are not always connected either directly or indirectly with law enforcement.
6. Politics and economics dictate the priorities given to particular types of crime and the amount of enforcement attention paid to these types of crime.
7. Immeasurable inaccuracies are associated with crime, its incidence, and its reporting by victims.
8. Immeasurable errors can be found among law enforcement agencies concerning the amount of crime detected, investigated, and solved.
9. There is substantial **spuriousness** in the research literature about crime and the impact of law enforcement agencies on the incidence of crime.
10. Better training methods for law enforcement officers do not necessarily equate with more effective crime fighting or reductions in the amount of crime.
11. Sweeping generalities about law enforcement and its effectiveness, regardless of whether we are discussing local, county, state, or federal governmental organizations, are usually without adequate foundation and are unwarranted.

These assumptions have been drawn from a variety of sources, including Cartwright (2000), Correia (2000), Garoupa (2000), Grabosky (1988), Normandeau and Leighton (1991), Smith and Alpert (2000), Southgate and Merrlees-Black (1991), and the Texas Criminal Justice Council (1972). If we accept most or all of these assumptions, then this means that outright law enforcement organizational assessments of effectiveness are probably too general to be of predictive utility to anyone. This also means that our analyses of effectiveness are perhaps more profitably focused at the interpersonal and/or individual levels of analysis, where behaviors of officers or groups of officers are more easily observed and measurable.

What Is Expected of Law Enforcement?

A preliminary inspection of a reasonably large number of textbooks dealing with police and law enforcement organizations ought to yield some clear and concise definitions of the expectations to have for law enforcement agencies at virtually any unit or level of analysis we choose. One good book is *Police Management* (2/e) by Roy R. Roberg and Jack Kuykendall (1998). Roberg and Kuykendall are quite specific about how police goals and objectives can be measured. For instance, they say that one police goal might be to reduce robberies by 10 percent during the coming year. They also quantify effectiveness by asking how much time and money the organization has expended to accomplish a specific goal. They say that to become more effective, an organization must have an increase in the number of goals and objectives accomplished or come closer to realizing them (1998:9). Interestingly, they also indicate that productivity of police organizations is not only the ability of these agencies to reduce the crime rate, but also to reduce citizen fear levels and improve citizen attitudes. Are reductions of citizen fear levels and improving citizen attitudes true measures of law enforcement effectiveness?

Another work consulted was *Police Administration* (5/e) by James J. Fyfe, Jack R. Greene, William F. Walsh, O.W. Wilson, and Roy Clinton McLaren (1997). This work contains *no* references to law enforcement goals, although a few references are made to effectiveness. Some of the examples chosen to illustrate police organization effectiveness were interesting. Comments such as "Neighborhood safety has in-

creased over the past year" and "Our community is one of the safest cities in America" were cited on p. 369. Fyfe et al. couched police productivity into economic terms: (1) how police services are produced, (2) what the costs of these services are, (3) how costs vary by type of service provided, and (4) what the impact of different services is on the problems they seek to address or the goals they seek to achieve (1997:369–370).

Actually, a better idea about police organizational goals was provided in a later discussion in the same book titled "What Is Good Policing?" (p. 376). Fyfe et al. preface their discussion by calling our attention to a persistent problem when it comes to defining law enforcement effectiveness and goals. They say, "The most desirable processes and outcomes of municipal police services have been difficult to specify largely because there is little clear agreement about either. We share an abstract notion, for instance, that the police should enforce the law . . . but it is often unclear how we want them to go about doing this or what we expect them to accomplish in doing it" (1997:376).

Perhaps David Bayley (1993:15) comes closest to providing us with measurable phenomena to gauge law enforcement effectiveness. Bayley categorizes police performance measures into three major categories: (1) hard, (2) soft, and (3) indirect. The hard measures are crime rates, criminal victimizations, the ability of the public to undertake routine activities, real estate values, the number of disorder situations interrupted, the number of community crime problems solved, and the amount of information volunteered to police about crimes. Soft measures include fear of crime, confidence in the police, commitment to neighborhoods, satisfaction with police actions, complaints about police service, willingness to assist police, and community solidarity. Indirect measures include the numbers of police officers, the number of uniformed officers on the street, the proportion of detectives to uniformed police officers, the ratio of supervisors to police officers, the response times to calls for service, arrests, clearance rates, the number of community watch and crime prevention meetings, the number of neighborhood watch groups, and speed in answering telephones.

Maybe our smaller-scale analyses of police groups and individual officers might be best after all. For instance, Rich (1999) conducted a study of the Neighborhood Problem Solving (NPS) system in Hartford, Connecticut. This was a program designed to improve citizen perceptions of community safety and improve police-community relations by creating maps based on reported crime conditions at different times. The overall usefulness of NPS in Hartford depended on neighborhood-based problem-solving committees, community organizers, cooperative city officials, and police officers. Extensive use was made of reported crime information and map formulation, particularly arrest information and citizen reports of crimes. Based on the reports of interviewed citizens and police officers, the program seemed successful.

In another small-scale study, an evaluation was made of the School Resource Officer Program (SRO) in Topeka, Kansas (Chen, Chang, and Tombs, 1999). A joint effort by the police and local school districts was begun in 1993 and aimed to provide educational leadership in preventing school violence and crime while also addressing substance abuse issues. Student perceptions of school safety and attitudes toward police were assessed. Changes in student behavior were closely monitored over several years and questionnaires were completed by 162 students and 17 SRO officers. Generally, the program was perceived as influential in changing student behavior, decreasing the incidence of illegal drug use, and creating a closer alliance between students and police (Chen, Chang, and Tombs, 1999).

In a more crime reduction–related study, an investigation was made of the use of high-tech closed-circuit television equipment in several English towns. Closed-circuit television systems (CCTVs) were installed in several key high-crime areas of Burnley, Lancashire, in northwest England. These were designated as "focal" beats according to police. Other areas were designated as "displacement" beats, since they were immediately adjacent to the focal beats. A third type of beat was studied and known simply as "other." It was believed that if crime decreases occurred in CCTV focal areas, there would be obvious spillover of crime into displacement beats adjacent to them. During the first several months that CCTVs were installed in focal beats, crime declined appreciably. Furthermore, the crime rate did not increase in the displacement beats. Crime rates continued at regular levels in "other" beats. This led researchers to conclude that installing CCTVs in certain areas would function as crime deterrents (Armitage, Smyth, and Pease, 1999).

The motto "To Protect and Serve" appears on a majority of police cruisers throughout the United States. Certainly, we would agree that one major function of all law enforcement agencies is to enforce the criminal laws. Numerous subsidiary functions of police agencies can be cited as well, however. An endless list of services are expected of law enforcement officers. An FBI agent may be expected to pitch in and assist in locating a lost child in Chandler, Arizona. An off-duty police officer visiting Washington, DC, from Eureka, California, may be expected to assist and provide some degree of backup in the event that U.S. Capitol police are confronted with a deranged person intending to shoot his way into a federal building. Examples of such law enforcement assistance across jurisdictional boundaries are endless.

What Can Be Done to Improve the Effectiveness of Law Enforcement Agencies?

Much is being done within all types of law enforcement agencies to improve their effectiveness. Managerial effectiveness seminars are being offered to assist those in supervisory capacities to become more proficient at what they do. Leadership training seminars are being offered on a regular basis for those seeking promotion to higher ranks. More sophisticated training techniques are being used by various law enforcement training academies to acquaint officers with the latest crime-fighting gear and weaponry.

But we are presently in an era of wanting to get a "bigger bang for our buck." The importance of the economics of administration is not lost on those in charge of law enforcement agency purse strings. The cost-effectiveness of just about everything law enforcement officers do is closely and consistently assessed by higher-ups. Efficiency means to operate effectively at the lowest possible cost to taxpayers and the organization itself.

In England, for instance, cost-effectiveness analysis (CEA) is currently considered the best approach for police forces to assess the value and efficiency of police services to the public (Stockdale, Whitehead, and Graham, 1999). Three types of evaluative policing—cost-benefit analysis, cost-effectiveness analysis, and performance indicators—were assessed over time in 43 different departments in England and Wales. Similar conclusions have been reached concerning Canadian law enforcement (Normandeau and Leighton, 1991) and Australian law enforcement (Grabosky, 1988). Also, powerful forces are at work in the United

States that suggest strong economic control of law enforcement quality and quantity (Forst and Manning, 1999).

Ultimately, it may prove fruitful for law enforcement agencies at all levels to invest more time and effort in programs designed to involve private citizens in their law enforcement activities. Not enough can be said about having a cooperative public in your corner, promoting your agency's goals and objectives. Whether this public involvement is related to community policing (Beito, 1999) or to paying greater attention to domestic violence issues (Melton, 1999), community participation stimulates organizational effectiveness at all levels.

In a general sense, the following kinds of things can be done to improve law enforcement effectiveness:

1. Utilize the latest technological developments for crime detection and prevention
2. Devise more effective programming with an emphasis on greater social skills and human relations for law enforcement academy training
3. Create greater opportunities for ethnic and racial diversity in selection and recruitment practices in all agencies
4. Emphasize multilingual ability as a recruit requirement or at least as a desirable characteristic for new recruits in any agency
5. Promote greater interagency information exchanges concerning criminals and crimes
6. Incorporate greater educational emphasis in training programs, with a special emphasis on due process rights of citizens and their rights under different constitutional amendments
7. Require officers to become familiar with the latest changes in U.S. Supreme Court decisions relating to law enforcement and evidentiary matters in criminal prosecutions
8. Require greater involvement in anger management courses for officers, including alternative ways of coping with stressful encounters with citizens
9. Encourage greater involvement in community activities for officers in all agencies
10. Work toward promoting greater respect for the law from within agencies at all levels in order to reduce corruption or misconduct (although it is unrealistic to expect that corruption and misconduct will ever vanish)
11. Create powerful review commissions and review boards with real powers to dole out sanctions when officers violate their codes of conduct or the laws they are expected to enforce

MEASURING THE EFFECTIVENESS OF PROSECUTORS AND COURTS

As was the case with law enforcement, the *Sourcebook of Criminal Justice Statistics* and other documents publish a great deal of information annually about criminal prosecutions and courts. For instance, we know how many cases of particular types are prosecuted, how many are plea-bargained, how many go to trial and are won or lost, how many judges are recalled or sanctioned, and what the conviction rates of prosecutors in different jurisdictions are. It is fairly easy to count the numbers of prosecuted cases, the numbers of convictions, the numbers of sentences, the sentence lengths, the use of probation and parole, and the nature and use of alternative or intermediate sanctions and their consequences. We also can easily determine the recidivism rates of persons placed on probation or parole, and thus, we have a reasonable idea of the relationship between incarceration lengths, places of incarceration (jails or prisons), and offender recidivism.

We have very specific information about the different types of sentencing systems used in the various states and federal government. We know if certain sentencing schemes have greater deterrent value than others, and we also know if judicial decision making is controlled in more or less rigorous ways under these different schemes. The fact is that there are numerous ways of counting things related to criminal prosecutions and judicial decision making.

But as we found out when attempting to assess law enforcement agency effectiveness, the criteria that are generally applicable to *all* courts and *all* prosecutors are often elusive and/or abstract. Again, it may be profitable for us to examine prosecutors in specific jurisdictions or particular types of courts at different points in time rather than to engage in broad or sweeping generalizations of prosecutors or court systems. Several examples from the research literature are instructive in this regard.

In recent years, because of the substantial increase in the use of illegal drugs, specialized courts have been created in different jurisdictions to handle drug cases exclusively. These courts are known as drug courts. Several drug court programs were launched in 1993 in

Florida's First Judicial Circuit, encompassing Escambia and Okaloosa Counties (Peters and Murrin, 2000). The drug courts established in Florida (and elsewhere subsequently) are designed for nonviolent offenders with a history of drug involvement and of limited criminal justice involvement. During a four-year period, 226 drug court participants were compared with an equal number of other drug offenders processed by courts outside of these Florida counties and with other types of offenders involving non–drug-related offenses. The drug court participants were given comprehensive psychosocial assessments and participated in a one-year multimodel treatment program consisting of individual and group counseling, peer support groups, community support and aftercare groups, and referral to mental health and other ancillary services. Subsequent comparisons between the two groups (e.g., the drug court graduates and the non–drug court graduates) disclosed that the drug court graduates were less likely to be arrested and had fewer arrests during a 30-month follow-up compared with matched sets of probationers and nongraduates. Drug court graduates also had lower rates of substance abuse compared with other groups of arrested offenders who had drug involvement. At least in the Florida experiment, the specialized drug courts and sentencing practices of judges appeared successful in realizing the goals of reducing recidivism of offenders relating to illicit drug use and remaining law abiding. Thus, these drug courts were deemed effective.

In an earlier investigation of DWI/DUI offenders in Maryland, Hardenbergh et al. (1990) studied 2,000 DWI/DUI offenders who had been convicted by judges from 1985 to 1987. Follow-ups through 1989 showed that 20 percent of these offenders were rearrested for DWI/DUI offenses. The study did not consider these recidivism figures impressive. The researchers recommended specific steps to be taken by judges in future dispositions of DWI/DUI cases: (1) Local jurisdictions should develop, and judges should use, DWI detention facilities in conjunction with follow-up aftercare and supervision; (2) local jurisdictions should make available, and judges should use as a sentencing option, alcohol ignition interlock devices on vehicles registered to offenders; (3) Maryland should pursue options to curtail the frequent use of jury trials in circuit court; (4) consideration should be given to legislating a three-tiered DWI offense, so that habitual offenders would be charged with a felony in circuit court; and (5) the district court should establish time standards and realistic goals for reducing delay in DWI/DUI cases. In fact, the original study data could be regarded as extremely successful, inasmuch as 80 percent of the DWI/DUI cases *did not result in further recidivism.* Sometimes researchers themselves are their worst critics when they do not deserve to be. In this Maryland study, most investigators would probably regard the program used as a success because of the high nonrecidivism rate! Judges would receive high ratings for their judgments involving dispositions of alcohol- and drug-related traffic offenses.

In another study, Norman and Wadman (2000) wanted to know if samples of Utah prosecutors and judges actually read the contents of presentence investigation reports (PSIs) prepared for different kinds of offenders prior to recommending or imposing sentences. A sample of 227 district court judges and prosecutors were asked if they actually read the full contents of PSI reports, which contain valuable and important information about the factors related to the current offense; the offender's prior record, if any; culpability in relation to the crime; harm done to victims; and risk assessment characteristics such as gang affiliation and substance abuse problems. Nearly half (45 percent) of all respondents indicated that they merely skimmed the PSI reports of convicted offenders and did not familiarize themselves fully with the report contents. Thus, both prosecutors and judges were affected by inaccuracies of various kinds, including unfair readings of the offenses and other aspects that resulted in a lack of objectivity. The PSI report information would have been quite helpful to prosecutors in formulating more appropriate sentencing recommendations as well as to judges in deciding on the sentences actually imposed on convicted offenders. In this particular study, we might assign the grade of "F" to those prosecutors and judges who admitted to not reading a critical piece of sentencing information, the PSI report. This was an integral part of their jobs as prosecutors and judges, and they failed to do their jobs properly. How much damage actually was caused to convicted offenders as the result of this significant neglect of their duties is unknown, but we can speculate that at least *some* damage was caused by this negligence. At least in this Utah case, this is serious indictment against those judges and prosecutors and the performance quality shown their jobs.

Are judges effective when they impose restitution orders that remain unpaid? In a study of restitution orders imposed by judges in Allegheny County, Pennsylvania, Outlaw and Ruback (1999) studied 904 probation and court records from 1994. They determined that judges generally imposed restitution orders on convicted offenders when damages were easy to calculate. Offenders were also more likely to pay restitution when they had the financial ability to pay. They also paid restitution more regularly when the victim was a business, such as Sears or Target. Those failing to make restitution most often were rearrested, but not because of their inability to pay. Rather, rearrest was closely associated with not being integrated into the community and with being unmarried, unemployed, and young. The clear implication of this research was that judges were not using their punishment powers prudently; that is, they were not devising creative sentences for those unable to pay restitution. After all, alternative means are available for offenders to work off restitution orders, including various forms of community service and nonmonetary forms of victim compensation.

In each of these cases, investigators examined procedures and protocol that were or were not followed by different courtroom actors. The results were or were not effective, depending on what was eventually found. But one value of these smaller-scale studies is that they direct our attention to specific ways in which prosecutors and judges can be evaluated to determine if they are effective. Is it reasonable for us to have general and universal expectations of prosecutors and judges throughout the United States, regardless of the jurisdiction?

What Is Expected of Prosecutors and Judges?

From previous descriptions of the roles of prosecutors and judges, we think we have a fairly good idea of what is expected of them. Several core functions of prosecutors in almost every U.S. jurisdiction can be delineated. The functions of prosecutors at the local, state, and federal levels include, but are not limited to, the following: (1) deciding or screening cases slotted for prosecution, (2) representing the government in presenting cases against suspects before the grand jury, (3) conferring with police participating in the initial arrest and ensuring the suspect's right to due process, (4) evaluating the sufficiency of evidence against the accused, (5) conferring with defense attorneys in pretrial conferences in an effort to avoid a trial proceeding, and (6) presenting the case against the defendant in court.

If we examine the duties and responsibilities of U.S. attorneys and their assistants in federal district courts, we discover the following list of functions:

1. Prosecute all offenses against the United States
2. Prosecute or defend for the government all actions, suits, or proceedings in which the United States is concerned
3. Appear on behalf of the defendants in civil actions and suits or proceedings pending in his or her district against collectors or other officers of the revenue or customs for any act done by them or for the recovery of any money exacted by or paid to these officers
4. Institute and prosecute proceedings for the collection of fines, penalties, and forfeitures incurred for violation of any revenue law
5. Make such reports as the attorney general may direct

A similar core set of expectations for judges exists in most jurisdictions. These functions or expectations are as follows: (1) They are required to decide conflicting contentions of law and disputed issues of fact, (2) they are required to formulate sanctions and remedial orders, and (3) they are required to supervise the activity of persons subject to the authority of the court.

In federal district courts, federal judges are expected to do the following:

1. Hear all civil actions in which the matter exceeds $10,000 and arises under the laws, Constitution, or treaties of the United States
2. Try diversity of citizenship matters and determine amounts in controversy and costs
3. Entertain bankruptcy matters and proceedings
4. Hear interpleaders or third-party complaints
5. Enforce ICC orders
6. Hear commerce and antitrust suits
7. Hear cases involving patents, copyrights, trademarks, and charges of unfair commercial competition
8. Hear internal revenue cases and customs duty matters
9. Judge tax matters by states
10. Hear civil rights cases
11. Hear matters in which the United States is a plaintiff or defendant

These expectations are clear enough. We can decide if prosecutors fail to perform one or more of their functions. We can determine if judges fail to act in ways directed by their offices. Since a majority of prosecutorial and judicial selections in the United States today are conducted through either partisan or nonpartisan elections, the public may be able to measure how effectively particular court actors are doing their jobs by reelecting them or by electing others to take their places. But it is not always that easy. Incumbent prosecutors and judges tend to have several advantages over their opponents, and thus, with persistent frequency, even incompetent or corrupt prosecutors and judges get reelected.

In the case of judges, the Center for Judicial Conduct Organizations conducts annual surveys of all state agencies that are mandated by legislative action to receive, investigate, and dispose of complaints regarding judicial misconduct, including judicial corruption. In 1997, for instance, there were 12,906 state judges that had complaints filed against them for a variety of reasons. About 2,318 complaints had been carried over from 1996, and thus 10,588 new complaints were received. By the end of 1997, 2,330 complaints were unresolved. The number of *dismissed complaints* during 1997 was 9,856, or 76 percent of all complaints. Informal sanctions short of removal from office were lodged against 551 (24 percent) of the judges whose cases had not been dismissed (including those in which the formal complaints had been dismissed), and 111 judges (4.7 percent) had vacated their offices by the end of 1997 (Maguire and Pastore, 2000:450–451). Only eight judges were suspended from their state offices during 1997, and only four judges were actually removed from office that same year. About 140 judges received private censure from their state judicial organizations, whereas about 65 judges received some form of public censure. Therefore, if the public wants to lodge complaints against judges for misconduct or corruption, the outcomes clearly favor judges.

For both prosecutors and judges, some cases have moved forward to indictments against these public officials for abuses of their offices. In 1996, for instance, 984 indictments were brought against judges and prosecutors, resulting in 902 convictions, a conviction rate of 91.6 percent. The conviction rate against federal judges and prosecutors who were indicted during 1996 was nearly 100 percent. For state or local judicial officials and prosecutors, the rate of convictions was about 45 percent (Maguire and Pastore, 2000:457). But a significant gap can be seen in the numbers of complaints against judges and prosecutors and the number of indictments of them. Complaints seldom lead to indictments.

How Can We Improve the Effectiveness of Prosecutors and Judges?

Improving the effectiveness of prosecutors and judges may be accomplished by the following general mechanisms:

PROSECUTORS

1. More selective screenings of cases for prosecution
2. More selective screenings of those running for prosecutorial offices, including more stringent background requirements and qualifications
3. Development of a review process for cases lost to determine if evidence against accused defendants was sufficient initially to justify the prosecution
4. Greater public accountability through independent complaint review boards similar to those for law enforcement agencies
5. Removal of immunity of prosecutors from lawsuits brought by defendants
6. Greater resources to hire more prosecutors to prosecute those cases meriting prosecution
7. Establishment of a public information medium to alert citizens to the extensive use of plea bargaining and how it is used specifically in each jurisdiction in order to heighten the accountability of prosecutors who enter into questionable plea bargain agreements
8. Mandatory review of all plea agreements by judges with the stipulation that prosecutors show how their cases could have been proved beyond a reasonable doubt in court if the case had gone to trial

JUDGES

1. Establishment of independent citizen complaint review boards (similar to those for law enforcement agencies) with real power to sanction judges when complaints are filed against them
2. Requirements that judges have formal legal expertise in order to qualify for their elected or appointed positions
3. Mandatory educational courses for judges on a continuing basis to enable them to keep up with

current legal developments relating to their state supreme court and U.S. Supreme Court decisions

4. Removal of immunity of judges from lawsuits brought by defendants

5. Expansion of the numbers of judges in different jurisdictions to process the increasing number of cases prosecuted

6. Caseload limitations for all judges, requiring election or appointment of additional judges when caseloads for existing judges are exceeded

MEASURING THE EFFECTIVENESS OF CORRECTIONS

For many critics of corrections, the word *corrections* is a misnomer. This is because in a majority of instances, those who enter the corrections process as convicted offenders are never corrected. Approximately 60 to 65 percent of those released into probation or parole programs each year commit new crimes or have their probation or parole programs revoked within a 24-month to 36-month period (Maguire and Pastore, 2000). The positive side is that about 35 to 40 percent of those released into these programs each year do not recidivate, or at least if they do commit new offenses, they are not detected or caught by police.

But if we were to measure the effectiveness of corrections, we would probably give it a low grade. There are numerous correctional programs throughout the United States. Many federal and state institutions have state-of-the-art facilities and programs aimed at helping inmates to improve their educational, vocational, social, and emotional skills. Community-based corrections, accommodating the lion's share of convicted offenders, boasts thousands of programs designed to provide various forms of educational, vocational, psychological, and social assistance for those in need. However, if we step back and take a long view of the correctional landscape, we might be disappointed generally by what we see. Again, a lesser unit or level of analysis might be more useful to measure the effectiveness of corrections.

The following pages encompass a brief investigation of corrections and its different components. We can look at corrections from an institutional view, which includes prisons and jails. This provides a rather simplistic analysis:

INSTITUTIONAL CORRECTIONS
Prisons
Jails

But these broad categorizations fail to capture certain intricacies of prison and jail organization. We might find the following detail more informative:

INSTITUTIONAL CORRECTIONS
Prisons (State or Federal)
Admin Max or Maxi-Maxi
Maximum Security
Medium Security
Minimum Security
Jails (City, County, or State Operated)
Mega Jails
Large Jails
Medium Jails
Small Jails
Holding Facilities
Drunk Tanks

In a similar manner, we can divide noninstitutional corrections into the following categories:

NONINSTITUTIONAL CORRECTIONS
Probation
Parole

But this simplified and overly broad categorization fails to include the intricacies of community-based corrections. A more detailed breakdown is as follows:

NONINSTITUTIONAL CORRECTIONS
Alternative Dispute Resolution
Diversion
Standard
Conditional
Probation
Standard
Conditional
Intensive Supervised Probation (Intensive Probation Supervision)
Home Confinement
Electronic Monitoring
Home Confinement with Electronic Monitoring
Boot Camps

Preparole, Prerelease

Work Release

Study Release

Furloughs

Parole (Supervised Release)

Halfway Houses

Intensive Supervised Parole (Intensive Parole Supervision)

Home Confinement

Electronic Monitoring

Home Confinement with Electronic Monitoring

Boot Camps

These lists are not exhaustive. For *all* of the noninstitutional programming mentioned, we also can include the following additional elements: fines, day fines, community service, victim restitution, restorative justice, day reporting programs, participation in individual or group counseling, participation in educational or vocational programming, employment, observance of curfews, and drug and alcohol checks.

Indeed, it is a much more complex picture of corrections than we originally imagined. What is it that we say "fails" if recidivism rates are too high? Which programs do we include? Which administrators are at fault (Wright, 1994)? It is clear that in order to criticize corrections, our criticisms must be couched in rather specific terms and refer to specific subparts of whatever it is we are criticizing. There are, of course, some exceptions. An ambitious study was conducted of the effectiveness of correctional treatment for sexual offenders, violent offenders, and drug addicts by Emth Beenakkers (2000). Beenakkers conducted his study by reviewing the "North American literature" concerning these subjects, somewhat of a meta-analysis, a research technique in which a broad spectrum of applicable literature is studied to find parallels in various studies of the same subject. Beenakkers concluded that programs based on cognitive-behavioral principles appeared to be more effective. Successful features of these programs included a theoretically sound concept, program integrity, competent staff in a structured setting, thorough assessment that targets the offender's specific criminogenic needs, intensive service for high-risk delinquents, and relapse prevention and aftercare. Beenakkers's survey is not clear about what program integrity actually is, nor is it obvious which programs are founded on cognitive-behavioral principles. None

of this material is put into a measurable, useful operational context. Essentially, the survey provides a sweeping set of generalizations gleaned from the literature of others that is of questionable application value. Some examples of meta-analysis may be less useful than others that provide more specific information about measurable data. Meta-analyses will be studied in more detail later in this chapter.

It is beyond the scope of this book to do a detailed critique of each and every one of these institutional and noninstitutional programs for convicted (and nonconvicted) offenders. Rather, the point is to recognize the incredible diversity of corrections that exists before we make sweeping generalizations about it. Some examples from the research literature illustrate analyses of correctional effectiveness of some limited scope.

A study of the effectiveness of prison rehabilitation programs was undertaken by Lin (2000). Data were examined based on an inspection of rehabilitation programs in existence at four different federal correctional institutions and one state prison, with 354 interviews gathered from staff members and inmates. These interviews were supplemented with direct observation of these settings by Lin and her assistants. She studied literacy and high school equivalency classes, vocational training, pay-for-performance assignments in prison industries, and intensive drug treatment. Interestingly, Lin found mixed results, mostly because of the diverse views taken of the programs by different prison personnel. For instance, she said that staff members tried to understand their jobs as a series of related tasks all bent toward the same purpose. In cases in which programs were believed by staff to be incompatible with that purpose (given particular inmate involvement), the program goals tended to be subverted, abandoned, or neglected. Thus, Lin found both successful and unsuccessful programs in the five prison settings she studied. Success was measured in different ways, but graduating from different activities with passing grades or high marks from instructional or vocational staff was regarded as a suitable evaluative criterion. Was Lin's study representative or typical of *all* prison rehabilitation programs in the United States? No. In fact, her research only scratched the surface, considering the several thousand state and federal prisons in the United States that could have been studied with a larger research staff and considerably more funding.

Some studies examine correctional effectiveness purely on the basis of dollars and cents. A study by

Pratt and Winston (1999) was conducted to study the efficiency hypothesis of public choice theory in a juvenile corrections setting. The hypothesis holds that private entities will be more efficient providers of correctional services than their public counterparts. Data were collected from 635 public and 2,126 private juvenile institutions across the United States from published sources. These researchers concluded that based on their examination of this secondary-source information, private correctional facilities for juveniles were no more cost-effective than public facilities. However, specific types of private institutions (e.g., low-security, non–detention center institutions such as halfway houses and shelters) tended to be more cost-effective under private management. Did these institutions cure any delinquents? What were the recidivism rates of follow-up studies? These and other similar questions were left unanswered because the focus of the study was strictly on the operating costs of these institutions, whether public or private. What does it mean to be "a more efficient provider of correctional services"? Does this mean hiring correctional officers and teachers who will work for less pay and attempt to deliver services of comparable quality to those types of employees holding out for higher pay? Does this mean that the laundry and medical costs of certain types of facilities housing equal numbers of juvenile offenders are lower for particular types of institutions (private) than others (public)? What does any of this have to do with rehabilitating juvenile offenders or reducing delinquency? In what respects are these institutions effective, and at what?

It is clear that evaluating the effectiveness of corrections requires specificity, and a great deal of it. In the 1990s and into the 2000s, a research technique known as **meta-analysis** has been applied increasingly as a means of reviewing large numbers of research investigations and drawing tentative conclusions about them. The Beenakkers (2000) study reported previously was conducted using meta-analysis. Meta-analysis seeks to understand programs and their relative effectiveness by examining large numbers of them at a single point in time. For instance, Latessa, Jones, and Fulton (1999) conducted a meta-analysis of 28 Ohio juvenile justice programs. They were interested in learning about effective intervention and its relation to delinquency reduction. Effective intervention was defined by these researchers as (1) intensive; (2) offering behavioral services focused on higher-risk offenders; (3) having a qualified, fair,

firm staff enforcing behavioral strategies; (4) targeting criminogenic needs and aiming to disrupt criminal networks; (5) addressing relapse prevention in the community; and (6) providing high levels of advocacy and brokerage. They found that of the 28 programs studied, 39 percent (11 programs) met fewer than half of these criteria for effectiveness. Over 35 percent of the programs (10 programs) conformed to at least 60 percent of these principles, however. Several previously evaluated programs showed marked improvement from prior years.

What Is Expected of Corrections?

Several approaches can be used to answer the question of what is expected of corrections. What does the general public expect? What do convicted offenders expect? What do prison and jail administrators expect? What do managers of probation and parole offices as well as the officers themselves expect? What do community-based correctional officials and workers expect? What do city, county, state, and government general accounting agencies expect (Casarez, 1995)?

A legislative report was released in 1989 that pertained to correctional expenditures for the state of Tennessee (Tennessee Select Oversight Committee on Corrections, 1989). The Tennessee Select Oversight Committee on Corrections reported that in 1988, Tennessee spent nearly $50 million for the housing of over 4,000 felons in local jails, representing a substantial increase from expenditures of $13 million for 2,000 prisoners in 1984. Calling attention to its increasing scarcity of resources, the committee recommended that Tennessee should establish a coherent system of punishments that allocates the resources of the state and local governments so that the state prison system can be reserved for the most serious and dangerous offenders. Their commentary also included the observation that continued use of certain local systems (e.g., community-based corrections) for diversion is a wise use of resources and eliminates an unnecessary duplication of capital and operational costs. The report concluded that a successfully implemented system of voluntary contracts could divert at least 2,500 felons from the state system, thereby achieving savings for both state and local governments. They recommended also that new methods of sentencing should be implemented, including intensive discipline, work, and treatment, and that these programs should be evaluated for their impact on recidivism and cost-effectiveness. Thus, at least this Tennessee committee was concerned almost exclusively with the dollar cost of housing varying numbers of inmates and alternative means of supervising them. Is this an example of what is expected of corrections?

In a more recent study, Jones and Harris (1999) devised an empirically based typology for placing delinquent youths most effectively in Philadelphia, Pennsylvania. These researchers believed that their newly devised typology would enable juvenile corrections authorities to make more effective placements of juveniles in different types of facilities, thus raising the predictability of program effectiveness for affected juveniles. Their typology, labeled Pro-Des, is an outcome-based personality assessment system using four standardized, self-reported personality scales that comprise 14 subscales and form the basis of the typology. Thus, this study focused on devising a better measure of program placement for youthful offenders as a means of improving treatment or intervention program effectiveness. We might view the work of Jones and Harris as one means to achieve a measurable correctional objective, something related to rehabilitation and/or reintegration.

A more direct investigation of what is known about the effectiveness of adult correctional programs in Canada and the United States was undertaken by Phipps et al. (1999). Phipps and her colleagues focused on those factors most closely associated with reducing recidivism among adult offenders. They investigated both institutional and community-based correctional programs, focusing on substance abuse treatment, education, employment, sex offender treatment, cognitive behavioral treatment, life skills training, and intensive supervision. Their results were mixed. They found that only some of the programs actually reduced predicted recidivism by about 10 to 15 percent. Other programs simply had not been evaluated sufficiently or rigorously enough to make any determination of their impact on offender recidivism. The conclusion reached by Phipps and her colleagues was that most programs had not been evaluated, which makes it impossible to answer questions about which correctional programs are effective.

In at least one study, researchers evaluated the effectiveness of counseling services for a sample of adjudicated juvenile delinquents (Kadish et al., 1999). The Juvenile Counseling and Assessment Program (JCAP) of the Juvenile Court of Clarke County, Pennsylvania, involved 55 adjudicated youths, ages 9 to 17, who participated in individual and group counseling over a 4-month to 6-month period. The program exposed youths to anger management training, social skills training, and lifestyle and career decision training, and it helped them to deal with situations that may have caused them to get into trouble in past years. The sample was compared with a matched control group of other adjudicated offenders who did not participate in JCAP. Only 25 percent of the JCAP youths were found to have reoffended in a follow-up period, compared with a recidivism rate of 64 percent for the non-JCAP youths. In this instance, the various interventions appeared successful at reducing recidivism rates, and by substantial margins. Certainly this is a correctional goal and one that appears to be achieved, at least in the present research.

In general, the goals of corrections are (1) retribution, (2) deterrence or prevention, (3) incapacitation or isolation, (4) rehabilitation, (5) reintegration, and (6) control. These have not necessarily been listed in the order of their priority for any correctional system or program. Nevertheless, some are more important than others under certain circumstances. For instance, incapacitation or isolation is a very important expectation of corrections for those offenders who are likely to endanger others (Henderson, Raugh, and Phillips, 1997). Many prisons such as the maximum-security federal penitentiary at Marion, Illinois, isolate prisoners in solitary confinement for 23½ hours per day. These offenders are considered the "baddest of the bad" and undeserving of the privilege of mingling with other prisoners in common social areas such as recreational yards.

Reintegration is definitely expected of those offenders who participate in work or study release programs or who are granted furloughs from prisons shortly before they are to be paroled back into society. Reintegration is also a key expectation of halfway houses and other community-based facilities (Hurley et al., 1996).

Within correctional institutions, rehabilitation has not been entirely abandoned. For about 20 percent of all prisoners in U.S. penitentiaries, opportunities exist for employment in prison industries. Many prisoners engage in constructive and useful activities that improve their job skills and make them more employable when they are released in future years. Various vocational, educational, and individual/group therapy programs are operated in prisons and in some large jails as means of enabling offenders to become rehabilitated. Although prisoners do not have an absolute right to rehabilitation, the opportunity for some of them to become rehabilitated while in prison nevertheless exists (Florida Office of Program Policy Analysis and Government Accountability, 1996b).

In community-based corrections, including probation and parole services, one primary expectation is that offenders will be controlled to some degree. But it is absolutely impossible for *any* community program to control offender behavior 24 hours a day, seven days a week. Thus, community-based agencies and probation and parole officials, including judges and parole boards, attempt to make effective placement of persons who are most likely to succeed and become law abiding. But as we have seen, a 65 percent recidivism rate is associated with most community programs within a three-year follow-up period. No program is foolproof. Therefore, a major objective of corrections is to reduce the likelihood of recidivism, and not to eliminate it entirely.

How Can Corrections Effectiveness Be Improved?

Correctional effectiveness can be improved in different ways, including the following:

1. Make educational and vocational programming a mandatory part of an inmate's prison sentence

2. Expand correctional budgets to provide adequate personnel to deliver the services required to fulfill inmate needs

3. Upgrade the educational requirements of all persons working with inmates and/or clients in institutional and community-based corrections

4. Require mandatory educational instruction on the latest developments in correctional law for corrections officers

5. Require mandatory anger management training and instruction on ethnic diversity for corrections officers

6. Enforce minimal educational and correctional training requirements for all corrections personnel, including volunteers and paraprofessionals who interact with clients in community-based corrections settings

7. Require mandatory refresher courses and programs for corrections personnel on a regular basis in order to introduce the latest correctional concepts and strategies for offender management

8. Establish rigorous selection requirements for any personnel who work with inmates or clients, including intensive psychological screenings and qualifying interviews

9. Establish inmate/client complaint review boards to investigate inmate or client complaints against programs, staff, or other inmates

10. Conduct regular performance evaluations of staff and administration based on independent reviews and observations by external sources, including groups of citizens and public officials, and make continuation of employment contingent on favorable performance reviews

11. Create an accountability mechanism for each institutional and community-based facility to conduct regular evaluations of staff and administrative performance

12. Provide sufficient resources within institutions and communities to enable inmates and clients who want to work an opportunity to do so

13. Establish effective networks of businesspersons and community representatives to place offenders once they are relocated within their communities

14. Furnish all inmates/clients with sufficient support services and opportunities for self-improvement

15. Segregate mentally ill or incapacitated offenders from the general inmate population and work with these persons on a one-to-one basis in order to enhance their treatment and personal improvement

16. Develop job assistance bureaus within and outside prisons to enable those looking for work to find it

17. Develop powerful incentives for advancement of corrections personnel featuring educational and professional advancement through attendance and/or participation in workshops, conferences, and other meetings of relevance to practitioners

18. Establish accreditation procedures, such as those promulgated by the American Correctional Association, as means of creating and perpetuating standards of excellence at all administrative levels

HEIGHTENING THE ACCOUNTABILITY OF CRIMINAL JUSTICE ACTORS AND AGENCIES

Perhaps the most important component in any strategy to improve organizational performance, effectiveness, or efficiency and maximize goal attainment is heightening the accountability of both offices and individuals in these organizations, whatever they may be (Florida Office of Program Policy Analysis and Government Accountability, 1996a; Hurley et al., 1996; Petersilia, 1999; Volcansek, 1993). Accountability means that someone or some office is responsible to another person or office for the work performed or the level of efficiency or effectiveness achieved.

When family court judges make child custody decisions that favor one party over another, the losing party sometimes claims that family court judges need to be more accountable for their actions. When prison or jail inmates are assaulted, raped, or killed, someone may say that correctional officers or the correctional administration itself needs to be more accountable for their or its actions. When prosecutors fail to get convictions against organized crime figures or persons who have been charged with especially heinous offenses, the public outcry often includes rhetoric about heightening the accountability of prosecutors. Judges who downgrade serious charges to less serious ones and approve generous plea bargain agreements also should be more accountable, according to critics of plea bargaining. When probationers or parolees or home confinement/electronically monitored clients commit violent crimes while free within their communities, the public wants to hold those responsible (i.e., the probation officers, the parole officers, the community-based correctional staffs) more accountable.

In law enforcement, for example, although there have been more egregious incidents since then, the Rodney King beating in 1992 by officers of the Los Angeles Police Department led to the establishment of the Christopher Commission, whose mission it was to assign responsibility and accountability for the incident (Hanson et al., 1992). Ultimately, several officers were convicted of violating Rodney King's civil rights under color of law. Subsequently, numerous civil and criminal actions have been initiated against police officers and police administrators in many jurisdictions throughout the United States. Many of these actions have been commenced by persons or relatives of persons who believe that one or more of their constitutional rights have been violated by the police. These suits name either specific police officers or specific police agencies or both, and many suits allege that these agencies and their representatives have misused their authority or applied excessive force against citizens (Lynch, 1999; Major City Chiefs Administrators, 1994).

Various steps have been taken and procedures have been implemented to hold police officers and their administrators to account when citizen complaints of police abuse are alleged (Coles, Thacher, and Sheingold, 1998; Lersch and Mieczkowski, 2000). But the general impact of citizen complaint review boards and other mechanisms of accountability that have been established to investigate and punish police misconduct and/or corruption has been ineffective (DeLeon-Granados and Wells, 1998; Fyfe, 1998; Green, 1999; Iris, 1998). But relatively little has been done to protect the public against police abuses of authority, except under the most blatant circumstances (Human Rights Watch, 1998; Lersch, 1998a, 1998b; Walker, 1998; Walker and Graham, 1998).

One solution that appears to be working in some jurisdictions is the creation of workshops in which facilitators bring together police and citizen groups for open discussions of issues relevant to police abuse of authority. The intent of these action education workshops is to heighten law enforcement accountability (Keleher, 1997).

Also in some jurisdictions, police officers and other sworn law enforcement personnel who have been found guilty of abuses of their authority have been decertified as officers. Decertification is the equivalent of losing one's license to carry firearms or hold law enforcement positions (Puro, Goldman, and Smith, 1997). The decertification process seems to work in selected jurisdictions. For instance, a study was conducted of the cases of 3,884 officers who were referred to the decertification process during the period from 1990 to 1995 (Trautman, 1997). Disciplinary measures were meted out to 3,104 of these officers, and 2,296 officers were totally decertified. The decertified officers had an average of seven years of service as police officers. The most frequent reasons for decertification included filing false statements or reports, larceny, and sex offenses.

Heightening the accountability of prosecutors and the judiciary is an even more difficult task. In 1996, for instance, over 95 percent of all state prosecutors were elected officials, and many of them had been reelected several times (DeFrances and Steadman, 1998). Judicial appointments were largely made through partisan and nonpartisan elections, and the terms of judicial appointments were fairly lengthy (Blankenship, Sparger, and Janikowski, 1994). Under extraordinary circumstances, some judges have been recalled (Wold and Culver, 1987). But as we saw earlier, it is difficult to sanction the judiciary effectively. The vast majority of complaints filed against prosecutors and judges are routinely dismissed by investigative bodies and oversight committees (Maguire and Pastore, 2000). One monitoring method used in selected jurisdictions in the United States has been dubbed the court watchers method. **Court watchers** are persons who sit in courtrooms and observe judicial decision making. Subsequently, they make reports to central locations of judicial decisions and this information is analyzed and a determination is made that certain judges are handing out disparate sentences. These reports are transmitted to the media, who may or may not give these reports credibility or coverage (Court Watchers, 1982).

Prosecutors have almost unlimited discretion in their charging decisions. Seldom do prosecutors' charging decisions get reviewed by any investigative panel to ensure that they have fulfilled the requirements of the law. Because of the highly political nature of their appointments, it is likely that a strong element of subjectivity exists when deciding which cases to pursue and which ones to drop. Judges are even more insulated from public criticism. The judicial system of appeals is founded on the principle that a lower-court decision is considered the correct one by a higher, appellate court. Thus, appellants find it very difficult to overcome the presumption of a judge's correctness in decision making and sentencing when appealing cases to higher courts.

One major concern about the judiciary arises from victims' interest groups. For instance, Turman (1998) has articulated 14 different judiciary recommendations that relate in one way or another to victims and victims' rights. Selected recommendations include the following: (1) Judges should play a leadership role in ensuring that police, prosecutors, defense counsel, judges, and court administrators receive joint training so that all have a comprehensive picture of what happens to a victim as he or she navigates through the criminal justice system; (2) judges should order restitution from offenders to help compensate victims for the harm they have suffered; and (3) codes of judicial conduct should be amended to reflect the fact that crime victims play a pivotal role in the criminal justice system.

Many attempts have been made to reform the judiciary and how it is organized. But investigators have found that making recommendations and seeing them implemented effectively are two entirely different concepts (Matsch, 1996). Research has concluded that appointment methods for judicial selection are no better than election methods in placing qualified judges on the bench. Thus, it is incumbent on policy makers to publicly proclaim the limitations of judicial selection in order to create reasonable expectations regarding judicial performance (Blankenship, Spargar, and Janikowski, 1994).

In corrections, staff accountability can be heightened by reviewing the progress of offender-clients in community-based agencies and the frequency of inmate complaints directed toward prison staff in institutional corrections. But for both law enforcement, especially the rank and file, and the large contingent of correctional officers, powerful unions exist that create effective barriers and often shield these officers from needed sanctions.

CODES OF ETHICS AND STANDARDS OF PROFESSIONAL RESPONSIBILITY

We have examined codes of ethics devised for law enforcement officers in earlier chapters. All law enforcement officers who graduate from academy training are sworn to uphold the law and observe articulated ethical standards of conduct while performing their duties. In fact, the existence of a code of ethics was described earlier as one indicator of professionalism.

The development of a code of ethics for police officers is not new. Orlando W. Wilson, a former police chief, criminology professor, consultant, and author, promoted a code of ethics from the beginning of his career in 1921 in California (Bopp, 1975). Wilson is considered to be the father of the Law Enforcement Code of Ethics. He founded the first police college cadet academy program, pioneered state-sponsored training courses and minimum standards for police personnel, and initiated psychological testing for selecting new police recruits. Despite his efforts, police officers in different agencies throughout the United States have sometimes not taken these codes of ethics seriously. From time to time, critics of police conduct feel inclined to remind officers and the general public of the existence of this code of ethics and how much it should be respected and followed (Felkenes, 1984; Law Enforcement Association on Professional Standards, Education, and Ethical Practice, 1972).

Some persons actively oppose the development of codes of ethics for their professions. This does not mean that they do not believe in ethics or do not think that ethics should guide decision making, but rather, that alternative ways of ensuring correct behavior exist besides codes of ethics. For instance, Michael Davis (1991) says that we do not need ethical codes for police officers merely because police use unnecessary force. He says that closer supervision, harsher discipline, less pressure from above for results, and alternative methods for handling problem situations would reduce police brutality more than any code that simply restates ordinary morality. Davis makes some good suggestions. He recommends that police officers should perform less undercover work, which seems to make officers more susceptible to corruption and graft over time. Furthermore, officers should work shorter and less irregular hours. Ultimately, argues Davis, police officers will become more interested in the professional responsibilities of their fellow officers rather than in their own conduct, which will be more controlled and law abiding.

Codes of ethics are not restricted to law enforcement agencies, however. Among prosecutors and judges, a code of ethical conduct also exists (Carr, 1995). The American Bar Association has promulgated rules of conduct that most prosecutors and judges are expected to observe (Hewitt, Gallas, and Mahoney, 1990). Although the American Bar Association has no direct removal authority, it still can make recommendations and observations to citizen groups and public officials in power to perhaps influence prosecutorial and judicial conduct.

The American Bar Association together with the National District Attorneys Association have evolved a Code of Professional Responsibility. Thus, if prosecutors make improper prosecutorial remarks during an argument to a jury during a trial, they may suffer a verbal rebuke from the judge. But other than that, they suffer little or no formal sanctions. One sanction that discourages errors is more frequent reversal of criminal convictions in which prosecutorial and/or judicial misconduct has adversely affected the verdict (Page, 1993; Volcansek and deFranciscis, 1996). Trial courts also can become more active in supervising the conduct of counsel and can curtail the fair reply doctrine. Prosecutors who continually transgress the limits of proper argument can be condemned by their peers. Furthermore, continuing legal education for both prosecutors and judges can discourage improper prosecutorial argument (Celebrezze, 1987).

Some people within the legal community are of the opinion that the incidence of unethical prosecutor-

ial practices is small, and thus, there is a tendency to ignore these unethical practices when they do occur. Judges are too often relied on to rectify prosecutorial errors of misconduct. But often these matters are beyond the scope of judicial review (Freedman, 1967). Six common practices raise questions about prosecutorial professional responsibility: (1) cases in which the primary motive for prosecution relates to matters other than the crime for which the defendant is being prosecuted; (2) various plea bargaining tactics that are beyond court supervision; (3) condoning and covering up police abuses; (4) suppression of evidence, introduction of misleading evidence, and coercion of witnesses; (5) attempts to preclude resolution of important issues by depriving the courts of jurisdiction; and (6) taking advantage of ineffective assistance of counsel, as in the case of novice public defenders.

In the arena of corrections, the American Correctional Association (ACA) has devised a code of ethics for its membership. The membership of the American Correctional Association consists of both educators and practitioners. But the code of ethics itself is directed largely at corrections officers and corrections professionals who interact with inmates and community-based correctional clients. Among other things, this code of ethics encourages respecting a client's civil rights, promoting the welfare of those served by institutions and agencies, and promoting a safer and more healthy work environment. Behavioral admonitions, which are an integral part of this code, include refraining from using corrections positions in ways that exploit inmates and clients, refraining from engaging in activities that compromise one's integrity (such as accepting illegal gifts or gratuities in exchange for favors performed because of one's position), refraining from discriminating against others because of race or ethnicity, and reporting any unethical or illegal conduct observed by either other officers or administrators (American Correctional Association, 1994).

In fact, most state correctional departments have adopted codes of ethics apart from those encouraged by the ACA. But it is one thing to articulate a code of ethics and another thing to enforce such a code (Nieto, 1998). Unethical conduct is often covert and difficult to detect (Silbert, 1986; Swift, 1984). When it is detected, it is often unreported, since there is a similar code of silence among correctional personnel as that which exists among police officers. Until or unless these codes of silence and barriers to effective ethical codes are eliminated, codes of ethics are relevant only for those persons willing to abide by them.

INTEGRATING THE COMMUNITY WITH CRIMINAL JUSTICE AGENCIES

A third general strategy for improving the effectiveness of any criminal justice agency is to use and even maximize the use of community resources in law enforcement, prosecution and the courts, and corrections. The community itself can do a great deal to enhance existing law enforcement services and staffing. Community crime prevention programs such as neighborhood watch programs and Operation Identification are important steps toward assisting the police in their mission to serve and protect community residents.

Community support also is needed in community-based correctional programs (Draine and Solomon, 1999; Spergel et al., 1999). Persons can become involved as either volunteers or paraprofessionals in different types of programs for probationers and parolees. Simply assisting someone with filling out a job application can do much to enhance a parolee's chances of reintegrating more successfully into the community, for example. If incarcerated offenders are granted entry into work or study release programs or furloughs, the public can do a great deal to ease their acceptance back into the community. Corrections needs a great deal of help from local community residents in an effort to assist in offender reintegration (O'Leary, 1987; Petersilia, 1998). We have seen that community-based programs generally have better success rates for participating offenders compared with institution-based programs. One reason for this difference is the impact of interacting with community residents (Minnesota Probation Standards Task Force, 1993).

SUMMARY

Evaluation research is any investigation that attempts to answer practical and applied questions. Any investigation designed to show the effectiveness of an intervention, treatment, or program also is considered evaluation research. Such research extends throughout all criminal justice areas, including law enforcement, prosecution and the courts, corrections, and the juvenile justice system. For purposes of verifying the success of programs, treatments, or interventions, researchers often conduct replication research, which involves conducting new research projects under different circumstances to see if similar results are obtained.

The results of evaluating whether or not organizations are effective depends on the criteria we use to measure effectiveness as well as the missions and goals of the agencies and institutions under investigation. Organizational effectiveness is closely associated with goal attainment. If organizations have formal mission statements, they are effective to the extent that their missions are being fulfilled by organizational activities. Law enforcement effectiveness is often assessed by tracking crime trends. But much more is expected of law enforcement than decreasing crime. Police officers perform diverse services for the public. Law enforcement effectiveness is improved through utilizing the latest technological developments for crime detection and prevention. The performance of law enforcement officers improves through greater training in racial and ethnic diversity and social skills. Officers are encouraged to become involved in various community projects and foster better public relations.

Prosecutors and the courts are frequently evaluated by the number of convictions obtained and cases processed. But prosecutors and judges must strive to ensure that defendants' due process rights are rigorously observed. Prosecutors must screen cases closely, and judges should act to ensure that all participants in court actions receive fundamental fairness in their processing and adjudication. Only the best and most qualified persons should be selected as prosecutors and judges. Prosecutorial or judicial misconduct should be minimized and dealt with swiftly when such misconduct is detected.

Corrections involves many expectations. Both institutional and community corrections are expected to rehabilitate offenders or at least prevent them from harming others. Corrections institutions and agencies are assessed in terms of the amount of recidivism exhibited by former inmates or clients. Generally, corrections can be improved through better institutional and community programming to assist offenders to become more reintegrated into their communities. Corrections personnel should be selected in ways that ensure that only the most qualified applicants for correctional positions are chosen. Regular performance evaluations of staff should be conducted in order to ensure that they have the educational skills necessary to do quality correctional jobs and can maximize their assistance to clients or inmates.

Almost every professional organization has evolved a code of ethics and standards of professional responsibility against which an individual's behavior can be measured. The police, prosecutors, courts, and corrections all have devised ethical codes of conduct in order to gauge their behaviors in relation to others.

Many people have proposed that different criminal justice agencies and organizations become more closely integrated with communities in order to share the responsibilities of rehabilitating and reintegrating correctional clients. Community support is needed especially in community corrections, in which extensive networking among different support services is necessary to maximize agency assistance to clients.

QUESTIONS FOR REVIEW

1. What is evaluation research? What are some primary objectives of evaluation research? Does evaluation research determine whether programs are good or bad? Why or why not?

2. How do we know that organizations are effective? What are some different criteria we can use to determine whether organizations are effective or ineffective?

3. How do we know that law enforcement is effective? What is wrong with making sweeping generalizations about law enforcement effectiveness?

4. What do researchers believe are commonly held expectations of law enforcement agencies? Do law enforcement agencies appear to be doing what is expected of them? Why or why not?

5. How can the effectiveness of law enforcement agencies be improved?

6. Why are prosecutors and judges difficult to sanction if they engage in misconduct?

7. What steps can be taken to hold judges and prosecutors more accountable for their decision making?

8. What are some general problems with making generalizations about corrections and corrections effectiveness?

9. What is meant by meta-analysis, and how can it be used to tell us about program effectiveness?

10. What are some ways that corrections, both institutional and within the community, can be improved?

SUGGESTED READINGS

Eisenberg, Michael (1999). *Three-Year Recidivism Tracking of Offenders Participating in Substance Abuse Treatment Programs.* Austin, TX: Texas Criminal Justice Policy Council.

Lynch, Gerald W. (ed.) (1999). *Human Dignity and the Police: Ethics and Integrity in Police Work.* Springfield, IL: Charles C Thomas.

Merlo, Alida V., and Peter J. Benekos (2000). *What's Wrong with the Criminal Justice System: Ideology, Politics, and the Media.* Cincinnati, OH: Anderson Publishing Company.

• CASE STUDIES •

1. THE BEATING

In Chicago, Illinois, in 1999, a man named Morgan Washington, 32, was beaten to death by two police officers as he sat in his car on a Chicago street. Allegedly, he refused to show officers whatever he was holding in his hand. Washington died as the result of severe blows to the head and neck. Subsequently, both police officers involved were charged with second-degree murder in Washington's death. The white officers, Mike Johnson and Burt James, were charged in a federal indictment with killing Washington, a black man. James went on trial first in federal district court and was subsequently acquitted by an all-white jury. Defense attorneys had argued in James's case that Washington died as the result of cocaine intoxication, although no evidence was presented to show that Washington had been using cocaine at the time of his beating or death.

Considerable media attention was given to the case following James's acquittal on the second-degree murder charges, and the media speculated that rioting would occur among Chicago's large black population if Johnson also was acquitted. At Johnson's trial, prosecutors presented evidence that Johnson and James had used their flashlights to beat Washington as he sat outside a suspected crack house. Johnson was convicted in October 2000. U.S. District Court Judge Morris Rubik threw out Johnson's conviction, however, because of the prejudice of jury members who had watched a racially charged film, *Remember the Titans,* during the trial. An attorney for Johnson, Jason Young, said, "A great deal of art can become political propaganda if taken out of context." Johnson's wife, Betty, said, "We found justice today. I'm just so thrilled that finally we found some justice here."

Federal prosecutors said that the Johnson ruling would be appealed. A retrial was already scheduled for James in February 2001. Johnson said, "I know I didn't do anything wrong and I'm looking forward to a second chance." After the federal judge's ruling, Johnson took a taxi from a federal prison in Allenwood, Pennsylvania, to catch a plane at a nearby airport. He had been held in confinement in Pennsylvania instead of Illinois, since authorities feared for his safety.

Questions for Discussion

1. Should federal district court judges have the power to set aside guilty verdicts by federal juries?

2. Substantial evidence was presented at both trials concerning Washington's condition at the time of his beating, including the fact that he did not have any cocaine in his body and none was found at the crime scene. Should this information have been persuasive enough for jurors to decide that Washington was beaten to death without justification? Why or why not?

3. There are clear racial overtones in this case. Was the all-white jury who heard James's case truly a jury of his peers? How can judges and other court officers ensure fundamental fairness in jury selection in racially charged trials?

4. What grounds can you cite for prosecutors to prevail in overturning the federal judge's decision to set aside the guilty verdict of the jury in Johnson's trial?

5. To what extent did media coverage of these two cases influence the two different outcomes?

2. THE CHASE

The television series *Real Stories of the Highway Patrol* was on location filming some action sequences in Lexington, Kentucky. A camera crew was in the cruiser of Kentucky state trooper Bernard Schiff. Suddenly, at 1:00 A.M., a drunk driver went speeding by. Schiff began his pursuit. The pursuit was videotaped in its entirety.

As Schiff chased the fleeing drunk-driving suspect, the speeds ranged from 50 to 100 mph. Even at 1:00 A.M., there was considerable traffic on the Kentucky highway. At different points, Schiff would yell out, "Die," whenever he would see the fleeing car lose control or spin around curves in a dangerous manner. Eventually, the driver plowed into the side of an oncoming car driven by Mindy Jacobs, 21, who was returning home after working a late shift at Kmart. Her car smashed into a telephone pole and she was killed instantly. The fleeing car made good its escape, only to be stopped by another collision farther down the road. By that time, three other police vehicles were in hot pursuit. When Schiff saw Jacobs smash against the telephone pole, he cried out, "I killed that girl, man, I killed her, goddamn it!" All of this was recorded on videotape. The incident happened on October 3, 2000. Since then, the drunk driver, George Goodman, was convicted of vehicular homicide and sentenced to 10 years in prison. The Jacobs family is suing the Kentucky Highway Patrol for the wrongful death of their daughter. Among other things, the presence of the television video camera is blamed in part for inspiring the trooper to pursue Goodman.

Subsequently, the producers of *Real Stories of the Highway Patrol* have shut down their operations. The cameramen who were with trooper Schiff at the time are nowhere to be found now. The videotape of the incident has been suppressed. *Real Stories of the Highway Patrol* continues to air on nightly broadcasts, but these are reruns.

Most police departments have policies governing hot pursuit of speeding motorists. In some jurisdictions, hot pursuits of fleeing cars are discouraged, since they may cause more trouble than the speeding offense itself. And the punishment, if death results, is substantially more excessive than if the suspect were apprehended and convicted without incident. There is no question that chasing suspects in any form is a dangerous tactic. Hot pursuit is a form of deadly force, intended to lead to the capture of those who pose a danger either to themselves or to others. More than a few police officers will not pursue drivers who speed up in response to being chased. These officers know that innocent motorists may be seriously injured or killed if they continue their pursuit. Chasing a gang of bank robbers who are shooting back at you is one thing, but chasing a speeding car in which the driver may be intoxicated is an entirely different matter, according to various experts.

Questions for Discussion

1. Is the hot pursuit of drunk drivers justified under any circumstances?
2. What policies would you adopt to regulate police conduct in high-speed chases?

3. Do you think that the presence of video crews may have caused trooper Schiff to continue his chase of the fleeing suspect?
4. Should videotaping of such pursuits be permitted under any circumstances? What do you think?
5. Whose fault was the death of Mindy Jacobs? Do you think the Kentucky Highway Patrol was negligent for failure to train its officers in high-speed pursuit situations? Why or why not?

Glossary

Absolute immunity The assumption that government officials are completely protected from lawsuits brought by probationers, parolees, or inmates for the officials' actions.

Accreditation A prescribed program generally receiving the approval of a recognized group of professionals, in which desired program components are identified and used to compare programs in terms of their effectiveness. In law enforcement and corrections, any professional organizational approval of curriculum, training procedures, and instruction designed to train personnel to perform their jobs in a capable manner.

Achievement motivation theory Elaborated by David McClelland (1985); holds that persons engage in goal-setting behavior in which the goals involve challenging work. Through aggressive action toward goal attainment and through a problem-solving process, persons obtain important feedback from significant others, such as supervisors and other workers, about the quality of their work performance. The ultimate result for high achievers is the attainment of desired goals, such as promotions, advancements, and tangible recognition and rewards.

Achievement-oriented leadership A leadership style that involves goal-setting behavior and also reflects task-oriented leadership.

Adjudication Legal resolution of a dispute; when a juvenile is declared delinquent or a status offender, the matter has been resolved; when an offender has been convicted or acquitted, the matter at issue (guilt or innocence) has been concluded by either a judge or jury.

Adjudicatory hearing Formal proceeding involving a prosecuting attorney and a defense attorney in which evidence is presented and a juvenile's status or condition is determined by the juvenile court judge.

Administration of justice Covers such areas as police management, criminal procedure, pretrial services, arraignment and trial, prosecution and defense, court organization, pleadings, sentencing, appeals, probation, and parole.

Administrative component That part of an organization charged with coordinating, facilitating, and supporting the activities of the rest of the organizational participants.

Administrative succession The degree of turnover among organizational administrators during a given time interval, such as a year or longer.

Admin max Maximum-security prison such as the federal penitentiary at Florence, Colorado; intended to hold only the most violent prisoners, who pose the greatest danger to other inmates and who are considered flight risks.

Adultification Process of transforming the juvenile court into a criminal court–like atmosphere created, in part, by a proliferation of constitutional safeguards extended to juveniles that also pertain to adults.

Affirmative action A formal program to correct previous discriminatory hiring practices through aggressive recruitment and promotion of previously disadvantaged groups.

Age of majority Chronological date when one reaches adulthood, usually either 18 or 21, when juveniles are no longer under the jurisdiction of the juvenile courts but rather, the criminal courts; also *age of consent*.

Aggravating circumstances Events about crime that may intensify the severity of punishment, including bodily injury, death to the victim, or the brutality of the act.

Alienative involvement One type of participation in Amitai Etzioni's compliance-involvement typology that suggests that persons who are forced or coerced into doing something will become resentful and object to becoming involved; consequences include poor work performance, low job satisfaction, and less organizational loyalty.

Alternative dispute resolution (ADR) Procedure by which a criminal case is redefined as a civil one and the case is decided by an impartial arbiter, in the process of which both parties agree to amicable settlement. Usually reserved for minor offenses.

Assistant United States attorneys (AUSAs) Subordinates to U.S. attorneys in U.S. districts; appointed by U.S. attorney and responsible for prosecuting crimes against the federal government.

Assumption Statement of fact about the real world or events; examples of assumptions include "All societies have laws" or "The greater the deviant conduct, the greater the group pressure on the deviant to conform to group norms."

Auburn State Penitentiary Prison constructed in Auburn, New York, in 1816. Pioneered use of tiers, in which inmates were housed on different floors or levels, usually according to their offense seriousness. Introduced congregate system, in which prisoners had opportunities to mingle with one another for work, dining, and recreation, and first used stereotypical striped uniforms for prisoners.

Auburn system Prison system developed in New York during the nineteenth century that emulated the Auburn State Penitentiary and depended on mass prisons that held prisoners in congregate fashion on various tiers that were differentiated according to offense seriousness. Compared with the Pennsylvania system.

Authoritarian model Prison management style characterized by a high degree of centralization of power and decision making.

Authority The power to delegate duties and responsibilities, usually vested in superordinates or supervisors, in relation to subordinates or lower-level participants; influence to cause others to conform to one's wishes.

Bailiffs Court officers who maintain order in the court while it is in session. Bailiffs oversee jury during a trial proceeding, sometimes have custody of prisoners while they are in the courtroom. Also known as messengers.

Beat patrolling Police patrol style originating in the early 1900s and designed to bring officers into closer physical contact with area residents. Beats are small geographical areas of neighborhoods or cities patrolled by individual officers, usually on foot.

Bench trials Tribunals in which guilt or innocence of defendant is determined by a judge rather than a jury.

Blended sentencing statute Any type of sentencing procedure in which either a criminal or juvenile court judge can impose *both* juvenile and/or adult incarcerative penalties.

Bobbies British police, named after Sir Robert "Bobby" Peel, the British Home Secretary in the 1820s.

Border Patrol (BP) Established in 1924 and currently employing 450 officers; originally created for the purpose of policing the borders between the United States and Canada and Mexico. Under the McCarran-Walter Act of 1952, BP was charged with three goals: (1) the reunification of families, (2) the immigration of persons with needed labor skills, and (3) the protection of the domestic labor force.

Bow Street Runners A small organization of paid police officers who attempted to apprehend criminals in England, originating in 1754.

Bridewell Workhouse First correctional institution in England. Confined both children and adults considered to be idle and disorderly.

Bureau of Alcohol, Tobacco, and Firearms (BATF) Originated as a subunit of the Internal Revenue Service in 1862 when certain alcohol and tobacco tax statutes were created; originally called the Alcohol, Tobacco, and Tax Unit, organization was later named the Alcohol, Tobacco, and Firearms Division within the IRS. In 1972, it became the current BATF under the direct control of the Department of Treasury; its general mission in combating crime is to reduce the illegal use of firearms and explosives; also seeks to curtail arson-for-profit schemes, and its agents investigate scenes of fires with mysterious origins.

Bureaucracy Organizational model that vests individuals with authority and spheres of competence in a predetermined hierarchy with abstract rules and selection by test.

Bureaucratic-lawful model A model that involves the bureaucratization of prisons and the establishment of elaborate chains of command linking prison administrators with their subordinates.

Bureaucratic model Way of viewing an organization as characterized by the following features: impersonal social relations, appointment and promotion on the basis of merit, previously specified authority obligations that are inherent in the position, a hierarchy of authority, abstract rules or laws covering task assignments and decisions, and specialization of position.

Bureaucratization The extension of the bureaucracy's spheres of activities and power either in its own interests or those of some of its elite. It tends toward greater regimentation of different areas of social life and some extent of displacement of its service goals in favor of various power interests or orientations.

Bureaus of Identification (BCIs) Similar to the FBI, agents of these state bureaus perform routine criminal investigation functions; when state police become involved in such operations, they usually perform supporting functions such as assisting state investigative agents; may assist agents by making arrests of criminal suspects, interviewing witnesses, and gathering and securing evidence from crime scenes.

Burnout Usually the result of stress, a syndrome of emotional exhaustion, depersonalization, and reduced personal accomplishment; a progressive loss of idealism, energy, and purpose; a state of physical, emotional, and mental exhaustion marked by physical depletion and chronic fatigue, feelings of helplessness and hopelessness, and the development of a negative self-concept and negative attitudes toward work, life, and other people.

Calculative involvement Disposition of persons who believe that they will be rewarded for complying with a superior's request to do something; rewards may be tangible or intangible (e.g., better working hours, pay, supervision, recognition, promotion, or advancement).

California Personality Inventory (CPI) Psychological device or instrument that purportedly measures personality dimensions such as anxiety, sociability, personal adjustment, and social adjustment.

Calls for service Reports of crime from citizens or requests for any other type of police assistance within the scope of police authority, duties, and responsibilities.

Centralization The power given to organizational subunits, departments, or separate operating units that could be retained by the central organizational hierarchy at the same level as the subunits to which it is distributed; focused control and an integrated and efficient organization.

Certification The process by which a state treats a juvenile as an adult for purposes of a criminal prosecution; the functional equivalent to a transfer or waiver.

Chain of command Pattern of authority relations in any organization showing vertical and horizontal power relations of different positions and roles relative to other positions or roles.

Chancellors Agents of the king of England who settled disputes between neighbors, such as property boundary issues, trespass allegations, and child misconduct.

Chancery courts Tribunals of equity rooted in early English common law in which civil disputes are resolved. Also responsible for juvenile matters and adjudicating family matters such as divorce. Has jurisdiction over contract disputes, property boundary claims, and exchanges of goods disputes.

Change agents Persons who have some amount of expertise concerning individual, interpersonal, or organizational problems. They may be consultants who are asked to solve organizational problems. They provide possible solutions to problems, and organizational members rely on their advice to remedy existing problems.

Charge reduction bargaining Negotiation process between prosecutors and defense attorneys involving dismissal of one or more charges against defendants in exchange for guilty plea to remaining charges, or in which prosecutor downgrades the charges in return for a plea of guilty.

Charismatic authority Evident in the relation of a leader to followers in which the leader possesses the gift of grace or divine gift. Leaders such as Alexander the Great and Napoleon have been attributed with this type of authority. Their commands to subordinates were typically obeyed without question; followers would conform to a degree paralleling religious zeal or sacred devotion.

Child savers Groups who promoted rights of minors during the nineteenth century and helped create a separate juvenile court. Their motives have been questioned by modern writers who see their efforts as a form of social control and class conflict.

Circuit courts Originally, courts that were held by judges who followed a circular path, hearing cases periodically in various communities. Now refers to courts with several counties or districts within their jurisdiction.

Circuit courts of appeal In federal courts, intermediate appellate court between U.S. district court and U.S. Supreme Court for hearing appeals from either the defense or prosecution; in state courts, intermediate courts between trial courts and state supreme courts for hearing trial court appeals.

Circuit riders Judges who rode from jurisdiction to jurisdiction in remote locations of states or federal territories to hold trials on a regular basis, such as once a month or once every six months.

Civilian complaint review boards Panels of citizens that judge acts of misconduct committed by police officers and recommend appropriate sanctions.

Classical model (Also known as *machine model*) This model views organizations as machines, and states that just as we build a mechanical device with given specifications for accomplishing tasks, so also do we construct an organization according to a blueprint to achieve a given purpose.

Client Any person, unconvicted or convicted of a crime, who is under the direct supervision of a community corrections agency, whether it is a probation or parole office or a community services organization.

Client system Either an individual, group, or an organization experiencing a problem that may be remedied by the services and intervention of a change agent.

Closed-system models Descriptive indicator of organizations that rely almost wholly on internal organizational processes to account for organizational behavior.

Code of ethics Regulations formulated by major professional societies that outline the specific problems and issues that are frequently encountered in the types of research carried out within a particular profession. Serves as a guide to ethical research practices.

Coercive power The ability to administer negative valences or remove or decrease positive valences.

Colquhoun, Patrick (1745–1820) An influential London magistrate who originated some unique ideas about the functions of police beginning in 1792. He was a legal reformist who believed that police should be used to establish and maintain order, control and prevent crime, and set an example of good conduct and moral sense for the citizenry; he also believed that existing enforcement methods, at least in London, were outmoded and improper and wanted to inculcate his officers with some professionalism. He believed that his officers should be funded by the particular jurisdiction.

Common law Authority based on court decrees and judgments that recognize, affirm, and enforce certain usages and customs of the people. Laws determined by judges in accordance with their rulings.

Community corrections Locally operated services offering minimum security, limited release, work release alternatives to prisoners about to be paroled. May also serve probationers.

Community corrections act (CCA) Statewide mechanism included in legislation by which funds are granted to local units of government and community agencies to develop and deliver front-end alternative sanctions in lieu of state incarceration.

Community residential centers Facilities for assisting offenders who are on probation in their cities or towns; offers counseling, employment assistance, and other services and treatments.

Community service orders Judicially imposed restitution for those convicted of committing crimes; some form of work must be performed to satisfy restitution requirements.

Compliance-involvement typology An explanation of organizational behavior that examines the application of different kinds of power to obtain conformity with one's wishes. Different types of power exercised by superiors in relation to subordinates elicit different reactions and feelings from those affected.

Conditional disposition Decision by juvenile court judge authorizing payment of fines, community service, restitution, or some other penalty after an adjudication of delinquency has been made.

Congregate system Introduced at Auburn State Penitentiary in New York, where prisoners could work and eat together in common work and recreational areas; prisoners were segregated at night.

Constables Favored noblemen of the king who commanded neighborhood groups; forerunners of modern-day police officers.

Contingency theory The view that effective leadership depends on the circumstances and work environment of the leader or administrator. If the work is highly structured and clearly spelled out by rules, such as those specified by the rules of criminal procedure in the courtroom environment, then mangers (e.g., judges, court officers, and others) orient themselves toward subordinates in a task-directed fashion.

Court clerks Court officers who may file pleadings, motions, or judgments, issue process, and may keep general records of court proceedings.

Court of civil appeals In various states, appellate court hearing civil cases from lower-level trial courts before cases are subsequently appealed to state supreme courts.

Court of criminal appeals Any state appellate court authorized to hear criminal appeals from state trial courts; an intermediary court of appeal between state trial courts and the state supreme court.

Court of last resort The last court that may hear a case. In the United States, the federal Supreme Court is the court of last resort for many kinds of cases.

Court reporter Court official who keeps a written word-for-word and/or tape-recorded record of court proceedings.

Courts of common pleas Early courts designed to try minor cases under prevailing common law.

Courts of record Courts in which a written record is kept of court proceedings.

Court watchers Persons who sit in courtrooms and observe judicial decision making as one way of heightening judicial accountability; they make periodic reports of judicial decision making, particularly sentencing disparities, to the news media or other agencies who use this information in different ways.

Creaming Denotes taking only the most qualified offenders for succeeding in a rehabilitative program. These offenders are low risk, unlikely to reoffend.

Creative sentencing A broad class of punishments as alternatives to incarceration that are designed to fit the particular crimes. May involve community service, restitution, fines, becoming involved in educational or vocational training programs, or becoming affiliated with other "good works" activity.

Criminal-exclusive blend Form of sentencing by a criminal court judge in which either juvenile or adult sentences of incarceration can be imposed, but not both.

Criminal-inclusive blend Form of sentencing by a criminal court judge in which both juvenile and adult sentences can be imposed simultaneously.

Criminal justice Interdisciplinary field studying nature and operations of organizations providing justice services to society.

Criminal justice organization Any one of numerous organizations that comprise the processing of defendants charged with crimes; conventionally includes law enforcement, prosecution, the courts, and corrections.

Criminal justice system An interrelated set of agencies and organizations designed to control criminal behavior, to detect crime, and to apprehend, process, prosecute, punish, and/or rehabilitate criminal offenders. The process-based aspect suggests that the interrelatedness implied by "system" may not be strong (e.g., judges might not contact jail or prison officials to inquire if sufficient space is available when offenders are sentenced to jail or prison terms).

Criminology The study of crime, the science of crime and criminal behavior, the forms of criminal behavior, the causes of crime, the definition of criminality, and the societal reaction to crime. An empirical social-behavioral science that investigates crime, criminals, and criminal justice.

Curfew violators Juveniles who violate laws and ordinances of communities prohibiting youths on the streets after certain evening hours, such as 10:00 P.M.; curfew itself is a delinquency prevention strategy.

Custodial dispositions Outcomes by juvenile judges following adjudication of juvenile as delinquent. Include nonsecure custody (in a foster home, community agency, farm, camp) or secure custody (in a detention center, industrial, reform school).

Day fine Monetary sanction geared to the average daily income of convicted offenders in an effort to bring equity to the sentencing process, or to compensate victims or the state (for court costs and supervisory fees). A day fine is calculated in a two-step process. First, courts use a unit scale or benchmark to sentence an offender to a certain number of day-fine units (e.g., 15, 30, 120), according to offense severity and without regard to income; and then the value of each unit is determined according to a percentage of the offender's daily income. Total fine amounts are calculated by multiplying the unit value by the number of units accompanying the offense.

Day fine programs Facilities operated in local, state, or federal jurisdictions in which offenders are assessed a certain amount of their earnings as a form of restitution to victims or victim compensation.

Day reporting A highly structured program in which offenders must check in at a local community facility on a regular basis, such as daily, for supervision, sanctions, and services.

Day reporting centers Facilities operated primarily during daytime hours for the purpose of providing diverse services to offenders in day reporting programs and their families. Offenders live at home and report to these centers regularly and often daily for supervision, sanctions, and services coordinated from a central focus.

Day watch Watch duty that citizens were obligated to perform in the 1500s in European towns and villages. Watches were assigned, day *and* night, on a rotating basis, comparable to modern-day shiftwork, and the watchmen alerted residents if they detected crimes in progress or any other community disturbance.

Debtors' prisons Incarcerative facilities established in the Middle Ages in England in which people owing money were held until they or their friends paid their debts.

Debureaucratization The reverse of bureaucratization, including the subversion of goals and activities of the bureaucracy in the interests of different groups with which it has close interaction (clients, patrons, interested parties); the specific characteristics of bureaucracy in terms of both its autonomy and its specific rules and goals are minimized, even up to the point at which its very functions and activities are taken over by other groups or organizations.

Decentralization The delegation of responsibilities from top management either to middle-level managers at the same headquarters or to managers of local offices.

Decertification The process of divesting arrest powers and law enforcement authority from a police officer or a sheriff's deputy for engaging in improper conduct or committing crimes; revoking one's power and authority as a law enforcement officer.

Decision-making power The amount of freedom an employee has to determine how the work should be performed.

Decision model Depiction of organization consisting of three important components. First, organizations are viewed as rational systems consisting of various parts. Each part, such as a department, makes decisions that affect relationships with other parts and with the organization as a whole. Second, organizational problems are accounted for, in part, by the quality of decisions pertaining to the utilization of organizational and individual resources. Third, the model has as its guiding theme the rational selection of the best action from several available alternatives with some calculated probability of predictable results.

Delegating style Mode of leadership that is task oriented and requires supervisors to tell subordinates what to do and delegates tasks to those who are emotionally mature enough to perform them.

Delinquency Any act committed by a child that would be a crime if committed by an adult. In some states, status offenses are considered delinquent conduct and subject to identical punishments, including incarceration. The offense itself is the delinquent act. Delinquency is status acquired through an adjudicatory proceeding by juvenile court.

Delinquent Child of not more than a specified age who has violated criminal laws or engages in disobedient, indecent, or immoral conduct, and is in need of treatment, rehabilitation, or supervision.

Demand waiver Action by juvenile to have his or her case transferred to the jurisdiction of a criminal court.

Dependent and/or neglected children Youths adjudged by the juvenile court to be without parent, guardian, or custodian or who need special care and treatment because the parent, guardian, or custodian is unable to provide for their physical or mental condition. Also used in cases in which the parent, guardian, or custodian wants to be relieved of legal custody for good cause, or if the children are without necessary care or support through no fault of the parent, guardian, or custodian.

Determinate sentencing Sanctioning scheme in which court sentences offender to incarceration for fixed period, and which must be served in full and without parole intervention, less any good time earned in prison.

Detroit Police Ministation Program Implemented in the early 1980s by Detroit (Michigan) Police Department, ministations or small substations staffed by police officers were placed in high-crime areas of Detroit; intent of program was to improve response time to calls for service from citizens when crimes were committed.

Directed leadership Mode of leadership in which leaders spell out exactly what is expected of their subordinates and detail how organizational goals can be achieved by subordinate behaviors.

Direct file Prosecutorial waiver of jurisdiction to a criminal court; an action taken against a juvenile who has committed an especially serious offense, by which that juvenile's case is transferred to criminal court for the purpose of a criminal prosecution.

Discretionary waivers Transfers of juveniles to criminal courts by judges at their discretion or in their judgment; also known as judicial waivers.

Dispositions Actions by criminal or juvenile justice court or agency signifying that a portion of the justice process is completed and jurisdiction is relinquished or transferred to another agency or signifying that a decision has been reached on one aspect of a case and a different aspect comes under consideration, requiring a different kind of decision.

Dissatisfiers Motivational factors contributing to work satisfaction and directly linked with working conditions, such as the nature of supervision, the supervisor-subordinate relation, salary, and work stress.

Distributed leadership Also known as multiple leadership, mode of exercising control over others in which specific persons in a group may have a special facility for calling the group to order, others may be able to quell a troublesome situation, others may be highly respected because of their judgment and character, and still others may be respected because of their expertise and because they have more facts to contribute than any other members.

Diversion Removing a case from the criminal justice system, although a defendant is required to comply with various conditions (e.g., attending a school for drunk drivers, undergoing counseling, performing community service). May result in expungement of record. Conditional removal of the prosecution of a case prior to its adjudication, usually as the result of an arrangement between the prosecutor and judge.

Division of labor Organized distribution of positions and work roles in any organization, usually involving a hierarchy of authority and planned and predictable communication patterns.

Dual-factor theory of motivation Concept that one's desire to work originates from satisfiers, or events in one's work environment that contribute to one's satisfaction, such as work content and intrinsic interest of work performed, the potential for advancement and recognition, and responsibility for important tasks; and from dissatisfiers, or those events in one's work environment that contribute to one's dissatisfaction.

Electronic monitoring The use of electronic devices (usually anklets or wristlets) that emit electronic signals to monitor offenders, probationers, and parolees. Purpose is to monitor an offender's presence in a given environment in which the offender is required to remain or to verify the offender's whereabouts.

Empirical generalizations Facts; observable regularities of human or social behavior.

Employee-maturity theory Mode of leadership stressing emotional and educational maturation of subordinates led; a collaborative relation between supervisors and subordinates, in which subordinates are given emotional consideration and are involved in decision making through feedback solicited by supervisors.

Equilibrium model Explanation of organization processes that stresses the importance of motivational factors to encourage member participation in organizational activities.

Equity theory Posits that workers desire equitable treatment when performing their jobs; workers compare themselves with others who perform similar work tasks; work output is a product of job input, and rewards as outcomes should be equivalent to the rewards of others who expend similar energy to reach the same goals; workers are content to the extent that they perceive that equity exists among all employees who perform similar work and are rewarded by the system equally.

Evaluation research Investigations that attempt to answer practical and applied questions; any investigation geared to test the efficacy of a strategy or intervention in relation to some event, such as delinquency or criminality.

Evarts Act Legislation introduced to establish a scheme for federal appellate review.

Exclusive jurisdiction Specific jurisdiction over particular kinds of cases. The U.S. Supreme Court has authority to hear matters involving the diplomats of other countries who otherwise enjoy great immunity from most other courts. Family court may have exclusive jurisdiction to hear child custody cases.

Expectancy theory Casts a worker's motivation to perform into a performance-outcome framework; employees are taught by their organizations that hard work and following the rules will lead to desirable outcomes, such as promotion, advancement, and greater recognition.

Expert power Power that is contingent on the amount of knowledge or expertise a superior has (or is believed to have by subordinates).

False positives Offenders who are predicted to be dangerous or to pose serious public risk according to various prediction devices and instruments, but who are not dangerous and do not pose public risks.

False negatives Offenders who are predicted to be nonviolent or not dangerous according to various risk prediction devices, but who turn out to be dangerous or pose serious public risk.

Family courts Judicial bodies of original jurisdiction that typically handle the entire range of family problems, from juvenile delinquency to divorce cases.

Federal district courts Also known as U.S. district courts, these are the basic trial courts involving federal civil and criminal cases.

Field training officers (FTOs). Senior police officers who train other officers in the field, overseeing their on-the-job training.

Fielding, Henry (1707–1754) Author-turned-politician who developed some interesting ideas about law enforcement; in 1748, he was appointed chief magistrate of the Bow Street court in London.

Fielding, Sir John Successor to Henry Fielding, his half brother. Sir John, who was blind, organized a small band of persons who could run fast and chase and apprehend criminals, known as the Bow Street Runners. This was a group of paid law enforcement personnel also called thief-takers, who received rewards from persons when they returned stolen property.

Financial/community service model Restitution model for juveniles that stresses the offender's financial accountability and community service to pay for damages.

Finders of fact Petit juries selected and comprised of one's peers; general function is to determine and weigh evidence against defendants and arrive at guilty or not guilty verdicts.

Fines Monetary punishments assessed for committing crimes.

Flat organizational structure Type of organizational hierarchical arrangement in which there are few levels of supervision.

Formal communication network Information transmission mode in an organization that relies almost exclusively on the prescribed hierarchy of authority; any information is distributed to organizational membership through official channels.

Formalization The extent to which communications and procedures in an organization are written down and filed;

a measure of the extent to which rules, procedures, instructions, and communications are written.

Formal organization A predetermined arrangement of departments and work roles governed by rules and related so as to achieve one or more goals; members are selected based on their expertise and qualifications for performing work roles.

Frame of reference Way of looking at an organization or problem affecting persons, groups, or organizations.

Frankpledge System requiring loyalty to the king of England and shared law and order responsibilities among the public. System directed that neighbors should form small groups to assist and protect one another if anyone is victimized by criminals.

Frumentarii First professional criminal investigative units in Western history, which had three principal duties: (1) supervise grain distribution to Rome's needy, (2) oversee the personal delivery of messages among government officials, and (3) detect crime and prosecute offenders.

Furlough An authorized unescorted or unsupervised leave granted to inmates for home visits, work, or educational activity, usually lasting from 24 to 72 hours. Temporary release program first used in Mississippi in 1918.

Gaols English jails originally established in the fifteenth century.

General jurisdiction Power of a court to hear a wide range of cases, both civil and criminal.

Goals model View of an organization that makes the following assumptions: (1) The organization exists to achieve stated goals; (2) the organization develops a rational procedure for goal attainment; and (3) the organization is assessed in terms of the effectiveness of goal attainment.

Grapevines Informal communication patterns that exist within the formal communication network. Informal leaders emerge who do not have the same degree of formal job status as formal leaders but who nevertheless exert significant influence on employees' attitudes toward their jobs. Every organization creates an informal structure, and the process of modifying organizational goals is effected through such structures.

Great man approach Similar to charismatic leadership, leadership notion that vests particular persons with significant power to influence others on the basis of their natural ability and will; similar to natural-born leader theory.

Group cohesiveness The tendency of group members to stick together; also measured by means of the number of times group members use "we" when referring to their group activities, the number of in-group sociometric choices, and the degree of willingness of group members to leave the group; the number of times that a work group will process grievances jointly before administrative higher-ups; the attraction of members to the group in terms of the strength of forces on the individual member to remain in the group and to resist leaving the group.

Guidelines-based sentencing Also known as presumptive sentencing, plan for sentencing based on recommended

ranges of months for different criminal offenses; judges must strongly consider guidelines of punishment outlined for particular offenses but may depart from guidelines if they write a rationale for doing so.

Halfway house Community-based centers or homes operated either publicly or privately, staffed by professionals, paraprofessionals, and volunteers, which are designed to provide housing, food, clothing, job assistance, and counseling to ex-prisoners and others in order to assist parolees in making the transition from prison to the community.

Harmful error Mistake made by judges that may be prejudicial to a defendant's case. May lead to reversals of convictions against defendants and to new trials.

Hawthorne effect Impact of being observed, in which observed individuals who know they are being observed will act differently than under conditions in which they do not know they are being observed.

Hawthorne studies Experiment performed in the 1920s at the Hawthorne plant of the Western Electric Company, involving bank wiring for telephones; workers were given special attention by observers and behaved differently compared with their behavior when not being observed.

Hierarchy of authority Predetermined arrangement of superior-subordinate relations involving the distribution of power in any organization. Lower-level employees or workers report or are responsible to higher-level employees or managers.

Hierarchy of needs Motivational scheme devised by Abraham Maslow; envisions basic physiological needs as the basis for developing other needs, including safety and security, belongingness, self-esteem, and self-actualization.

Home confinement Housing of offenders in their own homes with or without electronic monitoring devices. Reduces prison overcrowding and prisoner costs. Sometimes used as an intermediate punishment involving the use of offender residences for mandatory incarceration during evening hours after a curfew and on weekends; also called house arrest.

Horizontal complexity The lateral differentiation of functions that may be duplicated at all levels of authority in corporate organizations.

Horizontal differentiation Division of labor in which there is a proliferation of subunits at the same level; numerous departments at approximately the equivalent rank or status of other departments within an organization.

House arrest Use of one's residence as the primary place of confinement under a sentence of probation or parole; offenders must remain at their premises except when working, and they must make their premises open to inspection by probation or parole officers at all times.

Houses of refuge Institutions that provided services to youths as a means of separating juveniles from the adult correctional process. The first one was established in New York City in 1825.

Howard, John (1726–1790) Early English prison reformer and sheriff of Bedfordshire, England. Influenced by other

European countries such as France to lobby for prison reforms.

Hue and cry In the 1500s, warning shouted by village watchmen if crime was observed.

Human relations model View of organizations that focuses on persons, emphasizing (1) mutual interest, (2) individual differences, (3) motivation, and (4) human dignity.

Human relations school Body of thought emphasizing the importance of social contacts and influence in organizations. De-emphasizes adherence to rules and order maintenance, as suggested by bureaucracy. Focuses on emotional and affective factors as most important for encouraging employees to carry out organizational rules.

Human services approach Philosophy of some corrections officers, in either prisons or jails; they regard each inmate as a human being with feelings or emotions; actions toward inmates include how their needs can be met, apart from simply viewing them as objects to be guarded or confined.

Implicit plea bargaining Process by which a defendant pleads guilty with the expectation of receiving a more lenient sentence.

Indentured servant system Procedure in which persons paid for their passage to the American colonies from England by selling their services for a period of seven years. Also considered a "voluntary slave" migration pattern.

Indeterminate sentences Sentencing schemes in which a period is set by judges between the earliest date for a parole decision and the latest date for completion of the sentence. In holding that the time necessary for treatment cannot be set exactly, the indeterminate sentence is closely associated with rehabilitation.

Individual unit of analysis, level of analysis Study of organizations in which personality systems and attitudes are considered as primary factors in determining what is going on in organizations and why; key elements of analysis are persons and their dispositions and sentiments.

Influence Power on the part of any organizational member to obtain compliance from others.

Informal communication network Grapevine or information transmission that is unauthorized by the existing formal hierarchy of authority; rumor generated by social groups unrelated to the power hierarchy in an organization.

Initiating structure View of supervisory behavior that the leader facilitates group interaction toward goal attainment. This involves planning, scheduling, criticizing, and initiating ideas.

Inmate control model Method for inmate supervision in which prisoners form inmate government councils and establish organizations such as the California Union, a prisoner union patterned after those established in Scandinavian prisons.

Intake Process of screening juveniles who have been charged with offenses. Dispositions at intake include release to parents pending further juvenile court action, dismissal of charges against juvenile, detention, or treatment by some community agency.

Intake hearings Proceedings in which a juvenile probation officer conducts an informal investigation of the charges against a juvenile and determines if the juvenile should be moved forward into the juvenile justice system for further processing.

Intake officers Persons appointed by the juvenile court, usually juvenile probation officers, who conduct intake proceedings and screen youths for possible further processing in the juvenile justice system.

Intake screenings Proceedings involving an informal meeting with a juvenile probation officer or other juvenile court–appointed officer designed to determine if the juvenile should be advanced further into the juvenile justice system.

Intermediate punishments Sanctions imposed that are somewhere between incarceration and probation on a continuum of criminal penalties. May include home confinement and electronic monitoring.

Interpersonal unit of analysis, level of analysis Study of organizations in which the principal object of inquiry is the group; emphasis is on group structure and process as well as group influence on the organization itself and individuals within the group; small work groups are considered primary targets of inquiry for organizational researchers who use this level of analysis to research what is happening in organizations and why.

Jail City- or county-operated and -financed facility to contain those offenders who are serving short sentences or are awaiting further processing. Jails sometimes house more serious prisoners from state or federal prisons through contracts to alleviate overcrowding and also accommodate witnesses, juveniles, vagrants, and others.

Jailhouse lawyers Inmates in a prison or jail who learn about the law and become skilled enough to assist other prisoners in filing suits against prison or jail administration.

Job enrichment Implies infusing tasks with problem-solving activities and more complex and challenging duties that require thinking and creativity; seems to work better for those employees with greater amounts of education.

Job satisfaction The degree to which persons like their jobs or the actual work performed.

Job status Determined by one's position in the hierarchy of authority. People tend to evaluate one another in an organization according to the amount of power that they can wield over others. Higher or lower positions and/or greater or lesser amounts of power possessed determine one's status.

Judicial plea bargaining Recommended sentence by judge who offers a specific sentence and/or fine in exchange for a guilty plea.

Judicial review Authority of a court to limit the power of the executive and legislative branches of government by deciding if their acts defy rights established by the state and federal constitutions.

Judicial waivers Decision by juvenile judge to waive juvenile to jurisdiction of criminal court.

Judiciary Act of 1789 Act of Congress that provided for three levels of federal courts: (1) 13 federal district courts, each presided over by a district judge; (2) three higher circuit courts of appeal, each comprising two justices of the Supreme Court and one district judge; and (3) a Supreme Court, consisting of a chief justice and five associate justices.

Jury trials Tribunals in which guilt or innocence of defendant is determined by jury instead of by the judge.

Justice administration The description and elaboration of the structural, functional, and managerial processes involved in coordinating activities related to determining the incidence of criminal conduct, the detection and apprehension of alleged criminals, an assessment of the credibility of evidence against the accused, a formal judgment about that conduct, and how that conduct is punished.

Justices of the peace Minor judicial officials overseeing trivial offenses; courts, usually rural, possessing special original jurisdiction in most instances and certain quasijudicial powers.

Juvenile court A term for any court that has original jurisdiction over persons statutorily defined as juveniles and alleged to be delinquents, status offenders, or dependents.

Juvenile delinquency The violation of criminal laws by juveniles. Any illegal behavior or activity committed by persons who are within a particular age range and that subjects them to the jurisdiction of a juvenile court or its equivalent.

Juvenile delinquent Any minor who commits an offense that would be a crime if committed by an adult.

Juvenile-contiguous blend Form of blended sentencing by a juvenile court judge in which the judge can impose a disposition beyond the normal jurisdictional range for juvenile offenders; for example, a judge may impose a 30-year term on a 14-year-old offender, but the juvenile is entitled to a hearing when he or she reaches the age of majority to determine whether or not the remainder of the sentence shall be served.

Juvenile-exclusive blend Blended sentencing form in which a juvenile court judge can impose either adult or juvenile incarceration as a disposition and sentence but not both.

Juvenile-inclusive blend Form of blended sentencing in which a juvenile court judge can impose *both* adult and juvenile incarceration simultaneously.

Juvenile justice system The process through which juveniles are processed, sentenced, and corrected after arrests for juvenile delinquency.

Juvenile Any youth who has not reached the age of his or her majority, which is usually 18 or 21, depending on the jurisdiction; some states consider persons adults when they reach age 16 or 17.

Kales plan The 1914 version of the Missouri Plan, in which a committee of experts creates a list of qualified persons for judgeships and makes recommendations to the governor.

Labor turnover The number of persons who leave an organization according to some time interval, such as each year.

Latent social identities Personality dispositions and attitudes that individuals bring with them to the organization. Persons cannot separate themselves from their thoughts and beliefs outside of the work setting, and when they are working, their behavior is influenced by their previous experiences and encounters outside of the workplace.

Law Enforcement Assistance Administration (LEAA) An outgrowth of the President's Crime Commission during the period from 1965 to 1967, a time of great social unrest and civil disobedience. Created by Congress in 1968 and terminated in late 1970s. Designed to provide resources, leadership, and coordination to state and local law enforcement agencies to prevent and/or reduce adult crime and juvenile delinquency. Allocated millions of dollars to researchers and police departments, and many experiments were conducted with these monies, which led to innovative patrolling strategies in different communities.

Leader in a particular situation Explanation of why certain persons emerge as group or organizational leaders based on their particular abilities and skills relative to tasks assigned and regardless of their rank within the organizational hierarchy.

Leadership Ability of one person to evoke conformity to organizational rules or solicit compliance to directives from one or more others.

Leadership behavior Action of obtaining compliance from others in accordance with what one wants; may stem from personal qualities, one's ability to sanction or punish nonconformity, and any other number of factors.

Leadership styles Modes of conduct that emphasize how particular leaders will orient themselves toward subordinates. Leadership styles include (1) laissez-faire, (2) democratic, and (3) autocratic.

Learned leadership View that ability to invoke wanted behaviors from others can be acquired through gaining knowledge and education.

Legalistic model Model for law enforcement that emphasizes the importance of written procedure and limited individual officer discretion; promotes a "strictly-by-the-book," mentality that recognizes "only the facts" among law enforcement officers.

Legal-rational authority Best illustrated by referring to bureaucratic organizations: The authority of superiors in bureaucracies is legitimized by systems of abstract rules and norms and rights are bestowed on persons within an authority hierarchy by persons at a higher level and by rules that govern the particular position or role.

Legitimate authority Any method of obtaining compliance from others that is predetermined and/or approved by an organization or system. Max Weber identified three types of legitimate authority, including legal-rational authority, traditional authority, and charismatic authority.

Legitimate power Mode of obtaining compliance from others based on the subordinate's belief that the superior has the right to give orders.

Level of aspiration Goal or aim established by a worker in an organization; may be a position sought or particular salary level or fringe benefit.

Levels of analysis, units of analysis Three strata for examining organizational phenomena, in which the focus is on one of the following dimensions: (1) the individual; (2) the small, interpersonal work group; and/or (3) the formal organization.

Levels of authority Refers to the degree of vertical differentiation within an organization. *Levels* connotes layers of different positions, each layer constituting a homogeneous aggregate of employees.

Lifetime appointments Royal judges in England had served "at the King's pleasure during good behavior," or the equivalent of serving for life; this practice is still followed in all federal district and appellate courts in the United States and in some states, where judges are appointed for life or until they decide to retire.

Limited jurisdiction Court is restricted to handling certain types of cases such as probate matters or juvenile offenses. Also known as special jurisdiction.

Line personnel Operational personnel who carry out the primary goals of the organization; in police agencies, these workers consist of full-time or part-time sworn officers who respond to calls for service.

Machine model (Also known as *classical model*) This organizational conceptualization stresses the maximization of organizational effectiveness. Therefore, attention is directed to those aspects of organizations that can be rearranged and structured to fulfill this objective. Certain management principles should be applied, such as a division of labor, authority, discipline, unity of command and direction, subordination of individual interest to general interest, remuneration of personnel, centralization, a chain of command, order, equity, stability of tenure of personnel, initiative, and esprit de corps. One outcome of the application of these principles is the maximization of efficiency. Two variations of the machine model are scientific management and bureaucracy.

Malicious prosecution Prosecutorial action against someone without probable cause or reasonable suspicion.

Mandatory minimum sentencing Flat-time sentence that must be imposed in which a minimum amount of time must be served before an inmate becomes eligible for parole.

Mandatory waivers Automatic transfers of certain juveniles to criminal court on the basis of their age and/or the seriousness of their offense; for example, a 17-year-old in Illinois who allegedly committed homicide would be subject to mandatory transfer to criminal court for the purpose of a criminal prosecution. Juvenile court judge must deter-

mine that probable cause exists before executing a mandatory waiver for any particular juvenile offender.

Maslow's hierarchy of needs Essential psychological and biological needs that have been suggested by Abraham Maslow; needs include biological needs, safety needs, belongingness needs, esteem needs, and self-actualization needs; Maslow believed that these needs exist in a pyramid form, and that the most basic biological needs must be fulfilled before higher needs in the pyramid become important to the person (i.e., one must feel that he or she belongs before the need for esteem or self-actualization will be felt; one must satisfy biological needs of hunger and thirst before acquiring the need to belong); Maslow conjectured that need-fulfillment explained certain behaviors manifested by persons (i.e., certain acts could be interpreted as need-fulfilling behaviors).

Maxi-maxi prison Institution such as the federal penitentiary at Florence, Colorado, where offenders are confined in individual cells for up to 23 hours per day, under continuous monitoring and supervision, with no more than three prisoners per guard.

Maximum-security prisons Designation given to prisons in which inmates are maintained in the highest degree of custody and supervision. Inmates are ordinarily segregated from one another and have restricted visitation privileges.

Medium-security prisons Term applied to prisons in which some direct supervision of inmates is maintained, but prisoners are eligible for recreational activities and visitation privileges are more relaxed than in maximum-security prisons.

Megajails Any jail facility that has 1,000 or more beds.

Meta-analysis A methodological technique of surveying a large number of research articles for the purpose of determining commonalities or parallel findings in studies about the same or similar subject matter.

Metropolitan Police Act of 1829 Act that empowered Sir Robert Peel to select and organize the Metropolitan Police of London.

Metropolitan Police of London Organized in 1829 by Sir Robert Peel, a prominent British government official. Included duties that emphasized close interaction with the public and maintenance of proper attitudes and temperament.

Minimum-security prisons Term applied to prisons in which inmates are housed in efficiency apartments and permitted extensive freedoms and activities, under little supervision by correctional officers. Designated for nonviolent, low-risk offenders.

Ministations Small police stations strategically located in high-crime neighborhoods, staffed by one or more police officers; part of a program established by the Detroit Police Department in the early 1980s.

Minnesota Multiphasic Personality Inventory (MMPI) Instrument purportedly able to measure personality dimensions such as anxiety, sociability, personal adjustment, and social adjustment.

Mission statements Goals and orientation statements of organizations designed to disclose their purposes and responsibilities. Used to vest employees with direction and motivation.

Missouri Plan Method of selecting judges in which merit system for appointments is used. Believed to reduce political influence in the selection of judges.

Mitigating circumstances Factors about a crime that may lessen the severity of sentence imposed by the judge. Cooperating with police to apprehend others involved, youthfulness or old age of defendant, mental instability, and having no prior record are considered mitigating circumstances.

Models Conceptions of how organizations are structured or organized and function; views of organizations that enable researchers to determine and chart predictable patterns involving communication and power. Examples are bureaucracy, human relations, professional, and systems models.

Monotony Work routine and boredom from repetitiveness.

Moral involvement Disposition of persons who believe in complying with a superior's requests because it is the right and proper thing to do; persons who become involved in their work because of a moral sense of obligation or duty believe that their administrators or supervisors have a legitimate right to issue orders to them to behave in particular ways.

Motivational model Organizational view that specifies conditions that induce employees to work harder or produce more with proper incentives.

Multiple leadership Perhaps the most realistic view of leadership in organizations is considering various group needs and relying on several persons to fulfill leadership roles specifically designed to meet each need rather than depending on a single person to perform such an overwhelming diversification of tasks; a leadership division of labor in which some persons are responsible for certain tasks and others see to different tasks; no single person performs or assumes all leadership functions, but rather, these duties are distributed to various group members.

Natural-system model Model in which organizations are perceived as systems made up of independent parts, each part functioning so that the entire system is perpetuated and survives over time. The system draws its nourishment or energy from sources in its external environment. The system has built-in mechanisms for maintaining it and for regulating the relations between its component parts. In the context of the organic analogy, the system develops and grows, becoming increasingly complex. Each of the parts adjusts to the contributions of the other parts so that a type of homeostasis is generated. The major assumptions are that the organization is considered as a natural whole. The component structures of the system are emergent institutions that can be understood only in relation to the diverse needs of the total system. The component parts of an organization are interdependent. The organization is an end in itself. The realization of goals of the system as a whole is but one of several important needs to which the organization is oriented. The organization serves to link parts of the system and to provide avenues for controlling and integrating them. Organizational structures are viewed as spontaneously and homeostatically maintained and the system depends greatly on the conforming behavior of group members. Changes in organizational patterns are considered the results of cumulative, unplanned, adaptive responses to threats to the equilibrium of the system as a whole. Responses to problems are crescively developed defense mechanisms that are constantly shaped by shared values that are deeply internalized in the members.

Negligence Liability accruing to prison or correctional program administrators and probation or parole officers as the result of a failure to perform a duty owed clients or inmates or the improper or inadequate performance of that duty. May include negligent entrustment, negligent training, negligent assignment, negligent retention, or negligent supervision (e.g., providing probation or parole officers with revolvers and not providing them with firearms training).

Negligent assignment Placement of correctional officers, probation or parole officers, or other staff members in a position for which they are unqualified.

Negligent entrustment Administrators' failure to monitor guards supplied with items they have not yet been trained to use, such as firearms.

Negligent retention Maintaining officers determined unfit for their jobs in those jobs.

Negligent training Basis for civil lawsuit in which clear duty to train employees (e.g., to use firearms) is not met.

Nepotism The practice of hiring close friends or relatives, regardless of their qualifications, to fill positions in organizations; this practice is discouraged by the bureaucratic model, which seeks to select new recruits to organizations on the basis of merit rather than familial or friendship relations with those in charge of hiring decision making.

New York House of Refuge Established in New York City in 1825 by the Society for the Prevention of Pauperism to provide services for youths, including a school for status offenders that provided compulsory education with a strict prisonlike regimen that later was considered detrimental to youthful clientele.

Night watch Early English watchman program designed to report crime.

Night watchman A thirteenth-century untrained citizen who patrolled at night on the lookout for disturbances. Currently, usually a privately employed officer who maintains a vigilance on the premises of private or public buildings.

Nominal disposition Juvenile court outcome in which a juvenile is warned or verbally reprimanded but is returned to the custody of his or her parents.

Nonrational model Characterization of organizations that incorporates unplanned and spontaneous dimensions, in which order is attained apart from rules and regulations. Personality systems are primary, and individual differences account for employee performance and excellence rather than obedience to abstract rules under a bureaucratic model.

Nonsecure custody Type of juvenile disposition that involves some type of out-of-home placement, such as foster care or group homes; sometimes special camps are used in which juveniles can receive specialized attention from counselors and aides.

Normative power Type of power in which esteem and prestige symbols may be allocated for the benefit of subordinates to enlist their compliance.

Once an adult/always an adult Ruling that once a juvenile has been transferred to criminal court to be prosecuted as an adult, regardless of the criminal court outcome, the juvenile can never be subject to the jurisdiction of juvenile courts in the future; in short, the juvenile, once transferred, will always be treated as an adult if future crimes are committed, even if the youth is still not of adult age.

Open-system model Characterization of organizations that stresses their greater external environment and seeks to explain organizational behavior by using factors and events occurring both within and outside of the organization.

Organizational behavior Any characteristic referring to a dimension or feature of an organization that personifies it, such as an aggressive organization or an efficient organization.

Organizational chart A diagrammatic portrayal of the vertical and horizontal interrelatedness of all roles in an organization, from the highest level of administration to the lowest level and front-line employees. Each role is represented by a box, and interconnecting lines are drawn to show the superior-subordinate or horizontal relations between boxes (roles).

Organizational climate Somewhat like the personality for a person. The perceptions that people have of that climate produce its image in their minds. Some organizations are bustling and efficient, whereas others are easygoing. Some are quite human, but others are hard and cold. They change slowly, being influenced by their leaders and their environment.

Organizational complexity Two types of complexity have been identified: horizontal and vertical. Horizontal complexity is the lateral differentiation of functions that may be duplicated at all levels of authority in corporate organizations. Vertical complexity refers to the extent to which differentiated depth or organizational penetration exists below the most inclusive level (e.g., an organization that includes three or four different levels—national, regional, state, local—is more vertically differentiated and complex than one that has no additional levels below the national).

Organizational conflict The amount of friction between persons or departments within an organization; also refers to different departmental or personal goals that may be inconsistent with one another and in conflict.

Organizational control Refers to any variable that is central to the planning and coordinating of tasks within the overall division of labor of an organization. The initiation of directives to subordinate personnel and the formulation and implementation of policy decisions fall within the control realm.

Organizational effectiveness The degree to which any organization is able to achieve its goals or objectives.

Organizational flexibility The extent to which an organization can adapt to changes from within the internal environment and from the external environment; the adaptability of an organization to change.

Organizational goals Ends toward which organizations strive to achieve. Objectives and aims articulated by organizations in either written or unwritten form.

Organizational growth The increase in the number of employees in an organization over a specified time period, such as one year or longer; may also refer to an expansion of the division of labor or additional levels in the hierarchy of authority.

Organizational model Any explanation of what is occurring in an organization that focuses on specific features or characteristics of organizations as key explanatory factors.

Organizational size The number of personnel on the organization payroll; the total number of full-fledged members in the association.

Organizational structure Variables that tend to describe the arrangement of formalized positions or departments within an organization. They also describe the amount of differentiation and specialization within it. Three key variables pertaining to structure are (1) size, (2) complexity, and (3) formalization.

Organizational typologies Ways of describing or labeling differences among organizations. Certain relationships among variables may be true within one type of organization but not necessarily within another; typologies are considered useful because they contribute to explanations of differences between organizations.

Organizational unit of analysis, level of analysis Study of organizations in which the focus of a researcher's interest is the organization itself; the work group, interpersonal relations, and individuals within the organization are considered secondary to organizational factors, including organization size, structure, complexity, effectiveness, and change.

Original jurisdiction First authority over a case or cause, as opposed to appellate jurisdiction.

Paraprofessional Trained person who works as an assistant or lower-level employee in a professional occupation. In corrections, may work in a community agency or public organization and will have some work-related skills, but is not certified or has not completed any formal course of study culminating in a corrections certificate or degree.

Parolee Convicted offender who has been released from prison short of serving the full sentence originally imposed; usually must abide by conditions established by the parole board or paroling authority.

Parole officer (PO) Correctional official who supervises parolees.

Participating style Leadership mode devised by Hershey and Blanchard (1977) in which supervisors are task oriented and tell subordinates what to do, and a collaborative relation between subordinates and supervisors exists. Subordinates are given emotional consideration and are involved in decision making through feedback solicited by supervisors.

Participative leadership Mode of leadership that stresses involvement of subordinates in decisions affecting their work; supervisors solicit input from subordinates in the decision-making process; anticipated result is greater work satisfaction and commitment to organizational goals.

Path-goal theory Leadership view holding that there are goals sought by the organization and paths designated that are directly influenced by administrators; thus, administrators can influence goal attainment in specific ways by exercising different styles of leadership over subordinates.

Peace officers Any law enforcement officers at the state or local level whose primary responsibility is to enforce and preserve the public peace. May include sheriffs and their deputies, constables, and members of city police forces.

Peel, Sir Robert (1788–1850) British Home Secretary who created the Metropolitan Police of London in 1829; subsequently, British police became known as *bobbies* after Robert Peel.

Peace Officer Standards and Training (POST) Commission established to administer training programs for prospective law enforcement officers nationwide. Includes mandatory training requirements for newly hired police officers and those entering other aspects of law enforcement.

Penitentiary Act of 1779 Legislation passed by House of Commons in England authorizing creation of new facilities to house prisoners, where they could be productive. Prisoners would be well fed, well treated, well clothed, housed in safe and sanitary units, and trained to perform skills.

Pennsylvania system Devised and used in Walnut Street Jail in 1790 to place prisoners in solitary confinement. Predecessor to modern prisons. Used solitude to increase penitence and prevent cross-infection of prisoners. Encouraged behavioral improvements.

Petitioners Persons who bring a petition before the court.

Petitions Documents filed in juvenile court alleging that a juvenile is a delinquent, a status offender, or a dependent

and asking that the court assume jurisdiction over the juvenile or that the juvenile be transferred to a criminal court to be prosecuted as an adult.

Petit juries Finders of fact; juries of one's peers selected to determine guilt or innocence of defendants.

Philadelphia Society for Alleviating the Miseries of Public Prisons Society made up of prominent Philadelphia citizens, philanthropists, and religious reformers who believe prison conditions ought to be changed and made more humane. Established in 1787.

Plain error Error occurring during a trial that may substantially have affected the trial's outcome had it not occurred; standard used is legal impropriety affecting defendant's substantial rights that is sufficiently serious to bring about an unjust result.

Plea bargaining A preconviction deal-making process between the state and the accused in which the defendant exchanges a plea of guilty or *nolo contendere* (no contest) for a reduction in charges, a promise of sentencing leniency, or some other concession from full, maximum implementation of the conviction and sentencing authority of the court. Includes implicit plea bargaining, charge reduction bargaining, sentence recommendation bargaining, and judicial plea bargaining.

Police Deriving from the Greek word *polis,* meaning "city." Applied to anyone who has the authority to make arrests under the power and jurisdiction of the state; typically refers to uniformed officers who enforce local and state laws.

Police-community relations A generic concept including any program designed to promote or make more visible law enforcement strategies that are aimed at crime prevention and control and in which varying degrees of proactive citizen involvement are solicited.

Police discretion The autonomy in decision making and how police decide to enforce the law; the balancing mechanism between justice that is deserved by an individual and justice as equal treatment; professional individual and/or collective judgments that preserve and promote community and citizen safety, respect for the law, and citizen rights to due process and equal treatment under the law.

Police misconduct Any one of several different types of illegal and/or improper behavior of police officers, including acceptance of graft, falsifying police reports, and perjury.

Police professionalization Increasing formalization of police work and the rise in public acceptance of the police that accompanies it. A well-focused code of ethics, equitable recruitment and selection practices, and informed promotional strategies among many agencies.

Polygraph tests Apparatuses that record a person's blood pressure and various other sensory responses and record reactions by means of a moving pencil and paper. Designed to determine whether an individual is telling the truth during an interrogation. Also known as polygraphs. Results of tests are not admissible in court.

Poor Laws Seventeenth-century laws binding out vagrants and abandoned children as indentured servants.

POs Abbreviation for probation or parole officers.

Power The ability of a person to influence another person or persons to carry out orders; the capability one possesses to modify another's beliefs or behaviors.

Presumptive sentencing guidelines Statutory sentencing method that specifies normal sentences of particular lengths with limited judicial leeway to shorten or lengthen the term of the sentence.

Presumptive waivers Types of judicial waivers in which the burden of proof shifts from the state to the juvenile to contest whether or not a youth is transferred to criminal court.

Prime beneficiary typology Based on the principle of who benefits by the particular organizational activity. Four classes or types of beneficiaries are (1) members or rank-and-file participants; (2) owners, managers; (3) clients; and (4) general public; scheme created and described by Peter Blau and Richard Scott.

Prison State or federally operated facility to house long-term offenders; usually designed to house inmates serving incarcerative terms of one or more years. Self-contained facilities sometimes called total institutions.

Prison overcrowding Condition existing when the number of inmates housed in a prison exceeds the rated, operating, or design capacity.

Privatization Trend in prison and jail management and correctional operations generally in which private interests are becoming increasingly involved in the management and operations of correctional institutions.

Probation Condition of being placed in a nonincarcerative environment such as the community for a fixed period of time as a sentence in lieu of a sentence after being convicted of one or more crimes.

Probationary employees Rookies or new recruits who are in training for a given period; following their training, they become regular full-time employees or officers.

Probationer Convicted offender sentenced to a nonincarcerative alternative including supervised release in the community, restitution, community service, fines, or other conditions.

Probation officer (PO) Professional who supervises probationers.

Productivity Measured according to the particular organizational context within which employees are studied; may be the production of so many units of product per day or processing so much paperwork in a given time interval.

Professionalization Process of acquiring increased education, more in-service, "hands-on" training, practical work experience, as well as using higher selection standards (physical, social, and psychological) for officer or staff appointments.

Professionalization movement Pioneered by August Vollmer, who was chief of police of Berkeley, California, in the early 1900s. The movement stressed selecting officers according to test and on the basis of physical and psychological fitness; education was a key priority and a basis for advancements and promotions within police departments.

Professional model Explanation of organizations focusing on increased specialization within the organization as a means of attaining greater flexibility in managing organizational problems. Expanding the training of organizational members to deal with problematic events more flexibly is professionalizing them. Professional persons are typically identified as persons trained in professional schools, possessing complex skills and special knowledge, and equipped with internalized control mechanisms.

Prosecutor Court official who commences civil and criminal proceedings against defendants. Represents state or government interest, prosecuting defendants on behalf of a state or a government.

Prosecutorial misconduct Any immoral, unethical, or illegal acts associated with prosecutorial duties. For example, it is unethical for a prosecutor to pursue a case against a defendant if the prosecutor knows the defendant is innocent.

Psychological screening Selection of officers usually accomplished by both written and oral assessments of prospective recruits. Law enforcement agencies do not want to select recruits with emotional problems that could interfere with their work with the public, so tests are administered to evaluate characteristics such as emotional maturity and response to stress.

Quasi-judicial immunity Type of insulation from lawsuits enjoyed by probation officers who work directly for judges when preparing presentence investigation reports; officers may include erroneous information in their reports that may be harmful to probationers, but the officers enjoy some immunity within the scope of their duties under the power of the judges with whom they work.

Randolph Plan Sometimes called the Virginia Plan, consisting of superior and inferior courts, with the former having considerable appellate authority over the latter; evolved from England's royal court system.

Rational model Any characterization of an organization that stresses planned and coordinated activities and rules that lead to goal attainment and greater organizational effectiveness; examples are scientific management and bureaucracy.

Rattle watchmen In colonial America, persons equipped with noise-making rattles who were expected to shout and rattle their rattles in the event they observed crimes in progress or fleeing suspects.

Reeves Chief law enforcement officers of English shires or counties. Forerunners of county sheriffs.

Referent power Influence over others based on the degree of friendship felt by the subordinate toward the superior.

Referrals Any citations of a juvenile to juvenile court by a law enforcement officer, interested citizen, family member, or school official; usually based on law violations, delinquency, or unruly conduct.

Reform schools Antiquated term designating juvenile facilities geared to improve the conduct of those forcibly detained within.

Remunerative power Influence vested in the ability of the supervisor or superordinate to reward subordinates or others; obtaining compliance from others by enticing them with rewards.

Replication research Conducting a subsequent study based on the general guidelines of a previous study; an attempt to obtain the same results from a different sample by conducting fresh research at a later point in time; repetition of experiments or studies that utilize the same methodology.

Requests for proposals (RFPs) Public or private organization solicitations for research plans to investigate particular topics of interest to the organization. The U.S. Department of Justice and Office of Juvenile Justice and Delinquency Prevention Programs distribute these requests regularly, with guidelines and formats to follow; these solicitations lead to research proposal submissions that eventually may or may not be funded.

Restitution Stipulation by court that offenders must compensate victims for their financial losses resulting from crime. Compensation to victim for psychological, physical, or financial loss. May be imposed as a part of an incarcerative sentence.

Restorative justice Mediation between victims and offenders through which offenders accept responsibility for their actions and agree to reimburse victims for their losses; may involve community service and other penalties agreeable to both parties in a form of arbitration with a neutral third party acting as arbiter.

Reverse waiver Action by the criminal court to transfer direct file or statutory exclusion cases from the jurisdiction of criminal court back to juvenile court, usually at the recommendation of the prosecutor.

Reversible errors Errors committed by judges during trials that may result in reversals of convictions against defendants.

Reward power Influence over others based on the ability of one person to convey favors or benefits to others in exchange for their compliance.

Runaway Any juvenile who leaves his or her home for long-term periods without parental consent or supervision.

Role clarity The extent to which one knows what is expected of him or her in the performance of work tasks in an organization.

Role conflict Pertains to (1) conflict lying in the disparity between the demands of two roles that an individual performs; (2) conflict arising if a person assumes too many roles so that he or she cannot possibly fulfill all of the obligations involved; (3) conflict internal to a given role, in which a person accepts a role and finds that he or she does not have time to meet the demands and does not know how to get out of them, or a person accepts a role for which he or she has time but has neither the interest nor

the ability to carry out its obligations; and (4) conflict arising because of different expectations about how a role should be carried out.

Role specificity Refers to the perceived degree of familiarity with the requirements of one's work role in an organization; role clarity; role expectations.

Rule of fours Requirement that at least four U.S. Supreme Court justices must agree to hear a case before it is docketed or scheduled for appeal before them.

Satisfiers An integral part of Victor Vroom's dual-factor theory of motivation, those factors related directly to job content, such as the intrinsic interest in work performed, the potential for advancement and recognition, and the responsibility of the tasks.

Schouts and rattles Early New Yorkers who were equipped with actual noise-making rattles and who were expected to shout and rattle their rattles in the event they observed crimes in progress or fleeing suspects.

Scientific management Scheme for supervising workers devised by Frederick Taylor (1911), who believed that organizational effectiveness could be maximized by dividing all production-related tasks into a series of simple movements and operations. Each worker could be trained to perform a few simple operations, and the combined efforts of all workers laboring for the common good would maximize efficiency and productivity. Taylor believed also that the average worker is incapable of being self-motivated. Workers are interested in doing only whatever is minimally required by management. Therefore, in addition to redesigning and simplifying tasks, increased productivity could be achieved by establishing incentives to work harder during the work period.

Secure custody Any type of placement in a juvenile incarcerative facility for a period of time; considered the most serious punishment and a last resort by juvenile judges as a punishment for delinquent conduct.

Selling style Leadership mode emphasizing a collaborative relation between supervisors and subordinates, in which subordinates are given emotional consideration and involvement in decisions affecting their work through feedback solicited from supervisors.

Sentence recommendation bargaining Negotiation in which the prosecutor proposes a sentence in exchange for a guilty plea.

Sentencing hearings Optional hearing held in many jurisdictions in which defendants and victims can hear contents of presentence investigation reports prepared by probation officers. Defendants and/or victims may respond to report orally, in writing, or both. Hearing precedes sentence imposed by judge.

Service model Model designed to meet community needs and expectations and therefore shaped by them.

Shared-powers model Prototype of inmate supervision in which some degree of decision-making power is extended to inmates as well as to correctional officers and administrators. Reflecting the ideology of rehabilitation, the shared-powers model is apparent in those prisons with strong inmate councils that hear and decide inmate grievances and disputes. Prison officials acknowledge certain inmates as leaders, possessing the skills and influence to persuade other prisoners to comply with prison policies and rules. This perspective is viewed by some as democratizing prisons.

Sheriff Chief executive officer of counties; responsible for appointing jailers and other jail personnel and hiring deputies to enforce county laws.

Shires Early English counties.

Showing consideration View of supervisory behavior reflecting the degree to which the leader establishes two-way communication, mutual respect, and acknowledgment of the feelings of subordinates. Essentially, it represents a human relations orientation toward leadership.

Similarity of values The extent to which work groups share the same interests and attitudes about their work.

Solitary confinement A sentencing philosophy seeking to confine one offender away from other offenders by placing the prisoner in a cell with no communication with others. Also known as isolation, it originated in the Walnut Street Jail in Philadelphia, Pennsylvania, in the late 1700s. Another usage of this term is to segregate offenders from society through incarceration.

Span of control The number of persons or departments under the direct control of a supervisor or individual department. Span of control may also refer to the managerial or supervisory responsibilities and power relative to subordinates in different organizational units.

Special jurisdiction Indicates that the court is restricted to handling certain types of cases such as probating wills or adjudicating juvenile offenders.

Spuriousness Any association between two variables that may be explained away by introducing a third, more powerful variable in the original two-variable relation.

Staff personnel Support personnel consisting of the dispatchers, secretarial help, and other ancillary employees who facilitate the performance of police officer tasks, including communication, training, property, and records.

Stare decisis Legal precedent. Principle by which lower courts issue rulings consistent with those of higher courts, if the same types of cases and facts are at issue. The principle of leaving undisturbed a settled point of law or particular precedent.

Station house adjustments Decisions by police officers to deal informally with arrestees, often at the police station. Actions often do not involve arrests, but warnings.

Status offender Any juvenile who has committed an offense that would not be considered a crime if committed by an adult (e.g., a curfew violation would not be criminal action if committed by an adult, but such an act is a status offense if engaged in by a juvenile).

Status offense Any act committed by a juvenile that would not be a crime if committed by an adult; includes truancy, runaway behavior, and curfew violation.

Statutory exclusion Means that certain juveniles are automatically excluded from the juvenile court's original jurisdiction because of the crimes they have committed; also known as automatic waivers and legislative waivers.

Stress A nonspecific response to a perceived threat to an individual's well-being or self-esteem.

Superintendents Persons who are in administrative charge of prisons or penitentiaries.

Supervisory style Predominantly an independent variable in formal organizational research, connotes initiating activity for subordinates in the work setting. Leaders must obtain the compliance of lower-level participants in the organization. Different managers or leaders obtain compliance from subordinates in different ways, characterized as their "style."

Supportive leadership Any type of supervisory behavior that encourages greater employee involvement in decision making, in which administrators consider a worker's feelings and emotions and respect his or her knowledge of work to be performed.

Supreme court Any court of last resort in most kinds of cases at the state level; the federal court of last resort as specified by the United States Constitution is the U.S. Supreme Court.

Survival model Organizational view that indicates what an organization must do in order to endure over time.

Syntality The personality of a group.

Tall organizational structure Any hierarchy of authority with many supervisory levels.

Technology The mechanisms or processes by which an organization turns out its product or services.

Telling style Leadership mode that is task oriented and requires supervisors to tell employees or subordinates what to do; involves delegating tasks to subordinates who are emotional enough to perform them.

Texas model Also known as the "traditional" model of state court organization. Includes two "supreme" courts, one for civil appeals, one for criminal appeals, and has five tiers of district, county, and municipal courts.

Theory An integrated body of assumptions and propositions that are related in such a way as to explain and predict relations between two or more variables.

Theory X Advanced by Douglas McGregor, view of motivating workers assuming that persons have an inherent dislike of work and will avoid it if they can. Because of this human characteristic of dislike of work, most people must be coerced, controlled, directed, and threatened with punishment to get them to put forth sufficient effort toward the achievement of organizational objectives. This theory holds that the average human being prefers to be directed, wants to avoid responsibility, has relatively little ambition, and wants security above all.

Theory Y Explanation of worker motivation devised by Douglas McGregor, postulating that the expenditure of physical and mental effort in work is as natural as play or rest. External control and the threat of punishment are not the only means for bringing about effort toward organizational objectives. Workers will exercise self-direction and self-control in the service of objectives to which they are committed. Commitment to objectives is a function of the rewards associated with their achievement. The average human being learns, under proper conditions, not only to accept but to seek responsibility. The capacity to exercise a relatively high degree of imagination, ingenuity, and creativity in the solutions of organizational problems is widely, not narrowly, distributed in the population.

Theory Z Explanation of worker motivation devised by William Ouchi (1981) that emphasizes employee job security, participatory decision making, group responsibility and teamwork, increased product and services quality, slower evaluation and promotion policies, broader career paths, and a greater concern for employees' work and familial welfare.

Thief-takers Persons who were fleet of foot in early England, selected to pursue and apprehend fleeing criminals for a fee, or citizens who receive a reward for the apprehension of criminals.

Thomas's four wishes Scheme devised by social psychologist W.I. Thomas that described four needs or wishes persons have; these wishes are motivating factors to behave in certain ways; the wishes include the wish for response or love, recognition, new experience, and security; Thomas presumed that persons are motivated to achieve these needs and that this action explains their conduct.

Tiers Construction of prisons in layers or different floors, each containing offenders of varying levels of seriousness or dangerousness.

Tier system Method of establishing various floors for cells where prisoners of different types can be housed that was started at Auburn State Penitentiary in 1816.

Total quality management (TQM) A model of personnel management stressing high employee participation in the decision-making process. It also stresses teamwork, continuous learning and self-improvement, and the use of the scientific method and statistical quality control to evaluate and improve worker effectiveness. TQM is implemented through (1) developing effective leadership; (2) instilling greater worker commitment to work quality and services; (3) establishing a work atmosphere conducive to self-fulfillment, creativity, and pride in workmanship; (4) using scientific thinking; (5) creating open communication and emphasizing greater honesty and information sharing; and (6) being citizen oriented.

Traditional authority Type of power that adheres in kinship and follows rules of descent, such as cases in which the rights of the father pass to the oldest male child at the time of the father's death; power exerted through custom rather than through bureaucratic prescription.

Traditional model (1) Applied to organizations, views organizations as machines, and that just as we build a mechan-

ical device with given specifications for accomplishing tasks, so also do we construct an organization according to a blueprint to achieve a given purpose. (2) Applied to court organization, also known as the Texas model, featuring two courts of last resort, the supreme court, which hears cases of a civil nature and juvenile matters, and the court of criminal appeals, which has final appellate jurisdiction in criminal cases.

Trait approach Leadership theory that holds that leaders have inborn characteristics, qualities, or specific genetic attributes that vest them with power over others; assumes that such traits cannot be learned or transmitted socially.

Transfer Action by juvenile court to waive jurisdiction over a juvenile to the criminal court.

Truants Juveniles who absent themselves from school without a valid excuse.

Typologies Ways of viewing organizations that group them into different categories so that those sharing certain characteristics or qualities can be viewed as somewhat unique from other types of organizations with different sets of characteristics.

United States attorneys Presidential appointments, prosecutors who are responsible for controlling and supervising all criminal prosecutions and representing the government in any legal suits in which it is a party. U.S. attorneys may appoint committees to investigate other governmental agencies or offices if questions of wrongdoing are raised or if possible violations of the laws of the United States are suspected or detected.

United States Supreme Court Appellate court of last resort that also has both original jurisdiction and exclusive jurisdiction over all actions or proceedings against ambassadors or public ministers of foreign states and all controversies between two or more states.

Units of analysis Three levels of analysis for studying organizations, including the individual, the group, and the organization itself; abstractions used for theorizing and constructing explanations for what is going on in organizations and why.

Variables Any quantities that can assume more than one value; examples include gender, power, organizational size, complexity, and bureaucratization.

Venire List of prospective jurors drawn up from pools of registered voters, from vehicle drivers' licenses, or from tax assessors' records. Persons who are potential jurors in a given jurisdiction; these persons must reside within the particular jurisdiction in which the jury trial is held.

Veniremen Person who are selected for jury duty; the pool of citizens from which a jury will be selected.

Veniremen lists Compilations of prospective jurors made up from registered voters, those with drivers' licenses, and from tax assessors' records.

Vertical complexity The extent to which there is differentiated depth or organizational penetration below the most inclusive level (e.g., an organization that includes three or four different levels—national, regional, state, local—is more vertically differentiated and complex than one that has no additional levels below the national).

Vertical differentiation A proliferation of supervisory levels or numerous levels of supervision.

Victim/offender mediation model Process through which a criminal and the person suffering loss or injury from the criminal meet with a third-party, arbiter, such as a judge, attorney, or other neutral party, who decides what is best for all parties. All parties must agree to decision of third-party arbiter. Used for both juvenile and adult offenders.

Victim/reparations model Restitution model for juveniles in which juveniles compensate their victims directly for their offenses.

Virginia Plan Scheme deriving from England's royal court system, projecting superior and inferior courts; also called Randolph Plan.

Vollmer, August (1876–1955) In 1908, the chief of police of Berkeley, California, who demanded and incorporated greater formal professional and educational training for the police officers under his command; pioneered an academic regimen of police training, including investigative techniques, photography, fingerprinting, and anatomy, among other academic subject areas; used various forensics technologists to assist in this training.

Voluntary sentencing guidelines Recommended sentencing policies that are not required by law. They serve as a guide and are based on past sentencing practices, but the legislature has not mandated their use. Voluntary/advisory guidelines may use either indeterminate or determinate sentencing structures.

Volunteer Any citizen who donates time to assist in the community. In corrections, this may include assistance in the supervision, education, counseling, or training of probationers, parolees, or divertees.

Waivers Transfers of jurisdiction from the juvenile court to criminal court of particular juveniles so that they can be prosecuted and punished as adult offenders.

Walnut Street Jail Considered the first American prison seeking to correct offenders. Built in 1776 in Philadelphia, Pennsylvania. Also one of first penal facilities to segregate female from male offenders and children from adults. Introduced solitary confinement of prisoners, separated prisoners according to their offense severity, and operated on the basis that inmates could perform useful services to defray the costs of the confinement. Created one of first

prison industry programs; inmates also grew much of their own food through gardening.

Wardens Persons who are administrators of prisons or penitentiaries.

Watchman model Police style for organizational attainment with the following characteristics: stresses order maintenance, charged with keeping the peace, neither proactive nor reactive, and maintains order through physical presence and crime deterrence.

Watchmen Citizens in early England who were paid to observe in their neighborhoods for possible criminal activity.

Wickersham Commission Commission established in 1929 to investigate police agencies and the state of training and education among police officers. Generally critical of contemporary methods of police organization and operation. Conclusions published by the National Commission on Law Observance and Enforcement, chaired by George W. Wickersham.

Wilson, O.W. A former police chief in Wichita, Kansas, and Chicago, Illinois. First dean of the School of Criminology at the University of California–Berkeley in 1950. Successfully centralized police administration and created command decision making, not only in Berkeley, but in many other cities during the 1950s and 1960s.

Workhouses Early penal facilities designed to use prison labor for profit by private interests. Operated in English shires in mid-sixteenth century and later.

Work routine Monotonous and repetitive labor in organizational settings; doing the same things over and over again in a repetitive fashion; a work pattern.

Work/study release Community-based program in which persons about to be paroled work with limited supervision in the community at jobs during the day and return to a secure facility at night. Any program that provides for prison labor in the community, under conditions of relaxed supervision, and for which prisoners are paid adequate wages.

Writ of *mandamus* Order of a superior court commanding that a lower court, administrative body, or executive body perform a specific function. Commonly used to restore rights and privileges lost to a defendant through illegal means.

Writs of *certiorari* Orders of a superior court requesting that the record of an inferior court (or administrative body) be brought forward for review or inspection. Literally, "to be more fully informed."

REFERENCES

Adams, Stuart (1977). "Evaluating Correctional Treatments: Toward a New Perspective." *Criminal Justice and Behavior* **4:**323–339.

Adamson, Patrick B. (1991). "Some Comments on the Origin of the Police." *Police Studies* **14:**1–2.

Adamson, Raymond S., and Gene Deszca (1999). "Police Force Communications: Managing Meaning on the Firing Line." *Canadian Police College Journal* **14:**155–171.

Administrative Office of the U.S. Courts (2000). *Federal Courts, Organization, and Personnel.* Washington, DC: U.S. Government Printing Office.

Albrecht, Gary L. (1976). "The Effects of Computerized Information Systems on Juvenile Courts." *Justice System Journal* **2:**107–120.

Aldag, Ramon J., and Arthur P. Brief (1978). "Supervisory Style and Police Role Stress." *Journal of Police Science and Administration* **6:**362–367.

Alexander, David A., and Leslie G. Walker (1996). "The Perceived Impact of Police Work on Police Officers' Spouses and Families." *Stress Medicine* **12:**239–246.

Alfini, James J. (1981). "Mississippi Judicial Selection: Election, Appointment, and Bar Anointment." In *Courts and Judges,* James A. Cramer (ed.). Beverly Hills, CA: Sage.

Allinson, Richard (1983). "There Are No Juveniles in Pennsylvania Jails." *Corrections Magazine* **9:**13–20.

Alpert, Geoffrey P., and Roger G. Dunham (1990). *Police Pursuit Driving: Controlling Responses to Emergency Situations.* Westport, CT: Greenwood Press.

Alpert, Geoffrey P., and William C. Smith (1994). "Developing Police Policy: An Evaluation of the Control Principle." *American Journal of Police* **13:**1–20.

Altschuler, D.M. (1999). "Trends and Issues in the Adultification of Juvenile Justice." In *Research Results: Effective Community Correction,* P. Harris (ed.). Lanham, MD: American Correctional Association.

American Bar Association (1972). *Code of Judicial Conduct.* Chicago: American Bar Association.

American Bar Association (1975). *Standards Relating to Trial Courts.* Washington, DC: American Bar Association Commission on Standards of Judicial Administration.

American Correctional Association (1994). *The ACA Code of Ethics.* Lanham, MD: American Correctional Association.

American Correctional Association (1995). *The State of Corrections.* Laurel, MD: American Correctional Association.

American Correctional Association (1999). *1999 Directory: Juvenile & Adult Correctional Departments, Agencies & Paroling Authorities.* Lanham, MD: American Correctional Association.

American Correctional Association (2000). *2000–2001 National Jail and Adult Detention Directory.* Lanham, MD: American Correctional Association.

American Correctional Association (2001). *2001 ACA Directory.* Lanham MD: American Correctional Association.

American Federation of State, County, and Municipal Employees (1982). *Prisoners of Life: A Study of Occupational Stress Among State Corrections Officers.* Washington, DC: American Federation of State, County, and Municipal Employees.

American Judicature Society (1973). "State Court Progress at a Glance." *Judicature* **56:**427–430.

American Judicature Society (1983). *Report of the Committee on Qualification Guidelines for Judicial Candidates.* Chicago: American Judicature Society.

Anderson, B.D., et al. (1966). "Status Classes in Organizations." *Administrative Science Quarterly* **11:**264–283.

Anderson, Terry D. (2000). *Every Officer Is a Leader: Transforming Leadership in Police, Justice, and Public Safety.* Boca Raton, FL: St. Lucie Press.

Anderson, Theodore, and Seymour Warkov (1961). "Organizational Size and Functional Complexity: A Study of Administration in Hospitals." *American Sociological Review* **26:**23–38.

Angell, John E. (1971). "Toward an Alternative to the Classic Police Organization Arrangements: A Democratic Model." *Criminology* **9:**185–206.

Applewhite, P.B. (1965). *Organizational Behavior.* Englewood Cliffs, NJ: Prentice Hall.

Archambeault, William G., and Donald R. Deis, Jr. (1996). *Cost Effectiveness Comparisons of Private Versus Public Prisons in Louisiana: Executive Summary.* Baton Rouge, LA: School of Social Work, Louisiana State University.

Archambeault, William G., and Charles L. Weirman (1983). "Critically Assessing the Utility of Police Bureaucracies in the 1980s: Implications of Management Theory Z." *Journal of Police Science and Administration* **4:**420–429.

Argyle, Michael, Godfrey Gardner, and Frank Cioffi (1958). "Supervisory Methods Related to Productivity, Absenteeism, and Labor Turnover." *Human Relations* **11:**23–40.

Argyris, Chris (1960). *Understanding Organizational Behavior.* Homewood, IL: Dorsey Press.

Arkin, Sharon (1975). "Jobs for Addicts." *Manpower* **4:**19–24.

Armitage, Rachel, Graham Smyth, and Ken Pease (1999). "Burnley CCTV Evaluation." In *Surveillance of Public Space: CCTV, Street Lighting, and Crime Prevention*, Kate Painter and Nick Tilley (eds.). Monsey, NY: Criminal Justice Press.

Arnold, Charlotte S. (1993). "Respect, Recognition Are Keys to Effective Volunteer Programs." *Corrections Today* **55**:118–122.

Ash, Philip, Karen B. Slora, and Cynthia F. Britton (1990). "Police Agency Officer Selection Practices." *Journal of Police Science and Administration* **17**:258–269.

Assael, Henry (1969). "Constructive Role of Interorganizational Conflict." *Administrative Science Quarterly* **14**:573–583.

Auten, James H. (1985). "Police Management in Illinois: 1983." *Journal of Police Science and Administration* **13**:325–337.

Axon, Lee, and Robert H. Hann (1995). *Court Dispute Resolution Processes: The Application of Alternative Dispute Resolution in the Courts*. Ottawa, Can: Department of Justice, Research, Statistics, and Program Evaluation Directorate.

Bailey, William G. (1986). *Police Science, 1964–1984: A Selected, Annotated Bibliography*. New York: Garland Publishing Company.

Baker, Ralph, and Fred A. Meyer (1980). *The Criminal Justice Game: Politics and Players*. North Scituate, MA: Duxbury Press.

Baker, Stephen A. (1995). *Effects of Law Enforcement Accreditation: Officer Selection, Promotion, and Education*. Westport, CT: Praeger.

Bannerman, Elizabeth D. (1996). *Female Police Officers: The Relationship Between Social Support, Interactional Style, and Occupational Stress and Strain*. Ann Arbor, MI: University Microfilms International.

Barak-Glantz, Israel L. (1986). "Toward a Conceptual Schema of Prison Management Styles." *The Prison Journal* **60**:42–60.

Barker, Thomas (1986). "Peer Group Support." In *Police Deviance*, Thomas Barker and David L. Carter (eds.). Cincinnati, OH: Pilgrimage Press.

Barker, Thomas, Ronald D. Hunter, and Jeffrey P. Rush (1994). *Police Systems and Practices: An Introduction*. Upper Saddle River, NJ: Prentice Hall.

Barlow, David E., and Melissa Hickman Barlow (1994). "Cultural Diversity Rediscovered: Developing Training Strategies for Police Officers." *Justice Professional* **8**:97–116.

Barnard, Chester I. (1938). *The Functions of the Executive*. Cambridge, MA: Harvard University Press.

Bass, B.M. (1981). *Stogdill's Handbook of Leadership*. New York: Free Press.

Bayens, Gerald J., Jimmy J. Williams, and John Ortiz Smykla (1997). "Jail Type and Inmate Behavior: A Longitudinal Analysis." *Federal Probation* **61**:54–62.

Bayley, David H. (1985). *Patterns of Policing: A Comparative International Analysis*. New Brunswick, NJ: Rutgers University Press.

Bayley, David H. (1993). "Back from Wonderland, or 'Toward the Rational Use of Police Resources.'" In *Thinking About Police Resources*, N. Doob (ed.). Toronto, Can: University of Toronto, Centre for Criminology.

Bazemore, Gordon (1998). "Restorative Justice and Earned Redemption: Communities, Victims, and Offender Reintegration." *American Behavioral Scientist* **41**:768–813.

Bazemore, Gordon, Todd J. Dicker, and Ron Nyhan (1994). "Juvenile Justice Reform and the Difference It Makes: An Exploratory Study of the Impact of Policy Change on Detention Worker Attitudes." *Crime and Delinquency* **40**:37–53.

Bazemore, Gordon, and Lynette Feder (1997). "Judges in the Punitive Juvenile Court: Organizational, Career and Ideological Influences on Sanctioning Orientation." *Justice Quarterly* **14**:87–114.

Becker, Harold K., and Jack E. Whitehouse (1980). *Police of America: A Personal View, Introduction, and Commentary*. Springfield, IL: Charles C Thomas.

Becknell, Conan, G. Larry Mays, and Dennis M. Giever (1999). "Policy Restrictiveness and Police Pursuits." *Policing: An International Journal of Police Strategies and Management* **22**:93–101.

Bedea-Mueller, Sandra, and Theodore J. Hutler, Jr. (2000). "Transforming Corrections: Organizational Change in the Ocean County DOC." *Corrections Compendium* **25**:1–6, 16–18.

Beenakkers, Emth (2000). *Effectiveness of Correctional Treatment: A Literature Survey*. The Hauge, Neth: Netherlands Ministry of Justice.

Beito, Linda Royster (1999). *Leadership Effectiveness in Community Policing*. Bristol, IN: Wyndam Hall Press.

Belbot, Barbara A. (1995). *The Prison as a Political Community: An Analysis of Legal Issues in Classification*. Ann Arbor, MI: University Microfilms International.

Belcastro, Philip A., Robert S. Gold, and Justine Grant (1982). "Stress and Burnout: Physiologic Effects on Correctional Teachers." *Criminal Justice and Behavior* **9**:387–395.

Bennett, Brad R. (1992). "Transforming Police Leadership in the '90s." *Journal of Contemporary Criminal Justice* **8**:257–264.

Bennett, Richard R. (1997). "Job Satisfaction Among Police Constables: A Comparative Study in Three Developing Nations." *Justice Quarterly* **14**:295–323.

Bennis, Warren G. (1966). *Changing Organizations*. New York: McGraw-Hill.

Benson, Bruce L. (1998). *To Serve and Protect: Privatization and Community in Criminal Justice*. New York: New York University Press.

Benson, Bruce L., David W. Rasmussen, and David L. Sollars (1995). "Police Bureaucracies, Their Incentives, and the War on Drugs." *Public Choice* **83**:21–45.

Betsalel, Kenneth Aaron (1990). "Police Leadership and the Reconciliation of Police-Minority Relations." *American Journal of Police* **9**:63–77.

Biggam, Fiona H., and Kevin G. Power (1996). "The Personality of the Scottish Police Officer: The Issue of Positive and Negative Affectivity." *Personality and Individual Differences* **20**:661–667.

Biggam, Fiona H., et al. (1997). "Self-Perceived Occupational Stress and Distress in a Scottish Police Force." *Work and Stress* **11**:118–133.

Bilchik, Shay (1996). *State Responses to Serious and Violent Juvenile Crime.* Pittsburgh, PA: National Center for Juvenile Justice.

Bilchik, Shay (1998). *Mental Health Disorders and Substance Abuse Problems Among Juveniles.* Washington, DC: U.S. Department of Justice.

Bilchik, Shay (1999). *Juvenile Justice: A Century of Change.* Washington, DC: U.S. Department of Justice.

Biles, David, and Julia Vernon (eds.) (1994). *Private Sector and Community Involvement in the Criminal Justice System.* Canberra, Aus: Australian Institute of Criminology.

Bishop, Bill (1993). "New York's Crime War: The Empire Strikes Out!" *APPA Perspectives* **17**:13–14.

Bittner, Egon (1970). *The Functions of the Police in Modern Society.* Washington, DC: National Institutes of Mental Health, Center for Studies of Crime and Delinquency, U.S. Government Printing Office.

Bizzack, John W. (1993). *Professionalism and Law Enforcement Accreditation: The First Ten Years.* Lexington, KY: Autumn House Publishing.

Black, Henry Campbell (1990). *Black's Law Dictionary.* St. Paul, MN: West Publishing Company.

Blakely, Curtis R., and Vic W. Bumphus (1996). "Private Correctional Management: A Comparison of Enabling Legislation." *Federal Probation* **60**:49–53.

Blanchard, K., P. Zigarmi, and D. Zigarmi (1985). *Leadership and One Minute Manager.* New York: William Morrow and Company.

Blankenship, Michael B., Jerry B. Spargar, and W. Richard Janikowski (1994). "Accountability v. Independence: Myths of Judicial Selection." *Criminal Justice Policy Review* **6**:69–79.

Blankenship, Michael B., et al. (1997). "Jurors' Comprehension of Sentencing Instructions: A Test of the Death Penalty Process in Tennessee." *Justice Quarterly* **14**:325–351.

Blau, Peter M. (1955). *The Dynamics of Bureaucracy.* Chicago: The University of Chicago Press.

Blau, Peter M. (1968). "The Hierarchy of Authority in Organizations." *American Journal of Sociology* **73**:453–467.

Blau, Peter M. (1970). "Decentralization in Bureaucracies." In *Power in Organizations,* Mayer N. Zald (ed.). Nashville, TN: Vanderbilt University Press.

Blau, Peter M., and W. Richard Scott (1962). *Formal Organizations: A Comparative Approach.* San Francisco: Chandler.

Blowers, Anita Neuberger (1995). "Improving the Writing Skills of Jail Officers." *American Jails* **8**:41–46.

Blumenson, Eric, and Eva Nilsen (1998). "Policing for Profit: The Drug War's Hidden Economic Agenda." *University of Chicago Law Review* **65**:35–114.

Bohm, Robert M. (1986). "Crime, Criminal and Crime Control Policy Myths." *Justice Quarterly* **3**:193–214.

Boland, Mary L. (1997). *A Crime Victim's Guide to Justice.* Naperville, IL: Sourcebooks, Inc.

Bonjean, Charles M., and Michael D. Grimes (1970). "Bureaucracy and Alienation: A Dimensional Approach." *Social Forces* **48**:365–373.

Bonifacio, Philip (1991). *The Psychological Effects of Police Work: A Psychodynamic Approach.* New York: Plenum.

Bopp, William J. (1975). *In Quest of Police Profession: A Biography of Orlando W. Wilson.* Ann Arbor, MI: Xerox University Microfilms.

Borodzicz, Edward Piotr (1996). "Security and Risk: A Theoretical Approach to Managing Loss Prevention." *International Journal of Risk Security and Crime Prevention* **1**:131–143.

Boyd, John S., and Thomas J. Tiefenwerth (1995). "Jail Training on the Road in Texas." *American Jails* **9**:59–60.

Bradley, David, Neil Walker, and Roy Wilkie (1986). *Managing the Police: Law, Organization, and Democracy.* Brighton, UK: Harvester Press.

Bradley, J.M. (1986). "Training Doesn't Have to Be Expensive to Be Good." *FBI Law Enforcement Bulletin* **55**:11–14.

Brandl, Steven G., and Frank G. Horvath (1991). "Crime Victim Evaluation of Police Investigative Performance." *Journal of Criminal Justice* **19**:109–122.

Breci, Michael Gene (1986). *Police Response to Domestic Disturbances.* Ann Arbor, MI: University Microfilms International.

Breci, Michael Gene, and Ronald L. Simons (1987). "An Examination of Organizational and Individual Factors That Influence Police Response to Domestic Disturbances." *Journal of Police Science and Administration* **15**:93–104.

Brennan, Tim, and David Wells (1992). "The Importance of Inmate Classification in Small Jails." *American Jails* **6**:49–52.

Brereton, David, and Andrew Ede (1996). "The Police Code of Silence in Queensland: The Impact of the Fitzgerald Inquiry Reforms." *Current Issues in Criminal Justice* **8**:107–129.

Brewer, Neil (1995). *Handbook of Effective Supervisory Behavior.* Payneham, South Australia: Australian National Police Research Unit.

Brewer, Neil, and Carlene Wilson (eds.) (1995). *Psychology and Policing.* Hillsdale, NJ: Lawrence Erlbaum.

Brief, Arthur P., Ramon J. Aldag, and Richard A. Wallden (1978). "Correlates of Supervisory Style Among Policemen." *Criminal Justice and Behavior* **3**:263–271.

Britton, Dana M. (1997). "Perceptions of the Work Environment Among Correctional Officers: Do Race and Sex Matter?" *Criminology* **35**:85–105.

Britz, Marjie T. (1997). "The Police Subculture and Occupational Socialization: Exploring Individual and Demographic Characteristics." *American Journal of Criminal Justice* **21**:127–146.

Brown, Jennifer, Gary Cooper, and Bruce Kirkcaldy (1996). "Occupational Stress Among Senior Police Officers." *British Journal of Psychology* **87**:31–41.

Brown, M. Craig, and Barbara D. Warner (1992). "Immigrants, Urban Politics, and Policing in 1900." *American Sociological Review* **57**:293–305.

Brown, Paul W. (1987). "Probation Officer Burnout: An Organizational Disease/An Organizational Cure." *Federal Probation* **51**:17–21.

Bryan, Darrell (1995). "Emergency Response Teams: A Prison's First Line of Defense." *Corrections Compendium* **20**:1–4.

Buerger, Michael E. (1998). "Police Training as a Pentecost: Using Tools Singularly Ill-Suited to the Purpose of Reform." *Police Quarterly* **1**:27–63.

Bureau of Justice Assistance (1998). *1996 National Survey of State Sentencing Structures.* Washington, DC: U.S. Department of Justice.

Bureau of Justice Statistics (1992). *State and Local Police Departments, 1990.* Washington, DC: U.S. Department of Justice.

Bureau of Justice Statistics (1999a). *Law Enforcement Management and Administrative Statistics, 1997.* Washington, DC: U.S. Department of Justice.

Bureau of Justice Statistics (1999b). *Local Police Departments, 1997.* Washington, DC: U.S. Department of Justice.

Bureau of Justice Statistics (1999c). *Sheriffs' Departments, 1997.* Washington, DC: U.S. Department of Justice.

Burke, Kenneth (1935). *Permanence and Change.* New York: New Republic.

Burke, Ronald J. (1987). "Burnout in Police Work: An Examination of the Cherniss Model." *Group and Organizational Studies* **12**:174–188.

Burke, Ronald J., and Eugene Deszca (1986). "Correlates of Psychological Burnout Phases Among Police Officers." *Human Rights* **39**:487–502.

Burke, Ronald J., and Catherine Kirchmeyer (1990a). "Initial Career Orientations, Stress, and Burnout in Policeworkers." *Canadian Police College Journal* **14**:28–36.

Burke, Ronald J., and Catherine Kirchmeyer (1990b). "Present Career Orientations, Stress and Burnout in Policeworkers." *Canadian Police College Journal* **14**:50–57.

Burns, Henry (1975). *Corrections Organization and Administration.* St. Paul, MN: West Publishing Company.

Burstein, Carolyn (1980). "Criminal Case Processing from an Organizational Perspective: Current Research Trends." *Justice System Journal* **5**:258–273.

Burton, Velmer S., Jr., James Frank, Robert H. Langworthy, and Troy A. Barker (1993). "The Prescribed Roles of Police in a Free Society: Analyzing State Legal Codes." *Justice Quarterly* **10**:683–695.

Burton, Velmer S., Jr., Edward J. Latessa, and Troy Barker (1992). "The Role of Probation Officers: An Examination of Statutory Requirements." *Journal of Contemporary Criminal Justice* **8**:274–282.

Butts, Jeffrey A., and Howard N. Snyder (1997). *The Youngest Delinquents: Offenders Under Age 15.* Washington, DC: Office of Juvenile Justice and Delinquency Prevention.

Buzawa, Eve (1984). "Determining Patrol Officer Job Satisfaction: The Role of Selected Demographic and Job-Specific Attitudes." *Criminology* **22**:61–81.

Buzawa, Eve, Thomas Austin, and James Bannon (1994). "The Role of Selected Sociodemographic and Job-Specific Variables in Predicting Patrol Officer Job Satisfaction: A Reexamination Ten Years Later." *American Journal of Police* **13**:51–75.

Buzawa, Eve, Gerald Hoteling, and Andrew Klein (1998). "What Happens When a Reform Works? The Need to Study Unanticipated Consequences of Mandatory Processing of Domestic Violence." *Journal of Police and Criminal Psychology* **13**:43–54.

Byrne, James M., Arthur J. Lurigio, and Joan Petersilia (eds.) (1992). *Smart Sentencing: The Emergence of Intermediate Sanctions.* Newbury Park, CA: Sage.

Cahalan, Margaret W. (1986). *Historical Corrections Statistics in the United States, 1850–1984.* Washington, DC: U.S. Department of Justice.

Call, Jack E. (1995a). "Prison Overcrowding Cases in the Aftermath of *Wilson v. Seiter.*" *Prison Journal* **75**:390–405.

Call, Jack E. (1995b). "The Supreme Court and Prisoners' Rights." *Federal Probation* **59**:36–46.

Camp, Camille G., and George M. Camp (1999a). *The Corrections Yearbook 1998.* Middletown, CT: Criminal Justice Institute, Inc.

Camp, Camille G., and George M. Camp (1999b). *The Corrections Yearbook 1999.* Middletown, CT: Criminal Justice Institute, Inc.

Campbell, Frederick L., and Ronald L. Akers (1970). "Size and the Administrative Component in Occupational Associations." *Sociological Quarterly* **11**:435–451.

Canada Solicitor General (1977). *A Report on Canadian Correctional Services and Management.* Ottawa: Canada Solicitor General.

Cannizzo, Thomas A., Jr., and Peter Liu (1995). "The Relationship Between Levels of Perceived Burnout and Career Stage Among Sworn Police Officers." *Police Studies* **18**:53–68.

Cantelon, Sharon, and Donni LeBoeuf (1997). *Keeping Young People in School: Community Programs That Work.* Washington, DC: U.S. Department of Justice.

Caplow, Theodore (1964). *Principles of Organization.* New York: Harcourt, Brace, and World.

Carey, Alex (1967). "The Hawthorne Studies: A Radical Criticism." *American Sociological Review* **32**:403–416.

Carey, Raymond (1972). "Correlates of Satisfaction with the Priesthood." *Administrative Science Quarterly* **17**:185–195.

Carlan, Philip E. (1999). "Occupational Outcomes of Criminal Justice Graduates: Is the Master's Degree a Wise investment?" *Journal of Criminal Justice Education* **10**:39–55.

Carlson, Eric W., et al. (1977). *Halfway Houses: National Evaluation Program: Phase 1 Summary Report.* Columbus, OH: Ohio State University Program for the Study of Crime and Delinquency.

Carlson, Richard O. (1961). "Succession and Performance Among School Superintendents." *Administrative Science Quarterly* **6**:210–227.

Carp, Robert A., and Ronald Stidham (1993). *Judicial Process in America* (2/e). Washington, DC: Congressional Quarterly, Inc.

Carr, James G. (ed.) (1995). *Criminal Law Review 1995.* Deerfield, IL: Clark Boardman Callaghan.

Carter, David L. (1986). "A Taxonomy of Prejudice and Discrimination by Police Officers." In *Police Deviance,* Thomas Barker and David L. Carter (eds.). Cincinnati, OH: Pilgrimage.

Carter, David L., and Allen D. Sapp (1991). *Police Education and Minority Recruitment: The Impact of a College Requirement.* Washington, DC: Police Executive Research Forum.

Cartwright, William (ed.) (2000). *Mexico: Facing the Challenges of Human Rights and Crime.* Chicago: International Human Rights Institute, Transnational Publishers.

Carzo, Rocco, Jr., and John Yanouzas (1969). "Effects of Flat and Tall Organizational Structure." *Administrative Science Quarterly* **14**:178–191.

Casarez, Nicole B. (1995). "Furthering the Accountability Principle in Privatized Federal Corrections: The Need for Access to Private Prison Records." *University of Michigan Journal of Law Reform* **28**:249–303.

Cattell, Raymond B. (1951). "Concepts and Methods for Measuring Leadership in Terms of Group Syntality." *Human Relations* **4**:161–184.

Celebrezze, Frank D. (1987). "Prosecutorial Misconduct: Quelling the Tide of Improper Comment to the Jury." *Prosecutor* **21**:51–56.

Chaiken, Jan M. (1981). *The Impact of Fiscal Limitation on California's Criminal Justice System.* Santa Monica, CA: Rand Corporation.

Champion, Dean J. (1988a). "Private Counsels and Public Defenders: A Look at Weak Cases, Prior Records, and Leniency in Plea Bargaining." *Journal of Criminal Justice* **17**:253–263.

Champion, Dean J. (1988b). "The Severity of Sentencing: Do Federal Judges Really Go Easier on Elderly Offenders?" In *Older Offenders: Perspectives in Criminology and Criminal Justice,* Belinda McCarthy and Robert Langworthy (eds.). New York: Praeger Publishers.

Champion, Dean J. (1994). *Measuring Offender Risk: A Criminal Justice Sourcebook.* Westport, CT: Greenwood Press.

Champion, Dean J., and G. Larry Mays (1991). *Transferring Juveniles to Criminal Court.* New York: Praeger Publishers.

Champion, Dean J., and George E. Rush (1996). *Policing in the Community.* Upper Saddle River, NJ: Prentice Hall.

Cheek, Frances, and Marie di Stefano Miller (1982). "Reducing Staff and Inmate Stress." *Corrections Today* **44**:72–76.

Chen, Shu, Kunlun Chang, and Barbara S. Tombs (1999). *An Evaluation of School Response Officer School Program in Kansas.* Topeka, KS: Kansas Criminal Justice Coordinating Council.

Chereb, Sandra (1996). "Judges Must Train to Take the Bench." *Reno Gazette-Journal,* May 25, 1996:1B, 5B.

Chin, Gabriel J., and Scott C. Wells (1998). "The 'Blue Wall of Silence' As Evidence of Bias and Motive to Lie: A New Approach to Police Perjury." *University of Pittsburgh Law Review* **59**:233–299.

Chinoy, Ely (1952). "The Tradition of Opportunity and the Aspirations of Automobile Workers." *American Journal of Sociology* **57**:453–459.

Chinoy, Ely (1955). *Automobile Workers and the American Dream.* Garden City, NY: Doubleday.

Chowdhry, Kamla, and A.K. Pal (1957). "Production Planning and Organizational Morale: A Case Study from India." *Human Organization* **15**:11–16.

Church, Thomas W., and Milton Heumann (1989). "The Underexamined Assumptions of the Invisible Hand: Monetary Incentives As Policy Instruments." *Journal of Policy Analysis and Management* **8**:641–657.

Cicourel, Aaron V. (1995). *The Social Organization of Juvenile Justice* (Reprint ed.). New Brunswick, NJ: Transaction.

Clynch, Edward J., and David W. Neubauer (1981). "Trial Courts As Organizations: A Critique and Synthesis." *Law and Policy Quarterly* **3**:69–94.

Cohen, Howard (1985). "A Dilemma for Discretion." In *Police Ethics: Hard Choices for Law Enforcement,* William C. Heffernan and Timothy Stroup (eds.). New York: John Jay Press.

Cohn, Alvin W. (1998). "Reducing Opportunities for Civil Litigation." *American Jails* **12**:31–36.

Cohn, Yona (1977). "Delinquency Prevention: A System Approach." *Juvenile Justice* **28**:15–24.

Cole, Richard B., and Jack E. Call (1992). "When Courts Find Jail and Prison Overcrowding Unconstitutional." *Federal Probation* **56**:29–39.

Coleman, John L. (1995). *Operational Mid-Level Management for Police* (2nd ed.). Springfield, IL: Charles C Thomas.

Coles, Catherine, David Thacher, and Peter M. Sheingold (1998). *National COPS Evaluation: Organizational Change Case Study.* Washington, DC: Urban Institute.

Colson, Charles, et al. (1989). "Alternatives to Reduce Prison Crowding." *Journal of State Government* **62**:59–94.

Cominsky, Marvin, Philip C. Patterson, and William E. Taylor III (1987). *The Judiciary: Selection, Compensation, Ethics, and Discipline.* New York: Quorum Books.

Commission on Accreditation for Law Enforcement Agencies (1983). *Standards for Law Enforcement Agencies: The Standards Manual of the Law Enforcement Agency Accreditation Program.* Fairfax, VA: Commission on Accreditation for Law Enforcement Agencies.

Conley, John A. (ed.) (1979). *Theory and Research in Criminal Justice: Current Perspectives.* Cincinnati, OH: Anderson Publishing Company.

Cook, Stephen S. (1995). "Mediation As an Alternative to Probation Revocation Proceedings." *Federal Probation* **59**:48–52.

Cooper, Robin King (1986). *Occupational Stress in Police Work.* Ann Arbor, MI: University Microfilms International.

Cordner, Gary W. (1978). "A Review of Work Motivation Theory and Research for the Police Manager." *Journal of Police Science and Administration* **6**:286–292.

Cordner, Gary W. (1989). "Police Agency Size and Investigative Effectiveness." *Journal of Criminal Justice* **17**:145–155.

Cornelius, Gary F. (1994). *Stressed Out: Strategies for Living and Working with Stress in Corrections.* Laurel, MD: American Correctional Association.

Cornelius, Gary F. (1995). "Reducing Inmate Management Problems with the 'Human Services' Approach." *American Jails* **9**:62–63.

Cornelius, Gary F. (1997). *Jails in America: An Overview of Issues.* Lanham, MD: American Correctional Association.

Correctional Association of New York (1993). *Court Case Processing in New York: Problems and Solutions.* New York: Correctional Association of New York.

Correia, Mark E. (2000). "The Conceptual Ambiguity of Community in Community Policing: Filtering the Muddy Waters." *Policing: An International Journal of Police Strategies and Management* **23**:218–232.

Corwin, Ronald G. (1969). "Patterns of Organizational Conflict." *Administrative Science Quarterly* **14**:507–521.

Courtright, Kevin E., Bruce L. Berg, and Robert J. Mutchnick (1997). "The Cost of Effectiveness of Using House Arrest with Electronic Monitoring for Drunk Drivers." *Federal Probation* **61**:19–22.

Court Watchers (1982). *Court Watch Manual: A Citizen's Guide to Judicial Accountability.* Washington, DC: Court Watchers.

Coyle, Andrew (1991). *Inside: Rethinking Scotland's Prisons.* Edinburgh, Scot: Scottish Child.

Cramer, James A. (1981). *Courts and Judges.* Beverly Hills, CA: Sage Publications.

Crank, John P. (1993). "Legalistic and Order-Maintenance Behavior Among Police Patrol Officers: A Survey of Eight Municipal Police Agencies." *American Journal of Police* **12**:103–126.

Crank, John P. (1996). "The Construction of Meaning During Training for Probation and Parole." *Justice Quarterly* **13**:265–290.

Crank, John P., and Michael A. Caldero (2000). *Police Ethics: The Corruption of Noble Cause.* Cincinnati, OH: Anderson Publishing Company.

Crank, John P., and Robert Langworthy (1997). "Fragmented Centralization and the Organization of the Police." *Policing and Society* **6**:213–229.

Crank, John P., and L. Edward Wells (1991). "The Effects of Size and Urbanism on Structure Among Illinois Police Departments." *Justice Quarterly* **8**:169–185.

Crawford, Adam (1994). "Social Values and Managerial Goals: Police and Probation Officers' Experiences and Views of Inter-Agency Co-Operation." *Policing and Society* **4**:323–339.

Dahrendorf, Ralf (1959). *Class and Conflict in Industrial Society.* Stanford, CA: Stanford University Press.

Dantzker, Gail, Arthur J. Lurigio, and Susan Hartnett (1995a). "Preparing Police Officers for Community Policing: An Evaluation of Training for Chicago's Alternative Policing Strategy." *Police Studies* **18**:745–770.

Dantzker, Gail, Arthur J. Lurigio, and Susan Hartnett (1995b). *Preparing Police Officers for Community Policing: An Evaluation of Training for Chicago's Alternative Policing Strategy.* Evanston, IL: Northwestern University, Center for Urban Affairs and Policy Research.

Dantzker, Mark Lewis (1989). *The Effect of Education on Police Performance: The Stress Perspective.* Ann Arbor, MI: University Microfilms International.

Dantzker, Mark Lewis (1993). "Designing a Measure of Job Satisfaction for Policing: A Research Note." *Journal of Crime and Justice* **16**:171–181.

Dantzker, Mark Lewis (1994). "Measuring Job Satisfaction in Police Departments and Policy Implications: An Examination of a Mid-Size, Southern Police Department." *American Journal of Police* **13**:77–101.

Dantzker, Mark Lewis (1997). "Police Officer Job Satisfaction: Does Agency Size Make a Difference?" *Criminal Justice Policy Review* **8**:309–322.

Dantzker, Mark Lewis, and Betsy Kubin (1998). "Job Satisfaction: The Gender Perspective Among Police Officers" *American Journal of Criminal Justice* **23**:19–31.

Dantzker, M.L., and M.A. Surrette (1996). "The Perceived Levels of Job Satisfaction Among Police Officers: A Descriptive View." *Journal of Police and Criminal Psychology* **11**:7–12.

Das, Dilip K. (1986). "Police and Community in America: Influences from Across the Atlantic." *Police Studies* **9**:138–147.

Davis, Goliath John (1984). *Work Group Cohesion and Job Stress Among Police Officers.* Ann Arbor, MI: University Microfilms International.

Davis, Keith (1962). *Human Relations at Work.* New York: McGraw-Hill.

Davis, Keith, and William G. Scott (1969). *Human Relations and Organizational Behavior: Readings and Comments* (3/e). New York: McGraw-Hill.

Davis, Michael (1991). "Do Cops Really Need a Code of Ethics?" *Criminal Justice Ethics* **10**:14–28.

Davis, Robert C., and Pedro Mateu-Gelabert (1999). *Respectful and Effective Policing: Two Examples in South Bronx.* New York: Vera Institute of Justice.

Daviss, Ben (1982). "Burnout: No One Can Imagine What the Costs Really Are." *Police Magazine of New York* **5**:9–11, 14–18.

Daviss, Ben (1983). "From Urban Sprawl to Country Drawl." *Police* **6**:50–57.

DeFrances, Carol J., and Greg W. Steadman (1998). *Prosecutors in State Courts, 1996.* Washington, DC: Bureau of Justice Statistics.

Delbecq, Andre (1968). "How Informal Organization Evolves: Interpersonal Choice and Subgroup Formation." *Business Perspectives* **24**:17–21.

DeLeon-Granados, William, and William Wells (1998). "'Do You Want Extra Police Coverage w/Those Fries?' An Exploratory Analysis of Relationship Between Patrol Practices and Gratuity Exchange Principle." *Police Quarterly* **1**:71–85.

Dembo, Richard, et al. (1999). "Engaging High Risk Families in Community-Based Intervention Services." *Aggression and Violent Behavior* **4**:41–58.

Denhardt, Robert B.I. (1968). "Bureaucratic Socialization and Organizational Accommodation." *Administrative Science Quarterly* **13**:441–450.

Detroit Police Department (1983). *Mini-Station Personnel Training Manual.* Detroit, MI: Mini-Station Administration Unit.

Diggs, David W., and Stephen L. Pieper (1994). "Using Day Reporting Centers As an Alternative to Jail." *Federal Probation* **58**:9–12.

Donahue, Michael E. (1992). "Crisis in Police Ethics: Is Professionalization the Answer?" *American Journal of Police* **11**:47–70.

Donnelly, S.M. (1980). *Community Service Orders in Federal Probation.* Washington, DC: National Institute of Justice.

Draine, Jeffrey, and Phyllis Solomon (1999). "Describing and Evaluating Jail Diversion Services for Persons with Serious Mental Illness." *Psychiatric Services* **50**:56–61.

Draper, Jean D., and George B. Strother (1963). "Testing a Model for Organizational Growth." *Human Organization* **22**:180–194.

Drapkin, Martin, and Gary T. Klugiewicz (1994a). "Use of Force Training in Jails, Part I." *American Jails* **7**:9–12.

Drapkin, Martin, and Gary T. Klugiewicz (1994b). "Use of Force Training in Jails, Part II." *American Jails* **7**:93–98.

Drummond, Douglas S. (1976). *Police Culture.* Beverly Hills, CA: Sage.

Dubois, Philip L. (1990). "Voter Responses to Court Reform: Merit Judicial Selection on the Ballot." *Judicature* **73**:238–247.

Duffee, David (1975). *Correctional Policy and Prison Organization.* New York: Sage Publications.

Dufford, Priss (1986). *Police Personal Behavior and Human Relations: For Police, Deputy, Jail, Corrections, and Security Personnel.* Springfield, IL: Charles C Thomas.

Dunlap, Karen (2000). "Project Announcement: Implementing Effective Crime Prevention Practices and Programming." *APPA Perspectives* **24**:17.

Durham, Alexis M., III (1994). *Crisis and Reform: Current Issues in American Punishment.* Boston: Little, Brown.

Durkee, Daniel (1996). "Local Detention Education and Training: A Program Developed by the Criminal Justice Center, Lansing Community College." *American Jails* **10**:58–60.

Durkheim, Émile (1951). *Suicide.* Glencoe, IL: Free Press.

Dyer, William G. (1960). "Looking at Conflict." *Adult Leadership* **9**:79–80.

Dynia, Paul A. (1990). *Misdemeanor Trial Law: Is It Working?* New York: New York City Criminal Justice Agency.

Eisenberg, Terry, Deborah Kent, and Charles R. Wall (1973). *Police Personnel Practices in State and Local Governments.* Washington, DC: The Police Foundation.

Eisenberg, Terry, Deborah Kent, and Charles R. Wall (1974). *Police Personnel Practices in State and Local Governments.* Washington, DC: International Association of Chiefs of Police and the Police Foundation.

Eisenstadt, S.N. (1959). "Bureaucracy, Bureaucratization, and Debureaucratization." *Administrative Science Quarterly* **4**:302–320.

Eisenstein, James, and Herbert Jacob (1977). *Felony Justice: An Organizational Analysis of Criminal Courts.* Boston: Little, Brown and Company.

Elchardus, Jean Marc, et al. (1994). "The Problems of Therapeutic Interventions." *Revue Internationale Criminologie et de Police Technique* **47**:389–507.

Emerick, Jeanette E. (1996). "Raising Morale Through Communication." *American Jails* **10**:53–60.

Ethridge, Philip A., and Stephen W. Liebowitz (1994). "The Attitudes of Sheriffs in Texas." *American Jails* **8**:55–60.

Etter, Gregg W., and Michael L. Birzer (1997). "Community-Oriented: Why Training the Jail Officers?" *American Jails* **11**:66–71.

Etzioni, Amitai (1959). "Authority Structure and Organizational Effectiveness." *Administrative Science Quarterly* **4**:43–67.

Etzioni, Amitai (1961). *Complex Organizations.* New York: Holt.

Etzioni, Amitai (1964). *Modern Organizations.* Englewood Cliffs, NJ: Prentice Hall.

Evans, Barry J., Greg J. Coman, and Robb O. Stanley (1992). "The Police Personality: Type A Behavior and Trait Anxiety." *Journal of Criminal Justice* **20**:429–441.

Falcone, David N. (1998). "The Illinois State Police As an Archetypal Model." *Police Quarterly* **1**:61–83.

Farkas, Mary Ann (1999). "Correctional Officer Attitudes Toward Inmates and Working with Inmates in a 'Get Tough' Era." *Journal of Criminal Justice* **27**:495–506.

Farmer, James A. (1988). "Relationship Between Job Burnout and Perceived Inmate Exploitation of Juvenile Correctional Workers." *International Journal of Offender Therapy and Comparative Criminology* **32**:67–74.

Farr, Kathryn Ann (1993). "Shaping Policy Through Litigation: Abortion Law in the United States." *Crime and Delinquency* **39**:167–183.

Faunce, William A. (1958). "Automation in the Automobile Industry: Some Consequences for In-Plant Social Structure." *American Sociological Review* **23**:401–407.

Fayol, H. (1949). *General and Industrial Management.* London, UK: Sir Isaac Pitman and Sons, Inc.

Feld, Barry C. (1993). "Juvenile (In)justice and the Criminal Court Alternative." *Crime and Delinquency* **39**:403–424.

Feld, Barry C. (1998). "Abolish the Juvenile Court: Youthfulness, Criminal Responsibility, and Sentencing Policy." *The Journal of Criminal Law and Criminology* **88**:68–136.

Felkenes, George T. (1984). "Attitudes of Police Officers Toward Their Professional Ethics." *Journal of Criminal Justice* **12**:221–230.

Felkenes, George T., and James R. Lasley (1992). "Implications of Hiring Women Police Officers: Police Administrators' Concerns May Not Be Justified." *Policing and Society* **3**:41–50.

Felkenes, George T., and Peter Charles Unsinger (1992). *Diversity, Affirmative Action and Law Enforcement*. Springfield, IL: Charles C Thomas.

Fiedler, Fred E. (1967). *A Theory of Leadership Effectiveness*. New York: McGraw-Hill.

Fishkin, Gerald Loren (1987). *Police Burnout: Signs, Symptoms, and Solutions*. Gardena, CA: Harcourt Brace Jovanovich/Law Distributors.

Flanagan, Timothy J., W. Wesley Johnson, and Katherine Bennett (1996). "Job Satisfaction Among Correctional Executives: A Contemporary Portrait of Wardens of State Prisons for Adults." *Prison Journal* **76**:385–397.

Flango, Victor E. (1994a). "Court Unification and Quality of State Courts." *Justice System Journal* **16**:33–55.

Flango, Victor E. (1994b). "Federal Court Review of State Court Convictions in Noncapital Cases." *Justice System Journal* **17**:153–170.

Fleischman, Adam L., and Alexander B. Aikman (1993). "Total Quality Management: Where the Courts Are Now." *State Court Journal* **17**:17–22.

Fleishman, Edwin A., and E.F. Harris (1962). "Patterns of Leadership Behavior Related to Employee Grievances and Turnover." *Personnel Psychology* **15**:43–56.

Florida Office of Program Policy Analysis and Government Accountability (1996a). *Policy Review of the Department of Corrections' Correctional Officer Staffing*. Tallahassee, FL: Florida Office of Program Policy Analysis and Government Accountability.

Florida Office of Program Policy Analysis and Government Accountability (1996b). *Policy Review of Inmate Idleness Reduction Activities Administered by the Department of Corrections*. Tallahassee, FL: Florida Office of Program Policy Analysis and Government Accountability.

Florida Probation and Parole Services (1984). *Preliminary Report on Community Control*. Tallahassee, FL: Florida Department of Corrections.

Flynt, Charles, and Mickey Ellenbecker (1995). "The Certification Experience at Winona State University." *American Jails* **9**:57–58.

Form, William H., and J.A. Geschwender (1962). "Social Reference Basis of Job Satisfaction: The Case of Manual Workers." *American Sociological Review* **27**:351–362.

Forst, Brian, and Peter K. Manning (1999). *The Privatization of Policing: Two Views*. Washington, DC: Georgetown University Press.

Fosdick, Raymond B. (1920). *American Police Systems*. New York: Macmillan.

Fournet, G.P., M.K. Distefano, and M.W. Pryer (1966). "Job Satisfaction: Issues and Problems." *Personnel Psychology* **19**:165–183.

Frank, Susan J., and Darlene M. Atkins (1981). "Policy Is One Thing: Implementation Is Another: A Comparison of Community Agencies in a Juvenile Justice Referral Network." *American Journal of Community Psychology* **9**:581–604.

Franz, Verl, and David M. Jones (1987). "Perceptions of Organizational Performance in Suburban Police Departments: A Critique of the Military Model." *Journal of Police Science and Administration* **15**:153–161.

Frazer, Christopher (1993). *Privatise the Prosecutors: Efficiency and Justice in the Criminal Courts*. London, UK: Centre for Policy Studies.

Freedman, Monroe H. (1967). "The Professional Responsibility of the Prosecuting Attorney." *Criminal Law Bulletin* **3**:544–549.

Freedman, Warren (1989). *Summary Judgment and Other Preclusive Devices*. Westport, CT: Quorum Press.

Freeman, Robert M. (1999). *Correctional Organization and Management: Public Policy Challenges, Behavior, and Structure*. Boston: Butterworth-Heinemann.

French, J.R.P., Jr., and B. Raven (1959). *The Bases of Social Power*. Ann Arbor, MI: Institute for Social Research.

French, J.R.P., Jr., J. Israel, and D. Aos (1960). "An Experiment in Participation in a Norwegian Factory." *Human Relations* **13**:3–19.

Friedlander, Frank, and E. Walton (1964). "Job Characteristics As Satisfiers and Dissatisfiers." *Journal of Applied Psychology* **48**:388–392.

Friedmann, Georges (1955). *Industrial Society: The Emergence of the Human Problems of Automation*. New York: Free Press.

Fry, Louis W., and Leslie J. Berkes (1983). "Paramilitary Police Model: An Organizational Misfit." *Human Organization* **42**:225–234.

Fulton, Betsy, Paul Gendreau, and Mario Paparozzi (1995). "APPA's Prototypical Intensive Supervision Program: ISP as It Was Meant to Be." *APPA Perspectives* **19**:25–41.

Fyfe, James J. (1998). "Good Judgment: Defending Police Against Civil Suits." *Police Quarterly* **1**:91–117.

Fyfe, James J., et al. (1997). *Police Administration* (5/e). New York: McGraw-Hill.

Gaines, Larry K. (1978). *An Examination of Organizational Models in Traditional and Innovative Police Departments*. Ann Arbor, MI: University Microfilms International.

Gardner, Ralph (1981). "Guard Stress." *Corrections Magazine New York* **7**:7–14.

Garoupa, Nuno (2000). "The Economics of Organized Crime and Optimal Law Enforcement." *Economic Inquiry* **38**:278–288.

Geary, David Patrick (1985). *Community Relations and the Administration of Justice*. New York: Wiley.

Georgopoulos, Basil S., and A.S. Tannenbaum (1957). "Study of Organizational Effectiveness." *American Sociological Review* **22**:534–540.

Getzels, J.W., and E.G. Guba (1954). "Role, Role Conflict, and Effectiveness: An Empirical Study." *American Sociological Review* **19**:164–175.

Gibb, Cecil A. (1969). "Leadership." In *The Handbook of Social Psychology*, Gardner Lindzey and E. Aronson (eds.). Reading, MA: Addison Wesley.

Gido, Rosemary L. (ed.) (1998). "Evolution of the Concepts Correctional Organization and Organizational Change." *Criminal Justice Policy Review* **9**:5–139.

Giles, Sims Jean (1983). *Wife Battering: A Systems Theory Approach*. New York: Guilford Press.

Gill, Peter (1998). "Police Intelligence Processes: A Study of Criminal Intelligence Units in Canada." *Policing and Society* **8**:339–365.

Glaser, Daniel (1977). "Concern with Theory in Correctional Evaluation Research." *Crime and Delinquency* **23**:173–179.

Glensor, Ronald W., and Alissa J. Stern (1995). *Dispute Resolution and Policing: A Collaborative Approach Toward Effective Problem Solving*. Washington, DC: Police Executive Research Forum.

Gluckstern, Norma B., and Ralph W. Packard (1977). "The Internal-External Change-Agent Team: Bringing Change to a Closed Institution: A Case Study of a County Jail." *Journal of Applied Behavioral Science* **13**:41–52.

Goebel, Julius, Jr. (1971). *Antecedents and Beginnings to 1801*, Vol. I of *The Oliver Wendell Holmes Devise History of the Supreme Court of the United States*. New York: Macmillan.

Goerdt, John A., and John A. Martin (1989). "The Impact of Drug Cases on Case Processing in Urban Trial Courts." *State Court Journal* **13**:4–12.

Goerdt, John A., et al. (1989). *Examining Court Delay: The Pace of Litigation in 26 Urban Trial Courts, 1987*. Washington, DC: National Center for State Courts.

Golash, Deirdre (1992). "Race, Fairness and Jury Selection." *Behavioral Sciences and the Law* **10**:155–177.

Goldman, Roger, and Steven Puro (1987). "Decertification of Police: An Alternative to Traditional Remedies for Police Misconduct." *Hastings Constitutional Law Quarterly* **15**:45–80.

Goldsmith, Andrew J. (1988). "New Directions in Police Complaints Procedures: Some Conceptual and Comparative Departures." *Police Studies* **11**:60–71.

Goldsmith, Jack, and Sharon S. Goldsmith (1974). *The Police Community: Dimensions of an Occupational Subculture*. Pacific Palisades, CA: Palisades Publishers.

Goldstein, Herman (1967). "Administrative Problems in Controlling the Exercise of Police Authority." *Journal of Criminal Law, Criminology, and Police Science* **58**:160–172.

Golembiewski, Robert T., and Scob Kim Byong (1990). "Burnout in Police Work: Stressors, Strain, and the Phase Model." *Police Studies* **13**:74–80.

Goodstein, Lynne, and Doris Layton MacKenzie (eds.) (1989). *The American Prison: Issues in Research and Policy*. New York: Plenum.

Gordon, Jill A. (1999). "Do Staff Attitudes Vary By Position? A Look at One Juvenile Correctional Center." *American Journal of Criminal Justice* **24**:81–93.

Gorton, Ronald Joseph (1997). *Organizational Change and Managerial Control During the Contemporary Post-Reform Period of the Texas Prison System*. Ann Arbor, MI: University Microfilms International.

Gottfredson, Don M. (1999). *Effects of Judges' Sentencing Decisions on Criminal Careers*. Washington, DC: U.S. Department of Justice.

Gouldner, Alvin W. (1954). *Patterns of Industrial Bureaucracy*. New York: Free Press.

Gouldner, Alvin W. (1959). "Organizational Analysis." In *Sociology Today*, Robert K. Merton et al. (eds.). New York: Basic Books.

Grabosky, P.N. (1988). *Efficiency and Effectiveness in Australian Policing*. Woden, Aus: Australian Institute of Criminology.

Graves, W. (1996). "Police Cynicism: Causes and Cures." *FBI Law Enforcement Bulletin* **65**:17–20.

Gray, William, and Lucille R. Gray (1974). "Court Clinic Therapy: Theory and Practice." *International Journal of Offender Therapy and Comparative Criminology* **18**:143–152.

Gray, William, Donald Cochran, and Lucille R. Gray (1976). "General Systems Theory in Psychotherapy." *International Journal of Offender Therapy and Comparative Criminology* **20**:107–116.

Green, Mark (1999). *Investigation of the New York City Police Department's Response to Civilian Complaints of Police Misconduct: Interim Report*. New York: Office of the New York City Public Advocate and the Accountability Project.

Greene, Jack R. (1989). "Police Officer Job Satisfaction and Community Perceptions: Implications for Community-Oriented Policing." *Journal of Research in Crime and Delinquency* **26**:168–183.

Greene, Jack R., et al. (1999). "Doing Research in Public Housing: Implementation Issues from Philadelphia's 11th Street Corridor Community Policing Program." *Justice Research and Policy* **1**:67–95.

Gross, Edward (1969). "The Definition of Organizational Goals." *British Journal of Sociology* **20**:277–294.

Gulick, L., and L. Urwick (eds.) (1937). *Papers on the Science of Administration*. New York: Institute of Public Administration, Columbia University.

Hage, Jerald, and Michael Aiken (1969). "Routine, Technology, Social Structure, and Organizational Goals." *Administrative Science Quarterly* **14**:366–377.

Hageman, Mary Jeanette (1985). *Police-Community Relations*. Beverly Hills, CA: Sage.

Hagemann, Otmar (1995). "Adequate Wages in Prison: The Hamburg Model." *Monatsschrift fuer Kriminologie und Strafrechtsreform* **78**:341–351.

Haire, Mason (1959). *Modern Organization Theory*. New York: Wiley.

Hall, Donna L. (1995). "Job Satisfaction Among Male and Female Public Defense Attorneys." *Justice System Journal* **18**:121–139.

Hall, John C., et al. (1982). *Major Issues in Juvenile Justice Information and Training: The Out-of-State Placement of Children*. Washington, DC: National Institute for Juvenile Justice and Delinquency Prevention.

Hall, Richard H. (1972). *The Formal Organization.* New York: Basic Books.

Hall, Richard H., J. Eugene Haas, and Norman J. Johnson (1967). "Examination of the Blau-Scott and Etzioni Typologies." *Administrative Science Quarterly* **12:**118–139.

Hallett, Michael, and Dennis Powell (1995). "Backstage with 'COPS': The Dramaturgical Reification of Police Subculture in American Crime Info-Tainment." *American Journal of Police* **14:**101–129.

Hanna, Donald G. (1987). *The Police Chief's Handbook on Developmental and Power Management.* Springfield, IL: Charles C Thomas.

Hansen, Evan (1995). "Jail Supervision in the '90s." *American Jails* **9:**37–41.

Hanson, Wes, et al. (1992). "Ethics in Law Enforcement." *Ethics Easier Said Than Done* **17:**34–56.

Hargrave, George E., Dierdre Hiatt, and Tim W. Gaffney (1986). "A Comparison of MMPI and CPI Test Profiles for Traffic Officers and Deputy Sheriffs." *Journal of Police Science and Administration* **14:**250–258.

Harlow, Caroline Wolf (1998). *Profile of Jail Inmates 1996.* Washington, DC: U.S. Department of Justice.

Harper, Hill, et al. (1999). "A Cross-Cultural Comparison of Police Personality." *International Journal of Comparative and Applied Criminal Justice* **23:**1–15.

Harris, Louis M., and J. Norman Baldwin (1999). "Voluntary Turnover of Field Operations Officers: A Test of Confluency Theory." *Journal of Criminal Justice* **27:**483–493.

Harrison, E. Frank, and Monique A. Pelletier (1987). "Perceptions of Bureaucratization, Role Performance, and Organizational Effectiveness in a Metropolitan Police Department." *Journal of Police Science and Administration* **15:**262–270.

Harvard Law Review Association (1994). *A Uniform System of Citation.* Cambridge, MA: Harvard Law Review Association.

Harvey, E. (1968). "Technology and the Structure of Organizations." *American Sociological Review* **33:**247–259.

Heck, William P. (1992). "Police Who Snitch: Deviant Actors in a Secret Society." *Deviant Behavior* **13:**253–270.

Heffernan, William C., and Richard W. Lovely (1991). "Evaluating the Fourth Amendment Exclusionary Rule: The Problem of Police Compliance with the Law." *University of Michigan Journal of Law Reform* **24:**311–369.

Heim, Ted (1993). "The Washburn Experience: The University Role in Training Jail Personnel." *American Jails* **7:**18–20.

Henderson, George (ed.) (1981). *Police Human Relations.* Springfield, IL: Charles C Thomas.

Henderson, James D., W. Hardy Raugh, and Richard L. Phillips (1997). *Guidelines for the Development of a Security Program* (2/e). Lanham, MD: American Correctional Association.

Henderson, Thomas A., et al. (1991). *Alternative Approaches to the Comprehensive Adjudication of Drug Arrestees (CADA).* Arlington, VA: National Center for State Courts.

Hendricks, James E., and Bryan Byers (eds.) (1996). *Crisis Intervention in Criminal Justice/Social Service* (2/e). Springfield, IL: Charles C Thomas.

Hendricks, James E., and Jerome B. McKean (1995). *Crisis Intervention: Contemporary Issues for On-Site Intervenors* (2/e). Springfield, IL: Charles C Thomas.

Hepburn, John R. (1985). "The Exercise of Power in Coercive Organizations: A Study of Prison Guards." *Criminology* **23:**145–164.

Hepburn, John R., and Paul E. Knepper (1993). "Correctional Officers As Human Services Workers: The Effect on Job Satisfaction." *Justice Quarterly* **10:**315–337.

Herbert, Steve (1998). "Police Subculture Reconsidered." *Criminology* **36:**343–370.

Hershey, P., and K. Blanchard (1977). *Managing Organizational Behavior.* Englewood Cliffs, NJ: Prentice Hall.

Herzberg, Frederick (1966). *Work and the Nature of Man.* New York: World Publishing.

Herzberg, Frederick (1968). "One More Time: How Do You Motivate Employees?" *Harvard Business Review* **46:**53–62.

Herzberg, Frederick, et al. (1957). *Job Attitudes: Review of Research and Opinion.* Pittsburgh, PA: Psychological Service of Pittsburgh.

Herzberg, Frederick, et al. (1959). *Motivation to Work.* New York: Wiley.

Heumann, Milton (1978). *Plea Bargaining: The Experiences of Prosecutors, Judges, and Defense Attorneys.* Chicago: University of Chicago Press.

Hewitt, W.E., G. Gallas, and B. Mahoney (1990). *Courts That Succeed: Six Profiles of Successful Courts.* Williamsburg, VA: National Center for State Courts.

Hickson, D.J. (1966). "Convergence in Organizational Theory." *Administrative Science Quarterly* **11:**224–237.

Hilgendorf, E.L., and B.L. Irving (1969). "Job Attitude Research: A New Conceptual and Analytical Model." *Human Relations* **22:**415–426.

Hilte, Ken (1998). "Writing Policy and Procedure." *American Jails* **12:**33–36.

Hinings, C.R., et al. (1967). "An Approach to the Study of Bureaucracy." *Sociology* **5:**83–112.

Hoath, David R., Frank W. Schneider, and Meyer W. Starr (1998). "Police Job Satisfaction As a Function of Career Orientation and Position Tenure: Implications for Selection and Community Policing." *Journal of Criminal Justice* **26:**337–347.

Hochstedler, Ellen, and Christine M. Dunning (1983). "Communication and Motivation in a Police Department." *Criminal Justice and Behavior* **10:**47–69.

Hogue, Mark C., Tommie Black, and Robert T. Sigler (1994). "The Differential Use of Screening Techniques in the Recruitment of Police Officers." *American Journal of Police* **13:**113–124.

Holter, Harriet (1965). "Attitudes Toward Employee Participation in Company Decision-Making Processes: Processes:

A Study of Nonsupervisory Employees in Some Norwegian Firms." *Human Relations* **18:**297–321.

Homans, George (1950). *The Human Group.* New York: Harcourt, Brace, and World.

Homans, George (1961). *Social Behavior: Its Elementary Forms.* New York: Harcourt, Brace, and World.

House, Robert J., and John B. Miner (1969). "Merging Management and Behavioral Theory: The Interaction Between Span of Control and Group Size." *Administrative Science Quarterly* **14:**451–465.

House, Robert J., and T.R. Mitchell (1975). "Path-Goal Theory of Leadership." In *Studies of Social Power,* D. Cartwright (ed.). Ann Arbor, MI: Institute for Social Research.

Howell, Walter (1999). "Philadelphia's 'Adopt-a-School' Partnership to Prevent Delinquency." *Corrections Today* **61:**26–28.

Hsia, Heidi M., and Marty Beyer (2000). *System Change Through State Challenge Activities: Approaches and Products.* Washington, DC: U.S. Department of Justice.

Hudnut, William H. (1985). "The Police and the Polis: A Mayor's Perspective." In *Police Leadership in America: Crisis and Opportunity,* W.A. Geller (ed.). New York: Praeger Publishers.

Hudzik, John K. (1987). "Surviving the Loss of Federal Dollars and Mandate: The Case of State Planning Agencies." *Journal of Criminal Justice* **15:**105–120.

Hughes, Charles Evans (1966). *The Supreme Court of the United States.* New York: Columbia University Press.

Hughes, Robert (1987). *The Fatal Shore.* New York: Alfred Knopf.

Hulin, Charles L., and Milton R. Blood (1968). "Job Enlargement, Individual Differences, and Worker Responses." *Psychological Bulletin* **69:**41–55.

Human Rights Watch (1998). *Shielded from Justice: Police Brutality and Accountability in the United States.* New York: Human Rights Watch.

Hunt, J.G., and J.W. Hill (1969). "The New Look in Motivation Theory for Organizational Research." *Human Organization* **28:**100–109.

Hunt, Raymond G., and John M. Magenau (1993). *Power and the Police Chief: An Institutional and Organizational Analysis.* Newbury Park, CA: Sage Publications.

Hunter, Robert J., and Timothy S. Sexton (1997). "The Business of Jails: A Case Study." *American Jails* **11:**77–83.

Hurley, Pat, et al. (1996). *Special Task Force: Correctional Camp Security: Final Report.* Columbus, OH: Office of Management Systems, Bureau of Research, Ohio Department of Rehabilitation and Correction.

Hurst, Hunter, III (1999). *Workload Measurement for Juvenile Justice System Personnel: Practices and Needs.* Washington, DC: U.S. Department of Justice.

Hurst, Timothy E., and Mallory M. Hurst (1997). "Gender Differences in Mediation of Severe Occupational Stress Among Correctional Officers." *American Journal of Criminal Justice* **22:**121–137.

Hutchinson, Virginia (1999). "NIC Jails Division: Helping Jails Meet Diverse Challenges." *American Jails* **12:**15–20.

Indik, B.P. (1964). "Relationship Between Organizational Size and the Supervision Ratio." *Administrative Science Quarterly* **9:**301–312.

Inkster, Norman D. (1992). "The Essence of Community Policing." *The Police Chief* **59:**28–31.

International Association of Chiefs of Police (1988). *Developing Neighborhood Oriented Policing in the Houston Police Department.* Gaithersburg, MD: International Association of Chiefs of Police.

International Association of Chiefs of Police (1995). "Final Report: Association's Ad Hoc Committee on Accreditation Completes CALEA Review." *The Police Chief* **60:**157–161.

International City/County Management Association (1991). *Police Personnel Practices: Education, Participation, and Scheduling.* Washington, DC: International City/County Management Association.

Iris, Mark (1998). "Police Discipline in Chicago: Arbitration or Arbitrary?" *Journal of Criminal Law and Criminology* **89:**215–244.

Jacobs, Mark D. (1990). *Screwing the System and Making It Work: Juvenile Justice in the No-Fault Society.* Chicago: University of Chicago Press.

Jacoby, Joan E., Leonard R. Mellon, and Walter F. Smith (1982). *Policy and Prosecution.* Washington, DC: U.S. Government Printing Office.

Jacoby, Joan E., Edward C. Rutledge, and Heike P. Gramckow (1993). *Expedited Drug Case Management Programs: Issues for Program Development: Executive Summary.* Washington, DC: U.S. Department of Justice.

Jaffe, Harry Joe (1989). "The Presentence Report, Probation Officer Accountability, and Recruitment Practices: Some Influences of Guideline Sentencing." *Federal Probation* **53:**12–14.

Janes, Richard W. (1993). "Total Quality Management: Can It Work in Federal Probation?" *Federal Probation* **57:**28–33.

Jasinski, Jana L., Nancy L. Asdigian, and Glenda Kaufman Kantor (1997). "Ethnic Adaptations to Occupational Strain: Work-Related Stress, Drinking, and Wife Assault Among Anglo and Hispanic Husbands." *Journal of Interpersonal Violence* **12:**814–831.

Jayewardene, C.H.S., T.J. Juliani, and C.K. Talbot (1983). "Supply Side Corrections or Human Resource Management: A New Strategy for Parole and Probation." *International Journal of Comparative and Applied Criminal Justice* **7:**99–108.

Jepson, Bradette (1997). "Supervising Youthful Offenders." *Corrections Today* **59:**68–69.

Jermier, John M. (1979). *Participativeness and the Agents of Control: Frontline Decision Behavior in an Urban Police Bureaucracy.* Ann Arbor, MI: University Microfilms International.

Jermier, John M., and L.J. Berkes (1979). "Leader Behavior in a Police Command Bureaucracy." *Administrative Science Quarterly* **24:**1–23.

Jester, Jean C. (1982). *An Analysis of the Relationship Between Technology and Organizational Structure in Community Supervision Agencies*. Ann Arbor, MI: University Microfilms International.

Johnson, David R. (1995). *Illegal Tender: Counterfeiting and the Secret Service in Nineteenth-Century America*. Washington, DC: Smithsonian Institution Press.

Johnson, Elmer H. (1994). "Opposing Outcomes of the Industrial Prison: Japan and the United States Compared." *International Criminal Justice Review* **4**:52–71.

Johnson, Robert (1996). *Hard Time: Understanding and Reforming the Prison* (2nd ed.). Belmont, CA: Wadsworth Publishing Company.

Johnston, Les (1992). "Regulating Private Security." *International Journal of the Sociology of Law*, **20**:1–16.

Jonakait, Randolph N. (1987). "The Ethical Prosecutor's Misconduct." *Criminal Law Bulletin* **23**:550–567.

Jones, Mark, and Rolando V. del Carmen (1992). "When Do Probation and Parole Officers Enjoy the Same Immunity as Judges?" *Federal Probation* **56**:36–41.

Jones, Mark, and Darrell L. Ross (1997a). "Electronic House Arrest and Boot Camp in North Carolina." *Criminal Justice Policy Review* **8**:383–403.

Jones, Mark, and Darrell L. Ross (1997b). "Is Less Better? Boot Camp, Regular Probation, and Rearrest in North Carolina." *American Journal of Criminal Justice* **21**:147–161.

Jones, Peter R., and Philip W. Harris (1999). "Developing an Empirically Based Typology of Delinquent Youths." *Journal of Quantitative Criminology* **15**:251–276.

Josi, Don A., and Dale K. Sechrest (1998). *The Changing Career of the Correctional Officer: Policy Implications for the 21st Century*. Boston: Butterworth-Heinemann.

Joubert, Paul E. (1976). *Social Structure, Crime, and Imprisonment: A Causal Analysis*. Ann Arbor, MI: University Microfilms International.

Kadish, Sanford H. (1994). "Supreme Court Review." *Journal of Criminal Law and Criminology* **84**:679–1175.

Kadish, Tara E., et al. (1999). "Counseling Juvenile Offenders: A Program Evaluation." *Journal of Addictions and Offender Counseling* **19**:88–94.

Kahn, Robert L. (1960). "Productivity and Job Satisfaction." *Personnel Psychology* **13**:275–287.

Kaiser, Gunther (1984). *Prison Systems and Correctional Laws: Europe, the United States, and Japan: A Comparative Analysis*. Dobbs Ferry, NY: Transnational.

Kales, A.H. (1914). *Unpopular Government in the United States*. Chicago: University of Chicago Press.

Kammer, James J., Kevin I. Minor, and James B. Wells (1999). "An Outcome Study of the Diversion Plus Program for Juvenile Offenders." *Federal Probation* **61**:51–56.

Kane, Robert J. (2000). "Permanent Beat Assignments in Association with Community Policing: Assessing the Impact of Police Officers' Field Activity." *Justice Quarterly* **17**:259–280.

Kania, Richard R. (1982). *Discipline in Small Police Forces: An Ethnographic Examination of Bureaucratic Social Control*. Ann Arbor, MI: University Microfilms International.

Katz, Daniel, and Robert L. Kahn (1966). *The Social Psychology of Organizations*. New York: Wiley.

Keleher, Terry (1997). *Justice by the People: Action Education Workshops for Community Safety and Police Accountability*. Berkeley, CA: Chardon Press.

Kelly, Patricia A. (ed.) (1987). *Police and the Media: Bridging Troubled Waters*. Springfield, IL: Charles C Thomas.

Kelly, William R., and Sheldon Ekland-Olson (1991). "The Response of the Criminal Justice System to Prison Overcrowding: Recidivism Patterns Among Four Successive Parolee Courts." *Law and Society* **25**:601–620.

Kennedy, Sharon (1999). "Responsivity: The Other Classification Principle." *Corrections Today* **61**:48–55.

Kerle, Kenneth E. (1995). "Jail Supervision—Past and Present." *American Jails* **9**:5.

Kerle, Kenneth E. (1998). *American Jails: Looking to the Future*. Boston: Butterworth-Heinemann.

Kerstetter, Wayne A. (1981). "Patrol Decentralization: An Assessment." *Journal of Police Science and Administration* **9**:48–60.

Kerstetter, Wayne A., and Kenneth A. Rasinski (1994). "Opening a Window into Police Internal Affairs: Impact of Procedural Justice Reform on Third-Party Attitudes." *Social Justice Research* **7**:107–127.

Kiel, K. Douglas, et al. (1994). "Election, Selection, and Retention." *Judicature* **77**:290–321.

Kingsnorth, Rodney (1969). "Decision-Making in a Parole Bureaucracy." *Journal of Research in Crime and Delinquency* **6**:210–218.

Kinsman, Gary, and Deborah Brock (1986). "Patriarchal Relations Ignored: A Critique of the Badgley Report on Sexual Offences Against Children and Youth." *Canadian Criminology Forum* **8**:15–29.

Kirkcaldy, Bruce D., Gary L. Cooper, and Jennifer M. Brown (1995). "The Role of Coping in the Stress-Strain Relationship Among Senior Police Officers." *International Journal of Stress Management* **2**:69–78.

Kirschman, Ellen (1997). *I Love a Cop: What Police Families Need to Know*. New York: Guilford Press.

Klein, Mitchell S.G. (1984). *Law, Courts, and Society*. Englewood Cliffs, NJ: Prentice Hall.

Kleinig, John (ed.) (1996). *Handled with Discretion: Ethical Issues in Police Decision Making*. Lanham, MD: Rowman and Littlefield.

Knepper, Paul, and Shannon M. Barton (1996). "Informal Sources of Delay in Child Management Proceedings: Evidence from the Kentucky Court Improvement Project." *Juvenile and Family Court Journal* **47**:23–37.

Knowles, Lyle, and Kenneth Hickman (1984). "Selecting a Jury of Peers: How Close Do We Get?" *Journal of Police Science and Administration*, **12**:207–212.

Koren, Lawrence (1995). "Jail Officers and Education: A Key to Professionalization." *American Jails* **9**:43–48.

Kornfeld, Alfred D. (1995). "Police Officer Candidate MMPI-2 Performance: Gender, Ethnic and Normative Factors." *Journal of Clinical Psychology* **51**:536–540.

Kouzes, J.M., and B.Z. Posner (1987). *The Leadership Challenge: How to Get Extraordinary Things Done in Organizations.* San Francisco: Jossey-Bass.

Krapac, D. (1996). "The Position of the Victim in Criminal Justice." *European Journal of Crime, Criminal Law, and Criminal Justice* 3:230–240.

Kraska, Peter B., and Victor E. Kappeler (1995). "To Serve and Pursue: Exploring Police Sexual Violence Against Women." *Justice Quarterly* 12:85–111.

Krupp, Sherman (1961). *Patterns in Organizational Analysis.* New York: Holt.

Kuykendall, Jack L., and David E. Burns (1983). "The Black Police Officer: An Historical Perspective." *Criminal Justice* 19:41–45.

Lambert, Eric G., Shannon M. Barton, and Nancy Lynne Hogan (1999). "The Missing Link Between Job Satisfaction and Correctional Staff Behavior: The Issue of Organizational Commitment." *American Journal of Criminal Justice* 24:95–116.

Lancefield, Kay, C.J. Lennings, and Don Thomson (1997). "Management Style and Its Effect on Prison Officers' Stress." *International Journal of Stress Management* 4:205–219.

Landau, Simcha F. (1969). "Essential Problems in the Functioning of the Prison As a Formal-Bureaucratic Organization." *Delinquency and Society* 4:16–25.

Langworthy, Robert H. (1985). "Administrative Overhead in Municipal Police Departments." *American Journal of Police* 4:20–37.

Lashley, Rickey D. (1995). *Police Work: The Need for a Nobler Character.* Westport, CT: Praeger.

Lasley, James R., and Michael K. Hooper (1998). "On Racism and the LAPD: Was the Christopher Commission Wrong?" *Social Science Quarterly* 79:378–389.

Latessa, Edward J., Dana Jones, and Betsy Fulton (1999). *An Evaluation of Selected Juvenile Justice Programs in Ohio Using the Correctional Program Assessment Inventory: Final Report.* Cincinnati, OH: Division of Criminal Justice, University of Cincinnati.

Law Enforcement Association on Professional Standards, Education, and Ethical Practice (1972). *Police Ethical Practice.* St. Louis, MO: Law Enforcement Association on Professional Standards, Education, and Ethical Practice.

Lederman, Cindy S. (1999). "The Juvenile Court: Putting Research to Work for Prevention." *Juvenile Justice* 6:22–31.

Lee, M. (1901). *A History of Police in England.* London, UK: Methuen and Company.

Lehman, Joseph D. (1993). "A Commissioner's Appreciation: Pennsylvania Volunteers Build Bridges Between Our Prisons and the Community." *Corrections Today* 55:84–86.

Lehtinen, Marlene W., and Gerald W. Smith (1974). "The Relative Effectiveness of Public Defenders and Private Attorneys: A Comparison." *NLADA Briefcase* 32:13–20.

Lennings, C.J. (1997). "Police and Occupationally Related Violence: A Review." *Policing* 20:555–566.

Lersch, Kim Michelle (1998a). "Predicting Officer Race in Internal and External Allegations of Misconduct." *International Journal of Comparative and Applied Criminal Justice* 22:249–258.

Lersch, Kim Michelle (1998b). "Police Misconduct and Malpractice: A Critical Analysis of Citizens' Complaints." *Policing* 21:80–96.

Lersch, Kim Michelle, and Tom Mieczkowski (2000). "An Examination of the Convergence and Divergence of Internal and External Allegations of Misconduct Filed Against Police Officers." *Policing: An International Journal of Police Strategies and Management* 23:54–68.

Levi, Margaret (1977). *Bureaucratic Insurgency: The Case of Police Unions.* Lexington, MA: Lexington Books.

Lewis, J. Dean (1999). "An Evolving Juvenile Court: On the Front Lines with Judge J. Dean Lewis." *Juvenile Justice* 6:3–12.

Lewis, William G. (1989). "Toward Representative Bureaucracy: Blacks in City Police Organizations, 1975–1985." *Public Administration Review* 49:257–267.

Likert, Rensis (1961). *New Patterns of Management.* New York: McGraw-Hill.

Lin, Ann Chih (2000). *Reform in the Making: The Implementation of Social Policy in Prison.* Princeton, NJ: Princeton University Press.

Lindquist, Charles A., and John T. Whitehead (1986a). "Burnout, Job Stress, and Job Satisfaction Among Southern Correctional Officers: Perceptions and Causal Factors." *Journal of Offender Counseling Services and Rehabilitation* 10:5–26.

Lindquist, Charles A., and John T. Whitehead (1986b). "Correctional Officers As Parole Officers: An Examination of a Community Supervision Sanction." *Criminal Justice and Behavior* 13:197–222.

Lippitt, Gordon L. (1955). "What Do We Know About Leadership?" *National Education Association Journal* 15:556–557.

Litterer, Joseph A. (1965). *The Analysis of Organizations.* New York: Wiley.

Littrell, W. Boyd (1979). *Bureaucratic Justice: Police, Prosecutors, and Plea Bargaining.* Beverly Hills, CA: Sage Publications.

Litwak, Eugene (1961). "Models of Bureaucracy Which Permit Conflict." *American Journal of Sociology* 67:177–184.

Llynn, Richard E. (1980). *Omni House: Youth Service Bureau: A Study of the Stages of Organizational Growth and Development.* Ann Arbor, MI: University Microfilms International.

Lombardo, Lucien X. (1978). *The Correction Officer: A Study of a Criminal Justice Worker in His Work Place.* Ann Arbor, MI: University Microfilms International.

Londard, V.A., and Harry W. More (1993). *Police Organization and Management* (8/e). Westbury, NY: Foundation Press.

Lorr, Maurice, and Stephen Stack (1995). "Personality Profiles of Police Candidates." *Journal of Clinical Psychology* 50:200–207.

Los Angeles County Sheriff's Department (1992). *Mission Statement.* Los Angeles: Los Angeles County Sheriff's Department.

Los Angeles Independent Commission (1991). *Report.* Los Angeles: Los Angeles Independent Commission on the Los Angeles Police Department.

Lowin, Aaron, et al. (1969). "An Experimental Investigation of Leadership Traits." *Administrative Science Quarterly* **14:**238–253.

Lund, Dennis Wayne (1988). *Police Directed Preventive Patrol: Its Effect upon Personnel Motivation.* Ann Arbor, MI: University Microfilms International.

Lundman, Richard J. (1979). "Origins of Police Misconduct." In *Critical Issues in Criminal Justice,* R.G. Iacovetta and Dae H. Chang (eds.). Durham, NC: Carolina Academic Press.

Luthans, F. (1985). *Organizational Behavior Modification and Beyond.* Glenview, IL: Scott, Foresman.

Lynch, Gerald W. (ed.) (1999). *Human Dignity and the Police: Ethics and Integrity in Police Work.* Springfield, IL: Charles C Thomas.

Lyons, Donna, and James Turpin (1997). "Trends in State Juvenile Legislation—1996." *Corrections Today* **59:**104–105.

Maahs, Jeffrey R., and Rolando V. del Carmen (1996). "Curtailing Frivolous Section 1983 Inmate Litigation: Laws, Practices, and Proposals." *Federal Probation* **59:**53–61.

Mactavish, Marie (1992). "Are You an STJ? Examining Correctional Managers' Leadership Styles." *Corrections Today* **56:**162–164.

Maguire, Kathleen, and Ann L. Pastore (2000). *Bureau of Justice Statistics Sourcebook of Criminal Justice Statistics 1999.* Albany, NY: The Hindelang Criminal Justice Research Center, State University of New York at Albany.

Mahoney, Barry, and Holly C. Bakke (1995). *Criminal Caseflow Management Improvement in Essex County (Newark, New Jersey), 1990–1994.* Denver, CO: Justice Management Institute.

Mahoney, Thomas A., and William Weitzel (1969). "Managerial Models of Organizational Effectiveness." *Administrative Science Quarterly* **14:**357–365.

Maier, Norman R.F. (1965). *Psychology in Industry* (2/e). Boston: Houghton Mifflin.

Maier, Norman R.F. (1973). *Psychology in Industry* (3/e). Boston: Houghton Mifflin.

Major City Chiefs Administrators (1994). *Maintaining Integrity in Law Enforcement Organizations: Selected Readings.* Washington, DC: FBI Academy.

Manning, Peter K. (1977). *Police Work: The Social Organization of Policing.* Cambridge, MA: MIT Press.

March, James G., and Herbert A. Simon (1958). *Organizations.* New York: Wiley.

Marcson, S. (1960). *The Scientist in American Industry: Some Industrial Determinants in Manpower.* Princeton, NJ: Industrial Relations Section, Princeton University.

Markey, Vicki K., Sunny Ariessohn, and Margaret Mudd (1997). "Outcome-Based Supervision for Pregnant, Substance-Abusing Offenders." *APPA Perspectives* **21:** 21–23.

Marlette, Marjorie (1990). "Furloughs Tightened—Success Rates High." *Corrections Compendium* **15:**6–21.

Marley, C.W. (1973). "Furlough Programs and Conjugal Visiting in Adult Correctional Institutions." *Federal Probation* **37:**19–25.

Martin, John A., and Nancy C. Maron (1991). "Courts, Delay, and Interorganizational Networks: Managing Essential Tension." *Justice System Journal* **143:**268–288.

Maslach, Christina (1982a). "Understanding Burnout: Definitional Issues in Analyzing a Complex Phenomenon." In W.S. Paine (ed.). *Job Stress and Burnout.* Beverly Hills, CA: Sage.

Maslach, Christina (1982b). *Burnout: The Cost of Caring.* Englewood Cliffs, NJ: Prentice Hall.

Maslow, Abraham (1954). *Motivation and Personality.* New York: Harper.

Mastrofski, Stephen D., et al. (1999). *Policing Neighborhoods: A Report from St. Petersburg.* Washington, DC: U.S. Department of Justice.

Matsch, Richard P. (1996). "Court Management: Balancing People and Processes." *Federal Probation* **60:**58–59.

Mayo, Elton (1945). *The Social Problems of an Industrialized Civilization.* Cambridge, MA: Harvard University Press.

Mays, G. Larry, and William A. Taggart (1985). "The Impact of Litigation on Changing New Mexico Prison Conditions." *Prison Journal* **65:**38–53.

Mays, G. Larry, and William A. Taggart (1986). "Court Delay: Policy Implications for Court Managers." *Criminal Justice Policy Review* **1:**198–210.

McAulay, R. Peter (1989). "The Impact of Management Practices on Corruption." *Police Studies* **12:**171–174.

McCleary, Richard (1978). *Dangerous Men: The Sociology of Parole.* Beverly Hills, CA: Sage Publications.

McClelland, David (1985). *Human Motivation.* Glenview, IL: Scott, Foresman.

McConkey, Kevin M., Gail F. Huon, and Mark G. Frank (1996). *Practical Ethics in the Police Service.* Payneham, Aus: National Police Research Unit.

McCoy, Candace (ed.) (1997). "Comparative Perspectives." *Justice System Journal* **19:**1–243.

McGregor, Douglas (1960). *The Human Side of Enterprise.* New York: McGraw-Hill.

McGuire, Edward R. (1997). "Structural Change in Large Municipal Police Organizations During the Community Policing Era." *Justice Quarterly* **14:**547–576.

McLaren, Suzanne (1997). "Heart Rate and Blood Pressure in Male Police Officers and Clerical Workers on Workdays and Non-Workdays." *Work and Stress* **11:**160–174.

McLaughlin, Charles Vance (1984). *Police Selection Practices in Large Pennsylvania Municipal Police Departments.* Ann Arbor, MI: University Microfilms International.

McMullan, John L. (1984). *The Canting Crew: London's Criminal Underworld, 1550–1700.* New Brunswick, NJ: Rutgers University Press.

Meagher, M. Steven, and Nancy A. Yentes (1986). "Choosing a Career in Policing: A Comparison of Male and Female Perceptions." *American Journal of Police* **14:**320–327.

Melton, Heather C. (1999). "Police Responses to Domestic Violence." *Journal of Offender Rehabilitation* **29:**1–21.

Mendelsohn, Harold, and Garrett J. O'Keefe (1981). *Public Communications and the Prevention of Crime: Strategies for Control.* Denver, CO: University of Denver Center for Mass Communications Research and Policy.

Mericle, J. Gayle (1994). *Countersurveillance: Exploring Local Level Deepcover Narcotics Enforcement.* Ann Arbor, MI: University Microfilms International.

Merton, Robert K. (1940). "Bureaucratic Structure and Personality." *Social Forces* **18:**560–568.

Merton, Robert K. (1957). *Social Theory and Social Structure.* Glencoe, IL: Free Press.

Meyer, Jon'a, and Tara Gray (1997). "Drunk Drivers in the Courts: Legal and Extra-Legal Factors Affecting Pleas and Sentences." *Journal of Criminal Justice* **25:**155–163.

Meyer, Marshall W. (1972). *Bureaucratic Structure and Authority: Coordination and Control in 254 Government Agencies.* New York: Harper and Row.

Miller, Linda S., and Karen M. Hess (1994). *Community Policing: Theory and Practice.* Minneapolis/St. Paul: West Publishing Company.

Minnesota Probation Standards Task Force (1993). *Minnesota Probation: A System in Crisis.* St. Paul, MN: Minnesota Probation Standards Task Force.

Misner, Robert L. (1996). "Recasting Prosecutorial Discretion." *Journal of Criminal Law and Criminology* **86:**717–777.

Mitchell, George A. (1999). *Privatizing Parole and Probation in Wisconsin: The Path to Fewer Prisons.* Thiensville, WI: Wisconsin Policy Research Institute.

Mitchell, George A., and David Dodenhoff (1998). *The Truth About Sentencing in Wisconsin: Plea Bargaining, Punishment, and the Public Interest.* Thiensville, WI: Wisconsin Policy Research Institute.

Montana, Richard (1992). *Survey of Civilian Complaint Systems.* New York: New York City Police Department, Civilian Complaint Investigative Process.

Moore, David B. (1991). "Origins of the Police Mandate: The Australian Case Reconsidered." *Police Studies* **14:**107–120.

Morash, Merry, and Robin N. Haarr (1995). "Gender, Workplace Problems, and Stress in Policing." *Justice Quarterly* **12:**113–140.

More, Harry W. (1992). *Special Topics in Policing.* Cincinnati, OH: Anderson Publishing Company.

Morgan, Kathryn D., Barbara A. Belbot, and John Clark (1997). "Liability Issues Affecting Probation and Parole Supervision." *Journal of Criminal Justice* **25:**211–222.

Morley, Harvey N., and Robert S. Fong (1995). "Can We All Get Along? A Study of Why Strained Relations Continue to Exist Between Sworn Law Enforcement and Private Security." *Security Journal* **6:**85–92.

Morris, R. Aldridge (1971). "An Analysis of the Relationship Between Intelligence, Personality, Occupational Motivation, and Job Satisfaction in a Sample of Residential Care Workers." *Community Schools Gazette* **65:**107–116.

Morton, Joann B. (ed.) (1991). *Change, Challenge, and Choices: Women's Role in Modern Corrections.* Laurel, MD: American Correctional Association.

Mumford, Enid (1970). "Job Satisfaction: A New Approach Derived from an Old Theory." *Sociological Review* **18:**71–101.

Munro, Jim L. (1974). *Administrative Behavior and Police Organizations.* Cincinnati, OH: Anderson Publishing Company.

Munro, Jim L. (1976). *Classes, Conflict, and Control: Studies in Criminal Justice Management.* Cincinnati, OH: Anderson Publishing Company.

Musser, Denise Casamento (1999). "Kansas's Grassroots Juvenile Justice Reform." *Corrections Today* **60:**152–154.

Myers, M.S. (1964). "Who Are Your Motivated Workers?" *Harvard Business Review* **42:**73–88.

Nalla, Mahesh K., Michael J. Lynch, and Michael J. Leiber (1997). "Determinants of Police Growth in Phoenix, 1950–1988." *Justice Quarterly* **14:**115–143.

Nasheri, Hedieh (1998). *Betrayal of Due Process: A Comparative Assessment of Plea Bargaining in the United States and Canada.* Lanham, MD: University Press of America.

National Advisory Commission on Criminal Justice Standards and Goals (1973). *Report of the National Advisory Commission on Criminal Justice Standards and Goals.* Washington, DC: U.S. Government Printing Office.

National Advisory Commission on Criminal Justice Standards and Goals (1977). *Police Chief Executive.* Washington, DC: U.S. Government Printing Office.

National Center for State Courts (1990). *Night Court: Is It a Solution to Hennepin County (MN) Jail Overcrowding: Final Report.* Overland Park, KS: National Center for State Courts, Midwestern Regional Office.

National Center for State Courts (1995). *State Court Caseload Statistics, 1993.* Williamsburg, VA: National Center for State Courts.

National Center for State Courts (1997). *State Court Accountability Report.* Williamsburg, VA: National Center for State Courts.

National Drug Court Institute (1999). *DUI/Drug Courts: Defining a National Strategy.* Washington, DC: National Drug Court Institute.

National Institute of Justice (1991). *Private Security: Patterns and Trends.* Washington, DC: National Institute of Justice.

National Institute of Law Enforcement and Criminal Justice (1980). *Arson Prevention and Control: Program Model.* Washington, DC: U.S. Government Printing Office.

Nay, Richard Edward (1990). *Social Support and Its Relationship to Job Stress and Burnout in Correctional Officers.* Ann Arbor, MI: University Microfilms International.

Naylor, R.T. (1999). "Wash-Out: A Critique of Follow-the-Money Methods in Crime Control Policy." *Crime, Law and Social Change* **32:**1–57.

Nelson, James F. (1992). *Drugs, Prosecutors, Predicate Felons, and Prison Beds.* Albany, NY: New York State Office of Justice Systems Analysis.

Newcomb, Theodore M., Ralph H. Turner, and P.E. Converse (1965). *Social Psychology: The Study of Human Interaction.* New York: Holt.

New Jersey Attorney General's Office (1978). "A Status Report on the War Against Organized Crime in New Jersey: Some Recommendations for the Future." *Criminal Justice Quarterly* **6**:50–74.

New York State Division of Criminal Justice Services (1992). *Drugs, Prosecutors, Predicate Felons, and Prison Beds: A Description of Changes in Felony Arrests and Felony Case Processing Decisions in New York State.* Albany, NY: Office of Justice Systems Analysis.

Nieto, Marcus (1998). *Probation for Adult and Juvenile Offenders: Options for Improved Accountability.* Sacramento, CA: California Research Bureau.

Noonan, John T., Jr., and Kenneth I. Winston (eds.) (1993). *The Responsible Judge: Readings in Judicial Ethics.* Westport, CT: Praeger.

Norman, Michael D., and Robert C. Wadman (2000). "Utah Presentence Investigation Reports: User Perceptions of Quality and Effectiveness." *Federal Probation* **64**:7–12.

Normandeau, Andre, and Barry Leighton (eds.) (1991). "Police and Society in Canada." *Canadian Journal of Criminology* **33**:241–585.

North Carolina Bar Association (1971). *North Carolina Penal System Study Committee—Interior Report.* Raleigh, NC: North Carolina Bar Association.

Nossaman, Jeff (1996). "Community Service: Inmates Giving Back to the Communities." *American Jails* **10**:75–78.

O'Brien, Barbara S. (1985). *Stress in Corrections Officers: Iowa Department of Corrections Study.* Washington, DC: U.S. National Institute of Corrections.

Ogburn, Kevin R. (1993). "Volunteer Program Guide." *Corrections Today* **55**:66–70.

O'Leary, Vincent (1987). "Probation: A System of Change." *Federal Probation* **51**:8–11.

O'Shea, Timothy C. (1999). "Community Policing in Small Town Rural America: A Comparison of Police Officer Attitudes in Chicago and Baldwin County, Alabama." *Policing and Society* **9**:59–76.

Ostrom, Brian, and Neal Kauder (1999). "Drug Crime: The Impact on State Courts." *Caseload Highlights* **5**:1–8.

O'Toole, Michael (1993). "The Changing Role of Local Jails." *Corrections Today* **55**:8.

O'Toole, Michael (1997). "Jails and Prisons: The Numbers Say They Are More Different Than Generally Assumed." *American Jails* **11**:27–31.

Ouchi, W. (1981). *How American Business Can Meet the Japanese Challenge.* Reading, MA: Addison Wesley.

Outlaw, Maureen C., and Barry R. Ruback (1999). "Predictors and Outcomes of Victim Restitution Orders." *Justice Quarterly* **16**:847–869.

Page, Robert W. (1993). "Family Courts: An Effective Judicial Approach to the Resolution of Family Disputes." *Juvenile and Family Court Journal* **44**:3–60.

Pallone, Nathaniel J., and James J. Hennessy (1999). "Black and Whites As Victims and Offenders in Aggressive Crime in the U.S.: Myths and Realities." *Journal of Offender Rehabilitation* **30**:1–33.

Palmer, John W. (1996). *Constitutional Rights of Prisoners* (5th ed.). Cincinnati, OH: Anderson Publishing Company.

Palumbo, Dennis J., Michael Musheno, and Michael Hallett (1994). "The Political Construction of Alternative Dispute Resolution and Alternatives to Incarceration." *Evaluation and Program Planning* **17**:197–203.

Parker, Treadway C. (1963). "Relationships Among Measures of Supervising Behavior, Group Behavior, and Situational Characteristics." *Personnel Psychology* **16**:319–334.

Parsons, Talcott (1951). *The Social System.* Glencoe, IL: Free Press.

Parsons, Talcott (1956a). "Suggestions for a Sociological Approach to the Theory of Organizations." *Administrative Science Quarterly* **1**:63–85.

Parsons, Talcott (1956b). "Suggestions for a Sociological Approach to the Theory of Organizations—Part II." *Administrative Science Quarterly* **1**:225–239.

Patel, Jody, and Curt Soderlund (1994). "Getting a Piece of the Pie: Revenue Sharing with Crime Victims Compensation Programs." *APPA Perspectives* **18**:22–27.

Payne, Brian K., and Randy R. Gainey (1998). "A Qualitative Assessment of the Pains Experienced on Electronic Monitoring." *International Journal of Offender Therapy and Comparative Criminology* **42**:149–163.

Peach, F.J. (1999). *Corrections in the Balance: A Review of Corrective Services in Queensland.* Brisbane, Aus: Queensland Government.

Peak, Kenneth J. (1993). *Policing America: Methods, Issues, and Challenges.* Englewood Cliffs, NJ: Regents/Prentice Hall.

Pelletier, Daniel, Sylvain Coutu, and Annie Lamonde (1996). "Work and Gender Issues in Secure Juvenile Delinquency Facilities." *International Journal of Offender Therapy and Comparative Criminology* **40**:32–43.

Pelz, Donald C. (1952). "Influence: A Key to Effective Leadership in the First Line Supervisor." *Personnel* **29**:209–217.

Perrott, Stephen B., and Donald M. Taylor (1995). "Attitudinal Differences Between Police Constables and Their Supervisors: Potential Influences of Personality and Work Environment." *Criminal Justice and Behavior* **22**:326–339.

Perrow, Charles (1967). "A Framework for the Comparative Analysis of Organizations." *American Sociological Review* **32**:194–209.

Perryman, M. Ray (1981). "A Neglected Institutional Feature of the Labor Sector of the U.S. Economy." *Journal of Economic Issues* **15**:387–395.

Peters, Roger H., and Mary R. Murrin (2000). "Effectiveness of Treatment-Based Drug Courts in Reducing Criminal Recidivism." *Criminal Justice and Behavior* **27**:72–96.

Petersilia, Joan (1998). "A Decade of Experimenting with Intermediate Sanctions: What Have We Learned?" *Federal Probation* **62**:3–9.

Phipps, Polly, et al. (1999). *Research Findings on Adult Corrections Programs: A Review.* Olympia, WA: Washington State Institute for Public Policy.

Pizzi, William T. (1999). *Trials Without Truth: Why Our System of Criminal Trials Has Become an Expensive Failure and What We Need to Do to Rebuild It.* New York: New York University Press.

Plotnikoff, Joyce, and Richard Woolfson (1998). *Policing Domestic Violence: Effective Organisational Structures.* London, UK: Policing and Reducing Crime Unit, UK Home Office.

Polansky, Larry (ed.) (1993). "What's New In Court Technology?" *Judge's Journal* **13:**4–104.

Polizzi, Danielle M., Doris Layton MacKenzie, and Laura J. Hickman (1999). "What Works in Adult Sex Offender Treatment? A Review of Prison- and Non-Prison–Based Treatment Programs." *International Journal of Offender Therapy and Comparative Criminology* **43:**357–374.

Pollock, Joycelyn M. (ed.) (1997). *Prisons: Today and Tomorrow.* Gaithersburg, MD: Aspen Publishers.

Pollock-Byrne, Joycelyn M. (1989). *Ethics in Crime and Justice: Dilemmas and Decisions.* Pacific Grove, CA: Brooks/Cole Publishing Company.

Pollock, Joycelyn M., and Ronald F. Becker (1995). "Law Enforcement Ethics: Using Officers as a Teaching Tool." *Journal of Criminal Justice Education* **6:**1–20.

Pontell, Henry N., and Wayne N. Welsh (1994). "Incarceration As a Deviant Form of Social Control: Jail Overcrowding in California." *Crime and Delinquency* **40:**18–36.

Poole, Eric D., and Mark R. Pogrebin (1997). "Jail Duty and Jail Work: A Look at the Differences Between Deputy Sheriffs and Corrections Officers." *American Jails* **11:**63–70.

Potter, James T. (1991). "Future Trends in Intake and Discharge." *American Jails* **5:**47–50.

Poulos, Tammy Meredith (1992). *A Woman's Place Is on Patrol: Female Representation in Municipal Police Departments.* Tallahassee, FL: Florida State University.

Poulos, Tammy Meredith, and William G. Doerner (1996). "Women in Law Enforcement: The Distribution of Females in Florida Police Agencies." *Women and Criminal Justice* **8:**19–33.

Pratt, Travis C., and Melissa R. Winston (1999). "The Search for the Frugal Grail: An Empirical Assessment of Public vs. Private Correctional Facilities." *Criminal Justice Policy Review* **10:**447–471.

President's Commission on Law Enforcement (1967). *President's Commission on Law Enforcement and the Administration of Justice.* Washington, DC: U.S. Government Printing Office.

Price, Barbara Raffel (1974). "A Study of Leadership Strength of Female Police Executives." *Journal of Police Science and Administration* **2:**219–226.

Price, Barbara Raffel (1985). "Sexual Integration in American Law Enforcement." In *Police Ethics: Hard Choices in Law Enforcement,* William C. Heffernan and Timothy Stroups (eds.). New York: John Jay Press.

Pringle, P. (1955). *Hue and Cry.* London, UK: Museum Press.

Provine, Doris Marie (1986). *Judging Credentials: Nonlawyer Judges and the Politics of Professionalism.* Chicago: University of Chicago Press.

Puro, Steven, Roger Goldman, and William C. Smith (1997). "Police Decertification: Changing Patterns Among the States." *Policing* **20:**481–496.

Queensland Criminal Justice Commission (1995). *Beat Policing: A Case Study.* Brisbane, Aus: Queensland Criminal Justice Commission.

Rackmill, Stephen J. (1996). "Printzlien's Legacy, the 'Brooklyn Plan,' A.K.A. Deferred Prosecution." *Federal Probation* **60:**8–15.

Radelet, Louis A., and David L. Carter (1994). *The Police and the Community* (5/e). New York: Macmillan.

Reader, W.D. (1996). "The Laws of Unintended Results." *Akron Law Review* **29:**477–489.

Reaves, Brian A. (1996). *Local Police Departments, 1993.* Washington, DC: U.S. Department of Justice.

Reaves, Brian A. (1997). *Federal Law Enforcement Officers, 1996.* Washington, DC: Bureau of Justice Statistics.

Reaves, Brian A., and Andrew L. Goldberg (1998). *Census of State and Local Law Enforcement Agencies, 1996.* Washington, DC: Bureau of Justice Statistics.

Reaves, Brian A., and Andrew L. Goldberg (2000). *Local Police Departments, 1997.* Washington, DC: U.S. Department of Justice.

Reaves, Brian A., and Timothy C. Hart (2000). *Federal Law Enforcement Officers, 1998.* Washington, DC: U.S. Department of Justice.

Reese, James T. (1987). *Behavioral Science in Law Enforcement.* Washington, DC: U.S. Department of Justice, Federal Bureau of Investigation.

Regoli, Robert M. (1975). *Toward an Understanding of Police Cynicism.* Ann Arbor, MI: Xerox University Microfilms.

Reisig, Michael Dean (1996). *An Analysis of American Higher-Custody State Prisons: The Effects of Individual-Level, Organizational, and External Factors on Different Measures.* Ann Arbor, MI: University Microfilms International.

Reith, C. (1952). *The Blind Eye of History.* London, UK: Faber and Faber.

Rice, George H., Jr., and Dean W. Bishoprick (1971). *Conceptual Models of Organization.* New York: Appleton-Century-Crofts.

Rich, Thomas F. (1999). *Mapping and Crime Analysis by Community Organizations in Hartford, CT.* Cambridge, MA: Abt Associates.

Richardson, J. (1970). *The New York Police.* New York: Oxford University Press.

Rison, Richard Hall (1996). *Analysis and Development of a Prison Activation Model: The Creation of a Federal Multi-Security Prison and Hospital Complex for Female Offenders.* Ann Arbor, MI: University Microfilms International.

Roberg, Roy R., and Jack Kuykendall (1998). *Police Management* (2/e). Los Angeles: Roxbury Publishing Company.

Roberts, John W. (1997). *Reform and Retribution: An Illustrated History of American Prisons.* Lanham, MD: American Correctional Association.

Robertson, Elizabeth, and Joseph F. Donnermeyer (1998). "Patterns of Drug Use Among Nonmetropolitan and Rural Adults." *Substance Use and Misuse* 33:210–2129.

Robinson, David, Frank J. Porporino, and Linda Simourd (1996). "Do Different Occupational Groups Vary on Attitudes and Work Adjustment in Corrections?" *Federal Probation* 60:45–53.

Robinson, David, Frank J. Porporino, and Linda Simourd (1997). "The Influence of Educational Attainment on the Attitudes and Job Performance of Correctional Officers." *Crime and Delinquency* 43:60–77.

Roethlisberger, Fritz J. (1941). *Management and Morale.* Cambridge, MA: Harvard University Press.

Roethlisberger, Fritz J., and William J. Dickson (1939). *Management and the Worker.* Cambridge, MA: Harvard University Press.

Rogers, Joseph W. (1998). "Seven Ideal Criteria for the Constructive Evaluation of Discipline for Parents, Teachers, and Juvenile Probation Officers." *Juvenile and Family Court Journal* 49:27–37.

Rogers, Robert (1993). "Solitary Confinement." *International Journal of Offender Therapy and Comparative Criminology* 37:339–349.

Rollo, Joseph A., and George Kalas (1975). "An Analysis of the Role Expectations of Prison Superintendents in the Virginia Department of Corrections." *Georgia Journal of Corrections* 4:55–64.

Ross, J.C., and A. Zander (1957). "Need Satisfactions and Employee Turnover." *Personnel Psychology* 10:327–338.

Ross, Jeffrey Ian (1993). *The Politics and Control of Police Violence in New York City and Toronto.* Ann Arbor, MI: University Microfilms International.

Rousch, David W., and Michael A. Jones (1996). "Juvenile Detention Training: A Status Report." *Federal Probation* 60:54–60.

Rousch, David W., and B. Thomas Steelman (1981). "A Team Approach to Detention Staff Development." *Juvenile and Family Court Journal* 32:33–43.

Roy, Donald F. (1960). "Banana Time: Job Satisfaction and Informal Interaction." *Human Organization* 18:158–168.

Rubenstein, Alberta H., and Chadwick J. Haberstroh (1966). *Some Theories of Organization.* Homewood, IL: Dorsey Press.

Ruchelman, Leonard (1973). *Who Rules the Police?* New York: New York University Press.

Rush, George E. (1997) *Inside American Prisons and Jails.* Indian Village, NV: Copperhouse Publishing.

Russell, Gregory D., and Susan MacLachlan (1999). "Community Policing, Decentralized Decision Making, and Employee Satisfaction." *Journal of Crime and Justice* 22:31–54.

Ryan, Timothy, and Charles C. Plummer (1999). "Jail Accreditation: A Panacea or Problem?" *Corrections Today* 61:157.

Saari, David J. (1982). *American Court Management: Theories and Practices.* Westport, CT: Quorum Books.

Sanfilippo, Rudy (1969). *Management Development: Key to Increased Correctional Effectiveness.* Washington, DC: U.S. Government Printing Office.

Sayles, Leonard (1958). *Behavior of Industrial Work Groups.* New York: Wiley.

Schmidt, Freidrich (1989). *Organizational Factors Influencing Probation Supervision Effectiveness.* Ann Arbor, MI: University Microfilms International.

Schmidt, Wayne W. (1985). "Section 1983 and the Changing Face of Police Management." In *Police Leadership in America,* William A. Geller (ed.). New York: Praeger.

Schmidtke, A., S. Fricke, and D. Lester (1999). "Suicide Among German Federal and State Police Officers." *Psychological Reports* 84:157–166.

Schneider, Frank W. (1991). "Police Organizational Effectiveness: The Manager's Perspective." *Canadian Police College Journal* 15:153–165.

Schugam, Martin Serle (1983). *Systemic Trends and the Weighing of Systemic and Composite Issues in Juvenile Corrections Policy Making: A Case Study Analysis.* Ann Arbor, MI: University Microfilms International.

Scogin, Forrest, Joseph Schumacher, and Jennifer Gardner (1995). "Predictive Validity of Psychological Testing in Law Enforcement Settings." *Professional Psychology Research and Practice* 26:68–71.

Scott, W.H. (1966). "Professionals in Bureaucracies: Areas of Conflict." In *Professionalization,* H.M. Vollmer and D.L. Mills (eds.). Englewood Cliffs, NJ: Prentice Hall.

Seaman, Thomas W. (1978). *Exploration of the Systemic Model As a Basis for Planning and Evaluating Crime Control Practices.* Ann Arbor, MI: University Microfilms International.

SEARCH Group Inc. (1990). *Original Records of Entry.* Washington, DC: U.S. Bureau of Justice Statistics.

Segrave, Kerry (1995). *Policewomen: A History.* Jefferson, NC: McFarland and Company.

Selke, William L. (1978). *A Systems Model Approach to Evaluating Social Programs: The Case of Youth Service Bureaus.* Ann Arbor, MI: University Microfilms International.

Selye, Hans (1976). *The Stress of Life* (2/e). New York: McGraw-Hill.

Selznick, Phillip (1943). "An Approach to a Theory of Bureaucracy." *American Sociological Review* 28:399–411.

Selznick, Phillip (1966). *TVA and Grass Roots: A Study in the Sociology of Formal Organizations.* Berkeley, CA: University of California Press.

Senese, Jeffrey D. (1991). "Jail Utilization Over Time: An Assessment of the Patterns in Male and Female Populations." *Criminal Justice Policy Review* 5:241–255.

Senese, Jeffrey D., et al. (1992). "Evaluating Jail Reform: Inmate Infractions and Disciplinary Response in a Traditional and a Podular/Direct Supervision Jail." *American Jails* 6:14–23.

Seymour, James D., and Richard Anderson (1998). *New Ghosts, Old Ghosts: Prisons and Labor Reform Camps in China.* Armonk, NY: M.E. Sharpe.

Shadmi, Erella (1994). "Controlling the Police: A Public and Integrative Approach." *Policing and Society* **4:**119–129.

Shanahan, Donald T. (1978). *Patrol Administration: Management by Objectives* (2nd ed.). Boston: Allyn and Bacon.

Shapiro, C. (1982). "Creative Supervision: An Underutilized Antidote." In W. Paine (ed.). *Job Stress and Burnout: Research, Theory, and Intervention Perspectives.* Beverly Hills, CA: Sage.

Sharbaro, Edward, and Robert Keller (eds.) (1995). *Prison Crisis: Critical Readings.* Albany, NY: Harrow and Heston.

Sharp, John (1994). *Behind the Walls: The Price and Performance of the Texas Department of Criminal Justice.* Austin, TX: Texas Comptroller of Public Accounts.

Shepherd, Robert E., Jr. (1999). "The Juvenile Court at 100 Years: A Look Back." *Juvenile Justice* **6:**13–21.

Sherman, Lawrence W. (1974). *Police Corruption: A Sociological Perspective.* Garden City, NY: Anchor Books.

Shichor, David (1993). "The Corporate Context of Private Prisons." *Crime, Law, and Social Change* **20:**113–138.

Shigley, Richard T. (1987). "The Emerging Professional Education Model for Police and the Minnesota Experience." Unpublished paper presented at the Academy of Criminal Justice Sciences meeting, St. Louis, MO (March).

Shillingstad, Jay W., et al. (1995). "Supervision Can Make a Difference: Seven Success Stories." *Federal Probation* **59:**9–17.

Sigurdson, Herbert R. (1996). "A Difference That Made a Difference in the Administration of Justice." *American Jails* **10:**9–21.

Silbert, Earl J. (1986). "The Crime Fraud Exception to the Attorney-Client Privilege and Work-Product Doctrine, the Lawyer's Obligations of Disclosure, and the Lawyer's Response to Accusations of Wrongful Conduct." *American Criminal Law Review* **23:**351–378.

Simmel, Georg (1903). "The Number of Members As Determining the Sociological Form of the Group." *American Journal of Sociology* **8:**1–46.

Simmons, Calvin, John K. Cochran, and William R. Blount (1997). "The Effects of Job-Related Stress and Job Satisfaction on Probation Officers' Inclinations to Quit." *American Journal of Criminal Justice* **21:**213–229.

Simon, Herbert A. (1947). *Administrative Behavior.* New York: Macmillan.

Simon, Herbert A. (1957). *Models of Man.* New York: Wiley.

Simon, Herbert A., D.W. Smithburg, and V.A. Thompson (1950). *Public Administration.* New York: Knopf.

Skolnick, Jerome H. (1994). *Justice Without Trial: Law Enforcement in a Democratic Society* (3/e). New York: Macmillan.

Sloan, John J., and J.L. Miller (1990). "Repeat Player Police Officers and Prosecutorial Charge Reduction Decisions: A Note." *American Journal of Police* **9:**163–168.

Smith, Michael R., and Geoffrey P. Alpert (2000). "Pepper Spray: A Safe and Reasonable Response to Suspect Verbal Resistance." *Policing: An International Journal of Police Strategies and Management* **23:**233–245.

Snellenburg, Sidney C., and John W. Dickey (1989). *Innovative Approaches to Reduce Congestion and Court Delay: Final Report.* Blacksburg, VA: Virginia Polytechnic Institute and State University.

Snow, Robert L. (1992). "Accreditation: A 21st Century Necessity?" *Law and Order* **40:**84–88.

Snyder, Howard N. (1988). *Court Careers of Juvenile Offenders.* Pittsburgh, PA: National Center for Juvenile Justice.

Snyder, Howard N. (1999a). *Juvenile Arrests 1998.* Washington, DC: U.S. Department of Justice.

Snyder, Howard N. (1999b). "Violent Juvenile Crime: The Number of Juvenile Offenders Declines." *Corrections Today* **61:**96–100.

Society for Human Resource Management (1996). *1996 Workplace Violence Survey.* Alexandria, VA: Society for Human Resource Management.

Solomon, Rayman L. (1984). "The Politics of Appointment and the Federal Court's Role in Regulating America: U.S. Courts of Appeals Judgeships from T.R. to F.D.R." *American Bar Foundation Journal* **2:**285–343.

Souryal, Sam S. (1977). *Police Administration and Management.* St. Paul, MN: West Publishing Company.

Souryal, Sam S. (1995). *Police Organization and Administration.* Cincinnati, OH: Anderson Publishing Company.

Southerland, Mittie Davis (1984). *The Active Valuing of Education by Police Organizations.* Ann Arbor, MI: University Microfilms International.

Southerland, Mittie Davis (1989). "First-Line Police Supervision: Assessing Leadership Styles." Paper presented at the annual meeting of the Southern Criminal Justice Association, Jacksonville, FL (October).

Southerland, Mittie Davis (1990). "First-Line Supervision: Organizational Performance and Officer Satisfaction." Paper presented at the annual meeting of the Academy of Criminal Justice Sciences, Denver, CO (March).

Southgate, Peter, and Catriona Merrlees-Black (1991). *Traffic Policing in Changing Times.* London, UK: Her Majesty's Stationery Office.

Spector, P. (1996). *Industrial and Organizational Psychology: Research and Practice.* New York: John Wiley.

Speedy Trial Act Study Committee (1989). *North Carolina Report of the Speedy Trial Study Committee.* Raleigh, NC: Speedy Trial Act Study Committee.

Spencer, Herbert (1898). *Principles of Sociology,* Vol. I. New York: Appleton.

Spergel, Irving, et al. (1999). *Evaluation of the Little Village Gang Violence Reduction Project: The First Three Years (Executive Summary).* Chicago: Illinois Criminal Justice Information Authority.

Stamper, Norman H. (1988). *Executive Leadership and Executive Management in Big-City Police Departments: The Pro-*

fessed Values vs. the Observed Behavior of American Police Chiefs. Ann Arbor, MI: University Microfilms International.

Stamper, Norman H. (1992). *Removing Managerial Barriers to Effective Police Leadership*. Washington, DC: Police Executive Research Forum.

Standing Bear, Zug Galafa (1986). *Police Leadership Styles: An Empirical Investigation of the Relationships Between Perceived Leader Effectiveness and Prescriptive Leadership*. Ann Arbor, MI: University Microfilms International.

St. Clair, James D., et al. (1992). *Report of the Boston Police Department Management Review Committee*. Boston: Management Review Committee.

Steinberg, Laurence, and Elizabeth Cauffman (1999). "A Developmental Perspective on Serious Juvenile Crime: When Should Adults Be Treated As Adults?" *Federal Probation* **63:**52–57.

Steinman, Michael (1984). "Rationalizing Police Operations: Some Explanatory Factors." *Journal of Criminal Justice* **12:**221–233.

Stenning, Philip C., and Clifford D. Shearing (1991). "Policing." In *Criminology: A Reader's Guide*, Jane Gladstone, Richard Ericson, and Clifford Shearing (eds.). Toronto, Can: Centre of Criminology, University of Toronto.

Stevenson, Teresa Maureen (1988). *Stress Among Police Officers: Burnout and Its Correlates*. Ann Arbor, MI: University Microfilms International.

Steward, Mark (1997). "Kids or Killers? Promising Programs." *Corrections Today* **59:**90–93.

Stewart, Lynn, et al. (1995). "Offender Treatability." *Forum on Corrections Research* **7:**5–47.

Stitt, B. Grant, and Robert H. Chaires (1993). "Plea Bargaining: Ethical Issues and Emerging Perspectives." *Justice Professional* **7:**69–81.

Stockdale, J.E., C.M.E. Whitehead, and P.J. Graham (1999). *Applying Economic Evaluation to Policing Activity*. London, UK: Policing and Reducing Crime Unit, UK Home Office.

Stogdill, Ralph M. (1971). "The Sociometry of Working Relationships in Formal Organizations." *Sociometry* **12:**75–82.

Stogdill, Ralph M. (1974). *Handbook of Leadership: A Survey of Theory and Research*. New York: Free Press.

Stogdill, Ralph M., and A.E. Coons (1957). *Leadership Behavior: Its Description and Measurement*. Columbus, OH: Bureau of Business Research, Ohio State University.

Stohr, Mary K., et al. (1994). "Staff Management in Correctional Institutions: Comparing DiIulio's 'Control Model' and 'Employee Investment Model' Outcomes in Five Jails." *Justice Quarterly* **11:**471–497.

Stohr, Mary K., et al. (1995). "Staff Management in Correctional Institutions: 'Control Model' and 'Employee Investment Model' Outcomes in Five Jail Settings." *American Jails* **9:**28–36.

Stojkovic, Stan (1984). *Social Bases of Power in a Maximum-Security Prison: A Study of the Erosion of Traditional Authority*. Ann Arbor, MI: University Microfilms International.

Stroup, Timothy (1985). "Affirmative Action and the Police." In *Police Ethics: Hard Choices in Law Enforcement*, W.C. Heffernan and T. Stroup (eds.). New York: John Jay.

Stymne, Bengt (1968). "Interdepartmental Communication and Intraorganizational Strain." *Acta Sociologica* **11:**82–100.

Sullivan, Tommy T. (1977). "The Importance Given Selected Job Characteristics by Individuals Who Possess a Criminal Justice Degree." *Criminal Justice Review* **2:**93–100.

Suny, Ellen Yankee (1987). "Subpoenas to Criminal Defense Lawyers: A Proposal for Limits." *Oregon Law Review* **65:**215–308.

Surette, Ray (1979). "Organizational Models and Prisons: A Synthesis." *New England Journal on Prison Law* **6:**113–127.

Surette, Ray, and Alfredo Richard (1995). "Public Information Officers: A Descriptive Study of Crime News Gatekeepers." *Journal of Criminal Justice* **23:**325–336.

Sviridoff, Michele, et al. (1997). *Dispensing Justice Locally: The Implementation and Effects of the Midtown Community Court*. Washington, DC: U.S. National Institute of Justice and State Justice Institute.

Swanson, Charles R., Leonard Territo, and Robert W. Taylor (1993). *Police Administration: Structures, Processes, and Behaviors* (3/e). New York: Macmillan Publishing Company.

Swift, Joel H. (1984). "Model Rule 3.6: An Unconstitutional Regulation of Defense Attorney Trial Publicity." *Boston University Law Review* **64:**1003–1054.

Sykes, Gresham (1958). *The Society of Captives: A Study of Maximum Security Prisons*. Princeton, NJ: Princeton University Press.

Szostak, Edward W. (1996). "Jails and the Management of Other Agencies' Prisoners." *American Jails* **10:**22–24.

Takagi, Paul T., and Robert M. Carter (1967). "Persistent Problems and Challenges in Correctional Supervision." *Criminologica* **5:**36–46.

Takata, Susan Reiko (1983). *Discretionary Justice Within Local Parole Systems in California: A Comparative Organizational Analysis Between Los Angeles and San Francisco Counties*. Ann Arbor, MI: Microfilms International.

Tartaglini, Aldo J., and David A. Safran (1996). "Occupational Functioning of Correctional Officers: Job-Related, Organizational, and Social Considerations." *American Jails* **10:**42–44.

Taylor, Frederick W. (1911). *The Principles of Scientific Management*. New York: Harper.

Tennessee Select Oversight Committee on Corrections (1989). *State and Local Corrections: A Coordinated Strategy for Tennessee*. Nashville, TN: Tennessee Select Oversight Committee on Corrections.

Territo, Leonard, James B. Halsted, and Max L. Bromley (1998). *Crime and Justice in America: A Human Perspective* (5/e). Boston: Butterworth-Heinemann.

Terry, W. Clinton, III (ed.) (1999). *The Early Drug Courts: Case Studies in Judicial Innovation*. Thousand Oaks, CA: Sage.

Tewksbury, Richard (1994). "On the Margins of Two Professions: The Experiences of Job Satisfaction and Stress

Among Post-Secondary Correctional Educators." *American Journal of Criminal Justice* **18**:61–77.

Tewksbury, Richard, and Lise Marie Vannostrand (1996). "Environmental and Interactional Barriers to Job Satisfaction for Postsecondary Correctional Educators." *Prison Journal* **76**:275–292.

Texas Criminal Justice Council (1972). *Criminal Justice Plan for Texas—1972*. Austin, TX: Texas Criminal Justice Council.

Thomann, Daniel A., Lois Pilant, and Sheldon Kay (1994). "Police Women in the 1990s." *Police Chief* **61**:31–55.

Thomas, Charles W., Gary A. Kreps, and Robin J. Cage (1977). "An Application of Compliance Theory to the Study of Juvenile Delinquency." *Sociology and Social Research* **61**:156–175.

Thomas, Jim (1980). *The Relationship of Federal Funding to Criminology and Policing Research in the Social Sciences*. Ann Arbor, MI: University Microfilms International.

Thomas, Robert L. (1987). *A Study of Stress Perception Among Select Federal Probation Officers and Supervisors*. Ann Arbor, MI: University Microfilms International.

Thomas, Robert L. (1988). "Stress Perception Among Select Federal Probation and Pretrial Services Officers and Their Supervisors." *Federal Probation* **52**:48–58.

Thomas, W.I. (1923). *The Unadjusted Girl*. Boston: Little, Brown.

Thompson, Anthony C. (1999). "Stopping the Usual Suspects: Race and the Fourth Amendment." *New York University Law Review* **74**:956–1013.

Thompson, James D. (1967). *Organizations in Action*. New York: McGraw-Hill.

Thompson, Joel A., and G. Larry Mays (eds.) (1991). *American Jails: Public Policy Issues*. Chicago: Nelson-Hall.

Thomson, Doug (1980). "Accountability in Small Probation Agencies." *Journal of Probation and Parole* **12**:1–19.

Toch, Hans (1995a). "Democratizing Prisons." *Prison Journal* **74**:62–72.

Toch, Hans (1995b). "Inmate Involvement in Prison Governance." *Federal Probation* **59**:34–39.

Tolstoy, Leo N. (1928). "The Tsar and the Elephants." In *The Great Fables of All Nations*, M. Komroff (ed.). New York: Tudor Publishing Company.

Tonry, Michael (1999). "Parochialism in U.S. Sentencing Policy." *Crime and Delinquency* **45**:48–65.

Tonry, Michael, and Kathleen Hatlestad (1997). *Sentencing Reform in Overcrowded Times: A Comparative Perspective*. New York: Oxford University Press.

Tonry, Michael, and Norval Morris (1992). *Modern Policing*. Chicago: University of Chicago Press.

Torbet, Patricia, and Linda Szymanski (1998). *State Legislative Responses to Violent Juvenile Crime: 1996–1997 Update*. Washington, DC: U.S. Department of Justice.

Torbet, Patricia, et al. (1996). *State Responses to Serious and Violent Juvenile Crime*. Washington, DC: Office of Juvenile Justice and Delinquency Prevention.

Torres, Donald A. (1985). *Handbook of Federal Police and Investigative Agencies*. Westport, CT: Greenwood Press.

Torres, Donald A. (1987). *Handbook of State Police, Highway Patrols, and Investigative Agencies*. Westport, CT: Greenwood Press.

Townsend, Vincent, and Perry Eichor (1995). "Jails, Inmate Phone Service, and Call Rates . . . A Political Time Bomb Waiting to Explode?" *American Jails* **8**:27–39.

Trautman, Neal (1997). "The National Law Enforcement Officer: Disciplinary Research Project." *Law and Order* **45**:34–37.

Triplett, Ruth, and Janet L. Mullings (1999). "Examining the Effect of Work-Home Conflict on Work-Related Stress Among Correctional Officers." *Journal of Criminal Justice* **27**:371–385.

Trojanowicz, Robert, and Bonnie Bucqueroux (1990). *Community Policing: A Contemporary Perspective*. Cincinnati, OH: Anderson.

Trompetter, Philip S. (1993). "Pre-Employment Psychological Screening of Violence-Prone Peace Officer Applicants." *Journal of California Law Enforcement* **27**:32–55.

Troxell, J.P. (1954). "Elements of Job Satisfaction." *Personnel* **31**:199–205.

Trumbo, Donald A. (1961). "Individual and Group Correlates of Attitudes Toward Work-Related Change." *Journal of Applied Psychology* **45**:338–344.

Turman, Kathryn M. (1998). *New Directions from the Field: Victims' Rights and Services for the 21st Century: Judiciary*. Washington, DC: U.S. Department of Justice.

Twill, Sarah E., et al. (1998). "Changes in Measured Loneliness, Control, and Social Support Among Parolees in a Halfway House." *Journal of Offender Rehabilitation* **27**:77–92.

Ulmer, Jeffrey T. (1995). "The Organization and Consequences of Social Pasts in Criminal Courts." *Sociological Quarterly* **36**:587–605.

Ulmer, Jeffrey T., and John H. Kramer (1998). "The Use and Transformation of Formal Decision-Making Criteria: Sentencing Guidelines, Organizational Contexts, and Case Processing Strategies." *Social Problems* **45**:248–267.

Umbreit, Mark S. (1994). "Victim Empowerment Through Mediation." *APPA Perspectives* **18**:25–28.

U.S. Code Annotated (2001). *United States Code Annotated*. St Paul, MN: West Publishing Company.

U.S. Commission on the Advancement of Federal Law Enforcement (2000). *Law Enforcement in a New Century and a Changing World: Improving the Administration of Federal Law Enforcement*. Washington, DC: U.S. Commission on the Advancement of Federal Law Enforcement.

U.S. Department of Justice (1987). *Principles of Good Policing: Avoiding Violence Between Police and Citizens*. Washington, DC: U.S. Government Printing Office, Community Relations Service.

U.S. Department of Justice (1999). *Correctional Populations in the United States*. Washington, DC: U.S. Department of Justice.

U.S. Federal Bureau of Prisons (1994). *State of the Bureau: Emergency Preparedness and Response*. Washington, DC: U.S. Federal Bureau of Prisons.

U.S. Federal Courts Study Committee (1990). *Report of the Federal Courts Study Committee.* Philadelphia, PA: U.S. Federal Courts Study Committee.

U.S. General Accounting Office (1997). *Federal Offenders: Trends in Community Corrections.* Washington, DC: U.S. General Accounting Office.

U.S. General Accounting Office (1998). *Law Enforcement: Information on Drug-Related Police Corruption.* Washington, DC: U.S. General Accounting Office.

U.S. General Accounting Office (2000). *Racial Profiling: Limited Data Available on Motorist Stops.* Washington, DC: U.S. General Accounting Office.

U.S. National Institute of Law Enforcement and Criminal Justice (1980). *Arson Prevention and Control: Program Model.* Washington, DC: Abt Associates.

Utton, Mary W. (1994). "From Diversity to Unanimity: The Case of the New Mexico Children's Code." *APPA Perspectives* **18:**6–8.

Van Voorhis, Patricia (1993). "Psychological Determinants of the Prison Experience." *Prison Journal* **73:**72–102.

Van Voorhis, Patricia, Francis T. Cullen, and Brandon Applegate (1995). "Evaluating Interventions with Violent Offenders: A Guide for Practitioners and Policymakers." *Federal Probation* **59:**17–27.

Violanti, John M., and Douglas Paton (eds.) (1999). *Police Trauma: Psychological Aftermath of Civilian Combat.* Springfield, IL: Charles C Thomas.

Virginia Commission on Youth (1993). *Report on the Study of Serious Juvenile Offenders.* Richmond, VA: Commonwealth of Virginia.

Virginia Department of Criminal Justice Services (1998). *Report on Evaluation of the Richmond City Continuum of Juvenile Justice Services Pilot Program.* Richmond, VA: Virginia Department of Criminal Justice Services.

Virginia State Crime Commission (1994). *Police Accountability.* Richmond, VA: Virginia State Crime Commission, House Document No. 51.

Viteles, Morris S. (1953). *Motivation and Morale in Industry.* New York: Norton.

Vogel, Brenda (1995a). "Meeting Court Mandates: The CD-ROM Solution." *Corrections Today* **57:**158–160.

Vogel, Brenda (1995b). "Ready or Not, Computers Are Here." *Corrections Today* **57:**160–162.

Vogel, Mary E. (1999). "The Social Origins of Plea Bargaining: Conflict and the Law in the Process of State Formation, 1830–1860." *Law and Society Review* **33:**161–246.

Volcansek, Mary L. (1993). *Judicial Impeachment: None Called for Justice.* Champaign, IL: University of Illinois Press.

Volcansek, Mary L., and Maria-Elisabetta deFranciscis (1996). *Judicial Misconduct: A Cross-National Comparison.* Gainesville, FL: University Press of Florida.

Vroom, Victor H. (1960). *Some Personality Determinants of the Effects of Participation.* Englewood Cliffs, NJ: Prentice Hall.

Vroom, Victor H. (1964). *Work and Motivation.* New York: Wiley.

Wachtel, Julius (1982). *Police Undercover Work: Issues and Practice.* Ann Arbor, MI: University Microfilms International.

Waddington, P.A.J. (1999). "Police (Canteen) Sub-Culture." *British Journal of Criminology* **39:**287–309.

Waite, Robert G. (1993). *From Penitentiary to Reformatory . . . The Road to Prison Reform—New South Wales, Ireland, and Elmira, New York, 1840–1970.* Westport, CT: Greenwood Press.

Walker, Charles R. (1950). "The Problem of the Repetitive Job." *Harvard Business Review* **28:**54–58.

Walker, Samuel (1979). "Professionalism at the Crossroads: Police Administration in the 1980s." In *Critical Issues in Criminal Justice,* R.G. Iacovetta and D.H. Chang (eds.). Boston: Houghton Mifflin.

Walker, Samuel (1983). "Employment of Black and Hispanic Police Officers." *Academy of Criminal Justice Sciences Today* **10:**1–5.

Walker, Samuel (1992). *The Police in America: An Introduction* (2/e). New York: McGraw-Hill.

Walker, Samuel (1998). "Complaints Against the Police: A Focus Group Study of Citizen Perceptions, Goals, and Expectations." *Criminal Justice Review* **22:**207–226.

Walker, Samuel, and Nanette Graham (1998). "Citizen Complaints in Response to Police Misconduct: The Results of a Victimization Survey." *Police Quarterly* **1:**65–89.

Walker, Samuel, and Betsy Wright (1995). *Citizen Review of the Police, 1994: A National Survey.* Washington, DC: Police Executive Research Forum.

Wallace, Harvey, Cliff Roberson, and Craig Steckler (1995). *Fundamentals of Police Administration.* Englewood Cliffs, NJ: Prentice Hall.

Walsh, Anthony (1997). *Correctional Assessment, Casework and Counseling* (2/e). Lanham, MD: American Correctional Association.

Walsh, Arlene (1998). "Jail: The First Link in Our Chain of Collaboration." *American Jails* **12:**51–59.

Walsh, William Francis (1984). *The Analysis of the Variation in Patrol Officer Felony Arrest Rates.* Ann Arbor, MI: University Microfilms International.

Walters, Stephen (1996). "The Determinants of Job Satisfaction Among Canadian and American Correctional Officers." *Journal of Crime and Justice* **19:**145–158.

Warchol, Greg L., Dennis M. Payne, and Brian R. Johnson (1999). "Federal Forfeiture Law, Policy, and Practice." *Justice Professional* **11:**403–423.

Washington, Jeffrey (1987). "ACA Revaluates Small Jail Standards." *Corrections Today* **45:**15.

Watson, Goodwin (1966). *Social Psychology: Issues and Insights.* New York: Lippincott.

Weatherburn, Don (1993). *Grappling with Court Delay.* Sydney, Aus: Bureau of Crime Statistics and Research.

Weatherburn, Don, and Bronwyn Lind (1996). "Sentence Disparity, Judge Shopping and Trial Court Delay." *Australian and New Zealand Journal of Criminology* **29:**147–165.

Weber, Max (1947). *The Theory of Social and Economic Organization*. New York: Oxford University Press.

Weekes, John R., Guy Pelletier, and Daniel Beaudette (1995). "Correctional Officers: How Do They Perceive Sex Offenders?" *International Journal of Offender Therapy and Comparative Criminology* **39:**55–61.

Weisheit, Ralph A., Edward L. Wells, and David N. Falcone (1994). "Community Policing in Small Town and Rural America." *Crime and Delinquency* **40:**549–567.

Weiss, Robert P. (1987). "The Community and Prevention." In *The Handbook on Crime and Delinquency Prevention*, Elmer H. Johnson (ed.). Westport, CT: Greenwood Press.

Welch, Michael, and Danielle Gunther (1997a). "Jail Suicide and Prevention: Lessons from Litigation." *Crisis Intervention and Time Limited Treatment* **3:**229–244.

Welch, Michael, and Danielle Gunther (1997b). "Jail Suicide Under Legal Scrutiny: An Analysis of Litigation and Its Implications for Policy." *Criminal Justice Policy Review* **8:**75–97.

Welsh, Brandon C., and David P. Farrington (2000). "Correctional Intervention Programs and Cost-Benefit Analysis." *Criminal Justice and Behavior* **27:**115–133.

Wernimont, P.F. (1966). "Intrinsic and Extrinsic Factors in Job Satisfaction." *Journal of Applied Psychology* **50:**41–50.

West, J.P., E.M. Berman, and M.E. Milakovich (1994). "Implementing TQM in Local Government: The Leadership Challenge." *Public Productivity and Management Review* **17:**175–192.

Weston, Paul B. (1978). *Supervision in the Administration of Justice: Police, Corrections, Courts*. Springfield, IL: Charles C Thomas.

Whitehead, John T., and Charles A. Lindquist (1985). "Job Stress and Burnout Among Probation/Parole Officers." *International Journal of Offender Therapy and Comparative Criminology* **29:**109–119.

Whitehead, John T., and Charles A. Lindquist (1986). "Correctional Officer Job Burnout: A Path Model." *Journal of Research in Crime and Delinquency* **23:**23–42.

Whitmore, Robert C. (1995). "Tasks and Duties of Superintendents and Wardens in Pennsylvania." *American Jails* **9:**53–58.

Wicklund, Carl (1997). "Juvenile Justice Reform: An Arizona Experience." *APPA Perspectives* **21:**12–14.

Wiggins, Earl Lorenzo (1989). *Correctional Officer's Susceptibility to Stress: An Analysis of the Type A and Type B Behavioral Pattern*. Ann Arbor, MI: University Microfilms International.

Williams, Gerald L. (1989). *Making the Grade: The Benefits of Law Enforcement Accreditation*. Washington, DC: Police Executive Research Forum.

Williams, James L., Daniel G. Rodeheaver, and Denise W. Huggins (1999). "A Comparative Evaluation of a New Generation Jail." *American Journal of Criminal Justice* **23:**223–246.

Williams, James W. (2000). "Interrogating Justice: A Critical Analysis of the Police Interrogation and Its Role in the Criminal Justice System." *Canadian Journal of Criminology* **42:**209–240.

Williams, Jimmy J. (1995a). "Race of Appellant, Sentencing Guidelines, and Decisionmaking in Criminal Appeals: A Research Note." *Journal of Criminal Justice* **23:**83–91.

Williams, Jimmy J. (1995b). "Type of Counsel and the Outcome of Criminal Appeals: A Research Note." *American Journal of Criminal Justice* **19:**275–285.

Williams, Julie (2000). "Mentoring for Law Enforcement." *FBI Law Enforcement Bulletin* **69:**19–25.

Wilson, Carlene, and Karen Beck (1995). *The Impact of the Redesign of the Job of General Duties Patrol on the Motivation, Job Satisfaction, and Organizational Commitment of Patrol Officer*. Payneham, Aus: Australia National Police Branch.

Wilson, James Q. (1968). *Varieties of Police Behavior*. Cambridge, MA: Harvard University Press.

Wilson, O.W., and Roy C. McLaren (1977). *Police Administration* (4/e). New York: McGraw-Hill.

Winfree, Thomas L., Jr., and Greg Newbold (1999). "Community Policing and the New Zealand Police: Correlates of Attitudes Toward the Work World in a Community-Oriented National Police Organization." *Policing: An International Journal of Police Strategies and Management* **22:**489–617.

Winfree, Thomas L., Jr., David Guiterman, and G. Larry Mays (1997). "Work Assignments and Police Work: Exploring the Work World of Sworn Officers in Four New Mexico Police Departments." *Policing* **20:**419–441.

Witham, Donald C. (1985). *The American Law Enforcement Chief Executive: A Management Profile*. Washington, DC: Police Executive Research Forum.

Witte, Ann D. (1973). *Work Release in North Carolina: The Program and the Process*. Chapel Hill, NC: Institute of Government.

Witte, J.J., Lawrence G. Travis III, and Robert H. Langworthy (1990). "Participatory Management in Law Enforcement." *American Journal of Police* **7:**29–50.

Wold, John T., and John H. Culver (1987). "The Defeat of the California Justices: The Campaign, the Electorate, and the Issue of Judicial Accountability." *Judicature* **70:**348–355.

Woods, Gerald (1993). *The Police in Los Angeles: Reform and Professionalization*. New York: Garland.

Woodward, Joan (1965). *Industrial Organizations: Theory and Practice*. London, UK: Oxford University Press.

Wooldredge, John (1998). "Inmate Lifestyles and Opportunities for Victimization." *Journal of Research in Crime and Delinquency* **35:**480–502.

Wooldredge, John, and Jill Gordon (1997). "Predicting the Estimated Use of Alternatives to Incarceration." *Journal of Quantitative Criminology* **13:**121–142.

Worthy, James (1950). "Organizational Structure and Employee Morale." *American Sociological Review* **15:**169–179.

Wright, Kevin N. (1994). *Effective Prison Leadership*. Binghamton, NY: William Neil Publishing.

Wright, Kevin N. (1998). "Reinventing Corrections." *Corrections Management Quarterly* **2:**1–88.

Wright, Kevin N., et al. (1997). "Job Control and Occupational Outcomes Among Prison Workers." *Justice Quarterly* **14:**525–546.

Wycoff, M.A., and Wesley G. Skogan (1994). "The Effect of a Community Policing Management Style on Officers' Attitudes." *Crime and Delinquency* **40:**371–383.

Yeager, Peter C. (1981). *The Politics of Corporate Social Control: The Federal Response to Industrial Water Pollution.* Ann Arbor, MI: University Microfilms International.

Yee, Adelia, and James Turpin (1999). "Juvenile Justice Legislation." *Corrections Compendium* **24:**1–6.

Zaleznik, Abraham, et al. (1958). *Motivation, Productivity, and Satisfaction of Workers.* Boston: Graduate School of Business Administration, Harvard University.

Zander, Alvin (1961). "The Nature and Consequences of Leadership." *Michigan Business Review* **13:**29–32.

Zasslaw, Jay G. (1999). "Young Women in the Juvenile Justice System." *APPA Perspectives* **23:**33–38.

Zeidler, Peter C. (1981). *The Police: The Environment and Crime: An Empirical Analysis.* Ann Arbor, MI: University Microfilms International.

Zhao, Jihong, and Nicholas Lovrich (1997). "Collective Bargaining and the Police: The Consequences for Supplemental Compensation Policies in Large Agencies." *Policing* **20:**508–518.

Zhao, Jihong, Quint Thurman, and Ni He (1999). "Sources of Job Satisfaction Among Police Officers: A Test of Demographic and Work Environment Models." *Justice Quarterly* **16:**153–173.

Zimmerman, Sheryl Itkin (1988). *Police Social Work in Twenty-Three Programs: Program Description and Analysis of Interdisciplinary Relations.* Chicago: University of Chicago Press.

Cases Cited

Apodaca v. Oregon, 406 U.S. 404, 92 S.Ct. 1628 (1972)
Baldwin v. New York, 399 U.S. 66 (1970)
Batson v. Kentucky, 476 U.S. 79 (1986)
Bell v. Wolfish, 441 U.S. 520 (1979)
Bettis v. Delo, 14 F.3d 22 (1994)
Blackburn v. Snow, 771 F.2d 556 (1985)
Blanton v. North Las Vegas, 489 U.S. 538, 109 S.Ct. 1289 (1989)
Breed v. Jones, 421 U.S. 519 (1975)
Burch v. Louisiana, 441 U.S. 357 (1979)
Duncan v. Louisiana, 391 U.S. 145 (1968)
Ex parte Crouse, 4 Whart. 9 (1839)
Fletcher v. Peck, 6 Cr. 87 (1810)
Gregg v. Georgia, 428 U.S. 153 (1976)
Hackett v. United States, 606 F.2d 319 (1978)
In re Gault, 387 U.S. 1 (1967)
In re Winship, 397 U.S. 358 (1970)
Johnson v. Louisiana, 406 U.S. 356 (1972)
Kent v. United States, 383 U.S. 541 (1966)
Marbury v. Madison, 1 Cr. 137 (1803)
McKeiver v. Pennsylvania, 403 U.S. 528 (1971)
Quinones v. Nettleship, 773 F.2d 10 (1985)
Rhodes v. Chapman, 452 U.S. 337 (1981)
Roe v. Wade, 410 U.S. 113 (1973)
Sample v. Borg, 675 F.Supp. 574 (1987)
Schall v. Martin, 99 S.Ct. 2403 (1984)
Sypert v. United States, 559 F.Supp. 546 (1983)
Timberlake v. Benton, 786 F.Supp. 676, M.D. Tenn. (1992)
Walker v. United States, 437 F.Supp. 1081 (1977)

Name Index

CASES CITED

SUBJECT INDEX

National Center for State Courts (NCSC)
http://www.ncsc.dni.us
Disseminates findings from studies of court caseloads; provides information about arrest statistics, court technology, and administrative data

National Center for Statistics and Analysis, National Highway Traffic Safety Administration
http://www.nhtsa.dot.gov/people/ncsa
Provides state data for traffic fatalities and their causes as well as driver demographics

National Center for Youth Law
http://www.youthlaw.org
Organization that addresses the problems of children including abuse, neglect, and poverty; oriented toward improving children's lives by increasing availability of housing to poor families with children and providing information about available services

National Council of Juvenile and Family Court Judges
http://www.ncjfcj.unr.edu
Organization whose purpose is to focus attention on the concept of a separate tribunal for children and to encourage the development of essential treatment programs for children with special needs

National Court Appointed Special Advocate Association (CASA)
http://www.nationalcasa.org
Organization concerned with making decisions about abused and neglected children's lives; assists in child abuse cases; works with other family assistance programs to facilitate better lives for children

National Criminal Justice Association (NCJA)
http://www.acsp.uic.edu/ncja/nasbo.htm
Reports on state juvenile justice expenditures

National Criminal Justice Commission (NCJC)
http://www.ncianet.org/ncia/
Disseminates information about public safety issues and crime

National Criminal Justice Reference Service
http://www.ncjrs.org
A federally sponsored information clearinghouse for people involved with research, policy, and practice related to the criminal and juvenile justice system and drug control

National District Attorneys Association
http://www.ndaa.org
Largest national professional association specifically devoted to the needs of prosecutors; influences public policies affecting the safety of U.S.'s communities by advocating prosecutorial views with various governmental agencies

National Indian Justice Center
http://www.nijc.indian.com/
Indian-owned and operated non-profit corporation designed to establish an independent national resource for tribal courts; attempts to design and deliver legal education, research, and technical assistance programs that seek to improve tribal court systems and the administration of justice in Indian communities

National Institute of Corrections
http://www.nicic.org/inst/
Provides information about all aspects of U.S. corrections and corrections statistics

National Institute of Justice (NIJ)
http://www.ojp.usdoj.gov/nij
A research agency that supports research and conducts evaluation research and demonstration programs

National Institute of Justice Data Resources Program
http://www.nacjd@icpsr.umich.edu
Provides information about grant monies for research involving any criminal justice topic

National Institute for Standards and Technology (NIST)
http://www.first.org
Disseminates information about computer crimes, legal issues, and privacy matters

National Judicial College
http://www.judges.org
Conducts short courses for trial court judges and administrative law personnel

National Law Enforcement and Corrections Technology Center
http://www.nlectc.org
Publishes and disseminates information about computers and computer software, weapons and ammunition, and various forms of communication equipment

National Network of State Polls
http://www.unc.edu/depts/nnsp/archives.htm
A confederation of organizations that conducts state-level surveys

National Security Agency
http://www.NSA.GOV.8080/
Provides information about cryptologic history, news releases about information systems security, and educational and employment opportunities

National Sheriffs' Association
http://www.sheriffs.org
National organization of sheriff's office personnel, including corrections professionals, police chiefs, and other persons interested in county law enforcement

National Transportation and Safety Board
http://www.ntsb.gov
Provides statistical information about aviation accidents and fatalities; investigates accidents of airlines, trains, and automobiles

National White-Collar Crime Center (NWCCC)
http://www.iir.com/nwccc/nwccc.htm
Collects and disseminates information about white-collar crime in the United States

NCOVR Data Center
http://www.ncovr.heinz.cmu.edu
Organization designed to facilitate a central location for the accumulation and dissemination of scientific knowledge and to reduce the overhead of doing research; has implemented a data warehouse with large and small data sets for access to the general public and researchers

Office for Victims of Crime
http://www.ojp.usdoj.gov/ovc/
Organization that oversees diverse programs that benefit victims of crime; also supports training programs and educates criminal justice professionals regarding the rights and needs of crime victims; provides substantial funding to state victim assistance and compensation programs

Office of Community Oriented Policing Services (COPS)
http://www.usdoj.gov/cops
Generates information about the use of community oriented policing in different U.S. neighborhoods; collects information and funds research relating to community policing

Office of Justice Programs
http://www.ojp.usdoj.gov/
Works to develop, operate, and evaluate a wide range of criminal and juvenile justice programs

Office of Juvenile Justice and Delinquency Prevention (OJJDP)
http://www.ojjdp.ncjrs.org
Agency with broad responsibilities to collect and disseminate information about juveniles and the juvenile justice system; funds research relating to juvenile delinquency and how it can be prevented or controlled